AMERICAN HISTORY
A Survey
Volume I: To 1877

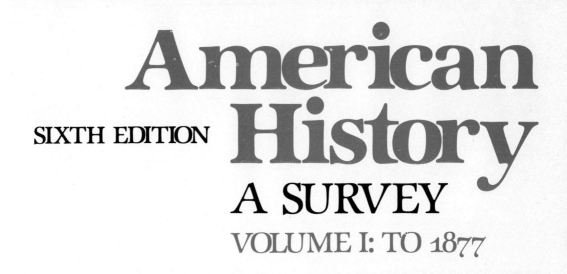

American History

SIXTH EDITION

A SURVEY

VOLUME I: TO 1877

Richard N. Current
University of North Carolina at Greensboro

T. Harry Williams
late of Louisiana State University

Frank Freidel
University of Washington

Alan Brinkley
Harvard University

ALFRED A. KNOPF   NEW YORK

THIS IS A BORZOI BOOK
PUBLISHED BY ALFRED A. KNOPF, INC.

Sixth Edition
9876543
Copyright © 1959, 1961, 1964, 1966, 1971, 1975,
1979 by Richard N. Current, T. Harry Williams,
Frank Freidel
Copyright © 1983 by Richard N. Current,
T. H. W., Inc., Frank Freidel, Alan Brinkley

Library of Congress Cataloging in
Publication Data

Main entry under title:
American history: a survey.
    Rev. ed. of: American history / Richard N. Cur-
rent, T. Harry Williams, Frank Freidel. 5th ed.
c1979.
    Includes bibliographies and index.
    1. United States—History. I. Current, Richard
Nelson.   II. Current, Richard Nelson. American
History.
E178.1.A492 1983b   973   82-17291
ISBN 0-394-33079-X (pbk.: v. 1)
ISBN 0-394-33080-3 (pbk.: v. 2)

Manufactured in the United States of America

Published 1961; reprinted five times
Second edition, 1966; reprinted three times
Third edition, 1971; reprinted four times
Fourth edition, 1975; reprinted four times
Fifth edition, 1979; reprinted three times

Color essay "The American Landscape": Photo
section—photo selection and text by Paula Franklin. Map section—cartographic research and text
by Michael Conzen, University of Chicago; maps
by David Lindroth.

Cover design and construction by Jack Ribik

Cover photograph by James McGuire

Text design by Leon Bolognese

PREFACE

This book attempts to tell a remarkable story: the story of the American people, from their first settlements in the wilderness many centuries ago to the present day. It is a story in part of triumph, of the creation with startling speed of the wealthiest and most powerful society in the history of the world. It is also a story of travail and injustice, of the oppression of the powerless by the powerful, of the careless exploitation of resources, and of the frustrations of international power. And it is, as well, the story of striving, of a people suffused with ideals and struggling constantly—sometimes successfully, sometimes not—to shape a nation and a world that would embody their dreams.

No single work can hope to tell the full story of any nation. In the case of the United States, a country of almost unparalleled diversity, in which change has occurred with such constant and dizzying speed as to make historical time seem to accelerate, that task is particularly difficult. The authors of this volume, therefore, have chosen to emphasize those themes that seem best to embody the heart of the American experience. First, we have recounted in detail the public life of the United States: the creation of the nation's political institutions, the changing expectations of the people involved in those institutions, and the continually evolving role the institutions have played in shaping the fabric of national life. Second, we have examined the development of America's role in the world, from its position as a weak dependency of the British Empire, through its years as a generally isolated nation with little influence in world affairs, to its rise to international preeminence. Third, we have examined the story of the development of the American economy from its simple agrarian beginnings, through its triumphant rise to industrial greatness, to its present troubled condition. And fourth, we have described the way in which the American people have lived: the cultural and social arrangements they have developed for themselves, the impact of political and economic changes upon those arrangements, and the efforts of diverse and often antagonistic groups to find ways of living together within a single society.

It is in this last effort that this sixth edition of *American History: A Survey* differs most significantly from that of its five predecessors. For in the more than twenty years since the first publication of this book, American historical scholarship has undergone something approaching a revolution: the rise of a new social history. Issues that in earlier eras remained obscure adjuncts to the dominant political and diplomatic history of the nation have now emerged as central themes in the writing of American history: the lives and habits of ordinary people; the plight of the majority of the American people who are women and of the substantial minorities who are black, Hispanic, Indian, and otherwise; the process by which America was settled by successive waves of immigrants, and the process by which those immigrants adapted to their new surroundings; the rise and transformation of the city; and the wrenching changes in the nature of agrarian society. This new edition, which represents the most thorough revision since the initial publication of this book, has attempted to incorporate the important new scholarship in all these fields into its pages, while retaining its thorough and careful coverage of the political and diplomatic history of the United States.

The two decades since the initial publication of this book have seen other changes in historical scholarship. They have, for one thing, produced a history of their own; and in this edition we have greatly expanded and deepened our coverage of the recent past. They have, in addition, called into question many of the assumptions that had guided the writing of American history in the past. So while we have in this book avoided taking a particular political or ideological stance, we have also made an effort to reexamine our earlier accounts of major developments in light of newer interpretations. Our coverage of the twentieth century, in particular, has been almost entirely recast and rewritten; but we have made major changes as well in our treatment of the colonial period of American life, of the late nineteenth century, and of many other subjects.

Those familiar with earlier editions of this work will notice other differences as well: the thorough reworking and expansion of the essays entitled "Where Historians Disagree"; completely new bibliographical essays, with critical commentary; changes in our selection of pictures, maps, charts, and other graphics; the addition of a vivid new cartographic essay illustrating the social and demographic evolution of the United States; and a new color art essay highlighting the many facets of the changing American landscape. The result of these, and other, revisions in this sixth edition is, we hope, a study of the American past that will convey more of the richness and complexity of our national life and that will illuminate more clearly how the study of history can enhance our understanding of our own time.

As always, we are deeply grateful to the many people who have contributed to the work on this new edition. In particular, we appreciate the careful, detailed critiques of the text by the scholars who generously agreed to assist us. Because some of these critics have asked not to be identified to us by name, we have chosen not to identify any of them specifically here. But we hope they will know of our gratitude for their invaluable efforts. We thank as well those students and teachers who have used this book over the past several years and who have offered us their comments, criticisms, and corrections—often unsolicited. We hope they will continue to inform us of their reactions to this book in the future, by sending their comments to us in care of the College Department, Alfred A. Knopf, 201 East 50th Street, New York, N.Y. 10022. Finally, we are grateful to the many people at Alfred A. Knopf who have worked to make this book the success it has been for more than two decades, and to those who have worked to make this new edition possible. In particular, we appreciate the efforts of David Follmer, James Kwalwasser, John Sturman, Liz Israel, June Smith, Lynn Goldberg, and Evelyn Katrak, whose indefatigable copy editing of this vast manuscript has removed many inelegancies and inconsistencies.

RICHARD N. CURRENT
Greensboro, North Carolina

FRANK FREIDEL
Seattle, Washington

ALAN BRINKLEY
Cambridge, Massachusetts

AUGUST 1982

CONTENTS

WHERE HISTORIANS DISAGREE

ILLUSTRATIONS

MAPS

CHARTS

AMERICAN HISTORY
A Survey
Volume I: To 1877

The American Landscape
Artistic Perspectives

PLATE 1. Short Bull. *Sun Dance*. Courtesy of American Museum of Natural History, New York.

"Our mother the earth" was how Indians typically described the land that nourished them. "The two-leggeds and the four-leggeds lived together like relatives," said a Plains holy man, "and there was plenty for them and for us." Among all the varied Indian peoples of America, rituals celebrated the unity of nature and humankind. One of these ceremonies was the sun dance of the Dakota Sioux, depicted on canvas in Plate 1. Although it is a late example of Indian art—earlier versions would have been done on hide and omitted horses, which were unknown in the New World until the arrival of the Europeans—it symbolizes an old culture whose attitude toward nature clashed with that of the Europeans who first arrived in the seventeenth century.

PLATE 2. Anonymous. *A New York Farm, with the Catskills in the Background*. New York State Historical Association.

One of the first colonists from the Old World, William Bradford, described America as "a hideous and desolate wilderness" that had to be tamed by cultivation. Prosperous farms displayed not only their owners' industry but also their triumph over hostile surroundings. Few colonial artists depicted the look of the American countryside. Those who did—including the painters of an upstate New York farm scene (Plate 2) and a South Carolina plantation (Plate 3)—showed the natural setting of hills and woods purely as a backdrop for the human settlements that were changing the face of the continent.

Not until the nineteenth century did American artists begin to paint the land for its own sake, to see it as landscape. Their work is typified by Asher B. Durand's *Kindred Spirits* (Plate 4). Durand (1796–1886)

PLATE 3. Thomas Coram. *View of Mulberry (House and Street)*. Oil on paper, 10 x 17.6 cm. (visible). Carolina Art Association/Gibbes Art Gallery, Charleston, South Carolina.

PLATE 4. Asher Brown Durand. *Kindred Spirits.* Oil on canvas, 44¼ x 36¼″. New York Public Library.

PLATE 5. George Inness. *The Lackawanna Valley* (1855). Oil on canvas, 33⅞ x 50¼″. Gift of Mrs. Huttleston Rogers, 1945, National Gallery of Art, Washington, D.C.

PLATE 7. Albert Bierstadt. *The Rocky Mountains* (1863). Oil on canvas, 73½ x 120¾″. The Metropolitan Museum of Art, Rogers Fund, 1907.

PLATE 6. Fitz Hugh Lane. *The Fort and Ten Pound Island, Gloucester, Massachusetts* (1847). Courtesy, The Kennedy Galleries, Inc.

and his fellows, working primarily in the mountains of New York and New England, belonged to a movement that was dubbed the Hudson River school. They were strongly influenced by Ralph Waldo Emerson, who wrote in his essay *Nature* (1836) that humanity may learn to worship God by contemplating natural beauty. By depicting the wonders of their own country, the Hudson River artists made the American wilderness a symbol of national pride in an intensely nationalistic period. Fittingly, *Kindred Spirits* shows nature poet William Cullen Bryant and Thomas Cole, leader of the Hudson River school, in a setting at once impressive and benign.

The nineteenth century thus emerged as the heyday of landscape painting in America, and gifted artists recorded many facets of the American scene. George Inness (1825–1894) is noted for his sweeping views of the spacious, fertile countryside of the agricultural Northeast. *The Lackawanna Valley*

(Plate 5) also reflects the growing role of railroads, which had begun to alter the landscape of the United States.

The New England coast attracted a number of painters, among them Fitz Hugh Lane (1804–1865). His harbor scene at Gloucester, Massachusetts (Plate 6), indicates the continuing importance of commerce and fishing in this region. Lane and others of the so-called luminist school (including Martin Johnson Heade and Frederick Church) were particularly interested in the dramatic contrasts in light that occur where sky, sea, and shore meet.

For drama, however, nothing could match the splendid vistas of the Far West. As the American frontier moved toward the Pacific coast, the magnificent scenery of the Rockies and other Western peaks seemed appropriate symbols of American achievement. In their day, the vast canvases of Albert Bierstadt (1830–1902), such as *The Rocky Mountains* (Plate 7), were extremely

PLATE 8. Thomas Eakins. *Max Schmitt in a Single Scull* (1871). Oil on canvas, 32¼ x 46¼". The Metropolitan Museum of Art, Purchase, 1934, Alfred N. Punnett Fund and Gift of George D. Pratt.

popular and sold for unprecedented sums (see pp. 499–500).

By the late nineteenth century, the United States had produced two painters of first-rate stature. Thomas Eakins (1844–1916) studied in Europe, like most American artists of his time, but returned to America to live. Known particularly for his unsparing portraits of fellow Philadelphians, he devoted the same scrutiny and technical skill to his outdoor scenes. The clarity of early spring light lends a special quality to his painting of his friend Max Schmitt rowing on the Schuylkill River (Plate 8). Eakins,

PLATE 9. Winslow Homer. *Palm Trees, St. John's River, Florida* (1890). Watercolor. The Kennedy Galleries, Inc.

also a keen sportsman—he was the first se- rious American artist to depict the world of sports—painted himself sculling in the mid- dle distance. The bridges in the background are a reminder of the industrialization and increasingly complex transportation net- works that were transforming much of the nation.

The other master of this period was Winslow Homer (1836–1910), whose sub- jects ranged from rural scenes to spectacu- lar seascapes. One of the few American painters of the time who did not study abroad, he served his apprenticeship as a staff artist for *Harper's Weekly*, sketching at the front during the Civil War. In Homer's later years, he became fascinated by more exotic, tropical settings. His watercolor of shimmering water and feathery palms in Florida (Plate 9) was done in a loose, free

style not unlike the impressionism then flourishing in France.

Impressionism had a number of Ameri- can followers, most notably James Abbott McNeill Whistler and Mary Cassatt, expa- triates who spent most of their lives in Eu- rope. Another, J. Alden Weir (1852–1919), preferred the United States. In *U.S. Thread Company Mills, Willimantic, Connecticut* (Plate 10), Weir lends a New England factory town a gentle, almost pastoral beauty.

The 1920 census revealed that, for the first time, more Americans lived in urban areas than in rural ones. Thus the American landscape was increasingly a cityscape, to be recorded in myriad ways.

One group of painters, formed in the 1890s, aimed at portraying city life, espe- cially that of New York, with objectivity and immediacy. These artists—who in-

PLATE 10. Julian Alden Weir. *U.S. Thread Company Mills, Willimantic, Connecticut.* Oil on canvas, 20 x 24''. The Metropolitan Museum of Art, Collection of Mr. and Mrs. Raymond J. Horowitz.

PLATE 11. John Sloan. *The City from Greenwich Village* (1922). Oil on canvas, 26 x 33¾". The National Gallery of Art, Washington, D.C.

cluded Robert Henri, William Glackens, George Luks, and John Sloan—called themselves The Eight but were derisively nicknamed the Ashcan school because of their stress on the commonplace. In *The City from Greenwich Village* (Plate 11), Sloan (1871–1951) views the metropolis from an immigrant section that had recently become a favored quarter for artists, writers, and bohemian hangers-on. In its dramatic use of darkness and pinpoints of light, Sloan's work shows that the Ashcan painters could both present the prosaic and the journalistic and achieve a kind of urban poetry.

But Ashcan realism enjoyed only a brief vogue. As early as 1913, at the famous Armory show in New York City, Americans were exposed to the innovations of such post-impressionists as Cézanne, Gauguin, Picasso, Matisse, and Léger. Many critics and most of the general public reacted with dismay, if not downright hostility: the exhibition was reviled as "a lunatic asylum" whose gospel was "stupid license and self-assertion" (see p. 560).

For some artists, however, the new styles were a revelation. Among them was John Marin (1870–1953), who had already come under the influence of the post-impressionists. While the Ashcan painters worked very much in the realistic tradition, Marin became one of the most successful of all American abstractionists. For example, when Brooklyn Bridge officially opened in 1883, its great towers and steel cables symbolized the nation's industrial strength. And in Marin's painting of the bridge (Plate 12), its actual appearance is less important than the feelings it engendered. The jumbled colors and broken forms of his spontaneous watercolor—a medium that Marin gave new power—seem to explode with energy.

The modernism exemplified by Marin had many detractors. It seemed, among other things, too private and too far removed from everyday reality. It was often linked to city sophistication and thus deemed out of touch with the "real" America. A number of painters who reacted against it are grouped together as regionalists, although they had no formal unity. Their goal was the realistic depiction of the American land and its people. Regionalism is associated primarily with the agricultural Midwest of the 1930s. During the trauma of the Great Depression, a restatement of traditional values in the context of rural life offered welcome reassurance to many people. Favorite subjects included farm activities, folk legends, and American history, particularly the winning of the West.

While all the regionalists tried to rediscover America in picturesque depictions of grass-roots culture, their subject matter varied, and so did their styles. Grant Wood (1892–1942), in scenes of his native Iowa, used smooth, conventionalized forms that tend to make the real world of fields and humble farms take on the aspect of a toy universe. No wind disturbs the trees in *Stone City, Iowa* (Plate 13), and a timeless calm immobilizes the people and animals.

Baptism in Kansas (Plate 14), by John Steuart Curry (1897–1946), shows regionalism in a different mode. Here style is secondary to narrative and sincerity of feeling. The religious fervor of the participants, rather than being diminished by the bleak

PLATE 12. John Marin. *Brooklyn Bridge* (1910). Watercolor, 18½ x 15⅛". The Metropolitan Museum of Art, Alfred Stieglitz Collection, 1949.

PLATE 13. Grant Wood. *Stone City, Iowa* (1930). Oil on wood panel, 30¼ x 40″. Joslyn Art Museum, Omaha, Nebraska.

PLATE 14. John Steuart Curry. *Baptism in Kansas* (1928). Oil on canvas, 40 x 50″. Collection of the Whitney Museum of American Art, New York.

PLATE 15. Thomas Hart Benton. *Boom Town* (1928). Oil on canvas, 45 x 54". Memorial Art Gallery of the University of Rochester, Marion Stratton Gould Fund.

Plains setting, is heightened by bright clouds (and a pair of improbable birds).

Still another approach to regionalism was that of Thomas Hart Benton (1889–1975), whose many farm scenes, whether of rice harvesting in Louisiana or plowing in Missouri, emphasize the dignity of labor and the joy of life lived outdoors. *Boom Town* (Plate 15) shows the other side of the coin—the pollution and congestion that followed industrialization and new forms of transportation into the heartland.

PLATE 16. Georgia O'Keeffe. *Ranchos Church* (c. 1930). Oil on canvas, 24 x 36". The Phillips Collection, Washington, D.C.

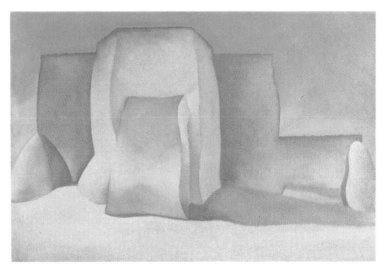

Although associated with the Southwest, Georgia O'Keeffe (1887–   ) is not considered a regionalist, for she is more interested in the interrelationship of forms as forms than in rendering a particular place at a particular time. Even so, her *Ranchos Church* (Plate 16) seems firmly rooted in the sands of New Mexico.

Despite the regionalists' emphasis on the nation's rural charms, the United States of the mid-twentieth century had become an industrial giant, its horizons bristling with

PLATE 19. Horace Pippin. *Cabin in the Cotton, III.* Collection, Roy N. Neuberger.

PLATE 20. Marsden Hartley. *Smelt Brook Falls* (1937). Oil on board, 71.1 x 55.9 cm. The St. Louis Art Museum, Elizabeth McMillan Fund.

factories, refineries, and high-tension wires. Charles Sheeler (1883–1965) turned to these complex forms for his inspiration, rendering them with a sharp, almost antiseptic, purity. (Indeed, he and O'Keeffe are sometimes referred to as precisionists.) Like most of his works, *Western Industrial* (Plate 17) is devoid of human reference.

For several artists of this period, landscape served to express personal feelings and inner moods. Loneliness pervades the paintings of Edward Hopper (1882–1967). His isolated figures, as in *Gas* (Plate 18), seem weighed down by brooding silence. Horace Pippin (1888–1946), the grandson of slaves, depicted various aspects of the black experience (as in Plate 19) with the straightforwardness and lack of sentimentality characteristic of naive painting. For Mars-

PLATE 21. Willem de Kooning. *Door to the River* (1960). Oil on canvas, 80 x 70″. Collection of Whitney Museum of American Art. Gift of the Friends of the Whitney Museum of American Art. Photograph by Geoffrey Clements.

den Hartley (1877–1943), nature symbolized the tragedy of the human condition. *Smelt Brook Falls* (Plate 20), a scene in his native Maine, conveys a sense of the blunt, almost crude, power of natural forces.

Landscape as we know it seemed to disappear almost entirely in the work of the abstract expressionists, who, in the late 1940s, abandoned representation in favor of dramatic daubs and dribbles of color. Their huge, emotionally intense canvases made the United States the leader of the art world for the first time. In spite of the highly personal nature of their paintings, several abstract expressionists hinted at landscapes in their titles, such as *Door to the River* (Plate 21) by Dutch-born Willem de Kooning (1904–   ). The sweeping brushstrokes and the rhythmic movement of its painted surface characterize de Kooning's work.

The immediate environment of the modern world was not to be ignored, however. The artifacts of the affluent consumer society, from soup cans to automobiles, gave rise in the late 1950s to a playful movement known as Pop Art. The work of Roy Lichtenstein (1923–   ) echoes mass-production printing techniques by employing in exaggerated form the dots characteristic of commercial photography. In his hands, even a mountain range (Plate 22) takes on the flatness of a comic strip.

In the 1970s, some artists returned to realism with a vengeance, depicting everyday aspects of contemporary life with a heightened naturalism, known as photorealism, superrealism, or sharp-focus realism. *The Magic Chef* (Plate 23), by John Baeder (1938–   ), typifies this movement's meticulous attention to banal subjects, in this case a stretch of the highway culture that has come to clutter the outskirts of many

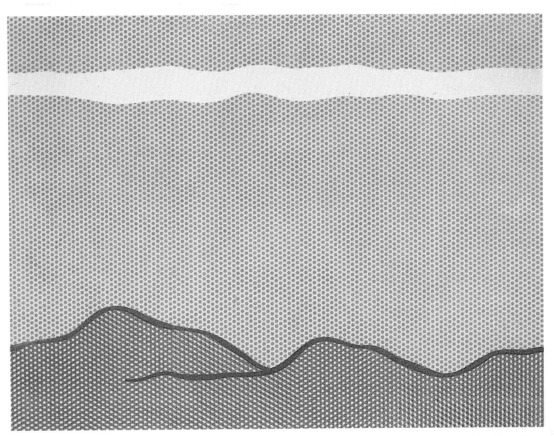

PLATE 22. Roy Lichtenstein. *Purple Range* (1966). Oil and magna on canvas, 36 x 48". Courtesy, Leo Castelli Gallery, New York. Private collection.

PLATE 23. John Baeder. *Magic Chef Cafe* (1975). Oil on canvas, 48 x 72". Collection, Denver Art Museum, Denver, Colorado.

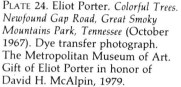

PLATE 24. Eliot Porter. *Colorful Trees. Newfound Gap Road, Great Smoky Mountains Park, Tennessee* (October 1967). Dye transfer photograph. The Metropolitan Museum of Art. Gift of Eliot Porter in honor of David H. McAlpin, 1979.

American towns. The perfection of detail creates an eerie effect.

Clearly, the American landscape has undergone sweeping changes as the United States has grown from a sparsely populated wilderness into a highly urbanized, industrial society. But, despite the defacement or destruction of much that was beautiful, the United States has not lost its visual splendors. Few record them with such fidelity as contemporary nature photographers, who might well be termed the true landscape artists of today.

Photography became respected as an art form in America with the work of Alfred Stieglitz early in the twentieth century (see p. 543). And several painters—including Charles Sheeler, himself a fine photographer—were strongly influenced by the tonalities of black-and-white photography. Like painting, photography lends itself to varied treatments, including romantic impressionism and studio abstractions. A highly developed pictorial imagination informs the work of such modern masters as Eliot Porter (1901–   ). His *Colorful Trees* (Plate 24), capturing the glow of a Tennessee hillside in autumn, is a powerful reminder that natural beauty is still a vital component of the American landscape.

The American Landscape

Geographical Perspectives

MAP 1

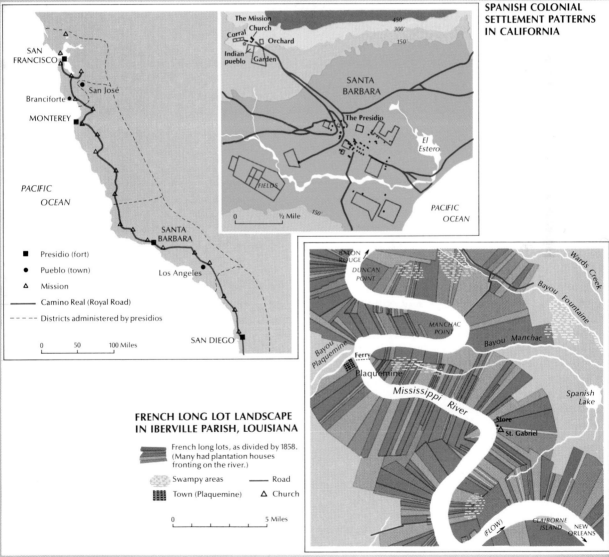

SPANISH COLONIAL SETTLEMENT PATTERNS IN CALIFORNIA

SAN FRANCISCO

San José

Branciforte

MONTEREY

PACIFIC OCEAN

SANTA BARBARA

Los Angeles

SAN DIEGO

- ■ Presidio (fort)
- ● Pueblo (town)
- △ Mission
- —— Camino Real (Royal Road)
- ----- Districts administered by presidios

0   50   100 Miles

The Mission
Church
Corral
Orchard
Indian pueblo
Garden
SANTA BARBARA
The Presidio
El Estero
FIELDS
PACIFIC OCEAN
450
300'
150'
150'
0   ½ Mile

FRENCH LONG LOT LANDSCAPE IN IBERVILLE PARISH, LOUISIANA

French long lots, as divided by 1858. (Many had plantation houses fronting on the river.)

Swampy areas — Road

Town (Plaquemine) △ Church

0   5 Miles

BATON ROUGE
DUNCAN POINT
Wards Creek
Bayou Fountaine
MANCHAC POINT
Bayou Manchac
Bayou Plaquemine
Ferry
Plaquemine
Mississippi River
Store
St. Gabriel
Spanish Lake
(FLOW)
CLAIBORNE ISLAND
NEW ORLEANS

MAP 2

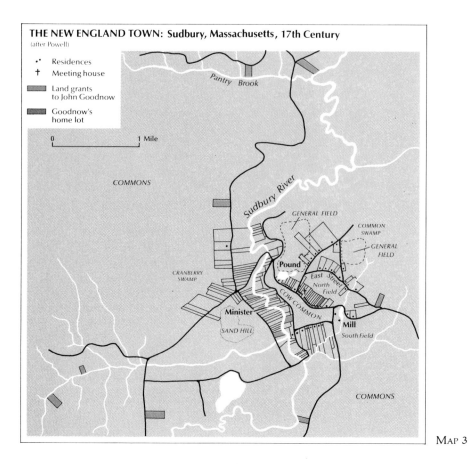

THE NEW ENGLAND TOWN: Sudbury, Massachusetts, 17th Century
(after Powell)

•· Residences
† Meeting house
▬ Land grants to John Goodnow
▬ Goodnow's home lot

0   1 Mile

COMMONS

Pantry Brook

Sudbury River

GENERAL FIELD

COMMON SWAMP

GENERAL FIELD

CRANBERRY SWAMP

Pound

East Street

North Field

COW COMMON

Minister

SAND HILL

Mill

South Field

COMMONS

MAP 3

The area that now forms the United States contains a rich array of contrasting regions—each with distinctive climate, landforms, and vegetation. And these regional differences have been compounded by the fact that the land was settled by groups of people from many different countries and cultures. Thus, the way in which the American landscape has developed is a reflection of varied goals and backgrounds, in addition to diverse natural conditions.

Despite the speed and scope of social change in modern times, many features discernible today, especially along the Atlantic coast and in parts of the Southwest, owe their distinctiveness to early colonization ventures. In the continental interior, the mixing of population streams and the diffusion of technology have not masked the divergent cultural landscapes that resulted from distinct resource environments. The westward movement of the nation and the progressive industrialization of its economy led to profound changes in population patterns, both in settled farming regions and in urban areas. More recently, settlement patterns have continued to evolve as a result of the enlarged scale of government, population movements, business organization, and social control.

Colonial Beginnings

Of all the major European colonization strategies in what later became the United States, Spain's was the most centralized, politically integrated, and geographically systematized—though often imperfectly realized. California exemplified the Spanish scheme for frontier settlement (Map 1): a string of missions and their surrounding Indian agricultural colonies with a few towns (*pueblos*) of Mexican settlers, all bound together under the protection of four military centers (*presidios*) that served an administrative function. The Spanish colonial network was far-flung, and its population was sparse. Even Santa Barbara, which had both a presidio and a mission, was quite a small settlement.

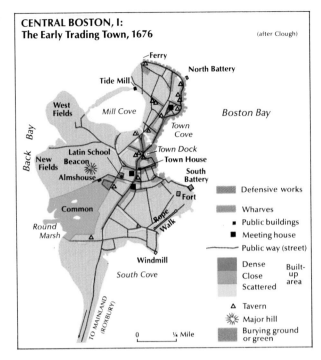

CENTRAL BOSTON, I:
The Early Trading Town, 1676
(after Clough)

Ferry
North Battery
Tide Mill
West Fields
Mill Cove
Boston Bay
Back Bay
Town Cove
Latin School
Beacon
Town Dock
Town House
New Fields
Almshouse
South Battery
Common
Fort
Round Marsh
Rope Walk
Windmill
South Cove
TO MAINLAND (ROXBURY)

0   ¼ Mile

Defensive works
Wharves
■ Public buildings
■ Meeting house
Public way (street)
Dense } Built-up area
Close
Scattered
△ Tavern
✷ Major hill
Burying ground or green

MAP 4

The French colonial network was also thin on a continental scale, but the French were able to create some larger and more autonomous pockets of colonization. Their land-grant system of individual "long lots," which were oriented to major rivers, has left an indelible mark on the cultural landscape of several parts of the United States, most notably the Mississippi bottomlands south of Baton Rouge, Louisiana (Map 2).

English colonizers arrived in North America with several different formulas for settlement. The Puritans produced the social and geographical unit called the New England town (Map 3; see also pp. 74–76). Adapted from the agricultural villages of England, it was distinguished by its system of local, communal government and by its expectations of economic self-sufficiency.

MAP 5

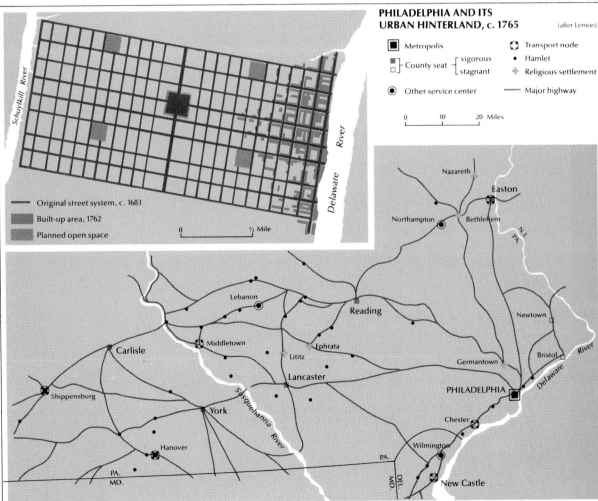

PHILADELPHIA AND ITS URBAN HINTERLAND, c. 1765
(after Lemon)

■ Metropolis
County seat { vigorous / stagnant
◉ Other service center
○ Transport node
• Hamlet
✚ Religious settlement
Major highway

0   10   20 Miles

Schuylkill River
Delaware River

Original street system, c. 1683
Built-up area, 1762
Planned open space

0   ½ Mile

Nazareth
Easton
Northampton
Bethlehem
N.J.
PA.
Lebanon
Reading
Newtown
Carlisle
Middletown
Ephrata
Lititz
Germantown
Bristol
River
Shippensburg
Lancaster
PHILADELPHIA
Delaware
York
Chester
Hanover
Wilmington
PA.
MD.
PA.
DEL.
MD.
New Castle
Susquehanna River

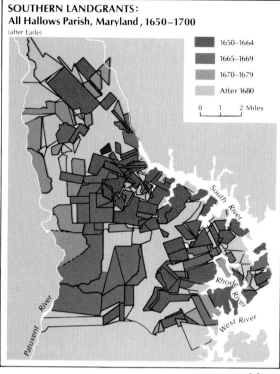

SOUTHERN LANDGRANTS:
All Hallows Parish, Maryland, 1650–1700
(after Earle)

■	1650–1664
■	1665–1669
■	1670–1679
■	After 1680

0   1   2 Miles

South River
Rhode River
West River
Patuxent River

MAP 6

Because New England lacked a major agricultural staple, trade soon became vital to the region, and Boston developed early as an international port and commercial center (Map 4). Docks, craft industries, and urban institutions soon gave the town a unique aspect, although the agricultural basis of its land and road communication patterns persisted for some time.

In the Middle Colonies, town founding by great proprietors such as William Penn was more centralized. Penn's intentions for Philadelphia were as prescriptive as Boston's experience had been haphazard (Map 5). Prior to the Revolution, Philadelphia's actual built-up area involved only the few city blocks near the Delaware River, but Penn's original plan was kept in mind as the city expanded further. So dominant was Philadelphia's urban growth that settlements in its shadow failed to grow during the colonial period. Nevertheless, a fertile

MAP 7

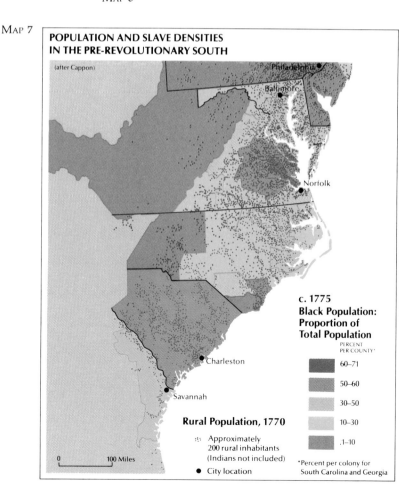

**POPULATION AND SLAVE DENSITIES
IN THE PRE-REVOLUTIONARY SOUTH**

(after Cappon)

Philadelphia
Baltimore
Norfolk
Charleston
Savannah

**c. 1775
Black Population:
Proportion of
Total Population**
PERCENT
PER COUNTY*

■	60–71
■	50–60
■	30–50
■	10–30
■	.1–10

Rural Population, 1770

∴ Approximately
200 rural inhabitants
(Indians not included)

● City location

*Percent per colony for
South Carolina and Georgia

0   100 Miles

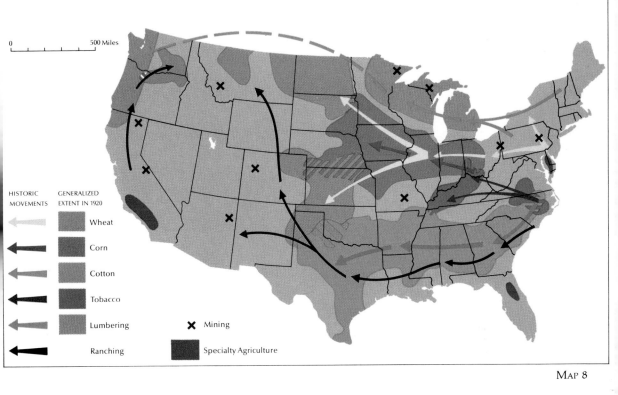

0   500 Miles

HISTORIC MOVEMENTS	GENERALIZED EXTENT IN 1920

Wheat

Corn

Cotton

Tobacco

Lumbering   ✘   Mining

Ranching   Specialty Agriculture

MAP 8

hinterland stimulated the early emergence of a regional system of towns with a variety of urban functions.

In the South, circumstances were less favorable to town growth. Instead, the emphasis on a few staple crops such as tobacco led to the rise of a plantation economy (see pp. 72–74). Characteristic of early tidewater settlement was the pattern of land grants in All Hallows Parish, Maryland, where most farms had direct access to water transport (Map 6). Metes-and-bounds surveys, which use natural landmarks rather than a rectilinear system, produced irregular, individualistic, and sometimes overlapping ownership tracts that contrasted markedly with the orderly structure of New England towns. Another distinct characteristic of the South was its increasing reliance on slave labor, especially in the most densely settled districts of Virginia and the Carolinas (Map 7; see also pp. 42–43).

Resource Frontiers

The regional agricultural specializations that had emerged during the colonial period intensified as settlers took grains, tobacco, cotton, and other crops across the Appalachian Mountains (Map 8). During the nineteenth century, wheat, corn, and cotton belts developed and extended westward as population, climate, and market prices determined the zones of optimum planting. Some regions passed through several phases of specialization, such as northern Illinois, with first cattle, then wheat, and then corn; others saw but one, such as northern Wisconsin, with lumbering only.

The settlements produced by these specializations were equally varied. Areas of grain and livestock farming quickly became thickly settled: small and medium-sized holdings, owned mainly by independent farmers, were set in landscapes of road and rail networks, towns of all sizes, and nu-

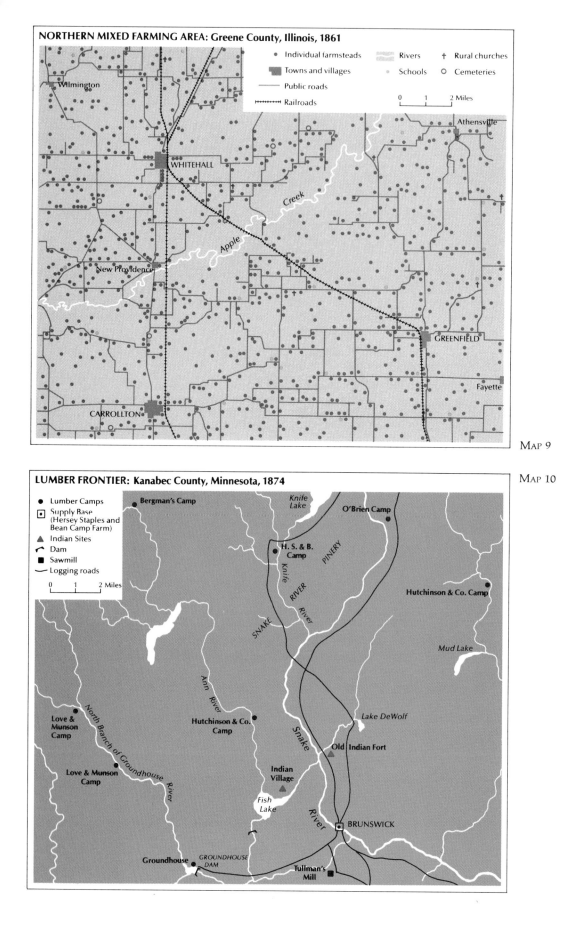

MAP 9

NORTHERN MIXED FARMING AREA: Greene County, Illinois, 1861

- Individual farmsteads
- Towns and villages
- Public roads
- Railroads
- Rivers
- Schools
- Rural churches
- Cemeteries

0   1   2 Miles

Wilmington

Athensville

WHITEHALL

Apple   Creek

New Providence

GREENFIELD

Fayette

CARROLLTON

MAP 10

LUMBER FRONTIER: Kanabec County, Minnesota, 1874

- Lumber Camps
- Supply Base (Hersey Staples and Bean Camp Farm)
- Indian Sites
- Dam
- Sawmill
- Logging roads

0   1   2 Miles

Bergman's Camp

Knife Lake

O'Brien Camp

H. S. & B. Camp

PINERY

Knife   RIVER

Hutchinson & Co. Camp

SNAKE   River

Mud Lake

Ann   River

Love & Munson Camp

North Branch of Groundhouse River

Hutchinson & Co. Camp

Snake   River

Lake DeWolf

Old Indian Fort

Love & Munson Camp

Indian Village

Fish Lake

BRUNSWICK

Groundhouse   GROUNDHOUSE DAM

Tullman's Mill

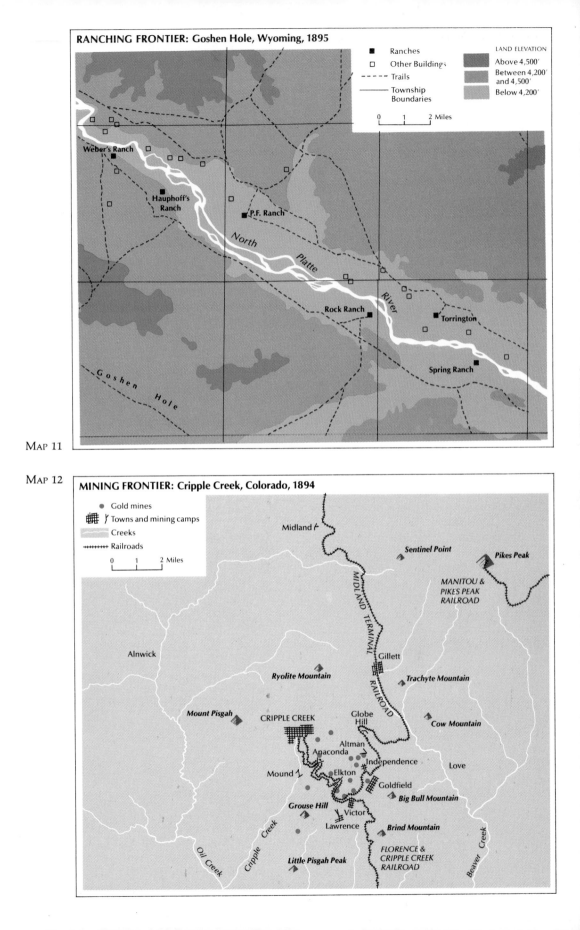

MAP 11

RANCHING FRONTIER: Goshen Hole, Wyoming, 1895

■ Ranches
□ Other Buildings
– – – Trails
——— Township Boundaries

LAND ELEVATION
Above 4,500'
Between 4,200' and 4,500'
Below 4,200'

0   1   2 Miles

Weber's Ranch
Hauphoff's Ranch
P.F. Ranch
North Platte River
Rock Ranch
Torrington
Spring Ranch
Goshen Hole

MAP 12

MINING FRONTIER: Cripple Creek, Colorado, 1894

● Gold mines
Towns and mining camps
Creeks
++++++ Railroads

0   1   2 Miles

Midland
Sentinel Point
Pikes Peak
MANITOU & PIKES PEAK RAILROAD
Alnwick
MIDLAND TERMINAL RAILROAD
Gillett
Ryolite Mountain
Trachyte Mountain
Mount Pisgah
CRIPPLE CREEK
Globe Hill
Cow Mountain
Altman
Anaconda
Independence
Love
Mound
Elkton
Goldfield
Big Bull Mountain
Grouse Hill
Victor
Brind Mountain
Oil Creek
Cripple Creek
Lawrence
FLORENCE & CRIPPLE CREEK RAILROAD
Little Pisgah Peak
Beaver Creek

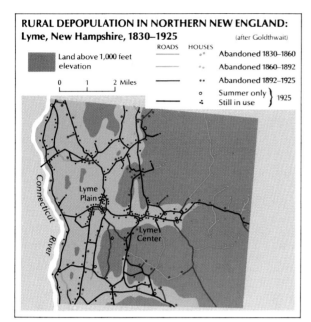

RURAL DEPOPULATION IN NORTHERN NEW ENGLAND:
Lyme, New Hampshire, 1830–1925
(after Goldthwait)

	ROADS	HOUSES	
Land above 1,000 feet elevation		.°	Abandoned 1830–1860
		°.	Abandoned 1860–1892
0 1 2 Miles		..	Abandoned 1892–1925
		o	Summer only ⎱ 1925
		.:	Still in use ⎰

MAP 13

Agrarian Change in Settled Areas

As the frontier pushed westward, older regions of the United States continued to undergo change. One cause of change was the new territory itself: cheap land and virgin soil to the west drew farm youths out of northern New England (as did new factory jobs to the south), resulting in considerable population loss in that region (Map 13; see also pp. 266–267, 321). In the South, the agents of rural change were the dislocations of the Civil War and Reconstruction and the abolition of slavery (pp. 466–467). Many once-profitable, compactly organized plantations were transformed into decentralized operations in which physically dispersed small farms were held together by ties such as sharecropping agreements (Map 14).

merous rural social-service institutions (Map 9). On the extensive lumber frontier, in contrast, isolated camps were connected by streams and logging roads to a few supply towns in a vast sea of forests. Kanabec County, Minnesota, was a good example (Map 10). Even more extensive was the ranching frontier of the Far West. Here cattle and cowboys roamed over hundreds of square miles of public domain, tied loosely to ranch settlements that monopolized major watercourses, as in eastern Wyoming (Map 11). And typical mining landscapes in the late nineteenth century represented still more remote conditions, though often concentrating large numbers of miners around mineral-rich strikes, such as the area near Pikes Peak, Colorado (Map 12; see also pp. 495–496).

As Maps 9–12 show, these various frontiers created contrasting settlement patterns that reflected differing kinds of resources, topographic conditions, and economic systems. These differences fostered an enormous diversity of geographical settings in which social patterns were shaped during the course of American expansion.

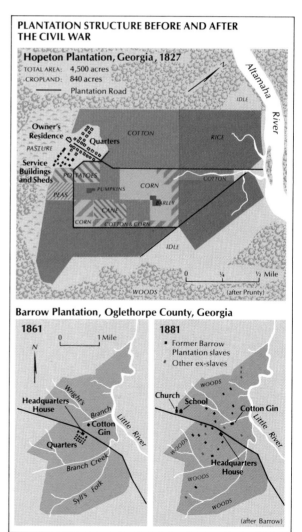

PLANTATION STRUCTURE BEFORE AND AFTER THE CIVIL WAR

Hopeton Plantation, Georgia, 1827
TOTAL AREA: 4,500 acres
CROPLAND: 840 acres
—— Plantation Road

(after Prunty)

Barrow Plantation, Oglethorpe County, Georgia

1861

1881
• Former Barrow Plantation slaves
• Other ex-slaves

MAP 14

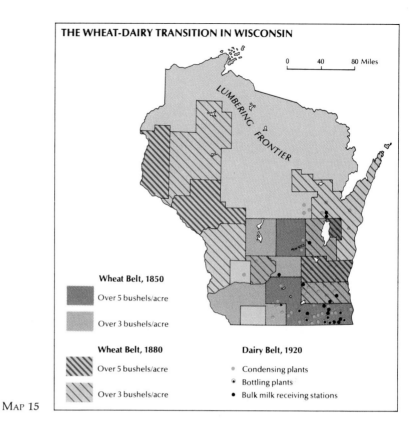

THE WHEAT-DAIRY TRANSITION IN WISCONSIN

0   40   80 Miles

LUMBERING FRONTIER

Wheat Belt, 1850

Over 5 bushels/acre

Over 3 bushels/acre

Wheat Belt, 1880

Over 5 bushels/acre

Over 3 bushels/acre

Dairy Belt, 1920

◦ Condensing plants

◉ Bottling plants

● Bulk milk receiving stations

MAP 15

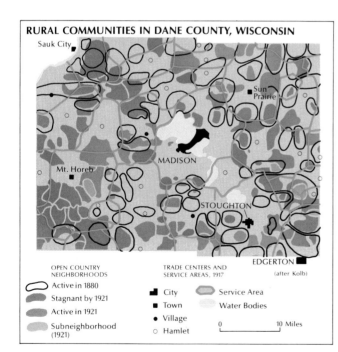

RURAL COMMUNITIES IN DANE COUNTY, WISCONSIN

Sauk City

Sun Prairie

MADISON

Mt. Horeb

STOUGHTON

EDGERTON

OPEN COUNTRY
NEIGHBORHOODS

Active in 1880

Stagnant by 1921

Active in 1921

Subneighborhood
(1921)

TRADE CENTERS AND
SERVICE AREAS, 1917   (after Kolb)

■ City   Service Area

■ Town   Water Bodies

● Village

○ Hamlet   0   10 Miles

MAP 16

Even in newer states like Wisconsin, the passing of the highly prosperous wheat frontier left many people searching for a new agricultural specialization. Between the 1880s and 1920, eastern and southern parts of the state developed an emphasis on dairying, which required intensive labor and a complex marketing network that linked local farms to the nearby cities of Chicago and Milwaukee (Map 15). As a result, the fabric of rural society changed, too. Farm families that had lived in longstanding country neighborhoods now felt the pull of small towns, which offered an increasing number of institutions and services (Map 16).

SPECIALIZED MANUFACTURING TOWNS: Lowell, Massachusetts, 1832

Lawrence Mfg. Co.
Merrimack Mfg. Co.
Suffolk Mfg. Co.
Tremont Mfg. Co.
The Mansion
EPISC. CONG.
Belvidere Village
RIVER STREET
METH. CONG.
Town House
Lowell Mfg. Co.
Hamilton Mfg. Co.
Locks
Pawtucket Falls
CATH.
Middlesex Mfg. Co.
BAP.
Locks
Appleton Mfg. Co.
Pawtucket
CONG.
Massack Falls
Guard Locks
Brewery
UNIV.
METH.
Canal
Railroad
Merrimack River
Concord River
Hales Mills
Whipples Powder Mills

■ Factories	▬ Hotels
▭ Contemplated factories	✚ Churches
▬ Boarding houses	┼┼┼┼ Railroad
▪▪▪ Other company housing	⁃⁃⁃ Other buildings (mostly residences)
■ The Mansion	
■ Town House	𝒹 Locks

0   ¼ Mile

MAP 17

Urban Developments During Industrialization

While new towns were changing the face of the countryside during the later part of the nineteenth century, major American cities were evolving as well. The potent forces behind urban change were industrialization and the associated transportation revolution. As early as the 1820s, specialized manufacturing cities like Lowell, Massachusetts, were created from nothing to accommodate huge factory-scale production (Map 17; see also pp. 267–268). Lowell's design reflected the supremacy of its textile mills; civic and cultural institutions were little more than afterthoughts. In larger and more diversified centers, the demands of both growth and new commercial functions created a distinctive new land-use zone—the multifunctional central business district, which became more efficient with the evolution of specialized subdistricts for finance, markets, ware-

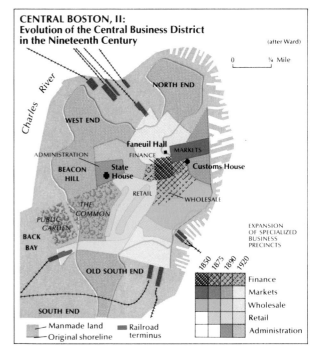

CENTRAL BOSTON, II:
Evolution of the Central Business District in the Nineteenth Century   (after Ward)

0   ¼ Mile

Charles River
NORTH END
WEST END
Faneuil Hall
MARKETS
ADMINISTRATION
FINANCE
Customs House
BEACON HILL
State House
RETAIL
WHOLESALE
THE COMMON
PUBLIC GARDEN
BACK BAY
EXPANSION OF SPECIALIZED BUSINESS PRECINCTS
OLD SOUTH END
SOUTH END
1850 1875 1890 1920

	Finance
	Markets
	Wholesale
	Retail
	Administration

▬ Manmade land   ▬ Railroad terminus
— Original shoreline

MAP 18

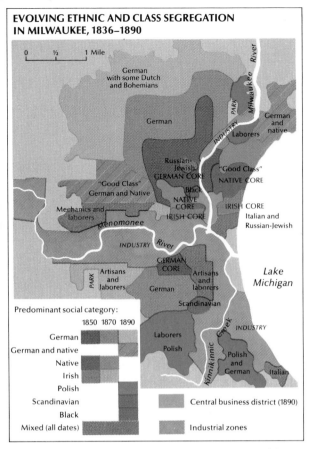

EVOLVING ETHNIC AND CLASS SEGREGATION IN MILWAUKEE, 1836–1890

0   ½   1 Mile

German with some Dutch and Bohemians

German

PARK

Milwaukee River

INDUSTRY

German and native

Laborers

Russian-Jewish GERMAN CORE

"Good Class" NATIVE CORE

"Good Class" German and Native

Black NATIVE CORE

IRISH CORE

Mechanics and laborers

Menomonee

IRISH CORE

Italian and Russian-Jewish

INDUSTRY

River

GERMAN CORE

PARK

Artisans and laborers

German

Artisans and laborers

Scandinavian

Lake Michigan

INDUSTRY

Kinnikinnic Creek

Laborers

Polish

Polish and German

Italian

Predominant social category:

	1850	1870	1890
German			
German and native			
Native			
Irish			
Polish			
Scandinavian			
Black			
Mixed (all dates)			

Central business district (1890)

Industrial zones

Map 19

housing, and so on (Map 18). This central district became even more important with the advent of railroads, which began to link cities together in the years before the Civil War.

The growth of central business districts was just one manifestation of the urban transformation. Another was the segregation of neighborhoods by ethnic group and social class. Partly because of streetcars, first horse-drawn and later electrified, which opened up new areas to daily commuting, cities developed many residential districts where one or more social group predominated; movement in and out of these districts mirrored ethnic assimilation and class mobility (Map 19). Especially noteworthy were the new districts of middle-class suburban housing, like the Garden District of New Orleans, that were made possible by the rapid growth of streetcar service (Map 20).

In the West, railroads were at once the promoters, predictors, and managers of growth. In the Dakotas, for example, whole networks of towns were planted and nurtured by the Chicago, Milwaukee and St.

Map 20

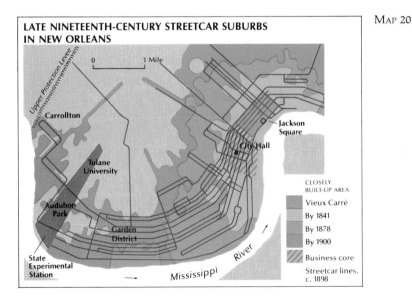

LATE NINETEENTH-CENTURY STREETCAR SUBURBS IN NEW ORLEANS

0   1 Mile

Upper Protection Levee

Carrollton

Jackson Square

City Hall

Tulane University

Audubon Park

Garden District

State Experimental Station

Mississippi River

CLOSELY BUILT-UP AREA

Vieux Carré

By 1841

By 1878

By 1900

Business core

Streetcar lines, c. 1898

Paul Railway Company, with different localities earmarked for different levels of future urban development (Map 21).

Modern Transformations

By World War I, as a result of such developments, the national urban system was complex and extensive. Almost every area of the country had a well-defined city system (Map 22). The pattern of major cities reflected the continued dominance of the older Eastern seaport cities, the maturation of Midwestern commercial and industrial cities (to form the nation's traditional Northeastern manufacturing belt), and the rise of Southern and Western centers of regional service and long-distance trade.

One of the most vexing consequences of urbanization has been political fragmentation at the local level. Chicago's growth, for example, has been frustrated by suburban resistance to annexation by the metropolis (Map 23). As a result, the efforts to solve

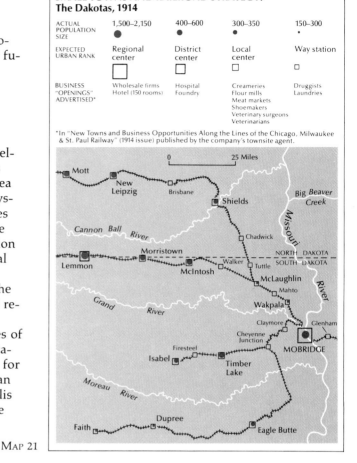

SMALL TOWNS AND RAILROAD STRATEGY:
The Dakotas, 1914

ACTUAL POPULATION SIZE	1,500–2,150	400–600	300–350	150–300
EXPECTED URBAN RANK	Regional center	District center	Local center	Way station
BUSINESS "OPENINGS" ADVERTISED*	Wholesale firms Hotel (150 rooms)	Hospital Foundry	Creameries Flour mills Meat markets Shoemakers Veterinary surgeons Veterinarians	Druggists Laundries

*In "New Towns and Business Opportunities Along the Lines of the Chicago, Milwaukee & St. Paul Railway" (1914 issue) published by the company's townsite agent.

MAP 21

MAP 22

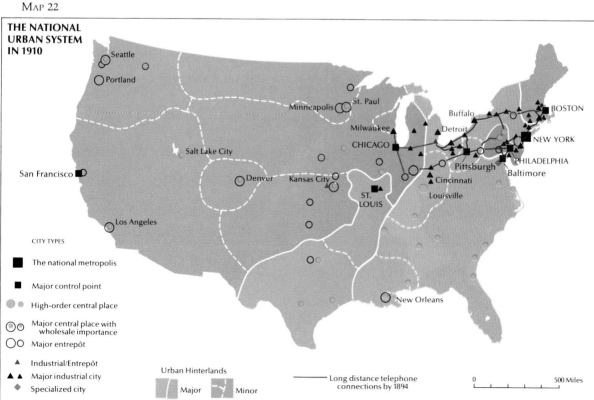

THE NATIONAL URBAN SYSTEM IN 1910

CITY TYPES

■ The national metropolis

■ Major control point

● High-order central place

◉● Major central place with wholesale importance

○○ Major entrepôt

▲ Industrial/Entrepôt

▲▲ Major industrial city

◆ Specialized city

Urban Hinterlands
Major   Minor

Long distance telephone connections by 1894

0   500 Miles

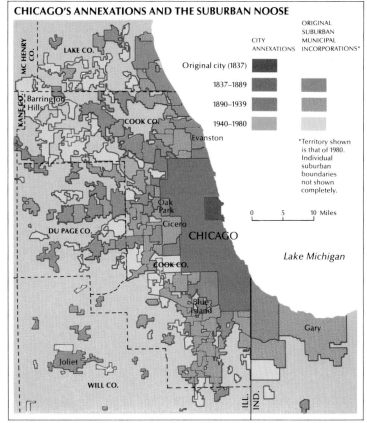

MAP 23

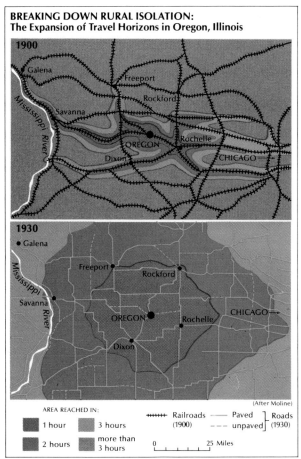

BREAKING DOWN RURAL ISOLATION:
The Expansion of Travel Horizons in Oregon, Illinois

(After Moline)

AREA REACHED IN:

- 1 hour
- 2 hours
- 3 hours
- more than 3 hours

++++ Railroads (1900)

— Paved (1930) Roads
--- unpaved (1930)

0 | | | | | 25 Miles

MAP 24

problems that affect entire metropolitan areas have led to both inefficiency and conflict, although many suburban dwellers have maintained a controlling voice in their immediate local environments.

The transportation revolution that spurred urban growth also transformed the rural scene. In the nineteenth century, railroads had strengthened the links between rural settlements and the outside world, and within decades, these bonds were vastly intensified by the automobile. For example, in 1900, travel to and from the town of Oregon, Illinois, was heavily dependent on train routes and schedules. By 1930, though, the car had brought a far greater territory within the same potential travel time at the convenience of the family (Map 24). Auto travel had become so widespread by 1950 that large cities developed not only huge commuting regions but also outer, exurban rings. By 1970, the urban centers of the Eastern seaboard were well on the way toward complete physical merger in one long

MEGALOPOLIS MATURES, 1950–1970

(after Browning)

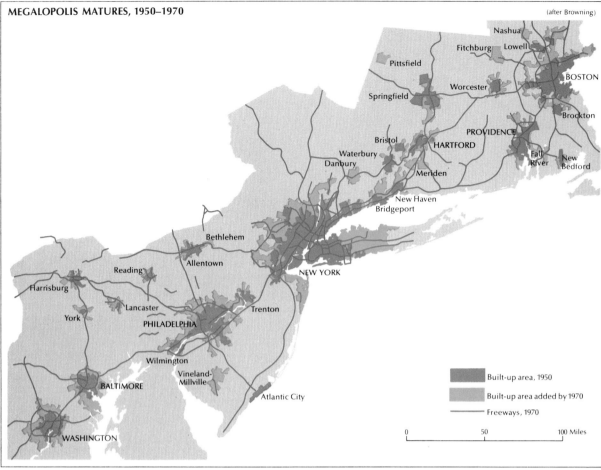

Nashua
Fitchburg Lowell
Pittsfield
BOSTON
Worcester
Springfield
Brockton
PROVIDENCE
Bristol
HARTFORD
Waterbury
Danbury
Fall
River
New
Bedford
Meriden
New Haven
Bridgeport
Bethlehem
Allentown
Reading
NEW YORK
Harrisburg
Lancaster
Trenton
York
PHILADELPHIA
Wilmington
Vineland-
Millville
BALTIMORE
Atlantic City
WASHINGTON

	Built-up area, 1950
	Built-up area added by 1970
——	Freeways, 1970

0   50   100 Miles

MAP 25

MAP 26

RISE OF CORPORATE FARMING AND IRRIGATION DEPENDENCY

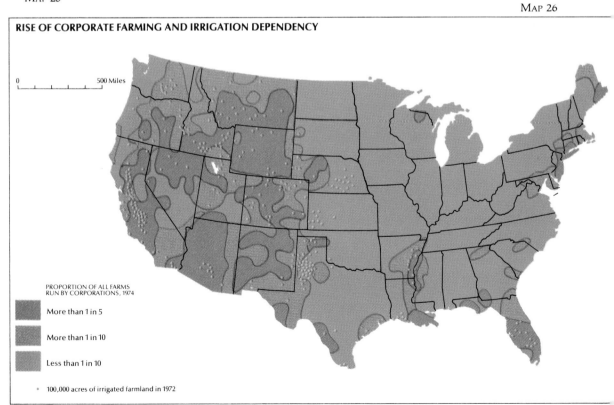

0   500 Miles

PROPORTION OF ALL FARMS
RUN BY CORPORATIONS, 1974

More than 1 in 5

More than 1 in 10

Less than 1 in 10

• 100,000 acres of irrigated farmland in 1972

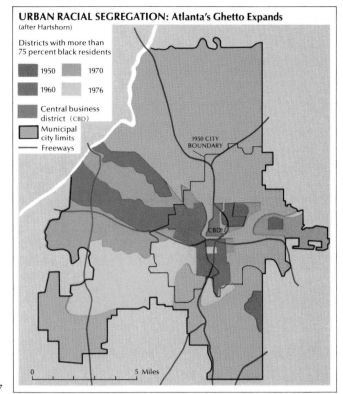

URBAN RACIAL SEGREGATION: Atlanta's Ghetto Expands
(after Hartshorn)

Districts with more than
75 percent black residents

1950   1970

1960   1976

Central business
district (CBD)

Municipal
city limits

Freeways

1950 CITY
BOUNDARY

CBD

0   5 Miles

MAP 27

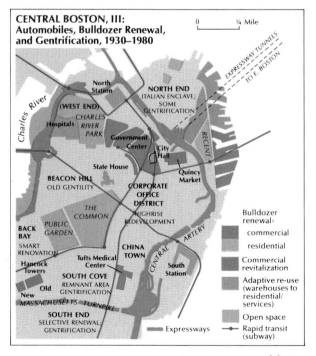

CENTRAL BOSTON, III:
Automobiles, Bulldozer Renewal,
and Gentrification, 1930–1980

0   ¼ Mile

EXPRESSWAY TUNNELS
TO E. BOSTON

North
Station

NORTH END
ITALIAN ENCLAVE;
SOME
GENTRIFICATION

Charles River

(WEST END)
CHARLES
RIVER
PARK

Hospitals

Government
Center

City
Hall

RECENT

State House

Quincy
Market

BEACON HILL
OLD GENTILITY

CORPORATE
OFFICE
DISTRICT

HIGHRISE
REDEVELOPMENT

THE
COMMON

CENTRAL ARTERY

BACK
BAY

PUBLIC
GARDEN

CHINA
TOWN

SMART
RENOVATION

Tufts Medical
Center

South
Station

Hancock
Towers

SOUTH COVE

Old   REMNANT AREA
New   GENTRIFICATION

MASSACHUSETTS TURNPIKE

SOUTH END
SELECTIVE RENEWAL;
GENTRIFICATION

Bulldozer
renewal:

commercial

residential

Commercial
revitalization

Adaptive re-use
(warehouses to
residential/
services)

Open space

Expressways

Rapid transit
(subway)

MAP 28

belt that has been called Megalopolis (Map 25).

Another trend that has affected many agricultural communities is the application of industrial methods to farming. In the West, for example, large-scale irrigation has extended crop production to regions that were previously too dry—and has heightened problems of overall water supply (Map 26). And the heavy capitalization needs of modern farming have resulted in the rise of corporate farming (agribusiness), heavily concentrated in the irrigated West, the cotton and sugar areas of the lower Mississippi basin, and the specialty crop areas of Florida and the Eastern seaboard.

Since World War II, no social problem in urban America has been more pressing than persistent residential segregation by race. Complex forces (see p. 863), including the movement of middle-class whites to suburban and exurban areas, have encouraged the growth of black and Hispanic ghettoes to the point that they constitute significant portions of the central cities (Map 27). And the inner cities have undergone other important changes in this same

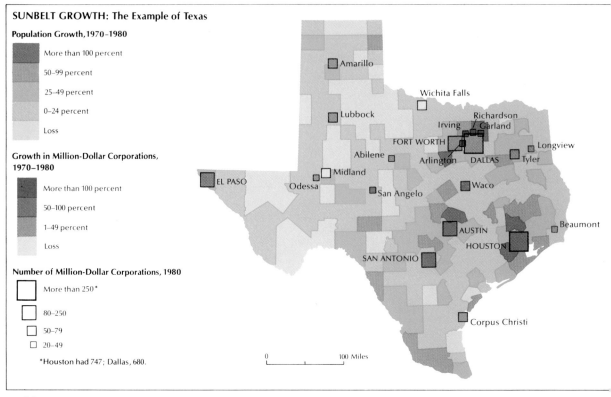

SUNBELT GROWTH: The Example of Texas

Population Growth, 1970–1980

- More than 100 percent
- 50–99 percent
- 25–49 percent
- 0–24 percent
- Loss

Growth in Million-Dollar Corporations, 1970–1980

- More than 100 percent
- 50–100 percent
- 1–49 percent
- Loss

Number of Million-Dollar Corporations, 1980

- More than 250*
- 80–250
- 50–79
- 20–49

*Houston had 747; Dallas, 680.

Amarillo

Wichita Falls

Lubbock

Richardson

Irving / Garland

FORT WORTH

Abilene

Longview

Arlington DALLAS Tyler

Midland

EL PASO Odessa

San Angelo

Waco

Beaumont

AUSTIN

HOUSTON

SAN ANTONIO

Corpus Christi

0   100 Miles

Map 29

period—urban renewal, expressway construction, and, most recently, commercial revitalization and gentrification (Map 28; see also p. 970). In Boston, for example, major redevelopments since the 1930s have dramatically changed what was the nineteenth-century city center; little more than the street system remains from the colonial period. But such vitality will be difficult for cities like Boston to maintain in the face of population shifts not only to the suburbs but also to more economically healthy regions; much urban-regional growth since 1970 has favored the "Sunbelt" (Map 29; see also pp. 969–970).

Today, then, the American landscape is in a state of flux. Will the older Northeastern cities regain their former economic buoyancy? Are the booming cities of the Sunbelt destined to suffer problems associated with speedy growth and equally rapid decline? Whatever the answers, there is little doubt that contrasts in American settlement patterns will remain as a legacy of geographical diversity, historical background, and many agents of change.

PART ONE

The New World, to 1775

For thousands of centuries—centuries in which human races were evolving, forming communities, and building the beginnings of national civilizations in Africa, Asia, and Europe—the continents we know as the Americas stood empty of mankind and its works. The human species was not born to the Western Hemisphere. It had to find it. And it did so in two great waves of immigration: the first from Asia, beginning between 25,000 and 40,000 years ago; the second from Europe and Africa, beginning in the sixteenth century. For humans at least, the Americas were indeed what awestruck Europeans of 400 years ago called them: the New World.

The story of this new world is unlike that of any other part of the globe. It is a story of immigrants: of men and women of courage, vision, ambition, often greed; of people enchanted by the promise of an unknown land or driven by a desire to escape the hardships of the land they knew. It is a story of thousands, and then millions, who left behind everything that was comfortable, familiar, and predictable to seek a future in a world that was strange, sometimes hostile, and always challenging. It is a story of the creation of a civilization where none existed.

About the earliest wave of human settlement in the New World we know little. The first men and women arrived in America many millennia ago, in what is now western Alaska. They were, presumably, nomadic hunters from eastern Siberia, and they crossed the narrow Bering Strait to the new land a few at a time, year after year, spreading southward until they had peopled much of North, Central, and South America. In some places, they created brilliant civilizations. South America, whose population had climbed to at least 6 million by the fifteenth century, produced the elaborate society of the Incas in Peru. In Central America and Mexico, where 3 million people lived by 1500, the Mayas and then the Aztecs created two of the world's most dazzling cultures. Isolated from contact with the flourishing civilizations of other continents, these early Americans continued to lack some of mankind's most basic tools and technologies. At the beginning of the sixteenth century, no American society had yet discovered the wheel. But there did emerge in the New World sophisticated and successful forms of social organization.

In other regions, including most of the territories that now constitute the United States, the accomplishments of the earliest inhabitants were more modest. Many continued to live as hunters, moving in tribes from place to place in search of prey. Some were by the fifteenth century beginning to establish primitive agricultural societies and, in a few places, permanent settlements that vaguely resembled cities. But in all the lands north of Mexico, still only about a million people resided. And so whereas the first Europeans to arrive in South and Central America encountered strong, well-established national cultures, those who traveled to the lands farther north found a sparsely populated wilderness in which civilization was as yet only slightly advanced.

It was this second wave of settlement, spearheaded first by the Spanish and Portuguese and then by the French, the Dutch, and above all the British—and by the African tribespeople they forcibly transported with them—that produced the American civilizations we now know. In the areas of Hispanic settlement, those civilizations emerged through a long, slow blending of European culture with that of native societies. In most of North America, European settlers made little effort to absorb the existing population. Instead, they isolated themselves from the natives, destroyed them when they thought it necessary, and attempted to create a society entirely their own.

They did not intend it to be a new civilization. They hoped, rather, to re-create in the New World the societies they had left behind in the Old—improved versions of them, perhaps, but not radically different. Gradually, however, the task proved impossible. In countless ways, large and small, often unnoticed, life in the new land forced the settlers to alter their established customs, patterns, and ideas. Always they found it necessary to adjust to conditions for which their prior experiences had not prepared them. And in the process there emerged an American civilization that, for all its familiar features, differed fundamentally from its European forebears.

It is the perilous, often heroic, and occasionally foolhardy efforts of these early settlers to create a society for themselves in an alien land, and the long, slow process of adaptation to the New World of their descendants, that constitute the story of the first phase of American history. Out of these struggles emerged the institutions, the customs, and the beliefs that would shape much of the nation's future.

From the Old World to the New

NOVA BRITANNIA.

OFFERING MOST

Excellent fruites by Planting in
VIRGINIA.

Exciting all ſuch as be well affected
to further the ſame.

LONDON
Printed for SAMVEL MACHAM, and are to beſold at
his Shop in Pauls Church-yard, at the
Signe of the Bul-head.
1 6 0 9.

Nova Britannia, 1609
This title page for a pamphlet by Robert Johnson, which extols the virtues of settlement in the New World, is indicative of the excitement that the possibilities of colonization in America created among Englishmen in the early seventeenth century. Most accounts of the "excellent fruites" of life in Virginia were, like this one, written by men who had never seen the New World. The actual settlers of the first English plantations in America had a far more dismal story to tell of conditions there. (New York Public Library/Picture Collection)

Europeans were almost entirely unaware of the existence of the Americas before the fifteenth century. A few early wanderers—Leif Ericson, an eleventh-century Norseman, and perhaps others—had glimpsed parts of the New World and had given evidence that Europeans were capable of crossing the ocean to find it. But even had their discoveries become common knowledge (and they did not), there would have been little incentive for others to follow. Europe in the Middle Ages (A.D. 500–1500) was not an adventurous civilization. Divided into innumerable small duchies and kingdoms, its outlook was overwhelmingly provincial. Dominated by subsistence agriculture, its commerce was limited; few merchants looked beyond the boundaries of their own regions. Although the Roman Catholic church exercised a measure of spiritual authority over most of the Continent, and although the Holy Roman Empire provided at least a nominal political center, power was for the most part so widely dispersed that no single leader was capable of launching great ventures.

Gradually, however, both the economic and the political life of Europe changed, so that by the late fifteenth century interest in overseas exploration had grown. Commerce began to flourish as Europeans became aware of the exotic cloths, dyes, and spices of Asia and as a new merchant class emerged to develop the new trade with the East. Advances in navigation and shipbuilding spurred the expansion of maritime trade; and in western Europe, whose access to the riches of Asia was limited because of the long, arduous land journey east, the dream of finding a sea route to the Orient—by sailing west across what most assumed was the empty and relatively narrow Atlantic Ocean—began to grow.

Paralleling the commercial revolution was a dramatic change in the political organization of Europe. In the western areas of the Continent in particular, where the authority of the distant pope and the even more distant Holy Roman emperor were necessarily weak, strong nation-states were beginning to emerge. Kings and queens of broad authority and substantial wealth were consolidating their power and becoming eager to use it to enhance the commercial growth of their nations. They listened avidly to those merchants and sailors who spoke of the benefits of a western sea route to Asia. And by the late fifteenth century, they were ready to finance daring voyages of discovery—voyages that would reveal, to the astonishment of nearly everyone, a vast new world.

THE SPANISH EMPIRE

The first European discovery of the American continents, and the first European settlements there, originated from the countries of the Iberian peninsula: first Portugal and then, with much greater result, Spain. Because of geography, both nations had a natural interest in navigation and the sea. And because of strong central governments, both had ample incentive for exploration. Although at first the New World appeared to them little more than an irritating obstacle to the Orient, by the early sixteenth century they were creating a vast and profitable new empire there. Unlike the British, who would establish an empire of their own in North America a century later, the early Spanish and Portuguese colonists saw their new territories less as places to build new societies than as places to exploit for quick and easy wealth. And their presence in South America, Central America, and Mexico, therefore, took on a fundamentally different character from that of the colonies farther north that would ultimately become the United States.

Voyages of Discovery

At first, it was Portugal that devoted the most energy and resources to exploration. Its maritime supremacy owed a great deal to one man, Prince Henry the Navigator, who devoted his life to nautical studies and to the promotion of exploration. Concentrating upon the western coast of Africa, with the visionary aim of establishing a Christian empire to aid in war against the Moors, and with the more practical object of finding gold, Prince Henry sent out expedition after expedition, some of his mariners going as far south as Cape Verde. After his death in 1460, his work was carried on by intrepid explorers advancing still farther south. At last, in 1486, Bartholomeu Díaz went clear around the southern tip of the continent, and in 1497–1498 Vasco da Gama proceeded all the way to India. In 1500, the next fleet bound for India, that of Pedro Cabral, was blown off its southward course and happened upon the coast of Brazil. So America would have been discovered within a decade even if Columbus had never made his famous voyage of 1492.

Christopher Columbus, who was born and reared in Genoa, Italy, obtained most of his seafaring knowledge and experience in the service of the Portuguese. He was not the first man to consider reaching the East by sailing west, but he was the first to act on the idea. Columbus was an industrious student of geography, and his wide readings convinced him that the Atlantic could provide easier passage to the Orient than either the existing land routes to the East or the arduous sea route around southern Africa. But in reality, Columbus's optimism rested on several basic misconceptions. He concluded that the world was far smaller than it actually is. And he believed that the Asian continent extended farther eastward than it actually does. He assumed, therefore, that the western ocean was narrow enough to be crossed on a relatively brief voyage. It never occurred to him that anything lay between Europe and the lands of Asia.

Columbus failed to convince the leaders of Portugal of the feasibility of his plan; instead, the Portuguese concentrated on establishing their route to the East around Africa and gradually lost interest in the idea of a westward crossing. So Columbus turned from Portugal to Spain. Although the Spaniards were not yet as advanced a maritime people as the Portuguese, they were proud, energetic, and ambitious. They were being unified under the strongest monarchy in Europe, the product of the marriage of the two most powerful regional rulers, Ferdinand of Aragon and Isabella of Castile.

Columbus appealed to Queen Isabella for support—men, money, and ships—for his proposed western voyage. The project would, he told her, extend the sway of Christianity to new lands and expand the power and glory of Spain. At first, however, the queen was more interested in consolidating both Christianity and her own power at home. Not until 1492 did she feel secure enough to turn her gaze to foreign ventures. In that year, the Moorish stronghold of Granada fell to the Spanish armies, and the last Mohammedans were driven from the country. That same year, Spanish Jews—the only other significant non-Christian element in the population—were forced either to convert to Christianity or to leave Spain. Confident now of her position within her own nation, Isabella finally granted Columbus his request.

Commanding ninety men and three ships—the *Niña*, the *Pinta*, and the *Santa Maria*—Columbus sailed west into the Atlantic on what he thought was a straight course for Japan. Ten weeks later, he sighted land and assumed he had reached his target. In fact, he had landed on Watling Island in the Bahamas. When he pushed on and landed in Cuba, he assumed he had reached China. He returned to Spain in triumph, bringing with him several natives as evidence of his achievement. (He called the natives "Indians" because they were, he believed, from the East Indies in the Pacific.)

Columbus did not, however, bring back to Spain any news of the great khan's court in China; nor did he carry any samples of the famous wealth of the Indies. And so a year

The Landing of Columbus
This nineteenth-century depiction of Christopher Columbus and other members of his
expedition setting foot in the Western Hemisphere for the first time (on Watling Island, or San
Salvador, in the West Indies), undoubtedly idealizes both the piety and the costumery of the
exhausted group. But the combination of patriotic zeal (as symbolized by the flag of the
Spanish monarchy) and Catholic enthusiasm (as denoted by the crucifix) was crucial to
inspiring and sustaining the early expeditions to the New World. (Library of Congress)

later, he tried again, this time with a much
larger expedition. As before, he headed into
the Caribbean, discovering several other islands and leaving a small colony on one of
them: Hispaniola. On a third voyage, in 1498,
he cruised along the northern coast of South
America. When he passed the mouth of the
Orinoco River, he concluded for the first time
that what he had discovered was not in fact
an island off the coast of China, as he had assumed, but a separate continent; such a large
freshwater stream could, he realized, emerge

only from a large body of land. Still, he remained convinced that Asia was only a short
distance away. And although he failed in his
efforts to sail around the northwestern coast
of South America through to the Indies (he
was blocked by the Isthmus of Panama), he
returned to Spain believing he had explored
at least the fringes of the Far East. He continued to believe that until the day he died.

At first a hero, Columbus ended his life in
obscurity. And in the end he was even denied
the honor of giving his name to the land he

had discovered. That honor went instead to a Florentine merchant, Amerigo Vespucci, a passenger on a later Portuguese expedition to the New World who wrote a series of vivid (if largely fictitious) descriptions of the lands he visited.

Yet Columbus, for all his misconceptions, deserved the fame that ultimately came to him. He dispelled the terrors of the unknown ocean and led the way to the New World. The explorers of many nations who followed him were only carrying on the work he had begun. Just as he had done on his final voyage, they concentrated their efforts mainly on the search for a water passage that would lead through or around the new lands and on to the riches of the Far East. They never found the kind of passage they sought (because it did not exist until 1914, when the Panama Canal was opened), but they revealed the outlines of both continents and

made known the vastness of the territory available for European use.

Spain, turning to the sea as a result of Columbus's initiative, replaced Portugal as the foremost exploring nation. Vasco de Balboa fought his way across the Isthmus of Panama (1513) and gazed upon the great ocean that separated America from China and the Indies. Seeking access to that ocean, Ferdinand Magellan, a Portuguese in Spanish employ, found the strait that now bears his name at the southern end of South America, struggled through the stormy narrows and into the ocean, so calm by contrast that he christened it the Pacific, then proceeded to the Philippines. There Magellan fell at the hands of natives, but his expedition went on to complete the first circumnavigation of the globe (1519–1522). By 1550, Spaniards had explored the coasts of North America as far north as Oregon and Labrador.

THE LANDS THAT COLUMBUS SAW ON HIS FOUR VOYAGES

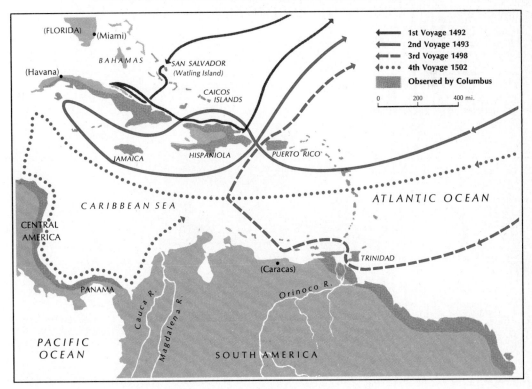

The Colonizing Impulse

Gradually, Spanish explorers in the New World stopped thinking of America simply as an obstacle to their search for a route to the East. They began instead to consider it a possible source of wealth rivaling and even surpassing the original Indies. On the basis of Columbus's discoveries (and with the aid of a papal decree), the Spanish claimed for themselves the whole of the New World, ex- cept for a chunk of it (Brazil) that they left to the Portuguese. And by the mid-sixteenth century, they were well on their way to es- tablishing a substantial American empire.

Awaiting the Spaniards were the riches of the native Aztec and Inca empires. The Aztecs were not the first to establish a great civilization in Middle America. In Yucatan and Central America, the Mayas had built elaborately carved stone temples and pyra- mids, bred corn from a kind of wild grass,

---

Tenochtitlán—The Aztec Capital

This is a model reconstructing the central square of Tenochtitlán. This city, located on the site of present-day Mexico City, had a population of about 100,000 in 1502, when the last of the emperors, Montezuma II, began his reign. His empire, covering much of central and southern Mexico, was a rather loose association of city-states from which he collected heavy tribute. The Aztecs developed a complex and magnificent civilization, made up largely of elements adapted from the Mayas and other neighboring peoples. In Tenochtitlán there were surgeons and physicians who are believed to have been as skillful as the best in contemporary Europe, and there were hospitals and nurses. There were also human sacrifices. To appease the Aztec gods, young men and women captives were slaughtered on top of the pyramids. These structures, like those of the Mayas, were comparable in size to the pyramids of ancient Egypt but were used as temples rather than burial monuments. When Hernando Cortés, the Spanish conqueror of Mexico, entered Tenochtitlán in 1519, he found in the central square a rack that held the skulls of about 100,000 sacrificial victims. (Courtesy of The American Museum of Natural History)

devised an accurate calendar from astronomical observations, and invented a number system similar to the Arabic and superior to the Roman. The Mayan civilization had declined when, about 1200, the Aztecs moved into the Valley of Mexico and established their capital on the present site of Mexico City, from which they sent out war parties to subdue neighboring peoples and extract tribute from them. From Cuzco in the mountains of Peru, the Incas ruled a more highly centralized and even larger empire, one of the largest of all history, and they constructed thousands of miles of paved roads (or rather pathways, for they had no wheeled vehicles) to hold their empire together.

The early Spanish colonists, beginning with those Columbus brought on his second voyage, settled on the islands of the Caribbean, where they tried without much luck to enslave the Indians and uncover gold. Then (during the same years, 1519–1522, that Magellan's fleet was on its way around the world) Hernando Cortés, one of the greatest and most brutal of the Spanish *conquistadores* (conquerors), ruthlessly destroyed the Aztec empire and looted its treasure. The news of silver to be found in Mexico turned the attention of the Spaniards to the mainland. From the island colonies and from the mother country, fortune hunters descended upon Mexico in a movement comparable in some ways to the nineteenth-century gold rushes elsewhere in the world. When Francisco Pizarro conquered Peru and revealed the wealth of the Incas (1532–1538), the way was opened for a similar advance into South America.

Exploration and colonization in Spanish America was primarily a work of private enterprise, carried on by individual leaders, with little direct support from the government at home. Before a man could undertake the job, he had to get a royal license. By its terms, the king was to have a fifth of the wealth to be produced in the new colony, and the colonizer was to have a tenth—in addition to a generous estate, other lands to divide among his followers, and the right for himself and for them to the use of native labor. But he had to equip and finance his own expedition and take the risk of loss or ruin. He might succeed and make a fortune, or through shipwreck or other accident he might lose everything including his life, as many an adventurer did.

The colonial population came only in small part from Spain itself and scarcely at all from other countries in Europe; for few Spaniards were able or willing to emigrate, and foreigners with a few exceptions were excluded from the colonies. Colonial officials were supposed to bring their wives with them, but among the ordinary settlers men outnumbered women by at least ten to one. Naturally, then, most of the Spanish men married Indian women, and a sizable mixed population grew up. There was nevertheless a manpower shortage, which the Spaniards tried to overcome by forcing the Indians to work for wages. The first experiments with forced labor, as on the island of Hispaniola, resulted in the near extermination of the natives, but Indians continued to work in the mines or on the ranches of the mainland for centuries. As workers on the plantations of the islands and coastal areas, African slaves began to be imported as early as 1502. The African slave trade had been established in Europe by the Portuguese more than fifty years before that.

Most of the first Spaniards to arrive in the New World were interested in only one thing: getting rich. More specifically, they were eager to exploit the American stores of gold and silver. And in that, they were fabulously successful. For three hundred years, beginning in the sixteenth century, the mines in Spanish America yielded more than ten times as much gold and silver as all the rest of the mines in the world. They made Spain for a time the wealthiest and most powerful nation on earth.

Yet of more lasting importance to the future of the New World were the efforts of other Spaniards to create a profitable agricultural economy in America. Those who searched for gold and silver left little behind; those who came to farm helped to establish elements of European civilization in America that would become permanent features of society there. They transferred their language and learning, their tools and mechanical arts, from the homeland to the colonies.

Spanish St. Augustine
St. Augustine, Florida, the oldest city in what
is now the United States, was founded in
1565 by the Spanish explorer Pedro Menendez de Aviles on the site of an old Indian village and near a spot where Ponce de Leon
had landed more than fifty years before. St.
Augustine (named for the saint on whose
name day Menendez entered the harbor)
withstood numerous assaults from the British
before it was finally lost to them in 1763.
After the American Revolution, the city returned to Spanish control, under which it remained until the United States annexed Florida in 1821. (Library of Congress)

They transplanted grains and fruits and vegetables, including wheat, oranges, lemons,
grapes, bananas, olives, and sugar cane. They
introduced domestic animals such as cows,
pigs, mules, and especially horses. The animals soon multiplied and ran wild even beyond the frontiers of the colonies, becoming
accessible to the native tribes of North
America and revolutionizing their way of
life. Above all, perhaps, the Spaniards

brought with them their religion. Priests or
friars accompanied every colonizing venture.
Every settlement became a Christian community. And the gospel of the Catholic church
ultimately extended throughout South and
Central America.

By the end of the sixteenth century, the
Spanish Empire had grown to become one of
the largest in the history of the world. It included the islands of the Caribbean and the
coastal areas of South America that had been
the targets of the first Spanish expeditions. It
extended to Mexico and southern North
America, where the next wave of European
invaders had moved in. The Spanish fort established in 1565 at St. Augustine, Florida,
became the first permanent European settlement in the present-day United States; Spanish missionaries ventured even farther north
in the following years—at times reaching as
far as the Chesapeake Bay. And the Spanish
Empire spread southward and westward as
well: into the land mass of South America—
Chile, Argentina, and Peru—which had been
the target of a third Spanish military thrust.
When in 1580 the Spanish and Portuguese
monarchies united (if only temporarily), Brazil came under Spanish jurisdiction as well.
From California, Florida, and Mexico to Cape
Horn at the tip of South America, Spain's
power stood unchallenged.

It was, however, a colonial empire very
different from the one that would emerge in
North America beginning in the early seventeenth century. Although the Spanish ruled
the New World, they did not people it. In the
first century of settlement, fewer than a quarter of a million European settlers established
themselves in the Spanish colonies. The bulk
of the population of over 9 million people
consisted of natives. The Spanish, in other
words, imposed a small ruling class upon a
large existing population; they did not create
a self-contained European society in the New
World as the British would do in the north.
As the years passed, moreover, the lines
dividing European settlers from the native
population—lines that would seldom be
breached in North America—grew progres-
sively less distinct. Frequent intermarriage—
not only of Europeans with Indians, but of
Europeans and Indians with blacks—pro-

duced a racially mixed society. And although racial distinctions continued to have a bearing upon social status, there was not the same inviolable barrier between whites and nonwhites in South America that would later emerge in the north. Latin American slavery, therefore, although often no less brutal than its northern counterpart, was generally far less rigid and in many cases ultimately less lasting than the North American system.

There were also important political differences between the Spanish Empire in America and the later British version. Although some of the earliest Spanish ventures in the New World had operated largely independent of the throne, by the end of the sixteenth century the monarchy had established an elaborate hierarchical structure by which its authority extended directly into the governance of local communities. Colonists had few opportunities to establish political institutions independent of the Crown. The British administration of North America, by contrast, would be far looser and more casual; and European settlers there would quickly develop a political system in which the Crown often played only an indirect, even nominal role.

There was, finally, an economic difference. The Spanish were far more successful than the British would be in extracting great surface wealth from their American colonies. But for the same reason, they concentrated far less energy on making their colonies profitable agricultural and commercial ventures. The problem was compounded by the unusually strict and inflexible commercial policy of the Spanish government. To enforce the collection of duties and to provide protection against pirates, the government required all trade with the colonies to be carried on through a single Spanish port and only a few colonial ports, in fleets making but two voyages a year. The system stifled economic development of the New World. The British colonies, on the other hand, ultimately produced a large, flexible, and flourishing commercial economy that would sustain prosperity in North America long after the depletion of the gold and silver supplies had begun to debilitate the economies to the south.

ENGLAND LOOKS TO THE WEST

England's first documented contact with the New World came only five years after Spain's. In 1497, John Cabot (like Columbus a native of Genoa) sailed to the northeastern coast of North America under the auspices of King Henry VII. He became the first European to leave a record of having viewed the continent and may therefore have some claim to being its discoverer. Other Englishmen, continuing Cabot's unsuccessful search for a northwest passage through the New World to the Orient, explored other areas of North America during the sixteenth century.

But while England claimed dominion over lands its explorers surveyed, a century passed before Englishmen made any serious efforts to establish colonies there. Only after a series of important changes within England itself could the establishment of an American empire begin.

The Lure of Expansion

Renaissance England, like much of the rest of Europe, was undergoing both an economic and a cultural transformation in the sixteenth century. It was a combination of changes in the nation's economy and in its social outlook that produced interest in overseas settlement.

Part of the attraction of the New World was, of course, its newness. To many Englishmen, therefore, it came to seem a place where mankind could start anew, where a perfect society could be created unencumbered by the flaws and inequities of the Old World. This dream of America as a place of unique opportunity—for liberty, abundance, security, and peace—emerged in England only a few years after Columbus's discovery. The dream found a classic expression in Sir Thomas More's *Utopia*, published in Latin in 1516 and translated into English thirty-five years later. The book described a mythical society on an imaginary island supposedly discovered by a companion of Amerigo Vespucci in the waters of the New World. Life in Utopia was as nearly perfect as human beings guided by reason and good will could make it. The Utopians lived comfortably enough, but they scorned the mere accumulation of material things; and while all were expected to keep busy, none was oppressed or overworked. They enjoyed complete freedom of thought but were careful not to offend one another in the expression of their beliefs. True lovers of peace, they went to war only to defend their neighbors and thereby ensure their own ultimate safety. In presenting such a picture of an ideal community, the book commented indirectly upon the social and economic evils of More's England.

For Tudor England, despite its literary glory (it produced, among much else, the works of Shakespeare) and its swashbuckling spirit, was an economically troubled nation. The bulk of the population suffered not only from the frequent European wars and the almost constant religious strife of their era, but from a harsh economic transformation of their country. The population of England grew steadily in the sixteenth century—from 3 million in 1485 to 4 million in 1603—but the food supply did not increase proportionately. Instead, many landowners were converting their lands from fields for growing crops to pastures for raising sheep. Because neither cotton nor silk had yet emerged as a major source of cloth, the worldwide demand for wool was high. Land tilled at one time by serfs and later by rent-paying tenants, much of it better suited to sheep raising than to the production of food, was steadily enclosed for sheep runs and taken away from the farmers.

Thousands of evicted tenants roamed the countryside in gangs, to the alarm of more fortunate householders, whose feelings are preserved in the nursery rhyme: "Hark, hark! the dogs do bark: the beggars are coming to town." The Elizabethan government passed rather ineffectual laws for halting enclosures, relieving the worthy poor, and compelling the able-bodied or "sturdy beggars" to work. Relatively few of these could find reemployment in raising or manufacturing wool. All the while the cost of living rose, mainly because of an increased money supply arising from the output of Spanish gold and silver mines in America. England, it seemed, contained either too many sheep or too many people.

Amid the widespread distress, a rising class of merchant capitalists prospered from the expansion of foreign trade as they turned from the export of raw wool to the export of woolen cloth. These merchant capitalists gathered up the raw material, put it out for spinning and weaving in individual households, and then sold the finished product both in England and abroad.

At first, each exporter did business on his own, though he might belong to the Company of Merchant Adventurers. This company regulated the activities of its members, secured trading privileges for them, and provided protection for their voyages. In time, chartered companies sprang up, each with a monopoly from the sovereign of England for trading in a particular region. Among them were the Muscovy Company (1555), the Levant Company (1581), the Barbary Company (1585), the Guinea Company (1588), and the East India Company (1600). Some of these were regulated companies, similar to the Merchant Adventurers, each member doing business separately. Others were joint-stock companies, much like modern corporations, with stockholders sharing risk and profit on either single ventures or, as became more common, on a permanent basis. These investors often made fantastic profits from the exchange of English manufactures, especially woolens, for exotic goods, and they felt a powerful urge to continue with the expansion of their profitable trade.

To further this drive, spokesmen for the merchant capitalists developed a set of ideas about the proper relation of government and business—ideas supporting the argument that (notwithstanding the sufferings of the dispossessed) the whole nation benefited from the activities of the overseas traders. The trade of England as a whole, it was said, was basically like that of any individual or

EXPLORATIONS OF SIXTEENTH-CENTURY AMERICA

firm: transactions were worthwhile if sales exceeded purchases in value. The difference in value would have to be paid in money (gold and silver), and the inflow of money into England would stimulate business and strengthen the national economy by raising commodity prices and lowering interest rates. Merchant capitalists depended upon loans to carry on their business, and interest was now considered as a cost of production, whereas in medieval times it had been regarded as sinful usury. According to their theory, the government should act to encourage a "favorable" balance of trade—that is, an excess of exports over imports.

This economic philosophy, restated by

Thomas Mun in his book *England's Treasure by Forraign Trade* (1664), came to be known in the eighteenth century as "mercantilism." It guided the economic policies not only of England but also of Spain, France, and other nation-states.

At first, this mercantilistic program thrived on the basis of England's flourishing wool trade with the European continent, and particularly with the great cloth market in Antwerp. Beginning in the 1550s, however, that glutted market collapsed, and English merchants found themselves obliged to look elsewhere for overseas trade. The establishment of colonies seemed to be a ready answer to the problem. Colonies would also, Englishmen came to believe, serve other useful purposes: the alleviation of poverty and unemployment by siphoning off surplus population, for example. The Oxford clergyman Richard Hakluyt, who published a series of explorers' narratives and an essay (1584) on "western planting," made himself the outstanding propagandist for the establishment of colonies. He and others argued that colonies would provide an additional market for English manufacturers and that the colonial demand would give employment in the mother country to the poor who lived there "idly to the annoy of the whole state." Colonial commerce would bring from the colonies products for which England previously had depended upon foreigners—products such as lumber, naval stores, and above all, silver and gold.

In addition to these economic motives for colonization, there were political and religious ones as well. In 1529, King Henry VIII, angered by the refusal of the pope to grant him a divorce, broke England's ties with the Catholic church and established himself as the head of the Christian faith in his country. After his death, however, the survival of Protestantism remained for a time in doubt, especially when Henry's daughter Mary ascended the throne and restored England's allegiance to Rome. Mary also cemented an alliance between her nation and Spain, an alliance that discouraged Englishmen from exploring the New World for fear of antagonizing the Spanish monarchy.

In 1558, Mary's sister, Elizabeth, became England's queen. She quickly severed once again the nation's connection with the Catholic church and, along with it, the alliance with Spain. Not only did this remove one of the most significant inhibitions to colonization; it added a new motive. English settlements in America could become useful bases for attacking the Spanish Empire, with which England was now engaged in a bitter commercial and naval rivalry.

There was yet another reason for the growing interest in the colonies. The Church of England, in the form it took under Elizabeth I, by no means satisfied all her subjects. It was too Protestant to suit those Englishmen who continued to adhere to the Roman Catholic faith; and it seemed too "popish" to those who most bitterly opposed the ways and influence of Rome. Among these were the Puritans, who, affected in varying degrees by the teachings of John Calvin, wished to "purify" the church. The majority of the Puritans were content to remain within the Anglican fold but hoped to simplify the forms of worship and lessen the power of the bishops, who were appointed by the throne. A minority, the Separatists, were determined to worship as they pleased in their own independent congregations. Like all subjects, however, they were forbidden by law to absent themselves from regular Anglican services or to hold unauthorized religious meetings, and they were taxed to support the established church.

The discontent of the Puritans and other dissenters increased after the death of Queen Elizabeth, the last of the Tudors, and the accession of James I, the first of the Stuarts, in 1603. A Scotsman, James I was looked upon as a foreigner. He was a learned man but a poor politician—the "wisest fool in Christendom," it was said. Convinced that kings ruled by divine right, he made it clear to his subjects at the outset that he intended to govern as he pleased. He soon antagonized the Puritans, who included most of the rising businessmen, by resorting to illegal and arbitrary taxation and also by favoring English Catholics and supporting "high-church" forms of elaborate ceremony. More and more religious nonconformists began to look for places of refuge outside the kingdom.

A variety of factors, then, combined to spur English interest in colonization in the late sixteenth century. There was the mercantile system, which depended on overseas trade and found itself suddenly without sufficient markets. There was a bloated population with many surplus laborers, who served as a potential source of settlers for new colonies. There was a new Protestant monarch and thus new rivalry with Spain, creating interest in challenging the Spanish monopoly in America. And there was a growing number of religious dissenters, unhappy with the Church of England and growing interested in escaping from its grip. By the turn of the century, all these factors were turning England's gaze to the West.

The Wilderness Setting

Awaiting the first English colonists in America was a land and a people. The land was far vaster and more rugged than anything the Englishmen had encountered at home; and its people were both racially and culturally alien to them. Both of these aspects of the North American environment played crucial roles in shaping the English colonies.

Three thousand miles and more from England, the colonies were to be separated from the mother country, and yet connected with it, by the Atlantic Ocean. The sea crossing took from four to twelve weeks or more, in closely packed and often disease-ridden ships that sailed at irregular intervals depending on wind and weather. The distance and the difficulty of ocean travel put the colonists very much upon their own resources once they had landed on the American shore. Nevertheless, the nature of the shoreline and of the terrain behind it inclined them toward the sea, and they kept in touch with the homeland by means of the same ocean they had crossed.

Along much of its extent the coast was, and is, indented with a number of bays and harbors, into each of which flows one or more rivers, giving access to and from the interior. For instance, the Charles leads to Boston harbor at its mouth, the Hudson to New York harbor, the Delaware to Delaware Bay, the Susquehanna and the Potomac and the York and the James (among others) to the Chesapeake Bay, and the Ashley and the Cooper to Charleston harbor. At a time when travel and transportation by water were easier and more economical than by land, the rivers with their tributaries largely determined the lines of settlement and the course of trade.

The area in which the colonies were located is divided lengthwise into three belts at different levels: the coastal plain, the piedmont plateau, and the Appalachian highland. The plain, very narrow in New England but increasing southward from New York to a width of 200 miles in Georgia, is so low that the rivers transversing it flow backward with the incoming tides, and hence it is known (in the South) as the "tidewater" region. The piedmont, 150 miles across at its widest, is several hundred or more feet higher than the plain and is set off from it by the "fall line," an imaginary line drawn through the points at which the rivers descend to the lowland over falls or rapids. From the piedmont, the Appalachian Mountains rise to elevations as high as 6,000 feet in New Hampshire and North Carolina. The mountain barrier is unbroken from New England to Georgia except along the course of the Hudson and Mohawk rivers, but between the various parallel ranges are valleys that allow fairly easy movement along the highland southwestward from Pennsylvania.

Depending upon latitude, elevation, and distance from the sea, the climate in what was English America varies a great deal from place to place, providing most though not all kinds of weather to be found within the Temperate Zone. There is a remarkable contrast between the steamy summers of the South Carolina coast and the snowy winters of the New England interior. Yet the climate on the whole was fairly similar to what Englishmen had known at home, similar enough that they could easily adapt themselves to it.

Soils in America resembled those in England enough to permit the growing of most of the familiar crops, in one place or another. But the soils varied considerably, from the silted river bottoms of the tidewater to the sandy pine barrens on the edge of the upcountry in the South, and from the rich lands of the Susquehanna Valley to the thin topsoil of glacier-scoured New England in the North. Subsoil minerals abounded, especially in the mountains, but most of them—coal, oil, gas—were left for later exploitation. Available in the colonial period were widely scattered deposits of iron ore, both in the mountains and in the lowland bogs. But at that time the most valuable natural resource, other than the soil itself, was the wood that grew upon it and that then served hundreds of industrial uses.

To the first colonists, America was trees. From the Atlantic to the Appalachians and beyond stretched a great forest, unbroken except for occasional small clearings made by the elements or by the Indians, and thick with tall pines, maples, oaks, and countless other varieties of trees as well as shrubs. Even before sighting land the early voyagers to America could sometimes smell the fresh and invigorating forest scent, and once they had disembarked they found themselves in a veritable Garden of Eden, full of birds and beasts for game; flowers, berries, and fruits; and infinite resources of wood. All this made a refreshing contrast with comparatively treeless England, rapidly being deforested to meet the needs of agriculture and industry.

And yet the friendly forest—so green and beautiful, so rich in materials for food and shelter and manufactures of many kinds—also had its uninviting and even hostile aspects. In its shadows lurked the wolves and panthers that devoured the settlers' livestock. In it too lived native tribes who, although at times helpful and welcoming to the newcomers, at other times were hostile and threatening. The forest stood in the way of the frontiersman eager to cultivate the soil, and he had to convert woods into fields by the slow and laborious effort of girdling or else chopping down the trees, burning the dead or downed timber, and eventually uprooting the stumps.

Apart from the great forest, the geographical fact that most distinguished the new country from the old and most influenced the economic development of the colonies was sheer space, the vast extent of

the land. Not that all the land was readily accessible. The need for clearing the forest, the presence of hostile tribes, the dependence upon water transport, and ultimately the difficulty of crossing the mountain barrier—all these considerations hindered the actual occupation of the land. Hence the English settlements, scattered though they might seem, remained on the whole fairly compact throughout the colonial period, at least in comparison with the Spanish and French settlements in the New World, though not in comparison with the crowded towns and countryside of the Old World. There, populations teemed and lacked sufficient room. In America, land was plentiful and people were relatively scarce.

The Woodlands Indians

The native residents of this sparsely populated land were different both from the Europeans who would soon arrive and, to some extent, from each other. The North American Indians (as they would forever be known as a result of Christopher Columbus's misconception) had the general features of their Asian ancestors—yellow or brown skin, straight and coarse black hair, and high cheekbones—but there were minor variations in physical appearance among the numerous tribes. There were greater differences in modes of living and ways of speaking. Hundreds of languages were spoken, but most of them belonged to one or another of about a dozen linguistic stocks. Men of different tribes with related languages could not always understand each other, any more than Frenchmen could understand Spaniards. Nor were such tribes necessarily alike in their cultural patterns.

In 1600, along the Atlantic seaboard south of the St. Lawrence River, there lived about 125,000 Indians. They were most heavily concentrated in southern New England and around the Chesapeake Bay. The largest group, as classified by language type, were the Algonquins, who were scattered from Canada south to Virginia. Next in numbers were the Iroquois, centering in New York and forming a wedge between the northern

Work of the Forest Indians
A Frenchman, J. F. Lafitau, visited North America, studied the customs of the Indians, and described them in a book that was published in Paris in 1724. This one of his sketches shows members of a southeastern tribe weaving, preparing hides, cooking, grating roots, and making corn meal by pounding and winnowing corn. (Bibliothèque Nationale, Paris)

and southern Algonquins. The Iroquois included the "five nations"—Seneca, Cayuga, Onondaga, Oneida, and Mohawk—and also, far to the south, the Cherokees and the Tuscaroras. Still farther south roamed the tribes of the third-largest language group, the Muskogees. These were the Chickasaws, Choctaws, Creeks, and Seminoles.

Most of the tribes carried on a primitive form of agriculture. They made clearings by cutting into trees to kill them and by setting fires in the forest. Among the dead and blackened trunks they planted pumpkins, squash, beans, and corn—crops they had learned of indirectly from the Indians of Mexico and South America. A tribe abandoned its clearing and made a new one when the yields fell, or when the accumulated filth of the village became too deep to endure. The Indian "old fields," especially in New England, attracted incoming settlers as convenient places to begin settlement, and the

newcomers eagerly adopted the cultivation of native crops, above all corn. Without the clearings and the crops that the Indians provided, the Englishmen would have had much greater difficulty than they did in getting a start in the New World.

None of the Indians of the eastern woodlands (or, for that matter, of the entire continent north of Mexico) showed a talent for political organization at all comparable to that of the Aztecs or the Incas. The nearest thing to it was found in the Iroquois league of five nations (which became six nations in 1713, when the Tuscaroras moved north and joined the league). Other tribes had their own separate and rudimentary governments and were often at war with one another or with the Iroquois. From time to time they made alliances or temporary confederations.

The primitive tribal system offered both advantages and disadvantages for the invading Englishmen. On the one hand, the divisions and rivalries among the natives helped the whites to deal with them. If the Indians had been united, they could possibly have driven out the invaders. On the other hand, the disunity of the tribes prevented the English from making such a quick and easy conquest as the Spaniards had made when they got control of Mexico and Peru by simply killing or capturing the native imperial rulers.

To Englishmen, the Indians were of interest as customers for English goods and as suppliers of woodland commodities, especially hides and skins. Thus trade brought the white man and the Indian into contact with one another in a continuing and meaningful way. This commerce generally benefited the English settlers, but it greatly weakened the natives. Indians obtained guns, knives, blankets, and iron pots from the white traders. But they were also introduced to alcohol, which proved debilitating to tribal

life; and they became increasingly dependent upon the Europeans and their commerce, to the detriment of their ability to survive on their own.

Viewed from a distance in England, the American Indian at times seemed like a strong and innocent creature, a noble savage, awaiting only an opportunity to be civilized and Christianized. Some of the colonists continued to look upon the Indian in that light after their arrival in America. By 1619, about fifty missionaries had traveled into the wilds to convert native souls. But most colonists either harbored no such good will toward the natives from the beginning, or changed their image of them quickly. When Indians proved resistant to European efforts to "civilize" them, when in fact they fought against the English incursions into their lands, the white settlers concluded that they were wild beasts fit only to be slaughtered.

AMERICAN INDIANS: APPROXIMATE LOCATIONS OF THE PRINCIPAL
TRIBES IN THE SEVENTEENTH CENTURY

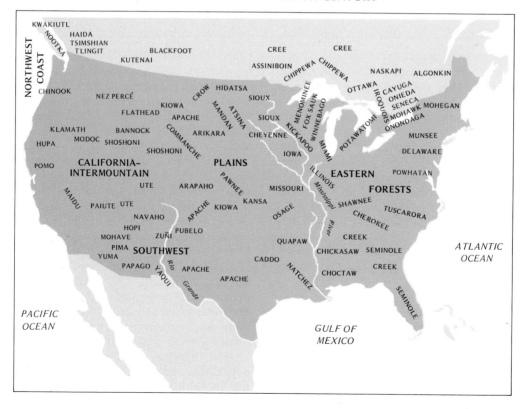

Such assumptions came readily to the English, for they fitted easily into the context of their only prior experience at colonization: Ireland. In the course of the sixteenth century, waves of English invaders had moved across Ireland, capturing territory and attempting to subdue the population. When the Irish resisted, the English quickly came to think of them as vicious savages, a people who could not be tamed and who certainly could not be assimilated into English culture. They must therefore be suppressed, isolated, and if necessary, destroyed.

In English America, therefore, where the same attitudes quickly took root, there was to be no fusion of Indian and European peoples and cultures as there was in the Spanish Empire. From the beginning, the English colonists attempted to transplant their own society to the New World; and unlike the Spanish (and the French), they often came as family groups. Hence the white male settlers of North America had much less occasion to intermarry with the natives than did their Spanish counterparts.

Nevertheless, the Indian civilization had a profound and lasting influence upon the creation of American society. Colonists learned much about agriculture from the natives; the American language became replete with words borrowed from Indian tongues and place names derived from Indian titles; American literature and American thought became colored by numerous elements of Indian lore.

On the whole, however, because the whites viewed the North American Indians not as possible allies in their quest to settle the New World but as an obstacle to that quest, the Indians gradually became the target of a campaign of exploitation, abuse, and ultimately destruction. That campaign would continue into the late nineteenth century and would end with the native population of North America virtually powerless in its own land. Just as the European settlers would attempt to tame and develop the natural wilderness, so they would try to pacify and destroy the Indian population. They would succeed at both, and North America would ultimately become a white man's (and later, as well, a black man's) land.

European Rivals

The English encountered not only native Indian tribes when they arrived in the wilderness, but also rival Europeans. To the south and southwest were the scattered North American outposts of the Spanish Empire, which despite the peace it had negotiated with England in 1604, continued to look on the English as intruders. The English in their settlements along the coast could not for many years feel entirely safe from attack by Spanish ships.

To the north and northwest were beginning to appear the outposts of another and eventually even more dangerous rival, France. The French founded their first permanent settlement in America at Quebec in 1608, less than a year after the English had started their first at Jamestown. New France grew in population very slowly. Few Roman Catholics felt any inclination to leave their beloved homeland, and the discontented Protestants who desired to emigrate were excluded from the colony. To the English in America, however, the French presented a danger disproportionate to their numbers, largely because of their influence upon the Algonquin Indians.

In the Indian trade, the English had the advantage of cheaper goods but the French had an offsetting advantage. While the English in the region generally bought from the Iroquois, who as middlemen secured furs from more remote tribes, the French bypassed the Iroquois and dealt directly with the Algonquins. *Coureurs de bois*, foot-loose and fearless fur traders and trappers, penetrated deep into the interior, made friends with the Indians, lived among them, and married Indian women. Thus the French gained the backing of the Hurons and other Algonquin tribes.

At the same time the French antagonized the Algonquins' traditional foes, the Iroquois. When Samuel de Champlain, founder of Quebec, discovered Lake Champlain and came upon a band of Iroquois (1609), some of his men fired. Terrified by their first experience with guns, the Indians fled. Thus began a historic enmity between the Iroquois and the French. The anti-French feeling of the Iroquois persisted because the Iroquois as middlemen resented the competition of the French in the fur trade. For many years the Iroquois were to look upon their English customers as allies.

Besides the Spanish and the French, the English were soon to find in the New World another European rival, the Dutch. Shortly after the planting of the first two English colonies, at Jamestown and Plymouth, the Dutch began to wedge themselves in be-

tween, when the Dutch West India Company established posts on the Hudson, Delaware, and Connecticut rivers.

The New World, in other words, offered to the English—as it offered to other European peoples—both matchless opportunities and major perils. In the first years of settlement, the perils would often seem to outweigh the opportunities. Gradually, however, the English learned how to live successfully in America.

THE FIRST ENGLISH SETTLEMENTS

The first English attempts to colonize the New World were sporadic, private efforts. There was little planning or direction from the government; instead, the early colonies resulted from the array of economic and social pressures that had been building in England through much of the late sixteenth century. Those pressures not only encouraged the development of colonies; they also helped determine what those colonies would be like.

Three conditions in particular shaped the character of the first English settlements. First, the colonies were business enterprises. They were financed and directed by private companies, to which the colonists were directly responsible. However much the early settlers might have dreamed of a better life in the New World, therefore, one of their first concerns was to produce a profit for their corporate sponsors. Second, because the colonies were tied only indirectly to the Crown (which chartered the private companies but took little interest in them thereafter), they would from the start begin to develop their own political and social institutions. And third, the English colonies, unlike those of the Spanish to the south, would be "transplantations" of societies from the Old World to the New. (Hence the term "plantation," which was used to describe most of the first settlements.) There would be no effort to blend European society with the society of the natives, as there was in many of the Spanish colonies. The English would, as far as they could, isolate themselves from the

Indians and create enclosed societies that would be entirely their own.

Early Attempts

The pioneers of English colonization were Sir Humphrey Gilbert and his half-brother Sir Walter Raleigh, though neither of them succeeded in founding a permanent colony. Both were friends of Queen Elizabeth. While Drake and other "sea dogs" were harrying the Spaniards in the New World and on the seas, Gilbert kept insisting at court that English bases in America would give still greater opportunities for sapping the power of Spain. In 1578, he obtained from Elizabeth a patent granting him, for six years, the exclusive right "to inhabit and possess at his choice all remote and heathen lands not in the actual possession of any Christian prince."

That same year, Gilbert and Raleigh, with seven ships and nearly 400 men, set out to establish a base in the New World. Storms turned them back before they had crossed the ocean. Gilbert waited five years while he sought to raise enough money to try again. Then, in 1583, he sailed with a second and smaller expedition, reached Newfoundland, and took possession of it in the queen's name. He proceeded southward along the coast, looking for a good place to build a military outpost that might eventually grow into a profitable colony, of which he would be proprietor. Once more a storm defeated him; this time his ship sank, and he was lost at sea.

Sir Walter Raleigh
Raleigh was a prominent figure in many aspects of the life of Elizabethan England. He served in the British military effort in Ireland in the 1570s, became a popular and influential favorite in the court of Queen Elizabeth in the 1580s, and served in Parliament in the 1590s—before finally falling into the disgrace that would ultimately lead to his execution in 1618. And Raleigh was also important as one of the major forces behind early English efforts to explore and colonize the New World. (Library of Congress)

The next year, Raleigh, securing from Elizabeth a six-year grant similar to Gilbert's, sent out men to look over the American coast. They returned with two Indians and with glowing reports of an island the natives called Roanoke, and of its environs (in what is now North Carolina). With her permission Raleigh named the area "Virginia" in honor of Elizabeth, the "Virgin Queen." He expected financial aid in return, but she said she could not afford it. So he had to raise money from private investors to finance another voyage to Roanoke. The hundred men he sent out in 1585 spent a year in America, exploring as far north as the Chesapeake Bay, which they recommended as the best location for a settlement.

In 1587, Raleigh sponsored still another expedition, this one carrying ninety-one men, seventeen women (two of them pregnant), and nine children as colonists. He directed them to the Chesapeake Bay, but the pilot nevertheless landed them on Roanoke Island. Here one of the women gave birth to Virginia Dare, the first American-born child of English parents. A relief ship, delayed until 1590 by the hostilities with Spain, found the island utterly deserted. What had become of the "lost colony" is still a mystery.

The colonizing efforts of Gilbert and Raleigh taught lessons and set examples for later and more successful promoters of colonization. After sending out his ill-fated settlers, Raleigh again sought financial aid from merchants, to whom he sold rights of trading with his proposed colony. He realized that the undertaking was too big for the purse of one man alone. Some of the colonizers after him raised funds for their ventures by forming companies and selling stock, but others, as individuals or unincorporated groups, continued to depend on their own resources.

After the accession of James I, Raleigh was accused of plotting against the king, deprived of his monopoly, imprisoned, and eventually executed. None of his successors received grants so vast and undefined as both his and Gilbert's had been. Thereafter the Crown, in theory the owner as well as the sovereign of lands to be occupied by Englishmen, granted and regranted territory to companies or proprietors, on terms that imposed varying conditions and set boundaries that often were conflicting and vague.

A group of London merchants, to whom Raleigh had assigned his charter rights, planned to renew his attempts at colonization in Virginia, which still consisted of an undefined stretch along the Atlantic seaboard. A rival group of merchants, who lived in Plymouth and other West Country towns, were also interested in American ventures. They were already sponsoring voyages of exploration to the coast farther north, up to New-foundland, where West Country fishermen had been going for many years.

In 1606, James I issued a new charter, which divided America between the two groups. The London Company got the exclusive right to colonize in the south (between the 34th and the 41st parallels), and the Plymouth Company the same right in the north (between the 38th and the 45th parallels). These areas overlapped, but neither company was allowed to start a colony within a hundred miles of the other. Each company, as soon as it had begun actual colonization, was to receive a grant of land a hundred miles wide and a hundred miles deep. The settlers themselves were to retain all the "liberties, franchises, and immunities" that belonged to Englishmen at home.

Through the efforts of the London Company (or Virginia Company of London, its full name), the first enduring English colony was about to be planted in America. The merchants, taking the East India Company as their model, intended at the outset to found not an agricultural settlement but a trading post. To it they expected to send English manufactures for barter with the Indians, and from it they hoped to bring back American commodities procured in exchange or produced by the labor of their own employees.

Jamestown

The first English settlers on the North American continent arrived in the spring of 1607. They were the 100 men (the survivors of a group of 144 who had embarked from England) of the London Company's first expedition; and their three ships (the *Godspeed*, the *Discovery*, and the *Susan Constant*) sailed into the Chesapeake Bay and up the James River, on whose banks they established their colony.

They chose their site poorly. Under instructions from the company to avoid the mistakes of Roanoke (whose residents were assumed to have been murdered by Indians) and select an easily defended location, they chose an inland setting that they believed would offer them security. But the site was low and swampy, intolerably hot and humid in the summer and prey to outbreaks of malaria. It was surrounded by thick woods, which were hard to clear for cultivation. And it was soon threatened by hostile Indians of a confederation led by the imperial chief Powhatan.

The result could hardly have been more disastrous. For seventeen years, one after another wave of settlers attempted to make Jamestown a habitable and profitable colony. Every effort failed. The town became instead a place of misery and death; and the London Company, which had sponsored it in the hope of vast profits, saw itself drained of funds and saddled with endless losses. All that could be said of Jamestown at the end of this first period of its existence was that it had survived.

The colonists, too many of whom were adventurous gentlemen and too few of whom were willing laborers, ran into serious difficulties from the moment they landed. They faced an overwhelming task in trying to sustain themselves, and the promoters in London complicated the task by demanding a quick return on their investment. When the men in Jamestown ought to have been growing food, they were required to hunt for gold and to pile up lumber, tar, pitch, and iron ore for export. By January 1608, when ships appeared with additional men and supplies, all but thirty-eight of the first arrivals were dead.

Jamestown, already facing extinction, was carried through the crisis mainly by the efforts of twenty-seven-year-old Captain John Smith, hero of his own narratives of hairbreadth escapes from both Turks and Indians but a sensible and capable man. Leadership in the colony had been divided among the several members of a council who quarreled continually until Smith, as council president, asserted his will. He imposed work and order on the community. During the next winter, fewer than a dozen (in a population of about 200) succumbed. By the summer of 1609, when Smith was deposed from the council and returned to England for the treatment of a serious powder burn, the colony was showing promise of survival, though in fact its worst trials were yet to come.

Captain John Smith
Long before John Smith gained fame as the leader and, as many believe, the savior of the English settlement at Jamestown, Virginia, he had engaged in numerous foreign escapades as a roving adventurer. According to his own immodest accounts, he spent years in eastern Europe fighting in wars against the Turks and was even a slave in Turkey for a time. After returning to England from Virginia in 1609, Smith made at least one additional journey to North America, visiting New England on behalf of a group of London merchants in 1614. In his later years, he wrote numerous books about his experiences, the last of which he completed in 1631, the year of his death.
(Library of Congress)

Already the promoters in London were making a strenuous effort to build up the Virginia colony. To raise money and men, they sold company stock to "adventurers" planning to remain at home, gave shares to "planters" willing to migrate at their own expense, and provided passage for poor men agreeing to serve the company for seven years. Under a new communal plan, the company would hold all land and carry on all

trade for a seven-year period. The settlers would contribute their labor to the common enterprise and draw upon a company storehouse for their subsistence. At the end of the period, the profits would be divided among the stockholders. The London merchants obtained a new charter (1609), which increased their power over the colony and enlarged its area (to a width of 400 miles north and south and a length extending all the way "from sea to sea, west and northwest"). In the spring of 1609, the company sent off to Virginia a "great fleet" of nine vessels with about 600 men, women, and children aboard.

Disaster followed. One of the Virginia-bound ships sank in a hurricane, and another ran aground on one of the Bermuda islands. Many of those who reached Jamestown, still weak from their long and stormy voyage, succumbed to fevers before winter came. That winter of 1609–1610 turned into a "starving time" worse than anything before. While Indians killed off the livestock in the woods and kept the settlers within the palisade, these unfortunates were reduced to eating "dogs, cats, rats, snakes, toadstools, horsehides," and even the "corpses of dead men," as one survivor recalled. When the migrants who had been stranded on Bermuda arrived at Jamestown the following May, they found about 60 scarcely human wretches still alive (there had been nearly 500 people there the previous summer). No one could see much point in staying, and soon all were on their way downriver, leaving the town to its decay.

Yet the colony was to begin again. The refugees met a relief ship coming up the river and were persuaded to go back to Jamestown. This ship was part of a fleet bringing supplies and the colony's first governor, Lord De La Warr. He reestablished the settlement and imposed strict discipline, then went home because of illness, while new relief expeditions with hundreds of colonists began to arrive. De La Warr's successors Thomas Dale and Thomas Gates continued his harsh rule, sentencing offenders to be flogged, hanged, or broken on the wheel. Under Dale and Gates the colony spread, with new settlements lining the river above and below Jamestown. The communal system of labor was not functioning very well, for despite the governors' strictness the lazy often evaded work, "presuming that howsoever the harvest prospered, the general store must maintain them." Before the seven years of the system were up, Dale changed it to allow the private ownership and cultivation of land in return for part-time work for the company and contributions of grain to its storehouses. Meanwhile the cultivators were discovering, in tobacco, a salable crop.

Tobacco had come into use in Europe soon after Columbus's first return from the West Indies, where he had seen the Cuban natives smoking small cigars (*tabacos*), which they inserted in the nostril. In England Sir Walter Raleigh popularized the smoking habit, and the demand for tobacco soared despite objections on both hygienic and economic grounds. Some critics denounced it as a poisonous weed, the cause of many diseases. King James I himself led the attack with *A Counterblaste to Tobacco* (1604), in which he urged his people not to imitate "the barbarous and beastly manners of the wild, godless, and slavish Indians, especially in so vile and stinking a custom." Other critics were concerned because England's tobacco imports came from the Spanish colonies and resulted in the loss of English gold. In 1612, the Jamestown planter John Rolfe began to experiment with the West Indian plant. It grew well in Virginia soil and, though rated less desirable than the Spanish-grown, found ready buyers in England. Tobacco cultivation quickly spread up and down the James.

When the seven-year communal period was up (1616), the company had no profits to divide, but only land and debts. Still, the promoters were generally optimistic because of their success with tobacco. In 1618, they launched a last great campaign to attract settlers and make the colony profitable. They offered a "headright" of fifty acres to anyone who paid his own or someone else's passage to Virginia, and another fifty for each additional migrant whose way he paid. Thus a wealthy man could send or take servants to work for him and receive, in return, a sizable plantation. The company expected to add to its income by charging the headright landholder a small quitrent (one shilling a year

for every fifty acres). Old investors and settlers were given grants of one hundred acres apiece. To make life in the colony more attractive, the company promised the colonists the rights of Englishmen (as provided in the original charter of 1606), an end to the strict and arbitrary rule, and even a share in self-government. To diversify the colonial economy, the company undertook to transport ironworkers and other skilled craftsmen to Virginia.

On July 30, 1619, in the Jamestown church, delegates from the various communities met as the House of Burgesses to consider, along with the governor and his council, the enactment of laws for the colony. This was a major portent of the future—the first meeting of an elected legislature, a representative assembly, within what was to become the United States. A month later, there occurred in Virginia another event with a less happy outcome. As John Rolfe recorded, "about the latter end of August" a Dutch ship brought in "20 and odd Negroes." These black persons were brought, it seems, not as slaves but as servants to be held for a term of years and then freed, like the white servants with whom the planters already were familiar. But whether or not anyone realized it at the time, a start had been made toward the enslavement of Africans within what was to be the American republic.

For several years the Indians had given the Virginia colonists little trouble. A kind of truce had resulted from the capture of the great chief Powhatan's daughter Pocahontas and her marriage (1614) to John Rolfe. Going with her husband on a visit to England, Pocahontas as a Christian convert and a gracious woman stirred up interest in projects to civilize the Indians. She died while abroad. Then Powhatan also died, and his brother Opechancanough replaced him as head of the native confederacy. Under Opechancanough, the Indians pretended to be friendly while laying plans to eliminate the English intruders. On a March morning in 1622, the tribesmen called on the white settlements as if to offer goods for sale, then suddenly turned to killing and were not stopped until 347 whites of both sexes and all ages, including Rolfe, lay dead or dying. The surviving

Indian Attack on Virginia
The arduous early years of white settlement in Virginia were marked not only by the demoralization and apparent indolence of the settlers, but by periodic conflict with hostile Indian tribes. This 1662 illustration of an Indian attack on a Virginia community suggests the terror with which whites viewed the native threat. Whites are depicted here as virtually helpless, while half-naked "savages" slaughter men, women, and children indiscriminately. War canoes filled with still more Indians can be seen heading toward shore in the background, reflecting the whites' awareness that—in the mid-seventeenth century, at least—they were still greatly outnumbered. (New York Public Library, Rare Book Division, Astor, Lenox, and Tilden Foundations)

Englishmen struck back with merciless revenge and gave up all thought of civilizing the aborigines.

The massacre was the final blow to the already staggering London Company, which had poured virtually all its funds into its profitless company and now faced imminent bankruptcy. In 1624, James I revoked the company's charter; and the colony at last came under the control of the Crown. So it would remain until 1776.

The worst of Virginia's troubles were now over. The colony had weathered a series of disasters and had established itself as a permanent settlement. It had developed a cash crop that promised at least modest profits. It had established a rudimentary representative government. And it could now realistically hope for future growth and prosperity. But these successes had come at a high cost. By 1624, the white population of Virginia stood at 1,300. In the preceding seventeen years, more than 8,500 white settlers had arrived in the colony. Over 80 percent of them, in other words, had died.

Plymouth Plantation

While the London Company was starting the colonization of Jamestown, the Plymouth Company attempted to found a colony far to the north, at the mouth of the Kennebec River (on the coast of what is now Maine). But in a year the surviving colonists returned to England. The Plymouth Company made no further effort to colonize. The most it did was to send Captain John Smith, after his return from Jamestown, to look over its territory. He drew a map of the area, wrote an enthusiastic pamphlet about it, and named it "New England." Eventually the Plymouth merchants reorganized as the Council for New England and, with a new, sea-to-sea land grant from the king, proceeded to deal in real estate on a tremendous scale.

The first enduring settlement in New England—the second in English America—resulted from the discontent of a congregation of Puritan Separatists. From time to time Separatists had been imprisoned and even executed for persisting in their defiance of the government and the Church of England. A band of them in the hamlet of Scrooby looked to Holland as a country where they might worship as they pleased, though it was against the law to leave the realm without the king's consent. Slipping away a few at a time, members of the Scrooby congregation crossed the English Channel and began their lives anew in Holland. Here they were allowed to meet and hold their services without interference. But, as aliens, they were not allowed to join the Dutch guilds of craftsmen, and so they had to work long and hard at unskilled and poorly paid jobs. They were

further troubled as their children began to speak Dutch, marry into Dutch families, and lose their Englishness. Some of the Puritans decided to move again, this time across the Atlantic, where they might find opportunity for happier living and also for spreading "the gospel of the Kingdom of Christ in those remote parts of the world."

Leaders of this group got permission from the London Company to settle as an independent community with land of its own in Virginia. They tried, and failed, to get from James I a guarantee of religious freedom, but they were assured that he would "not molest them, provided they carried themselves peaceably." This was a historic concession on the part of the king, for it opened English America to settlement by dissenting Protestants. The next step was to arrange financing. Several English merchants agreed to advance the necessary funds, on the condition that a communal plan like that of Jamestown be put into effect, with the merchants to share the profits at the end of seven years.

The migrating Puritans "knew they were pilgrims" when they left Holland, their leader and historian, William Bradford, later wrote. The sailing from Plymouth was delayed, and it was not until September that the *Mayflower*, with thirty-five "saints" (Puritan Separatists) and sixty-seven "strangers" aboard, finally put out to sea. Their destination was probably the mouth of the Hudson River, in the northeast corner of the London Company's Virginia grant, but when they sighted Cape Cod in November, it was too late in the year to go on. After reconnoitering, they chose a site in an area that John Smith had labeled "Plymouth" on his map. Since this area lay outside the London Company's territory, they would be without a government once ashore, and some of the "strangers" began to show a lawless spirit. One of the "saints" therefore drew up an agreement, which forty-one of the passengers signed. This Mayflower Compact was like the church covenant by which the Separatists formed congregations, except that it set up a civil government, and it professed allegiance to the king. Then, on December 21, 1620, the Pilgrims landed at Plymouth Rock.

The Mayflower Compact [1620]

In the name of God, Amen. We, whose names are underwritten, the Loyal Subjects of our dread Sovereign Lord King James, by the Grace of God, of Great Britain, France, and Ireland, King, Defender of the Faith, & Having undertaken for the Glory of God, and Advancement of the Christian Faith, and the Honour of our King and Country, a Voyage to plant the first colony in the northern Parts of Virginia; Do by these presents, solemnly and mutually in the Presence of God and one another, covenant and combine ourselves together into a civil Body Politick, for our better Ordering and Preservation, and Furtherance of the Ends aforesaid; And by Virtue hereof do enact, constitute, and frame, such just and equal Laws, Ordinances, Acts, Constitutions, and Offices, from time to time, as shall be thought most meet and convenient for the general Good of the Colony; unto which we promise all due Submission and Obedience.

They settled on cleared land that had been an Indian village until, several years earlier, an epidemic had swept the place. During the first winter, half of the colonists perished from scurvy and exposure, but the rest managed to put the colony on its feet. Among the neighboring Indians, whose military power had been weakened by the recent plague, the Pilgrims discovered friends— Squanto, Samoset, Massasoit—who showed them how to obtain seafood and cultivate corn. After the first harvest, the settlers invited the Indians to join them in an October festival, the original Thanksgiving. They could not aspire to rich farms on the sandy and marshy soil, but they soon developed a profitable trade in fish and furs. From time to time new colonists arrived from England, and in a decade the population reached the modest total of 300.

The people of "Plymouth Plantation" were entitled to elect their own governor, and they chose the great-hearted William Bradford again and again. As early as 1621 he cleared their land title with a patent from the Council for New England, but he never succeeded in his efforts to secure a royal charter giving them indisputable rights of government. Terminating the communal labor plan ahead of schedule, the governor distributed land among the families, thus making "all hands very industrious." He and a group of fellow "undertakers" assumed the colony's debt to its financiers in England and, with earnings from the fur trade, finally paid it off, even though the financiers had not lived up to their agreement to keep on sending supplies.

The Pilgrims remained poor; as late as the 1640s they had only one plow among them. Yet they clung to the belief that God had put them in the New World for a reason. Governor Bradford wrote in retrospect: "As one small candle may light a thousand, so the light here kindled hath shone to many, yea in some sort to our whole nation."

SUGGESTED READINGS

The European explorations of America are the subject of an unusually rich and sweeping literature. Of special importance is the work of Samuel Eliot Morison, in particular, *Admiral of the Ocean Sea*, 2 vols. (1942), a classic biography of Columbus, and *The European Discovery of America: The Northern Voyages* (1971) and *The Southern Voyages* (1974). See also J. H. Parry, *The Age of Reconnaissance* (1963); and David B. Quinn, *North America from Earliest Discovery to First Settlements* (1977). Accounts of the Spanish conquests and early Spanish settlements include Charles Gibson, *Spain in America* (1966); James Lockhart, *Spanish*

Peru, 1532–1560: A Colonial Society (1968); James Lang, *Conquest and Commerce: Spain and England in the Americas* (1975); and J. H. Elliott, *The Old World and the New, 1492–1650* (1970). The latter two titles include treatment of English colonization as well.

For the European background of colonization, see W. H. McNeill, *The Rise of the West* (1963); and J. H. Parry, *Europe and the New World, 1415–1715* (1949) and *The Age of Reconnaissance* (1963). For England, see Wallace Notestein, *The English People on the Eve of Colonization, 1603–1630* (1954), a good introductory account. Peter Laslett, *The World We Have Lost* (1965), is a pioneering study of the social and demographic forces at work in premodern England, a subject that receives attention as well in Carl Bridenbaugh, *Vexed and Troubled Englishmen, 1590–1642* (1968). Treatments of the religious background of English colonization include Patrick Collinson, *The Elizabethan Puritan Movement* (1967); C. H. George and Katherine George, *The Protestant Mind of the English Reformation* (1961); Michael Walzer, *The Revolution of the Saints* (1965), a challenging and controversial interpretation; and Keith Thomas, *Religion and the Decline of Magic* (1971). Other important studies of Tudor–Stuart England include Lawrence Stone, *The Crisis of the Aristocracy* (1965); and Mildred Campbell, *The English Yeoman Under Elizabeth and the Early Stuarts* (1942).

A good introductory account of American Indians, both before and after the arrival of Europeans, is Wilcomb E. Washburn, *The Indian in America* (1975). Other useful studies include Kenneth MacGowan and J. A. Hester, Jr., *Early Man in the New World* (1950); Harold E. Driver, *Indians of North America*, 2nd ed. (1970); and Francisco Guerra, *The Pre-Columbian Mind* (1971). Important studies of interaction between the Indians and the new settlers include Gerald B. Nash, *Red, White, and Black*, rev. ed. (1982); Alfred W. Crosby, Jr., *The Columbian Exchange: Biological and Cultural Consequences of 1492* (1972); and Henry Warner Bowden, *American Indians and Christian Missions* (1982).

For the first English colonizing efforts, see A. L. Rowse, *Sir Walter Raleigh* (1962); and David B. Quinn, *The Roanoke Voyages, 1584–1590*, 2 vols. (1955). The history of the early Jamestown settlement can be examined through the writings of its early leaders in *Travels and Works of Captain John Smith*, 2 vols. (1910). Modern studies include Bradford Smith, *Captain John Smith* (1953); Philip L. Barbour, *The Three Worlds of Captain John Smith* (1964); Alden T. Vaughn, *American Genesis* (1975); and Wesley Frank Craven, *The Dissolution of the Virginia Company* (1932).

Plymouth Plantation can also be studied through the writings of one of its founders: William Bradford, *Of Plymouth Plantation*, a landmark of American literature published in many editions, of which the best is that of Samuel Eliot Morison (1952). See also George Langdon, *Pilgrim Colony* (1966); and John Demos, *A Little Commonwealth* (1970), an important social history of the settlement.

Transplanted Englishmen

2

The Landing at Savannah
English colonists and Indians mingle on the shore of the Savannah River in Georgia as supplies and belongings are unloaded. The founding of Savannah in February 1733 marked the creation of the last English colony in North America, more than a century after the first permanent English settlement had been established at Jamestown. Georgia was the only Southern colony to prohibit slavery during its early years, but pressure from slave-holding Carolinians who began to settle in the new province led to a repeal of the prohibition in 1749.
(Culver Pictures)

From these fragile beginnings—Jamestown in the South, Plymouth Plantation in the North—the English settlements grew and spread until by the late seventeenth century they covered virtually the whole of the eastern seaboard, from Massachusetts to South Carolina. Few of the settlers thought of the colonies as a single society, much less a single nation. Each was a distinct entity, united with its fellow colonies by little more than geographical proximity and a common tie to England. Founded by different groups for different purposes, peopled by different religious sects and social classes, the settlements engaged in a wide range of economic pursuits and created different institutions.

Yet despite all the variations among them, the American colonies shared one important characteristic: all were part of the emerging British Empire. All felt the effects of the political turbulence that rocked England through most of the seventeenth century; and all were affected when the British government began attempting to tighten its administration of its colonies. Politically, at least, the English settlements in the New World were, a full century before the American Revolution, encountering similar experiences and producing similar responses.

THE GROWTH OF NEW ENGLAND

Although it was in Virginia that Englishmen had established their first permanent colony, it was in New England that English settlement most rapidly spread and flourished in the first half of the century. In this, the future of the region was shaped less by the Pilgrim Separatists, who were its first settlers, than by the Puritans. More worldly and more wealthy than the Pilgrims, the Puritans came to America not only to escape from the sins (and the religious repression) of England but to create a prosperous, well-ordered economy. Far from seeking to isolate themselves from the rest of the world, they sought to serve as a model for it—hoping, by example, to inspire a transformation of English society into something resembling their own.

To Massachusetts Bay

The interest of the English Puritans in migrating to America was much enhanced in the 1620s by events within England. There, a protracted and often bitter struggle was in progress between king and Parliament; and for a time, religious dissenters suffered severely from the results. The death of Eliza-beth I in 1603 had brought to the throne the autocratic James I, whose attempts to assert the divine right of kings and whose harshness toward Puritans created serious tensions. The situation worsened upon his death in 1625, when he was succeeded by his son, Charles I. Charles was even more aggressively autocratic than his father; and his efforts to restore Roman Catholicism to England and to destroy religious nonconformity launched the nation on the road that in the 1640s would lead to civil war. For the Puritans, who were particular targets of Charles's wrath (many of them were imprisoned for their beliefs), the climate of England was becoming intolerable. And the king's dissolution of Parliament in 1629 (it was not to be recalled until 1640) ensured that there would be no political redress.

In the midst of this political and social turmoil, a group of Puritan merchants were organizing a new enterprise designed to take advantage of opportunities in America. At first, their interest was largely an economic one. They obtained a grant of land in New England for most of the area now comprising Massachusetts and New Hampshire; they acquired a charter to establish the Massachusetts Bay Company and to establish a colony in the New World; and they bought equipment and supplies from a defunct fishing and trading company that had attempted (and failed) to establish a profitable enterprise in North America. In 1629, they were ready to dispatch a substantial group of settlers to New England.

Among the members of the Massachusetts Bay Company, however, were some Puritans who saw the enterprise as something more than a business venture. Distressed by the inhospitable atmosphere of England under Charles I, they began to consider the possibility of emigrating themselves, of creating in New England a refuge for Puritans. Members of this faction within the company met secretly in the summer of 1629 and agreed to move en masse to America if the other members of the company would transfer control of the enterprise to them. When those investors who preferred to remain in England concurred and sold their stock to the prospective emigrants, no obstacle remained.

The new owners of the company elected as their governor John Winthrop, a gentleman of means, university-educated, with a deep piety and a remarkably forceful character. Winthrop had been instrumental in organizing the migration; and he commanded the expedition that sailed for New England in 1630: seventeen ships and 1,000 people, the largest single migration of its kind in the seventeenth century. Winthrop carried with him the charter of the Massachusetts Bay Company. The colonists would be responsible to no company officials in England; they would be responsible only to themselves.

Unlike the two previous English settlements in America—Jamestown and Plymouth—the Massachusetts migration produced more than one new town. Although the port of Boston, at the mouth of the Charles River, became the company's headquarters and the colony's capital, settlers moved almost simultaneously into a number of other new communities in eastern Massachusetts: Charlestown, Newtown (Cambridge), Roxbury, Dorchester, Watertown, Ipswich, Concord, Sudbury, and others.

The Massachusetts Bay Company soon

John Winthrop
Unlike some English settlers in America, John Winthrop—longtime governor of the Massachusetts Bay Colony—did not travel to the New World to escape limited circumstances at home. Born to a socially prominent family, he studied at Trinity College, Cambridge, and became a prosperous lawyer. But his strong Puritan religious views motivated him to leave England and establish a new society in America, a society he likened—in a famous statement he made just before arriving in New England—to a "city upon a hill," a godly community that would serve as an example to the rest of the world. (Library of Congress)

was transformed into the Massachusetts colonial government. According to the terms of the company charter, the "freemen" (the stockholders) were to meet as a General Court to choose officers and adopt rules for the corporation. After their arrival in America, the freemen proceeded to elect officials and pass laws for the colony. At their first meeting the freemen, eight of them, voted to concentrate power in their own and the governor's hands. At their next meeting, in 1631, they increased the number of freemen (the word now meaning voters or citi-

Boston Harbor
The founders of Boston (and of the Massachusetts Bay Colony of which it was the capital)
envisioned the new town as a peaceful, united, religious community whose harmony would
serve as an example to the world. But they also hoped to create a thriving commercial center
that would contribute to their own and the empire's prosperity. This early view of Boston
harbor, showing the north battery, built in 1646, suggests the growing commercial orientation
of the city even in its early years. (Library of Congress)

zens, not necessarily stockholders) by more
than a hundred, so as to include about half of
the family heads in the colony. Winthrop
continued to dominate colonial politics, but
in 1634 he agreed to an arrangement by
which the freemen would elect from year to
year the governor, the deputy governor, the
council of governor's assistants, and two
"deputies" from each town—all of whom
would constitute the General Court. In 1644
this became a bicameral legislature, with a
lower House of Deputies and an upper chamber consisting of the governor and his council.

Unlike the Separatist founders of Plymouth, the Puritan founders of Massachusetts
had come with no intention of breaking away
from the Church of England. They only
wished, at first, to rescue the church from
what they saw as the evil influence of Rome.
Nevertheless, they soon were acting as if they
were religiously independent. As the prominent preacher John Cotton said, the church in
every town had "complete liberty to stand
alone." Each congregation chose its own

minister and regulated its own affairs. Thus
there arose in Massachusetts—as well as in
Plymouth—what came to be known as the
Congregational church.

These Massachusetts Puritans were not
necessarily grim, joyless, or "puritanical,"
despite their belief in predestination. They
enjoyed the ordinary pleasures of life, and
they appreciated beauty in plain and simple
forms. They strove to lead a useful, conscientious life of thrift and hard work. They
honored material success, for if a person did
well it was possible evidence that God favored him as one of the elect. If his ways
were upright, this was another possible indication of divine grace. Many were hopeful
that they were among the chosen, but no one
could be sure. So people searched their
hearts, and those of their neighbors so far as
possible, to look for signs of their salvation.

"We here enjoy God and Jesus Christ,"
Winthrop wrote to his wife soon after his ar-
rival; "is this not enough?" He and the other
Massachusetts founders saw themselves as

Day of Doom [1662]

The earliest book-publishing centers in English America were Cambridge and Boston. From their presses came more than 200 titles between 1640 and 1700. The very first of these was The Whole Book of Psalms, *popularly known as the "Bay Psalm Book." Another best seller, published in 1662 and reprinted many times thereafter, was* The Day of Doom, Or a Poetical Description of the Great and Last Judgment, *written by Michael Wigglesworth, a Harvard graduate and Puritan divine. Two of its 224 dreary stanzas describe the eternal punishment of the damned as follows:*

> Whom having brought, as they are taught,
>   unto the brink of Hell,
> (That dismal place far from Christ's face
>   where Death and Darkness dwell;
> Where God's fierce ire kindleth the fire,
>   and vengeance feeds the flame
> With piles of Wood, and Brimstone Flood,
>   that none can quench the same,)
>
> With Iron bands they bind their hands
>   and cursed feet together,
> And cast them all, both great and small,
>   into that Lake for ever,
> Where day and night, without respite,
>   they wail, and cry, and howl
> For tort'ring pain, which they sustain
>   in Body and in Soul.

starting a holy commonwealth, a model—a "city upon a hill"—for the corrupt world to see. The problem was to keep it holy. In this effort, the preachers and the politicians worked together. The ministers did not run the government, but they supported it, and they exerted great influence upon the church members who alone could vote or hold office in it. The government in turn protected the ministers, taxed the people (members and nonmembers alike) to support the church, and enforced the law requiring attendance at services. In this Puritan oligarchy, the dissidents had no more freedom of worship than the Puritans themselves had had in England.

The Lord seemed to smile upon the Massachusetts enterprise. After the first winter (1629–1630), when nearly 200 died and many others decided to leave, the colony grew and prospered. The nearby Pilgrims helped with food and advice. Incoming settlers, many of them well-to-do, brought needed tools and other goods, which they exchanged for the cattle, corn, and other produce of the established colonists.

Throughout the 1630s, while Charles I ruled England without a Parliament, Puritans escaped to America from his tyranny in such numbers that by 1643 the colony had a population of about 15,000. In the 1640s, however, the migration slowed when civil war broke out in England. After a Puritan government seized power, many who might otherwise have emigrated chose to remain at home; and others who had come to America in more perilous times returned to England. For a while, those leaving Massachusetts exceeded those who were arriving. Yet the colony survived, and despite the decline in immigration (which was, in any case, only temporary), the population continued to grow through natural increase.

Exodus from the Bay Colony

Meanwhile, an outpouring from Massachusetts Bay to various parts of New England (and to other places in English America) had begun. This exodus was motivated generally by one or both of two considerations: the unproductiveness of the stony soil around Boston and the oppressiveness of the Massachusetts government. Not all the incoming settlers were saints, and as the population increased, the proportion of those who could vote or hold office declined. To the Puritan authorities, opposition to their church seemed like a threat to the government, like both heresy and treason. Independent thinkers—and Puritanism somehow bred them—had little choice but to give in or get out. Such thinkers were responsible for new settlements north and south, in New Hampshire and Rhode Island. Families seeking richer lands as well as greater religious and political independence began new settlements in the west, in Connecticut.

The Connecticut Valley, one hundred miles beyond the settled frontier, contained fertile meadows that invited pioneering despite the presence of warlike Indians and the claims of the already fortified Dutch. By the early 1630s, a few Englishmen were already living there. The valley appealed in particular to Thomas Hooker, a minister of Newtown (Cambridge), who questioned the fairness of government by the Massachusetts General Court, arguing that "a general council, chosen by all" would be "most suitable to rule and most safe for the relief of the whole people." When, in 1634, Newtown petitioned the General Court for permission to occupy the Connecticut Valley before it was "possessed by others," Governor Winthrop and his associates turned down the request. In 1635, a number of families from other Massachusetts towns moved west with the General Court's approval, on the understanding that they would "continue still under this government." The next year, Hooker led his congregation through the wilds and—in defiance of Winthrop and his government—established the town of Hartford.

Disregarding the claims of the Dutch, the English grantees, and the Massachusetts General Court, the people of Hartford and two other newly founded upriver towns, Windsor and Wethersfield, decided to set up a colonial government of their own. In 1639, they adopted a constitution known as the Fundamental Orders of Connecticut. This provided for a government similar to that of Massachusetts Bay but gave a larger proportion of the people the right to vote and hold office.

A separate colony, the project of a Puritan minister and a wealthy merchant from England, grew up around New Haven on the Connecticut coast. The Fundamental Articles of New Haven (1639) set up a Bible-based government even stricter than that of Massachusetts Bay, but eventually the governor of Connecticut obtained a royal charter (1662) that not only authorized the Hartford colony but also extended its jurisdiction over the New Haven settlements.

Rhode Island had its origin in the religious dissent of Roger Williams, a likable but troublesome young minister of Massachusetts Bay. Even John Winthrop, who considered him a heretic, called Williams a "sweet and amiable" man, and William Bradford described him thus: "A man godly and zeal-

COLONIES THAT GREW OUT OF MASSACHUSETTS BAY

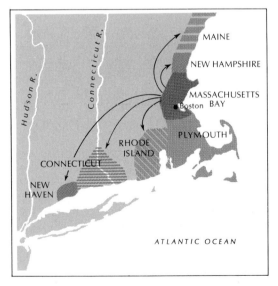

ous, having many precious parts, but very unsettled in judgment." Williams was an extreme Separatist who at first advocated not religious freedom but rather a church made even more pure and strict. Making friends with the neighboring Indians, he concluded that the land belonged to them and not to the king or to the Massachusetts Bay Company. The colonial government considered Williams a dangerous man and decided to deport him, but he escaped before they could. He took refuge with Narragansett tribesmen during a bitter winter, then bought a tract of land from them and in 1636, with a few of his friends, created the town of Providence on it.

By that time another menace to the established order had appeared in Massachusetts Bay. Anne Hutchinson, a strong-minded and charismatic woman from a substantial Boston family, attracted many more followers than Williams with her heretical doctrine that the Holy Spirit dwelled within and guided every true believer. If this were so, the Bible would have no more authority than anyone's personal revelation, and both the church and the government would be exposed to anarchy, or so it seemed to Governor Winthrop and his associates. Anne Hutchinson's followers were numerous and influential enough to prevent Winthrop's reelection as governor in 1636, but the next year he returned to office and set the orthodox ministers to proving that she was a heretic. In 1638, after a trial at which Winthrop himself presided, Hutchinson was convicted of sedition and banished as "a woman not fit for our society." With her family and some of her followers, she moved to a point on Narragansett Bay not far from Providence.

In time, other communities of dissidents arose in that vicinity. They quarreled with one another and with Roger Williams, who, having paid the Indians for the land, looked upon himself as its proprietor. As he matured, he modified some of his views on religion. He began to advocate complete freedom of worship and separation of church and state. Eventually he turned into a "seeker," one who respected but doubted all religions while he sought the true one. Rhode Island reflected his changing ideas. In 1644, he got from Parliament a charter authorizing a gov-

ernment for the combined settlements. The government, though based on the Massachusetts pattern, did not restrict the vote to church members nor did it tax the people for church support. A royal charter of 1663 confirmed this arrangement and added a guarantee of "liberty in religious concernments."

New Hampshire and Maine had become the separate possessions of two proprietors, Captain John Mason and Sir Ferdinando Gorges. In 1629, they divided their grant from the Council for New England along the Piscataqua River. Despite lavish promotional efforts, especially on the part of Gorges, few settlers were drawn to these northern regions until the religious disruption of Massachusetts Bay. In 1639, John Wheelwright, a disciple of Anne Hutchinson, led some of his fellow dissenters to Exeter, New Hampshire. Thereafter a number of towns in that province and in Maine were peopled by orthodox and unorthodox Puritans from Massachusetts or by new colonists from abroad. The Massachusetts Bay Company extended its authority over the whole territory in the north but ultimately lost its cases against the heirs of both Mason and Gorges in the highest courts of England. New Hampshire was then set up as a separate colony in 1679, the Gorges family having sold their rights to it. Maine remained a part of Massachusetts until admitted to the Union as a state in 1820.

Settlers and Natives

As the European settlement of New England expanded, the colonists became embroiled in a struggle that would characterize American history for more than two centuries: the battle between whites and Indians. Almost from the beginning, the Puritans had viewed the natives as "pernicious creatures" who should be either "civilized" by conversion to Christianity and European ways or, failing that, exterminated. Occasionally, an exceptional colonial leader would advocate tolerance and respect for the Indian: Roger Williams in Rhode Island; or John Eliot, a missionary who translated the Bible into an Indian language. For the most part, however, the English attitude toward the natives was stern, disapproving, and often brutal.

In 1637, members of the Pequot tribe, exasperated by the continuing European incursions into their lands and the antagonistic attitudes of the new settlers, began hostilities in the Connecticut Valley. White frontiersmen responded in what would become a familiar pattern: they marched against a palisaded Pequot stronghold and set it afire. About 400 Indians died—burned to death in the flaming stockade or killed by the white attackers as they attempted to escape. Those who survived were hunted down, captured, and sold as slaves. The Pequot tribe was almost wiped out. Other tribes would face a similar fate in the years that followed.

It was not that the European settlers of America were intrinsically more cruel or violent than the native population. Indians too were often appallingly brutal in their wars against the whites. But several factors made the relationship between whites and Indians in the ensuing years disastrous for the Indians: the automatic assumption of the European colonists that the natives were inferior savages whose civilization deserved no respect; the European commitment to expansion into and development of the wilderness, which put the whites in direct conflict with the Indians, whose way of life depended upon preservation of the natural world; and, eventually, the superior strength and numbers of the whites, which ultimately made the inevitable conflicts hopeless mismatches and left the American Indians with a tragic choice—accept white society or perish. The triumphant march of white civilization across the continent was in part a result of the courage, resourcefulness, and idealism of white settlers; but it would also rest upon their success in subduing and often nearly exterminating a bewildered native population.

The bloodiest and most prolonged encounter between whites and Indians in the seventeenth century began in 1675: a nightmare that would be remembered for generations as King Philip's War. As in Connecticut nearly forty years before, an Indian tribe—in this case the Wampanoags, under the leadership of a chieftain known to the white settlers as King Philip—rose up in retaliation against the encroachments of the English settlers into what they considered their lands. For three years, they inflicted terror upon a string of Massachusetts towns, destroying or depopulating twenty of them and causing the deaths of one-sixteenth of the white males in the colony. As before, however, the whites ultimately prevailed. Massachusetts leaders requested assistance from the so-called "praying" Indians of the region—thousands of natives who had been converted to Christianity by missionaries and who had settled in or near the towns of the whites. One of these Indians shot and killed King Philip, and gradually the rebellion was crushed. Some Wampanoag leaders were executed; others were sold into slavery in the West Indies. And the power of the Wampanoags and their allied tribes was forever destroyed.

Yet these victories by the white colonists did not end the danger to their settlements. This was in part because other Indians in other tribes survived, capable of launching future wars. It was also because the New England settlers faced competition not only from the natives but also from the Dutch and the French, who claimed the territory on which some of the outlying settlements were established. The French, in particular, would pose a constant threat to the English and would later support hostile Indians in their attacks on the New England frontier.

THE CHESAPEAKE COUNTRY

While Puritan settlers were expanding the area of settlement in New England, other English immigrants were peopling a large region farther south, in the vicinity of the Chesapeake Bay. After its disastrous beginnings at Jamestown, the colony of Virginia began in the 1620s and 1630s rapidly to expand. And alongside it there emerged a new colony—Maryland—which, though founded under different auspices and for different reasons, developed in markedly similar ways.

The Massachusetts Bay Colony had been established as a planned society, and the development of New England in the seventeenth century continued to reflect a sense of collective interest and shared social purpose. The Chesapeake Bay colonies did not. "The most noticeable feature of the Chesapeake settlements," the historian Wesley Frank Craven has written, "is the absence of a common purpose and goal except such as was dictated principally by the requirements of individual interest."

Maryland and the Calverts

Like Massachusetts, Maryland emerged in part from the desire of a religious minority in England to establish a refuge from discrimination. In this case, the minority was not dissenting Protestants but Roman Catholics. The new colony was the idea of George Calvert, the first Lord Baltimore. Calvert was a recent convert to Catholicism, as well as a shrewd businessman. And he envisioned establishing a colony both as a great speculative venture in real estate and as a retreat for English Catholics oppressed by the Anglican establishment at home. He experimented first with a settlement in Newfoundland, now part of Canada; but after spending a frigid winter there, he traveled to the Chesapeake and determined to relocate his colony there. Returning to England, he began the long process of winning a charter from King Charles I; and although he died before his efforts bore fruit, the charter was finally issued in 1632 to his son and the second Lord Baltimore, Cecilius Calvert.

The Maryland charter was remarkable not only for the extent of the territory it granted to Calvert—an area that encompassed parts of Pennsylvania, Delaware, and Virginia, in addition to present-day Maryland—but for the powers it bestowed upon him. He and his heirs were to hold their province as "true and absolute lords and proprietaries," and were to acknowledge the ultimate sovereignty of the king only by paying an annual fee to the Crown. The Calverts could establish a government however they saw fit, adopt whatever methods they wished

for distributing land, and even revive a system of feudal dependency in Maryland—awarding property to men who would become the vassals of the proprietor.

Since the London Company (which still claimed its land rights in Virginia) objected to the Calvert grant, Lord Baltimore remained at home to defend his interests at court. He appointed his brother Leonard Calvert governor and sent him with another brother to see to the settlement of the family's province. In March of 1634 the *Ark* and the *Dove*, bearing two or three hundred passengers, most of them Protestants, entered the Potomac and turned into one of its eastern tributaries. On a high and dry bluff, these first arrivals laid out the village of St. Mary's, while the neighboring Indians, already withdrawing to avoid native enemies, assisted by selling land and providing stocks of corn. The early Marylanders knew no massacres, no plagues, no starving time.

Spending a large part of the family fortune in the development of their American possessions, the Calverts had to attract many thousands of settlers if their venture was to pay. They encouraged the immigration of Protestants as well as Roman Catholics, and since relatively few of the latter were inclined to leave England, the Protestant settlers (mostly Anglicans) soon far outnumbered the Catholics. Realizing that Catholics would always be a minority in the colony, the Calverts insisted from the beginning on religious toleration. To appease the non-Catholic majority, Calvert appointed a Protestant as governor in 1648. A year later, he sent over from England the draft of an "Act Concerning Religion," which assured freedom of worship to all Christians. Nevertheless, politics in Maryland remained plagued for years by tensions between the Catholic minority (including the proprietor) and the Protestant majority.

As in other colonies, government in Maryland quickly took on a form in many ways similar to government in England. At the insistence of the first settlers, the Calverts agreed in 1635 to the calling of a representative assembly—known as the House of Delegates—whose proceedings were based on the rules of Parliament. Within fifteen years, the colony had a bicameral legislature, with an upper house that consisted of the governor and his council.

In other respects, however, the distribution of power in Maryland differed sharply from that in other colonies. Under the royal charter that the Calverts had secured from the Crown, the proprietor retained absolute authority to distribute land as he wished; and Lord Baltimore initially granted large estates to his relatives and to other English aristocrats, so that from the start there existed in Maryland a distinct upper class. By 1640, the severe labor shortage in the colony had forced a modification of the land grant procedure; and Maryland, like Virginia, adopted a "headright" system—a grant of a hundred acres to each male settler, another hundred for his wife and each servant, and fifty for each of his children. But the great landlords of the colony's earliest years remained powerful even as the population grew larger and more diverse.

Turbulent Virginia

Having survived the starving time of the early days at Jamestown, the Virginia colony grew rapidly in the mid-seventeenth century, increasing both its population and the complexity and profitability of its economy. It also grew more politically contentious, as the emerging factions within the state began to compete for the favor of the government.

Virginia had been a royal colony, with its governor appointed by the king, ever since the collapse of the London Company in 1624. One of those royal governors, Sir William Berkeley, dominated the politics of the colony for more than thirty years. He arrived in Virginia in 1642 at the age of thirty-six with an appointment from King Charles I; and with but one interruption he remained in control of the government until the 1670s, at times popular, at times faced with serious challenges.

The colonists responded enthusiastically to Berkeley's policies during the first years of his tenure. The governor helped to open up the interior of Virginia by sending out explorers who crossed the Blue Ridge Moun-

tains. He directed a force that put down the Indians in 1644, when old Chief Opechancanough led them in a bloody attack comparable to the massacre of twenty-two years earlier. Opechancanough was captured and, against Berkeley's orders, was shot and killed. The defeated Indians agreed to a treaty ceding all the land between the York and the James rivers to the east of the fall line, and prohibiting white settlement to the west of that line.

This attempt to protect Indian territory—like many such attempts later in American history—was a failure from the start. Virginia was growing fast, especially after Cromwell's victory in the English civil war (see p. 41) and the flight of many of the defeated Cavaliers to the colony. By 1650, its population (16,000) was twice as large as it had been in 1640; and by 1660, five times as large (40,000). As the choice lands along the tidewater were taken up, new arrivals and servants completing their terms or escaping from their masters pressed on beyond the falls into the piedmont. By 1652, three counties had been formed in the territory recently set aside for the Indians. Clashes frequently occurred between the Indians and the frontiersmen.

When Cromwell seized power in England, Berkeley had to give up the governorship of Virginia; but King Charles II reappointed him after the Stuart Restoration. Once back in office, Berkeley, by the force of his personality, and by corrupting the council and the House of Burgesses, made himself practically an autocrat. Originally, the Virginia government had been remarkably democratic. When the first burgesses were elected in 1619, all men aged seventeen or older were entitled to vote. After 1670, the vote was restricted to landowners and elections were seldom held, the same burgesses remaining in office year after year. Each county continued to have only two representatives, even though the new counties contained many more people than some of the old ones of the tidewater area. Thus the more recent settlers on the frontier were underrepresented or not represented at all. A pattern was emerging in Virginia that would repeat itself time and again in other parts of America. New settlements in the west (or the

The Virginia House of Burgesses
This engraving depicts the first meeting of the colonial assembly of Virginia—the House of Burgesses—in 1619. Established by Governor George Yeardley, it was the first local representative assembly in the New World. Through most of the colonial era, the House of Burgesses represented (and was composed of) only relatively prosperous landowners of Virginia. The common people of the colony had virtually no political influence. (Culver Pictures)

"back country," as it was known) were growing larger and more prosperous, developing interests and political demands of their own. But more established elites near the coast continued to ignore the demands of the back country's citizens for representation and assistance. A situation was building that promised to produce social conflict.

Bacon's Rebellion

And in 1676, it did. Nathaniel Bacon, a young, handsome, and ambitious graduate of Cambridge University, arrived in Virginia in 1673. His wealth and his family background enabled him to purchase a good farm in the back country and to obtain a seat on the gov-

ernor's council. He established himself, in other words, as a member of the back country gentry—an influential, propertied elite that was emerging in the western region of the state just as other elites had emerged earlier in the east. Yet the new back country gentry was different in crucial ways from its tidewater counterpart. Isolated geographically from the colonial government, western aristocrats sensed themselves cut off from real political power. As part of a new, still half-formed frontier economy, their position was always precarious, and it became even more so as Virginia began to suffer serious economic difficulties in the 1670s. There were, in short, growing regional tensions between eastern and western Virginia.

These frustrations and resentments came to a head in response to Berkeley's policies for dealing with Indians on the Virginia frontier. Property owners in the back country had long chafed at the governor's attempts to hold steady the line of settlement in an effort to avoid antagonizing the Indians. It was, they believed, an effort by the eastern aristocracy to protect its dominance by restricting western expansion. (It was also, in part, an effort by Berkeley to protect his own lucrative trade with the Indians.) Gradually, Bacon established himself as the leader of an opposition faction in western Virginia, which—in defiance of Berkeley—attempted to seize additional lands from the natives.

The result was predictable: a bloody confrontation between white settlers and Indians in 1676, in the course of which several hundred whites (including Bacon's overseer) were killed. Bacon and other concerned landholders demanded that the governor send the militia out to pursue and destroy the Indian marauders. Berkeley, however, continued to attempt to dampen the conflict. He ordered the militia merely to guard the edge of settlement, to engage in no aggressive actions against the Indians. Bacon, outraged, now organized an army of his own and launched a vicious but ultimately unsuccessful pursuit of the Indian challengers. When Berkeley heard of this unauthorized military effort, he dismissed Bacon from the council and proclaimed him and his men to be rebels.

At that point began what became known as Bacon's Rebellion—the largest and most powerful insurrection against established authority in the history of the colonies, one that would not be surpassed until the Revolution. When Berkeley, in an effort to increase his popular support, called for a new election of members of the House of Burgesses, Bacon ran and was overwhelmingly elected. He then marched with his army to Jamestown to demand his seat. And there the young rebel, not yet thirty years old, confronted the governor, who was now seventy. Berkeley's first impulse was to have Bacon arrested; but fearful of the consequences of hanging such a "darling of the people," he soon pardoned him, promised him a commission to fight the Indians, and restored him to his position on the council. When Bacon, temporarily pacified, departed with his army, the assembly passed a series of reforms, known as Bacon's Laws, to lessen the authority of the governor and to give greater powers of self-government to the counties.

Convinced now that he had undermined Bacon's popular support, Berkeley withheld the promised commission and renewed the charge that Bacon was a rebel. Once again, Bacon led his army on a march from the frontier to Jamestown—this time gathering wide popular support as he came. Ultimately he forced Berkeley to flee, burned the capital, and—in the midst of widespread social chaos throughout the colony—stood on the verge of taking command of Virginia. Instead, he died of dysentery. Berkeley soon managed to regain control, at which point he saw to the repeal of Bacon's Laws and the execution of thirty-seven of the rebels.

Bacon's Rebellion was significant for several reasons. It revealed the bitterness of the competition among rival elites—and between easterners and westerners in particular—in the still half-formed society of the colonies. But it also exposed something Bacon himself had never intended to unleash: the potential for instability in the large population of free, landless men—most of them former indentured servants—who formed the bulk of Bacon's constituency. The problems of such men were severe, and their grievances were great; and while Bacon had for a time maintained his popularity among them by exploiting their hatred of Indians, ultimately he found himself, without really meaning to, leading a movement that directed much of its animosity toward the landed gentry (of which Bacon himself, ironically, was a part). In the years following Bacon's Rebellion, therefore, property owners in both eastern and western Virginia remained uneasy about the potential for revolution among the white lower class. As a result, they turned increasingly to the African slave trade to fulfill their need for labor. Enslaved blacks might pose dangers too, but the events of 1676 suggested that the perils of importing a large white working class were even greater.

THE RESTORATION COLONIES

Political turmoil in England in the mid-seventeenth century inhibited further efforts at colonization for a time. After Lord Baltimore received his grant in Maryland in 1632, no new settlement projects began for approximately thirty years. Instead, the English were preoccupied with a chaotic civil war at home.

The English Civil War

England's problems had begun during the rule of James I, who was far more aggressive than his predecessor (Elizabeth I) in asserting the absolute power, the "divine right," of the monarchy. James died in 1625, having created significant political tensions but without yet having come to blows with Parliament. His son, Charles I, was not so fortunate. Even more extreme than his father, both in his autocratic tendencies and in his Roman Catholic sympathies, he antagonized his subjects by ruling as an absolute monarch from 1629 to 1640. During this period he refused to call Parliament into session, imposed high-church reforms upon the country, and imprisoned Puritan leaders. Finally, in need of money, the king called Parliament into session in the hope that its members would vote him additional taxes. But Charles antagonized the new Parliament by dismissing it twice in two years; and in 1642, the members organized a military force and began the English Civil War.

The conflict between the Cavaliers (the supporters of the king) and the Roundheads (the forces of Parliament, who were largely Puritans) lasted seven years. Finally, in 1649, the Roundheads defeated the king's forces, captured Charles himself, and—in an action that horrified not only much of continental Europe at the time but future generations of Englishmen—beheaded the monarch. To replace him, they elevated the stern Roundhead leader Oliver Cromwell to the position of "protector," from which he ruled for the next nine years. But when Cromwell died in 1658, the Protectorate fell upon hard times. His son and heir proved unable to maintain his authority; and two years later, King Charles II, son of the beheaded monarch, returned from exile and claimed the throne.

One result of the Stuart Restoration was the resumption of colonization in America. Charles II quickly began to reward faithful courtiers with grants of land in the New World; and in the twenty-five years of his reign, he issued charters for four additional colonies: Carolina, New York, New Jersey, and Pennsylvania. The new colonies were, without exception, proprietary ventures (modeled on Maryland rather than on Virginia and Massachusetts), thus exposing a basic change in the nature of American settlement. No longer did private companies take an interest in launching colonies, realizing at last that there were no quick profits to be had in the New World. In their place were emerging ventures with different aims: not quick commercial success, but permanent settlements that would provide proprietors with land and power.

The Carolinas

Carolina (after *Carolinus*, Latin for "Charles"), was, like Maryland, carved in part from the original Virginia grant. It was awarded by Charles II to a group of eight of his favorites, all prominent politicians active in colonial affairs. One was the Virginia governor, Sir William Berkeley. But the man who was to do the most for the development of Carolina was Sir Anthony Ashley Cooper, about to become the Earl of Shaftesbury. In successive charters (1663, 1665) the eight proprietors received joint title to a vast territory stretching south to the Florida peninsula and west to the Pacific Ocean. Like Lord Baltimore, they were given almost kingly powers over their grant.

Like him, they expected to profit as landlords and land speculators, reserving tremendous estates for their own development, selling or giving away the rest in smaller tracts, and collecting annual payments as quitrents from the settlers. Though committed to the advancement of the Church of England, the Carolina proprietors welcomed customers whether Anglican or not. Indeed, the charter guaranteed religious freedom to all who would worship as Christians. The proprietors also promised political freedom—at least as much of it as was to be found anywhere else in America—with laws to be made by a representative assembly. They hoped to attract settlers from the existing American colonies and thus to avoid the expense of financing expeditions from England.

The proprietors, four of whom had investments in the African slave trade, also intended to introduce slaves into the colony so as to profit both from selling them and from using their labor. Early settlers were offered a bonus of extra land for every black bondsman or -woman they brought in. Black slavery existed from the outset in Carolina, with no transitional period of temporary servitude as in Virginia.

The leading proprietor, the Earl of Shaftesbury, desired a planned society and a uniform pattern of settlement for the colony. With the aid of the philosopher John Locke, he drew up the Fundamental Constitution for Carolina in 1669. The territory was to be divided into 12,000-acre squares, with counties consisting of forty squares apiece. In each county, eight of the squares would belong to the proprietors, or "seigneurs," eight others would go to newly created nobles, who would bear the title of "landgrave" or "cacique," and the remaining twenty-four would be distributed among ordinary settlers, or "leet-men." At the bottom of this stratified society would be the blacks, whose subjection would be complete, regardless of their possible conversion to Christianity: "Every freeman of Carolina shall have absolute power and authority over his Negro slaves, of what opinion or religion soever." Proprietors, nobles, and other landholders would have a voice in the colonial parliament in proportion to the size of their landholdings.

While the Fundamental Constitution, with occasional revisions, remained in effect (at least on paper) for thirty years, Carolina was slow to develop; and when it did, it took a pattern much less regular and artificial. In

THE CAROLINAS AND GEORGIA

fact, the colony developed along two natural but quite different lines in its two widely separated areas of settlement—the one in its northeastern corner, around Albemarle Sound; and the other far to the southwest, on the Ashley and Cooper rivers and in their hinterland.

The northern part of Carolina, the first part to be settled, suffered in the early years from geographical handicaps, the coastal region being isolated by the Dismal Swamp, and by the lack of natural harbors usable for oceangoing ships. As a Carolina proprietor, Virginia's Governor Berkeley worked hard to induce Virginians to take up land on the other side of the colonial boundary, and gradually the Albemarle settlements grew. Virginians were inclined to look on the new Carolinians as a lazy and immoral set of runaway servants, debtors, thieves, and pirates. Actually, most of these people—like many in the Virginia they had left behind—were honest but poor tobacco-growing farmers, though they showed the marks of their primitive backwoods existence, having few roads and practically no villages, churches, schools—or slaves.

The southern part of Carolina was favored with an excellent harbor at the point where the Ashley and Cooper rivers joined. Here in 1670 a fleet arrived, bringing colonists whom the Earl of Shaftesbury had sent out after realizing that settlers from existing colonies were not going to flock in. Then, in 1680, he saw to the laying out of the city of Charleston, which soon had wharves, fortifications, and fine houses. Settlers took up land along the two rivers, down which they began to send large quantities of corn, lumber, cattle, pork, and (in the 1690s) some rice to Charleston, for shipment to Barbados in the British West Indies. To Charleston also came furs, hides, and Indian slaves obtained by traders who were advancing farther and farther into the interior.

In Charleston and its vicinity there developed a stratified society that embodied the spirit, though not the letter, of Shaftesbury's Fundamental Constitution. Many of the early inhabitants had moved there from the declining sugar plantations of Barbados and other West Indian islands. These people, already familiar with African slavery, brought their blacks with them. Large planters, often with homes in Charleston as well as plantations nearby, and city merchants occupied more or less the position of the nobles in the Shaftesbury plan. Ordinary farmers, many of them located at some distance inland, corre-

sponded roughly to the "leet-men." The wealthy planters and merchants dominated the region's economy, social life, and politics. Charleston became the capital of Carolina in 1690, when the governor took up his residence there, leaving a deputy to take charge of the Albemarle settlements.

Already there were in fact two Carolinas, each having a distinctive way of life, long before the colony was formally divided (1729) into North and South Carolina, with completely separate governments.

New Netherland and New York

In 1664, one year after making his Carolina grant, Charles II bestowed on his brother, the Duke of York, all the territory lying between the Connecticut and Delaware rivers. But unlike other such grants, this one faced a major challenge from prior claims upon the region. Some of the territory presumably belonged to the Massachusetts Bay Company by virtue of the sea-to-sea grant it had secured decades before. A far more serious challenge, however, lay in the Dutch claim to the entire area, and in the existence of Dutch settlements at strategic points within it.

Early Charleston
Charleston (originally Charles Town), South Carolina, was founded on its present site in 1680, ten years after English settlers under William Sayle arrived in South Carolina and established a settlement about seven miles away. The city became the most important port and the largest urban center in the Southern colonies in the years before the American Revolution, and it remained important as a trading center for the South after independence.
(Brown Brothers)

The Dutch republic, after winning independence from Spain, had launched upon its own career of overseas trading and empire building in Asia, Africa, and America. On the basis of Hudson's explorations, the Dutch staked an American claim and proceeded promptly to exploit it with a busy trade in furs. To add permanence to the business, the Dutch West India Company began to encourage settlement, transporting whole families on such voyages as that of the *New Netherland* in 1624, and later offering vast feudal estates to "patroons" who would bring over immigrants to work the land. So developed the colony of New Netherland. It centered on New Amsterdam, with its blockhouse on Manhattan Island, and included thinly scattered settlements on the Hudson, the Delaware, and the Connecticut, with forts for their protection. In 1655, the Dutch extended their sway over the few Swedes and Finns settled along the lower Delaware. In the Connecticut Valley, they had to give in to the superior numbers of the English moving out from Massachusetts Bay.

Three Anglo-Dutch wars arose from the commercial and colonial rivalry of England and the Netherlands throughout the world. In America in particular, the English resented the foreign stronghold that wedged apart their own northern and southern colonies and provided smuggling bases for the Dutch. In 1664, troop-carrying vessels of the English navy put in at New Amsterdam and extracted a surrender from the arbitrary and unpopular governor, Peter Stuyvesant. During the final

The Stadt Huys, New Amsterdam
The government building, together with the adjoining buildings in a typically Dutch style, made New Amsterdam look much like a town in Holland. It continued to have much the same appearance when this drawing was made, about 1679, after the English had established control and renamed the place New York. From the *Journal of a Voyage to New York, 1679–1682,* by Jasper Dankers and Peter Stuyler. (Courtesy of the Long Island Historical Society)

conflict, the Dutch reconquered and briefly held their old provincial capital (1673–1674), then lost it again for good.

New York, formerly New Netherland, already the property of the Duke of York and renamed by him, was his to rule virtually as an absolute monarch. Since he was himself a Roman Catholic, and since his province included Anglicans from England and Puritans from New England as well as Calvinists from Holland, he found it expedient to be religiously and politically broad-minded.

Like other proprietors before him, instead of going to America he delegated powers to a governor and a council. The Duke's Laws, which the first governor issued, were based on some of the laws of Massachusetts and Connecticut. They provided for no town meetings but for the election of certain local officials and the gubernatorial appointment of others. These laws also directed each town to set up a church and to give tax support both to it and to any other church that residents of the town might organize. Thus there was to be a variety of established churches. On the duke's instructions, a later governor, who took office in 1683, consulted with representatives of the people and with them adopted a Charter of Liberties and Privileges, which guaranteed the rights of Englishmen and called for an elected assembly.

The duke's concessions failed to satisfy all New Yorkers. Many people complained about the inequality of property holding and political power. The duke confirmed the Dutch patroonships already in existence, the most notable of them being Rensselaerswyck with its 700,000 acres around Albany, and he gave comparable estates to Englishmen in order to create a class of influential landowners loyal to him. Wealthy English and Dutch landlords, shipowners, and fur traders, along with the duke's political appointees, actually dominated the colonial government.

The system of landholding turned away from New York some settlers who preferred living on their own farms to working as tenants on someone else's estate. Under English rule the population nevertheless grew much faster than under the Dutch regime. By 1685, when the duke ascended the throne as James II, New York contained about four times as many people (around 30,000) as when he had taken it over some twenty years before. Most of them still lived within the Hudson Valley, close to the river itself, with the largest settlement at its mouth, in the town of New York. The colony had become predominantly English in both population and customs, yet Dutch traditions lingered on.

On the north and west the duke's dominions were extended as far as Lake Ontario by means of a protectorate over the Iroquois. On the east, however, his territory was trimmed in a boundary compromise with Massachusetts and Connecticut. On the south it was enlarged somewhat by his claim (based on conquest from the Dutch) to land west of the lower Delaware, but it was diminished even more by his generosity in parting with his possessions. He gave what became New Jersey to a pair of political allies, both Carolina proprietors, Sir George Carteret and Sir John Berkeley. The latter sold his half interest to two enterprising members of the Society of Friends, thus bringing the Quakers into the business of colonization. The duke gave what would become Delaware to another Quaker: William Penn, perhaps the greatest colonizer of all.

The Quaker Colonies

The Society of Friends originated in mid-seventeenth-century England in response to the preachings of George Fox, a Nottingham shoemaker, whose followers came to be known as Quakers from his admonition to them to "tremble at the name of the Lord." The essence of Fox's teachings was the doctrine of the Inner Light, the illumination from God within each soul, which when rightly heeded could guide human beings along the paths of righteousness.

Of all the Protestant sectarians of the time, the Quakers were the most anarchistic and the most democratic. They had no church government except for their monthly, quarterly, and annual meetings, at which the congregations were represented on a local, regional, and national basis. They had no traditional church buildings, only meeting-houses. They had no paid clergy, and in their worship they spoke up one by one as the spirit moved them. Disregarding social distinctions such as those of sex and class, they treated women as equals and addressed one another with the "thee" and "thou" then commonly used in speaking to servants and inferiors. Defying other accepted conventions, they refused to participate in taking oaths or in fighting wars. The Quakers were unpopular enough as a result of these beliefs and practices, and they increased their unpopularity by occasionally breaking up other religious groups at worship. Many of them were jailed from time to time.

Naturally, like the Puritans earlier, George Fox and his followers looked to America for asylum. A few of them went to New England. But there (except in Rhode Island), they were greeted with fines, whippings, and orders to leave, and three men and a woman who persisted in staying were actually put to death. Many migrated to north-ern Carolina, and there, as the fastest-growing religious community, they soon were influential in colonial politics. Yet the Quakers desired a colony of their own, and Fox himself visited America (1671–1672) to look over the land. As the head of a sect despised in England, however, he could not get the necessary grant without the aid of someone influential at the court. Fortunately for his cause, his teachings had struck the hearts of a number of wealthy and prominent men, one of whom in particular made possible a large-scale effort to realize the Quaker dream.

William Penn—whose father was Sir William Penn, an admiral in the Royal Navy and a landlord of valuable Irish estates—received a gentleman's education at his father's expense but could not overcome his mystical inclinations despite his father's discipline. Converted to the doctrine of the Inner Light, the younger Penn took up evangelism and, though always moderate and soft-spoken, was repeatedly put in prison, where he wrote

Quakers Going to Meeting
The meetinghouse, at which these members of the Society of Friends are arriving on a summer day, was in a Welsh settlement near Cambria, Pennsylvania. Though made in the early nineteenth century, this print depicts a scene not very different from that in similar communities of the previous century. (Library of Congress)

Penn's Treaty with the Indians
William Penn entered into a number of treaties with the Indians for the purchase of land. These treaties were scrupulously observed by the Pennsylvania Quakers. Benjamin West's painting, one of the best known of his many historical canvases, probably represents negotiations that were carried on in June 1683. (Library of Congress)

a powerful tract, *No Cross, No Crown*. With George Fox he visited the European continent and found Quakers there, as in the British Isles, who longed to emigrate.

New Jersey, half of which was owned by two of his fellow Quakers, received Penn's attention first, when its proprietors asked him for help with their debts. In their behalf Penn helped to divide the province into East and West Jersey. Carteret, as one of the original proprietors, kept the east, and the Quakers the west. West Jersey soon began to fill up with Friends from England, while East Jersey was populated mostly by Puritans from New England. Before long Penn, together with other wealthy Quakers, purchased the eastern property from Carteret (1682), and eventually the two Jerseys were reunited as one colony (1702), second in Quaker population only to Pennsylvania itself.

Pennsylvania—which Charles II insisted on naming for his old ally the admiral—was based on a grant of the king in 1681. Penn had inherited his father's Irish lands and also his claim to a small fortune owed by the king. Charles II, possessing more real estate than ready cash, paid the debt with a grant of territory, between New York and Maryland, which was larger than England and Wales combined and which (unknown to him) contained more value in soil and minerals than any other province of English America. Within this fabulous estate Penn was to have the rights of both landlord and ruler while acknowledging the feudal suzerainty of the king by the token payment of two beaver skins a year.

Like the Calverts, the Carolina proprietors, and the Duke of York, Penn intended to make money from land sales and quitrents and from private property to be worked for him. He promptly sold several large tracts to rich Quaker associates and one tract of 15,000 acres to a group of German immigrants. Through his informative and honest advertising—as in his pamphlet entitled *A Brief Account of the Province of Pennsylvania*, which was translated into several European languages—Penn made Pennsylvania the best-known and most cosmopolitan of all the colonies. But he and his descendants were to find almost hopeless the task of collecting quitrents.

Penn was much more than a mere real estate promotor, and he undertook in Pennsylvania what he called a Holy Experiment. Colonies, he said, were the "seeds of nations," and he proposed to plant the seeds of brotherly love. He devised a liberal Frame of Government with a representative assembly. He personally sailed to Pennsylvania in 1682 to oversee the laying out, between the Delaware and the Schuylkill rivers, of the city he appropriately named Philadelphia ("Brotherly Love"), which with its rectangular streets, like those of Charleston, helped to set the pattern for most later cities in America. Penn believed, as had Roger Williams, that the land belonged to the Indians, and he was careful to see that they were reimbursed for it, as well as to see that they were not debauched by the fur traders' alcohol. With the Indians, who honored him as a rarity, an honest white man, his colony had no trouble during his lifetime. It prospered from the outset because of his thoughtful planning and also because of favorable circumstances, including the mildness of the climate and the fertility of the soil. The settlers were well-to-do and well equipped, and they received assistance from the people of other colonies and from the Swedes, Dutch, and Finns already there—for Pennsylvania when Penn first saw it was already home to significant numbers of immigrants.

Delaware, after its transfer to Penn from the Duke of York (1682), was treated as a part of Pennsylvania (and was known as "the lower counties") but was given the privilege of setting up its own representative assembly. The three counties did so in 1703, and thereafter Delaware was considered a separate colony, though until the Revolution it continued to have the same governor as Pennsylvania.

The Founding of Georgia

The establishment of the Restoration proprietary colonies expanded English settlement along the length of the Atlantic coast from New England to South Carolina. Although the population of each colony continued to grow, pushing the frontier of settlement steadily westward, for several decades there were no attempts to enlarge the English realm in America farther north or south. Not until 1733 did another new colony emerge: Georgia, the last English colony on the mainland of what would become the United States.

Georgia was unique in its origins. It was founded neither by a corporation (as Massachusetts and Virginia had been) nor by a wealthy proprietor (as in the case of Maryland, the Carolinas, Pennsylvania, and others). Its guiding purpose was neither the pursuit of profit nor the desire for a religious refuge. Instead, Georgia emerged from the work of a group of unpaid trustees. And while its founders were not uninterested in economic success, their primary motives were military and philanthropic. They wanted to erect a military barrier against the Spaniards on the southern border of English America; and they wanted to provide a refuge for impoverished Englishmen, a place where men and women without prospects at home could come and begin a new life.

The need for a military buffer between South Carolina and the Spanish settlements in Florida was growing urgent in the first years of the eighteenth century. There had been tensions between the English and the Spanish ever since the first settlement at Jamestown; and although in a treaty of 1676, Spain had recognized England's title to lands already occupied by Englishmen, conflict between the two colonizing powers continued. In 1686, Spanish forces from Florida attacked and destroyed an outlying South Carolina settlement south of the treaty line. And when Spain and England resumed their war in Europe in 1701, hostilities erupted in America again. The war ended in 1713, but another European conflict with repercussions for the New World was continually expected.

General James Oglethorpe, a hero of the late war with Spain, was therefore keenly aware of the military advantages of an English colony south of the Carolinas. Yet his interest in settlement rested even more on his philanthropic interests. As head of a parliamentary committee investigating English prisons, he had grown appalled by the plight of honest debtors rotting in confinement. Such prisoners, and other poor Englishmen in danger of succumbing to a similar fate, could, he believed, become the farmer-soldiers of the new colony in America.

A 1732 charter from King George II transferred the land between the Savannah and Altamaha rivers to the administration of Oglethorpe and his fellow trustees for a period of twenty-one years. In their colonization policies they were to keep in mind the needs of military security. Landholdings were limited in size so as to make settlement compact. Blacks—free or slave—and Roman Catholics were excluded to forestall the danger of wartime insurrection and of collusion with enemy coreligionists. And the Indian trade was strictly regulated, with rum prohibited, to lessen the risk of Indian complications.

Oglethorpe himself led the first expedition, building a fortified town at the mouth of the Savannah River in 1733, and later constructing additional forts south of the Altamaha. Only a few debtors were released from jail and sent to Georgia, but hundreds of needy tradesmen and artisans from England and Scotland and religious refugees from Switzerland and Germany were brought to the new colony at the expense of the trustees, who raised funds from charitable individuals as well as from Parliament. Though other settlers came at their own expense, immigrants were not attracted in large numbers during the early years. Newcomers generally preferred to settle in South Carolina, where there were no laws against big plantations, slaves, and rum. Before the twenty-one years of the trusteeship were up, these restrictions were repealed, and after 1750, Georgia developed along lines similar to those of South Carolina.

THE DEVELOPMENT OF EMPIRE

The English colonies in America had originated as quite separate projects; and for the most part they grew up independent of one another, with little thought that they belonged—or ought to belong—to a unified imperial system. Yet the growing commercial success of the colonial ventures was by the mid-seventeenth century producing pressure in England for a more rational, uniform structure to the empire. Reorganization, many claimed, would increase the profitability of the colonies and the power of the English government to supervise them. Above all, it would contribute to the success of the mercantile system, which had become the foundation of the English economy.

Mercantilism

One of the arguments for colonization in the first place had been that colonies would increase the wealth of the mother country and lessen its dependence on other nations. According to the mercantile theory, England would prosper and grow strong by exporting more and more to foreigners and importing less and less from them. Colonies would aid by providing a market for its manufactured goods and a source of supply for raw materials it could not produce at home. To get the full benefit, England would have to exclude foreigners (as Spain had done) from its colonial trade.

On the whole, such a mercantile system would meet the needs of the colonies as well as those of the mother country. The colonies stood to gain by concentrating on the crude products of the field and forest, and exchanging these products for the finer goods of manufacturers abroad who had the capital and skilled labor to produce them economically. In actual practice, the colonies did turn out products that the mother country needed for its own consumption or for resale to foreigners—such products as tobacco, furs, lumber, and naval stores. But the colonies also produced surpluses of some commodities—wheat, flour, and fish—that competed with commodities produced in the mother country. And whether the goods were complementary or competitive, the colonial producers sometimes found that they could make a better bargain with Spaniards, Frenchmen, or Hollanders than with Englishmen. Hence a considerable trade early developed between the English colonists and foreigners, especially the Dutch.

At first the English government, distracted as it was by the conflict between king and Parliament, made only halfhearted efforts to regulate the colonial trade in accordance with mercantilist principles. Once Oliver Cromwell was in power, he secured laws from Parliament (1650, 1651) to keep Dutch ships out of the English colonies. After the Restoration, under Charles II, the government went much further, adopting legislation that had the positive aim of directing colonial trade as well as the negative one of excluding foreigners from it.

This legislation consisted of three Navigation Acts. The first of them (1660) closed the colonies to all trade except that carried in English ships, which were defined as ships built in England or the colonies and manned by sailors of whom three-fourths were Englishmen or colonists. This law also required that certain enumerated items, among them tobacco, be exported from the colonies only to England or to an English possession. The second act (1663) provided that all goods sent from Europe to the colonies had to go by way of England and that taxes could be put on the goods during their transshipment. The third act (1673) was designed to prevent colonists from evading the export control (in regard to the enumerated items) by clearing from one colonial port for another and then actually heading for a foreign port. The new act levied a duty on cargoes bound for the intercolonial coastal trade. It also provided for the appointment of customs officials to collect the duties and administer the Navigation Acts. These acts, with later amendments

and additions, were to form the legal basis of England's mercantile system for a century.

The Dominion of New England

If the Navigation Acts were to be strictly enforced, the king would have to do more than dispatch customs officials to America. He would have to set up in London an agency that would permit him a more direct oversight of colonial affairs and more direct control over colonial governments.

Only in Virginia, a "royal colony" since 1624, did the king as yet have the right to appoint the governor. In Massachusetts, a "corporate colony," the people elected their own governor, as they also did in Plymouth. In Maryland, a "proprietary colony," the appointing power had been delegated to the proprietor. When Charles II created other proprietary colonies—Carolina, New York, New Jersey, Pennsylvania—he himself followed the Maryland example. And when he gave royal charters to Connecticut and Rhode Island, he accepted these two as "corporate colonies" by allowing them to go on choosing their officials. Moreover, he and his predecessors had permitted the development of an assembly representing the people (or some of the people) in each of the colonies—royal, corporate, or proprietary. And the assemblies were claiming more and more power for themselves.

For help in enforcing the new trade regulations, Charles II could not place much reliance on the colonial governments. Least of all could he depend on Massachusetts, which dared to behave practically like an independent republic, even usurping the sovereign's prerogative of coining money. The Puritan oligarchs, whose religion in itself was obnoxious to him, persisted in maintaining their own established church instead of the Church of England, thus violating the terms of the Massachusetts Bay Company's charter, which obliged the colony to conform to English law. Many of the Massachusetts merchants, disregarding the Navigation Acts as well, evaded the payment of duties and made smuggling a regular business.

After a royal investigation commission had visited the Bay Colony and reported back to London the extent of the colony's illegal business, Charles II decided to take action to control and chastise Massachusetts in particular and tighten control over the American empire in general. In 1675 he set up a special committee, the Lords of Trade (consisting of some of his official advisers on the Privy Council), to make recommendations for imperial reform. The Lords of Trade recommended that the king participate more directly in colonial government. He did so, and at the same time struck a blow at Massachusetts when, in 1679, he denied it authority over New Hampshire and chartered a separate, royal colony whose governor he would himself appoint.

Charles II wished to make a royal colony of Massachusetts as well, but its corporate charter was one he could not revoke without a lawsuit. He soon had grounds for action. When the Lords of Trade ordered Massachusetts to see that the Navigation Acts were obeyed, the General Court replied that, in view of the charter's provisions for self-government, Parliament had no power to legislate for the colony. When the Lords of Trade sent over a customs official to see to the enforcement of the acts, the General Court not only refused to recognize him but arrested the local agents he appointed. Finally the king started legal proceedings that led, in 1684, to revocation of the charter.

His brother and successor, James II, went much further when he came to the throne in 1685. He combined Massachusetts and the rest of the New England colonies into one Dominion of New England, and later he added New York and New Jersey to it. Within this dominion he eliminated the existing assemblies, and over it he placed a single governor, Sir Edmund Andros, with headquarters in Boston. An able but stern and tactless administrator, Andros thoroughly antagonized the people as he proceeded to levy taxes and enforce the Navigation Acts. When colonists protested on the basis of their rights as Englishmen—especially their right to be taxed only with the consent of their representatives—he retorted that they had no such rights.

The "Glorious Revolution"

James II was not only making himself unpopular in America; he was winning powerful enemies in England by attempting to exercise autocratic control over Parliament and the courts and by appointing Catholics (of whom he himself was one) to high office. By 1688, his popular support had all but vanished; and Parliament was emboldened to invite his Protestant daughter Mary and her husband, William of Orange, ruler of the Netherlands and Protestant champion of Europe, to assume the throne. James II did not resist, perhaps remembering what had happened to his father, Charles I. Instead, he fled to France; and William and Mary became joint sovereigns. By this "Glorious Revolution," as the English called it, the long struggle between king and Parliament was finally settled in Parliament's favor.

Soon after the Bostonians heard of the movement to overthrow James II in England, they determined to overthrow his viceroy in New England. A mob set out after Andros and other royal officials. Andros escaped but later surrendered and was imprisoned.

The Massachusetts leaders now hoped to get back their old corporate charter, but they were to be disappointed. Despite the persuasive efforts of Increase Mather, an outstanding Puritan divine who was on a lobbying mission in London, the new sovereigns, William and Mary, combined Plymouth with Massachusetts and claimed the land as a royal colony (1691). Under the new charter, they themselves appointed the governor; but they restored the General Court with its elected lower house and allowed the General Court to choose the members of the upper house. This charter also did away with the religious test for voting and officeholding. Though there remained a property requirement, the great majority of Massachusetts men could meet it. Thus the Massachusetts government, no longer a Puritan oligarchy, began to be fairly democratic. Quakers, Baptists, and other sectarians now were free to worship as they pleased in what once had been the exclusive land of the Puritans, though all had to pay tithes in support of the established (Congregational) church.

Andros had been ruling New York through a lieutenant governor, Captain Francis Nicholson, who enjoyed the support of the wealthy merchants and fur traders of the province. The same groups had shared political power while New York was a proprietary colony of the Duke of York and after it became a royal colony upon the duke's accession to the English throne as James II. The groups that were excluded from a fair share in the government—farmers, mechanics, small traders, and shopkeepers—already had a long accumulation of grievances when news came of James's fall and Andros's arrest. Rebellious militiamen seized the New York City fort, and Lieutenant Governor Nicholson sailed away to England.

The leadership of the New York rebels fell to Jacob Leisler, who had come from Germany, succeeded as a merchant, and married into a prominent Dutch family, but had never gained acceptance as one of the colony's ruling class. Leisler's followers proclaimed him commander in chief, and he declared his loyalty to William and Mary. He claimed, as intended for him, the dispatches arriving from the king and queen and addressed to "Our Lieutenant-Governor and Commander-in-Chief of our Province of New York, or in his absence to such as for the time being take care to keep the peace and administer the laws." Assuming the title of lieutenant governor, Leisler with the aid of the militia kept the peace and administered the laws for two years (1689–1691), until William and Mary finally appointed a new governor, who was given authority to call an elected assembly. When, ahead of the new governor, a British officer appeared with a contingent of troops, Leisler refused to surrender the fort to him. Leisler afterward yielded, but the delay gave his political enemies, soon back in power, a pretext for charging him with treason. He and one of his sons-in-law were hanged, drawn, and quartered.

In Maryland, the people at first assumed (erroneously) that the Catholic Lord Baltimore had sided with the Catholic James II and had opposed the accession of William and Mary. So in 1689, an old opponent of the proprietor's government, John Coode, started a new revolt as head of an organization calling itself "An Association in Arms for the Defense of the Protestant Religion, and for Asserting the Right of King William and Queen Mary to the Province of Maryland and All the English Dominions." The insurgents drove out Lord Baltimore's officials and, through an elected convention, chose a committee to run the government for the time being. In 1691, William and Mary used this opportunity to deprive the proprietor of his authority and to transform Maryland into a royal colony. (It became a proprietary colony again in 1715, after the fifth Lord Baltimore joined the Anglican church.)

Thus the Glorious Revolution of 1688 in England touched off revolutions, mostly bloodless, in the colonies. Under the new regime, the representative assemblies that had been abolished were revived, and the scheme for colonial unification from above was abandoned. Several of the provinces, however, were now royal colonies in which the king appointed the governor and over which he potentially had greater direct control than he once had had. The colonists had not yet challenged the ultimate authority of the king. "What had been won (possibly the word should be 'preserved')," Wesley Frank Craven has written, "was the practical right of the colonists to determine very largely for themselves questions of public policy fundamentally affecting their domestic life. In this large measure of self-government the colonists were to find with time good cause for remembering the Revolution as a glorious one and, by remembering it, fresh and potent defenses for their rights of self-government."

SUGGESTED READINGS

The classic, and still the fullest, account of the early English colonies in North America is Charles M. Andrews, *The Colonial Period in American History*, 4 vols. (1934–1938). Other general accounts include Clarence L. Ver Steeg, *The Formative Years, 1607–1763* (1964); and John E. Pomfret and F. M. Shumway, *Founding the American Colonies, 1583–1660* (1970).

The founding of Boston and the Massachusetts Bay Colony is examined in Samuel Eliot Morison, *Builders of the Bay Colony* (1930); Darrett Rutman, *Winthrop's Boston* (1965); and R. E. Wall, *Massachusetts Bay: The Crucial Decade, 1640–1650* (1972). Particularly valuable in shedding light both on the political life of Massachusetts Bay and on the religious issues that underlay it is Edmund S. Morgan, *The Puritan Dilemma: The Story of John Winthrop* (1958). Alden T. Vaughn, *New England Frontier: Puritans and Indians* (1965), examines the interaction between colonists and natives. Bernard Bailyn, *The New England Merchants in the Seventeenth Century* (1955), is a valuable study of commerce.

New England Puritanism has inspired some of the most extensive and most provocative of all American historical literature. The classic works remain those of Perry Miller, among them *The New England Mind: The Seventeenth Century* (1939), *The New England Mind: From Colony to Province* (1953), *Orthodoxy in Massachusetts* (1933), and *Errand into the Wilderness* (1956). More recent studies of Puritanism include Edmund S. Morgan, *Visible Saints* (1963) and *The Puritan Family* (1966); Sacvan Bercovitch, *The American Jeremiad* (1978) and *The Puritan Origins of the American Self* (1975); David Hall, *The Faithful Shepherd* (1972); Robert Middlekauff, *The Mathers* (1971); and Larzer Ziff, *Puritanism in America* (1973). Dissenters from Puritan orthodoxy are discussed in Edmund S. Morgan, *Roger Williams: The Church and the State* (1967); Kai Erikson, *Wayward Puritans* (1966), a study of the ideas of Anne Hutchinson that should be supplemented by Emery Battis, *Saints and Sectaries* (1962); and W. K. B. Stoever, *A Faire and Easy Way to Heaven* (1978). J. V. James, *Colonial Rhode Island* (1975); M. J. A. Jones, *Congregational Commonwealth: Connecticut, 1636–1662* (1968); and Paul R. Lucas, *Valley of Discord* (1976), examine two of the colonies created by the exodus from Massachusetts.

A good introduction to the Chesapeake colonies is Wesley Frank Craven, *The Southern Colonies in the Seventeenth Century* (1949). A brilliant examination of colonial Virginia is Edmund S. Morgan, *American Slavery, American Freedom* (1975). See also W. F. Craven, *White, Red, and Black: The Seventeenth Century Virginian* (1971); and Richard L. Morton, *Colonial Virginia*, 2 vols. (1960). For Bacon's Rebellion, see, in addition to the relevant chapters in Morgan, Wilcomb E. Washburn, *The Governor and the Rebel* (1958); and T. J. Wertenbaker, *Torchbearer of the Revolution* (1940). For Maryland, see M. P. Andrews, *The Founding of Maryland* (1933).

An important study of the English Civil War is Christopher Hill, *The World Turned Upside Down* (1972). The founding of the Restoration colonies receives attention in the general works mentioned above, particularly Andrews. For more specific treatment, see H. T. Merrens, *Colonial North Carolina* (1964); M. E. Sirmans, *Colonial South Carolina* (1966); Verner Crane, *The Southern Frontier, 1670–1732* (1929); and Clarence L. Ver Steeg, *Origins of a Southern Mosaic* (1975). Michael Kammen, *Colonial New York* (1975), Thomas J. Condon, *New York Beginnings* (1968), Van Cleaf Bachman, *Peltries or Plantations* (1969), and George L. Smith, *Religion and Trade in New Netherland* (1973), examine the early history of New York. See also Patricia Bonomi, *A Factious People* (1971), for a valuable account of politics in early New York. Edwin B. Bronner, *William Penn's Holy Experiment* (1962), and Mary Maples Dunn, *William Penn: Politics and Conscience* (1967), shed light on the founding of Pennsylvania. James T. Lemmon, *The Best Poor Man's Country* (1972), is a valuable social history of the settlement of the colony. J. E. Pomfret is the author of two studies of colonial New Jersey: *The Province of West New Jersey, 1609–1702* (1956) and *The Province of East New Jersey* (1962). For Georgia, consult T. R. Reese, *Colonial Georgia: A Study in British Imperial Policy in the Eighteenth Century* (1963); and K. Coleman, *Colonial Georgia* (1976).

The most comprehensive study of the eighteenth-century British imperial system is Lawrence Gipson's remarkable fifteen-volume work, *The British Empire Before the American Revolution* (1936–1970). Important studies of imperial administration of more modest length include Stephen S. Webb, *The Governors-General* (1979), which challenges the traditional assumption that mercantilism was the primary motivating force behind the empire; Michael Kammen, *Empire and Interest* (1970); Thomas C. Barrow, *Trade and Empire* (1967); I. K. Steele, *The Politics of Colonial Policy* (1968); and James Henretta, *Salutary Neglect* (1972). Michael Hall, *Edward Randolph and the American Colonies* (1960), examines the career of a colonial official. Viola Barnes, *The Dominion of New England* (1923), has long been the standard work on the imperial reorganization. Lawrence Harper, *The English Navigation Laws* (1939), examines problems of enforcement. The best general account of the events of 1688–1689 is David S. Lovejoy, *The Glorious Revolution in America* (1972).

3

Life in Provincial America

An Eighteenth-Century Sampler
This needlepoint sampler, done by a ten-year-old girl in 1773, is typical of many such works, which were among the most popular art forms of the seventeenth and eighteenth centuries. This sampler suggests some of the changes that American society was experiencing on the eve of the Revolution. The fine dress of the embroidered characters stands in contrast to the much simpler garb of earlier generations of Americans. But the pious inscription indicates the continuing importance of religion.
(The Bettmann Archive)

As the extent of settlement in North America grew, and as the economies of the colonies flourished, a distinctive way of life began to emerge. In some respects it resembled the society of England, from which most of the early settlers had come. But in other ways, American civilization was developing characteristics of its own.

There were three obvious reasons for the divergence between the culture of the colonies and that of the homeland. First, English society had not been transplanted whole to the New World. Those who came to America were not typical Englishmen. They were usually more discontented or more adventurous than the majority of their countrymen. Second, they found in the New World an environment in which certain elements of the English inheritance flourished, but in which others withered or never took root. Third, some of the early colonists—and many more as time went on—were not Englishmen at all. Beginning with the Dutch settlements in New York, the area that would become the United States became a magnet for immigrants from many lands: Scotland, Ireland, the European continent. And

beginning with the first importation of slaves into Virginia, America became the destination for thousands of forcibly transplanted Africans. English culture continued to predominate, but American society took its eventual shape from a wide range of influences.

Just as the colonies were becoming increasingly different from England, so were they different from one another. Not until the mid-eighteenth century did the colonists begin to call themselves "Americans." Until then, they would have identified themselves either as Englishmen or as citizens of their particular colonies. There was good reason for the lack of commonality, for the pattern of society of some areas of North America seemed to resemble that of others scarcely at all. The civilization of Puritan New England differed markedly from that of the mid-Atlantic colonies; it differed even more from the plantation economy of the South. And although Americans would ultimately discover that they had enough in common to join together to form a single nation, these regional differences continued to affect their society well beyond the colonial period.

THE COLONIAL POPULATION

The first Americans were the Indians, and for many years after the beginning of European colonization, they continued to outnumber the new settlers in North America. Even within areas in which English settlements took root, the colonists were often in the minority. Gradually, however, the European population grew—through continued immigration and through natural increase—until by the late seventeenth century whites (and their black servants) became the dominant group in the population of the Atlantic coast.

The Early Population

A few of the early settlers were members of the English upper classes: usually the younger sons of the lesser gentry, men who stood to inherit no land at home and aspired to establish estates for themselves in America. For the most part, however, the colonial population was conspicuous for its lack of representatives of the aristocracy. Instead, the dominant element was free English laborers. Some came to the New World independently. The

This Indenture MADE the *Thirteenth* Day of *May* in the Year of our Lord one thousand, seven hundred and *eighty four* BETWEEN *Alex.r Beard of Broughshane in the County of Antrim Taylor* by Consent of his Father of the one Part, and *John Duckey of Cullybackey in the said County* — *Gentleman* of the other Part, WITNESSETH, that the said *Alexand.r Beard* doth hereby covenant, promise and grant, to and with the said *John Duckey* — *his* — Executors, Administrators and Assigns, from the Day of the Date hereof until the first and next Arrival at *Philadelphia* — in America, and after for and during the Term of *Three* — Years to serve in such Service and Employment as the said *John Duckey* — or *his* Assigns shall there employ *him* according to the Custom of the Country in the like Kind. In Consideration whereof the said *John Duckey* doth hereby covenant and grant to and with the said *Alex.r Beard* to pay for *his* Passage, and to find allow *him* Meat, Drink, Apparel and Lodging, with other Necessaries, during the said Term; and at the End of the said Term to pay unto *him* the usual Allowance, according to the Custom of the Country in the like Kind. IN WITNESS whereof the Parties above-mentioned to these Indentures have interchangeably put their Hands and Seals, the Day and Year first above written.

Signed, Sealed, and Delivered,
   in the Presence of

Peter Dillon
John. Weir

Alexr Beard

John Duckey

An Eighteenth-Century Indenture
This contract, dated May 13, 1784, was made late in the history of indentured servitude and typifies the standardized form that developed. Note that it is printed, with spaces left blank to be filled in. In this particular case, the contract was made between the master and his servant before either of them sailed for America. Originally, a contract was written in two identical parts on a single sheet, which was torn in two, leaving an indented or indentured edge—hence the term "indenture."

religious dissenters who formed the bulk of the population of early New England, for example, generally arranged their own passage, brought their families with them, and established themselves from the start on their own land. Others—many more in the Southern and later in the mid-Atlantic colonies—came as indentured servants.

The system of temporary servitude in the New World developed naturally out of existing practices in England, where a youth commonly bound himself to a master as an apprentice for a term of seven years, during which time he would presumably learn a trade. In America, the term of service was usually briefer—four to five years; and the expectation of training was generally lower. But the conditions of the agreement were otherwise basically the same. In return for service to his master, a servant was entitled to passage to America, food and shelter, and—upon completion of his term—such benefits as clothing, tools, and occasionally land.

Most of these indentured servants came to the colonies voluntarily, but not all. Beginning as early as 1617, the English government occasionally dumped shiploads of convicts in America to be sold into servitude, although some criminals, according to Captain John Smith, "did chuse to be hanged ere they would go thither, and were." The government also transported prisoners taken in battles with the Scots and the Irish in the 1650s, as well as other groups deemed undesirable: orphans, vagrants, paupers, and those who were "lewd and dangerous." Still other involuntary immigrants were neither dangerous nor indigent but simply victims of kidnapping, or "impressment."

It was not difficult to understand why the system of indentured servitude proved so appealing to those in a position to employ servants in colonial America. It provided a means of coping with the severe labor shortage in the wilderness; and in the Chesapeake country it offered an additional incentive: a master received a grant of land (or "headright") for every servant he brought to the New World. For the servants themselves, the attractions were not always so clear. Those who came voluntarily often did so to escape troubles in England; others came in the hope of establishing themselves on land or in trades of their own when their terms of service expired. Yet the reality often differed sharply from the hope.

As the number of freed indentured servants grew, becoming by the late seventeenth century one of the largest elements of the population, serious problems began to develop. Some managed to establish themselves quite successfully as farmers, tradesmen, or artisans. Others, however, found themselves without employment and without prospects; and there grew up in some areas a large floating population of young single men—such as those who formed the backbone of Bacon's Rebellion—who traveled restlessly from place to place in search of work or land. These "herds of roving bachelors," as some have called them, became the source of social turbulence not only in Virginia, but in many areas.

Even those free laborers who did find employment or land for themselves, and settled down with families, often did not stay put for very long. The phenomenon of families simply pulling up stakes and moving to another, more promising location every several years was one of the most prominent characteristics of the colonial population.

Indentured servitude remained an important source of population well into the eighteenth century, but its character changed in several ways. After 1700, the flow of white servants to the Southern colonies (where most had headed in the seventeenth century) all but ceased. Instead, they traveled to the mid-Atlantic settlements—Pennsylvania and New York, in particular—where working conditions were more attractive and opportunities more numerous, and where they were not displaced by black slaves. By now, the system had become flexible enough that a prospective indenture did not need to arrange his terms of service with his master in advance. Many eighteenth-century immigrants came as so-called free willers, or redemptioners, who gave their indentures to the captain of the ship they boarded as payment for their passage. When they arrived in America, the captain would auction off their contracts to waiting landowners.

Birth and Death

At first, new arrivals in most colonies—whatever their background or status—could anticipate great hardship: inadequate food, frequent epidemics, and—in an appallingly large number of cases—early death. By the second half of the seventeenth century, however, conditions in most places had improved; and the population began to expand rapidly, not only through immigration but, more important, through natural increase.

Several factors contributed to the improvement. The most obvious was that as time went on, the settlers cleared more land, built better shelter, and learned to provide for themselves more adequately. Also important was the slow development of immunity to indigenous diseases, a process that was particularly important in the swampy Chesapeake colonies and was known as "seasoning." Conflicts with Indians continued to pose a danger to the European settlers, but in some areas the whites had managed to pacify or eliminate the natives.

Equally important, however, were two other factors. One was the relative youthfulness of the colonial population. Far more young people migrated from England than did older men and women. Thus, there were relatively more women of childbearing age; and the population as a whole tended to be hardier than that of England. There was also a steady improvement in the sex ratio through the seventeenth century. In the early years of settlement, more than three-quarters of the white population of the Chesapeake consisted of men. And even in New England, which from the beginning had attracted more families (and thus more women) than the Southern colonies, 60 percent of the inhabitants were male in 1650. Whatever effects this uneven ratio may have had on the status of women in America (and some have argued that it improved their status greatly), it had a debilitating effect upon the birth rate. Gradually, however, more women began to arrive in the colonies. Not until well into the eighteenth century did the ratio begin to match

that in England (where women were a majority); but by the late seventeenth century, the proportion of males to females in all the colonies was becoming more balanced. The population, as a result, was becoming better able to reproduce itself.

Perhaps the most remarkable feature of the colonial population was its longevity. In New England, in particular, the average life expectancy was remarkably high. In Andover, Massachusetts (a town that has been the subject of a thorough demographic study), the first generation of male settlers lived to an average age of seventy-one, the women to seventy. The next generation's life expectancy declined somewhat—to sixty-five for men—but remained far higher than the English equivalent.

The result of all these factors—immigration, rising birth rates, low death rates—was

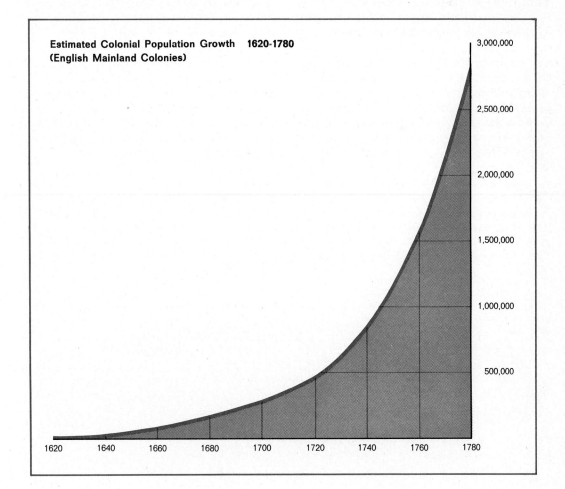

Estimated Colonial Population Growth 1620-1780 (English Mainland Colonies)

a remarkably rapid increase in the colonial population. By the end of the seventeenth century, the European population in the English colonies of North America had grown to over a quarter of a million. Virginia grew almost tenfold in the last half of the century; New England more than quadrupled its population through natural increase alone, and continued immigration swelled the region further.

The Beginnings of Slavery

The demand for black servants to supplement the always scarce Southern labor supply existed almost from the first moments of settlement. The supply of African laborers, however, remained relatively restricted during much of the seventeenth century because of the nature of the slave trade.

That trade had begun in the sixteenth century, when Portuguese ships began visiting the west coast of Africa. There they captured native tribesmen and shipped them across the Atlantic to the new colonies in South America. The commerce grew more extensive, more sophisticated, and more horrible in the seventeenth century. Flourishing slave marts grew up on the African coast, where native chieftains made large supplies

of blacks available by capturing enemy tribesmen in battle and bringing them—tied together in long lines, or "coffles"—out of the jungle and to the ports. Then, after some haggling on the docks between the European traders and the African suppliers, the unfortunate victims were packed into the dark, filthy holds of the ships for the horrors of the "middle passage"—the journey to America. For weeks, occasionally months, the black prisoners were kept chained in the bowels of the slave ships, unable to stand, hardly able to breathe, supplied with minimal food and water. Those who died en route—and there were many—were simply thrown overboard. Slave traders accepted such deaths as an inevitable result of the system. They tried to cram as many Africans as possible into their ships to ensure that enough would survive to yield a profit at journey's end. Once in the colonies, the slaves were auctioned off to white landowners and transported—terrified and bewildered—to their new homes.

The first black laborers arrived in English North America before 1620; and as English seamen began to establish themselves in the slave trade, the flow to the colonies gradually increased. In the beginning, virtually all the arriving blacks were brought from the West Indies. Not until the 1670s did traders start importing them directly from Africa to North

---

A Slave Ship
The plan of the *Brookes,* an eighteenth-century English vessel built specially for the slave trade, shows how little space was wasted. Pictured here is only one of two lower decks. The slaves were packed in so tightly that they had no room to stand or even to sit. During part of the day (except in bad weather) they were allowed on the main deck to get food, air, and exercise. (New York Public Library)

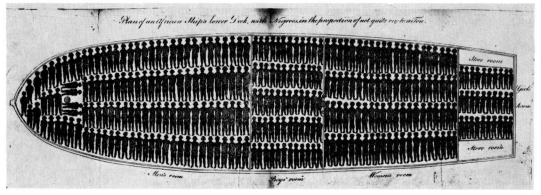

"Facts" Versus Interpretations

Unlike some other fields of scholarship, history is not an exact science. Although we can establish with some certainty many of the basic "facts" of history—that the United States declared its independence in 1776, for example; or that the North won the Civil War; or that the first atomic bomb was detonated in 1945—wide disagreement remains, and will always remain, about the *significance* of such facts. There are as many different ways of viewing a historical event as there are historians viewing it. In reading any work of history, therefore, it is important to ask not only what facts the author is presenting, but how he or she is choosing and interpreting those facts.

Historians disagree with one another for many reasons. People of different backgrounds, for example, often bring different attitudes to their exploration of issues. A black historian might look at the American Revolution in terms of its significance for the members of his race and thus draw conclusions about it that would differ from those of a white historian. A Southerner might view Reconstruction in terms different from a Northerner. Social, religious, racial, ethnic, and sexual differences among historians all contribute to the shaping of distinctive points of view.

Historians might disagree, too, as a result of the methods they use to explore their subjects. One scholar might choose to examine slavery by using psychological techniques, while another might reach different conclusions by employing quantitative methods and making use of a computer. Because history is an unusually integrative discipline—that is, because it employs methods and ideas from many different fields of knowledge, ranging from science to the humanities, from economics to literary criticism—the historian has available an enormous range of techniques, each of which might produce its own distinctive results.

One of the greatest sources of disagreement among historians is personal ideology—a scholar's assumptions about the past, the present, politics, society. Historians who accept the teachings of Karl Marx and others—that economics and social classes lie at the root of all historical processes—will emphasize such matters in their examination of the past. Others might stress human ideas, or the influence of particular men, or the workings of institutions and bureaucracies. A critic of capitalism, for example, might argue that American foreign policy after World War II was a reflection of economic imperialism. A critic of communism would be more likely to argue that the United States was responding to Soviet expansionism.

Perhaps most important, historical interpretations differ from one another according to the time in which they are written. It may not be true, as many have said, that "every generation writes its own history." But it is certainly true that no historian can entirely escape the influence of his or her own time. Hence, for example, historians writing in the relatively calm 1950s often emphasized very different issues and took very different approaches from those who wrote in the turbulent 1960s, particularly on such issues as race and foreign policy. A scholar writing in a time of general satisfaction with the nation's social and political system is likely to view the past very differently from one writing in a time of discontent. Historians in each generation, in other words, emphasize those features of the past that seem most relevant to contemporary concerns.

All of this is not to say that present concerns dictate, or should dictate, historical views. Nor is it to say that all interpretations are equally valid. On some questions, historians do reach general agreement; some interpretations prove in time to be without merit, while others become widely accepted. What is most often the case, however, is that each interpretation brings something of value to our understanding of the past. The life of the world, like the life of an individual, has so many facets, such vast complexities, so much that is unknowable, that there will always be room for new approaches to understanding it. Like the blind man examining the elephant, in the fable, the historian can get hold of and describe only one part of the past at a time. The cumulative efforts of countless scholars examining different aspects of history contribute to a view of the past that grows fuller with every generation. But the challenge and the excitement of history lies in the knowledge that that view can never be complete.

America. Even then, however, the flow remained small, mainly because a single group—the Royal African Company of England—maintained a monopoly on the trade and managed as a result to keep prices high and supplies low.

A turning point in the history of the black population in America was 1697, the year that the Royal African Company's monopoly was finally broken. With the trade now opened to English and colonial merchants on a competitive basis, prices fell and the number of blacks arriving greatly increased. By the end of the century, about 25,000 slaves lived in America (approximately 10 percent of the population). But because blacks were so heavily concentrated in a few Southern colonies, they were already beginning to outnumber whites in some areas.

By 1760, the number of blacks had increased tenfold since the turn of the century—to approximately a quarter of a million. A relatively small number (16,000 in 1763) lived in New England; there were slightly more in the middle colonies (29,000). The vast majority, however, continued to live in the South. As a result, the flow of free white laborers to that region had all but stopped, and blacks had become permanently established as the basis of the Southern work force.

It was not entirely clear at first that the status of black laborers in America would be fundamentally different from that of white indentured servants. In the rugged conditions of the seventeenth-century South, it was often difficult for whites and blacks to maintain strictly separate roles. In some areas—South Carolina, for example, where the number of black arrivals swelled more quickly than anywhere else—whites and blacks lived and worked together for a time on terms of relative equality. Some blacks were freed after a term of servitude; others were treated much like white hired servants.

Gradually, however, relations between the races evolved in such a way that a rigid distinction became established between black and white. (See "Where Historians Disagree," page 63.) White servants were necessarily freed after a term of servitude; their masters were required by contract to release them. There was no such necessity to free black workers, and the assumption slowly spread that blacks would remain in service permanently. Another incentive for making the status of blacks rigid was that the children of slaves provided white landowners with a self-perpetuating labor force. White assumptions about the inferiority of the black race contributed further to the growing rigidity of the system; even when blacks began converting in large numbers to Christianity, most whites continued to consider them a lesser breed, capable of little more than manual labor. There were, in short, many incentives for whites to keep blacks in bondage, and virtually none to free them. The result was the evolution of a system of permanent servitude, a system made legal in the early eighteenth century when colonial assemblies began to pass "slave codes" limiting the rights of blacks and ensuring almost absolute authority to white masters.

New Immigration

Besides the Africans, other non-English peoples came in large numbers to the colonies after the end of the seventeenth century, while immigration from England itself fell off. Recovering from a prolonged depression in the 1630s, England thereafter began to develop more and more industries that demanded workmen, so that the talk of overpopulation ceased to be heard. Instead of encouraging emigration from its own shores, the government tried to check the loss of English manpower by prohibiting the departure of skilled artisans, while continuing to unload the unemployable or the undesirable upon the defenseless colonies. Although, during the eighteenth century, the colonies received relatively few newcomers from England, the populations of several of them were swelled by vast numbers of arrivals from France, Germany, Switzerland, Ireland, and Scotland.

Of these immigrants the earliest, though not the most numerous, were the French Calvinists, or Huguenots. Under the Edict of Nantes (1598), they had enjoyed liberties and privileges that enabled them to constitute

The Origins of Slavery

Historians have long disagreed about the nature of the institution of slavery in nineteenth-century America. In recent years, however, they have also offered several different views of the factors that led to the creation of the institution in the first place.

Among the first historians to examine the process by which the slave system evolved in the seventeenth and early eighteenth centuries were Oscar and Mary Handlin. Writing in 1950, they pointed out that many residents of the American colonies (and of England) lived in varying degrees of "unfreedom," that there was nothing unusual or new about a dependent labor force. What was new was the transformation of black servitude into a permanent system, based on race, with the condition of slavery passed from one generation to the next. The Handlins identified this transition from "servant" to "slave" as a legal process by which colonial legislatures sought to increase the available labor force. Imposing slavery on European immigrants would have discouraged laborers from migrating. But since Africans were imported by force, there was no reason to mitigate the conditions of their servitude. Slavery, in short, emerged out of traditional forms of "unfreedom," transformed by the peculiar nature of life in the New World.

Winthrop Jordan, in White over Black (1968), offered a very different view of how slavery developed in America. Rejecting the argument of the Handlins that it was primarily a legal process, Jordan emphasized the long tradition of slavery in Western culture—a tradition with which the English settlers in America were familiar. And he showed, too, how Europeans had for centuries viewed people of color—and particularly black Africans—as inferior beings preeminently fit to serve whites. Slavery did not evolve slowly from a system of relative racial equality. Blacks and whites were viewed and treated differently from the beginning; and the institution that finally emerged was a natural reflection of the deep-seated racism that the white settlers had brought with them. David Brion Davis, similarly, argued in The Problem of Slavery in Western Culture (1966) that American slavery emerged not so much from the legal or economic conditions of the colonies as from a deeply embedded set of cultural assumptions. Davis placed less emphasis than Jordan on racism; he argued, instead, that the notion of slavery was an integral part of Western culture and that African servitude in America was not profoundly different from other forms of slavery in other societies.

Several historians in the 1970s returned to an emphasis on the particular conditions within the American colonies that helped produce the slave system. But unlike the Handlins, they saw the legal process by which slavery emerged as secondary to other issues. Peter Wood, in Black Majority (1974), emphasized the economic benefits that the black labor force provided whites in colonial South Carolina. African workers were better suited than Europeans to do the arduous work of rice cultivation, and landowners therefore encouraged the importation of slaves for economic reasons. At first, blacks and whites worked together, and differentiations in status were relatively vague. By the early eighteenth century, however, whites were becoming uneasy about the presence of a black majority in the colony. And the hardening of the slave system, through legislation and in practice, reflected white fears of black resistance or revolt.

Edmund S. Morgan's American Slavery, American Freedom (1975) described the simultaneous development of slavery and freedom in the New World as the central paradox of American history. In an intensive examination of colonial Virginia, Morgan suggested that the early colonists did not intend to create a permanent system of human bondage. By the late seventeenth century, however, the flourishing tobacco economy had created a growing need for cheap labor. The existence of a large, dependent white labor force was unappealing to the colonists—not only because such a labor force was difficult to recruit and control but because it contradicted the dream of the early settlers of a free and equal society. African slavery, therefore, answered both an economic need and an ideological one. It was a way to have a dependent labor force that could be reconciled with democratic ideals. Blacks were simply considered a different species of people, unentitled to the freedoms that early Americans believed were the natural right of all white citizens.

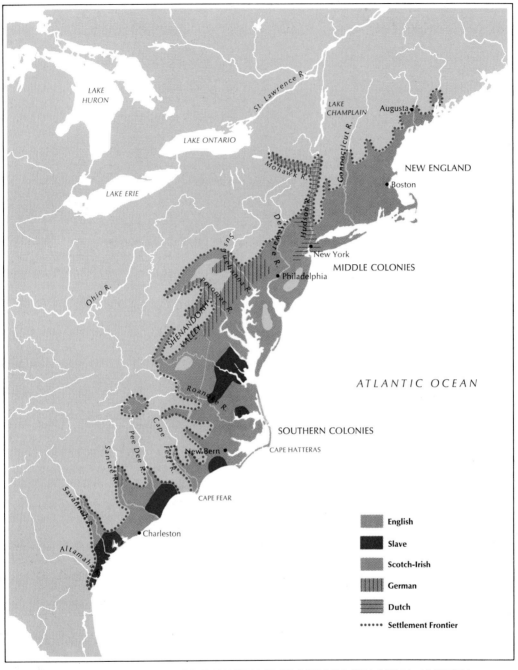

DISTRIBUTION OF MAJOR IMMIGRANT GROUPS IN COLONIAL AMERICA

practically a state within the state in Roman Catholic France. In 1685, however, the edict was revoked, and singly and in groups the Huguenots took the first opportunity to leave the country, until a total of about 300,000 had left for England, the Netherlands, America,

and elsewhere, only a small minority of them going to the English colonies.

Like the French Protestants, many German Protestants suffered from the arbitrary enactments of their rulers; and German Catholics as well as Protestants suffered even more from the devastating wars of the Sun King of France, Louis XIV. The Rhineland of southwestern Germany, the area known as the Palatinate, was especially exposed to the slaughter of its people and the ruin of its farms. For the Palatine Germans, the unusually cold winter of 1708–1709 came as the last straw, and more than 12,000 of them sought refuge in England. The Catholics among them were shipped back to Germany, and the rest were resettled in England, Ireland, or the colonies.

Arriving in New York, approximately 3,000 of them tried to make homes in the Mohawk Valley, only to be ousted by rapacious colonial landlords. Some of the Palatines moved farther up the Mohawk, but most of them made their way to Pennsylvania, where they received a hearty welcome. After that, the Quaker colony was the usual destination of Germans, who sailed for America in growing numbers, including some Moravians and Mennonites with religious views similar to those of the Quakers. But quite a few of the German Protestants went to North Carolina, especially after the founding of New Bern (1710) by a company of 600 German-speaking Swiss.

The Scotch-Irish, the most numerous of the newcomers, were not Irishmen at all, though they came from Ireland. In the early seventeenth century, King James I, to further the conquest of Ireland, had seen to the peopling of the northern county of Ulster with his subjects from the Scottish Lowlands, who as good Presbyterians might be relied upon to hold their ground against the Irish Catholics. These Ulster colonists—the Scotch-Irish—eventually prospered despite the handicap of a barren soil and the necessity of border fighting with the Irish tribesmen. Then, after about a century, the English government destroyed their prosperity by prohibiting the export of their woolens and other products, and at the same time threatened their religion by virtually outlawing it and

insisting upon conformity with the Anglican church. As the long-term leases of the Scotch-Irish terminated, in the years after 1710, the English landlords doubled and even tripled the rents. Rather than sign new leases, thousands upon thousands of the ill-used tenants embarked in successive waves of emigration.

Often coldly received at the colonial ports, most of the Scotch-Irish pushed out to the edge of the American wilderness. There they occupied land with scant regard for ownership, believing that "it was against the laws of God and nature that so much land should be idle while so many Christians wanted it to labor on and to raise bread." There they also fought the Indians, as earlier they had fought the Irish.

The Scots and the Irish who migrated to America had no direct connection with the Scotch-Irish immigrants. Scottish Highlanders, some of them Roman Catholics frustrated in the rebellions of 1715 and 1745, went to more than one of the colonies, but mostly to North Carolina. Presbyterian Lowlanders, afflicted with high rents in the country and unemployment in the towns, left in large numbers shortly before the American Revolution. The Irish had migrated in trickles over a long period, and by the time of the Revolution they were about as numerous as the Scots, though less conspicuous, many of them having lost their Roman Catholic religion and their identity as Irishmen.

All these various immigrants contributed to the remarkable growth of the colonies. In 1700, the colonial population totaled a quarter of a million or less; by 1775, it was nearly ten times as large—more than 2 million. The number practically doubled every twenty-five years. Important as the continuing immigration was, the rapid growth of the colonial population was mainly due to natural increase, to the excess of births over deaths. In the colonies, with their abundance of land and opportunity, large families were an asset.

THE COLONIAL ECONOMY

Although colonial Americans engaged almost from the beginning in a wide range of economic pursuits, it was farming that dominated all areas of settlement throughout the seventeenth and eighteenth centuries. Beyond that basic similarity, however, the

Tobacco Preparation, Eighteenth Century
When tobacco was harvested, the stalks were hung in a well-ventilated barn to cure. After several months, in damp weather when the leaves were pliable, they were stripped from the stalks, sorted, and tied into "hands," then packed tightly in hogsheads. These were stored in public warehouses until examined by official inspectors. Eventually, the hogsheads were carried by boat or wagon or were rolled to the nearest ship landing. Ships from England ascended the rivers of the tobacco country to pick up cargoes. From William Tatham, *An Historical and Practical Essay on the Culture and Commerce of Tobacco* (London, 1800).

economies of the different regions varied markedly from one another; and even within colonies, different areas grew in different ways. In the South, economic life revolved around the cultivation of marketable crops through the plantation system. In the North, where farming was—especially in New England—usually less profitable, the economy was more diverse and included an important commercial sector.

The Southern Economy

In the Chesapeake region, where Europeans arrived first, tobacco early established itself as the basis of the colonial economy. One reason was the soil, which proved particularly suitable for the crop. Another was the long and irregular shoreline, with its many inland rivers and streams, which made it possible for planters to transport their crops easily. Demand for tobacco in England and continental Europe expanded quickly once the substance was introduced there, and for a time at least the market for the product flourished.

It was not, however, a stable market. Tobacco farmers soon began to experience the same problem that would afflict American farmers in other areas repeatedly for centuries: overproduction. The result was a series of severe declines in the price of the crop, beginning in 1640, followed by recoveries of varying degrees of completeness. The boom-and-bust cycle would continue for the rest of the century and into the next. At times, the colonial governments would attempt to limit production so as to ensure a stable price. Virginia passed the first such law in 1640, ordering farmers to plant less. But the ordinance was difficult to enforce; and it had no effect at all upon neighboring Mary-land, where tobacco production continued unabated.

Most of the Chesapeake planters believed that the way to protect themselves from the instability of the market was not to grow less tobacco but to grow more. The result was that those who could afford to expanded their landholdings, enlarged their fields, and acquired additional laborers. Through most of the seventeenth century, farms remained relatively small. But after 1700, great tobacco plantations employing hundreds of slaves were quick to emerge. The small farm of a hundred acres, cultivated by the family of the owner with perhaps two or three slaves, was now overshadowed by great estates. The Maryland plantation of Charles Carroll of Carrollton, reputedly the wealthiest man in the colonies, covered 40,000 acres and contained 285 slaves. Other plantations, in Maryland, Virginia, and the tobacco-growing

---

Virginia Tobacco Land [1686]

In 1686 the Reverend John Clayton of Yorkshire, England, visited the Virginia tobacco country. Two years later he reported to the Royal Society of London (a society of Englishmen and colonials devoted to scientific inquiry):

And yet in truth 'tis only the barrenest parts that they have cultivated, by tilling and planting only the highlands, leaving the richer vales unstirred, because they understand not anything of draining. So that the richest meadow lands, which is one third of the country, is boggy, marsh, and swamp, whereof they make little advantage, but lose in them abundance of their cattle, especially at the first of the spring, when the cattle are weak, and venture too far after young grass. Whereas vast improvements might be made thereof, for the generality of Virginia is sandy land with a shallow soil, so that after they have cleared a fresh piece of ground out of the woods, it will not bear tobacco past two or three years, unless cowpenned [and thus manured]. . . . Therefore every three or four years they must be for clearing a new piece of ground out of the woods, which requires much labour and toil, it being so thick grown all over with massy timber. Thus their plantations run over vast tracts of ground, each ambitious of engrossing as much as they can, that they may be sure to have enough to plant, and for their stocks and herds of cattle to range and to feed in. Plantations of 1,000, 2,000 or 3,000 acres are common, whereby the country is thinly inhabited, the living solitary and unsociable, trading confused and dispersed, besides other inconveniences. Whereas they might improve 200 or 300 acres to more advantage, and would make the country much more healthy. For those that have 3,000 acres have scarce cleared 600 acres thereof, which is peculiarly termed the plantation, being surrounded with the 2,400 acres of wood, so that there can be no free or even motion of the air.

regions of North Carolina, eventually attained similar size.

Elsewhere in the South, the economy developed along different lines. South Carolina and Georgia were unsuitable for the growing of tobacco, and they relied instead on rice production. The low-lying coastline with its many tidal rivers made it possible to establish, through the construction of dams and dikes, rice paddies that could be flooded and then drained. Rice cultivation was arduous work—performed standing knee deep in the mud of malarial swamps, under a blazing sun, surrounded by insects—a task so difficult and unhealthful that white laborers generally refused to perform it. Hence the far greater dependence of planters in South Carolina and Georgia on slaves than their Northern counterparts. Yet it was not only because blacks could be compelled to perform these difficult tasks that whites found them so valuable. It was also because they were much better at the work than whites. They showed from the beginning a far greater resistance to some of the local diseases that killed or incapacitated many white workers. And they proved far more adept— perhaps because many had come from similar climates in Africa—at performing the basic agricultural tasks required.

Beginning in the 1740s, indigo became another important crop in the southernmost colonies. Introduced by Eliza Lucas, the daughter of a West Indian planter, it could be grown on high ground, so that it did not interfere with the rice cultivation. It had the advantage, too, of occupying slaves during some of the periods when the rice crop did not demand attention. The brilliant blue dye that indigo produced found immediate favor in England, which had traditionally been dependent on foreign sources for such coloring substances.

Because of this early dependence on large-scale cash crops, the Southern colonies developed far less of a commercial or industrial economy than the colonies to the north. The trading in tobacco and rice was handled largely by merchants based in London and, later, in the Northern colonies. Few cities of more than modest size developed in the South; no substantial local merchant communities emerged. A pattern was established that would characterize the Southern economy, and differentiate it from that of other regions, for more than two centuries.

The Northern Economy

The economies of the Northern colonies— the settlements stretching from Pennsylvania into Maine—were even more varied than those of their Southern counterparts. In the North, as in the South, agriculture continued to dominate, yet it was a far more diverse agriculture. And in addition to farming, there gradually emerged an important commercial sector of the economy, with far-reaching effects on the future of the region.

One reason that agriculture did not remain the exclusive economic pursuit of the North was that conditions for farming were far less favorable than in the South. In New England, in particular, colder weather and hard rocky soil made it almost impossible for colonists to develop a successful commercial farming system. Instead, most settlers cultivated relatively small areas of land, growing food, raising animals, and in general attempting to make themselves self-sufficient. Modest cash crops—scrawny livestock, apples, and corn—enabled New Englanders to trade for those things they could not grow or make for themselves. One exception to the normal New England farm scene was to be found on the shores and islands of Narragansett Bay in Rhode Island. There, rich and extensive farms existed, on which colonists bred fine sheep, cattle, and horses. It was one of the few areas of the region where black slaves were common.

Conditions for agriculture were far better in the middle colonies, where the soil was excellent and the weather slightly more temperate. Farmers in New York and Pennsylvania concentrated less on growing crops for their own use than on cultivating staples for sale both at home and abroad. Their wheat production made their region the chief supplier to much of New England and to parts of the South. Despite the favorable conditions and the ready markets, however, agricultural production in some areas lagged far behind its potential. In New York, the engrossment of land into great estates, some of them thousands and even hundreds of thousands of acres large, discouraged production. Few people were willing to work as tenants when they could get farms of their own in other colonies. In Pennsylvania, by contrast, German immigrants succeeded in increasing production greatly by applying the methods of intensive cultivation they had learned in the old country. They took pride in their neat, substantial barns and in their carefully manicured farms. Yet they too were troubled by shortages of labor, and they compensated in part by using women to work in the fields—a practice that other immigrant groups on occasion found appalling.

From time to time, entrepreneurs in New England and the middle colonies attempted to augment their agricultural economy with industrial enterprises. Beginning with an unsuccessful effort to establish an ironworks in Saugus, Massachusetts, in the mid-seventeenth century, colonists embarked on innumerable ventures. Some succeeded; far more failed. Several obstacles blocked the development of a flourishing industrial sector of the colonial economy. The continuing labor shortages made it difficult to recruit a work force. And technology in the colonies was so little advanced as to make any but the simplest industrial processes impossible. In the eighteenth century, when such technology might have been imported from Europe and when the population was reaching a point that might have sustained more elaborate ventures, trade regulations imposed by the British discouraged many potential enterprises. Not until the nineteenth century would manufacturing begin to become central to the Northern economy.

Nevertheless, the colonists did manage to establish a wide range of industrial activities on a modest scale. At the simplest level, almost every colonist engaged in a certain amount of "industry" at home: carpentry, spinning, weaving, making soap and candles, and other tasks basic to the life of the family. Beyond these private efforts, craftsmen and artisans established themselves in colonial towns as cobblers, blacksmiths, riflemakers, cabinetmakers, silversmiths, printers, and so forth. In some areas, entrepreneurs harnessed the waterpower of the many streams and rivers to run small mills—some for grinding grain, others for processing cloth, still others for milling lumber. And in several places, large-scale shipbuilding operations began to flourish. The largest industrial enterprise anywhere in English North America was that of the German ironmaster Peter Hasenclever, in northern New Jersey. Founded in 1764 with British capital, it employed several hundred laborers, many of them imported from ironworks in Germany. Few other such enterprises appeared in the colonies, however, because of restrictions in the Iron Act of 1750, a measure passed by Parliament restricting colonists from engaging in metal processing. Similar prohibitions applied to the manufacture of woolens (through the Woolen Act of 1699) and hats (through the Hat Act of 1732), although Americans often disregarded the legislation.

More important than manufacturing to the economy of the Northern colonies were the so-called extractive industries: those that exploited the natural resources of the continent. At first, it was trapping that seemed to hold out the most promise for the New England economy. A flourishing fur trade grew up during the first decades of settlement; but by the mid-seventeenth century the supply of fur-bearing animals had been nearly exhausted, and the trade all but ceased. For the next century and more, the colonists relied instead on lumbering—which took advantage of the vast forests of the New World; fishing—which proved particularly profitable in the waters off New England; and mining—which exploited iron and other mineral reserves throughout the colonies. These extractive industries provided what manufacturing and agriculture often failed to give the colonists: commodities that could be exported to England in exchange for manufactured goods. And they helped, therefore, to produce the most distinctive feature of the Northern economy—a thriving commercial class.

The Rise of Commerce

The inability of any one colony, or any one region, to attain genuine economic self-sufficiency made the development of some level of commerce inevitable. The form that commerce took, however, reflected not only economic necessity but a wide array of arcane legal restrictions and the financial peculiarities of the seventeenth- and eighteenth-century world.

Perhaps the most remarkable feature of colonial commerce in the seventeenth century was that it was able to survive at all. American merchants faced such bewildering and intimidating obstacles, and lacked so many of the basic institutions of trade, that they managed to stay afloat only with difficulty. There was, first, no commonly accepted medium of exchange. The colonies had almost no specie (gold or silver coins). They experimented at times with different forms of paper currency—tobacco certificates, for example, which were secured by tobacco stored in warehouses; or land certificates, secured by property. Such paper was not, however, acceptable as payment for any goods from abroad; and it was, in any case, ultimately outlawed by Parliament. For the most part, colonial merchants had to rely on a jerry-built system of barter, or on crude money substitutes such as beaver skins.

A second obstacle was the near impossibility of rationalizing trade. No merchant could be certain that the goods on which his commerce relied would be produced in sufficient quantity; nor could he be certain of finding adequate markets for them if they were. Few channels of information existed to inform traders of what they could expect in foreign ports; and vessels sometimes stayed at sea for several years, journeying from one market to another, trading one commodity for another, attempting to find some way to turn a profit. Engaged in this chaotic commerce, moreover, was an enormous number of small, competing companies, which made the problem of rationalizing the system even more acute.

Despite these and other problems, commerce in the colonies not only survived but grew. There was an elaborate coastal trade, through which the colonies did business with one another. And there was as well an expanding international trade, which linked the North American colonies in an intricate and confusing network of commerce with the European colonies in the West Indies, with the eastern coast of Africa, and with England and continental Europe. One pattern that emerged was often defined as a "triangular trade": the transporting of rum and other goods from New England to the Guinea Coast of Africa; the exchange of those goods for captive blacks, who were then shipped to the West Indies (hence the term "middle passage" for the the dread journey—it was the second of the three legs of the voyage); and the exchange of the slaves for sugar and molasses, which was then shipped back to New England to be distilled into rum. Yet the system in reality was seldom so simple. The "triangular" trade in rum, slaves, and sugar was frequently intertwined with other, equally important trade routes: between the Northern and Southern colonies, between America and England, between the West Indies and Europe.

Out of this confusing and highly risky system there emerged a group of adventurous businessmen who by the mid-eighteenth century were beginning to constitute a distinct merchant class. Concentrated in the port cities of the North (Boston, New York, Philadelphia, and other, smaller, trading centers), they had the advantage of protection from foreign competition, the British Navigation Acts having excluded all non-British ships from the colonial carrying trade. These merchants had access to a market in England for such colonial products as furs, timber, and American-built ships. To sell other goods— fish, flour, wheat, and meat, all of which England could produce for itself—they had to look elsewhere. Despite laws restricting colonial trade to England and its possessions, many merchants developed markets in the French, Spanish, and Dutch West Indies, where prices were often higher than in the British colonies. The profits from this trade enabled the colonies to import the manufactured goods they needed from Europe.

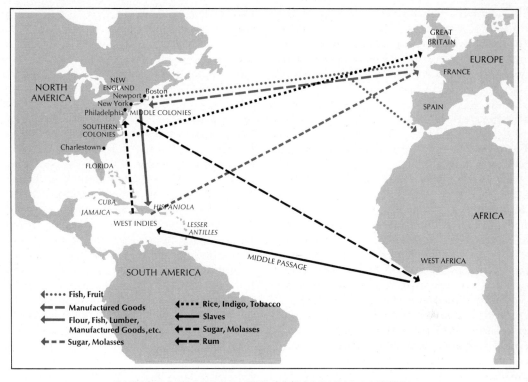

OVERSEAS TRADE ROUTES OF COLONIAL AMERICA

In the course of the eighteenth century, the colonial commercial system began to stabilize. In some cities, the more successful merchants expanded their operations so greatly that they were able to dominate some sectors of trade and curb some of the destabilizing effects of competition. Merchants managed, as well, to make extensive contacts in the English commercial world, securing their positions in certain areas of trade. But the commercial sector of the American economy remained open to newcomers, largely because it—and the society on which it was based—was expanding so rapidly.

PATTERNS OF SOCIETY

It was not only in the composition of its population and the structure of its economy that the society of the colonies differed from that of England. It was also in the nature of its most basic social institutions—the class structure, the community, and the family. The class system of England was unable to re-create itself in North America. Although there were sharp class distinctions in the colonies, there was no entrenched aristocracy as in England. And there were many more opportunities for social mobility—both up and down. There emerged, too, new forms of community whose structure reflected less the British model than the realities of the American wilderness. These forms varied greatly from one region to another, but several basic—and distinctly American—types emerged.

The Plantation

The plantation system of the American South illustrated clearly both the differences between the colonial and English class systems and the way in which colonial communities evolved in response to local conditions. The first plantations emerged in the early settlements of Virginia and Maryland, in response to the establishment of tobacco as the economic basis of the Chesapeake. Some colonists hoped to re-create in America the entrenched, landholding aristocracy of England; and in a few cases—notably in the great Maryland estates granted by Lord Baltimore to his relatives and friends—a semblance of such an aristocracy did emerge. For the most part, however, plantations were far from aristocratic places. In the early days in Virginia, they were little more than crude clearings on the frontier, where landowners and indentured servants worked side by side in conditions so horrible that death was an everyday occurrence. Even in later years, when the death rate declined and the landholdings became more established, plantations were seldom more than simple farms. Most landowners lived in rustic cabins or houses, with their servants or slaves nearby. A few planters expanded their holdings into large and truly wealthy estates, worked by hundreds of servants. But the more common plantation was of relatively modest size, with a work force of no more than thirty.

The economy of the plantation, like all agricultural economies, was a precarious one. In good years, a successful grower could earn great profits, enabling him to expand his operations and move closer to the position of a landed aristocrat. But without control over his market, the planter was also constantly at risk. When prices for his crops fell—as tobacco prices did, for example, in the 1660s—he could face the prospect of ruin. The plantation economy created many new wealthy landowners, but it also destroyed many.

Because plantations were often far from cities and towns—which were, in any case, relatively few in number in the South—they often became self-contained communities. Residents lived in close proximity to one another in a cluster of buildings that included the "great house" of the planter himself (a house that was usually, although not always, far from great), the service buildings, the barns, and the cabins of the slaves. Wealthier planters often created something approaching a full town on their plantations, with a school (for white children only), a chapel, and a large population. Smaller planters lived far more modestly, but still in a relatively self-sufficient world.

Among white farmers in the South, a distinct class system emerged. Even though the fortunes of planters could rise and fall quckly, at any given time there were always a few particularly wealthy landowners, who exercised far greater social and economic influence than their less prosperous neighbors. Within a particular area, a great landowner not only controlled the lives of those who worked his own plantation but the livelihood of independent farmers working small plots who depended on him to market their crops and supply them with credit. Some whites rented their farms from wealthy planters.

The black slaves, of course, lived very differently. On the smaller plantations, it was not always possible for a rigid separation to develop between masters and slaves. But where blacks lived together in substantial numbers, they began to develop a society and culture of their own—influenced by their white masters, to be sure, but also independent of them. Although whites did nothing to encourage marriage among slaves, usually hoping only that they would produce children rapidly, blacks themselves developed a strong and elaborate family structure. Families often lived together and worked together, tending the private gardens allotted to them for growing their own food. The slave family was so successful that the black population increased more rapidly in the early eighteenth century than the white. Blacks also developed languages of their own. In South Carolina, for example, the early slaves com-

Mount Vernon
George Washington's plantation on the shores of the Potomac River in Virginia was far from typical. Most Southern estates were more modest, both in their size and their grandeur. But Mount Vernon resembled other plantations in certain important ways: its strategic location along a major river, for easy water access to markets; its spatial organization, with the "great house" of the master serving as the center of a much larger social community; and above all, its labor system, which was based (despite Washington's personal qualms) on black slavery.
(The Granger Collection)

municated with one another in Gullah, a hybrid of English and African tongues, that not only reinforced the blacks' sense of connection with their ancestry but enabled them to engage in conversations their white masters could not understand. There emerged too a distinctive slave religion, which blended Christianity with African folklore, and it became a central element in the emergence of an independent black culture.

Most slaves worked as field hands, but there was a wide variety of other roles they could perform. Some were house servants and as a result often lived in what was, by black standards, great luxury. Others learned trades and crafts—blacksmithing, carpentry, and others—and became particularly valuable members of the plantation work force. These skilled craftsmen were at times hired out to other planters; some were even permitted to set up their own establishments in towns or cities, paying a share of their profits to their owners and, on occasion, buying their freedom. There was a small but significant free black population living in Southern cities by the time of the Revolution.

As an economic unit, the Southern plantation was both efficient and productive, helping the agricultural output of the region to expand greatly in the course of the colonial period. As a social unit, it achieved stability at the cost of human freedom. The relationship between blacks and whites on the plantation was a complex one—at times cruel, at times warm and kind; but whatever its particular character, it rested in the end on the enforced servitude of one race to another. And it relied on the racist assumptions of the master class that blacks were innately inferior to whites. The result was the emergence of two separate cultures in the South, closely tied to one another, yet separate: the culture of the white planter and the culture of the black slave.

The Puritan Community

A very different form of community emerged in Puritan New England, but one that was equally distinctively American. Since much of the Northeast was settled by large groups of immigrants arriving together (entire Puritan congregations often moving to the New World en masse), the characteristic community in New England was not the isolated farm, but the town. Each new settlement drew up a "covenant" among its members, binding all residents together in a religious and social commitment to unity and harmony. The structure of the towns generally reflected the spirit of the covenant. Colonists laid out a village, with houses and a meeting-house arranged around a central pasture, or "common." They also divided up the outlying fields and woodlands of the town, the size of a field and the desirability of its location depending on the family's numbers, wealth, and social station. But wherever his land might lie, the New England townsman lived with his neighbors close by, reinforcing the strong sense of community.

Once established, a town was generally left alone by the higher authorities of the colony. Residents held a yearly "town meeting" to decide important questions and to choose a group of "selectmen," who governed the town until the next general gathering. As a rule, all adult males were permitted to participate in the meeting. But important social distinctions remained, the most crucial of which was membership in the church. Only those residents who could give evidence of having been "saved," of being among the elect (the "visible saints") assured of salvation, were admitted to membership, although other residents of the town were required to attend church services.

Towns were usually fairly self-sufficient entities. Each established its own school, as required by colonial statute. A 1647 Massachusetts law—designed to circumvent "that old deluder Satan"—required every community of more than fifty households to hire a schoolmaster to teach reading and writing; a larger town—one of a hundred or more households—had to set up a Latin grammar school (the rough equivalent of a high school). Villages maintained relatively self-contained economies as well. Residents consumed most of what they produced, and they used the surplus to trade for those comparatively few goods they could not make for themselves.

Central to the Puritan community was the family. And central to each family was the father, who exercised nearly dictatorial power over family members. The English system of primogeniture—the passing of all property to the firstborn son—was not re-created in America. Instead, a father divided up the lands allotted to him among all his sons. His control of this inheritance was one of the most effective means of exercising power over the family. Often a son would reach his late twenties before his father would allow him to move into his own household and work his own land.

The early Puritan community, in short, was a tightly knit organism. The town as a whole was bound together by the initial covenant, by the centralized layout of the village, by the power of the church, and by the town meeting. The family was held together by a rigid patriarchal structure that limited opportunities for younger members to strike out on their own. Yet as the years passed and the communities grew, this rigid communal structure came under increasing strain. By the late seventeenth century, New England had ceased to be a purely agricultural society; a new commercial sector had been added to the economy, and new economic opportunities (and pressures) had intruded themselves

Confession of a Witch [1692]

Mrs. Mary Osgood, of Andover, Massachusetts, was examined for witchcraft, September 8, by a group of judges. They reported:

She confesses that, about 11 years ago, when she was in a melancholy state and condition, she used to walk abroad in her orchard; and upon a certain time she saw the appearance of a cat, at the end of the house, which yet she thought was a real cat. However, at that time, it diverted her from praying to God, and instead thereof she prayed to the devil; about which time she made a covenant with the devil, who, as a black man, came to her and presented her a book, upon which she laid her finger, and that left a red spot: and that upon her signing, the devil told her he was her God, and that she should serve and worship him, and she believes she consented to it. She says, further, that about two years agone, she was carried through the air, in company with deacon Frye's wife, Ebenezer Baker's wife, and Goody Tyler, to five mile pond, where she was baptised by the devil, who dipped her face in the water and made her renounce her former baptism, and told her she must be his, soul and body, forever, and that she must serve him, which she promised to do.

About six weeks later, on October 19, she was visited by Increase Mather, who reported:

Mrs. Osgood freely and relentingly said that the confession which she made upon her examination for witchcraft, and afterwards acknowledged before the honourable judges, was wholly false, and that she was brought to the said confession by the violent urging and unreasonable pressings that were used toward her; she asserted that she never signed the devil's book, was never baptised by the devil, never afflicted any of the accusers, or gave her consent for their being afflicted.

---

into even the most isolated communities. The family structure, too, was undergoing changes. For the first several generations, the available land within any town had been sufficient to satisfy the needs of younger members of a family. Even when a father had to divide his land among four or five sons, there was usually enough for all. By the third generation, however, when such lands were being subdivided for the third time, there was often too little to go around. Sons began to chafe at the prospect of remaining permanently under the control of their fathers, with no prospect of an independent estate. And towns as a whole were growing overcrowded. The result was that in community after community, groups of younger residents were breaking away and moving elsewhere to form towns of their own. Some journeyed only a few miles. Others moved to far distant areas. In either case, however, the original, communal nature of the community was challenged and eroded.

The result of this gap between the expectation of a united community and the reality of a diverse and divided one was often severe social and psychological strain. At the extreme, these tensions could produce bizarre and disastrous events. One example was the widespread hysteria in the 1680s and 1690s over witchcraft in New England. It reached its greatest extremes in Salem, Massachusetts, where the strange behavior of several children and the mysterious actions of two West Indian slaves steeped in voodoo lore produced hundreds of accusations of witchcraft. Nineteen residents of Salem were put to death before the trials finally ended in 1692.

On the surface, the witchcraft crisis was an example of wild superstition and social hysteria. A closer examination, however, reveals deeper origins. Research into the background of the phenomenon in Salem has indicated that the witchcraft turmoil there was in large part a result of severe social tensions in the town: tensions between those who were gravitating toward the new commercial economy of the town's thriving seaport and those who remained tied to the languishing agricultural economy of the community's western areas. Residents of the outlying areas of the town resented the favored position of their eastern neighbors. But since such jealousy could not be openly expressed in a "godly" community, it found expression instead in the form of accusations of witchcraft. The accusations were usually made by the relatively isolated and unsuccessful members of the community against people associated with its more prosperous segments. The Puritan vision of community—a vision of a "peaceable kingdom" united in a common purpose—was a heavy burden to bear, particularly when the realities of life tended to transform towns into something very different. Few communities reacted to these tensions as violently as Salem. But social change created uneasiness in towns throughout New England.

Cities

To call the commercial centers that emerged along the Atlantic coast in the eighteenth century "cities" would be to strain today's definition of that word. Even the largest colonial community was scarcely bigger than a modern small town. Yet by the standards of the eighteenth century, cities did indeed exist in America. The two largest ports—Philadelphia and New York—had populations of 28,000 and 25,000 respectively, which made them larger than most English urban centers. Boston (16,000), Charles Town (the modern Charleston, South Carolina, with a population of 12,000 in the 1770s), and Newport, Rhode Island (11,000), were also substantial communities by the standards of the day.

Colonial cities developed in response to both internal and external commercial demands. They served as trading centers for the farmers of their regions; and they were the marts of international trade as well. Their social, economic, and political leaders, therefore, were the merchants, who, despite the precariousness of their businesses, occasionally acquired substantial estates. Although in most colonial communities, disparities of wealth were generally not very great, in cities they sometimes came to seem enormous. Wealthy merchants and their families moved along crowded streets dressed in fine imported clothes, often riding in fancy carriages, coming in and out of large houses with staffs of servants. Moving beside them were the numerous minor tradesmen, workers, and indigents, dressed simply and living in crowded and often filthy conditions. It would be an exaggeration to claim that sharp class divisions emerged in the cities; but more than in any other area of colonial life (except of course in the relationship between masters and slaves) social distinctions were real and visible in urban areas.

There were other distinctive features of urban life as well. Cities were the centers of much of what industry there was in the colonies, such as the distilleries for turning imported molasses into exportable rum. They were the locations of the most advanced schools and sophisticated cultural activities and of shops where imported goods could be had. In addition, they were communities with social problems that were peculiarly urban: crime, vice, pollution, traffic. Unlike smaller towns, cities were required to establish elaborate corporate governments. They set up constables' offices and fire departments. They developed systems for supporting the urban poor, whose numbers grew steadily and became especially large in times of economic crisis.

Perhaps most important for the political future of the colonies, cities became places where new ideas could circulate and be discussed. Because there were printers, it was possible to have regular newspapers. Books and other publications from abroad introduced new intellectual influences. And the

Baltimore in 1752
Though founded in 1729, Baltimore remained a small settlement at the time this painting was made. The town had not developed as a port, since most of the Maryland tobacco growers shipped their crops from their own wharves along the rivers. (The Maryland Historical Society, Baltimore)

taverns and coffee houses of cities provided forums in which people could gather and debate the issues of the day. It was hardly surprising that when the revolutionary crisis began to build in the 1760s and 1770s, it manifested itself first in the cities.

THE MIND AND THE SPIRIT

Two powerful forces were competing for the American mind in the eighteenth century. One was the traditional intellectual and religious outlook of the sixteenth and seventeenth centuries, with its emphasis upon a personal God, intimately involved with the world, keeping watch over individual lives. The other was the new spirit of the Enlightenment, a movement that was sweeping both Europe and America and that stressed the importance of science and human reason. The old views made possible such phenomena as the belief in witchcraft and other superstitions; and they placed great value on a stern moral code in which intellect was less important than faith. The Enlightenment, by contrast, suggested that individuals had substantial control over their own lives and the course of their societies; that the world could be explained and therefore could be structured along rational scientific lines.

The intellectual climate of colonial America was shaped by the tension between these two impulses. Yet there was a significant intermingling of them as well, as the lives of two of the outstanding men of the eighteenth century suggest. No one better exemplified the worldly, scientific spirit of the Enlightenment than Benjamin Franklin, whose intellectual curiosity and scientific and political accomplishments made his career a triumph of human reason. Yet Franklin remained wedded to many traditional moral and religious precepts: a belief in an unchanging moral code, a deference to social distinctions, a strong religiosity. Similarly, no man was a clearer symbol of the survival of traditional beliefs than Jonathan Edwards, who personified the effort to restore the original intensity of the Puritan faith. Yet Edwards displayed as well a concern with modern scientific knowledge and secular education.

The Pattern of Religions

The American colonists brought their religions with them from abroad. But like so many other imported institutions, religion took on a new and distinctive pattern in the New World. In part, this was because of the sheer number of different faiths established in America. With the immigration of diverse sectarians from several countries, the colonies became an ecclesiastical patchwork. Toleration flourished to a degree unmatched in any European nation, not because Americans deliberately sought to produce it, but because conditions favored its growth. Since no single religious establishment predominated in the colonies—as the Church of England did in Britain or the Catholic or Lutheran faiths did in western Europe—Americans had little choice but to accept the existence of a variety of faiths in their midst.

The experience of the Church of England illustrated how difficult the establishment of a common religion would be in the colonies. By law, Anglicanism was established as the official faith in Virginia, Maryland, New York, the Carolinas, and Georgia. In these colonies everyone regardless of belief or affiliation was supposed to be taxed for the support of the church. Actually, except in Virginia and Maryland, the Church of England succeeded in maintaining its position as the established church only in certain localities.

To strengthen Anglicanism, in America and elsewhere, the Church of England in 1701 set up the Society for the Propagation of the Gospel in Foreign Parts. Missionaries of the SPG founded a number of new Anglican communions in the colonies, especially in Massachusetts and Connecticut. But Anglicanism never succeeded in becoming the dominant religious force in America that some members of the SPG envisioned.

Even in areas where a single faith had originally predominated, the forces of denominationalism soon began to be felt. In New England, for example, Puritans had originally believed themselves all to be part of a single faith: Calvinism. In the course of the eighteenth century, however, there was a growing tendency for different congregations to affiliate with different denominations. Some became Congregationalists; others identified themselves as Presbyterians. In belief, these two groups were essentially the same, but they differed in ecclesiastical organization, the Presbyterians having a more highly centralized government, with a governing body of presbyters (made up of ministers and lay elders) for the churches of each district. In the early eighteenth century, many of the Puritan churches of Connecticut, and most of those founded in other colonies by emigrants from New England, adopted the Presbyterian form of government. The number of Presbyterians in America was greatly increased by the immigration of the Scotch-Irish. At first, most of these people lacked churches and pastors. Francis Makemie, often called the father of Presbyterianism in America, organized the first American presbytery (1705) and for twenty years traveled up and down the coast from New York to South Carolina to set up churches for the churchless.

Another Calvinist group, numerous in parts of New York and New Jersey, was the Dutch Reformed. Originally, the American Baptists, of whom Roger Williams is considered the first, were also Calvinistic in their theology. Then, in Rhode Island and in other colonies, a bewildering variety of Baptist sects sprang up. They had in common a belief that infant baptism did not suffice and that rebaptism, usually by total immersion, was necessary. Some remained Calvinists, believers in predestination; others came to believe in salvation by man's free will.

Quite different from the Calvinists were the Quaker mystics and the German Pietists, such as the Mennonites, Dunkers, and Moravians. The Quakers (Society of Friends) abandoned their early fanaticism, which once had caused them to disturb other religious gatherings when they first settled in America. As their wealth increased, many of the Friends lost still more of their old-time fervor, the rich Philadelphia merchants dividing their allegiance between meetinghouse and countinghouse. Though politically dominant in Pennsylvania from the beginning, the Quakers did not use their power to compel conformity. Of all the colonies, Rhode Island and Pennsylvania were characterized by the greatest religious diversity and freedom. In Pennsylvania and other places where Germans settled, the Lutherans as well as the Pietist sects added variety to the colonial religious scene.

Protestants extended toleration to one another more readily than to Roman Catholics. To strict Puritans, the pope seemed no less than the Antichrist. Their border enemies in New France, being "papists," seemed agents of the devil bent on frustrating the divine mission of the wilderness Zion in New England. In most of the English colonies, however, the Roman Catholics were far too small a minority to occasion serious conflict. They were most numerous in Maryland, and even there they numbered no more than 3,000. Ironically, they suffered their worst persecution in that colony, which had been founded as a refuge for them and had been distinguished by its Toleration Act of 1649. According to Maryland laws passed after 1691, Catholics not only were deprived of political rights but also were forbidden to hold religious services except in private houses.

Even fewer than the Catholics, the Jews in provincial America totaled no more than about 2,000 at any time. The largest community lived in New York City, smaller groups in Newport and Charleston, and dispersed families in all the colonies. There was relatively little social discrimination against the Jews, but there was political discrimination: in no colony could they vote or hold office. In New England they enjoyed a certain esteem because of the Puritans' interest in the Old Testament and in Hebrew culture.

The Great Awakening

By the beginning of the eighteenth century, Americans had become deeply troubled by the apparent decline in religious piety in their society. In part, this was a result of the rise of denominationalism. With so many diverse sects existing side by side, some people were tempted to doubt whether any particular denomination, even their own, possessed a monopoly of truth and grace. More important, however, were other changes in colonial society. The movement of the population westward and the wide scattering of settlement had caused many communities to lose touch with organized religion. The rise of towns and the multiplication of material comforts led to an increasingly secular outlook in densely settled areas. The progress of science and free thought in Europe—and the importation of Enlightenment ideas to America—caused at least some colonists to adopt a rational and skeptical view of the world.

Concerns about declining piety were not new to the eighteenth century. They had surfaced as early as the 1660s in New England, where the Puritan oligarchy found itself faced with a steady deterioration of the power of the church. As the first generation of American Puritans died, the number of church members rapidly declined, for few of the second generation seemed to harbor enough religious passion to demonstrate the "saving grace" that was a prerequisite for membership.

The situation posed a difficult dilemma. If the Puritans continued to admit only "visible saints" to their church, membership would continue to shrink. If they opened the doors to others, the church would lose its purity. Their response was a compromise. The children of "saints" were permitted to be baptized as partial members of the church even without proof of a conversion experience. But what about the following generations, the unconverted children of these partial members? In 1662, a conference of ministers attempted to solve this problem by instituting the Halfway Covenant, which gave these men and women of the third and later generations the right to be baptized but not the right to partake of communion or vote in church affairs.

As time passed, this carefully drawn difference between full and half members was largely forgotten, and in most communities the church came to include all those who could take part in colonial politics as voters and officeholders. Qualification for membership in the church, in other words, became almost entirely secular. Orthodox Puritans continued to oppose the transformation that was enveloping the erstwhile land of the saints. Sabbath after Sabbath, ministers preached sermons of despair (known as "jeremiads") deploring the signs of waning piety. "Truly so it is," one minister lamented in 1674, "the very heart of New England is changed and exceedingly corrupted with the sins of the times." There was, he said, a growing spirit of profaneness, pride, worldliness, sensuality, gainsaying and rebellion, libertinism, carnality, formality, hypocrisy, "and a spiritual idolatry in the worship of God." Only in relative terms was religious piety actually declining in New England. By the standards of later times (or by the standards of other societies of the seventeenth century), the Puritan faith remained remarkably strong. It did not, however, remain the pervasive force it once had been for maintaining stability and social order.

By the early eighteenth century, similar concerns were emerging in other regions and among members of other faiths. Everywhere, it seemed, religious piety was in decline and opportunities for spiritual regeneration were dwindling. Such anxieties reflected (and were in large part caused by) concurrent concerns about social and economic changes in colonial society. Commercial pressures were rending the traditional fabric of many communities. Population growth was creating tensions, as members of the younger generation began to realize that they could not always expect to inherit enough land from their fathers to ensure future prosperity. Because of the strong patriarchal structure of early eighteenth-century America, there were few acceptable ways to give voice to these economic concerns and family tensions. Many uneasy colonists, therefore, channeled their anxieties into religion. The result was the first great American revival.

It was known as the Great Awakening. Although the first stirrings (or "freshenings") began in some places early in the century, the Great Awakening was truly launched in the 1730s and reached its climax in the 1740s. Then, for a time, a new spirit of religious fervor seemed for thousands of Americans to have reversed the trend away from piety. That the movement was not purely religious in origin is suggested by the identity of those who responded most frequently to it: residents of areas where social and economic tensions were greatest; younger sons of the third or fourth generation of settlers—those who stood to inherit the least land and who thus faced the most uncertain futures. The social origins of the revival were evident too in much of its rhetoric, which emphasized the potential for every individual to break away from the constraints of the past and start anew in his or her relationship to God (and, implicitly, to the world).

Wandering exhorters from abroad did much to stimulate the revivalistic spirit. John and Charles Wesley, founders of Methodism, which began as a reform movement within the Church of England, visited Georgia and other colonies in the 1730s with the intention of revitalizing religion and converting Indians and blacks. George Whitefield, a powerful open-air preacher from England and for a time an associate of the Wesleys, made several evangelizing tours through the colonies. Everywhere he went, Whitefield drew tremendous crowds, and it was said (with some exaggeration) that he could make his hearers weep merely by uttering, in his moving way, the word "Mesopotamia."

Though itinerants such as Whitefield contributed to the rousing of religious excitement, the Great Awakening could hardly have occurred without the work of regular ministers with an evangelizing bent. One of the most important of these was Theodore J. Frelinghuysen, a youthful German-born pastor of three Dutch Reformed congregations in central New Jersey. Frelinghuysen

"Sinners in the Hands of an Angry God" [1741]

Jonathan Edwards (1703–1758) was the most original and systematic theologian of colonial America. Edwards argued that God's grace is the only means by which anyone can be redeemed from the original sin committed by Adam; poor sinners could yield themselves up to God's grace if their hearts were "filled with love to him who has loved them." The extremes of terror and salvation that he posed were undeniably effective: when he preached this sermon at Enfield, Connecticut, in 1741, it produced great "breathing of distress, and weeping."

Your wickedness makes you as it were heavy as lead, and to tend downwards with great weight and pressure towards hell; and if God should let you go, you would immediately sink and swiftly descend and plunge into the bottomless gulf. . . .

O sinner! Consider the fearful danger you are in: it is a great furnace of wrath, a wide and bottomless pit, full of the fire of wrath, that you are held over in the hand of God. . . . You hang by a slender thread, with the flames of divine wrath flashing about it, and ready every moment to singe it, and burn it asunder. . . .

And now you have an extraordinary opportunity, a day wherein Christ has thrown the door of mercy wide open, and stands in the door calling and crying with a loud voice to poor sinners. . . .

And let everyone that is yet out of Christ, and hanging over the pit of hell, . . . now hearken to the loud calls of God's word and providence. This acceptable year of the Lord, a day of such great favours to some, will doubtless be a day of as remarkable vengeance to others. . . .

---

preached the necessity of spiritual rebirth not only to the Dutch Reformed but also to the Scotch-Irish Presbyterian settlers of the Raritan Valley. His emotional preaching divided his own parishioners. The older and more well-to-do among them were scandalized; the young and the poor rallied to his support.

The Puritans of New England also were divided on the issue of revivalism. Despite their long-standing concern about the decline of piety, most Congregational ministers in Massachusetts denounced the "errors" and "disorders" arising from revival meetings. Among the errors and disorders was the practice of uneducated men "taking upon themselves to be preachers of the word of God," creating confusion and tumult, and leading members away from their regular churches.

The outstanding preacher of the Great Awakening in New England was Jonathan Edwards—a Puritan of the Puritans and one of the most profound theologians in the history of American religious thought. From his pulpit in Northampton, Massachusetts, Edwards attacked the new doctrines of easy salvation for all. He called upon his people to return to the faith of their fathers. He preached afresh the old Puritan ideas of the absolute sovereignty of God, the depravity of man, predestination, the necessity of experiencing a sense of election, and election by God's grace alone. Describing hell as vividly as if he had been there, he brought his listeners to their knees in terror of divine wrath. Day after day the agonized sinners crowded his parsonage to seek his aid; at least one committed suicide.

The Great Awakening spread over the colonies like a religious epidemic. It was most contagious in frontier areas and among the comparatively poor and uneducated folk, especially in the South. In the Southern back country it affected the largest number of people, prevailed the longest, and had the most lasting consequences. The Presbyterian church was split by the formation of a large and rapidly growing group of revivalistic "New Light" Presbyterians. Converts flocked to various free-will Baptist sects; the Baptists were on the way to becoming eventually one of the two most numerous denominations in the United States.

The Great Awakening not only led to the division of existing congregations and the founding of new sects, but it also had a number of other results. Some of the revivalists denounced book learning as a snare and a delusion, a positive hindrance to salvation. But others saw education as a means of furthering their own brand of religion, and so they founded schools for the preparation of ministers. Many believed that revivalism, through its emphasis on righteous conduct, brought about an improvement in manners and morals. To some extent, too, it aroused a spirit of humanitarianism, a concern for the physical as well as the spiritual welfare of the poor and oppressed. The widely preached doctrine of salvation for all—of equal opportunity to share in God's grace—encouraged the notion of equal rights to share also in the good things on earth.

Though the Great Awakening had these important and lasting consequences, many of the converted soon backslid, and by the end of the colonial period English America contained fewer church members for its population than did any other Christian country of the time, and fewer than the United States has today.

Language and Letters

The divergence of American culture from its English origins was evident, too, in the development of a distinctive colonial language and literature. As early as the mid-seventeenth century, newcomers to the colonies noticed a gradual Americanization of the English language. New words originated in borrowings from the Indians (such as *skunk* and *squash*), from the French (*portage, prairie*), and from the Dutch (*boss, cookie*). Americanisms also arose from the combining of words already in the English language (*bullfrog, snowplow*), from the formation of new adjectives based on existing nouns (*kinky, chunky*), from the adoption of unfamiliar uses for familiar words (*branch,* meaning "stream"; *ordinary,* meaning "inn"), and from the retention of old English expressions that were being dropped in England (*cater-corner; bub,* for "boy"). After 1700, English travelers in America began to notice a strangeness in accent as well as vocabulary, and in 1756 the great lexicographer Dr. Samuel Johnson mentioned the existence of an "American dialect."

Dr. Johnson thought of Americans as barbarians, and some no doubt were. But from the beginning many had been concerned lest civilization be lost in the wilderness. They continued to provide schooling for their children as best they could, particularly in New England. In various colonies, the advancement of religion was one motive for education. The Quakers and other sects operated church schools. Here and there a widow or an unmarried woman conducted a "dame school," holding private classes in her home. In some of the cities, master craftsmen set up evening schools for their apprentices. At least a hundred such schools appeared between 1723 and 1770. To the end of the colonial period (and beyond it), numberless children with no school available were still being taught to read and write by their parents.

Far more people learned to read than ever attended school, yet a great many never learned to read at all. The literacy rate, never formally measured, seems to have been very low in some of the thinly settled areas, especially in the South. It was highest in the towns, especially in New England. Nevertheless, the Connecticut legislature stated in 1690 that many people in Connecticut were "unable to read the English tongue," and of the thirteen town proprietors of Manchester, New Hampshire, in 1716, eight could not write. On the whole, literacy doubtless improved during the eighteenth century, and by the time of the Revolution probably a majority of Americans could read.

Founded in 1704, the first regular newspaper in the colonies, though not a very newsy one, was the weekly Boston *News-Letter*, a small folded sheet of four pages with two columns to a page. By the 1760s, one or more weekly papers were being published in each of the colonies except New Jersey and Delaware, both of which were well enough supplied by the presses of New York and Philadelphia. Several monthly magazines, notably the *American Magazine* of Philadelphia, were started after about 1750, with hopes of wide circulation. One after another they appeared for a year or two and then expired. More successful and more widely read were the yearly almanacs. Originally mere collections of weather data, they turned into small magazines of a sort, containing a great variety of literary fare. *Poor Richard's Almanac*, now well remembered, was only one of many, though a superior one.

Its publisher, Benjamin Franklin, was one of a few colonial-born men of letters who wrote works of lasting literary merit. The titles of some of his essays—*Advice to a Young Man on Choosing a Mistress* (1745), *Reflections on Courtship and Marriage* (1746), *Observations Concerning the Increase of Mankind* (1755), and *Advice to a Young Tradesman* (1762)—suggest his pragmatic, worldly outlook. Quite different was the sternly logical and otherworldly view of Jonathan Edwards, whose treatise *On the Freedom of the Will* (1754) is often described as one of the most brilliant of American theological studies.

As a rule, colonial authors had no time for belles lettres, for fiction, poetry, drama, and the like. Writers concentrated on sermons, religious tracts, and subjects of urgent, practical concern. Puritans, Quakers, and many other Protestants condemned playacting as sinful. The first theaters opened in the South, one at Williamsburg in 1718 and the famous Dock Street Theater at Charleston in 1736. By the middle of the century, plays could be seen in all the larger seaport cities except Boston, where the Puritan ban remained.

Higher Learning

Nowhere was the intermingling of the influences of traditional religiosity and the new spirit of the Enlightenment clearer than in the colleges and universities that grew up in colonial America. Of the six colleges in operation by 1763, all but two were founded by religious groups primarily for the training of preachers. Yet in almost all, the influences of the new scientific, rational approach to knowledge could be felt.

Harvard, the first American college, was founded by the Puritans within five years of their arrival in Massachusetts. It began operating in Cambridge in 1636. Decades later, in 1693, William and Mary College was established in Williamsburg, Virginia, by Anglicans. And in 1701, conservative Congregationalists, dissatisfied with the growing religious liberalism of Harvard, founded Yale in New Haven, Connecticut. Out of the Great Awakening emerged the College of New Jersey, founded in 1746 and known later as Princeton (after the town in which it was located). One of its first presidents was Jonathan Edwards. Despite the religious basis of these colleges, students at all of them could derive something of a liberal education from the curricula, which included not only theology, but logic, ethics, physics, geometry, astronomy, rhetoric, Latin, Hebrew, and Greek. From the beginning, Harvard was intended not only to provide an educated ministry but also to "advance learning and perpetuate it to posterity." King's College, founded in New York in 1754 and later renamed Columbia, was even more devoted to the spread of secular knowledge. It had no theological faculty and was interdenominational from the start. The Academy and College of Philadelphia, which became the University of Pennsylvania, was from its birth in 1755 a completely secular institution, founded by a group of laymen under the inspiration of Benjamin Franklin. It offered courses in utilitarian subjects—mechanics, chemistry, agriculture, government, commerce, and modern languages—as well as in the liberal arts.

By the mid-eighteenth century, in other words, the colonies were (in comparison with most European nations) well supplied with colleges; and from them emerged a group of men steeped in the ideas and principles of the Enlightenment. Some Americans continued to travel to England for a university edu-

A North-West Prospect of Nassau-Hall, with a Front View of the Presidents House, in New-Jersey.

Nassau Hall at Princeton
At the left is Nassau Hall, completed in 1756, ten years after the founding of the College of New Jersey (which became Princeton University in 1896). It is the oldest building now standing on the Princeton campus. At the right is the president's house. From a drawing made in 1763. (Princeton University Library)

cation, and they brought home with them still more new theories and philosophies. After 1700, however, most colonial leaders received their entire education in America.

Until a medical school was opened in Philadelphia (1765), there was no opportunity for aspiring physicians to get academic training on this side of the Atlantic. Those who desired to attend a medical school had to go abroad, and usually they went to the University of Edinburgh. Most of the practicing physicians had no medical degrees. Some put in a sort of internship with an older practitioner, and others took up the healing art entirely on their own. Some colonial physicians and, surprising though it seems, churchmen like Cotton Mather and Jonathan Edwards advocated as earnestly as anyone in the world the most controversial medical in-

novation of their time—inoculation against smallpox. There was no law school in the colonies, and men prepared themselves for a legal career by independent study, by working with an established lawyer, or, in comparatively few cases, by attending one of the Inns of Court (law schools) in London.

In the colonial colleges, considerable attention was given to scientific subjects. Chairs in "natural philosophy," or physical science, were endowed at William and Mary and at Harvard. The most advanced scientific thought of Europe—Copernican astronomy and Newtonian physics—eventually made its way into American teaching. But scientific speculation and experiment were not the exclusively academic, professional occupations that they later became.

Mather, Edwards, and many other ministers, merchants, and planters in America were active as amateur scientists. The Royal Society of London, founded in 1662 for the advancement of science, elected a number of them as fellows. To this society, the American members and nonmember correspondents sent samples and descriptions of plants, animals, and remarkable phenomena. By means of their contributions, the colonial amateurs added a good deal to the accumulation of data upon which later scientific progress was to be based. They also sent in plans for mechanical inventions and helped to start the reputation of Americans as a mechanically ingenious people.

The greatest of colonial scientists and inventors, Benjamin Franklin, gained worldwide fame with his kite experiment (1752), which demonstrated that lightning and electricity are one and the same. Showing their respect for experimental science, Harvard, Yale, and William and Mary honored themselves by honoring Franklin as a Master of Arts. The University of St. Andrews in Scotland and Oxford University in England conferred doctoral degrees upon him. Thereafter he took satisfaction in being known as "Dr. Franklin." He interested himself in countless subjects besides electricity, and he was a theoretical or "philosophical" scientist as well as a practical one. He also was a promoter of science. In 1727, he and his Philadelphia friends organized the Junto, a club for the discussion of intellectual and practical matters of mutual interest. In 1744, he led in the founding of the American Philosophical Society, the first learned society in America.

Concepts of Law and Politics

The legal and political systems of the colonies experienced a process similar to that of their social and intellectual lives. Americans in the seventeenth and eighteenth centuries believed that they were re-creating in the New World the practices and institutions of the Old. In reality, they had—without meaning to, or even realizing it—created something very different.

Changes in the law in America resulted in part from the scarcity of English-trained lawyers, who were almost unknown in the colonies until after 1700. Not until a full generation after that did authorities in England try to impose the common law and the statutes of the realm upon the provinces. By then, it was already too late. Although the American legal system adopted most of the essential elements of the English system, including such ancient rights as trial by jury, significant differences had already become well established. Some were a result of ignorance of the laws of Britain, others of the inappropriateness of English practices for the conditions of the colonies. Whatever the reason, there were significant—and at times controversial—discrepancies.

Pleading and court procedures were simplified in America, and punishments were made less severe. Instead of the gallows or the prison, the colonists more commonly resorted to the whipping post, the branding iron, the stocks, and the ducking stool (for gossipy women). Crimes were redefined. In England, a printed attack on a public official, whether true or false, was considered libelous. In the colonies, at the trial (1734) of the New York publisher John Peter Zenger, who was powerfully defended by the Philadelphia lawyer Andrew Hamilton, it was held that criticisms of the government were not libels if factually true—a verdict that brought some progress toward freedom of the press. Legal philosophy itself was changed, as colonists came to think of law as a reflection of the divine will or the natural order, not as an expression of the power of an earthly sovereign. Provincial lawyers, who became an influential class during the eighteenth century, were less closely attached to English tradition than the legal profession in the United States was afterward to be.

Even more significant for the future of the relationship between the colonies and England were important differences that were emerging between the American and British political systems. Because the royal government that was in theory the ultimate authority over the colonies was so far away, Americans created a group of institutions of their own that gave them—in reality, if not in theory—a large measure of self-government. In most colonies, local communities grew accustomed to running their own affairs with minimal interference from higher authorities. Communities also expected to maintain strict control over their delegates to the colonial assemblies; and those assemblies came to exercise many of the powers that Parliament exercised in England (even though in theory Parliament remained the ultimate authority in America). Provincial governors had broad powers on paper, but in fact their influence was sharply limited. They lacked control over appointments and contracts; such influence resided largely in England or with local colonial leaders. They could never be certain of their tenure in office; because governorships were patronage appointments, a governor could be removed any time his patron in England lost favor. And in many cases, governors were not even familiar with the colo-

nies they were meant to govern; some were native Americans, but most were Englishmen who came to the colonies for the first time to assume their offices. The results of all this were that the focus of politics in the colonies became a local one; the provincial governments became accustomed to acting more or less independently of Parliament; and a set of assumptions and expectations about the rights of the colonists took hold in America but was not shared by policy makers in England. These differences caused few problems prior to the 1760s, because the British did little to exert the authority they believed they possessed. But when, beginning in 1763, the English government began attempting to tighten its control over the American colonies, a historic crisis resulted.

SUGGESTED READINGS

The most important reference for the study of the colonial population is Robert V. Wells, *The Population of the British Colonies in America Before 1776* (1975). A valuable local study, particularly interesting for its information on birth and death, is Philip Greven, *Four Generations* (1970), which examines colonial Andover, Massachusetts. Greven is also the author of an important examination of women and the family in the colonial period: *The Protestant Temperament: Patterns of Child-Rearing, Religious Experience, and the Self in Early America* (1977). See also J. William Frost, *The Quaker Family in Colonial America* (1972); and Christopher Jedrey, *The World of John Cleaveland: Family and Community in Eighteenth-Century New England* (1979). General social portraits of colonial society in the eighteenth century include James A. Henretta, *The Evolution of American Society, 1700–1815* (1973); and Richard Hofstadter, *America at 1750: A Social Portrait* (1971).

There are a number of significant studies of the origins of American slavery. In particular, see Edmund S. Morgan, *American Slavery, American Freedom* (1975), which studies the institution in Virginia; Peter Wood, *Black Majority* (1974), which examines South Carolina; and Winthrop Jordan, *White over Black* (1968), a sweeping study of American racial attitudes. David Brion Davis, *The Problem of Slavery in Western Culture* (1966), offers a broader view of the origins of the institution. On the colonial slave trade, see Philip D. Curtin, *The Atlantic Slave Trade* (1969). The standard study of white indentured servitude is Abbot E. Smith, *Colonists in Bondage* (1947). Gerald Mullin, *Flight and Rebellion* (1972), examines slave resistance in colonial Virginia. A significant study of colonial society in terms of race relations is Gary B. Nash, *Red, White, and Black*, rev. ed. (1982).

The complicated story of immigration to the colonies has not yet been told in a single, comprehensive work. Pieces of the puzzle can be examined in Albert B. Faust, *The German Element in the United States*, 2 vols. (1909); Ian C. C. Graham, *Colonists from Scotland: Emigration to North America, 1707–1783* (1956); James G. Leyburn, *The Scotch-Irish: A Social History* (1962); Frederic Klees, *The Pennsylvania Dutch* (1950); and R. J. Dickson, *Ulster Immigration to the United States* (1966). And for an overview, consult Marcus L. Hanson, *The Atlantic Migration, 1607–1860* (1940). See James Kettner, *The Development of American Citizenship* (1978), for a study of naturalization.

General studies of the colonial economy include the Henretta work mentioned above; Alice Hanson Jones, *Wealth of a Nation to Be* (1980), which examines the economic condition of the colonies on the eve of the Revolution; and Jackson Turner Main, *The Social Structure of Revolutionary America* (1965), which examines the impact of economic inequality on colonial society. The Southern plantation economy is examined in Carl Bridenbaugh, *Myths and Realities: Societies of the Colonial South* (1963); Edmund S. Morgan, *Virginians at Home* (1952); Thomas J. Wertenbaker, *The Planters of Colonial Virginia* (1922); and Lewis C. Gray, *History of Agriculture in the Southern United States to 1860*, 2 vols. (1933). Jacob M. Price, *France and the Chesapeake*, 2 vols. (1973), is an important study of the tobacco trade. Julia Spruill, *Women's Life and Work in the Southern Colonies* (1938), examines Southern family life. Harry R. Merrens, *Colonial North Carolina in the Eighteenth Century* (1964), is a useful local study.

The New England town has been the subject of a vast and rich literature. In addition to the studies of Puritanism cited in the readings for Chapter 2 and the Greven study of Andover listed above, see Kenneth Lockridge, *A New England Town* (1970), a study of Dedham, Massachusetts; Michael Zuckerman, *Peaceable Kingdoms* (1970), which challenges the prevailing modern view of the Puritan community as rife with social tension; Darrett Rutman, *Winthrop's Boston* (1965), which examines changes in the early seventeenth century; and Charles Grant, *Democracy in the Connecticut Frontier Town of Kent* (1961). Paul Boyer and Stephen Nissenbaum, *Salem Possessed* (1974), is an important study of witchcraft in Salem, linking the phenomenon to social tensions in the community. E. M. Cook, Jr., *The Fathers of Towns* (1976), examines colonial leadership. Sumner Chilton Powell, *Puritan Village* (1963), is one of the first of the "new" social histories of the New England towns, in this case Sudbury, Massachusetts. Richard Bushman, *From Puritan to Yankee* (1967), examines social and economic changes in Connecticut in the eighteenth century. Robert Gross, *The Minutemen and Their World* (1976), is an important study of Concord, Massachusetts, at the time of the Revolution.

Two works by Carl Bridenbaugh, *Cities in the Wilderness* (1938) and *Cities in Revolt* (1955), have long been the standard references on colonial urban life. A more recent work by Gary B. Nash, *The Urban Crucible* (1979), adds an important new dimension to the subject. G. B. Warden, *Boston, 1687–1776* (1970), examines the development of one of the first colonial towns into one of the first colonial cities. Stephanie G. Wolf, *Urban Village* (1976), examines aspects of city life in Germantown, Pennsylvania.

The rise of commerce is chronicled, in the studies of cities above, and also in Stuart Bruchey, *The Colonial Merchant* (1966); J. F. Shepherd and G. M. Walton, *The Economic Rise of Early America* (1979); James B. Hedges, *The Browns of Providence Plantation*, vol. 1 (1952), a study of a colonial merchant family; and Frederick B. Tolles, *Meeting House and Counting House: The Quaker Merchants of Colonial Philadelphia, 1682–1763* (1948). Bernard Bailyn, *The New England Merchants in the Seventeenth Century* (1955), is an important history of early commerce. Arthur Jensen, *The Maritime Commerce of Colonial Philadelphia* (1963), examines colonial trade in Pennsylvania; while Randolph S. Klein, *Portrait of an Early American Family* (1975), is a study of a Philadelphia merchant family.

The studies of Puritanism listed in the readings for Chapter 2 are among the most important works on colonial religion. For a general overview, see Sidney Ahlstrom, *A Religious History of the American People* (1972). W. W. Sweet, *Religion in Colonial America* (1942), is a primarily institutional history of the churches. Carl Bridenbaugh, *Mitre and Sceptre: Transatlantic Faiths, Ideas, Personalities, and Politics, 1689–1775* (1962), examines the interaction between religion and politics. Sidney Mead, *The Lively Experiment: The Shaping of Christianity in America* (1963), is an important general study. Studies of particular denominations include J. T. Ellis, *Catholics in America* (1965); J. R. Marcus, *Early American Jewry* (1951); and Janet Whitman, *John Woolman, American Quaker*

(1942). William C. McLoughlin, *New England Dissent, 1630–1833*, 2 vols. (1971), is an important study of the colonial Baptists.

An especially rich literature is available for the study of the Great Awakening. Among many other works, see Edwin S. Gaustad, *The Great Awakening in New England* (1957); J. M. Bumsted and John E. Van de Wetering, *What Must I Do to Be Saved? The Great Awakening in Colonial America* (1976); Alan Heimert, *Religion and the American Mind* (1966), which traces the divisions that emerged during the Great Awakening into the Revolutionary era and beyond. Perry Miller, *Jonathan Edwards* (1949), is an important analysis of the ideas of the preeminent American leader of the Awakening; Ola Winslow, *Jonathan Edwards* (1940), is an important biography. Conrad Wright, *The Beginnings of Unitarianism in America* (1955), traces the subject back to the early eighteenth century. J. W. Davidson, *The Logic of Millennial Thought* (1977), examines an important strand of theology.

Lawrence A. Cremin, *American Education: The Colonial Experience, 1607–1783* (1970), the first volume in a comprehensive history of American education, is the basic source. See also Bernard Bailyn, *Education in the Forming of American Society* (1960); James Axtell, *The School upon a Hill: Education and Society in Colonial New England* (1974); and Robert Middlekauff, *Ancients and Axioms* (1963). Samuel Eliot Morison examines the beginnings of America's first university in *The Founding of Harvard College* (1935). Kenneth Lockridge, *Literacy in Colonial New England* (1974), is a general examination of colonial learning.

On the general subject of colonial culture and the Enlightenment, Louis B. Wright, *The Cultural Life of the American Colonies* (1957), and Daniel J. Boorstin, *The Americans: The Colonial Experience* (1958), are important overviews. See also Richard Beale Davis, *Intellectual Life in the Colonial South*, 2 vols. (1978); Henry May, *The Enlightenment in America* (1976); and Howard Mumford Jones, *O Strange New World* (1964). Brook Hindle, *The Pursuit of Science in Revolutionary America* (1956), examines the institutions of scientific study. Carl Van Doren, *Benjamin Franklin* (1941), and V. W. Crane, *Benjamin Franklin and a Rising People* (1954), are standard biographies of the Enlightenment's leading American figure; but Franklin's own *Autobiography* is the best source. H. Leventhal, *In the Shadow of Enlightenment* (1976), examines occultism in eighteenth-century America.

An invaluable study of colonial politics is Bernard Bailyn, *The Origins of American Politics* (1968). Other important studies of law and government include Jack P. Greene, *The Quest for Power* (1963), which examines the colonial assemblies; J. R. Pole, *Political Representation in England and the Origins of the American Republic* (1966); Leonard W. Labaree, *Royal Government in America* (1930); and Robert Zemsky, *Merchants, Farmers, and River Gods* (1971), a study of politics in colonial Massachusetts. The intellectual context of colonial politics is discussed in Caroline Robbins, *The Eighteenth-Century Commonwealthman* (1959); and J. G. A. Pocock, *The Machiavellian Moment* (1975).

The Empire Under Strain

4

Paul Revere's Ride
This 1917 depiction of Revere's famous ride from Boston to Lexington on April 18, 1775, conveys the romance and excitement that Americans have always attached to the episode. Revere, along with another rider, William Dawes, rode through the night to warn the rebel militias of the approach of the British army. The two forces were to meet the following day in the first battle of the American Revolution. In addition to his famous political activities, Revere became known as one of the leading silversmiths and engravers of his era. The "Revere Bowl," which he designed, remains popular today.
(Library of Congress)

As late as the 1750s, few Americans could see any reason to object to their membership in the British Empire. The imperial system provided them with many benefits: opportunities for trade and commerce, military protection, political stability. And these benefits were accompanied by few costs. For the most part, the English government left the colonies alone. Americans had great latitude in governing their internal affairs. And while Britain did attempt to regulate the colonists' external trade, those regulations were usually so laxly administered that they could be easily circumvented. Some far-sighted Americans might predict that ultimately the colonies would develop to a point where a greater autonomy would become inevitable. But few expected such a change to occur soon.

By the mid-1770s, however, the relationship between the American colonies and their British rulers had become so strained, so poisoned, so characterized by suspicion and resentment, that the once seemingly unbreakable bonds of empire were on the verge of dissolution. And in the spring of 1775, the first shots were fired in a war that would ultimately win America its independence. How had it happened? And how so quickly?

In one sense, of course, it had not happened quickly at all. Ever since the first days of settlement in North America, the ideas and institutions of the colonies had been diverging from those in England in countless ways. Only because the relationship between America and Britain had been so casual had those differences failed to create serious tensions in the past. In another sense, however, the revolutionary crisis emerged from a series of important changes in the administration of the empire. Beginning in 1763, the English government embarked on a series of new policies toward its colonies—policies dictated by changing international realities and new political circumstances within England itself—that brought the differences between the two societies into sharp focus. In the beginning, most Americans reacted to the changes with relative restraint. They demanded the repeal of particular obnoxious laws, but they did not yet consider the possibility of open rebellion, much less independence. Gradually, however, as crisis followed crisis, a large group of Americans found themselves fundamentally disillusioned with the imperial relationship. By 1775, that relationship was, for all practical purposes, damaged beyond repair.

A LOOSENING OF TIES

After England's Glorious Revolution of 1688 and the collapse of the Dominion of New England, the English government (or the British government after 1707, when Great Britain was created by the union of England and Scotland) made no serious or sustained effort for more than seventy years to tighten its control over the colonies. During that time, it is true, additions were made to the list of royal colonies (New Jersey, 1702; North and South Carolina, 1729; Georgia, 1754) until they numbered eight, in all of which the king had the power of appointing governors and other colonial officials. During that time, also, Parliament passed new laws supplementing the original Navigation Acts and elaborating on the mercantilist program—laws restricting colonial manufactures, prohibiting paper currency, and regulating trade. Nevertheless, the British government itself remained uncertain and divided about the extent to which it ought to interfere in colonial affairs. The colonies were left, within broad limits, to go their separate ways.

A Tradition of Neglect

During the first half of the eighteenth century, though the colonies continued to be governed in the king's name, Parliament more and more asserted its supremacy over the king. Theoretically, Parliament represented the interests of the whole kingdom and indeed the whole empire. Actually, it represented best the interests of the great merchants and landholders in England. Most of them objected to any ambitious scheme for imperial reorganization that would require large expenditures, increase taxes, and diminish the profit of the colonial trade.

During the reigns of George I (1714–1727) and George II (1727–1760), both of whom were German-born, the real executive in England was beginning to be the prime minister and his fellow cabinet ministers, who held their places not by the king's favor but by their ability to control a majority in Parliament. The first of the prime ministers, Robert Walpole, believed that a relaxation of trade restrictions against the colonies would enable them to buy more English goods and would thus benefit England and its merchants. Walpole therefore deliberately refrained from attempting a very strict enforcement of the Navigation Acts. His policy of "salutary neglect" was to continue until after the outbreak of the French and Indian War.

Meanwhile, the day-to-day administration of colonial affairs remained decentralized and inefficient. In England, there was no separate and full-fledged colonial office. The nearest equivalent was the Board of Trade and Plantations, set up in 1696. The board, a mere advisory body, made recommendations to the Privy Council (the central agency of all administration), while the Privy Council, the war department, the lords of the admiralty, or the treasury officials made most of the actual decisions. All these agencies, except for the board itself, had responsibility for administering laws at home as well as overseas; none could concentrate on colonial affairs alone. To complicate matters further, there

was a certain amount of overlapping and confusion of authority among the departments. And very few of the London officials ever visited America and obtained firsthand knowledge of conditions there.

Some information could be obtained from colonial agents in England. Though the colonists did not elect official representatives to sit in Parliament, some of the assemblies sent unofficial representatives or lobbyists to London to encourage the passage of desired legislation and discourage the enactment of unwanted laws. The best known of these agents, Benjamin Franklin, looked out for the interests of not only Pennsylvania but also Georgia, New Jersey, and Massachusetts.

The conflicts of administrative authority in London, together with the ministerial policy of salutary neglect, weakened the hold of England upon the colonies, and so did the character of the officials who were sent to America. These included the officials placed in charge of each royal colony—governor, councillors, secretary, attorney general, receiver general, surveyor general, supreme court justices—and the agents of the London administrative departments, such as collectors of customs and naval officers, who were located in all the colonies. Some of these officeholders were able and devoted men, but the majority were not. There being no merit system, appointments often were made on the basis of bribery or favoritism rather than ability or integrity. Many an appointee remained in England and, with part of his salary, hired another man to take his place in America. Such a deputy, poorly paid as he was, found it hard to resist opportunities to augment his income with bribes. For example, a customs collector seldom hesitated, for a fee smaller than the duty itself, to pass the goods of a smuggling colonial merchant. Even honest and well-paid officials, desiring to get along with the people among whom they had to live, usually found it expedient to yield to popular resistance in the colonies.

This resistance to imperial authority centered in the colonial assemblies. By the 1750s they had established the right to levy taxes, make appropriations, approve appointments, and pass laws for their respective colonies. Their legislation was subject to veto by the

governor and to disallowance by the Privy
Council, but they could often sway the governor by means of their money powers, and
they could get around the Privy Council by
repassing disallowed laws in slightly altered
form. The assemblies came to look upon
themselves as little parliaments, each practically as sovereign within its colony as Parliament itself was in England. In 1754, the
Board of Trade reported to the king, regarding the members of the New York assembly:
they "have wrested from Your Majesty's
governor the nomination of all offices of government, the custody and direction of the
public military stores, the mustering and direction of troops raised for Your Majesty's
service, and in short almost every other part
of executive government."

Intercolonial Disunity

Despite their frequent resistance to British
authority and evasion of British laws, the colonists continued to think of themselves as
loyal British subjects. They had much to gain
from keeping their imperial connection.
They enjoyed access to the markets of the
empire, bounties on the production of certain
goods, the protection afforded by British
naval and military forces, and the pride of
belonging to the most powerful aggregation
of peoples on the globe.

In some respects, the colonists had more
in common with Englishmen than with one
another. To New Englanders, Virginia
seemed almost a foreign land, and to Virginians, New England was just as strange. A
Connecticut man denounced the merchants
of New York for their "frauds and unfair
practices," while a New Yorker condemned
Connecticut because of the "low craft and
cunning so incident to the people of that
country." An English traveler wrote: "Fire
and water are not more heterogeneous than
the different colonies in North America."

At the same time, however, a basis was
emerging for the eventual growth of a sense
of intercolonial community. The increase of
population, which produced an almost continuous line of settlement along the seacoast,
brought the people of the various colonies

The Need for Colonial Unity
Probably the first American editorial cartoon,
this sketch appeared in Benjamin Franklin's
newspaper, the *Pennsylvania Gazette* of Philadelphia, for May 9, 1754. The cartoon was
intended to illustrate the need for colonial
unity and, in particular, for the adoption of
Franklin's Albany Plan.

into closer and closer contact, as did the
gradual construction of roads, the rise of intercolonial trade, and the improvement of the
colonial post office. In 1691, the postal service
operated only from Massachusetts to New
York and Pennsylvania. In 1711, it was extended to New Hampshire in the north; in
1732, to Virginia in the south; and ultimately,
all the way to Georgia. After 1753, Franklin, a
deputy postmaster, improved the service,
providing weekly instead of biweekly posts
and speeding them up so that, for example,
mail was delivered from Boston to Philadelphia in about three weeks instead of six. Post
riders carried newspapers as well as letters
and thus enlarged and unified the colonial
reading public.

Still, the colonists were loath to cooperate
even when, in 1754, they faced a new threat
from old and dreaded enemies, the French
and their Indian allies. At the call of the
Board of Trade, a conference of colonial
leaders—with delegates from Pennsylvania,
Maryland, New York, and New England—
was meeting in Albany to negotiate a treaty
with the Iroquois. The delegates stayed on to
talk about forming a colonial federation for
defense. Benjamin Franklin proposed to his
fellow delegates a plan by which Parliament
would set up in America "one general government" for all the colonies, each of which

would "retain its present constitution" except for the powers to be given the general government. The new government would take charge of all relations with the Indians; the council, subject to his veto, would make laws and levy taxes for raising troops, building forts, waging war, and carrying on other Indian affairs.

War with the French and Indians was already beginning when this Albany Plan was presented to the colonial assemblies. Yet none of them approved it, and none except the Massachusetts assembly even gave it very serious attention. "Everyone cries, a union is necessary," Franklin wrote to the Massachusetts governor, "but when they come to the manner and form of the union, their weak noodles are perfectly distracted."

THE STRUGGLE FOR THE CONTINENT

The war in North America was but one part of a larger struggle between England and France for dominance in world trade and naval power. In America, it was known as the French and Indian War; to Europeans, it was the Seven Years' War. Its outcome confirmed the superior position of England, which emerged from the struggle in almost undisputed control of the settled regions of North America. Ironically, however, the end of the war also served to precipitate the long crisis that would result in Britain's loss of the greatest part of its newly secured empire.

New France

The French and the English had coexisted relatively peacefully in North America for many years. By the 1750s, however, the continent had come to seem too small to contain them both. As both English and French settlements expanded, the inherent suspicion with which each group viewed the other steadily grew. There were religious tensions between the Protestant English and the Catholic French. And there were increasing commercial tensions as well, as competition in the fishing and fur trades intensified. Ultimately, each national group began to feel that its survival in America depended on the elimination of the influence of the other.

The origins of the crisis lay in the expansion of the French presence in America in the late seventeenth century. It was then that the "Sun King," Louis XIV, embarked on a search for national unity and expanding world power that led him to take a renewed interest in colonial acquisitions. Jean Colbert, the king's finance minister and economic planner, conceived of an integrated empire consisting of four parts: France itself as the center and the source of capital and manufactured goods; its West Indian islands (especially Martinique and Guadeloupe) as suppliers of sugar and other exotic products; posts along the African coast as aids in carrying on the slave trade; and the settlements in Canada as a market for exports from France and a granary for provisioning the West Indies. The colonies were to be governed directly from Paris, much as if they were local subdivisions of France itself. New France was to have a governor, an intendant, and a bishop, each to be apponted by the king and each to serve as a check on the other two. In practice this arrangement led to jealousies and cross-purposes that often frustrated the colonial administration—except when some individual official in America had the character and will to assert his preeminence. Such a man was Jean Talon, the first of the intendants, and even more outstanding was Count Frontenac, the greatest of the governors (1672–1698).

Though Colbert intended to make Canada a compactly settled agricultural province, the aspirations of Talon and Frontenac for the glory of France caused them to expand New France beyond Colbert's limits; other forces also tended to disperse the colonial population. The lure of the forest and its furs drew immigrant peasants into the wilderness, where they often married Indian women and

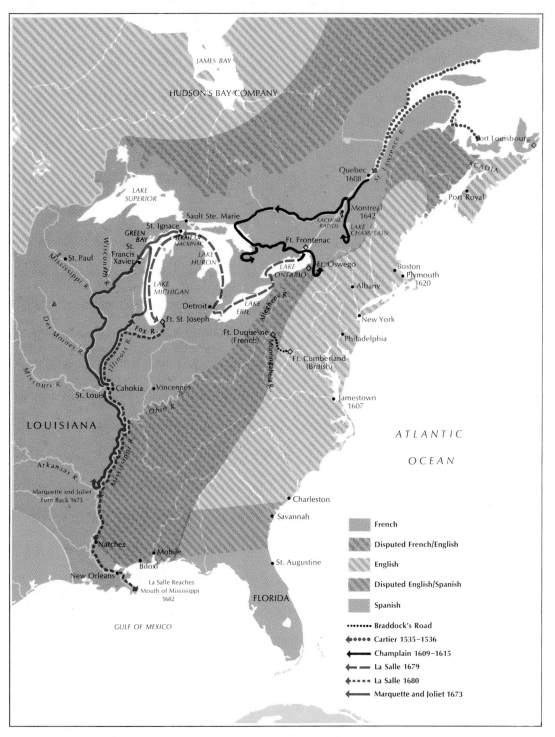

THE FRENCH IN AMERICA

adopted tribal ways. Another group, the Jesuits, were impelled onward by their missionary zeal in the search for savage souls to save. And the bottomlands of the Mississippi attracted farmers discouraged by the short growing season in Canada.

The nature of the Illinois country had been made known by adventuresome explorers. In 1673, Louis Joliet and Father Marquette journeyed together by canoe from Green Bay along the Fox, Wisconsin, and Mississippi rivers as far as the mouth of the Arkansas, then returned with assurance that the Mississippi empties into the Gulf of Mexico, not the Gulf of California, as previously thought. The next year René Robert Cavelier, Sieur de La Salle, a supremely romantic and at the same time shrewdly practical man, began the explorations that finally, in 1682, took him to the delta of the Mississippi, where he took possession of the surrounding country for the king of France, naming it Louisiana in the king's honor. Subsequently traders and missionaries wandered to the southwest as far as the Rio Grande, and the explorer La Vérendrye (1743) pushed westward from Lake Superior to a point within sight of the Rocky Mountains. Eventually, Frenchmen revealed the outlines of the whole continental interior.

To secure their hold upon the territory thus staked out, they founded a string of widely separated communities, strategically located fortresses, and far-flung missions and trading posts. On Cape Breton Island they established Fort Louisbourg, one of the most redoubtable strongholds in all the New World, to guard the approach to the Gulf of St. Lawrence. From both banks of the St. Lawrence River the strips of land ("seigneuries") of would-be feudal lords stretched to the edge of the clearings. On a high bluff above the river stood Quebec, the pride of the French Empire in America. Farther up the river was Montreal, even more "provincial" and less sophisticated than Quebec. Hundreds of miles to the west, near the juncture of Lake Superior with Lakes Michigan and Huron, was the tiny outpost of Sault Sainte Marie. Hundreds of miles to the southeast of this settlement, at the juncture of Lakes

Huron and Erie, was the well-fortified Detroit.

On the lower Mississippi were plantations much like those in the Southern colonies of English America, plantations worked by black slaves and supporting a race-conscious class of "Creoles" (white immigrants of French descent). Louisiana became relatively populous, and New Orleans, founded in 1718, soon grew into a city comparable in size with some of those on the Atlantic seaboard. To the east of New Orleans, along the Gulf of Mexico, were the towns of Biloxi (founded 1699) and Mobile (1702), completing the string of mainland settlements that stretched all the way around from Fort Louisbourg.

Anglo-French Conflicts

No serious trouble between English and French colonists occurred so long as their homelands remained at peace. Charles II and James II of England persisted in their friendship for Louis XIV of France even though Louis, with his wars of French aggrandizement, was violating the traditional English policy of maintaining a balance of power on the European continent. In the Treaty of Whitehall (1686), James II and Louis XIV pledged themselves to refrain from hostilities in America even if ("which God forbid") they should find themselves at war with one another in Europe. In just a few years, however, it was a dead letter.

When James II was deposed, he was replaced by Louis XIV's enemy, William III, who remained stadholder (chief magistrate) of the Netherlands as well as king of England, and who soon resumed his stubborn resistance to the European aggressions of the French. His successor, Queen Anne, with the aid of alliances William had formed before his death, carried on the struggle against France and its new ally, Spain.

These wars spread from Europe to America, where they were known to the English colonists as King William's War (1689–1697) and Queen Anne's War (1701–1713). The first, which involved few of the colonists except in northern New England, led to no decisive result. The second, which entailed border fighting with the Spaniards in the south as well as with the French and their Indian allies in the north, ended in one of the great international settlements of modern history—the Treaty of Utrecht (1713). At Utrecht, the English were awarded some sizable territorial gains in North America at the expense of the French: Acadia (Nova Scotia), Newfoundland, and the shores of Hudson Bay.

After about a quarter of a century of European and American peace, Britain went to war with Spain over the question of British trading rights in the Spanish colonies, and the British in Georgia came to blows with the Spaniards in Florida. The Anglo-Spanish conflict soon merged with a general European war when Frederick the Great of Prussia seized some of the territory of Maria Theresa of Austria. Louis XV of France joined the Prussians against the Austrians in the hope of getting the Austrian Netherlands (Belgium), and George II of England came to the aid of Maria Theresa so as to keep the French out of the Low Countries. Again New England and New France were involved in the hostilities—in what the English colonists referred to as King George's War (1744–1748). New Englanders captured the French bastion at Louisbourg on Cape Breton Island, but to their bitter disappointment they had to abandon it in accordance with the peace treaty, which provided for the mutual restoration of conquered territory.

This war and the two preceding it had arisen primarily from European causes, and only a small fraction of the people in the English colonies had taken any part. But the next conflict was different. Known to the colonists as the French and Indian War, it was in fact a "Great War for the Empire." Unlike the preliminaries, this climactic struggle originated in the interior of North America.

The Great War for the Empire

Within the American wilderness a number of border disputes arose, but the most serious of them concerned the ownership of the

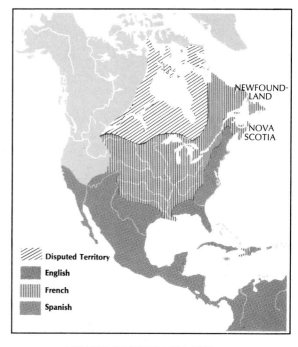

NORTH AMERICA IN 1700

Ohio Valley. The French, desiring to control this direct route between Canada and Louisiana, began to build a chain of fortifications to make good their claim. Pennsylvania fur traders and Virginia land speculators (the latter organized as the Ohio Company) looked to the country across the Alleghenies as a profitable field for their operations; and the British government, aroused to the defense of its territorial rights, gave instructions to the colonial governors to resist French encroachments. Acting on these instructions, the governor of Virginia sent George Washington, then only twenty-one, to lodge protests with the commanders of the French forts newly built between Lake Erie and the Allegheny River. These commanders politely replied that the land was French. In the meantime, a band of Virginians tried to forestall the French by erecting a fort of their own at the strategic key to the Ohio Valley— the forks of the Ohio, where the Allegheny and the Monongahela rivers join. A stronger band of Canadians drove the Virginians

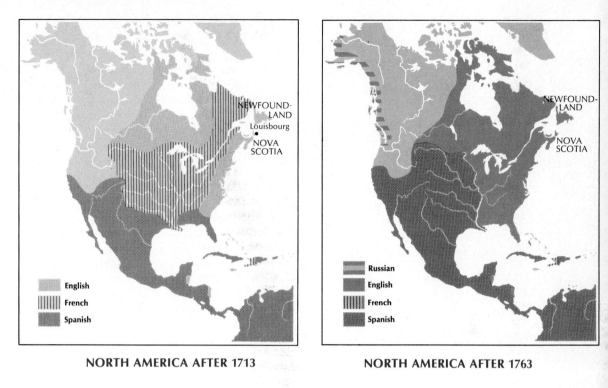

NORTH AMERICA AFTER 1713

English
French
Spanish

NORTH AMERICA AFTER 1763

Russian
English
French
Spanish

away, completed the work, and named it Fort Duquesne.

The colonial government of Virginia again dispatched Washington to deal with the dispute, not as a diplomat this time, but as the leader of a military relief force. Approaching Fort Duquesne, he met a French detachment in a brief but bloody skirmish. He then fell back to a hastily constructed stockade, Fort Necessity, where he was overwhelmed by troops from Fort Duquesne and compelled to surrender (July 4, 1754). The first shots of the French and Indian War had been fired.

For the English colonists, the war had begun inauspiciously, and it continued to go badly during the next few years. They received aid from the home government, but this aid was inefficiently and unintelligently applied. The British fleet failed to prevent the landing of large French reinforcements in Canada, and the newly appointed commander in chief of the British army in America, General Edward Braddock, failed to

retake the forks of the Ohio. Wise in the ways of European warfare but unused to the American woods, Braddock wore out his men by having them cut a long military road through the forest toward Fort Duquesne, and he exposed them to attack from the tree-hidden enemy by marching them in the accepted European formation. Seven miles from the fort he ran into a French and Indian ambush (July 9, 1755); he himself and large numbers of his men were killed, and the survivors fled all the way back to Fort Cumberland in Maryland. The frontier from Pennsylvania to Virginia was left exposed to Indian raids, and many frontier settlers withdrew to the east of the Allegheny Mountains.

After about two years of fighting in America, the governments of France and England finally declared hostilities, and a world war (known in Europe as the Seven Years' War, 1756–1763) began. France and England now changed partners, France allying itself with its former enemy, Austria, and England joining France's former ally, Prussia.

Henceforth battles were fought not only on the American mainland but also in the West Indies, in Europe, and in India.

In this global contest, the British had the advantage of the mightiest navy on the seas and, with Frederick the Great on their side, the finest army in Europe. In America, the people of the English colonies outnumbered those of the French colonies by approximately fifteen to one, but were by no means that much stronger militarily. The French had numerous and powerful Indian allies, many of them newly attracted to the French by the latter's early victories in the war. The English had few such allies; the Iroquois, traditionally friendly to the English and hostile to the French, now remained firmly neutral. Furthermore, the French government kept its colonists in a state of military discipline and readiness, and could count upon the loyal services of a high proportion of its colonial manpower. The British government, on the other hand, exercised much less control over its thirteen colonies, which often acted as if they were autonomous. Only when they were exposed to immediate danger did the English colonists wholeheartedly support the war effort.

At first, the overall direction of British strategy was weak. Then, in 1757, William Pitt, as prime minister, was allowed to act as practically a wartime dictator. Pitt reformed the army and the navy, replacing bureaucratic deadwood with young and eager officers. He gave generous subsidies to Frederick the Great, who thus was enabled to keep the French busy in Europe. And he turned to the offensive in America, with a determination to drive the French out of the continent.

With Pitt as organizer, the British regulars in America, together with colonial troops, proceeded to take one French stronghold after another, including Fort Duquesne in 1758. The next year, after a siege of Quebec, supposedly impregnable atop its towering cliff, the army of General James Wolfe struggled up a hidden ravine, surprised the larger forces of the Marquis de Montcalm, and defeated them in a battle in which both commanders were slain. The fall of Quebec marked the climax of the American phase of the war.

Some other phases of the war were less romantic, less high-minded. In the course of it the British resorted to such expedients as population dispersal. Fearing trouble from the French inhabitants of Nova Scotia, the British uprooted several thousand of them and scattered them throughout the English colonies; some of these Acadians eventually made their way to Louisiana, where they became the ancestors of the present-day Cajuns. Meanwhile the French and their Indian allies were committing worse atrocities, and hundreds of defenseless families along the English frontier fell before the hatchet and the scalping knife.

Peace finally came after the accession of George III and the resignation of Pitt, who disagreed with the new king and wished to continue hostilities. Yet Pitt's aims were largely realized in the treaty signed at Paris in 1763. By its terms, the French ceded to Great Britain some of their West Indian islands and all their colonies in India except two. The French also transferred Canada and all other French territory east of the Mississippi, except the island of New Orleans, to Great Britain. New Orleans and the French claims west of the Mississippi were ceded to Spain. Thus the French gave up all title to the mainland of North America. And the British emerged from the conflict with a dramatically enlarged empire.

THE NEW IMPERIALISM

With the treaty of 1763, England found itself truly at peace for the first time in more than fifty years. Undistracted by war, the British government could now turn its attention to the organization of its empire, which it had long neglected. In fact, it had virtually no choice; even if policymakers had wished to revert to the old colonial system with its half-hearted enforcement of the mercantilist program they would have found it virtually impossible to do so. Saddled with enormous debts from the many years of fighting, England was desperately in need of new revenues from its empire. And responsible for vast new lands in the New World, the imperial government could not long avoid expanding its involvement in its colonies.

Burdens of Empire

The English had themselves unwittingly made it more difficult to impose a tighter imperial governance by their actions during the French and Indian War. Aware that the American colonists opposed direct legislation of their affairs by Parliament, Britain had not attempted to tax or draft the colonists directly. It had, instead, called on the provincial assemblies to provide quotas of soldiers and supplies. This requisition system heightened the sense of self-importance that the assemblies already harbored. Most of them further asserted their autonomy by complying in a slow and niggardly way. Some, unwilling to be taxed by Parliament, refused as well to tax themselves; they issued paper money instead.

In Virginia, the legislature not only issued paper money but, when the price of tobacco rose, also passed a law to deprive the Anglican clergy (who were paid in tobacco) of the benefits of the price rise. When this law was disallowed (1759), one of the ministers sued his vestrymen for his full pay. At the trial of the "parson's cause," the young lawyer Patrick Henry, defending the vestrymen, denounced the Privy Council for its tyranny and told his fellow Virginians to ignore its action. Roused by Henry's oratory, the jurors awarded the parson damages of only one penny. Thus did they defy the authority of the British government.

In Massachusetts, the merchants disregarded the laws of the empire even more flagrantly. Throughout the war, these merchants persisted in trading with the enemy in Canada and in the French West Indies. British officials resorted to general search warrants—"writs of assistance"—for discovering smuggled goods and stamping out the illegal and unpatriotic trade. As attorney for the Massachusetts merchants, James Otis maintained that these searches violated the ancient rights of Englishmen and that the law of Parliament authorizing the warrants was therefore null and void. With eloquence as stirring as Henry's, Otis insisted that Parliament had only a limited power of legislating for the colonies.

These emerging disputes over taxation and finance were compounded at the end of the war by the new challenges of imperial expansion. The expansion created particular problems because there were fundamental differences of opinion about how best the empire should use its new lands—indeed about whether the empire should acquire the lands at all. The thirteen continental colonies were only a part of the British possessions scattered throughout the Americas and the world, and before 1763 they were not considered (except in their own eyes) as the most valuable part. Some of them, such as Virginia and Maryland with their tobacco production, fitted in fairly well with the aims of mercantilism; but on the whole the island colonies contributed a great deal more than those of the mainland to the profits of English merchants and the prosperity of the English homeland. The "sugar islands" in particular—Barbados and the Windward Islands, the Leeward Islands, Jamaica—yielded remarkable opportunities for the investment of English capital. They also complemented the economies of some of the mainland colonies by providing a market for the output of fisheries, farms, and forest industries.

Believing in a kind of commercial imperialism, most English merchants opposed the acquisition of territory for its own sake. But some Englishmen, and many more Americans, began to believe that land itself should be acquired for the empire because of the population the land would support, the taxes it would produce, and the sense of imperial greatness it would confer. Both William Pitt and Benjamin Franklin were among the advocates of this new territorial imperialism. Franklin wrote powerfully about the future greatness of the British Empire in America, stressing the need for vast spaces to accommodate the rapid and limitless growth of the American people. Old-fashioned mercantilists, however, continued to think of trade as the essence of empire, and of island and coastal possessions as bases for trade. The issue came to a head with the peacemaking at the end of the French and Indian War. Commercial imperialists urged that Canada be returned to France in exchange for the most valuable of its sugar islands, Guadeloupe. Territorial imperialists, Franklin among them, argued in favor of keeping Canada. The decision to retain Canada marked a change in the emphasis of imperial policy.

With the acquisition of Canada and other North American territory in 1763, the area of the British Empire was suddenly twice as great as it had been, and the problems of governing it were thus made many times more complex. Almost immediately, England faced a series of sharply conflicting pressures as it attempted to devise a policy for governing the new lands. Some argued that the empire should restrain rapid settlement and development of the western territories; to do otherwise would be to risk further costly conflicts with the Indians and might help encourage France to launch a new attack somewhere in America in an effort to recover some of its lost territories and prestige. Others wanted to restrict settlement so that the land would remain available for hunting and trapping. Still others wanted to see the new territories opened for immediate development; yet even they disagreed among themselves about who should control the western lands. Colonial governments made fervent, and often conflicting, claims of jurisdiction. Others argued that control should remain in England, that the territories should be considered entirely new colonies, unlinked to the existing settlements. There were, in short, a host of problems and pressures that the British could not ignore.

At the same time, the government in London was running out of options in its effort to find a way to deal with its staggering war debt. Landlords and merchants in England itself were objecting strenuously to increases in what they already considered excessively high taxes. The colonies, on the other hand, had contributed virtually nothing, the British believed, to the support of a war fought in large part for their benefit. The

necessity of stationing significant numbers of British troops on the western frontier even after 1763 was adding even more to the cost of defending the American settlements. And the half-hearted response of the colonial assemblies to the war effort suggested that in its search for revenue, England could not rely on any cooperation from the provincial governments. Only a system of taxation administered by London, the leaders of the empire believed, could deal effectively with England's needs.

The Role of George III

At this crucial moment in Anglo-American relations, with the imperial system in desperate need of redefinition, the government of England was thrown into turmoil by the ascension to the throne of a new king. George III assumed power in 1760 upon the death of his father. And he brought two particularly unfortunate qualities to the office. First, he was determined, unlike his two predecessors, to reassert the authority of the monarchy. Pushed by his ambitious mother, he removed from power the long-standing and relatively stable coalition of Whigs, who had governed the empire for much of the century. In their place, he created a new coalition of his own through patronage and bribes and gained an uneasy control of Parliament. Yet the new ministries that emerged as a result of these changes were inherently unstable, each lasting an average of only about two years in office. In addition to these dangerous political ambitions, the king had serious intellectual and psychological limitations. He suffered, apparently, from a rare mental disease that produced intermittent bouts of insanity. (Indeed, in the last years of his long reign he was, according to most accounts, a virtual lunatic, confined to the palace and unable to perform any official functions.) Yet even when George III was lucid and rational, which was most of the time in the 1760s and 1770s, he was painfully immature (he had been only twenty-two when he ascended to the throne) and insecure—striving constantly to prove his fitness for his position but time and again finding himself ill-

George III
To American patriots during the Revolution, George III appeared to be a vicious and brutal tyrant. In fact, the king was a man of limited ability trying desperately (and stubbornly) to fulfill a role for which he was ill equipped. He suffered intermittently from insanity beginning at least as early as 1780; by 1810, he was permanently incapacitated. For the last ten years of his sixty-year reign (1760–1820), he was a virtual invalid, barred from all official business, which was conducted by his son, his eventual successor. (Library of Congress)

equipped to handle the challenges he seized for himself. The king's personality, therefore, contributed both to the instability and to the intransigence of the British government during these critical years.

More immediately responsible for the problems that soon emerged with the colonies, however, was George Grenville, whom the king made prime minister in 1763. Grenville, a brother-in-law of William Pitt, did not share Pitt's sympathy with the American point of view. He agreed instead with the prevailing opinion within Britain that the colonists had been too long indulged and that

they should be compelled to obey the laws and to pay a part of the cost of defending and administering the empire. He fancied himself something of an efficiency expert, and he was indeed an able administrator. Furthermore, as chancellor of the exchequer and first lord of the treasury, he was well acquainted with matters of public finance. He promptly undertook to impose system upon what had been a rather unsystematic aggregation of colonial possessions in America.

The Western problem was the most urgent. With the repulse of the French, frontiersmen from the English colonies had begun immediately to move over the mountains and into the upper Ohio Valley. Objecting to this intrusion, an alliance of Indian tribes, under the remarkable Ottawa chieftain Pontiac, prepared to fight back. As an emergency measure, the British government issued a proclamation forbidding settlers to advance beyond a line drawn along the mountain divide between the Atlantic and the interior.

Though the emergency passed, the principle of the Proclamation Line of 1763 remained—the principle of controlling the westward movement of population. This was something new. Earlier, the government had encouraged the rapid peopling of the frontier for reasons of both defense and trade. In time, the official attitude had begun to change because of a fear that the interior might draw away so many people as to weaken markets and investments nearer the coast, and because of a desire to reserve land-speculating and fur-trading opportunities for English rather than colonial enterprisers. Then, having tentatively announced a new policy in 1763, the government soon extended and elaborated it. A definite Indian boundary was to be located, and from time to time relocated, in agreement with the various tribes. Western lands were to be opened for occupation gradually, and settlement was to be carefully supervised to see that it proceeded in a compact and orderly way.

To provide further for the defense of the colonies, and to raise revenue and enforce imperial law within them, the Grenville ministry meanwhile instituted a series of measures, some of which were familiar in princi-

ENGLISH MAINLAND COLONIES

ple and others fairly novel. Regular troops were now to be stationed permanently in the provinces, and by the Mutiny Act (1765) the colonists were called upon to assist in provisioning and maintaining the army. Ships of the navy were assigned to patrol American waters and look out for smugglers. The customs service was reorganized and enlarged, and vice-admiralty courts were set up in America to try accused smugglers without the benefit of sympathetic local juries. Royal officials were ordered to take up their colonial posts in person instead of sending substitutes. The Sugar Act (1764), designed in part to eliminate the illegal trade between the continental colonies and the foreign West Indies, lowered the high molasses duty of the Molasses Act of 1733 but imposed new duties on a number of items and made provision for more effective collection. The Currency Act (1764) forbade the colonial assemblies to issue any more paper money and required them to retire on schedule all the paper money issued during the war. And, most momentous of all, the Stamp Act (1765) imposed a tax to be paid on every legal document in the colonies, every newspaper, almanac, or pamphlet.

Thus the new imperial program with its firm reapplication of old mercantilist principles began to be put into effect. In a sense, it proved highly effective. British officials soon were collecting more than ten times as much annual revenue in America as before 1763. But the new policy was not a lasting success.

The Colonial View

The colonists still had much to gain by remaining within the empire and enjoying its many benefits. They continued, moreover, to harbor as many grievances against one another as against the authorities in London. In 1763, for example, a band of Pennsylvania frontiersmen known as the Paxton Boys descended on Philadelphia to demand defense money and changes in the tax laws, and bloodshed was averted only by concessions from the colonial government.

In 1771, a small-scale civil war broke out as a consequence of the Regulator movement in North Carolina. The Regulators were farmers of the Carolina upcountry who organized to oppose the extortionate taxes that the sheriffs collected. These sheriffs, along with other local officials, were appointed by the governor. At first the Regulators tried to redress their grievances peaceably, by electing their leaders to the colonial assembly. But since the western counties were badly underrepresented in the assembly, the Regula-

tors were unable to get control of it. They finally armed themselves and undertook to resist tax collections by force. To suppress the revolt, Governor William Tryon raised an army of militiamen, mostly from the eastern counties. The militiamen met and defeated the Regulators, some 2,000 strong, in the Battle of Alamance, in which nine on each side were killed and many others wounded. Afterward, six Regulators were hanged for treason.

Although such bloodshed was exceptional, the people of the colonies were divided by numerous conflicts of interest. After 1763, however, the policies of the British government increasingly offset the divisive tendencies within the colonies and caused Americans to look at the disadvantages of empire more closely than at its benefits. These policies appeared to threaten, in some degree or other, the well-being of nearly all classes in America.

Northern merchants would suffer from the various restraints upon their commerce, from the closing of the West to their ventures in land speculation and fur trading, from the denial of opportunities in manufacturing, and from the increased load of taxation. Southern planters, already burdened with debts to English merchants, not only would have to pay additional taxes but would also be deprived of the chance to lessen their debts by selling Western land, in which George Washington and others were much interested. Professional men—preachers, lawyers, and professors—considered the interests of merchants and planters to be identical with their own. Small farmers, clearly the largest group in the colonies, stood to lose as a result of reduced markets and hence lower prices for their crops, together with an increase in their taxes and their costs, not to mention the difficulty of getting paper-money loans. Town workers faced the prospect of narrowing opportunities, particularly because of the restraints on manufacturing and paper money.

At the end of the French and Indian War, the colonists already were beginning to feel the pinch of a postwar depression. Previously the British government, pouring money into their midst to finance the fighting, had stimu-

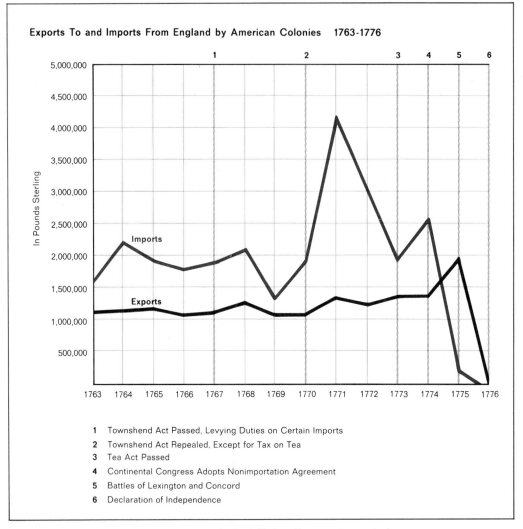

Exports To and Imports From England by American Colonies   1763-1776

Though the Stamp Act (1765) apparently had little effect on imports from England, the Townshend Act (1767) led to a considerable reduction in them in 1769. After this law's almost complete repeal (1770), imports rose dramatically in 1771. The Tea Act (1773) and the nonimportation agreement (1774) helped to bring on another decline, and the subsequent outbreak of hostilities resulted in an almost complete stoppage of trade.

lated a wartime boom. Now the government proposed to take money out of the colonies instead of putting it in. If the government's measures were strictly enforced, the immediate effect would be to aggravate the hard times. The long-term effect, many feared, would be to confine the enterprising spirit of the colonists and condemn them to a fixed or even a declining level of living.

In reality, most Americans soon found ways to live with (or circumvent) the new British policies. The economy of America was not, in fact, being destroyed. Nevertheless, economic anxieties contributed to the rising sense of unease, particularly in the cities—the places most directly affected by British policies and the places where resistance first arose. The periodic economic slumps that were occurring with greater and greater frequency, the frightening depression of the early 1760s, the growth of a large group within the population who were unemployed or semiemployed, and who were in either case a destabilizing element in the community: all combined to produce a feeling in some colonial cities—and particularly in Boston, the city suffering the worst economic problems—that something was deeply amiss. Only in an indirect way did these material concerns contribute to the revolutionary crisis. But unhappiness about the state of the economy almost certainly made Americans more likely to resist changes in the power of the imperial government.

Whatever the economic consequences of George III's and Grenville's programs, the political consequences were—in the eyes of the colonists, at least—far worse. While colonial democracy was far from complete, the colonists were used to a remarkably wide latitude in self-government. Nowhere else in the world at that time did so large a proportion of the people take an active interest in public affairs. The chief centers of American political activity were the provincial assemblies; and here the people (through their elected representatives) were able to assert themselves because the assemblies had established the right to give or withhold appropriations for the costs of government within the colonies. If, now, the British authorities should succeed in raising extensive revenues directly from America, the colonial voters and their representatives would lose control over public finance, and without such control their participation in politics would be very nearly meaningless.

Home rule was not something new and different that Americans were striving to get. It was something old and familiar that they desired to keep. They would lose it if the London authorities were allowed to carry out the program of raising revenues from colonial taxation and providing unconditional salaries for royal officials. The discontented Americans eventually prepared themselves to lay down their lives for a movement that was at the same time democratic and conservative—a movement to conserve the liberties they believed they already possessed.

STIRRINGS OF REVOLT

Thus by the mid-1760s, a hardening of positions had begun in both England and America that would bring the colonies into increasing conflict with the mother country. To the colonists, the victorious war for empire had given a heightened sense of their own importance and a renewed commitment to protecting their political autonomy. To the British, it had given a strengthened belief in the need to tighten administration of the empire and a strong desire to use the colonies as a source of revenue. The result was a progression of events that, more rapidly than anyone could have imagined, drove a deep wedge between the Americans and the English.

The Stamp Act Crisis

Prime Minister Grenville could not have devised a better method for antagonizing and unifying the colonies than the Stamp Act if he had tried. The new tax fell on all Americans, of whatever section, colony, or class. In particular, the stamps required for ships' papers and legal documents offended merchants and lawyers. Tavern owners, often the political oracles of their neighborhoods, now were supposed to buy stamps for their licenses; and printers—who were the most influential group in distributing information and ideas in colonial society—were required to buy stamps for their newspapers and other publications Thus the tax antagonized those who could play most effectively on public opinion.

The actual economic burdens of the Stamp Act were, in the end, relatively light. What made the law obnoxious to the colonists was not so much its immediate cost as the precedent it seemed to set. In the past, taxes and duties on colonial trade had always

Response to the Stamp Act

This October 31, 1765, issue of a Pennsylvania newspaper carries a death's head insignia on its masthead and heavy black rules down its columns to suggest public mourning—mourning for the loss of popular liberties as a result of the Stamp Act and mourning for the paper itself, which is announcing in this issue that it is ceasing publication rather than pay the hated tax. Eighteenth-century newspapers were, as this issue suggests, highly partisan and polemical. They became effective agents in spreading the ideology of the revolutionary struggle.

(New York Public Library, Rare Book Division, Astor, Lenox, and Tilden Foundations) been interpreted as measures to regulate commerce. Even the Sugar Act of 1764 did not appear to many Americans to differ fundamentally from the traditional nature of imperial duties. The Stamp Act, however, could be interpreted in only one way. It was a direct attempt by England to raise revenue in the colonies; and it was being done without the consent of the colonial assemblies. If this new tax were allowed to pass without resistance, the door would be open for far more burdensome taxation in the future.

Nevertheless, it occurred to few colonists that they could do anything more than grumble and buy the stamps, until the Virginia House of Burgesses sounded a "trumpet of sedition" that aroused Americans to action almost everywhere. In the House of Burgesses, a group of young aristocrats aspired to exert themselves against the oligarchy of tidewater planters who, with the royal governor, dominated Virginia politics. Foremost among these young malcontents was Patrick Henry, who was ambitious to enlarge the fame he had gained in the "parson's cause." Henry made a fiery speech in the House (May 1765), concluding with a hint that George III, like earlier tyrants, might lose his head. There were shocked cries of "Treason!" and, according to a man who was present, Henry apologized, though many years afterward he was quoted as having made the defiant reply: "If *this* be treason, make the most of it." In any case, he proceeded to introduce a set of resolutions declaring that Americans possessed all the rights of Englishmen, especially the right to be taxed only by their own representatives; moreover, that Virginians should pay no taxes except those voted by the Virginia assembly, and that anyone advocating the right of Parliament to tax Virginians should be deemed an enemy of the colony. The House of Burgesses did not adopt the most extreme of Henry's resolutions, but all of them were printed and circulated as the "Virginia Resolves," thus giving the impression in other colonies that the people of Virginia were more militant than they actually were.

Stirred by the Virginia Resolves, mobs in various places began to take the law into their own hands, and during the summer of 1765 riots broke out in various places, the worst of them in Boston. Men belonging to the newly organized Sons of Liberty went about terrorizing stamp agents and burning the stamps. The agents, themselves Americans, hastily resigned, and very few stamps were sold in the continental colonies. In Boston, the mob harried pro-British "aristocrats" such as the lieutenant governor, Thomas Hutchinson, whose house was wrecked (even though privately he had opposed passage of the Stamp Act).

At about the time that Patrick Henry presented his resolutions to the Virginia assembly, James Otis proposed to his fellow legislators in Massachusetts that they call an intercolonial congress for concerted action against the new tax. In October 1765, the Stamp Act Congress met in New York, with delegates from nine of the colonies present, and decided to petition both the king and the two houses of Parliament. Though admitting that Americans owed to Parliament "all due subordination," the congress denied that they could rightfully be taxed except by their provincial assemblies.

If the British government had tried to enforce the Stamp Act, the Revolutionary War might have begun ten years earlier than it did. The government was not deterred by resolves, riots, and petitions; but the Americans also used something more persuasive than any of these—economic pressure. Already, in response to the Sugar Act of 1764, many New Englanders had quit buying English goods. Now the colonial boycott spread, and the Sons of Liberty intimidated those colonists who were reluctant to participate in it. The merchants of England, feeling the loss of much of their colonial market, begged Parliament to repeal the Stamp Act, while stories of unemployment, poverty, and discontent arose from English seaports and manufacturing towns.

Having succeeded Grenville as prime minister, the Marquis of Rockingham tried to appease both the English merchants and the American colonists, and King George III himself finally was convinced that the act must be repealed. Opponents of repeal, strong and vociferous, insisted that unless the colonists were compelled to obey the

The Stamp Act Congress: Resolutions [1765]

I. That His Majesty's subjects in these colonies owe the same allegiance to the Crown of Great Britain that is owing from his subjects born within the realm, and all due subordination to that august body the Parliament of Great Britain.

II. That His Majesty's liege subjects in these colonies are intitled to all the inherent rights and liberties of his natural born subjects within the kingdom of Great Britain.

III. That it is inseparably essential to the freedom of a people, and the undoubted right of Englishmen, that no taxes be imposed on them but with their own consent, given personally or by their representatives.

IV. That the people of these colonies are not, and from their local circumstances cannot be, represented in the House of Commons in Great Britain.

V. That the only representatives of the people of these colonies are persons chosen therein by themselves, and that no taxes ever have been, or can be constitutionally imposed on them, but by their respective legislatures. . . .

Stamp Act, they would soon cease to obey any laws of Parliament. So Parliament passed the Declaratory Act, asserting parliamentary authority over the colonies "is in all cases whatsoever," and then repealed the Stamp Act (1766). In their rejoicing over the repeal, most Americans paid little attention to the sweeping declaration of Parliament's power.

The Townshend Program

The appeasement policy of the Rockingham government was not as well received in England as it was in America. English landlords protested that the government had "sacrificed the landed gentlemen to the interests of traders and colonists." They were, in other words, fearful that the retreat of the government from its policy of taxing the colonies would result in renewed taxes on them. Finally, the king bowed to popular clamor and dismissed the Rockingham ministry. To replace it, he called upon the aging but still powerful William Pitt to form a government. Pitt had been a strong critic of the Stamp Act and had a reputation in America as a friend of the colonists (although some Americans had looked askance at his acceptance of a peerage, as Lord Chatham). Once in office, however, Pitt was so hobbled by gout and at times so incapacitated by mental illness that the actual leadership of his administration fell to the chancellor of the exchequer, Charles Townshend—a brilliant politician but something of a playboy, as suggested by his popular nickname "Champagne Charlie."

Townshend had to deal almost immediately with the litany of imperial problems and colonial grievances left over from the Grenville ministry. With the Stamp Act repealed, the greatest American grievance involved the Mutiny (or Quartering) Act of 1765, which required the colonists to provide quarters and supplies for the British troops in America. To the British, this seemed only fair. After all, the troops were stationed in North America to protect the colonists from Indian or French attack and to defend the frontiers. Lodging the troops in coastal cities was simply a way to reduce the costs of supplying them. To the colonists, however, the presence of British troops not only in their communities but, under the provisions of the Mutiny Act, in their homes was both intrusive and threatening. They responded with defiance. The government of Massachusetts resisted first; its assembly refused to vote the mandated supplies to the troops. The New York assembly soon did the same thing, posing an even greater challenge to imperial authority, since the army headquarters were in New York City.

The Declaratory Act [1766]

Whereas several of the houses of representatives in his Majesty's colonies and plantations in America have of late, against law, claimed to themselves, or to the general assemblies of the same, the sole and exclusive right of imposing duties or taxes upon his Majesty's subjects in the said colonies and plantations; and have, in pursuance of such claim, passed certain votes, resolutions, and orders, derogatory to the legislative authority of parliament, and inconsistent with the dependency of said colonies and plantations upon the crown of Great Britain: ... be it declared ... That the said colonies and plantations in America have been, are, and of right ought to be subordinate unto and dependent upon the imperial crown and parliament of Great Britain; and that the King's majesty, by and with the advice and consent of the lords spiritual and temporal and commons of Great Britain in parliament assembled, had, hath, and of right ought to have full power and authority to make laws and statutes of sufficient force and validity to bind the colonies and people of America, subjects of the crown of Great Britain, in all cases whatsoever.

To enforce the Mutiny Act and raise revenues in the colonies, Townshend proposed two measures to Parliament. First, New York was to be punished by the suspension of its assembly until the law was obeyed there. By thus singling out New York, Townshend thought he would avoid Grenville's mistake of arousing all the colonies at once. Second, duties were to be levied on colonial imports of glass, lead, paint, paper, and tea. Townshend reasoned that the colonists could not logically object to taxation of this kind. For Benjamin Franklin, as a colonial agent in London trying to prevent the passage of the Stamp Act, had drawn a distinction between "internal" and "external" taxes and had denounced the stamp duties as internal taxation. While Townshend had laughed at this distinction, he was now recommending duties that, without question, were to be collected externally. In 1767, Parliament approved the so-called Townshend Duties and suspended the New York assembly.

Townshend's efforts to satisfy colonial grievances were, however, to no avail. The new duties were no more acceptable to Americans than the stamp tax. They recognized that even though these were ostensibly "external" taxes, their purpose was still to raise revenue from the colonists without their consent. And the suspension of the New York assembly, far from isolating New York, aroused the resentment of all the colonies. This assault on the rights of one provincial government could serve as a precedent for annihilation of all of them. Taking up New York's cause as well as its own, the Massachusetts assembly sent out a circular letter urging all colonies to stand up against every tax, external or internal, imposed by Parliament. At first, the Massachusetts circular evoked little response in some of the legislatures (and ran into strong opposition in Pennsylvania's). Then Lord Hillsborough, occupant of the new office of secretary of state for the colonies, issued a circular letter of his own in which he warned that assemblies endorsing the Massachusetts letter would be dissolved. Promptly the other colonies, even Pennsylvania, rallied to the support of Massachusetts.

Besides inducing Parliament to levy import duties and suspend the New York assembly, Townshend also took steps to enforce commercial regulations in the colonies more effectively than ever. The most fateful of these steps was the establishment of a board of customs commissioners in America. In doing so, he intended to stop the corruption in the colonial customhouses. His commissioners, with headquarters in Boston, virtually ended the smuggling at that place, though smugglers continued to carry on a busy trade in other colonial seaports.

Naturally the Boston merchants were the most indignant, and they took the lead in organizing another boycott. In 1768, the merchants of Philadelphia and New York joined those of Boston in a nonimportation agreement, and later some of the Southern merchants and planters also agreed to cooperate. Throughout the colonies, crude American homespun became suddenly fashionable, while English luxuries were frowned upon.

Before the consequences of his program were fully apparent, Townshend died, leaving the question of revising his import duties to his successor, Lord North. Hoping to break the nonimportation agreement and divide the colonists, Lord North secured the repeal (1770) of all the Townshend Duties except the tea tax.

The Boston Massacre

Boston had the most aggressive popular leader of any colony, Samuel Adams. The impoverished son of a once wealthy brewer, Adams had taken to politics after he himself had failed in business. As a resistance leader he had no equal in the colonies, and from the time of the Stamp Act troubles he was the guiding spirit of Massachusetts radicalism. Adams's success as a politician depended on his finding suitable topics for agitation, and the British government, having repeatedly supplied him with topics, obliged him again by locating the customs commissioners in Boston and then stationing troops there.

To the Boston "liberty boys," the presence of the customs commissioners was a standing invitation to violence, and before long the terrified officials were driven to take refuge in Castle William, out in the harbor. So that they could return safely to their duties, the British government placed four regiments (afterward reduced to two) within the city. The presence of the redcoats antagonized Samuel Adams and his followers more than ever. While his men ragged the soldiers and engaged them in brawls, Adams filled the newspapers with stories of rapes and other imagined atrocities committed by the

troops; and he spread throughout Boston a rumor that the soldiers were preparing for a concerted attack upon the citizens. On the night of March 5, 1770, a mob of dockworkers and other "liberty boys" fell upon the sentry at the customhouse. Hastily, Captain Preston of the British regiment lined up several of his men in front of the building to protect it. There was some scuffling, and one of the soldiers was knocked down. Other soldiers then fired into the crowd, killing five of its members.

These events quickly became known as the "Boston Massacre" through the efforts of Samuel Adams and his adherents, who published an account bearing the title *Innocent Blood Crying to God from the Streets of Boston* and giving the impression that the dead were victims of a deliberate plot. The soldiers, tried before a jury of Bostonians and defended by Samuel Adams's cousin John Adams, were found guilty of no more than manslaughter and were given only a token punishment. Nevertheless, through newspapers and pamphlets, Samuel Adams convicted the redcoats of murder in the minds of many contemporary Americans, and year after year on March 5 he revived the people's memory with orations recalling the events of 1770. Later generations accepted his version of the "massacre" and thus, without knowing it, honored his skill as the foremost propagandist of the pre-Revolutionary decade.

The Philosophy of Revolt

A superficial calm settled on the colonies for approximately three years after 1770. In reality, however, American political life remained restless and troubled. The reason was the power of ideas. The crises of the 1760s had helped to arouse an ideological excitement among large groups of colonists that continued in the 1770s, producing a political outlook that would ultimately serve to justify revolt. "The Revolution was effected before the war commenced," one of the greatest of the Founding Fathers, John Adams, afterward remarked. "The Revolution was in the minds and hearts of the people." Adams perhaps exaggerated. Few Americans were willing to

The "Bloody Massacre"

This broadside, "Engrav'd Printed & Sold by Paul Revere, Boston," pictures the Patriot version of the Boston incident of March 5, 1770. At the extreme right, Captain Thomas Preston, in command of the customhouse guards, leers as he orders his grinning men to fire on the unarmed citizens. The customhouse, Preston's headquarters, is sarcastically labeled "Butcher's Hall." Accompanying the picture were the names of the dead and eighteen lines of verse. One of the dead was Crispus Attucks, a tall, brawny, forty-seven-year-old man, reputed to be black, with some Indian blood, who had escaped from slavery and taken up the life of a sailor. When, in 1888, a monument was erected to the fallen, a poem was recited honoring Attucks as "leader and voice that day; /The first to defy and the first to die. . . ." (Courtesy of the Metropolitan Museum of Art, gift of Mrs. Russell Sage, 1910) consider complete independence from England until after the war had begun; and even those few (among them Samuel Adams) generally refrained from admitting that independence was their goal. But John Adams was certainly correct in arguing that well before the fighting began in 1775, a profound ideological shift had occurred in the way many Americans viewed the British government and their own.

The ideas that would support the Revolution emerged from many sources. Some were indigenous to America, drawn from religious (particularly Puritan) sources or from the political experiences of the colonies. But these native ideas were enriched and enlarged by the importation of powerful arguments from abroad. Of most importance, perhaps, were the "radical" ideas of those in Great Britain who stood in opposition to their government. Some were Scots, who viewed the English government as tyrannical. Others were embittered "country Whigs," who considered the existing system corrupt and oppressive. Drawing from some of the great philosophical minds of earlier generations—most notably John Locke—these English dissidents framed a powerful argument against their government; and that argument found a ready audience in the troubled colonies.

Central to this emerging ideology was a concept of what government should be. Because man was inherently corrupt and selfish, government was necessary to protect citizens from the evil in one another. But because any government was run by corruptible men, it must itself be protected against its members. In the eyes of most Englishmen and most Americans, the English constitution was the best system ever devised by man to meet these necessities. By distributing power among the three elements of society—the monarch, the aristocracy, and the common people—the English political system ensured that no individual or group could exercise authority unchecked by another. Yet by the mid-seventeenth century, both the English opposition and the colonists in America were becoming deeply concerned that this noble constitution was being destroyed. The king and his ministers were exercising such corrupt and autocratic authority, they believed,

that the balancing functions of the government were no longer being performed. The system was threatening to become a dangerous tyranny.

Compounding this concern was the resentment in America of Britain's claims to authority over the colonies. The English constitution, Americans believed, guaranteed them the individual liberties and political autonomy they claimed. Parliament's attempts to infringe upon those rights was further proof of the dangerous corruption infecting the British government, and evidence of a threatening conspiracy against liberty in progress in London. Americans were, in short, coming to the conclusion that they were remaining more faithful to the English constitution than the English were themselves; that it was they who were defending the traditional system and England that was attempting to destroy it.

Such arguments found little sympathy in England, largely because most Englishmen had a very different view of the nature of their constitution than did most Americans. To the English, the constitution, although it was greatly revered, was a flexible, constantly changing entity, an assortment of laws and customs that had evolved through many centuries and had remained elastic and vague. Far from being a fixed, clearly defined system of government, the constitution was a general sense of the "way things were done." To Americans, on the other hand, the constitution appeared to be a fixed and definite body of principles. Drawing from their experience with colonial charters, in which the shape and powers of government were permanently inscribed, many argued that the English constitution should be similarly fixed—written down so as to avoid disagreements. Rights that were basic to Englishmen (and, some argued, to all mankind) should not be left to the shifting sentiments of particular governments. They should be permanently and clearly guaranteed.

Of these rights the most fundamental, according to the colonists, was the right to be taxed only with their own consent. When Townshend levied his "external" duties, the Philadelphia lawyer John Dickinson maintained in the *Letters of a Pennsylvania Farmer* that even external taxation was legal only when designed to regulate trade and not to raise a revenue. But Americans did not like trade regulations either, when the regulations began to be enforced. Eventually the discontented colonists took an unqualified stand with the slogan "No taxation without representation."

This clamor about "representation" made little sense to Englishmen. Only about one in twenty-five of them was entitled to vote for a member of Parliament, and some populous boroughs in England had no representatives at all. According to the prevailing English theory, however, Parliament did not represent individuals or geographical areas. Instead, it represented the interests of the whole nation and indeed the whole empire, no matter where the members happened to come from. The unenfranchised boroughs of England, the whole of Ireland, and the colonies 3,000 miles away—all were thus represented in the Parliament at London.

That was the theory of "virtual" representation. But Americans believed in actual representation. They felt they could be represented in Parliament only if they sent their quota of members to it. Yet even that would not satisfactorily resolve the problems. Some Americans, among them James Otis, considered proposals for electing American representatives, but most of the colonists realized that if they were to participate in the actions of Parliament they would be bound by those actions, even though they would be outnumbered and outvoted. More important, American members of Parliament would be so isolated from the people who elected them that they would not be able to perform as true representatives. So most colonists reverted to the argument that they could be fairly represented only in their own colonial assemblies.

According to the American view of the empire, and according to the actual fact, these assemblies were little parliaments, as competent to legislate for their respective colonies as Parliament was for England. The empire was a sort of federation of commonwealths, each with its own legislative body, all tied together by common loyalty to the king (much as in the British Commonwealth of Nations today). This being their conception of the empire, the Americans protested bitterly against the pretensions of Parliament. Not until very late did they begin to criticize the king himself. And not until the colonies were ready to declare their independence in 1776 were they ready to repudiate the English constitution.

What made the conflict between England and America ultimately insoluble was a fundamental difference of opinion over the nature of sovereignty. By arguing that Parliament had the right to legislate for the empire as a whole, but that only the provincial assemblies could legislate for the individual colonies, Americans were in effect arguing for a division of sovereignty. Parliament would be the sovereign in some matters; the assemblies would be sovereign in others. To the British, such an argument was untenable and absurd. Sovereignty, they believed, was by definition unitary. In any system of government there must be a single, ultimate authority. And since the empire was, in their view, a single, undivided unit, there could be only one authority within it: the English government of king and Parliament. Thus when the colonists attempted to make a distinction between "internal" and "external" taxes, most English leaders listened with incredulity. There could be no such distinction, because it suggested that authority within the empire could be divided. Thus it was that the Anglo-American crisis ultimately presented the colonists with a stark choice. In the eyes of the English, there was no middle ground between complete subordination and complete independence. Slowly, cautiously, Americans found themselves moving toward independence.

That movement began with resistance, rather than with any sentiment for open revolt. Opposition to British policies in the 1760s had not taken the form of repudiation of England but of refusal to obey certain unjust laws. In that, the colonists were drawing from their own interpretation of the Bible and from the writings of John Locke. For generations, the preachers of New England had taught that no man need obey a government when it violated the will of God as set forth in the Scriptures. Now, to show that rebellion against tyranny was lawful in God's sight, they retold such Bible stories as the one about a king of Israel who burdened his people with unjust taxes and was overthrown.

John Locke (1632–1704) might have been shocked if he had lived to see the use that Americans made of his doctrines. In his *Two Treatises of Government* (1690) Locke attempted to justify the English revolution of 1688–1689 by which Parliament had won supremacy over the king. According to Locke's theory, men originally lived in a state of nature and enjoyed complete liberty, then agreed to a "compact" by which they set up a government to protect their "natural rights," especially their right to the ownership and enjoyment of private property. The government was limited by the terms of the compact and by "natural law." It was contrary to natural law for a government to take property without the consent of the owners, Locke wrote, and Americans noted in particular his sentence: "If any one shall claim a power to lay and levy taxes on the people by his own authority, and without such consent of the people, he thereby invades the fundamental law of property, and subverts the end of government." To Americans of the 1760s and 1770s it was clear that the British government was flouting the law of nature as well as the will of God. And, according to Locke, if a government should persist in exceeding its rightful powers, men would be released from their obligation to obey it. What was more, they would have the right to make a new compact and establish another government. The right to resist was, in other words, only the first step. If resistance proved ineffective, if a government proved to be so thoroughly corrupt and tyrannical that it could not be reformed, then citizens were entitled to revolt against it. They had a "right of revolution."

By the early 1770s, the relationship between America and England had become so poisoned by resentment and mutual suspicion, Americans had become so fearful of what they considered to be a "conspiracy against liberty" within the British government, that only a small distance remained to be traversed before the colonies would be ready to break their ties with the empire.

That distance was crossed quickly, beginning in 1773, when a new set of British policies shattered forever the imperial relationship.

The Tea Excitement

There had been occasional episodes of American resistance in the first years of the 1770s to break the relative stillness in America. Colonists had seized a British revenue ship on the lower Delaware River. And in 1772, angry citizens of Rhode Island had protested what they considered heavy-handed enforcement of trade regulations by boarding the British schooner *Gaspée*, setting it afire, and sinking it in Narragansett Bay. The British response to the *Gaspée* affair further inflamed American opinion. Instead of putting the accused attackers on trial in colonial courts, the British sent a special commission to America, with power to send the defendants back to England for trial. Once again, the British were challenging America's right to exercise independent authority.

What finally revived the revolutionary fervor of the 1760s to its old strength, however, was a new act of Parliament—one that the English government had expected to be relatively uncontroversial. It involved the business of selling tea. In 1773, Britain's East India Company, with large stocks of tea on hand that it could not sell, was on the verge of bankruptcy. In an effort to save it, the government passed the Tea Act of 1773, which gave the company the right to export its product directly to the colonies without paying any of the regular taxes that were imposed on the colonial merchants, who had traditionally served as the middlemen in such transactions. With these privileges, the company could undersell American merchants and monopolize the colonial tea trade.

The act proved inflammatory for several reasons. First, it angered the colonial merchants, who were influential in American society. Some were threatened with bankruptcy, with being replaced by a powerful monopoly. The East India Company's decision to grant franchises to certain American merchants for the sale of their tea created

Taking the Pledge
This British caricature, entitled "A Society of Patriotic Ladies, at Edenton in North Carolina," was published in London in March 1775. It ridicules the American buy-at-home movement. The women are emptying their tea canisters and signing a pledge, which reads: "We the Ladies of Edenton do hereby Solemnly Engage not to Conform to that Pernicious Custom of Drinking Tea, or that we the aforesaid Ladies will not promote the Wear of any Manufacture from England until such time that all Acts which tend to Enslave this our Native Country shall be Repealed." (Courtesy of the Metropolitan Museum of Art, bequest of Charles Allen Munn, 1924)

further resentments; those who were excluded from this lucrative trade were deeply embittered. More important, however, the Tea Act revived American passions about the issue of taxation without representation. The law provided no new tax on tea. But the original Townshend duty on the commodity—the only one of the original duties that had not been repealed—survived. Lord North assumed that most colonists would welcome the new law because it would reduce the price of tea to consumers by removing the middlemen. But agitators in America seized on the Tea Act and argued that it represented another insidious effort by the English to force the colonists to pay an unconstitutional tax. The colonists responded by boycotting tea, of which many of them—especially women—were extremely fond. They drank instead such substitutes as coffee and chocolate.

Meanwhile, with strong popular support, leaders in various colonies made plans to prevent the East India Company from landing its cargoes in colonial ports. In Philadelphia and New York determined men kept the tea from leaving the company's ships, and in Charleston they stored it away in a public warehouse. In Boston, having failed to turn back the three ships in the harbor, the followers of Samuel Adams staged a spectacular drama. On the evening of December 16, 1773, three companies of fifty men each, masquerading as Mohawks, passed through a tremendous crowd of spectators (which served to protect them from official interference), went aboard, broke open the tea chests, and heaved them into the water. As the electrifying news of the Boston "tea party" spread, other seaports followed the example and held tea parties of their own.

When the Bostonians refused to pay for the property they had destroyed, George III and Lord North decided on a policy of coercion, to be applied not against all the colonies but only against Massachusetts—the chief center of resistance. In four acts of 1774, Parliament proceeded to put this policy into effect. One of the laws closed the port of Boston; another drastically reduced the local and provincial powers of self-government in Massachusetts; still another permitted royal officers to be tried in other colonies or in England when accused of crimes; and the last provided for the quartering of troops in the colonists' barns and empty houses.

These Coercive Acts—or, as they were more widely known in America, Intolerable Acts—were followed by the Quebec Act, which was separate from them in origin and quite different in purpose. Its object was to provide a civil government for the French-speaking Roman Catholic inhabitants of Canada and the Illinois country. The law extended the boundaries of Quebec to include the French communities between the Ohio and Mississippi rivers. It also granted political rights to Roman Catholics and recognized the legality of the Roman Catholic church within the enlarged province. In many ways it was a liberal and much-needed piece of legislation.

To many Protestants in the thirteen colonies, however, the Quebec Act was anathema. They were already alarmed by rumors that the Church of England schemed to appoint a bishop for America with the intention of enforcing Anglican authority on all the various sects. To them the line between the Church of England and the Church of Rome had always seemed dangerously thin. When Catholics ceased to be actively persecuted in the mother country, alarmists in the colonies began to fear that Catholicism and Anglicanism were about to merge; and at the passage of the Quebec Act they became convinced that a plot was afoot in London to subject Americans to the tyranny of the pope. Moreover, those interested in western lands believed that the act, by extending the boundaries of Quebec, would reinforce the land policy of the Proclamation Line of 1763 and hinder westward progress.

Had it not been for the Quebec Act, Lord North might have come close to succeeding in his effort to divide and rule the colonies by isolating Massachusetts. As it was, the colonists generally lumped the Quebec law with the Massachusetts measures as the fifth of the "Intolerable Acts." From New Hampshire to South Carolina the people prepared to take a united stand.

COOPERATION AND WAR

Revolutions do not simply happen. They must be organized and led. Beginning in 1765, colonial leaders developed a variety of organizations for converting popular discontent into action—organizations that in time formed the basis for an independent government.

New Sources of Authority

The passage of authority from the royal government to the colonists themselves began on the local level, where the tradition of autonomy was already strong. In colony after colony, local institutions responded to the resistance movement by simply seizing authority on their own. At times, entirely new, extralegal bodies emerged semispontaneously and began to perform some of the functions of government. In Massachusetts in 1768, for example, Sam Adams called a convention of delegates from the towns of the colony to sit in place of the General Court, which the governor had dissolved. The Sons of Liberty, which Adams also helped to organize in Massachusetts and which sprang up elsewhere as well, also became a source of power; they served at times as disciplined mobs, vigilantes making certain that all colonists maintained boycotts and other forms of popular resistance. And in most colonies, committees of prominent citizens began meeting to perform additional political functions.

The most famous and most effective of these new groups were the committees of correspondence. Massachusetts took the lead (1772) with such committees on the local level, a network of them connecting Boston with the rural towns; but Virginia was the first to establish committees of correspondence on an intercolonial basis. These made possible cooperation among the colonies in a more continuous way than had the Stamp Act Congress, the first effort at intercolonial union for resistance against imperial authority. Virginia took the greatest step of all toward united action in 1774 when, the governor having dissolved the assembly, a rump session met in the Raleigh Tavern at Williamsburg, declared that the Intolerable Acts menaced the liberties of every colony, and issued a call for a Continental Congress.

Variously elected by the assemblies and by extralegal meetings, delegates from all the thirteen colonies except Georgia were present when, in September 1774, the Continental Congress convened in Philadelphia. The delegates divided into moderates and extremists, and the more extreme members seized the upper hand. At the outset they showed their strength by designating Carpenters' Hall as the meeting place. This was the headquarters of the Philadelphia Carpenters' Company, and some members complained that its selection was an unseemly attempt to curry favor with the city's artisans. In the ensuing sessions of the Congress, however, the extremists were unable to carry through a program quite so thorough as some of them would have liked.

A majority of the delegates in Carpenters' Hall agreed on five major decisions. First, in a very close vote, they defeated the plan of Joseph Galloway for a colonial union under British authority, a plan (much like the earlier Albany Plan) that included a legislative council made up of representatives from the colonial assemblies and a president-general to be appointed by the king. Second, they drew up a somewhat self-contradictory statement of grievances, conceding to Parliament the right to regulate colonial trade but demanding the elimination of all oppressive legislation passed since 1763, and they addressed a petition to George III as their "Most Gracious Sovereign." Third, they approved a series of resolutions from a Suffolk County (Massachusetts) convention recommending, among other things, that military preparations be made for defense against possible attack by the British troops in Boston. Fourth, they agreed to nonimportation, nonexportation, and nonconsumption as means of stopping all trade with Great Britain, and they formed a "Continental Association" to see that these agreements were carried out. Fifth, the delegates adjourned to meet again the next spring, thus indicating that they conceived of the Continental Congress as a continuing organization.

Through their representatives in Philadelphia the colonies had, in effect, reaffirmed their autonomous status within the empire and declared economic war to maintain that position. The more optimistic of the Americans supposed that economic warfare alone would win a quick and bloodless victory, but the more pessimistic had their doubts. "I expect no redress, but, on the contrary, increased resentment and double vengeance," John Adams said to Patrick Henry; "we must fight." And Henry replied, "By God, I am of your opinion."

During the winter, the Parliament in London debated proposals for conciliating the colonists. Lord Chatham (William Pitt) urged the withdrawal of troops from America, Edmund Burke the repeal of the Coercive Acts, but in vain; and not even Chatham and Burke thought of renouncing parliamentary authority over the colonies. Lord North, conceding less than Burke or Chatham, introduced a set of proposals of his own, and Parliament approved them early in 1775. The essence of these so-called Conciliatory Propositions was that the colonies, instead of being taxed directly by Parliament, should tax themselves at Parliament's demand. With this offer, Lord North intended to redivide Americans by appealing to the disgruntled moderates. But his offer was too grudging and too late. It did not reach America until after the first shots of war had been fired.

Lexington and Concord

For months, the farmers and townspeople of Massachusetts had been gathering arms and ammunition and training as "minutemen," ready to fight on a minute's notice. The Continental Congress had approved preparations for a defensive war, and these citizen-soldiers only waited for an aggressive move by the British regulars in Boston.

In Boston, General Thomas Gage, commanding the British garrison, knew of the warlike bustle throughout the countryside but thought his army too small to do anything until reinforcements should arrive. But some of his less cautious officers assured him that Americans were cowards. Major John Pitcairn, for example, insisted that a single "small action" with the burning of a few towns would "set everything to rights." When General Gage received orders to arrest the rebel leaders Sam Adams and John Hancock, known to be in the vicinity of Lexington, he still hesitated. But when he heard that the minutemen had stored a large supply of gunpowder in Concord (eighteen miles from Boston) he at last decided to act. On the night of April 18, 1775, he sent a detachment of about 1,000 men out from Boston on the road to Lexington and Concord. He intended to surprise the colonials with a bloodless coup.

But during the night the hard-riding horsemen William Dawes and Paul Revere warned the villages and farms, and when the redcoats arrived in Lexington the next day, several dozen minutemen awaited them on the common. Shots were fired and some of the minutemen fell, eight of them killed and ten more wounded. Advancing to Concord, the British burned what was left of the powder supply after the Americans had hastily removed most of it to safety. On the road from Concord back to Boston the 1,000 troops, along with 1,500 more who met them at Lexington, were harassed by the continual gunfire of farmers hiding behind trees, rocks, and stone fences. Before the day was over, the British had lost almost three times as many men as the Americans.

The first shots—the "shots heard round the world," as Americans later called them—had been fired. But who had fired them first? According to one of the minutemen at Lexington, Major Pitcairn had shouted to the colonists on his arrival, "Disperse ye rebels!" When this command was ignored, he had given the order to fire. British officers and soldiers told a different story. They claimed that the minutemen had fired first, that only after seeing the flash of American guns had they begun to shoot. The truth will never be known. The important thing was that the rebels succeeded in circulating their account

The Battle of Lexington
A contemporary engraving by Amos Doolittle pictures the American version of the affair of April 19, 1775, at Lexington. In the center is shown "the party who fired first," at the command of Major Pitcairn, on horseback. In the foreground are some of the fallen and the fleeing members of the "Provincial Company of Lexington" (minutemen). The more prominent buildings on the edge of the square, or green, are the public inn at the left of the large tree and the meetinghouse at the right of it. Behind the meetinghouse are companies of British regulars marching along the road to Concord. (Courtesy of the New York Public Library, Stokes Collection)

well ahead of the British version, adorning it with horrible tales of atrocities performed by the hated redcoats. The effect was to rally to the rebel cause thousands of colonists, North and South, who previously had been less than enthusiastic in support of it. Now that the English had, as they believed, opened fire on American citizens, the issue was clearly drawn.

It was not immediately clear to the Brit-ish, and even to many Americans, that the skirmishes at Lexington and Concord were the first battles of a war. Many saw them as simply another example of the tensions that had been afflicting Anglo-American relations for years; there seemed no reason to expect a large-scale conflict. But whether they recognized it at the time or not, the British and the colonists had taken the final step. The War for Independence had begun.

SUGGESTED READINGS

The coming of the American Revolution has spawned a vast literature and a large amount of historical controversy, which continues today. John Shy, *The American Revolution* (1973), is an excellent, although already out-of-date, bibliography. For general studies of the progress toward revolt, see John C. Miller, *Origins of the American Revolution* (1957); Merrill Jensen, *The Founding of a Nation* (1968); Edmund S. Morgan, *The Birth of the Republic* (1956), a concise account; and J. R. Alden, *A History of the American Revolution* (1969). Charles M. Andrews, *The Colonial Background of the American Revolution* (1924, rev. 1931), is a classic account by one of the most important chroniclers of the establishment of the colonies; Lawrence Henry Gipson, *The Coming of the Revolution, 1763–1775* (1954), summarizes the views of the preeminent historian of the British Empire in the eighteenth century. Ian R. Christie and Benjamin W. Labaree, *Empire or Independence, 1760–1776* (1976), and Ian R. Christie, *Crisis of Empire* (1966), are both useful general studies.

Lawrence Henry Gipson, *The British Empire Before the American Revolution,* 15 vols. (1936–1970), is the outstanding study of the nature of the imperial system and the changes in the 1760s. Relations between the colonies and England before the 1760s are discussed in Robert C. Newbold, *The Albany Congress and Plan of Union of 1754* (1955); Richard Pares, *War and Trade in the West Indies, 1739–1763* (1936); and Howard H. Peckham, *The Colonial Wars, 1689–1762* (1963), which includes discussion of the French and Indian War. Alan Rogers, *Empire and Liberty* (1974), is another useful study of the period of the war. The accession of George III and his influence on colonial relations can be examined in Lewis B. Namier, *England in the Age of the American Revolution,* rev. ed. (1961) and *The Structure of Politics at the Accession of George III,* rev. ed. (1961). A differing view, stressing the wider context of English politics, can be found in John Brewer, *Party Ideology and Popular Politics at the Accession of George III* (1976). See also Bernard Donoughue, *British Politics and the American Revolution: The Path to War, 1773–1775* (1965); and John Brooke, *King George III* (1972). Michael Kammen, *A Rope of Sand* (1968), examines the influence of the colonial agents and British politics on the colonies.

On the French, the Indians, and the West, see Thomas P. Abernethy, *Western Lands and the American Revolution* (1937), and J. M. Sosin, *Whitehall and the Wilderness* (1961), both of which discuss British policies. John R. Alden, *John Stuart and the Southern Colonial Frontier* (1944), David H. Corkran, *The Cherokee Frontier* (1962), R. S. Cotterill, *The Southern Indians* (1954), and Howrd H. Peckham, *Pontiac and the Indian Uprising* (1947), examine the relationship between the white settlers and the native tribes.

Some of the economic tensions of the 1760s and 1770s are discussed in Joseph Ernst, *Money and Politics in America, 1755–1775* (1973). Earlier examinations of economic influences on the Revolution include Arthur M. Schlesinger, *The Colonial Merchants and the American Revolution* (1917), which argues that merchants were instrumental in fomenting resistance; and Oliver M. Dickinson, *The Navigation Acts and the American Revolution* (1951), which de-emphasizes economic regulation as a cause. John Shy, *Toward Lexington* (1965), discusses the role of the presence of British troops in the process leading to revolution.

Most of the major events leading to conflict have been the subject of individual studies. David Ammerman, *In the Common Cause* (1974), examines the Coercive Acts and the response to them. Hiller B. Zobel, *The Boston Massacre* (1970), discusses one of the early conflicts. Edmund S. Morgan and Helen M. Morgan, *The Stamp Act Crisis* (1953), is an elegant account of the most important political event of the 1760s. Benjamin W. Labaree, *The Boston Tea Party* (1964), examines one of the last controversies before the outbreak of war.

The most important study of the ideas and principles that led to the American Revolution is Bernard Bailyn, *The Ideological Origins of the American Revolution* (1967). Ian R. Christie, *Wilkes, Wyvil, and Reform* (1962), and George Rudé, *Wilkes and Liberty* (1962), examine one of the most important British influences on American revolutionary ideology. Isaac Kramnick, *Bolingbroke and His Circle* (1968), examines another of the English ideological influences on Americans. Clinton Rossiter, *Seedtime of the Republic* (1953), traces later American ideas about liberty to the Revolutionary period. Pauline Maier, *From Resistance to Revolution* (1972), shows how political ideas led to the rise of resistance and how colonial leaders influenced the popular crowd. Dirk Hoerder, *Crowd Action in Revolutionary Massachusetts* (1977), is an alternative interpretation, stressing class consciousness. Nathan Hatch, *The Sacred Cause of Liberty* (1977), examines religious influences. Richard Merritt, *Symbols of American Community, 1735–1775* (1966), traces the rise of American nationalism. Gary B. Nash, *The Urban Crucible* (1979), examines the role of cities in the coming of the Revolution.

For events in individual states, see—among many others—Carl Becker, *The History of Political Parties in the Province of New York* (1909), an influential study arguing that the Revolution involved not only differences between the colonies and England but social tensions within the colonies themselves. Richard D. Brown, *Revolutionary Politics in Massachusetts* (1970), examines committees of correspondence. David Lovejoy, *Rhode Island Politics and the American Revolution* (1958), emphasizes the unifying influence of opposition to the British. Studies of other states include L. R. Gerlach, *Prologue to Independence* (1976), on New Jersey; Theodore Thayer, *Pennsylvania Politics and the Growth of Democracy* (1953); Ronald Hoffman, *A Spirit of Dissension* (1973), on Maryland; R. E. Brown and B. K. Brown, *Virginia, 1705–1786* (1964); and Charles S. Sydnor, *Gentlemen Freeholders* (1952), also on Virginia.

PART TWO

The New Nation, 1775-1820

The shots fired at Lexington and Concord represented only one of many steps along the road to the creation of an independent American nation. The first steps had been taken many years before 1775, when the first European settlements in the New World had begun to develop ideas and institutions different from those of the society they had left behind. And the steps continued for many years after 1775, as Americans fought first to win their independence, and then to build a new government and a new society.

This progression toward nationhood went through a series of vital stages after the outbreak of hostilities. First was the decision to demand independence. In the spring of 1775, that decision had not yet been made. Many Americans still believed that they were fighting simply to protect their proper position within the British Empire. To them, all that would have been necessary to resolve the conflict would have been a retreat by England from its unpopular policies. But as the war continued and expanded in the ensuing months—and as political agitation for a complete break with England grew—sentiment for independence gained favor. Finally, in July 1776, the leaders of the thirteen colonies, meeting in Philadelphia, declared America to be a new, autonomous nation.

Much remained to be done. To secure their independence, the American people had to fight a long and difficult war against the greatest military power in the world, a war that few objective observers believed they could win. For nearly seven years it continued, with the American cause at first on the verge of collapse. Gradually, however, the new nation gained strength; and finally, in 1781, it secured a decisive military victory over the British. Two years later, a peace treaty confirmed the end of the war. The British remained a far more formidable power than the Americans.

But English military power had proved poorly suited to the new kind of war being fought in North America. And the forces of the fledgling United States had displayed a spirit and persistence that few could have anticipated.

The War for Independence resolved the question of whether the new nation would survive. It did not, however, resolve the question of what it would be. In political terms, at least, the answer to that question emerged from an extraordinary process, beginning during the war itself and culminating in 1789, with the creation of a new federal government. There were few precedents in history for this self-conscious effort by Americans to create a political system for themselves, a system based on carefully argued ideas about the role of government and the nature of man. From the deliberations first of the individual states and then of the nation at large came one of the stablest and most enduring political systems in the world.

The framing of the Constitution, however, still did not complete the process of nation building. For the next three decades, the United States engaged in a series of intense and often bitter political conflicts, as competing factions fought with one another to determine the directions the new nation would take. Would the central government be strong or weak? Would the nation's economy be agrarian or industrial? Would the United States play an active role in the world or remain isolated from it? Such questions produced controversies that at times threatened to tear the new nation apart. And when, beginning in 1812, the United States found itself engaged in another war with Great Britain, the survival of the republic appeared precarious indeed.

By 1820, many of these initial controversies had been, if not fully resolved, then at least made manageable. And the threat from overseas had been for the moment dispelled. The American nation was not yet complete. It could be argued that it never would be. But the initial stage of development had come to an end. The United States sensed itself secure in its nationhood and ready for a period of rapid expansion and change—a period that would ultimately produce new crises of its own.

The American Revolution

5

George Washington Between 1772 and 1795, the Maryland-born artist and taxidermist Charles Willson Peale painted from life more than a dozen portraits of George Washington, under whom he served as a soldier during the Revolutionary War. This portrait, which conveys something of the moral as well as the physical grandeur of Washington, shows him in the uniform of commander in chief at his Princeton headquarters in 1776. (Charles Willson Peale, American, 1741–1827. Oil on canvas. 95 × 61¾". The Metropolitan Museum of Art, gift of Collis P. Huntington, 1896.)

Two struggles occurred simultaneously during the seven years of war that began in April of 1775. One was the military conflict with Great Britain. The second was a political conflict within America. Each had a profound effect upon the other.

The military conflict was, by the standards of later wars, a relatively modest one. Battle deaths on the American side totaled fewer than 5,000. The technology of warfare was so crude that cannons and rifles were effective only at extraordinarily close range; and fighting of any kind was virtually out of the question in bad weather. Yet the war in America was, by the standards of its own day, an unusually savage conflict, pitting not only army against army, but at times the population at large against a powerful external force. It was this shift of the war from a traditional, conventional struggle to a new kind of conflict—a revolutionary war for liberation—that made it possible for the United States finally to defeat the vastly more powerful British.

At the same time, Americans were wrestling with the great political questions that the conflict necessarily produced: first, whether to demand independence from Britain; then, how to structure the new nation they had proclaimed. Only the first of these questions had been resolved by the time of the British surrender at Yorktown in 1781. But even then, the United States had established itself—both in its own mind and in the mind of much of the rest of the world—as a nation with a special mission, a society dedicated to new, enlightened ideals. Thomas Paine, himself an important figure in shaping the Revolution, reflected the opinion of many when he claimed that the American War for Independence had "contributed more to enlighten the world, and diffuse a spirit of freedom and liberality among mankind, than any human event . . . that ever preceded it."

THE STATES UNITED

In the American Revolution, a war for autonomy on the part of the united colonies soon turned into a war for independence on the part of the United States. The still-unformed nation, with a population less than a third as large as the nine million of Great Britain, and with economic and military resources proportionately still smaller, faced a tremendous task of mobilizing for the war. The task was further complicated by divisions among the people, who persisted in disagreeing about war aims.

Defining American War Aims

Three weeks after the battles of Lexington and Concord, when the Second Continental Congress met in the State House in Philadel-phia, the delegates (again from every colony except Georgia, which was not represented until the following autumn) agreed in their determination to support the war but disagreed about its objects. At one extreme, the Adams cousins, John and Samuel, leaned toward independence (although they did not yet openly avow it); at the other extreme, John Dickinson of Pennsylvania hoped for an early reconciliation with Great Britain. Most of the delegates, holding views that ranged between those of Dickinson and the Adamses, disregarded Lord North's Conciliatory Propositions as insincere but voted reluctantly for one last appeal to the king: the so-called Olive Branch Petition. Then, on July 6, 1775, they adopted a Declaration of the Causes and Necessity of Taking Up Arms, announcing that the British government had left the American people with only two alternatives, "unconditional submission to the tyranny of irritated ministers or resistance by force," and that the people had decided to resist.

So, for the first year of the war, the Americans were fighting for a redress of grievances within the British Empire, not for independence. During that year, however, many of them began to change their minds, for various reasons. For one thing, they were making sacrifices so great—as in the Battle of Bunker Hill, the bloodiest engagement of the entire war and one of the most sanguinary anywhere in the eighteenth century—that their original war aims seemed incommensurate with the cost. For another thing, they lost much of their lingering affection for the mother country when Britain prepared to use Indians, black slaves, and foreign mercenaries (the hated "Hessians") against them. And, most important, they felt that they were being forced into independence when the British government replied to the Olive Branch Petition with the Prohibitory Act, which closed the colonies to all overseas trade and made no concession except an offer of pardon to repentant rebels. The Americans desperately needed military supplies to continue the war, and now they could get them from abroad in adequate amounts only if they broke completely with Great Britain and proceeded to behave in all respects as a sovereign nation.

These feelings in America were clarified and crystallized by the publication, in January 1776, of the pamphlet *Common Sense*. Its author, unmentioned on the title page, was Thomas Paine, who with letters of introduction from Benjamin Franklin had emigrated from England to America less than two years before. Long a failure in various trades, Paine now proved a brilliant success as a revolutionary propagandist. In his pamphlet, he argued with great fervor that it was simple common sense for Americans to separate from an England rotten with the corrupt monarchy of George III, brutal as an unnatural parent toward its colonies, responsible for dragging them in to fight its wars in the past, and no more fit as an island kingdom to rule the American continent than a satellite was

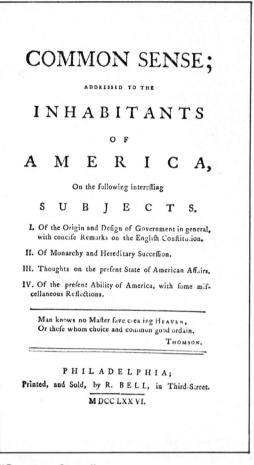

"Common Sense"
Title page of the first edition of Thomas Paine's pamphlet, published anonymously in Philadelphia on January 10, 1776. Afterward, Paine enlisted as a soldier and accompanied Washington's army on its retreat across New Jersey. During that time, he wrote a series of essays under the collective title *The Crisis* to arouse support for the Patriot cause. The first of the *Crisis* papers contains the sentence: "These are the times that try men's souls." After the American Revolution, Paine went to France and took an active part in the French Revolution, which began in 1789. In support of the French revolutionary cause he wrote *The Rights of Man* (1791–1792). He also wrote *The Age of Reason*, in which he attacked some aspects of conventional Christianity and expounded his own rationalistic beliefs. Returning to America in 1802, he spent his last years as a lonely, obscure man.
(Library of Congress)

fit to rule the sun. "O! ye that love mankind! ye that dare oppose not only the tyranny but the tyrant, stand forth!" Paine declared. Month after month the pamphlet was reprinted until many thousands of copies were in circulation, passing from hand to hand and being read and reread.

The Declaration of Independence

Despite the persuasive influence of *Common Sense,* the American people were still far from unanimous in their views of the proper aims of the war. The first half of 1776 saw, therefore, a bitter debate at many levels over the merits and disadvantages of independence. In the midst of this controversy, the Continental Congress was moving slowly and tentatively toward a final break. It opened American ports to the ships of all nations except Great Britain, entered into communication with foreign powers, and recommended to the various colonies that they establish governments without the authority of the empire, as in fact they already were doing. Congress also appointed a committee to draft a formal declaration and, on July 2, 1776, before approving the declaration, adopted a resolution "That these United Colonies are, and, of right, ought to be, free and independent states; that they are absolved from all allegiance to the British crown, and that all political connexion between them and the state of Great Britain is, and ought to be, totally dissolved." Two days later, on July 4, Congress approved the Declaration of Independence, which gave reasons for the action already taken.

The thirty-three-year-old Virginian Thomas Jefferson wrote the Declaration of Independence. His fellow committeemen Benjamin Franklin and John Adams revised the wording a little. And Congress made more drastic changes, striking out passages that condemned the British people and the slave trade. As Adams afterward observed, Jefferson said little new in the document. Its very virtue, in fact, lay in his noble phrasing of beliefs already widespread in America. He planned the document in two main parts. In the first part he restated the familiar contract

theory of John Locke, who had held that governments were formed to protect the rights of life, liberty, and property; but Jefferson gave the theory a more humane tone by referring instead to the rights of "life, liberty and the pursuit of happiness." In the second part he listed the alleged crimes of the king, who, with the backing of Parliament, had violated his contract with the colonists and thus had forfeited all claim to their loyalty.

The Declaration of Independence exerted an incalculable influence upon later history. With its democratic principle that "all men are created equal," it stimulated humanitarian movements of various kinds in the United States, and abroad it helped to inspire the French Revolution with its Declaration of the Rights of Man. More immediately, it led to increased foreign aid for the struggling rebels and prepared the way for France's intervention on their side. It steeled American Patriots to carry on without regard to offers of a peace short of the stated goal. And at the same time it divided Americans more cruelly and more extensively than ever before.

At the news of the Declaration of Independence, crowds gathered to cheer, fire guns and cannons, and ring church bells in Philadelphia, Boston, and other places. But there were many people in America who did not rejoice. Some had disapproved of the war from the beginning, and others had been willing to support it only so long as its aims did not conflict with their basic loyalty to the king. These people, numerous but in the minority, refused to cross the new line that had been drawn. Either openly or secretly they remained Loyalists, as they chose to call themselves, or Tories, as they were known to the Whig or Patriot majority.

The War Governments

The Declaration of Independence simply confirmed what circumstances had already ensured: that the American people, at war with Great Britain, would have to devise a means of governing themselves and supporting their military struggle. To meet these new demands, new institutions emerged at both the state and the national levels.

In the individual states, new governments had to be created to replace the royal governments that independence had eliminated. In the course of the war, therefore, all of the thirteen former colonies began to construct new political systems based on the principles that had gained favor in the years before the fighting began. By 1781, most states had produced written constitutions for themselves that established republican governments; some of these governments survived, with only minor changes, for decades to come.

At the national level, however, the process was more troubled and the result less satisfactory. No sooner had the Congress appointed a committee to draft a declaration of independence than it appointed another to draft a plan of union. And after much debate and many revisions, the Congress adopted the committee's plan in November 1777. The document was known as the Articles of Confederation. The new document did little more than confirm the weak, decentralized system already in operation. The Continental Congress would survive as the chief governing body of the nation, but its powers over the individual states would be extraordinarily limited. In any case, the Articles did not receive final ratification by the states until 1781—very near the end of the war. During most of the period of fighting, the Second Continental Congress remained the chief agency for directing and coordinating the war effort of the thirteen states. The war was won as much in spite of as because of its efforts. (See pp. 145–151 for discussion of the nature of the new state and national governments.)

Mobilizing for War

Congress and the states faced overwhelming tasks in raising and organizing armies, providing the necessary supplies and equipment, and paying the costs of war.

Supplies of most kinds were scarce at the outset, and shortages persisted to the end. America was a land of hunters and thus contained numerous gunsmiths. But these craftsmen were not able to meet the wartime demand for guns and ammunition; nor were they able to produce heavy arms. Some of the states offered bounties for the encouragement of manufactures, especially for the production of guns and powder; and Congress in 1777 established a government arsenal at Springfield, Massachusetts. Even so, Americans managed to manufacture only a small fraction of the equipment they used. They supplemented their own manufactures with materiel that fell into their hands on the seizure of forts such as Crown Point and Ticonderoga (in 1775), the surrender of British armies, and the capture of supply ships by American privateers. But they got most of their war materials through importations from Europe, particularly from France.

In trying to meet the expenses of war, Congress had no power to tax the people, and the states had little inclination to do so. Indeed, cash was scarce in the country, as it always had been. When Congress requisitioned money from the states, none of them contributed more than a tiny part of its share. At first Congress hesitated to requisition goods directly from the people, but it finally allowed army purchasing agents to take supplies from farmers and pay with certificates of indebtedness. Congress could not raise much money by floating long-term loans at home, since few Americans could afford war bonds and those few usually preferred to invest in more profitable ventures, such as privateering. So Congress had no choice but to issue paper money, and Continental currency came from the printing presses in large and repeated batches. The states added sizable currency issues of their own.

With goods and coin so scarce and paper money so plentiful, prices rose to fantastic heights and the value of paper money fell proportionately. One reason why Washington's men suffered from shortages of food and clothing at Valley Forge during the winter of 1777–1778 was that American farmers and merchants preferred to do business with the British forces occupying nearby Philadelphia, since the British could pay in gold or silver coin. To check the inflationary trend, Congress advised the states to pass laws for price control; but it soon saw the futility of such measures and recommended that they be dropped. Eventually, in 1780, Congress decided that the states should accept Continental currency from taxpayers at the rate of forty paper dollars to one silver dollar, then send it to Congress to be destroyed. If the currency was not turned in for taxes at a fortieth of its face value, it became utterly worthless. By this time Congress was able to meet the most pressing of its financial needs by borrowing from abroad.

Only a small proportion of eligible American men were willing to volunteer for the American armies once the first surge of patriotism at the start of the war had passed. The states had to resort to persuasion and force, to bounties and the draft, the bounties being commonly in the form of land scrip, since land was an asset with which the states were well supplied. Thus recruited, militiamen remained under the control of their respective states.

Foreseeing some of the disadvantages of separately organized militias, Congress called upon the states (while they were still colonies) to raise troops for a Continental army and agreed that it should have a single commander in chief. George Washington, forty-three years old, sober and responsible, possessed more command experience than any other American-born officer available. And he had political as well as military qualifications. An early advocate of independence, he was admired and trusted by nearly all Patriots. A Virginian, he had the support not only of Southerners but also of Northerners who feared that the appointment of a New Englander might jeopardize sectional harmony. As the unanimous choice of the delegates, he took command in June 1775.

Congress chose well. Throughout the war, Washington kept faithfully at his task,

despite difficulties and discouragements that would have daunted a lesser man. With the aid of foreign military experts such as the Marquis de Lafayette from France and the Baron von Steuben from Prussia, he succeeded in building and holding together the Continental army, a force of fewer than 10,000 men (not counting the militias of the separate states). The morale of the soldiers, who were getting short rations and low pay, became so bad that mutinies broke out (in 1781) among the Pennsylvania and New Jersey troops. Meanwhile, during the dark winter of Valley Forge, some congressmen and army officers, conspiring together in the so-called Conway Cabal, hinted at replacing Washington as commander in chief. He, on the other hand, complained often and bitterly against his employers, the delegates in Congress, who seemed to do too little in supplying him with manpower and equipment, and too much in interfering with his conduct of military operations.

The faults were not all on the side of Congress. Washington was not without shortcomings as a military commander; indeed, he lost more battles than he won. Yet for all his faults and failures, he was indisputably a great war leader. In a nation still unsure of either its purposes or its structure, with a central government both weak and contentious, Washington was the indispensable man whose steadiness, courage, and dedication to his cause provided the army—and the people—with a symbol of stability around which they could rally. He was not the most brilliant of the country's early leaders. But in the crucial years of the war, at least, he was the most successful in holding the new nation together.

THE WAR FOR INDEPENDENCE

On the surface, at least, all the advantages in the military struggle between America and Great Britain appeared to lie with the British. They possessed the greatest navy and the best-equipped army in the world. They had access to the resources of an empire. They had a coherent structure of command. The

Americans, by contrast, were struggling to create an army and a government at the same time that they were trying to fight a war.

Yet the United States had advantages that were not at first apparent. Americans were fighting on their own ground, far from the center of British might. They were willing to commit themselves to the conflict more fully than were the British, who were only half-heartedly supporting the war. And beginning in 1777, the Americans had the benefit of substantial aid from abroad, after the American war had merged with a world contest in which Great Britain faced the strongest powers of Europe—most notably France—in a struggle for imperial supremacy.

The American victory was not simply the result of these advantages, or even of the remarkable spirit and resourcefulness of the people and the army. It was a result, too, of a series of egregious blunders and miscalculations by the British in the early stages of the fighting, when England could (and probably should) have won. And it was, finally, a result of the transformation of the war—through three distinct phases—into a new kind of conflict that the British military, for all its strength, could not hope to win.

The First Phase: New England

For the first year of the fighting—from the spring of 1775 to the spring of 1776—the British remained uncertain about whether or not they were actually engaged in a war. Many English authorities continued to believe that what was happening in America was a limited, local conflict, that they were simply attempting to quell pockets of rebellion in the contentious area around Boston. Gradually, however, the colonial forces took the offensive and proved to England that the war was not confined to Massachusetts, that the entire territory of the American colonies was becoming a battleground.

After the British retreat from Concord and Lexington, the Americans besieged the army of General Gage in Boston. The Patriot forces suffered severe casualties in the Battle of Bunker Hill (actually fought on Breed's Hill, June 17, 1775), and were ultimately driven from their position there. But they inflicted even greater losses on the enemy and thereafter continued to tighten the siege. Far to the south, at Moore's Creek Bridge in North Carolina, a band of Patriots crushed an uprising of Tories (February 27, 1776) and thereby discouraged British plans for invading the Southern states with Loyalist aid. Far to the north the Americans themselves un-

THE WAR IN THE NORTH, 1775

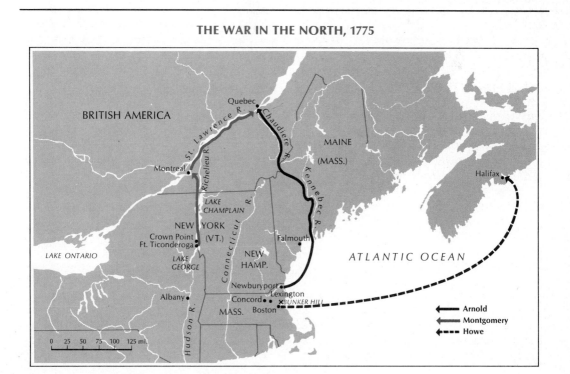

dertook an invasion of Canada. The fearless Benedict Arnold threatened Quebec after a winter march of incredible hardship. He was joined by Richard Montgomery, who took command of the combined forces. When they launched an attack, Montgomery was killed and Arnold wounded; though the latter kept up a siege for a time, the Quebec campaign ended in frustration. In the spring, a civilian commission headed by the seventy-year-old Franklin returned from the north without success in its efforts to secure the allegiance of Canada as the fourteenth state. Already, however, the British had given up their attempt to hold Boston and had departed with hundreds of Loyalist refugees (March 17, 1776) for Halifax. Within a year from the firing of the first shots, the enemy had been driven—temporarily—from American soil.

The British evacuation of New England was not so much a victory for the Americans (although their accomplishments so far had been impressive) as a reflection of changing English assumptions about the war. It was now clear that the conflict was not a local phenomenon in the area around Boston. The American campaigns in Canada, the agitation in the South, and the growing evidence of colonial unity all suggested that England must be prepared to fight a much larger conflict. It was clear, too, that Boston was not the best place from which to wage it. Not only was it in the center of the most fervently anti-British region of the colonies; it was also tactically undesirable—a narrow neck of land, easily isolated and besieged. The departure of the British marked, therefore, a shift in strategy more than an admission of defeat.

The Second Phase: The Mid-Atlantic Region

The next phase of the war, which lasted from 1776 until early 1778, was when the British were in the best position to win. Indeed, had it not been for a series of blunders and misfortunes, they probably would have crushed the rebellion then. For during this period the struggle became, for the most part, a traditional, conventional war. And in that,

the Americans were woefully overmatched.

The enemy soon regrouped after its retreat from Boston, and from the beginning it managed to put the Americans on the strategic defensive (a position they maintained for the rest of the war). During the summer of 1776, in the weeks immediately following the Declaration of Independence, the waters around the city of New York became filled with the most formidable military force Great Britain ever had sent abroad. Hundreds of men-of-war and troopships and 32,000 disciplined soldiers arrived, under the command of the affable Sir William Howe. Howe had no grudge against the Americans. He hoped to awe them into submission rather than shoot them; and he believed that most of them, if given a chance, would show that they were loyal to the king. In a parley with commissioners from Congress he offered the alternatives of submission with royal pardon or battle against overwhelming odds.

To oppose Howe's awesome array, Washington could muster only about 19,000 poorly armed and trained soldiers, including both Continentals and state troops; and he had no navy at all. Yet without hesitation, the Americans chose continued war—which meant inevitably a succession of defeats. The British pushed the defenders off Long Island, compelled them to abandon Manhattan Island, and drove them in slow retreat over the plains of New Jersey, across the Delaware River, and into Pennsylvania.

Warfare being for eighteenth-century Europeans a seasonal activity, the British settled down for the winter with occupation forces at various points in New Jersey and with an outpost of Hessians at Trenton on the Delaware. But Washington did not content himself with sitting still. On Christmas night 1776, he daringly recrossed the icy river, surprised and scattered the Hessians, and occupied the town. Then he advanced and drove off a force of redcoats at Princeton. Unable to hold either Princeton or Trenton, he finally took refuge for the rest of the winter in the hills around Morristown. As the campaign of 1776 came to an end, the Americans could console themselves with the thought that they had won two minor victories, that their main army was still intact, and that the in-

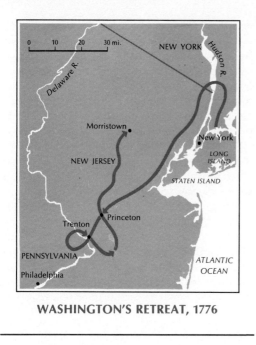

WASHINGTON'S RETREAT, 1776

vaders were really no nearer than before to the decisive triumph that Howe had so confidently anticipated.

For the campaign of 1777 the British devised a strategy that, if Howe had stuck to it, might have cut the United States in two and prepared the way for final victory by Great Britain. Howe would move from New York up the Hudson to Albany, while another force, in a gigantic pincers movement, would come down from Canada to meet him. One of Howe's ambitious younger officers, the dashing John Burgoyne, secured command of this northern force and elaborated on the plan by preparing for a two-pronged attack along both the Mohawk and the upper Hudson approaches to Albany.

Then, fortunately for the United States, Howe adopted a different plan for himself, intending to dispirit the Patriots and rally the Loyalists by seizing the rebel capital, Philadelphia. Taking the bulk of his forces away from New York by sea, Howe landed at the head of the Chesapeake Bay, brushed Washington aside at the Battle of Brandywine (September 11), and proceeded to occupy Philadelphia. Meanwhile, Washington, after an unsuccessful attack at Germantown (October 4), went into winter quarters at Valley

Forge, and the scattered Congress resumed its sittings in York, Pennsylvania.

Up north, Burgoyne was left to carry out his twofold campaign without aid from Howe. Sending Colonel Barry St. Leger with a fast-moving force up the St. Lawrence River toward Lake Ontario and the headwaters of the Mohawk, Burgoyne with his own army advanced directly down the upper Hudson Valley. He got off to a flying start, easily taking Fort Ticonderoga and an enormous store of powder and supplies, and causing such consternation that Congress removed General Philip Schuyler from command in the north and replaced him with Horatio Gates.

By the time Gates took command, Burgoyne already faced a sudden reversal of his military fortunes in consequence of two staggering defeats. In one of them, at Oriskany, New York (August 6), Nicholas Herkimer's force of German farmers checked a force of St. Leger's Indians and Tories, so that Benedict Arnold had time to go to the relief of Fort Stanwix and close off the Mohawk Valley to St. Leger's advance. In the other battle, at Bennington, Vermont (August 16), the Bunker Hill veteran John Stark with his New England militiamen severely mauled a detachment that Burgoyne had sent out to seek supplies. Short of materials, with all help cut off, Burgoyne fought several costly engagements and then withdrew to Saratoga, where Gates surrounded him. On October 17, 1777, he ordered what was left of his army, nearly 5,000 men, to lay down their arms.

Not only the United States but also Europe took note of the amazing news from the woods of upstate New York. The British surrender at Saratoga, a great turning point in the war, led directly to an alliance between the United States and France.

The British failure to win the war during this period, a period in which they had overwhelming advantages, was in large part a result of their own mistakes. And in assessing them, the role of William Howe looms large. From the beginning, it seems clear in retrospect, he was ill-suited to serve as commander in a war of revolution. Time and again, he showed not only serious deficiencies in tactical and strategic judgment, but a

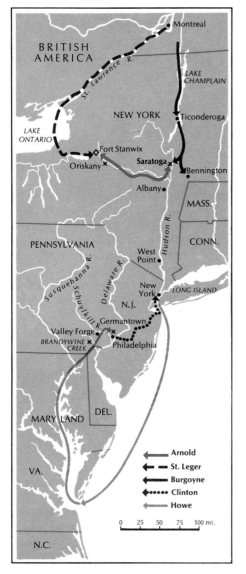

BRITISH CAMPAIGNS, 1777

win the war, that he was actually secretly in sympathy with the American cause. His family had close ties to the colonies; and he himself was linked politically to those forces within the British government that opposed the war. Others pointed to personal weaknesses: Howe's apparent alcoholism, his romantic attachments (he spent the winter of 1777–1778 in Philadelphia with his mistress when many were urging him to move elsewhere). But the most important problem, it seems clear, was lack of judgment.

Whatever the reasons, the failure of the British to crush the Continental army in the mid-Atlantic states, combined with the stunning American victory at Saratoga (which serves as another example of Howe's strategic incompetence), transformed the war and ushered it into a new and final phase.

Securing Aid from Abroad

Central to this transformation of the war was American success in winning the indirect assistance of several European nations, and the direct support of France, in the military struggle. Shortly after the beginning of the fighting, Congress appointed a secret committee, headed by Benjamin Franklin, to correspond with "our friends" in Great Britain and, more significantly, in "other parts of the world." Later Congress replaced this agency with a Committee for Foreign Affairs and then (1781) with a Department of Foreign Affairs, the immediate ancestor of the State Department. As far as possible, however, Congress as a whole conducted foreign relations.

Even before the Declaration of Independence, Congress drew up a treaty plan for liberal commercial arrangements with other countries and prepared to send representatives to the capitals of Europe for negotiating treaties—which necessarily would mean European recognition of the United States as one of the sovereign nations of the world. "Militia diplomats," John Adams called the early American representatives abroad; and unlike the diplomatic regulars of Europe, they knew little of the formal art and etiquette of Old World diplomacy. Since over-

lack of aggressive instincts. With the Continental army weakened and in disarray, Howe refrained from moving in for the final attack, although he had several opportunities. Instead, he repeatedly allowed Washington to retreat and regroup; and he permitted the American army to spend a long winter unmolested in Valley Forge, where—weak and hungry—they might have been easy prey for British attack.

Some believed that Howe did not want to

The Continental Army at Valley Forge
Many foreigners served as officers in the Continental army—too many, it seemed to General
Washington. Most of them received their commissions from Congress, not from the commander
in chief. Once he referred to the foreigners as "hungry adventurers." But he deeply appreciated
the assistance of a few of the volunteers from abroad, especially the Marquis de Lafayette and
the Baron von Steuben. A veteran of the Prussian army, Steuben came to the United States in
1777, and Washington appointed him inspector general, with overall charge of military
discipline, instruction, and supply. Steuben reorganized the Continental army, provided for
improved training and drill of soldiers, and wrote a manual of army regulations. The painting by
Edwin A. Abbey, which hangs in the Pennsylvania House of Representatives, shows Steuben
instructing troops in Washington's camp at Valley Forge, near Philadelphia, during the winter of
1777–1778. After the war, Steuben settled in New York. (Courtesy of the Pennsylvania Department
of Commerce)

seas communication was slow and uncertain
(it took from one to three months to cross the
Atlantic), these representatives abroad sometimes had to interpret the instructions of
Congress very freely and make crucial decisions entirely on their own.

Of all the possible foreign friends of the
United States, the most promising and the
most powerful were the French, who still resented their defeat at the hands of Great Britain in 1763. France under King Louis XVI,
who came to the throne in 1774, had an astute and determined foreign minister in the
Count de Vergennes, an expert practitioner
of Machiavellian principles. Vergennes soon
saw that France had a vital interest in the
outcome of the American war. If the colonies
should assert and maintain their independence, the power of Great Britain would be
seriously weakened by the loss of a good part

of its empire, and the power of France would
be correspondingly increased.

From the start of the troubles between
England and its colonies, the French had
maintained observers in America to report
the course of events. After the shooting had
begun, Americans and Frenchmen both put
out diplomatic feelers. In London, the Massachusetts colonial agent Arthur Lee met the
French dramatist and political genius Caron
de Beaumarchais, and the two discussed the
possibilities of secret assistance to the colonies. Beaumarchais reported to Vergennes,
and Vergennes dispatched an army officer to
America to encourage the rebellion, urge independence, and promise supplies. After
several meetings with Vergennes's spokesman, Franklin's committee of secret correspondence sent Silas Deane to France as a
"merchant" to make "commercial" arrange-

ments. In consequence of these arrangements, Beaumarchais shipped large quantities of munitions to America through a fictitious trading firm that he created. Whether these shipments were gift or loan later became a question of bitter dispute between Congress and Beaumarchais.

After the Declaration of Independence, Franklin himself went to France to get further aid and outright recognition of the United States. A natural diplomat, the equal if not the superior of the world's best at that time, Franklin immediately captivated Frenchmen of all classes—and many Frenchwomen as well. But Vergennes hesitated. At the first news of the American Declaration of Independence, he was inclined to make a treaty recognizing the United States. But he did not wish to act without Spain; and when reports came of Washington's defeat on Long Island, he decided to wait and watch the military developments in America. If and when the Americans should show that they had a real chance of winning, then France would intervene. Meanwhile Vergennes was willing to go on financing the American war. He initiated a series of subsidies, which in time amounted to nearly $62 million, and a series of loans that totaled over $6 million.

The news that Vergennes and Franklin were waiting for—the news from Saratoga—arrived in London on December 2 and in Paris on December 4, 1777. In London the knowledge of Burgoyne's surrender caused Lord North to decide in favor of a peace offensive, an offer of complete home rule within the empire for Americans if they would quit the war. In Paris, learning of Lord North's intentions from a British spy, Franklin let the word get out for Vergennes to hear. Vergennes worried. If the Americans should accept the British offer, his opportunity to weaken France's traditional enemy would be gone; and if they could not get what they wanted from France, they might accept. Without waiting for Spain to go along, Vergennes on February 6, 1778, signed two treaties with Franklin and Deane, one a treaty of commerce and amity, and the other, which was supposed to be secret, a treaty of conditional and defensive alliance, to take effect if Great Britain should go to war with France.

Congress and the king quickly ratified the treaties, and Congress received and feted a minister from France while the king welcomed Franklin as minister from the United States.

France soon drifted into war with Great Britain, and in 1779 Spain, with objectives of its own, declared war as an ally of France, although not of the United States. A year later the Netherlands, persisting in its profitable trade with both the French and the Americans, found itself also at war with Britain and agreed to a treaty with the United States.

Indirectly, all the countries arrayed in hostility to Britain contributed to the ultimate success of the United States by complicating England's task. The Netherlands provided direct loans to the Americans but was powerless to give military or naval support, and Spain gave unofficial subsidies but confined its military and naval activities to strictly Spanish objectives. France (for its own reasons, of course) was the true friend in need of the Americans. Not only did it furnish them with most of their money and munitions, but it also provided a navy and an expeditionary force that proved invaluable in the final, successful phase of the revolutionary conflict.

The Final Phase: The South

The last phase of the war was fundamentally different from either of the first two. After the defeat at Saratoga and the introduction of France into the conflict, the British government—never united in support of the war in the first place—made a series of decisions that changed the nature of Britain's involvement. Because England now had to worry once again about its European rivals, there was a strong incentive to limit the commitment to North America. Instead of a full-scale military struggle against the American army, therefore, the British chose a different strategy. They would attempt to enlist the support of those elements of the American population still loyal to the Crown; they would, in other words, work to undermine the Revolution from within. George III and some of his ministers continued to believe that those who supported independence in America were a tiny minority. The loyal majority, they hoped, could be aroused to rout the forces of rebellion. Since Loyalist sentiment was considered to be strongest in the Southern colonies, the main focus of the British effort shifted there; and it was thus in the South, for the most part, that the war was fought to its conclusion.

The new strategy proved a ludicrous failure. British forces spent three years (from 1778 to 1781) moving through the South, fighting small battles and large, and attempting to neutralize (or to use the terminology of a later American war, "pacify") the territory through which they traveled. (These efforts were no more successful than those of American troops two centuries later in Vietnam, where similar attempts to win the "hearts and minds" of a people engaged in a revolution ended in frustration.) The British badly overestimated the extent of Loyalist sentiment. While it was true that in Georgia and the Carolinas there were numerous Tories, some of them disgruntled members of the Regulator movement, it was also true that Patriot sentiment was far stronger than the British believed. In Virginia, support for independence was as fervent as in Massachusetts. And even in the lower South, Loyalists often feared to offer aid to the British because they realized they might face reprisals from the Patriots around them. There were also severe logistical problems facing the British in the South. Patriot forces could move at will throughout the region, living off the resources of the countryside, blending in with the civilian population and making the British unable to distinguish friend from foe. The British, by contrast, suffered all the disadvantages of an army in hostile territory.

It was this phase of the conflict that made the war truly "revolutionary"—not only because it introduced a new kind of warfare, but because it had the effect of mobilizing and politicizing large groups of the population who had previously remained aloof from the struggle. With the war expanding into previously isolated communities, with many civilians forced to involve themselves whether they liked it or not, the political climate of the United States grew more heated than ever. And support for independence, far from being crushed as the British had hoped, greatly increased.

That was the backdrop against which the important military encounters of the last years of the war occurred. In the North, where significant numbers of British troops remained, the fighting settled into a relatively quiet stalemate. Sir Henry Clinton replaced the hapless William Howe in 1778 and moved what had been Howe's army from Philadelphia back to New York. There, the British troops stayed for more than a year, with Washington using his army to keep watch around them. During 1778–1779, those American forces did relatively little fighting. Washington sent some troops west to strike back against hostile Indians who had been attacking and massacring white settlers. During that same winter, George Rogers Clark, with orders from the state of Virginia—not from either Washington or Congress—led a daring expedition over the mountains and captured the settlements in the Illinois country from the British and their Indian allies. Otherwise, there were few important engagements in the North.

During this period of relative calm, the American forces—and George Washington in particular—were shocked by the exposure of treason on the part of General Benedict Arnold. Arnold had been one of the early heroes of the war; but now, convinced that the American cause was hopeless, he conspired with British agents to betray the Patriot stronghold at West Point on the Hudson River. In the nick of time, the scheme was exposed and foiled; and Arnold fled to the safety of the British camp, where he spent the rest of the war.

The decisive fighting during these last years of the conflict, however, took place in the South. Sir Henry Clinton, by nature a timid strategist and, in any case, constrained by British policymakers from launching too bold an offensive, believed that a Southern offensive would destroy the American will to resist. Once the South was conquered, he believed, the rest of the country would soon fall as well. But he made several vital mistakes. First, of course, was his assumption that Southern Loyalists would rise up en masse to

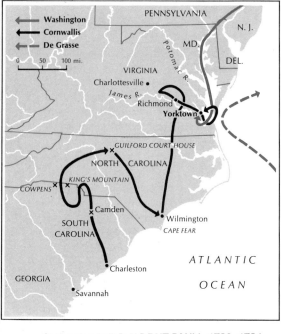

THE ROAD TO YORKTOWN, 1780–1781

1780) a combined force of militiamen and Continentals under Horatio Gates. Congress recalled Gates, and Washington gave the Southern command to Nathanael Greene, a former Quaker blacksmith of Rhode Island and probably the ablest of all the American generals of the time next to Washington himself.

Before Greene arrived in the war theater along the North and South Carolina line, the tide of battle already had begun to turn against Cornwallis. At King's Mountain (October 7, 1780), a band of Patriot riflemen from the backwoods killed, wounded, or captured an entire force of 1,100 New York and South Carolina Tories, upon whom Cornwallis had depended as auxiliaries. Once Greene arrived, he confused and exasperated Cornwallis by dividing the American forces into fast-moving contingents while refraining from a showdown in open battle. One of the contingents inflicted what Cornwallis admitted was "a very unexpected and severe blow" at Cowpens (January 17, 1781). At last, having received the reinforcements he awaited, Greene combined all his forces and arranged to meet the British on ground of his own choosing at Guilford Court House, North Carolina. After a hard-fought battle (March 15, 1781) Greene was driven from the field, but Cornwallis had lost so many men that he decided at last to abandon the Carolina campaign.

Cornwallis withdrew to Wilmington, North Carolina, to get supplies by sea; later he moved north to carry on raids in the interior of Virginia. But Clinton, concerned for the army's safety, ordered him to take up a position on the peninsula between the York and James rivers and wait for water transport to New York or Charleston. So Cornwallis retreated to Yorktown and began to build fortifications there.

Washington now made plans with the Count de Rochambeau, commander of the French expeditionary force in America, and with Admiral de Grasse, commander of a French fleet in American waters, for trapping Cornwallis. Washington and Rochambeau marched a Franco-American army from the New York vicinity to join Lafayette in Virginia while de Grasse sailed with additional

welcome and assist the British "liberators." They did not. But Clinton was also mistaken in his belief that British seapower would enable him to move troops from point to point along the coast with ease, and that the difficulty of overland travel would make American counteraction ineffectual. Clinton erred too in his choice of commanders. He placed in charge of the Southern offensive Lord Cornwallis, a man as rash as Clinton was cautious, and one capable of changing plans and disobeying orders in midcampaign.

The British did have some significant military successes during this period. On December 29, 1778, they captured Savannah, on the coast of Georgia; and five months later, on May 20, 1779, they took the port of Charleston, South Carolina. They even inspired some Loyalists to take up arms, and they managed to advance far into the interior. At every turn they were harassed, however, by Patriot guerrillas led by such resourceful fighters as Thomas Sumter, Andrew Pickens, and Francis Marion, the "Swamp Fox." Penetrating to Camden, well up the Wateree River in South Carolina, Cornwallis met and crushed (August 16,

The Surrender of Cornwallis
The surrender of the British army at Yorktown on October 19, 1781, did not officially end the Revolutionary War. Not until 1783, after difficult negotiations, was a formal treaty of peace with Great Britain signed. But Yorktown did mark the end of all major hostilities between the Americans and the British. In this 1846 print by Nathaniel Currier, Washington (in the foreground, on horseback) accepts the sword of Lord Cornwallis, while the Marquis de Lafayette (to the right of Washington) watches. As British soldiers stacked their weapons, a military band played "The World Turned Upside Down." (Library of Congress)

troops for the Chesapeake Bay and the York River. These joint operations, perfectly timed and executed, caught Cornwallis between land and sea. After a few shows of resistance, he asked for terms on October 17, 1781, four years to the day after the capitulation of Burgoyne. Two days later, as an American band played the old tune "The World Turn'd Upside Down," he surrendered his whole army of more than 7,000.

Except for a few skirmishes, the fighting was over; but the war was not yet won. British forces continued to hold the seaports of Savannah, Charleston, Wilmington, and New York. Before long, a British fleet met and defeated Admiral de Grasse's fleet in the West Indies, ending Washington's hopes for further seapower assistance. For more than a year, then, although there was no significant further combat between British and American forces, it remained possible that the war might resume and the struggle for independence might still be lost.

Winning the Peace

Until Yorktown, peace had been for Americans an illusory and at times a dangerous proposition; and the prospects even after that victory, though improved, were not ideal. The trouble was with Spain. That country had entered the war solely to recover lost terrritories in America and Europe, above all Gibraltar, and it had formed an alliance binding France to make no separate peace. The United States had promised in its treaty of alliance to conclude no peace without France. Now, if Spain should fight on until it won back Gibraltar, and if France should stick by Spain, and the United States by France, the Americans might be at war forever. That, however, was not the greatest danger to American interests. The danger was that Spain, to get Gibraltar or American territory, might enter into a deal with Great Britain at the expense of the United States and that France might feel compelled to go along with Spain. In making peace, the United States had as much to fear from its allies as from its enemy.

Indeed, for a time it had appeared that America's diplomatic future lay not in the hands of its own delegates, but in those of French Foreign Minister Vergennes. In 1779, the American government had named John Adams as its representative to any mediation or peace conference that might be arranged in Europe. Vergennes, who disliked Adams, had arranged, through his representative in Philadelphia, La Luzerne, to limit Adams's authority by adding Benjamin Franklin and John Jay to the American negotiating team. He had also pressured Congress to instruct its delegates to maintain close touch with the French government, to tell it everything, and to follow its advice. The United States thus could not negotiate peace without Vergennes's guidance and approval. When Austria and Russia made a joint offer of mediation in 1781—an offer that would ultimately lead to a general peace settlement—it appeared at first that the American response would be framed largely by the French.

Then the victory at Yorktown, by giving the Americans new bargaining power, rescued them from the worst of their dependence on Vergennes. In England, Cornwallis's defeat provoked outcries against continuing the war and raised demands for cultivating American friendship as an asset in international politics. Lord North resigned, and Lord Shelburne emerged from the political wreckage as prime minister. British emis-

saries appeared in France to talk informally with Franklin. He suggested what he called "necessary" terms of peace, including independence and the establishment of the Mississippi as the western boundary of the United States, and "desirable" terms, including the cession of Canada. But John Jay, recently arrived from his fruitless mission to Spain, objected to continuing the negotiations on the grounds that the Americans were being addressed not as plenipotentiaries of a sovereign nation but as "persons" from "colonies or plantations." The negotiations were delayed until Jay was satisfied.

All along Franklin, Jay, and Adams had kept Vergennes informed of their conversations with British agents, in accordance with the instructions from Congress. Then Jay learned that Vergennes's private secretary was off on a secret mission to England. Jay feared that Vergennes was going to make a separate peace by which Great Britain and Spain would divide between themselves the territory west of the Alleghenies and east of the Mississippi. Such a deal, as Franklin exclaimed, would have "cooped us up within the Allegheny Mountains." Though Jay was mistaken as to the details of the secret mission, he was right in thinking that Vergennes was suggesting separate negotiations that were to be kept from the American peacemakers and that might have proved disadvantageous to the United States. From that day on, Franklin, Jay, and Adams ceased to inform Vergennes of their diplomacy but went ahead on their own and soon drew up a preliminary treaty with Great Britain.

After the preliminary articles were signed (November 30, 1782), Jay and Adams left to Franklin the delicate task of telling Vergennes what had been done. Franklin admitted to Vergennes that the Americans perhaps had violated etiquette in failing to keep the French informed, but he trusted the incident would cause no rift in the Franco-American alliance. Cleverly Franklin observed: "The English, I just now learn, flatter themselves they have already divided us. I hope this little misunderstanding will therefore be kept a secret, and that they will find themselves totally mistaken." Vergennes, dealing with a fellow master of diplomacy, was doubtless

The Treaty of Paris [1783]

1. "His Britannic Majesty acknowledges the said United States . . . to be free, sovereign and independent States."
2. Boundaries shall run, as described in some detail, from Nova Scotia to and through the Great Lakes and the Lake of the Woods, "thence on a due west course to the river Mississippi, down the Mississippi to the thirty-first parallel, and then east to the Atlantic Ocean.
3. The people of the United States shall have fishing rights and liberties in the waters of British North America.
4. Creditors on either side "shall meet with no lawful impedient to the recovery of the full value, in sterling money, of all bona fide debts heretofore contracted."
5. Congress "shall earnestly recommend to the legislatures of the respective States" that they make restitution for confiscated Loyalist property.
6. There shall be no future confiscations or prosecutions on account of the part that anyone may have taken in the war.
7. Hostilities shall cease, and "His Britannic Majesty shall, with all convenient speed, and without causing any destruction, or carrying away any negroes or other property of the American inhabitants, withdraw all his armies, garrisons and fleets from the said United States, and from every post, place and harbour within the same."

glad to have an excuse for ending the war regardless of the wishes of his Spanish ally. Franklin coolly asked for another loan from France—and got it.

The final treaty was signed September 3, 1783, when Spain as well as France agreed to end hostilities. It included a number of provisions that Franklin, Jay, and Adams had opposed. Some of them were to lead to serious friction with Great Britain and Spain in the years ahead. Yet it also included essentially the "necessary" terms that Franklin originally had indicated, though not his "desirable" ones, such as the cession of Canada. On the whole, the peace was remarkably favorable to the United States in granting a clear-cut recognition of independence and a generous, though ambiguous cession of territory—from the southern boundary of Canada to the northern boundary of Florida and from the Atlantic to the Mississippi. With good reason the American people celebrated, as the last of the British occupation forces embarked from New York and General Washington at the head of his troops rode triumphantly in.

WAR AND SOCIETY

Historians have long debated the question of whether the American Revolution was a social as well as a political revolution. Some have argued that the colonists were struggling not only over the question of home rule, but over the question of "who should rule at home." Others claim that domestic social and economic concerns had little to do with the conflict. (See "Where Historians Disagree," pp. 140–141.) Whatever the motivations of Americans, however, there can be little doubt that the War for Independence had important effects on the nature of the economy and the society.

Loyalists and Minorities

The Revolution did not create a general assault on the wealthy and powerful in America. When the war ended, those who had been wealthy at its beginning were, for the most part, still wealthy. Those who had wielded social and political influence (which

The American Revolution

One of the oldest and most enduring controversies among American historians involves the nature of the American Revolution. Two broad schools of interpretation have emerged. One group of scholars has argued, and continues to argue, that the Revolution was primarily a political and intellectual event; that Americans in the 1770s were fighting to defend principles and ideals. Others have maintained, and still maintain, that much of the motivation for the Revolution was social and economic; that Americans were inspired to fight because of economic interests and social aspirations. Although there is a wide range of views and approaches within each of these schools, the question of "ideas" versus "interests" remains the crucial divide in interpretation.

The emphasis on ideology as the cause of the Revolution reflects, to some extent, the view of those who were involved in the event itself. Early histories of the Revolution, written by participants and contemporaries, invariably emphasized the high ideals of the Founding Fathers. That approach continued in an almost unbroken line throughout the nineteenth century, culminating in the work of the first great American historian, George Bancroft, who wrote in 1876 that the Revolution "was most radical in its character, yet achieved with such benign tranquillity that even conservatism hesitated to censure." Its aim, he believed, was to "preserve liberty" against the threat of British tyranny.

It was in the early twentieth century that historians first began seriously to examine the social and economic forces that may have contributed to the Revolution. Influenced by the reform currents of the progressive era, during which the power of economic interests came under scorching criticism, a number of scholars adopted the ideas of Carl Becker, who wrote in 1909—in a case study of New York—that not one but two questions were involved in the struggle. "The first was the question of home rule; the second was the question, if we may so put it, of who should rule at home." In addition to the fight against the British, in other words, there was also in progress a kind of civil war, a contest for power between radicals and conservatives that led to the "democratization of American politics and society." J. Franklin Jameson, expanding on Becker's views, argued in an extraordinarily influential book—*The American Revolution Considered as a Social Movement* (1926)—that the "stream of revolution, once started, could not be confined within narrow banks, but spread abroad upon the land. . . . Many economic desires, many social aspirations were set free by the political struggle, many aspects of society profoundly altered by the forces thus let loose."

Other progressive historians accepted the importance of economics as a cause of the Revolution but differed with Becker and Jameson over the form economic influences took. Arthur M. Schlesinger, for example, argued in an influential 1917 study that it was

often accompanied the possession of wealth) continued to wield it.

There were, however, exceptions; and among the most glaring was the case of the Loyalists. Estimates differ as to how many Americans remained loyal to England during the Revolution, but it is clear that there were many—up to a third of the white population. Their motivations were varied. Some were the officeholders in the imperial government, who stood to lose their positions as a result of the Revolution. Others were merchants whose trade was closely tied to the imperial system. (Most merchants, however, were supporters of the Revolution.) Still others were people who lived in isolation; they had not been exposed to the wave of discontent and resentment that had turned so many Americans against Britain and had simply retained their traditional loyalties. There were also cultural and ethnic minorities who feared that an independent America would the colonial merchants who were chiefly responsible for arousing American resistance to the British; and that although they spoke of principles and ideals, their real motives were economic self-interest: freedom from the restrictive policies of British mercantilism. In the event, however, the Revolution could not be controlled by the merchants and became a far more broadly based social movement than they had anticipated or desired.

Economic interpretations of the Revolution prevailed for several decades; but the relatively conservative political climate of the 1950s helped produce new studies that reemphasized the role of ideology. Robert E. Brown, in *Middle-Class Democracy and the American Revolution in Massachusetts* (1955), contended that long before 1776, Massachusetts was "very close to a complete democracy," and that the internal social conflicts that some historians ascribed to the era simply did not exist. Edmund S. Morgan, like Brown, argued in 1956 that most Americans of the Revolutionary era shared the same basic political principles, that the rhetoric of the Revolution could not be dismissed as propaganda—as Schlesinger had claimed—but should be taken seriously as the motivating force behind the movement. The preeminent statement of the importance of ideas in the conflict came from Bernard Bailyn in *The Ideological Origins of the American Revolution* (1967). After reading hundreds of Revolutionary pamphlets, Bailyn concluded that they "confirmed my rather old-fashioned view that the American Revolution was above all else an ideological, constitutional, political struggle and not primarily a controversy between social groups undertaken to force changes in the organization of the society or the economy."

By the time Bailyn's book was published, however, a new group of historians was reviving an economic approach to the Revolution. Influenced by the New Left of the 1960s, they claimed that domestic tensions between classes contributed in crucial ways to the development of the Revolutionary movement. Such historians as Jesse Lemisch and Dirk Hoerder pointed to the actions of mobs in colonial cities as evidence of the social concerns of resisting Americans. Joseph Ernst reemphasized the significance of economic pressures on colonial merchants and tradesmen. And Gary B. Nash, in *The Urban Crucible* (1979), emphasized the role of increasing economic tension and distress in colonial cities in creating a climate in which the Revolutionary movement could flourish. Many of the new economic interpretations of the Revolution argue not that the struggle was a direct expression of the economic self-interest of the participants, but that social and economic concerns were important in shaping the ideology of the conflict. "Everyone," Gary Nash has written, "has economic interests; and everyone . . . has an ideology." Only by exploring the relationships between the two, he maintained, can historians hope fully to understand either.

not offer them sufficient protection. And there were those who, expecting the British to win the war, were simply currying favor with the expected victors.

What happened to these men and women during the war is a turbulent and at times tragic story. Hounded by Patriots in their communities, harassed by legislative and judicial rulings, the position of many of them became intolerable. Up to 100,000 fled the country during the war. Those who could afford to—for example, the hated Tory governor of Massachusetts, Thomas Hutchinson—fled to England, where many lived in difficult and lonely exile. Others of more modest means moved to Canada, establishing the first English-speaking community in the province of Quebec. Some returned to America after the war and, as the early passions and resentments faded, managed to reenter the life of the nation. Others remained abroad for the rest of their lives.

Because so many of the Loyalists were people of means, they left behind substantial estates and vacated important positions of social and economic leadership. Even some who remained in the country saw their property confiscated and their positions forfeited. The result, of course, was new opportunities for Patriots to acquire land and influence, a situation that produced important social changes in many communities. It would be an exaggeration, however, to claim that the departure of the Loyalists was responsible for anything approaching a social revolution.

The war had a significant effect on the position of other minorities as well, and on certain religious groups in particular. No sect suffered more than the Anglicans, many of whose members were Loyalists and all of whom were widely identified with England. In Virginia and Maryland, where the church had benefited from tax support, the new Revolutionary governments disestablished it and thus eliminated the subsidy. In other states, Anglicans had benefited from aid from England, which also ceased with the outbreak of war. By the time the fighting ended, many Anglican parishes no longer even had clergymen, for there were few recruits to take the places of those who had died or who had left the country as Loyalist refugees. Since there had never been an American bishop or an intercolonial organization of the church, there was little institutional strength from which those Anglicans who remained could rebuild their church; and although Anglicanism survived in America, it was to remain permanently weakened from its losses during the Revolution. Also weakened were the Quakers in Pennsylvania and elsewhere, who won widespread unpopularity because of their pacifism. Their reluctance to support the war destroyed much of the social and political prestige they had enjoyed, and the church was never to recover fully.

While the war was weakening the Anglicans and the Quakers, it was doing much to improve the position of the Roman Catholic church. On the advice of Charles Carroll of Carrollton, a Maryland statesman and Catholic lay leader, most American Catholics supported the Patriot cause during the war.

The French alliance brought Catholic troops and chaplains to the country, and the gratitude with which most Americans greeted them did much to erode old hostilities toward Catholics, who in earlier times had often been denounced as agents of the devil. The church did not greatly increase its numbers as a result of the Revolution, but it did strengthen itself considerably as an institution. Shortly after the peace treaty was signed, the Vatican provided the United States with its own Catholic hierarchy. (Up to now, the American church had been controlled by the English bishops.) Father John Carroll (also of Maryland) was named head of Catholic missions in America in 1784 and, in 1789, the first American bishop. In 1808 he became Archbishop of Baltimore. Hostility toward Catholics had not disappeared forever from American life, but the church had established a solid footing from which to withstand future assaults.

For the most conspicuous of America's minorities—the black population—the war had limited, but nevertheless profound, significance. For some, it meant freedom. Because so much of the fighting occurred in the South during the last years of the war, many slaves came into contact with the British army, which—in the interests of disrupting and weakening the American cause—emancipated thousands of them and took them out of the country. For other blacks, the Revolution meant exposure to the idea, although not the reality, of liberty. In the towns and cities of the South, where large groups of both free and enslaved blacks lived, the ideology of the Revolution had a pronounced effect. Although most blacks could not read, few could avoid exposure to the new and exciting ideas; and in many cases, they attempted to apply those ideas to themselves. The result was a series of incidents in many communities in which blacks engaged in open resistance to white control. In Charleston, South Carolina, there was even a brief and ineffectual revolt. It would be many years before blacks would be in position to make more than sporadic efforts on behalf of their freedom; but the experience of the Revolution produced distinct stirrings of discontent.

The Rights of Women

The Revolutionary emphasis on liberty and the rights of man led some American women to question their position in society as well. "By the way," Abigail Adams wrote to her husband John Adams in 1776, "in the new code of laws which I suppose it will be necessary for you to make, I desire you would remember the ladies and be more generous and favorable to them than your ancestors. Do not put such unlimited power into the hands of husbands." Other women argued similarly for enhancing the status of their sex. Judith Sargent Murray, one of the leading essayists of the late eighteenth century, wrote in 1779 that women's minds were as good as those of men and that girls as well as boys therefore deserved access to education. Murray later served as one of the leading defenders of the works of the English feminist Mary Wollstonecraft, whose *Vindication of the Rights of Women* was published in America in 1792. After reading it, Murray rejoiced that "the Rights of Women" were beginning to be understood in the United States and that future generations of women would inaugurate "a new era in female history."

But the new era did not arrive. Some political leaders—Benjamin Franklin, Benjamin Rush, and Thomas Jefferson among them—voiced support for the education of women and for other feminist reforms. Yale students in the 1780s debated the question, "Whether women ought to be admitted into the magistracy and government of empires and republics." And there was for a time wide discussion of the future role of females in the new republic. But few concrete reforms were enacted into law or translated into practice.

Mercy Otis Warren
Mercy Otis Warren, born in Barnstable, Massachusetts, in 1728, was about thirty-five years old when John Singleton Copley painted this portrait of her. Mrs. Warren was to be a leading propagandist of the Revolution. Copley, of Boston, was an outstanding American portraitist and at first a sympathizer with the Patriot cause and an admirer of Samuel Adams, whose portrait he also painted. In 1774, however, Copley left America to continue his distinguished artistic career in England for the rest of his life. (Courtesy Museum of Fine Arts, Boston)

Yet while the Revolution ultimately did little to improve the legal position of women, it did contribute to an alteration of the role of women in the family and in the economy that had important long-range implications. Whereas in earlier times women had often been viewed as little better than servants in their husbands' homes, there was now a new emphasis on the capacity of wives to instruct their families in the tender virtues that members of their sex were believed instinctively to understand. Wives were far from equal partners in marriage, but their ideas and interests were increasingly considered worthy of respect. And far fewer women now suffered the indignity of "arranged" marriages—marriages to men chosen by their fathers rather than by the women themselves.

Part of this change was a result of the participation of women in the Revolutionary struggle itself. There had been influential women propagandists in the years of agitation against the British before 1775—most notably Mercy Otis Warren of Massachusetts. And in the course of the war, many women—either by choice or by necessity—assumed tasks that had long been considered the exclusive province of men. Some managed farms and businesses in the absence of their husbands. Others traveled with the Patriot army, helping to keep the soldiers fed and clothed and occasionally themselves engaging in battle. The legendary "Molly Pitcher," so named because she carried pitchers of water to soldiers on the battlefield, watched her husband fall during one encounter and immediately took his place at a field gun. After the war, most such women returned to traditional domestic roles. But a precedent had been established that in future years permitted a significant number of women to engage in income-producing activities inside the home (for example, weaving cloth for sale) and later outside it (teaching, industrial work, and more).

The War Economy

Inevitably, the Revolution produced important changes in the structure of the American economy. After more than a century of dependence on the British imperial system, American trade suddenly found itself on its own. No longer did it have the protection of the great British navy; on the contrary, English ships now attempted to drive American vessels from the seas. No longer did American merchants have access to the markets of the empire; those markets were now hostile ports—including, of course, the most important source of American trade: England itself.

Yet while the Revolution was responsible for much disruption in traditional economic patterns, it served in the long run to strengthen the American economy. Well before the war was over, American ships had learned to evade the British navy with light, fast, easily maneuverable vessels. Indeed, the Yankees began to prey on British commerce with hundreds of privateers. For many a shipowner, privateering proved to be more profitable than ordinary peacetime trade. More important in the long run, the end of imperial restrictions on American shipping opened up enormous new areas of trade to the new nation. Colonial merchants had been violating British regulations for years, but the rules of empire had nevertheless served to inhibit American exploration of many markets. Now, enterprising merchants in New England and elsewhere began to develop new commerce in the Caribbean and South America. By the mid-1780s, American merchants were developing an important new pattern of trade with the Orient, and by the end of that decade Yankee ships were regularly sailing from the eastern seaboard around Cape Horn to California, there exchanging manufactured goods for hides and furs, and then proceeding across the Pacific to barter for goods in China. There was also a substantial increase in trade among the American states.

When English imports to America were cut off—first by the prewar boycott, then by the war itself—there were desperate efforts throughout the states to stimulate domestic manufacturing of certain necessities. There was no great industrial expansion as a result, but there were several signs of the economic growth that was to come in the next century.

Americans began to make their own cloth—"homespun," which became both patriotic and fashionable—to replace the now unobtainable British fabrics. It would be some time before a large domestic textile industry would emerge, but the nation was never again to rely exclusively on foreign sources for its cloth. There was, of course, pressure to build factories for the manufacture of guns and ammunition. And there was a growing awareness that America need not forever be dependent on other nations for manufac-

tured goods. Having broken politically with the British Empire, citizens of the new nation began to dream of breaking economically with it too—of developing a strong economy to rival that of the Old World.

The war stopped short of revolutionizing the American economy. Not until the nineteenth century would that begin to occur. But it did serve to release a wide range of entrepreneurial energies that, despite the temporary dislocations, encouraged growth and diversification.

THE CREATION OF STATE GOVERNMENTS

At the same time that Americans were struggling to win their independence on the battlefield, they were also struggling to create new institutions of government for themselves, to replace the British system they had repudiated. The construction of these new political institutions occurred in several stages and continued over a period of more than fifteen years. Yet its most crucial phase occurred in the very first years after independence, during the war itself; and it occurred not at the national but at the state level.

The formation of state governments began early in 1776, even before the adoption of the Declaration of Independence. It was the most creative period of American political development; for in it was determined the basic structure of the republic, and in it were resolved many of the early problems of republicanism. At first, the new constitutions reflected primarily the fear of bloated executive power that had become so pronounced during the 1760s and early 1770s. Gradually, however, Americans began to become equally concerned about the instability of a government too responsive to the popular will. In a second phase of state constitution writing, therefore, they gave renewed attention to the idea of balance in government.

The Assumptions of Republicanism

If Americans agreed on nothing else when they began to build new governments for

themselves, they agreed that those governments would be republican. To them, that meant a political system in which all power was derived from the people, rather than from some supreme authority (such as a king) standing above them. The success of any government, therefore, depended on the nature of its citizenry. If the population consisted of sturdy, independent property owners, then the republic could survive. If it consisted of a few powerful aristocrats and a great mass of dependent workers, then it would be in danger. From the beginning, therefore, the ideal of the small freeholder became basic to American political ideology.

Another crucial part of that ideology was the concept of equality. The Declaration of Independence had given voice to that idea in its most ringing phrase: "all men are created equal." It was a belief that stood in direct contrast to the old European assumption of an inherited aristocracy. Every citizen, Americans believed, was born in a position of equality with every other citizen. It would be a person's innate talents and energies that would determine his role in society, not his position at birth. American equality, therefore, did not envision a society without social gradations. Some people would inevitably be wealthier and more powerful than others. But everyone would have to earn his success. There would be no equality of condition, but there would be full equality of opportunity.

In reality, of course, these assumptions could not always be sustained. The United

States was never able to become a nation in which all citizens were independent property holders. From the beginning, there was a sizable dependent labor force—the white members of which were allowed many of the privileges of citizenship while the black members were excluded from all political activity. American women remained both politically and economically subordinate, with few opportunities for advancement independent of their husbands. Nor was it possible to ensure full equality of opportunity. American society was more open and more fluid than that of most European nations; but it remained true that wealth and privilege were often passed from one generation to another. The conditions of a person's birth survived as a crucial determinant of success.

Nevertheless, in embracing the assumptions of republicanism, Americans were adopting a powerful, even revolutionary new ideology, one that would enable them to create a form of government never before seen in the world. Their experiment in statecraft became a model for many other countries and made the United States for a time the most admired and studied nation on earth.

The First State Constitutions

Two of the original thirteen states saw no need to produce new constitutions. Connecticut and Rhode Island already had corporate charters which provided them with governments that were republican in all but name; they simply deleted references to England and the king from their charters and adopted them as constitutions. In the other eleven states, however, it was necessary to create new governments. In doing so, Americans at first devoted their greatest efforts to avoiding what they considered to be the problems of the British system they were repudiating.

The first and perhaps most basic decision was that the constitutions were to be written down. In England, the constitution was not a document but a vague understanding about the way society should be structured. Americans believed that the vagueness of that understanding had allowed the British government to become corrupted. To avoid a

similar fate, they insisted that their own government rest on clearly stated and permanently inscribed laws, so that no individual or group could pervert them.

The second decision was that the power of the executive, which in England had grown so bloated and threatening, must be limited. Only one state went as far as to eliminate the executive altogether: Pennsylvania. But most states inserted provisions sharply limiting the power of the governor over appointments, reducing or eliminating his right to veto bills, and preventing him from dismissing or otherwise interfering with the legislature. Above all, every state forbade the governor or any other executive officer from holding a seat in the legislature, thus ensuring that the two branches of government would remain separate, that the English parliamentary system would not be re-created in America. The constitutions also added provisions protecting the judiciary from executive control, although in most states the courts had not yet emerged as fully autonomous branches of government.

In limiting the executive and expanding the power of the legislature, the new constitutions were moving far in the direction of direct popular rule. They did not, however, move all the way. Only in Georgia and Pennsylvania did the legislature consist of one house. In all the other states, there was an upper and a lower chamber; and in most cases, the upper chamber was designed to represent the "higher orders" of society. In all states, there were property requirements for voters—in some states, only the modest amount that would qualify a person as a taxpayer, in other states somewhat greater requirements. Among the white population, such requirements tended to have little impact, since property ownership was so widespread. But universal suffrage was not yet an accepted part of American government. Nor were the rights of women. Only in New Jersey were women allowed to vote, and eventually they lost that right even there.

The initial phase of constitution writing proceeded rapidly. Ten of the states completed the process before the end of 1776. Only Georgia, New York, and Massachusetts delayed. Georgia and New York completed the task by the end of the following year, but Massachusetts did not finally adopt its version until 1780. By then, the construction of state governments had moved into a new phase.

Revising State Governments

By the late 1770s, Americans were already growing concerned about what they perceived as the excessive factiousness and instability of their new state governments. Legislatures were the scene of constant squabbling. Governors were unable to exercise sufficient power to provide any real leadership. It was proving extraordinarily difficult to get the new governments to accomplish anything at all. To many observers, the problem began to appear to be one of too much democracy. By placing so much power in the hands of the people (and of their elected representatives in the legislature), the state constitutions were inviting disorder and political turbulence.

As a result, most of the states began to revise their constitutions to cope with these problems. Massachusetts was the first to act on the new concerns. By waiting until 1780 before finally ratifying its first constitution, Massachusetts allowed these changing ideas to shape its government; and the state produced a constitution that was to serve as a model for the efforts of others.

Two changes in particular characterized the Massachusetts and later constitutions. The first was a change in the process of constitution writing itself. In the first phase, the documents had usually been written by state legislatures. As a result, they could easily be amended (or violated) by those same bodies. By 1780, sentiment was growing to find a way to protect the constitutions from the people who had written them, to make it difficult to change the documents once they were approved. The solution was the constitutional convention: a special assembly of the people that would meet only for the purpose of writing the constitution and that would never (except under extraordinary circumstances) meet again. The constitution would, therefore, be the product of the popular will; but

once approved, it would be protected from the whims of public opinion and from the political moods of the legislature.

The second change was similarly a reflection of the new concerns about excessive popular power: a significant strengthening of the executive. In Massachusetts, the governor under the 1780 constitution became one of the strongest in any state. He was to be elected directly by the people; he was to have a fixed salary (in other words, he would not be dependent on the good will of the legislature each year for his wages); he would have expanded powers of appointment; and he would be able to veto legislation. Other states soon followed. Those states that had weak or nonexistent upper houses strengthened or created them. Most states increased the powers of the governor; and Pennsylvania, which had had no executive at all at first, now produced a strong one. By the late 1780s, almost every state had either revised its constitution or drawn up an entirely new one to make allowances for the belief in the need for stability.

The States in Operation

The new state governments—both under the first constitutions and under the later, revised ones—adopted a number of policies that increased opportunities for social and political mobility. In one way or another, they multiplied opportunities for land ownership and thus enlarged the voting population. For example, they eliminated the legal rights of primogeniture (the requirement that a father's estate be passed intact to his first son) and entail (whereby a man kept his estate intact from generation to generation by willing that it never be sold). In fact, neither practice had ever been widespread in America; but in a few places, the new laws did contribute to the erosion of landed aristocracies.

The new states also moved far in the direction of complete religious freedom. Most Americans continued to believe that religion should play some role in government; but they did not wish to give special privileges to any particular denomination. In some states, religious tests survived as a qualification for

The Virginia Statute of Religious Liberty: An Act for Establishing Religious Freedom [1785]

Thomas Jefferson was the author of this statute, passed by the Virginia General Assembly in October 1785. It was the first and clearest legislative expression of the idea of complete religious freedom in America.

I. WHEREAS Almighty God hath created the mind free; that all attempts to influence it by temporal punishments or burthens, or by civil incapacitations, tend only to beget habits of hypocrisy and meanness, and are a departure from the plan of the Holy author of our religion, who being Lord both of body and mind, yet chose not to propagate it by coercions on either, as was in his Almighty power to do; . . . that our civil rights have no dependence on our religious opinions, any more than our opinions in physics or geometry; that therefore the proscribing any citizen as unworthy the public confidence by laying upon him an incapacity of being called to offices of trust and emolument, unless he profess or renounce this or that religious opinion, is depriving him injuriously of those privileges and advantages to which in common with his fellow-citizens he has a natural right; . . . and finally, that truth is great and will prevail if left to herself, that she is the proper and sufficient antagonist to error, and has nothing to fear from the conflict, unless by human interposition disarmed of her natural weapons, free argument and debate, errors ceasing to be dangerous when it is permitted freely to contradict them.

II. Be it enacted by the General Assembly, that no man shall be compelled to frequent or support any religious worship, place or ministry whatsoever, nor shall be enforced, restrained, molested, or burthened in his body or goods, nor shall otherwise suffer on account of his religious opinions or belief; but that all men shall be free to profess, and by argument to maintain their opinion in matters of religion, and that the same shall in no wise diminish, enlarge or affect their civil capacities.

III. And though we well know that this Assembly, elected by the people for the ordinary purposes of legislation only, have no power to restrain the acts of succeeding Assemblies . . . yet as we are free to declare, and do declare, that the rights hereby asserted are of the natural rights of mankind, and that if any Act shall hereafter be passed to repeal the present, or to narrow its operation, such Act will be an infringement of natural right.

---

officeholding. (Atheists and, in a few places, Catholics were barred from office; but since there were few of either in most of the states in question, the requirements were largely meaningless.) More characteristic, however, was the erosion of the privileges that many churches had once enjoyed. New York and the Southern states, in which the Church of England had been tax-supported, soon saw to the complete disestablishment of the church; and the New England states stripped the Congregational church of many of its privileges. Boldest of all was Virginia, which in its Declaration of Rights announced the principle of complete toleration. And in 1786, Virginia enacted a Statute of Religious Liberty, written by Thomas Jefferson, which called for the complete separation of church and state.

More difficult to resolve was the question of slavery. The rhetoric of the Revolution—which emphasized the importance of liberty and the perils of slavery—could not help but direct attention to America's own institution of bondage. And in some places, it cast the institution into disrepute. In areas where slavery was weak—in New England, where there had never been many slaves, and in Pennsylvania, where the Quakers were outspoken in their opposition to slavery—it was abolished. Pennsylvania passed a general gradual-emancipation act in 1780; and the supreme court of Massachusetts ruled in 1783 that the ownership of slaves was impermissible under the state's bill of rights. Even in the South, there were some pressures to amend the institution (a result, in part, of the activities of the first antislavery society in America, founded in 1775). Every state but South Carolina and Georgia prohibited the further importation of slaves from abroad, and even South Carolina laid a temporary wartime ban on the slave trade. Virginia passed a law encouraging manumission (the freeing of slaves), and other states encountered growing political pressures to change the institution.

In the end, however, most of the pressures came to naught. Slavery survived in all the Southern and border states; and it would continue to survive for nearly a century more. The reasons were many. Racist assumptions about the natural inferiority of blacks persuaded many Americans that there was nothing incompatible in asserting the innate rights of man while denying those rights to blacks. And economic pressures made it difficult to free slaves. Many Southerners had enormous investments in their black laborers and were unwilling to consider losing them.

An equally important obstacle was that few Southerners—even such men as Washington and Jefferson, who expressed deep moral misgivings about slavery—could envision any alternative to it. If slavery were abolished, what would happen to the blacks? Some argued that they should be sent back to Africa, but that was clearly unrealistic. The black population was too large; and many slaves were now so many generations removed from Africa that they felt but little identification with it and had no wish to return. Few whites believed that blacks could be integrated into American society as

---

A Ruling Against Slavery in Massachusetts [1783]

In the case of Quork Walker, who was a slave suing his master, the chief justice of Massachusetts gave the following charge to the jury:

As to the doctrine of slavery and the right of Christians to hold Africans in perpetual servitude, and sell and treat them as we do our horses and cattle, that (it is true) has been heretofore countenanced by the Province Laws formerly, but nowhere is it expressly enacted or established. It has been a usage—a usage which took its origin from the practice of some of the European nations, and the regulations of British government respecting the then Colonies, for the benefit of trade and wealth. But whatever sentiments have formerly prevailed in this particular or slid in upon us by the example of others, a different idea has taken place with the people of America, more favorable to the natural rights of mankind, and to that natural, innate desire of Liberty, with which Heaven (without regard to color, complexion, or shape of noses) has inspired all the human race. And upon this ground our Constitution of Government, by which the people of this Commonwealth have solemnly bound themselves, sets out with declaring that all men are born free and equal—and that every subject is entitled to liberty, and to have it guarded by the laws, as well as life and property—and in short is totally repugnant to the idea of being born slaves. This being the case, I think the idea of slavery is inconsistent with our own conduct and Constitution; and there can be no such thing as perpetual servitude of a rational creature, unless his liberty is forfeited by some criminal conduct or given up by personal consent or contract.

equals. Even those most opposed to slavery usually shared the general assumptions about the unfitness of blacks for citizenship. In maintaining slavery, Jefferson once remarked, Americans were holding a "wolf by the ears." However unappealing it was to hold on to, letting go promised to be even worse.

There was, finally, a more subtle obstacle to the elimination of slavery. The economy of the South depended, most Southerners believed, on a large, servile labor force. Yet the ideals of republicanism required a homogeneous population of independent, property-owning citizens. Were slavery to be abolished, the South would find itself with a substantial unpropertied laboring class; and whether that class were black or white, its existence would raise troubling implications for the future of democracy. The social tensions that would inevitably ensue would, Southerners feared, ultimately destroy the stability of society.

Thus, just as in the early years of settlement, so during the Revolution: Americans encountered only vague, philosophical pressures to abolish slavery but powerful social and economic pressures to maintain it. As a result, slavery survived.

THE SEARCH FOR A NATIONAL GOVERNMENT

Americans were much quicker to agree on the proper shape of their state institutions than they were to decide on the form of their national government. At first, most believed that the central government should remain a relatively weak and unimportant force. Each state would be virtually a sovereign nation. The national government would serve only as a loose, coordinating institution, with little independent authority. Such beliefs reflected the assumption that a republic operated best in a relatively limited, homogeneous area; that were a republican government to attempt to administer too large and diverse a nation, it would founder. It was in response to such ideas that the Articles of Confederation emerged.

The Confederation

No sooner did the Continental Congress appoint a committee to draft a declaration of independence in 1776 than it appointed another to draft a plan of union. After much debate and many revisions, the Congress adopted the committee's proposal in November 1777 as the Articles of Confederation.

The Articles provided for a central government very similar to the one already in operation. Congress was to survive as the central—indeed the only—institution of national government. But its authority was to be somewhat expanded. It was to have the powers of conducting war, carrying on foreign relations, and appropriating, borrowing, and issuing money. But it could not regulate trade, draft troops, or levy taxes directly. For troops and taxes it would have to make requisitions of the states; it would, in effect, have to address formal requests to the state legislatures, which could and often did refuse them. There was to be no separate, single, strong executive (the "president of the United States" was to be merely the presiding officer at the sessions of Congress). Congress itself was to see to the execution of laws through an executive committee of thirteen, made up of one member from each state, through ad hoc and standing committees for specific functions, and through such administrative departments as it might choose to create. There were to be no Confederation courts, except for courts of admiralty, but disputes among the states were to be settled by a complicated system of arbitration. These states were to retain their individual sovereignty, each of the legislatures electing and paying the salaries of two to seven delegates to Congress, and each delegation, no matter how numerous, having only one vote. At least nine of the states (through their delegations) would have to approve any important measure, such as a treaty, before Congress could pass it, and all thirteen state legislatures would have to approve before the Articles could be ratified or amended.

The Articles of Confederation [1781]

1. [Article II] "Each state retains its sovereignty, freedom and independence, and every Power, Jurisdiction and right, which is not by this confederation expressly delegated to the United States, in Congress assembled."
2. [Article IV] The free inhabitants of each state "shall be entitled to all privileges and immunities of free citizens in the several states" and "full faith and credit" shall be given by each state to the judicial and other official proceedings of other states.
3. [Article V] Each state shall be represented in Congress by no less than two and no more than seven members, shall pay its own delegates, and shall have one vote (regardless of the number of members).
4. [Article VI] No state, without the consent of Congress, shall enter into diplomatic relations or make treaties with other states or with foreign nations, or engage in war except in case of actual invasion.
5. [Article VIII] A "common treasury" shall be supplied by the states in proportion to the value of their land and improvements; the states shall levy taxes to raise their quotas of revenue.
6. [Article IX] Congress shall have power to decide on peace and war, conduct foreign affairs, settle disputes between states, regulate the Indian trade, maintain post offices, make appropriations, borrow money, emit bills of credit, build a navy, requisition soldiers from the states, etc.—but nine states must agree before Congress can take any important action.
7. [Article X] A "Committee of the States," consisting of one delegate from each state, shall act in the place of Congress when Congress is not in session.
8. [Article XIII] No change shall be made in these Articles unless agreed to by Congress and "afterwards confirmed by the legislatures of every state."

Ratification was delayed by differences of opinion about the proposed plan. The people of all the small states insisted on equal state representation, but those of the large states thought they should be represented in proportion to their population. Above all, the states claiming Western lands wished to keep them, but the rest of the states demanded that all such territory be turned over to the Confederation government. The "landed" states founded their claims largely on colonial charters, The "landless" states, particularly Maryland, maintained that as the fruit of common sacrifices in war the Western land had become the rightful property of all the states. At last New York gave up its rather hazy claim, and Virginia made a qualified offer to cede its lands to Congress. Then Maryland, the only state still holding out against ratification, approved the Articles of Confederation, and they went into effect in 1781.

The Confederation government came into being in time to conclude the war and make the peace. Meanwhile, during the years of fighting from 1775 to 1781, the Second Continental Congress had served as the agency for directing and coordinating the war effort of the thirteen states.

In later years, it became popular to characterize the government under the Articles of Confederation, which existed from 1781 until 1789, as an almost total failure. Such judgments are not entirely fair. The Confederation did manage to solve some of the problems facing the new nation. It performed particularly creditably in organizing America's territories in the West. Yet the new government was far from a success. Lacking adequate powers to deal with interstate issues, lacking any effective mechanisms that would have permitted it to enforce its will on the states, and lacking sufficient stature in the eyes of the world to be able to negotiate effectively, the Confederation suffered a series of damaging setbacks.

The Disputed Treaty

Evidence of the low regard in which the new government was held abroad was the difficulty of the United States in persuading Great Britain (and to a lesser extent Spain) to live up to the terms of the peace treaty of 1783. That treaty had recognized the independence of the United States and granted the new nation a vast domain—on paper. But Americans found it hard to exercise their full sovereignty in fact.

Despite the treaty provision calling on the British to evacuate American soil, British forces continued to occupy a string of frontier posts along the Great Lakes within the United States. Secret orders to hold these forts went from the Colonial Office in London to the governor general of Canada on April 8, 1784, just one day before King George III proclaimed the peace treaty as being in final effect and called on all his subjects to obey its terms. The real reason for the secret orders was the Canadian and British desire to maintain points of contact with Indian tribes in the Northwest for the conduct of the fur trade and the continuance of defensive alliances with them. The avowed reason, which was an afterthought, was the alleged failure of the United States to carry out its treaty obligations, particularly in regard to private debts.

These debts, dating from pre-Revolutionary days, were owed by American citizens, mostly Southern planters, to merchants and other creditors in England. The American debtors had no intention of paying—many of them had supported the Revolution in order to throw off their old obligations. The treaty provided only that the United States should place no obstacle in the way of the collection of the debts, and the United States did place no obstacle in the way. True, the individual states interfered with debt collections, through the passage of debtor stay laws, the issuance of paper money as legal tender, and the rulings of courts sympathetic to local debtors.

According to the ill-founded British complaints, the United States was violating not only the article regarding private debts but also the one regarding Loyalist property. On this point the treaty said merely that Congress should recommend to the various states that they make restitution to certain categories of Loyalists whose possessions had been confiscated during the war. Congress did recommend, but the states did not respond. The British had not really expected them to. The article was put into the treaty as a gesture of the king's concern for the fate of his faithful subjects. Anticipating that the states would do little or nothing for Loyalist refugees, Parliament itself appropriated money for their relief.

To British allegations of bad faith, Americans countered with the charge that Great Britain, besides refusing to abandon the frontier posts, was disregarding the treaty provision that obligated it to compensate American slaveowners whose slaves had been carried off by the British armies at the end of the war. And the two countries disputed the meaning and application of still another article, the one defining the northeastern boundary of the United States. Over part of its course the boundary was supposed to follow the St. Croix River, but the river had two major branches, and the treaty did not specify which of the two was meant.

The peace arrangements led also to a boundary dispute between the United States and Spain. In its settlement with Spain, Great Britain gave back Florida (which had been British from 1763 to 1783), with the Atlantic and the Mississippi specified as its eastern and western limits but with no precise definition of its northern border. In the preliminary treaty with the United States, however, Great Britain had agreed secretly that if Britain itself were to keep Florida, the boundary would be set at latitude 32°28′, and that if Britain ceded it to Spain, the boundary would be located farther south, at the 31st parallel. Afterward, the United States insisted on the more southerly of these lines, but Spain demanded the additional northern strip as rightfully a part of Florida.

Failures in Foreign Affairs

Thus the peace with Great Britain failed to give Americans the benefits they desired and expected. Above all, American shippers and traders wanted commercial arrangements that would give them privileges of trading and shipping on equal terms with British subjects in all parts of the British Empire.

No longer colonists, these businessmen, it is true, now had opportunities for exploiting worldwide routes of trade, which before the war had been legally closed to them. But while commerce flourished in new directions, most American trade persisted as far as was possible in the old, prewar patterns. In the United States, the bulk of imports continued to come from British sources; for Americans were used to British goods, and British merchants knew and catered to American tastes, offered attractive prices, and extended long and easy credit. To earn the British funds needed to pay for these imports, Americans desired free access to more British markets than were open to them after the war.

In 1784, Congress sent John Adams as minister to London with instructions to get a commercial treaty and speed up the evacuation of the frontier posts. Taunted by the query whether he represented one nation or thirteen, Minister Adams made no headway in England, partly because Congress had no power to retaliate against the kind of commercial warfare that Great Britain was pursuing against the United States. Throughout the 1780s, the British government refused even to return the courtesy of sending a minister to the American capital.

The Spanish government, by contrast, was willing to negotiate its differences with the United States, and in 1785 its representative, Diego de Gardoqui, arrived in New York (where Congress had moved from Philadelphia) to deal with the secretary for foreign affairs, John Jay. After months of friendly conversations, Jay and Gardoqui initialed a treaty (1786). By its terms, the Spanish government would have granted Americans the right to trade with Spain but not with its colonies; would have conceded the American interpretation of the Florida boundary; and (in a secret article) would have joined in an alliance to protect American soil from British encroachments. The United States, besides guaranteeing Spanish possessions in America, would have agreed to "forbear" the navigation of the Mississippi for twenty years, though not to abandon the right of navigation. Jay found it hopeless, however, to secure the necessary nine state votes for the ratification of his treaty by Congress, since the delegates from the five Southern states objected bitterly (and correctly) that the interests of Southerners in Mississippi navigation were being sacrificed to the interests of Northerners in Spanish trade.

The Needs of the West

During and after the Revolution, an unprecedented number of American settlers moved into the areas that were the focus of postwar dispute. When the war began, only a few thousand lived west of the Appalachian divide; by 1790 their numbers had increased to 120,000. Most of the migrants made the mountain crossing under the auspices of able and far-seeing land promoters. The frontiersman usually had to depend on such speculators for his land title and for other favors, yet he was characteristically an individualist determined to make a future for himself. Such men and their families served as evidence of the tremendous potential for growth and development in the West.

But the United States could realize this potential only if the government were able to meet the needs of the frontier settler and keep him loyal to its distant authority. The settler needed protection from the Indians, access to outside markets for his surplus crops, and courts with orderly processes of law. In dealing with the West, Congress inherited responsibilities that formerly had baffled king and Parliament.

At first, Congress lacked clear-cut jurisdiction over the trans-Appalachian region, and for several years conflicts of authority persisted among Congress, the states, and the frontier settlements themselves. With Virginia's cession of control of its Western lands to Congress in 1781, the landed states had begun to yield their Western claims to the Confederation. But the process was a slow one, and one state after another found grounds on which to resist or delay its cession. Not until 1802 did the last of the states, Georgia, give up its claim. Meanwhile these

STATE CLAIMS TO WESTERN LANDS, 1781

states transferred the actual ownership of most of the land south of the Ohio River to private individuals and companies, and impatient settlers proceeded to set up their own state governments for Frankland (or Franklin, later Tennessee) and for Kentucky. North Carolina, meanwhile, attempted to incorporate Tennessee, and Virginia tried to make Kentucky a Virginia county.

Planning for the Territories

In 1784, having persuaded Virginia to make a new cession without specific restrictions,

Congress accepted Virginia's Western lands (not including Kentucky) and began to make policy for the national domain. The most momentous decision, already resolved upon, was that settlements in the territory should not be held in permanent subjection as colonies but should be transformed ultimately into states equal with the original thirteen. In the Ordinance of 1784, Congress temporarily adopted Thomas Jefferson's democratic plan for the transition to statehood of the territory between the Ohio River and the Great Lakes. This territory was to have been divided into ten districts, each to be self-governing from the start, to be represented by a delegate in Congress as soon as its population reached 20,000, and to be admitted as a state when its population equaled the number of free inhabitants of the smallest existing state.

Having thus prepared a scheme of territorial government, Congress in the Ordinance of 1785 provided a system of land survey and sale. The land to the north of the Ohio was to be surveyed and marked off in a rectangular pattern before any of it was sold. The land ordinance of Congress provided for east-west base lines, north-south "ranges," and townships with sides paralleling the ranges and base lines. Each township was to contain thirty-six square-mile sections. In every township four sections were to be set aside for the United States and one for a public school. The rest of the sections were to be sold at auction for not less than $1 an acre. Since there were 640 acres in a section, the prospective buyer of government land had to have at least $640—a very large sum by the standards of the day—in ready cash or in United States certificates of indebtedness.

These terms favored the large speculators too much and the ordinary frontiersman too little to suit Jefferson, who believed that the West ought to belong to actual settlers on the ground. But the large speculators desired still further advantages, and Congress, in a hurry to realize returns from its domain, soon gave in to lobbying groups composed of some of its own members and various former army officers. To the Ohio and Scioto companies and the associates of John Cleves Symmes, Congress disposed of several million acres at only a few cents an acre. Millions of acres besides had been reserved at the time of cession by Virginia and Connecticut as bounty lands for their Revolutionary soldiers. Thus, before the government surveys had been well started, most of the choicest land north of the Ohio River was already spoken for (as was all the land south of the Ohio, to which the ordinances of Congress did not apply).

To protect their interests in the Northwest, the directors of the Ohio and Scioto companies demanded a territorial government that would give less influence to the inhabitants than would the one outlined in Jefferson's Ordinance of 1784, and the companies' skillful lobbyist, Manasseh

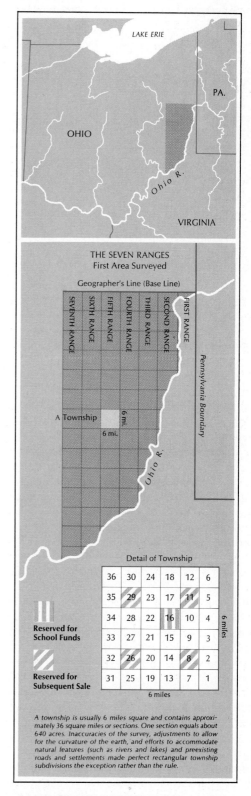

THE SEVEN RANGES
First Area Surveyed

Geographer's Line (Base Line)

SEVENTH RANGE
SIXTH RANGE
FIFTH RANGE
FOURTH RANGE
THIRD RANGE
SECOND RANGE
FIRST RANGE

Pennsylvania Boundary

A Township
6 mi.
6 mi.

Ohio R.

Detail of Township

36	30	24	18	12	6
35	29	23	17	11	5
34	28	22	16	10	4
33	27	21	15	9	3
32	26	20	14	8	2
31	25	19	13	7	1

6 miles

Reserved for School Funds

Reserved for Subsequent Sale

A township is usually 6 miles square and contains approximately 36 square miles or sections. One section equals about 640 acres. Inaccuracies of the survey, adjustments to allow for the curvature of the earth, and efforts to accommodate natural features (such as rivers and lakes) and preexisting roads and settlements made perfect rectangular township subdivisions the exception rather than the rule.

LAND SURVEY: ORDINANCE OF 1785

The Northwest Ordinance [1787]

1. Congress shall appoint a governor, a secretary, and three judges for the Northwest Territory. These officials shall adopt suitable laws from the original states. When the territory has "five thousand free male inhabitants of full age," they shall be allowed to elect representatives. These representatives, together with the governor and a legislative council of five, shall form a general assembly to make laws for the territory.

2. The inhabitants shall be entitled to the benefits of trial by jury and other judicial proceedings according to the common law.

3. "Religion, morality, and knowledge being necessary to good government and the happiness of mankind, schools and the means of education shall forever be encouraged."

4. "There shall be formed in the said territory not less than three nor more than five States. . . . And, whenever any of the said States shall have sixty thousand free inhabitants therein, such State shall be admitted, by its delegates, into the Congress of the United States, on an equal footing with the original States."

5. "There shall be neither slavery nor involuntary servitude in the said territory, otherwise than in the punishment of crimes whereof the party shall have been duly convicted."

Cutler, carried their case to Congress. Some of the congressmen themselves disliked Jefferson's idea of creating as many as ten new states north of the Ohio, since these states in time might gain political ascendancy. Soon Congress replaced the original law—which had never gone into actual effect—with the Ordinance of 1787. This famous "Northwest Ordinance" established one Northwest Territory for the time being, provided for its subsequent division into several territories, not fewer than three or more than five, and laid out three stages for the evolution of each territory into a state. In the first stage, Congress-appointed officials would govern the territory; in the second, an elected legislature would share power with them; and in the third, when the people numbered 60,000 or more, they might frame a constitution and apply for statehood. The Northwest Ordinance, embodying as it did the views of conservative Easterners, failed to satisfy the restless inhabitants of the Ohio country.

The Indian policy of Congress fell short of the requirements of land speculators as well as of frontier settlers. In 1785 and 1786 congressional commissioners made treaties with representatives of the Iroquois and other tribes, who thereby surrendered their claims to a stretch of land north of the Ohio in return for comparatively worthless trinkets. Repudiating the treaties, many of the tribesmen went on the warpath. Congress vainly instructed Colonel Josiah Harmar, commanding the federal troops in the Ohio country, to drive the Indians back, then in desperation called upon the aging hero George Rogers Clark to save the frontier. While the campaign against the Indians in the Northwest faltered, a new threat arose in the Southwest, where the Creeks under the half-breed Alexander McGillivray not only repudiated their treaties ceding land but also formed an alliance with the Spaniards to resist the advance of American frontiersmen.

Some of the frontier leaders in the Southwest, instead of fighting the Spaniards, turned to collaborating with them. These leaders and their followers thought for a time that they saw advantages for themselves in the possible creation of a Southwestern confederacy under Spanish tutelage. They might thus get what the United States seemed unable to give them—protection from the Indians, cheap or free land, and an outlet to Eastern and foreign markets through the navigation of the Mississippi. After the collapse of the Jay-Gardoqui negotiations, the "Spanish Conspiracy" began to hum, attracting not only unscrupulous adventurers like General James Wilkinson but also such prominent politicians as William Blount of Kentucky and John Sevier of Tennessee. At the same time, another underground separatist movement was afoot on the far northern frontier. The aspirations of Vermont for statehood having been frustrated by the rival claims of New York and New Hampshire to its soil, the Allen brothers intrigued with British agents to return the Green Mountain country to the British Empire.

Debts, Taxes and Daniel Shays

At the end of the war, foreign ships crowded into American seaports with cargoes of all kinds, and the American people bought extravagantly with cash or credit. In consequence, the wartime accumulations of specie were drained out of the country, consumer indebtedness to importing merchants was multiplied, and a postwar depression lasting from 1784 to 1787 was made worse than it might otherwise have been. The depression, with its money scarcity, bore heavily on debtors both public and private, complicating the financial problems of many citizens and of the Confederation and state governments.

The Confederation government had canceled most of its war debt to Americans by repudiating hundreds of millions of dollars in Continental currency. Yet it still owed a domestic debt estimated at about $34 million in 1783; and through continued borrowings from abroad, mostly from the Netherlands, its foreign debt increased to more than $10 million by 1788. During the 1780s, the government had to make do with uncertain and fluctuating revenues. It could only make requisitions on the states, which often complained of unfairness and refused to comply; as a whole, they paid an average of only about one-sixth of the total that was requested. This was barely enough to meet the government's ordinary operating expenses. To pay the interest on the foreign debt, the secretary of the treasury, Robert Morris, used

the proceeds from the new loans. Thus he maintained an excellent credit rating with Dutch and other foreign bankers. But he could not keep up with the domestic obligations, and the government lost credit at home. At a fraction of the face value, shrewd speculators bought up Confederation certificates of indebtedness from former Revolutionary soldiers and others who had lost hope of payment from Congress and who needed ready cash.

The states, too, came out of the war with large debts, and one by one they added to their obligations by taking over parts of the Confederation debt owed to their respective citizens. Taxable resources varied a good deal from state to state. The chief reliance everywhere was on the direct tax on land and its improvements, the income tax then being exceptional, although Maryland had one. The states supplemented their revenues by means of customs duties and harbor fees, although these tariff and navigation laws served also to protect the states' manufacturers and shippers from foreign competition.

Suffering seriously from the postwar deflation and from the tax burden on their land, the debtor farmers of the country demanded relief in the form of paper money; and seven of the states responded by issuing such currency. Of these seven, Rhode Island went to the greatest extremes, not only designating its paper as legal tender but compelling creditors to accept it or lose the right to collect their debts. While creditors fled from debtors eager to pay in Rhode Island currency, the highest court in the state, in the case of Trevett v. Weeden (1786), held that the monetary legislation was unconstitutional, and the legislature summoned the judges before it and censured them for their action.

The other six states refused to yield to the advocates of inflation and pursued policies of unrelieved taxation to support their public debts. To the state creditors—that is, the bondholders—all this was sound and honest public finance. But it seemed like robbery and tyranny to many of the poverty-stricken farmers, especially in New England, who felt that money was being extorted from them to

Shays's Rebellion
At its peak, Shays's Rebellion involved the
massing of discontented western Massachusetts farmers into something resembling an
army, which blocked the sitting of certain
courts and attacked (unsuccessfully) a federal
arsenal. But well before it was formally organized, the rebellion had been simmering
among debtors, who expressed their resentment of the creditor classes of the east in numerous, spontaneous acts of rebellion and
aggression—such as the brawl depicted here.
(Brown Brothers)

Mobs of distressed farmers rioted in various parts of New England. They caused the
most serious trouble in Massachusetts.
There, the malcontents of the Connecticut
Valley and the Berkshire Hills, many of them
Revolutionary veterans, found a leader in
Daniel Shays, himself a former captain in the
Continental army. Organizing and drilling
his followers, Shays put forth a program of
demands that included paper money, tax relief, a moratorium on debts, the removal of
the state capital from Boston to the interior,
and the abolition of imprisonment for debt.
During the summer of 1786, the Shaysites
concentrated on the immediate task of preventing the collection of debts, private or
public, and went in armed bands from place
to place to break up court sittings and sheriffs' sales. In Boston, members of the legislature, including Samuel Adams, denounced
Shays and his men as rebels and traitors.
When winter came these rebels, instead of
laying down their arms, advanced on Springfield to get more weapons from the arsenal
there. From Boston approached an army of
state militiamen financed by a loan from
wealthy merchants who feared a new revolution. In January 1787, this army met the ragged troops of Shays, killed several of them,
captured many more, and scattered the rest
to the hills in a blinding snowstorm.

As a military enterprise, Shays's Rebellion was a fiasco, yet it had important consequences for the future of the United States.
In Massachusetts, it resulted in a few immediate gains for the discontented groups.
Shays and his lieutenants, at first sentenced
to death, were soon pardoned, and some
concessions to Shays's earlier demands were
granted in the way of tax relief and the post-
ponement of debt payments. Far more significant, the rebellion also affected the country
as a whole by giving added urgency to the
movement for a new constitution.

swell the riches of the wealthy bondholders
in Boston and other towns. At a time when
cash was not to be had, these farmers were
called upon to pay in specie not only state tax
collectors but also mortgage holders and
other private creditors. Debtors who failed to
pay found their mortgages foreclosed and
property seized, and sometimes they found
themselves in jail.

SUGGESTED READINGS

There are several studies of the ideas underlying the
Declaration of Independence. Carl Becker, *The Declaration of Independence* (1922), is a classic work empha-

sizing the influence of John Locke on the Founding
Fathers. Morton White, *The Philosophy of the American
Revolution* (1978), is a more modern version of that

argument. Challenging both is Garry Wills, *Inventing America* (1978), a controversial study emphasizing the influence of Scottish radicals on Jefferson. For studies of Thomas Paine and his influence on the shaping of the American war aims, see Eric Foner, *Tom Paine and Revolutionary America* (1976), a provocative interpretation; and David Hawke, *Paine* (1974), a biography. Other studies of political thought during the Revolution include Peter Shaw, *The Character of John Adams* (1976) and *American Patriots and the Rituals of Revolution* (1981); John R. Howe, Jr., *The Changing Political Thought of John Adams* (1966); and Edmund S. Morgan, *The Meaning of Independence* (1976).

A good introduction to the vast literature on the military history of the Revolution is Willard Wallace, *Appeal to Arms* (1950); or John ꓭ. Alden, *The American Revolution* (1964). Piers Mackesy, *The War for America* (1964), and Don Higginbotham, *The American War for Independence* (1971), are fine, standard accounts, as is Howard H. Peckham, *The War for Independence* (1958). A fuller account can be found in Christopher Ward, *The War of the Revolution*, 2 vols. (1952). John Shy, *A People Numerous and Armed* (1976), is a brilliant study of the social influences on the military effort; Charles Royster, *A Revolutionary People at War* (1979), discusses political ideas and military behavior. G. W. Allen, *Naval History of the American Revolution*, 2 vols. (1913), remains the standard account. See also Samuel Eliot Morison, *John Paul Jones* (1959). Studies of Washington as commander include T. G. Frothingham, *Washington: Commander in Chief* (1930); the appropriate volumes of Douglas Southall Freeman, *George Washington*, 7 vols. (1948–1957); and James T. Flexner, *George Washington in the American Revolution* (1968).

Revolutionary diplomacy is described by Samuel F. Bemis, *The Diplomacy of the American Revolution* (1935). The peace negotiations are recounted in Richard B. Morris, *The Peacemakers* (1965). Gerald Sourzh describes the influence of America's preeminent diplomat in *Benjamin Franklin and American Foreign Policy*, rev. ed. (1969). See also L. S. Kaplan, *Colonies into Nation: American Diplomacy, 1763–1801* (1972). Clarence L. Ver Steeg, *Robert Morris* (1954), and E. J. Ferguson, *The Power of the Purse* (1961), examine the efforts to finance the Revolution.

Important studies of the Loyalists include Wallace Brown, *The King's Friends* (1965); and Robert M. Calhoon, *The Loyalists in Revolutionary America* (1973). The ideas of the Loyalists are examined in Mary Beth Norton, *The British Americans: The Loyalist Exiles in England 1774–1789* (1972); and William H. Nelson, *The American Tory* (1962). Bernard Bailyn, *The Ordeal of Thomas Hutchinson* (1974), is a sensitive biography of a leading Tory. See also Paul H. Smith, *Loyalists and Redcoats* (1964); and James W. St. G. Walker, *The Black Loyalists* (1976). For the experience of women during the Revolution, consult Mary Beth Norton, *Liberty's Daughters* (1980); Linda K. Kerber, *Women of the Republic* (1980); and Linda Grant DePauw, *Found-*

ing Mothers (1975). Carl Degler, *At Odds* (1980), is a sweeping study of women and the family in American history, beginning with the era of the Revolution. The broader social effects of the Revolution are considered in J. F. Jameson, *The American Revolution Considered as a Social Movement* (1962), which argues that the war worked to enhance social and economic democracy. Similar views are expressed in Staughton Lynd, *Class Conflict, Slavery and the United States Constitution* (1968); and Merrill Jensen, *The American Revolution Within America* (1974). Richard McCormick, *Experiment in Independence* (1950), a study of New Jersey in the 1780s, argues that there was little class conflict during the Revolutionary period. Jackson Turner Main, *The Social Structure of Revolutionary America* (1965), emphasizes inequality.

Some of the most significant literature on the Revolutionary period deals with the anomalous existence of slavery in a society fighting a war for "liberty." David Brion Davis, *The Problem of Slavery in the Age of Revolution* (1975), places the issue of slavery in America in a larger world context and traces attitudes toward the institution into the nineteenth century. Edmund S. Morgan, *American Slavery, American Freedom* (1975), suggests that the existence of slavery allowed white Southerners to avoid some of the troubling implications of their Revolutionary ideology. Arthur Zilversmit, *The First Emancipation* (1967), discusses early antislavery activity; and Benjamin Quarles, *The Negro and the American Revolution* (1961), discusses the impact of the struggle on blacks themselves. Duncan MacLeod, *Slavery, Race, and the American Revolution* (1974), is critical of the way the Founding Fathers handled the issue.

Gordon S. Wood, *The Creation of the American Republic* (1969), is the single most important modern study of the formation of state governments. Studies of political developments in individual states include Stephen E. Patterson, *Political Parties in Revolutionary Massachusetts* (1973); and Irwin Polishook, *Rhode Island and the Union, 1774–1795* (1969). Willi Paul Adams, *The First American Constitutions* (1980), is a broader study, as are three works by Jackson Turner Main: *Political Parties Before the Constitution* (1973), *The Sovereign States, 1775–1783* (1973), and *The Upper House in Revolutionary America, 1763–1788* (1967).

The classic account of national politics under the Articles of Confederation is John Fiske, *The Critical Period of American History, 1783–1789* (1883), a bleak portrait of the first national government. Modern studies of this period include Jack N. Rakove, *The Beginnings of National Politics* (1979), which is critical of the Articles; and Merrill Jensen, *The New Nation* (1950) and *The Articles of Confederation*, rev. ed. (1959), which provide more favorable views. H. James Henderson studies national party politics in *Party Politics in the Continental Congress* (1974). Jack Eblen, *The First and Second United States Empires* (1968), studies the administration of the territories from the 1780s into the twentieth century.

The Constitution and the New Republic

6

The Inauguration of Washington
Washington took the oath of office as the first president of the United States in 1789 in New York City. Already, however, he and other members of the new government were making plans for a new capital city. There was wide disagreement at first over where the new capital should be located; but in 1790, when Congress was in the midst of a divisive debate over federal assumption of state debts, Thomas Jefferson, James Madison, and other Southerners agreed to support assumption in return for Northern backing for a national capital in the South. The actual site— on the Potomac River, along the border between Maryland and Virginia—was, despite its swampy and humid character, particularly pleasing to George Washington (after whom the city was to be named), for it was only a few miles from his plantation at Mount Vernon. (Library of Congress)

By the late 1780s, enough Americans had grown dissatisfied with their weak national government—with its factiousness, its instability, its ineffectuality in the face of such crises as Shays' Rebellion—that they were ready to replace it with a stronger, more carefully constructed system. Beginning in 1786, they began to discuss what that new system should be; and in 1787, they created for the nation what the individual states had created for themselves years before: a written constitution and a government consisting of three independent branches.

The American Constitution, although it derived most of its principles from the state documents that had preceded it, is one of history's most remarkable political creations. Out of the contentious atmosphere of a fragile new nation, it created a system of government that would survive for more than two centuries as one of the stablest and most successful in the world. The Constitution was, the nineteenth-century English statesman William Gladstone once remarked, the "most wonderful work ever struck off at a given time by the brain and purpose of man." And although some could argue that Gladstone exaggerated, the American people in the years to come almost universally agreed. Indeed, to them the Constitution took on some of the characteristics of a sacred writing, a holy mystery. Its framers were viewed by later generations as men almost godlike in their wisdom. Its provisions, set out in a brief 7,000 words, were considered for years to come to be an unassailable "fundamental law," from which all public policies, all political principles, all solutions of controversies must spring.

Yet the adoption of the Constitution did not complete the creation of the American Republic. It only defined the terms in which debate over the future of government would continue. Because although most Americans came to agree that the Constitution was a nearly perfect document, they disagreed—at times fundamentally—on what that document said. Some believed that the founders had meant the federal government to exercise broad powers beyond those specifically enumerated in the Constitution—"implied powers," as they were called. Others argued that the framers had intended to limit federal power to the precise areas specified in the Constitution ("expressed powers"), that all other authority would remain at the state level. Out of this disagreement emerged the first great political battle of the new nation.

TOWARD A NEW GOVERNMENT

So unpopular and ineffectual had the Confederation Congress become by the mid-1780s that it began to lead an almost waiflike existence. In 1783, its members timidly withdrew from Philadelphia to escape from the clamor of army veterans demanding their back pay. They took refuge for a while in Princeton, New Jersey, then moved on to Annapolis, and in 1785 settled in New York.

Through all of this, the members of Congress were often conspicuous largely by their absence. Only with great difficulty was a quorum secured to permit ratification of the treaty with Great Britain ending the Revolutionary War. The Confederation's most important piece of legislation, the Northwest Ordinance, was voted on by a mere eighteen members, representing only eight states. In the meantime, a major public debate was beginning over the future of America's national government.

Advocates of Centralization

Weak and unpopular though the Confederation government was, it satisfied for a time a great many—probably a majority—of the people. They did not want a strong or prestigious central government. Having just fought the Revolutionary War to avert the danger of remote and, to them, tyrannical authority, they desired to keep the centers of political power close to home in the thirteen states.

Others, however, either disliked the Articles of Confederation from the outset or came eventually to desire something different. Disgruntled at the refusal of Congress to grant them half pay for life, some of the military men through their exclusive and hereditary Society of the Cincinnati hoped to control and invigorate the government, some of them even aspiring to a kind of army dictatorship. Artisans or "mechanics," the manufacturers of the time, preferred a uniformly high national tariff to the varying state tariffs. Merchants and shippers preferred a single and effective commercial policy to thirteen different and ineffective ones. Land speculators wished to see the "Indian menace" finally removed from their Western tracts, and creditors desired to stop the state issues of paper money. Investors in Confederation securities hoped to have the Confederation debt made good and the value of their securities enhanced. Large property owners in general looked for a reliable means of safety from the threat of mobs.

The issue was not whether the Confederation should be changed but how drastic the changes should be. Even its defenders reluctantly came to agree that the government needed strengthening at its weakest point—its lack of power to tax. To save the Articles of Confederation, its friends backed the impost amendment of 1782, which would have authorized Congress to levy customs duties. All the states ratified the amendment except Rhode Island, whose single veto was enough to kill it. The next year, a similar amendment was accepted by Rhode Island but defeated by New York. Later, the states' rights advocates proposed that the states make to Congress a temporary and qualified grant of taxing authority (not an amendment to the Articles), but most of the centralizers had by then begun to lose interest in such remedies. They were now beginning to insist on a much more thoroughgoing change.

The most resourceful of the reformers was the political genius, New York lawyer, onetime military aide to General Washington, and illegitimate son of a Scottish merchant in the West Indies—Alexander Hamilton. From the beginning, he had been dissatisfied with the Articles of Confederation, had seen little to be gained by piecemeal amendments, and had urged the holding of a national convention to overhaul the entire document. To this end, he took advantage of a movement for interstate cooperation that began in 1785 when a group of Marylanders and Virginians met in Alexandria to settle differences between the two states.

One of the Virginians, James Madison, who was as eager as Hamilton to see a stronger government, induced the Virginia legislature to invite all the states to send delegates to a larger conference on commercial questions. This group met at Annapolis in 1786, but representatives from only five states appeared. Hamilton, a delegate from New York, took satisfaction in seeing the conference adopt his report and send copies to the state legislatures and to Congress. His report recommended that Congress call a convention of special delegates from all the states to gather in Philadelphia the next year and consider ways to "render the constitution of the Federal government adequate to the exigencies of the union."

At that moment, in 1786, there seemed little possibility that the Philadelphia convention would be any better attended or would accomplish any more than the previous meeting at Annapolis. Only the leadership of Washington would make success possible. At the time, however, Washington's participation was far from certain. One of the wealthiest men in the country, but temporarily short of cash, he doubted whether he would undertake the trouble and expense of a trip to Philadelphia.

Alexander Hamilton
Many believed that Hamilton was the real head of the federal government during the first years of the Washington administration and that the president himself was little more than a figurehead. It was an impression Hamilton did nothing to discourage; on one occasion, he referred to Washington as "an aegis very necessary to me." Whether or not Hamilton's power was as great as was popularly supposed, he emerged as the clear leader of the faction within the new government that favored strong federal authority; and it was around him that the Federalist party began to develop. Hamilton served as secretary of the treasury from 1789 to 1795 and remained influential within the government in the following years even though he held no official post. In the election of 1800, he lobbied in Congress for the election of Thomas Jefferson (who was tied in the electoral voting with Aaron Burr). In 1804, he helped ensure Burr's defeat in a race for governor of New York. The embittered Burr challenged Hamilton to a duel that same year and mortally wounded him. (Library of Congress)

Then, early in 1787, the news of commotion and bloodshed in Massachusetts spread throughout the country and the world, news that seemed to foretell other and more dangerous insurrections than that of Shays. In Paris the American minister, Thomas Jefferson, was not alarmed. "I hold," he confided in a letter to James Madison, "that a little rebellion, now and then, is a good thing, and as necessary in the political world as storms in the physical." At Mount Vernon, however, Washington did not take the news so calmly. "There are combustibles in every State which a spark might set fire to," he exclaimed. "I feel infinitely more than I can express for the disorders which have arisen. Good God!"

James Madison
Although often overshadowed by the more charismatic Thomas Jefferson, Madison was at least as responsible for devising many of the theories that underlay the new republic. And with Jefferson, he served as a focal point for those opponents of Hamilton who worked in the late 1790s to unseat the Federalists and install leaders favoring a less powerful federal government. Yet Madison and Jefferson had not always been in full agreement. During the debate over the Constitution, Jefferson had favored the addition of a Bill of Rights. Madison, on the other hand, argued that a written declaration of rights should be avoided, that any such declaration could be construed as *limiting* rights rather than guaranteeing them. Madison's concerns found expression, finally, in the Ninth Amendment, which stated that "the enumeration in the Constitution of certain rights shall not be construed to deny or disparage others retained by the people." (Library of Congress)

Washington refused to listen to renewed suggestions that he make himself a military dictator. But after Congress had issued its calls for a constitutional convention, he borrowed money for the journey and, in May, left Mount Vernon for Philadelphia.

A Divided Convention

Fifty-five men, representing all the states except Rhode Island, attended one or more sessions of the convention that sat in the Philadelphia State House from May to September, 1787. Never before or since has there been a more distinguished gathering in America. These "Founding Fathers," as they were later to become known, instead of being gray-bearded ancients as the term implies, were on the whole relatively young men, many of them in their twenties and thirties and only one (Benjamin Franklin) extremely old; his eighty-one years raised the average age from forty-three to forty-four. Despite their comparative youth, the delegates were men of vast practical experience in business, plantation management, and politics; and they were well educated for their time, more than a third of them being college graduates. Most of them represented the great property interests of the country. Many feared what one of them called the "turbulence and follies" of democracy.

Most of the constitution makers agreed that the United States needed a stronger central government. There were differences of opinion, however, as to how much stronger the government should be, what specific powers it should have, and what structure it should be given. There were differences, in particular, over the relative influence the large and small states should exert in the new system, and over provisions for the protection and promotion of economic interests in different sections of the country.

Among the states, Virginia was then much the largest in population—more than twice as large as New York, more than four times as large as New Jersey, more than ten times as large as Delaware. Among the delegations at Philadelphia, the Virginians were also the best prepared for the work of the convention. And among the Virginians, James Madison (aged thirty-six) was the intellectual leader. Already, before the convention met, he had devised in some detail a plan for a new "national" government. The Virginians took the initiative from the moment the convention began.

Washington was easily elected to preside, and then a resolution was passed to keep the proceedings absolutely secret. Next, Edmund Randolph of Virginia proposed that "a *national* government ought to be established, consisting of a *supreme* Legislative, Executive, and Judiciary." This proposal being approved, Randolph introduced the plan that Madison already had worked out. The Virginia Plan, if adopted, would give the larger influence to the richer and more populous states. It would also mean abandoning the Articles of Confederation and building the government anew.

But the existing Congress had called the convention "for the sole and express purpose of revising the Articles of Confederation," and the states in commissioning their "deputies" had authorized them to do no more than revise the Articles. Some of the delegates—especially those from the smaller states—now raised doubts whether the convention properly could entertain such proposals as were embodied in the Virginia Plan. At first, however, these men had nothing to offer in its stead. After some delay, William Paterson of New Jersey submitted an alternative scheme for a "federal" as opposed to a "national" government. The New Jersey Plan was intended only to revise and strengthen the Articles.

The stage was now set for a full debate between large-state and small-state delegates—between advocates of a national system (nationalists—those who wished a powerful central government, on the European

---

The Virginia Plan [1787]

The following branches of government were recommended in the Virginia Plan:

1. A "National Legislature," with the states represented in proportion either to their "quotas of contribution" or to "the number of free inhabitants." Two branches, the members of the first to be elected by the people, the members of the second to be nominated by the state legislatures and elected by the first. Powers: to "legislate in all cases to which the separate states are incompetent," to "negative all laws passed by the several states, contravening in the opinion of the National Legislature the articles of Union," and to use force against recalcitrant states.
2. A single "National Executive" to be chosen by the National Legislature.
3. A "National Judiciary" to be chosen by the National Legislature.
4. A "Council of Revision," consisting of the National Executive and part of the National Judiciary, with power to "examine" and reject state and national laws before they went into effect.

The New Jersey Plan [1787]

The main features of the New Jersey Plan were:

1. The continuance of the existing one-house Congress, with one vote for each state, but with the following additional powers: to raise a revenue from import duties, stamp taxes, and postage; to regulate interstate and foreign commerce; and to provide for the collection of taxes within any state failing to pay its share of the requisitions upon the states.
2. A plural "Federal Executive" to be elected by Congress.
3. A "Federal Judiciary" to be appointed by the Executive.
4. The establishment of acts of Congress and federal treaties as the "supreme law" of the states, and the authorization of the Federal Executive to "call forth the power of the Confederated States . . . to enforce and compel an obedience."

nation-state model) and of a federal system (federalists—those who favored a looser confederation, in which power would be shared among the federal and state governments). The Virginia Plan went much too far to suit the federalists. To them, one of its worst features was the system of representation in the proposed two-house legislature. In the lower house, if the states were to be represented in proportion to their population, the largest state (Virginia) would have about ten times as many representatives as the smallest (Delaware). In the upper house, if its members were to be elected by the lower house, some of the smaller states at any given time might have no members at all. To the small-state delegates, both the Congress of the Articles of Confederation and the Congress of the New Jersey Plan at least had the merit of equal representation for all the states, regardless of size. But the New Jersey Plan gained the support of only a minority and, after much argument, was tabled.

The Virginia Plan was left as the basis for discussion. Its proponents realized that they would have to make concessions to the small-state men if the convention were ever to reach a general agreement. The majority soon conceded an important point by consenting that the members of the upper house should be elected by the state legislatures rather than by the lower house of the national legislature. Thus each state would be sure of always having at least one member in the upper house, but there remained the question of how many members each state should have.

There remained also the question of the number of representatives each state should have in the lower house. If the number was to depend on population, were slaves to be included in the population figure? The delegates from the states where slavery seemed a permanent institution—especially those from South Carolina—insisted that slaves should be counted as persons (though not, of course, entitled to vote) in determining a state's representation. But these delegates argued that slaves ought to be considered as property, not as persons, when it was proposed that the new legislature be allowed to levy a direct tax (such as a land or poll tax) on each state in proportion to its population. Men who came from states where slavery had disappeared or was expected to disappear argued that slaves should be included in calculating taxation but not representation. Thus an issue between slave and free states was added to the one between large and small states.

Differences Compromised

On these and other matters, the delegates bickered day after day. By the end of June, as both temperature and tempers rose to uncomfortable heights, the convention seemed in danger of breaking up, with nothing accomplished. If this should happen, the men at Philadelphia would "become a reproach and by-word down to future ages," said the venerable Franklin, the voice of calmness and conciliation throughout the summer. "And what is worse, mankind may hereafter, from this unfortunate instance, despair of establishing governments by human wisdom, and leave it to chance, war and conquest."

Through the calming influence of Franklin and others, especially Oliver Ellsworth of Connecticut, the delegates managed to settle the most serious of their disputes and go on with their work. A committee of twelve, with one member from each state, brought in a report that culminated in what afterward was known as the "Great Compromise" (adopted on July 16, 1787). One part of this report provided that the states should be represented in the lower house in proportion to their population, and that three-fifths of the slaves should be included in determining the basis for both representation and direct taxation. The three-fifths formula, though seemingly arbitrary, was based on the assumption that, in contributing his labor to the wealth of a state, a slave was on the average three-fifths as productive as a freeman. Another part of the Great Compromise provided that in the upper house, the states should be represented equally with two members apiece.

In the ensuing weeks, while committees busied themselves with various parts of the document that was beginning to take shape, the convention as a whole effected another compromise, this one having to do with the legislative power to impose tariffs and regulate commerce. The men from some of the Southern states feared that this power might be used for levying export duties on their crops, interfering with the slave trade, and making commercial agreements (as in the recent Jay-Gardoqui treaty) that would sacrifice the interests of rice and tobacco growers. The South Carolinians proposed that a two-thirds vote in the legislature be required not only to approve commercial treaties but also to pass commercial laws. Although it did not accept this proposal, the convention made concessions by forbidding the legislature to levy a tax on exports, to put a duty of more than ten dollars a head on imported slaves, or to prohibit slave importations until twenty years had elapsed.

Some differences of opinion the convention was unable to harmonize, and it disposed of them by evasion or omission. One concerned the question whether the new courts or some special agency should be empowered to review legislative acts and set them aside. The "council of revision," a part of the original Virginia Plan, was dropped, and no provision was added to confer the power of judicial review explicitly upon the courts.

The Constitution, as it finally took form at the end of summer in 1787, though an outgrowth of the Virginia Plan, was in some respects so different that Randolph himself refused to sign it. Yet it differed even more from the New Jersey Plan, and several refused on that account to give it their approval. Indeed, the completed document did not entirely satisfy any of the delegates. Nevertheless, thirty-nine of them affixed their signatures to it, doubtless with much the same feeling that Franklin expressed. "Thus I consent, Sir, to this Constitution," he said, *"because I expect no better, and because I am not sure that it is not the best."*

The Constitution of 1787

Madison, who was responsible for most of the actual drafting, observed that it was, "in strictness, neither a national nor a federal Constitution, but a composition of both."

Certainly it possessed some strongly national features. The Constitution and all laws and treaties made under it were to be the "supreme law" of the land, regardless of anything to the contrary in the constitution or laws of any state. Broad powers were granted to the central government, including the congressional powers of taxation, regulation of commerce, control of money, and the passage of laws "necessary and proper" for carrying out its specific powers. At the same time, the states were deprived of a number of the powers—such as the issuance of money and the passage of laws "impairing the obligation of contracts," for example, laws postponing the payment of debts—that they had been free to exercise under the Articles of Confederation. Now all state officials were to be required to take an oath of allegiance to the Constitution, and the state militias were to be made available, on call, for enforcing the new "supreme law." Nowhere were the former claims of the states to individual sovereignty recognized. Gone was the stipulation of the Articles that "each State shall retain every power, jurisdiction, and right not *expressly* delegated to the United States in Congress assembled." Lacking was any bill of rights to limit the central government as the state bills limited the state governments.

On the other hand, the Constitution was federal in setting up a government that presupposed the existence of separate states and left wide powers to them. For instance, the states were to be represented as separate and equal entities in one of the two branches of the new legislature.

Within the allotted sphere of its powers, the new government was authorized to act directly upon the power of the United States. It would not have to act upon them solely through the member states, as the previous Confederation government had done. Here, then, was something new and unique, something for which old terms were hardly adequate. It was a combination of two kinds of government, state and central, with each of them intended to be supreme within its respective sphere.

This system of divided authority marked the final resolution of an ideological struggle that had been in progress since the earliest days of the Revolutionary crisis: a struggle over the nature of sovereignty. Perhaps the greater obstacle to a resolution of America's disagreements with Great Britain had been the idea that sovereignty could not, by definition, be divided, that it must ultimately reside in a single place. In British eyes, that place had been Parliament, where the authority of king, Lords, and Commons meshed to produce a stable center of power. Thus American insistence that the colonial assemblies were sovereign in certain matters (for example, internal taxation) while Parliament remained sovereign in others (such as regulation of imperial trade) seemed to the English a logical impossibility.

The construction of the federal Constitution raised such issues again in different form. How could a national government exercise sovereignty concurrently with state governments? Where did ultimate sovereignty lie? The answer, Americans decided, was that all power, at all levels of government, flowed ultimately from the people. Thus neither the federal government nor the state governments were truly sovereign. All of them derived their authority from below. The logical obstacle to the distribution of authority among different branches or different levels of government was thus removed. The federal Constitution contained few major innovations in the internal structure of the central government. Most of its institutions were modeled on the state constitutions that had preceded it. But in resolving the issue of sovereignty and in producing the idea of federalism, the American Constitution well earned its position as one of history's most important political documents.

Next to the distinctive federal arrangement (the "division of powers"), the most striking feature of the new system was the complex organization and operation of the central government itself, with its checks and balances among the legislative, executive, and judicial branches (the "separation of powers"). There was the new Congress, with its two chambers, the Senate and the House of Representatives, each with members elected in a different way and for different terms, and each checking the other, since both must agree before any law could be passed. There was the single executive, the president, who was to be chosen by special electors, who themselves were to be chosen in whatever way the separate states might designate. The electors, meeting in isolated groups, state by state, were to cast their ballots as they saw fit, and if any man should receive a majority of the electoral votes, he would be president. It was assumed, however, that usually no man would get a majority, and then the final selection among the leading candidates would be up to the House of Representatives. Thus the election of a president would be far removed from the mass of the people. Yet the president, in addition to other powers, would have the power of vetoing acts of Congress. There was also the Supreme Court, which was still further removed from the ordinary voters, since the president with the consent of the Senate was to appoint the judges for life. And while nothing was said in the Constitution itself about the power of reviewing and disallowing presidential actions or congressional acts, the Supreme Court could be expected to have some authority over them.

This complicated structure resulted from accident—that is, from the compromising of contradictory views—as much as from deliberate planning. Nevertheless, the complexity was such as to give the framers hope that no single group or combination of groups in the country could ever gain absolute and unchecked power. A government so divided against itself ought to frustrate tyranny from whatever source. When the framers spoke of tyranny, they usually had in mind not only their memories of English oppression, but even more prominently their fears of the rule of mobs and demagogues—the threat of such leaders as Daniel Shays.

ADOPTION AND ADAPTATION

Since the delegates at Philadelphia had exceeded their instructions from Congress and the states, they had reason to doubt whether the Constitution would ever be ratified if

The Background of the Constitution

The debate among historians about the motives of those who framed the American Constitution mirrors in many ways the debate about the causes of the American Revolution. To some, the creation of the federal system was an effort to preserve the ideals of the Revolution by eliminating the disorder and contention that threatened the new nation. To others, supporters of the Constitution appear to have been men attempting to protect their own economic interests, even at the cost of betraying the principles of the Revolution.

The first and most influential exponent of the former view was John Fiske, whose book *The Critical Period of American History* (1888) painted a grim picture of political life under the Articles of Confederation. The nation was, Fiske argued, reeling under the impact of a business depression, the weakness and ineptitude of the national government, the threats to American territory from Great Britain and Spain, the inability of either Congress or the state governments to make good their debts, the interstate jealousies and barriers to trade, the widespread use of inflation-producing paper money, and the lawlessness that culminated in Shays' Rebellion. Only the timely adoption of the Constitution, Fiske claimed, saved the young republic from disaster.

Fiske's view met with little dissent until 1913, when Charles A. Beard, one of the greatest of American historians, published a powerful challenge to it in *An Economic Interpretation of the Constitution of the United States*. According to Beard, the 1780s had been a "critical period" not for the nation as a whole, but for certain conservative business interests who feared that the decentralized political structure of the republic imperiled their financial positions. Such men, he claimed, wanted a government able to promote industry and trade, protect private property, and perhaps most of all, make good the public debt—much of which was owed to them. The Constitution was, Beard claimed, "an economic document drawn with superb skill by men whose property interests were immediately at stake" and who won its ratification over the opposition of a majority of the people. Were it not for their impatience and determination, he argued in a later book (1927), the Articles of Confederation might have formed a perfectly satisfactory, permanent form of government. The Beard view of the Constitution influenced more than a generation of historians. Such scholars as Merrill Jensen continued to argue into the 1950s, in *The New Nation* (1950), that the 1780s were not years of chaos and despair, but a time of hopeful striving; that only the

they followed the procedures laid down in the Articles of Confederation, which required *all* of the state *legislatures* to approve alterations in the form of the government. So the convention changed the rules, specifying in the Constitution that the new government should go into effect among the ratifying states when only *nine* of the thirteen had ratified, and recommending to Congress that the Constitution be submitted to specially called state *conventions* rather than to the legislatures of the states.

The "Federalists" and the "Antifederalists"

The Congress in New York, completely overshadowed by the convention in Philadelphia, accepted the latter's work and submitted it to the states for their approval or disapproval. The state legislatures, again with the exception of Rhode Island, arranged for the election of delegates to ratifying conventions, and sooner or later each of these conventions got down to business. Meanwhile, from the economic interests of a small group of wealthy men can account for the creation of the Constitution.

But the 1950s also produced a series of powerful and persuasive challenges to the Beard thesis. Robert E. Brown, for example, argued in 1956 that "absolutely no correlation" could be shown between the wealth of the delegates to the Constitutional Convention and their position on the Constitution. Forrest McDonald, in *We the People* (1958), looked beyond the convention itself to the debate between the Federalists and the Antifederalists and concluded similarly that there was no consistent relationship between wealth and property on the one hand and support for the Constitution on the other. Instead, opinion on the new system was far more likely to reflect local and regional interests. Areas suffering social and economic distress were likely to support the Constitution; states that were stable and prosperous were likely to oppose it. There was no intercolonial class of monied interests operating in concert to produce the Constitution.

The cumulative effect of these attacks has been virtually to destroy Beard's argument; hardly any historians any longer accept his thesis without reservation. By the 1960s, however, a new group of scholars was beginning to revive an economic interpretation of the Constitution—one that differed from Beard's in important ways but that nevertheless emphasized social and economic factors as motives for supporting the federal system. Jackson Turner Main argued, in *The Antifederalists* (1961), that supporters of the Constitution, while not perhaps the united creditor class that Beard described, were nevertheless wealthier than critics of the document; that they were people of higher station (and thus had a greater concern for preserving the existing social order) than were the Antifederalists. Gordon Wood's important study, *The Creation of the American Republic* (1969), de-emphasized economic grievances but nevertheless suggested that profound social divisions found reflection in the debate over the state constitutions in the 1770s and 1780s; and that those same divisions helped shape the argument over the federal Constitution. The Federalists, in other words, were not a self-interested creditor class, but neither were they disinterested idealists. They were representatives of a widespread but far from unanimous popular belief that order and stability were more important to the republic than some of the more radical Revolutionary ideals.

Other historians have taken a somewhat different approach, stressing not so much class divisions or economic interests as generational differences. Stanley Elkins and Eric McKitrick argued in a 1961 article ("The Founding Fathers," *Political Science Quarterly*) that the Federalists tended to be younger men than the Antifederalists; that they saw the development of a strong, united nation as the key to their own futures. Pauline Maier, in *The Old Revolutionaries* (1980), offered portraits of early leaders of the resistance to Britain as they observed post-Revolutionary America, and she suggested similarly that the transition from one generation to the next produced profound changes in political outlook.

fall of 1787 to the summer of 1788, the merits and demerits of the new Constitution were debated in the legislatures, in mass meetings, and in the columns of newspapers, as well as in the convention halls. For the most part the struggle, though intense, was peaceful and deliberative, yet the opposing factions sometimes came to blows. In at least one place—Albany, New York—such clashes resulted in injuries and death.

Despite the reference of its preamble to "We the people," the Constitution was not literally ordained and established by the whole people of the United States. In the elections for the state conventions, approximately three-fourths of the adult white males in the country failed to vote for delegates, mainly because of indifference, and therefore exercised no real influence on the outcome. Of those who did vote, a large majority favored ratification. The voters, however, did not have a clear-cut choice between a "federal" and a "national" government. The issues were confused, both because of the "mixed" character of the Constitution itself and because of the terminology that was employed in the ratification debates. Since the idea of a strongly national government was thought to be unpopular, the advocates of the new Constitution chose to call themselves "Federalists" and to call their opponents "Antifederalists." These misnomers stuck, despite the insistence of opponents of ratification that they were "Federal Republicans," the true federalists of the time.

The friends of the Constitution had a number of advantages. They possessed a positive program and an appealing name, while the Antifederalists by that very word were made to stand for nothing constructive,

for chaos itself. The Federalists were the better-organized group and had the weight of fame and superior leadership on their side. They could point to the support of the two most eminent men in America, Franklin and Washington. And Washington himself declared that the choice lay between the Constitution and disunion. The Federalists also included some of the most profound political philosophers of any period or place in Hamilton, Madison, and Jay, who under the joint pseudonym "Publius" wrote a long series of newspaper essays expounding the meaning and virtues of the Constitution. Afterward published in book form as *The Federalist Papers*, these essays have been described as

---

The Federalist No. 1 [1787]

The series of essays known as The Federalist Papers *were published anonymously, over the single pen name "Publius." In fact, they were the work of three men: Alexander Hamilton, James Madison, and John Jay. This first essay, written by Hamilton, summarizes the purposes of the papers to come.*

After an unequivocal experience of the inefficacy of the subsisting federal government, you are called upon to deliberate on a new Constitution for the United States of America. The subject speaks its own importance; comprehending in its consequences nothing less than the existence of the UNION, the safety and welfare of the parts of which it is composed, the fate of an empire in many respects the most interesting in the world. It has been frequently remarked that it seems to have been reserved to the people of this country, by their conduct and example, to decide the important question, whether societies of men are really capable or not of establishing good government from reflection and choice, or whether they are forever destined to depend for their political constitutions on accident and force. If there be any truth in the remark, the crisis at which we are arrived may with propriety be regarded as the era in which that decision is to be made; and a wrong elec-

tion of the part we shall act may, in this view, deserve to be considered as the general misfortune of mankind. . . .

I propose, in a series of papers, to discuss the following interesting particulars:—*The utility of the* UNION *to your political prosperity—The insufficiency of the present Confederation to preserve that Union— The necessity of a government at least equally energetic with the one proposed, to the attainment of this object—The conformity of the proposed Constitution to the true principles of republican government—Its analogy to your own State constitution*—and lastly, *The additional security which its adoption will afford to the preservation of that species of government, to liberty, and to property.*

In the progress of this discussion I shall endeavor to give a satisfactory answer to all the objections which shall have made their appearance, that may seem to have any claim to your attention. . . .

PUBLIUS

the most authoritative of all constitutional commentaries and, indeed, as one of the greatest of all treatises on political science.

The opponents of ratification produced no comparable set of Antifederalist papers, but they made a vigorous case for themselves in their own speeches and newspaper propaganda. Necessarily, the Antifederalists resorted mainly to negative argument. The Constitution, they protested, was illegal—as indeed it was if judged by the Articles of Confederation, the existing fundamental law. The new government would increase taxes, obliterate the states, wield dictatorial powers, favor the "well born" over the common people, and put an end to individual liberty, the Antifederalists added. Of all their specific criticisms the most compelling was this: the Constitution lacked a bill of rights.

The Antifederalist concern about inclusion of a bill of rights revealed one of the most important sources of their opposition to the new Constitution: a basic mistrust of human nature and of the capacity of man to wield power. Reflecting the early Revolutionary fears of corruption and tyranny, many Antifederalists argued that any government that centralized authority in the hands of powerful men would inevitably produce despotism. Only by so weakening government, so dividing authority that no individual or group could gain great power, could society be protected against tyranny. The idea of a bill of rights, therefore, reflected a belief that no government could be trusted not to infringe on the liberties of its citizens; only by enumerating the natural rights of the people could there be any certainty that those rights would be protected.

For all the efforts of the Antifederalists, ratification proceeded during the winter of 1787–1788. Delaware, the first to act, did so unanimously, as did two others of the smallest states, New Jersey and Georgia. In the large states of Pennsylvania and Massachusetts the Antifederalists put up a determined struggle but lost in the final vote. By June 1788, when the New Hampshire convention at last made up its mind, nine of the states had ratified and thus had made it possible for the Constitution to go into effect.

A new government could hardly hope to

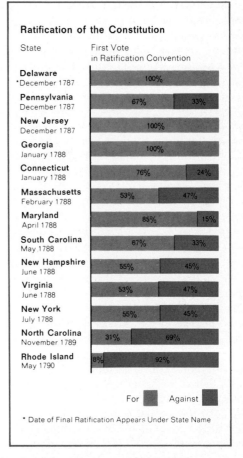

Ratification of the Constitution

State	First Vote in Ratification Convention	
Delaware *December 1787	100%	
Pennsylvania December 1787	67%	33%
New Jersey December 1787	100%	
Georgia January 1788	100%	
Connecticut January 1788	76%	24%
Massachusetts February 1788	53%	47%
Maryland April 1788	85%	15%
South Carolina May 1788	67%	33%
New Hampshire June 1788	55%	45%
Virginia June 1788	53%	47%
New York July 1788	55%	45%
North Carolina November 1789	31%	69%
Rhode Island May 1790	8%	92%

For ▪ Against ▪

* Date of Final Ratification Appears Under State Name

The Constitution was promptly and overwhelmingly approved by the ratifying conventions of some of the smaller states, such as Delaware, New Jersey, and Georgia. But it barely got by in the large states of Massachusetts, Virginia, and New York. It was approved by North Carolina and Rhode Island only after it had already gone into effect. The conventions in these two states waited until they were sure a bill of rights would be added.

succeed, however, without the participation of Virginia and New York, whose conventions remained closely divided. Before the end of the month, Virginia and then New York consented to the Constitution by narrow votes. The New York convention yielded to expediency—even some of the most staunchly Antifederalist delegates feared that the state's commercial interests would suffer if, once the other states gathered under the "New Roof," New York were to remain outside. Massachusetts, Virginia, and New York all ratified on the assumption, though not on the express condition, that certain desired amendments would be added to the Constitution, above all a bill of rights. Deciding to wait and see what became of these hopes for amendment, the North Carolina convention adjourned without taking action. Rhode Island, for the time being, did not even call a convention to consider ratification.

Completing the Structure

When the first elections under the Constitution were held, in the early months of 1789, the results showed that the new government was to be in the hands of its friends. Few if any of the newly elected congressmen and senators had been extreme Antifederalists; almost all had favored ratification, and many had served as delegates to the Philadelphia convention. The president-elect, George Washington, had presided at the convention; many who had favored ratification did so because they expected him to preside over the new government also. He received the votes of all the presidential electors, whom the states, either by legislative action or by popular election, had named. John Adams, who was a firm Federalist, though not a member of the convention, received the next highest number of electoral votes and hence was to be vice president.

For the time being, the seat of government was to continue to be the city of New York; the sensibilities of the geographical sections were thus neatly balanced, the president being from the South, the vice president from New England, and the capital in one of the middle states. Congressmen were so slow to reach New York that not until April was a quorum on hand to make an official count of the electoral vote and send a messenger to notify General Washington of his election. After a journey from Mount Vernon marked by elaborate celebrations along the way, Washington was inaugurated on April 30.

The responsibilities facing the first president and the first Congress were in some ways greater than those facing any president or Congress to follow. Though these men of 1789 had the Constitution as a guide, that document provided only a general plan that had yet to be applied to specific situations as they arose. It left many questions unanswered. What, for example, should be the rules of the two houses for the conduct of their business? What code of etiquette should govern the relations between the president on the one hand and Congress and the people on the other? Should the chief executive have some high-sounding title, such as "His Highness the President of the United States and Protector of Their Liberties"? (Vice President John Adams believed both he and the president ought to have dignified forms of address.) What was the true meaning of various ambiguous phrases in the Constitution? In answering these and other questions, Washington and his colleagues knew they were setting precedents that, in many cases, would give lasting direction to the development of the Constitution in actual practice.

By filling certain gaps in the Constitution, the first Congress served almost as a continuation of the Constitutional Convention. Most conspicuous was the drafting of a bill of rights, which proponents of the Constitution had promised in order to conciliate the Antifederalists. There were some who continued to have reservations about the propriety of enumerating rights. James Madison, for example, had long argued that including a list of human rights would have the effect of limiting those rights—that future governments would tend to act on the assumption that unless a right was written down it did not exist. Far healthier, Madison argued, was an assumption that the people retained *all* rights, except those specifically limited by the Constitution. But despite such reservations, virtually all supporters of the Constitution agreed by early 1789 that some sort of bill of rights would be essential to legitimize the new government in the eyes of its opponents.

Dozens of amendments intended to make up for the absence of an enumeration of rights had been proposed in the state ratifying conventions, and Congress now undertook the task of sorting these, reducing them

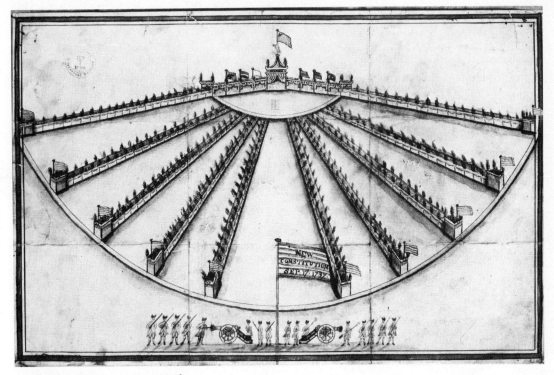

Ratification Banquet, New York
The New York convention ratified the Constitution on July 26, 1788. Three days earlier, confident that the convention was going to act favorably, 6,000 citizens of New York City gathered to celebrate. After parades, they took their places in a gigantic pavilion to feast and to listen to speeches. From a contemporary drawing. (Courtesy of the New-York Historical Society, New York City)

to a manageable number, and sending them to the states for ratification. Of the twelve sent out, ten were ratified, and they took effect in 1791. (Thus, what we know as the Bill of Rights is, in legal terms, simply the first ten amendments to the Constitution.) The first nine of them limited Congress by forbidding it to infringe on certain basic rights, such as freedom of religion, of speech, and of the press, immunity from arbitrary arrest, and trial by jury. The Tenth Amendment reserved to the states all powers except those specifically withheld from them or delegated to the federal government.

In regard to the structure of the federal courts, the Constitution had only this to say: "The judicial power of the United States shall be vested in one Supreme Court, and in such inferior courts as the Congress may from time to time ordain and establish."

Thus the convention had left up to Congress the number of Supreme Court judges to be appointed and the kinds of lower courts to be organized. In the Judiciary Act of 1789, Congress provided for a Supreme Court of six members, with one chief justice and five associate justices; for thirteen district courts with one judge apiece; and for three circuit courts, each to consist of one of the district judges sitting with two of the Supreme Court justices. In the same act, Congress gave the Supreme Court the power to make the final decision in cases involving the constitutionality of state laws. If the Constitution was in fact to be the "supreme law of the land," the various state courts could not be left to decide for themselves whether the state legislatures were violating that supreme law.

As for executive departments, the Constitution referred indirectly to them but did not specify what or how many they should be. The first Congress created three such departments—state, treasury, and war—and also established the offices of attorney general and postmaster general.

In appointing department heads and other high officials, President Washington selected men who were well disposed toward the Constitution (no Antifederalists), and who as a group would provide a balanced representation of the different sections of the country. To the office of secretary of the treasury he appointed Alexander Hamilton of New York, who had taken the lead in calling the Constitutional Convention and who, though only thirty-two, was an expert in public finance. For secretary of war he chose a Massachusetts Federalist, General Henry Knox. As attorney general he named Edmund Randolph of Virginia, sponsor of the plan on which the Constitution had been based. He picked as secretary of state another Virginian, Thomas Jefferson, who had been away from the country as minister to France.

From time to time, Washington called on these four men for advice, usually as individuals. They did not form a cabinet in the sense of a group of presidential counselors holding regular meetings (the cabinet in this sense began to develop during the presidency of Jefferson). When Washington took office he supposed, as did many others, that the Senate would act for certain purposes as an advisory council, since according to the Constitution the Senate was to give its advice and consent for the appointment of high officials and for the ratification of treaties. With only twenty-two members in the beginning, the Senate was small enough so that Washington could expect to consult personally with it. He changed his mind, however, after taking a treaty draft to the senators for their advice. They demanded that he leave the document for them to inspect and change at their leisure, and he refused, resolving never again to submit a treaty to the senators until its negotiation had been completed. Thus he set a precedent in treaty making that for the most part his successors have followed.

HAMILTON AGAINST JEFFERSON, FEDERALISTS AGAINST REPUBLICANS

The resolution of these initial issues stopped far short, however, of resolving the disagreements about the nature of the new government. On the contrary, for the first twelve years under the Constitution, American politics was characterized by a level of acrimony seldom matched in any period since. The framers of the Constitution had resolved disagreements among the various factions by making a series of vague compromises; as a result, the disagreements survived to plague the new government.

At the heart of the controversies of the 1790s was the same basic difference in philosophy that had lain at the heart of the debate over the Constitution. On one side stood a powerful group who believed that America required a strong, *national* government: that the country's mission was to become a genuine nation-state, with centralized authority, a complex commercial economy, and a proud

standing in world affairs. On the other side stood another group—a minority at first, but gaining strength during the decade—who envisioned a far more modest central government. It would be stronger than that under the Confederation, to be sure; but it would remain a far weaker instrument than the European equivalents. Moreover, American society should not, this group believed, aspire to be highly commercial or urban. It should remain predominantly rural and agrarian.

The two factions soon took on many of the attributes of political parties. The centralizers became known as the Federalists and gravitated to the leadership of Alexander Hamilton. Their opponents acquired the name Republicans and gathered under the leadership of James Madison and Thomas Jefferson. Yet neither was a party in the modern sense; indeed, neither believed that there was any place in a republican society for permanent parties. Instead, each considered the other a dangerous and unacceptable force; each strove not just for dominance but for total victory. Because the differences between the two philosophies seemed irreconcilable, the dispute at times took on the character of a struggle to the death.

Hamilton and the Federalists

Control of the new government lay from the beginning largely in the hands of the Federalists. It remained there for twelve years. One reason was George Washington, who had always envisioned a strong national government and who during his eight years as president did little to hamper the efforts of those attempting to consolidate its power. Yet Washington's role in enacting the Federalist program was in many respects a passive one, a result of his concept of the office he held. The president, Washington believed, should not be directly involved in political controversies. He should, rather, be an Olympian figure, above the fray—a symbol of American nationhood. Washington avoided any personal involvement in the deliberations of Congress; he made few efforts to mediate among contending factions; he remained aloof.

As a result, the dominant figure in his administration became his talented secretary of the treasury, Alexander Hamilton, a man who exerted more influence than anyone else on domestic and foreign policy both during his term of office and, to an almost equal extent, after his resignation in 1794. Of all the leading men of his time, Hamilton was one of the most aristocratic in personal tastes and political philosophy—ironically, perhaps, since his own origins had been exceedingly humble. Having risen above the common people himself, he looked back on them with distinct mistrust. Far from embracing republican ideals of the virtue of the people, he believed that a stable and effective government required an elite ruling class; authority should be lodged in the hands of the "enlightened few." As a result, he hoped to adapt the British system of rule by the king and the aristocracy as closely as possible to the United States. The alternative, he was certain, would be continuing disorder.

The new government could best be strengthened, Hamilton believed, by attracting the support of the wealthy men of the country. And since he believed that all men were motivated by self-interest, he assumed that the way to gain the support of the wealthy was to give them a stake in the success of the new government. He therefore planned a program of legislation that, among other things, was intended to cause the propertied classes to look to the federal government for profitable investments and for the protection and promotion of their interests.

If men of means were to have faith in the government, then it must keep faith with them by paying its debts and establishing its credit on a sound basis. Therefore, first of all, Hamilton proposed that the existing public debt be "funded," or in other words that the miscellaneous, uncertain, depreciated certificates of indebtedness that the old Congress had issued during and since the Revolution be called in and exchanged for uniform, interest-bearing bonds, payable at definite dates. Next, he recommended that the Revolutionary state debts be "assumed" or taken over by the United States, his object being to cause the state as well as the federal bondholders to look to the central government for eventual payment. He did not, in other words, envision paying off and thus eliminating the debt. He wanted instead to create a large and permanent national debt, new bonds being issued as old ones were paid off. The result, he believed, would be that creditors—the wealthy classes most likely to lend money to the government—would have a permanent stake in seeing the government survive.

Hamilton also planned the establishment of a national bank. At the time, there were only a few banks in the country, located in Boston, Philadelphia, and New York. A new, national bank would serve several purposes. It would aid business by providing loans and currency. It would aid the government by making a safe place available for the deposit of federal funds, by facilitating the collection of taxes and the disbursement of the government's expenditures, and by keeping up the price of government bonds through judicious bond purchases. The kind of institution that

Hamilton had in mind was to be "national" in the sense that it was to be chartered by the federal government, was to have a monopoly of the government's own banking business, and was to be government-controlled to some degree, one-fifth of the directors being appointed by the government.

The funding and assumption of the debts, together with the payment of regular interest on them, would cost a great deal of money, and so Hamilton had to find adequate sources of revenue. He thought the government should depend mainly on two kinds of taxes (in addition to the receipts to be anticipated from the sales of public land). One of these was an excise to be paid by distillers of alcoholic liquors. This tax would hit most heavily the whiskey distillers of the back country, especially in Pennsylvania, Virginia, and North Carolina. These were small farmers who converted part of their corn and rye crop into whiskey, so as to have a concentrated and valuable product that they could conveniently take to market by horseback or muleback over poor mountain roads.

The other tax on which Hamilton relied was the tariff on imports. Such a tax would not only raise a revenue but also protect and encourage American manufactures by raising the price of competing manufactured goods brought in from abroad. The worst defect of the old Articles of Confederation, according to its defenders as well as its critics, had been Congress's lack of power to levy customs duties. One of the first acts of the new Congress, in 1789, was the passage of a tariff law designed to foster industries while raising a revenue, but the average level of duties under this law was extremely low. Hamilton advocated a higher and more decidedly protective tariff. In his Report on Manufactures he glowingly set forth the advantages, as he saw them, of stimulating the growth of industry in the United States. Factories, he said, would make the nation more nearly self-sufficient in wartime, would increase prosperity by creating a home market for the produce of the farms, and would make possible the fuller utilization of all kinds of labor, including the labor of women and children, even those (to quote Hamilton himself) of "tender years."

The Federalists, in short, offered more than a vision of how to ensure the stability of the new government. They offered a vision of the sort of nation America should become—a nation with a wealthy, enlightened ruling class; one possessing a vigorous, independent commercial economy with a thriving industrial sector; a country able to play a prominent role in world economic affairs.

Enacting the Federalist Program

Between 1789 and 1792, Hamilton succeeded in persuading Congress to pass the necessary laws for erecting his financial system—but only after a bitter struggle with a rising opposition group.

As for the funding of the public debt, very few of the congressmen objected to the plan itself, for they agreed with Hamilton that the government must make its credit good. Many of them disagreed, however, with his proposal to fund the debt at par, that is, to exchange new bonds for old certificates of indebtedness on a dollar-for-dollar basis. These old certificates had been issued to merchants and farmers in payment for war supplies during the Revolution, or to officers and soldiers of the Revolutionary army in payment for their services. Many of these original holders had been forced to sell at a sacrifice during the hard times of the 1780s, to speculators who bought up the securities at a fraction of their face value.

Almost everyone agreed that the government should arrange to pay every cent it owed, but there was wide disagreement regarding to whom it should pay the money. Many congressmen believed that the original holders deserved some consideration, and James Madison, now a representative from Virginia, argued for a plan by which the new bonds would be divided between the original purchasers and the speculators. But the friends of Hamilton insisted that such a plan was impracticable and that the honor of the government required a literal fulfillment of its earlier promises to pay. Congress finally passed the funding bill in the form that Hamilton desired.

His assumption bill ran into even greater

difficulty. Its opponents had a strong case, for if the federal government took over the state debts, the people of one state would have to pay federal taxes for servicing the debts of other states, and some of these debts, such as that of Massachusetts, were much larger than others, such as that of Virginia. Naturally, Virginia representatives in Congress balked at the assumption bill.

Finally, the bill got the support of some of them and so managed to pass, but only because of a logrolling deal. The Virginians wanted the national capital to be perma-

nently located near them in the South. After Jefferson's return from France, Hamilton appealed to him. Jefferson held a dinner at which arrangements were made to barter Virginia votes for the assumption bill in return for Northern votes for a Southern location of the capital. In 1790, the capital was moved from New York back to Philadelphia for a ten-year period; after that, a new capital city was to be built on the banks of the Potomac River, on land to be selected by Washington himself.

When Hamilton's bank bill was intro-

The First Bank of the United States
The headquarters of the Bank of the United States, which was founded through Alexander Hamilton's efforts, were in Philadelphia. The bank building on Third Street was completed in 1795. It is a good example of Early Republican architecture, with its rather boxlike shape, its balustrade along the roof edge, its quoins at the angle of the walls, and its Roman pediment and columns in front. From a drawing and engraving by W. Birch & Son of Philadelphia, published in 1799.

Constitutionality of the Bank: Hamilton

It is conceded that *implied powers* are to be considered as delegated equally with *express ones*. Then it follows, that as a power of erecting a corporation may as well be *implied* as any other thing, it may as well be employed as an *instrument* or mean of carrying into execution any of the specified powers, as any other *instrument* or *mean* whatever. . . .

It is objected that none but necessary and proper means are to be employed; and the Secretary of State maintains that no means are to be considered as necessary but those without which the grant of the power would be *nugatory*. . . .

It is certain that neither the grammatical nor popular sense of the term requires that construction. According to both, necessary often means no more than *needful, requisite, incidental, useful,* or *conducive to*. . . .

If the end be clearly comprehended within any of the specified powers, and if the measure have an obvious relation to that *end*, and is not forbidden by any particular provision of the Constitution, it may safely be deemed to come within the compass of the national authority. . . .

A bank has a natural relation to the power of collecting taxes—to that of regulating trade—to that of providing for the common defence. . . . [Therefore] the incorporation of a bank is a constitutional measure. . . .

Constitutionality of the Bank: Jefferson

The incorporation of a bank, and the powers assumed by this bill, have not, in my opinion, been delegated to the United States by the Constitution.

I. They are not among the powers specially enumerated. . . .
II. Nor are they within either of the general phrases, which are the two following:
   1. To lay taxes to provide for the general welfare of the United States." . . . They [*Congress*] are not *to do anything they please,* to provide for the general welfare, but only *to lay taxes* for that purpose. . . . It was intended to lace them up straitly within the enumerated powers, and those with-

out which, as means, these powers could not be carried into effect. . . .
   2. The second general phrase is, "to make all laws *necessary* and proper for carrying into execution the enumerated powers." But they can all be carried into execution without a bank. A bank, therefore, is not *necessary,* and consequently not authorized by this phrase.

It has been much urged that a bank will give great facility or convenience in the collection of taxes. Suppose this were true; yet the Constitution allows only the means which are "necessary," not those which are merely "convenient," for effecting the enumerated powers.

duced in Congress, Madison and others opposed it on the grounds that it was unconstitutional, and although a majority voted for it, President Washington himself had his doubts. He therefore asked his official advisers for written opinions on the subject. In Hamilton's opinion, the establishment of a bank was a fitting exercise of the powers of Congress, though the Constitution nowhere explicitly gave Congress the right. But Jefferson, with the support of his fellow Virginian Randolph, argued that the Constitution should be construed in a strict sense and that Congress should be allowed no powers not clearly given to it. Washington found Hamilton's case more convincing, and he signed the bank bill when it came to him. The Bank of the United States began operations in 1791, under a charter that granted it the right to continue for twenty years.

Hamilton also had his way with the excise tax, though after its passage the law was altered somewhat, in response to protests from farmers, so as to bear less heavily on the smaller distillers. He did not succeed in getting from Congress a tariff as highly protective as he had hoped for, yet the tariff law of 1792 did raise the rates somewhat.

Once enacted, Hamilton's program operated as he had intended. The public credit quickly was restored; the bonds of the United States were soon selling at home and abroad at prices even above their par value.

At the same time, speculators got rich, and corruption was rife. Many congressmen had bought up large amounts of the old certificates of indebtedness, and these men profited by their own legislation in funding the debt at par. Directly or indirectly, properly or improperly, thousands of wealthy merchants in the seaports also gained from the Hamilton program.

The mass of the people—the farmers scattered over the countryside—profited much less. The financial program required taxes, and these came mostly from the farmers, who had to pay not only land taxes to their state governments but also the excise and, indirectly, the tariff to the federal government. The feeling grew that the Washington administration was not treating all the people fairly, and out of this feeling an organized political opposition arose.

The Republican Opposition

The Constitution had made no reference to political parties, and the omission had been no oversight. Most of the framers—and George Washington in particular—believed that organized parties were evil and should be avoided. It was inevitable that men would disagree on particular issues, but most believed that such disagreements should not lead to the formation of permanent factions.

"The public good is disregarded in the conflicts of rival parties," Madison had written in *The Federalist Papers* (in Number 10, perhaps the most influential of all the essays), "and . . . measures are too often decided, not according to the rules of justice and the rights of the minor party, but by the superior force of an interested and overbearing majority."

Yet not many years had passed after the ratification of the Constitution before Madison and others became convinced that Hamilton and his followers had become just such an "interested and overbearing majority." Not only had the Federalists enacted a program that many of these leaders opposed. More ominously, Hamilton had, in their eyes, worked to establish a national network of influence that embodied all the worst features of a party. The Federalists had used their control over appointments and the awarding of government franchises, and all the other powers of their offices, to reward their supporters and win additional allies. They had encouraged the formation of local associations—largely aristocratic in nature— to strengthen their standing in local communities. They were doing many of the same things, their opponents believed, that the corrupt British governments of the early eighteenth century had done.

Because the Federalists appeared to their critics to be creating such a menacing and tyrannical structure of power, there was no alternative but to organize a vigorous opposition. And the result was the emergence of an alternative political party: the Republicans. By the late 1790s, the Republicans were going to even greater lengths than the Federalists to create an apparatus of partisan influence. In every state, they had formed committees, societies, and caucuses; Republican groups were corresponding with each other across state lines; they were banding together to influence state and local elections. And they were justifying their actions by claiming that they and they alone represented the true interests of the nation—that they were fighting to defend the people against a corrupt conspiracy by the Federalists. Just as Hamilton believed that the network of supporters he was creating represented the only legitimate interest group in the nation, so the Republicans believed that their party organization represented the best interests of the people. Neither side was willing to admit that it was acting as a party; nor would either concede the right of the other to exist.

From the beginning, the preeminent figures among the Republicans were Thomas Jefferson and James Madison. Indeed, the two men were such intimate collaborators that it is sometimes difficult to distinguish the contributions of one from those of the other. Their political philosophies by this time were almost entirely alike. But Jefferson, as the more magnetic personality of the two, gradually emerged as the most prominent spokesman for the Republicans.

Jefferson, himself a farmer, believed that farmers were God's chosen people and that an ideal republic would consist of sturdy citizens, each tilling his own soil. Though he was an aristocrat by birth, he had faith in the good intentions of the ordinary farmer-citizens and thought that if properly educated, they could be trusted to govern themselves through the election of able and qualified men. But in the 1790s, he feared city mobs as "sores upon the body politic." He then opposed the development of extensive manufactures because they would lead to the growth of cities packed with propertyless workers. While Hamilton emphasized the need for order and stability, Jefferson stressed the primary importance of individual freedom.

As a member of President Washington's official circle, Jefferson differed so strongly with his colleague Hamilton on particular issues such as the Bank that he soon offered to resign. But Washington preferred to keep both men in office to preserve national unity if possible. His became a coalition government, though he himself agreed more often with Hamilton than with Jefferson. The two secretaries continued to work against each other, and each began to organize a following in Congress as well as in the country at large.

The Federalists of the 1790s were not entirely the same men as the Federalists of 1787–1788 who had campaigned for the ratification of the Constitution, nor were the Republicans exactly the same men as the old Antifederalists. There were numerous exceptions, the most noteworthy being Madison, who had played a leading role at the Constitutional Convention and in the ratification effort, then had broken with Hamilton on the questions of funding and the Bank, and had become one of the founders of the Republican party. Both parties had members in all sections of the country, but the Federalists were most numerous in the commercial centers of the Northeast, though also strong in such Southern seaports as Charleston, while the Republicans were most numerous in the rural areas of the South and the West.

Unlike the old Antifederalists, the new Republicans did not denounce the Constitution. On the contrary, they professed to be its special friends and champions and accused their opponents of violating it.

Republicans and Federalists differed in their social philosophies as well as in their economic interests and their constitutional views. Their differences in social outlook are seen in their reactions to the progress of the revolution in France. When that revolution first began, as a rather mild movement in favor of constitutional monarchy and the rights of man, practically all Americans hailed it as a step in the right direction. But when the revolution went to radical extremes, with attacks on organized religion, the overthrow of the monarchy, and eventually the guillotining of the king and queen, Americans adopted different views about the events in France, the Federalists denouncing and the Republicans applauding them. Indeed, many of the Republicans imitated the French radicals (the Jacobins) by cutting their hair short, wearing pantaloons, and addressing one another as "Citizen" Smith and "Citizeness" Jones. Republicans accused the Federalists of being aristocratic and even "monarchical." Federalists referred to the Republicans, in horrified tones, as "Jacobins" and as "Jacobinical rabble"—terms that then had much the same implication as the word "communist" was to have many years later.

When the time came for the election of 1792, the Republicans had no candidate to put up against Washington. Jefferson as well as Hamilton urged him to run for a second term, and the president consented, though he would have preferred to retire to his plantation at Mount Vernon.

For the moment at least, the conflict between the Federalists and the Republicans remained relatively contained. Although many Republicans were already certain that the Federalists posed a dire threat to the survival of liberty in America, as long as Washington remained president, and as long as Hamilton and his allies exercised reasonable restraint in pursuing their policies, the opposition was unable to mobilize enough public support to prevail. Thus although the political atmosphere grew increasingly acrimonious during Washington's second term, Hamilton and the Federalists continued for the most part to have their way.

ASSERTING NATIONAL SOVEREIGNTY

One of the most effective ways in which the Federalists consolidated their position—and attracted wide support to the new national government—was by dealing with two problems that the old Confederation had been unable to resolve. They helped to stabilize the Western frontier, and they improved America's position in world affairs. The failures of the Confederation in both those areas had been major incentives for framing the new Constitution. The Federalists moved actively, therefore, to prove that the new government was better able to succeed.

Securing the Frontier

Previously, during the 1780s, the old Congress had been powerless to tie the outlying parts of the country firmly to the United States, as farmers in western Massachusetts rose in revolt and settlers in Vermont, Kentucky, and Tennessee toyed with the idea of separating from the Union. Now, however, the Washington administration made the power of the federal government felt even on the farthest reaches of the frontier.

The federal authority was challenged when, in 1794, the farmers of western Pennsylvania refused to pay the whiskey excise and terrorized the would-be tax collectors, much as the colonists had done throughout America at the time of the Stamp Act. The so-called Whiskey Rebellion was not left to the authorities of Pennsylvania as Shays' Rebellion had been left to the authorities of Massachusetts. Urged on by Hamilton, Washington took drastic steps. Calling out the militias of three states, he raised an army of nearly 15,000, a larger force than he had commanded against the British during most of the Revolution, and he personally accompanied this army as far as the town of Bedford. At the approach of the militiamen, the farmers around Pittsburgh, where the rebellion centered, either ran for cover or stayed home and professed to be law-abiding citizens. The rebellion quickly collapsed.

While the whiskey rebels were intimidated into obedience, other frontiersmen were made loyal to the government by its acceptance of new states as members of the Union. First to be admitted were two of the original thirteen, North Carolina (1789) and Rhode Island (1790), both of which had ratified the Constitution when they found that a bill of rights was definitely to be added and that they could not conveniently go on as independent commonwealths. Then Vermont, which had had its own state government since the Revolution, was accepted as the fourteenth state (1791) after New York and New Hampshire finally agreed to give up their claims to sovereignty over it. Next came Kentucky (1792) with the consent of Virginia, which previously had governed the Kentucky counties as its own. After North Carolina finally ceded its Western lands to the Union, this area was given a territorial government similar to that of the Northwest Territory and after six years became the state of Tennessee (1796).

In the more remote areas of the Northwest and the Southwest, meanwhile, the government had to contend with the Indians and their foreign allies, British and Spanish, in order to get a firm grasp on all the territory belonging to the United States. The Indians of the Southwest—Cherokees, Creeks, Choctaws, and Chickasaws—were led by the colorful and vengeful Alexander McGillivray, a half-breed Creek chieftain who had fought as a Tory during the Revolution and who continued to hate Americans. In his efforts to resist the advance of American frontiersmen into the lower Mississippi Valley, McGillivray received the support and encouragement of Spain. In 1790, President Washington tried to buy peace with the Southwestern Indians by inviting McGillivray to New York and agreeing to pay him $100,000. Despite McGillivray's treaty with the United States, the Indians continued to accept subsidies from the Spaniards and to raid American settlements along the border. At last, in 1793–1794, the Tennesseans went on the warpath themselves, their militia invading the Indian country and chastising several of the tribes. Thus the Southwestern frontier was made safe for the time being.

In the Northwest, the government pursued a policy of force against the Indians, even at some risk of becoming involved in hostilities with the Indians' protector and ally, Great Britain. Two expeditions failed before a third one finally succeeded in the conquest of the Ohio country. Washington gave the frontier command to General Wayne, who, despite his nickname "Mad Anthony," was a careful planner as well as a dashing soldier. With over 4,000 men, including a large contingent of Kentucky sharpshooters, Wayne moved cautiously toward the Maumee River, building forts as he went. The British officials in Canada, who were providing the Indians with supplies, themselves ordered the construction of a fort about twenty miles from the mouth of the river, well within the boundary of the United States. Near the British fort, at a place where trees had been blown over by a windstorm, Wayne in the summer of 1794 met and decisively defeated the Indians in the Battle of Fallen Timbers, the British garrison prudently keeping out of the fight. Next summer the Indians agreed in the Treaty of Greenville to abandon to the white men most of what afterward became the state of Ohio.

Maintaining Neutrality

When Washington became president, Great Britain had not sent a minister to the United States, though all the other powers of Europe (except Russia) had entered into normal diplomatic relations with the young republic. In Congress, Madison and the Republicans argued that Great Britain, in refusing to make a commercial treaty with the United States, was waging economic warfare against the country, and that the United States should retaliate by imposing special customs duties and harbor dues, in excess of the regular rates, on British goods and ships. Though this legislation did not pass, the threat of it induced the British government, in 1791, to dispatch a regular minister to America.

A new crisis in foreign affairs faced the Washington administration when the French revolutionary government, after executing King Louis XVI, went to war in 1793 with Great Britain and its allies. Should the United States recognize the radical government of France by accepting a diplomatic representative from it? Was the United States obligated by the alliance of 1778 to go to war on the side of France? These questions Washington put to his official advisers, and both Hamilton and Jefferson recommended a policy of neutrality, though they presented quite different arguments for it. Washington decided to recognize the French government and to issue a proclamation announcing the determination of the United States to remain at peace. The proclamation (1793), although it did not mention the word "neutrality," was generally (and correctly) interpreted as a neutrality statement. The next year, Congress passed a neutrality act forbidding American citizens to participate in the war and prohibiting the use of American soil as a base of operations for either side.

The first challenge to American neutrality came from France. Not that the French revolutionaries asked for a declaration of war: they did not, for they supposed that the United States would be of more use to them as a nonbelligerent. Their purposes became apparent when their first minister to America arrived. Instead of landing at Philadelphia and presenting himself immediately to the president, the youthful and brash Citizen Edmond Genêt disembarked at Charleston. There he made plans for using American ports to outfit French warships, issued letters of marque and reprisal authorizing American shipowners to serve as French privateers, and commissioned the aging George Rogers Clark to undertake an overland expedition against the possessions of Spain, which at this point was an ally of Great Britain and an enemy of France. In all these steps, Genêt brazenly disregarded Washington's proclamation and flagrantly violated the Neutrality Act. When he finally reached Philadelphia, after being acclaimed by pro-French crowds on a tour through the interior, he got a stony reception from the president. He then assumed that the people were behind him, and he repeatedly appealed to them over the president's head. His conduct not only infuriated Washington and the Federalists but also embarrassed all except the most ardent Francophiles among the Republicans. At last, Washington demanded that the French government recall him, but by that time Genêt's party, the Girondins, were out of power in France and the still more extreme Jacobins in control, so it would not have been safe for him to return. Generously the president granted him political asylum in the United States, and he settled down to live to a ripe old age with his American wife on a Long Island farm. Meanwhile the neutrality policy had survived its first great test.

The second challenge, an even greater one, came from Great Britain. Early in 1794, the Royal Navy suddenly seized hundreds of American ships engaged in trade in the French West Indies. The pretext for these seizures was a British interpretation of international law—known as the Rule of 1756—which held that a trade prohibited in peacetime (as American trade between France and the French overseas possessions had been) could not be legally opened in time of war. At the news of the seizures, the prevalent opinion in the United States became as strongly anti-British as it had recently been anti-French, and the anti-British feeling rose still higher at the report that the governor general of Canada had delivered a warlike speech to the Indians on the Northwestern frontier. Hamilton grew concerned, for war would mean an end to imports from England, and most of the revenue for maintaining his financial system came from duties on those imports.

Jay's Treaty

To Hamilton and to other Federalists it seemed that this was no time for ordinary diplomacy. Jefferson had resigned in 1793 to devote himself to organizing a political opposition, and the State Department was now in the hands of an even more ardently pro-French Virginian, Edmund Randolph. Bypassing the State Department, Washington named as a special commissioner to England the staunch New York Federalist, former secretary for foreign affairs under the old Confederation, and current chief justice of the Supreme Court, John Jay. Jay was instructed to secure damages for the recent spoliations, withdrawal of British forces from the frontier posts, and a satisfactory commercial treaty, without violating the terms of the existing treaty of amity and commerce with France, signed at the time of the alliance in 1778.

The treaty that Jay negotiated (1794) was a long and complex document dealing with frontier posts, boundaries, debts, commerce, ship seizures, and neutral rights. It yielded more to Great Britain and obtained less for the United States than Jay had been authorized to give or instructed to get. When the terms were published in the United States, the treaty was denounced more than any treaty before or since, and Jay himself was burned in effigy in various parts of the country. The Republicans were unanimous in decrying it; they said it favored Great Britain and was unfair to France. Even some of the Federalists were outraged by its terms, those in the South objecting to its provision for the payment of the pre-Revolutionary debts. Opponents of the treaty went to extraordinary lengths to defeat it in the Senate, and French agents aided them and cheered them on. The American minister to France, James Monroe, and even the secretary of state, Edmund Randolph, cooperated closely with the French in a desperate attempt to prevent ratification. Nevertheless, after amending the treaty, the Senate consented.

There was much to be said for Jay's Treaty, despite its very real shortcomings. By means of it the United States gained valuable time for continued peaceful development, obtained undisputed sovereignty over all the

Jay's Treaty [1794]

Frontier Posts. "His Majesty will withdraw all his troops and garrisons from all posts and places within the boundary lines assigned by the treaty of peace to the United States."

Boundaries. Joint surveys will be made to locate the United States-Canadian boundary west of the Lake of the Woods and at the northeast, between Maine and New Brunswick.

Debts. The United States "will make full and complete compensation" for uncollectable debts owed by Americans to British creditors.

Commerce. There shall be freedom of commerce and navigation between the United States and Great Britain and the British East

Indies. (Article XII, permitting the United States to trade with the British West Indies also, but only in relatively small ships, was stricken out before ratification.)

Ship Seizures. The British government will compensate Americans for ships and cargoes illegally captured in the past, the amount of payment to be determined by arbitration.

Neutral Rights. American ships carrying enemy (French) property, when captured by the British, shall be taken to British ports and the enemy property removed. (This provision was inconsistent with the usual American principle that "free ships make free goods.")

Northwest, and secured a reasonably satisfactory commercial agreement with the nation whose trade was most important. More than that, the treaty led immediately to a settlement of the worst of the outstanding differences with Spain.

The Spanish foreign minister feared that the understanding between Great Britain and the United States might prove a prelude to joint operations between those two countries against Spain's possessions in North America. Spain was about to change sides in the European war, abandoning Great Britain for France, and it was therefore in Spain's interest to appease the United States. The relentless pressure of American frontiersmen advancing toward the Southwest made it doubtful whether Spain could long hold its

borderlands in any event. And so, when Thomas Pinckney arrived in Spain as a special negotiator, he had no difficulty in gaining nearly everything that the United States had sought from the Spaniards for more than a decade. Pinckney's Treaty (1795) recognized the right of Americans to navigate the Mississippi to its mouth and to deposit goods at New Orleans for reloading on oceangoing ships; fixed the northern boundary of Florida where Americans always had insisted it should be, along the 31st parallel; and bound the Spanish authorities to prevent the Indians in Florida from raiding across the border.

Thus before Washington had completed his second term in office, the United States had freed itself from the encroachments of both Great Britain and Spain.

THE DOWNFALL OF THE FEDERALISTS

These impressive triumphs did not, however, ensure the continued dominance of the Federalists in the national government. On the contrary, success seemed to produce problems of its own—problems that eventually led to their downfall. Having secured for the new government the virtually unanimous support of the American people, Hamilton

and his followers soon overreached themselves.

Since almost everyone agreed in the 1790s that there was no place in a stable republic for an organized opposition, the emergence of the Republicans as a powerful contender for the popular favor seemed to the Federalists a grave threat to national stability. When, beginning in the late 1790s, major international perils confronted the government as well, the temptation to move forcefully against the opposition became too great to resist. Facing what they believed was a stark choice between respecting individual liberties and preserving stability, the Federalists chose the latter. The result was political disaster. After 1796, the Federalists never won another election. The popular respect for the institutions of the federal government, which they had worked so hard to produce among the people, survived. But the Federalists themselves gradually vanished as a meaningful political force.

The Election of 1796

As the time approached for the election of 1796, some friends of Washington urged him to run again. Already twice elected without a single vote cast against him in the electoral college, he could be counted on to hold the Federalist party together and carry it to a third great victory. But Washington, weary of the burdens of the office and disgusted with the partisan abuse that was being heaped on him, longed to retire to Mount Vernon. Though he did not object to a third term in principle, he did not desire one for himself. To make his determination clear, he composed, with Hamilton's assistance, a long letter to the American people and had it published in a Philadelphia newspaper.

When Washington in this "Farewell Address" referred to the "insidious wiles of foreign influence," he was not writing merely for rhetorical effect. He had certain real evils in mind. Lately he had dismissed the secretary of state, Edmund Randolph, and had recalled the minister to France, James Monroe, for working hand in hand with the French to defeat Jay's Treaty. The French were still interfering in American politics with the hope of defeating the Federalists in the forthcoming presidential election.

There was no doubt that Jefferson would be the candidate of the Republicans, and he chose as his running mate the New York Republican leader, Aaron Burr. With Washington out of the running, there was some question as to who the Federalist candidate would be. Hamilton, the very personification of Federalism, was not "available" because his forthright views had aroused too many enemies. John Jay was too closely identified with his unpopular treaty, and Thomas Pinckney, though *his* treaty had been enthusiastically received, had the handicap of being a South Carolinian at a time when party leaders thought the next candidate should be a Northerner. John Adams, who as vice president was directly associated with none of the Federalist measures, finally got the nomination for president at a caucus of the Federalists in Congress, and Pinckney received the nomination for vice president.

With Washington stepping aside, the Federalist party became torn by fierce factional rivalries. Hamilton disliked Adams and preferred Pinckney, as did many other Federalists, especially in the South. New Englanders, on the other hand, had no particular liking for Pinckney and feared a plot to make him president instead of Adams. The result was a near disaster for the Federalists. They elected a majority of the presidential electors. But when the electors balloted in the various states, some of the Pinckney men declined to vote for Adams, and a still larger number of the Adams men declined to vote for Pinckney. So Pinckney received fewer votes than Jefferson, and Adams only three more than Jefferson. The next president was to be a Federalist, but the vice president was to be a Republican.

By virtue of his diplomatic services during the Revolution, his writings as a conservative political philosopher, and his devotion to the public weal as he saw it, John Adams ranks as one of the greatest American statesmen. Like most prominent members of the illustrious Adams family afterward, however, he lacked the politician's touch. Even Washington, remote and austere as he sometimes seems to have been, was adept at conciliating factions and maintaining party harmony. Unwisely, the new president chose to continue Washington's department heads in office. Most of them were friends of Hamilton, and they looked to him for advice, though he held no official post.

John Adams
John Adams (1735–1826) was the patriarch of one of the most extraordinary families in American history. He served brilliantly as a diplomat during the Revolution, as one of the most influential of the founders of the republic, as the first vice president, and as the second president of the United States. His son, John Quincy Adams, was one of the greatest of all American secretaries of state (under James Monroe), president of the United States (1825–1829), and for nearly twenty years until his death in 1848 a member of Congress from Massachusetts. Charles Francis Adams, son of John Quincy, served in Congress and as the brilliant minister to Great Britain during the Civil War. And among his sons were Charles Francis Adams, Jr., an important railroad magnate in the late nineteenth century; Brooks Adams, a renowned historian; and Henry Adams, an even greater historian and one of the most gifted and influential intellectuals of his generation. (The Bettmann Archive)

The Quasi War with France

As American relations with Great Britain and Spain improved in consequence of Jay's and Pinckney's treaties, relations with France,

now under the government of the Directory, went from bad to worse. Despite the victory of the Federalists in the election of 1796, the leaders of the Directory assumed that France had the sympathy and support of the mass of the American people and could undermine the Adams administration by frustrating it in foreign affairs. Therefore the French, asserting that they were applying the same principles of neutral rights that the United States and Great Britain had adopted in Jay's Treaty, continued to capture American ships on the high seas and, in many cases, to imprison the crews. When Minister Monroe left France after his recall, the French went out of their way to show their affection for him and for the Republican party. When the South Carolina Federalist Charles Cotesworth Pinckney, a brother of Thomas Pinckney, arrived in France to replace Monroe, the Directory considered him *persona non grata* and refused to receive him as the official representative of the United States.

War seemed likely unless the Adams administration could settle the difficulties with France. Some of the president's advisers, in particular his secretary of state, the stiff-backed New England Francophobe Timothy Pickering, favored war. Others urged a special effort for peace, and even Hamilton approved the idea of appointing commissioners to approach the Directory. Adams, himself a peace man, appointed a bipartisan commission of three: C. C. Pinckney, the recently rejected minister; John Marshall, a Virginia Federalist, afterward famous as the great chief justice of the United States; and Elbridge Gerry, a Massachusetts Republican but a personal friend of the president's. In France, in 1797, the three Americans were met by three agents of the Directory's foreign minister, Prince Talleyrand. Talleyrand's agents demanded a loan for France and a bribe for French officials before they would deal with Adams's commissioners. The response of the commissioners was summed up in Pinckney's laconic words: "No! No! Not a sixpence!"

When Adams received the commissioners' report, he sent a message to Congress in which he urged readiness for war, denounced the French for their insulting treatment of the

United States, and vowed he would not appoint another minister to France until he knew the minister would be "received, respected and honored as the representative of a great, free, powerful and independent nation." The Republicans, doubting the president's charge that the United States had been insulted, asked for proof. Adams then turned the commissioners' report over to Congress, after deleting the names of the three Frenchmen and designating them only as Messrs. X., Y., and Z. When the report was published, the "XYZ Affair" provoked an even greater reaction than Adams had bargained for. It aroused the martial spirit of most Americans, made the Federalists more popular than ever as the party of patriotism, and led to a limited and undeclared war with France (1798–1800).

With the cooperation of Congress, which quickly passed the necessary laws, Adams cut off all trade with France, abrogated the treaties of 1778, and authorized public and private vessels of the United States to capture French armed ships on the high seas. Congress set up a Department of the Navy (1798) and appropriated money for the construction of warships to supplement the hundreds of privateers and the small number of government vessels already built for the protection of American shipping in the Mediterranean against the Barbary pirates. The new United States Navy soon won a number of duels with French vessels of their own class and captured a total of eighty-five ships, including armed merchantmen.

Having abandoned neutrality, the United States now was cooperating so closely with Great Britain as to be virtually a cobelligerent, though technically at peace. When the British offered to lend a part of their fleet to the United States, President Adams declined to accept the loan, since he preferred to build up a navy of his own. Nevertheless, the British provided shot and shell to make up for the deficient American supplies, furnished officers to help with the training and direction of American crews, and exchanged signaling information so that British and American ships could communicate readily with one another.

Talleyrand finally began to see the wisdom of an accommodation with the Americans. He took notice of the rapprochement between the United States and Great Britain, the successes of the American navy, and the failure of the American people to show the expected enthusiasm for France. He was enlightened in regard to American public opinion by George Logan, a Philadelphia Quaker who, with no official authorization but with a letter of introduction from Vice President Jefferson, visited France to work for peace. After Logan returned, President Adams gave him a sympathetic hearing, even though the Federalists in Congress passed a law, the so-called Logan Act, to prohibit citizens from engaging in private and unofficial diplomacy with foreign governments in the future.

When, in 1800, Adams's new three-man commission arrived in France, Napoleon Bonaparte was in power as first consul. The Americans requested that France terminate the treaties of 1778 and pay damages for seizures of American ships. Napoleon replied that if the United States had any claim to damages, the claim must rest on the treaties, and if the treaties were ended, the claim must be abandoned. Napoleon had his way. The Americans agreed to a new treaty that canceled the old ones, arranged for reciprocity in commerce, and ignored the question of damages. When Adams submitted this treaty to the Senate, the extreme Federalists raised so many objections that its final ratification was delayed until after he had left office. Nevertheless, the "quasi war" had come to an honorable end, and the United States had at last freed itself from the entanglements and embarrassments of the "perpetual" alliance with France.

Repression and Protest

The outbreak of hostilities in 1798 had given the Federalists an advantage over the political opposition, and in the congressional elections of that year they increased their majorities in both houses. Meanwhile, their newly found power went to their heads. Some of them schemed to go on winning elections by passing laws to weaken and silence the opposition. They had as an excuse

Building the Navy
After the Revolutionary War, the United States abandoned the warships it had accumulated, and from 1783 to 1798 there was no American navy. Then, with the outbreak of undeclared hostilities with France, the Department of the Navy was established and a naval building program begun. In that age of wooden sailing ships, there were three main categories of war vessels: (1) ships of the line, or line-of-battle ships, which were the largest and most heavily armed (roughly corresponding to twentieth-century battleships or dreadnoughts); (2) frigates, which were smaller and faster and had fewer guns (comparable to modern cruisers); (3) corvettes, sloops of war, and other relatively small craft (somewhat like the light cruisers, destroyers, and gunboats of the present). At the outset, the United States Navy eschewed line-of-battle ships and placed its chief reliance on specially designed frigates that were faster, more maneuverable, and more heavily gunned than their European counterparts. In 1798, the frigates *United States, Constitution,* and *Constellation,* already partly built, were completed, and the *Philadelphia* and several others were started. The illustration shows work in progress on the *Philadelphia* in a Philadelphia shipyard. This frigate was not finished in time to be used against the French, but it saw action later in the war with Tripoli (1803). Tripolitan pirates captured the ship, and Americans, in a daring raid, destroyed her to prevent the enemy's using her against them. (The Historical Society of Pennsylvania)

---

the supposed necessity of protecting the nation from dangerous foreign influence in the midst of the undeclared war. By persecuting their critics, the Federalists produced a crop of Republican martyrs, gave rise to protests against their disregard of the Constitution, and provoked a reaction that helped to bring their party to defeat.

Since many Republican critics of the administration were foreigners by birth, especially Irish or French, the Federalists in Congress thought it desirable to limit the political rights of aliens and make it more difficult for them to become citizens. The Federalists struck at the civil liberties of both native Americans and the foreign-born in a pair of laws commonly known as the Alien and Sedition Acts—two of the most repressive pieces of legislation in American history.

The Alien Act was the less threatening of the two. It made it more difficult for foreigners to become American citizens and strengthened the president's hand in dealing with aliens. Far more ominous was the Sedition Act, which empowered the government to prosecute those who engaged in sedition against the government. In theory, only libelous or treasonous activities were subject to prosecution. In fact, however, the law had the capacity to become a potent vehicle for stifling any opposition. The Republicans responded to the new laws with anger and dismay, interpreting them as part of a Federalist campaign to destroy them. The Alien and Sedition Acts became, as a result, the spark that finally ignited the political passions that had been building for nearly a decade.

President Adams, who had signed the new laws, was nevertheless fairly cautious in implementing them. He did not act to deport any aliens, as he was empowered to do; and he prevented the government from launching a massive crusade against the opposition. Nevertheless, the legislation did have a significant repressive effect, enough to justify the fears of the Republicans that they were tyrannical in intent. The Alien Act, together with the Naturalization Act passed around the same time, discouraged immigration and encouraged some foreigners already in the country to leave. And the administration made use of the Sedition Act to arrest several dozen men; ten were convicted. Most of those prosecuted were Republican newspaper editors whose writings, although clearly critical of the Federalists, were not truly libelous or seditious at all. One of the editors had merely expressed the wish that, when a salute was fired in honor of the president, the wadding of the cannon had "struck him in the rear bulge of the breeches."

In seeking to oppose the Alien and Sedition Acts, the Republicans could not rely on the Supreme Court for relief. Indeed, the Court never yet had declared an act of Congress unconstitutional, and the Republicans denied that it had the power to do so. They believed, however, that the recent Federalist legislation, particularly the Sedition Act, was unconstitutional, for the First Amendment stated that Congress should pass no law abridging freedom of speech or of the press.

What agency of government should decide the question of constitutionality? The Republican leaders Jefferson and Madison concluded that the state legislatures should decide. They ably expressed their view in two sets of resolutions, one written (anonymously) by Jefferson and adopted by the Kentucky legislature (1798, 1799), and the other drafted by Madison and approved by the Virginia legislature (1798). These Kentucky and Virginia resolutions asserted that the federal government had been formed by a "compact" or contract among the states. It was a limited government, possessing only certain delegated powers. Whenever it exercised any additional and undelegated powers, its acts were "unauthoritative, void, and of no force." The parties to the contract, the states, must decide for themselves when and whether the central government exceeded its powers. And "nullification" by the states was the "rightful remedy" whenever the general government went too far. The resolutions urged all the states to join in declaring the Alien and Sedition Acts null and void and in requesting their repeal at the next session of Congress. But none of the other states went along.

The Republicans failed to win wide support for their efforts on behalf of nullification; they did, however, succeed in elevating their dispute with the Federalists to the level of a national crisis. By the late 1790s, the entire nation was as deeply and bitterly politicized as it would ever be in its history. The partisan divisions had become so intense that they created deep divisions within every community. Friends and families became bitterly divided. State legislatures at times resembled battlegrounds; loud and angry debates were almost constant, and on several occasions there were rowdy fistfights and brawls in the legislative chambers. Even the United States Congress was plagued with violent disagreements. In one celebrated incident, a Republican representative from Vermont and a Federalist representative from Connecticut got into a bitter fight in the chamber of the House of Representatives. Matthew Lyon, the Republican, responded to an insult from Roger Griswold, the Federalist, by spitting in Griswold's eye. Griswold attacked Lyon with his cane, Lyon fought back with a pair of fire tongs, and soon the two men were engaged in a wrestling match on the floor. Such incidents were not only embarrassing to the individuals involved; they served as a disturbing reminder to the public at large of the growing rancor and instability of the nation's politics. By 1800, it had begun to seem as though the nation was on the verge of dissolving into chaos.

The "Revolution" of 1800

In this troubled atmosphere, Americans went about the task of electing a president in the fall of 1800. The presidential candidates were the same as four years earlier: Jefferson was the Republican nominee, with Aaron Burr again his running mate; Adams campaigned for reelection as a Federalist, with Charles Pinckney as the party's candidate for vice president.

The campaign of that year was the most vicious in American history. Although Adams and Jefferson themselves were relatively restrained in their discussions of each other, supporters of each circulated scurrilous stories about the opposition. (It was during this campaign, for example, that a story of Jefferson's alleged romantic involvement with a black slave woman was first widely aired.) In addition to personal slander, each side argued strenuously that its opponents threatened the very existence of the republic. The Federalists accused Jefferson of being a dangerous radical and his followers of being wild men who, if they should come to power, would bring on a reign of terror comparable to that of the French Revolution at its worst. The Republicans pictured Adams as a tyrant, as one who was conspiring to become king; and they accused the Federalists of plotting to subvert human liberty and impose slavery on the people—accusations that mirrored the anti-British propaganda of the pre-Revolutionary years.

The contest was close, and the outcome in

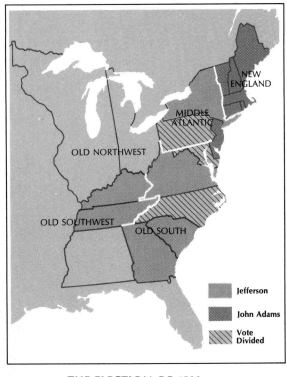

THE ELECTION OF 1800

the electoral college depended on the voting in one state, New York. In New York City the vice-presidential candidate, Burr, was the organizer of Republican victory. The Revolutionary veterans of the city had formed the Tammany Society to maintain their wartime fellowship and to combat the pretensions of the Society of the Cincinnati, the exclusive and aristocratic organization of Revolutionary officers. Though not himself a member of Tammany, Burr converted it into a political machine and, with its aid, carried the city for the Republicans by such a large majority as to carry the state also. The Republicans gained control of the legislature, and since New York was one of the states in which the legislature cast the electoral vote, the Republicans could count on that vote in the presidential election.

When the state electors cast their votes, Adams received a total of 65 and Pinckney 64. Jefferson got 73 and so did Burr. To avoid such a tie, Republican leaders had meant at least one of their electors to refrain from giving Burr his vote. But through a misunderstanding—some said that Burr himself was secretly responsible—the plan went awry. And so the election was not yet over: in accordance with the Constitution the decision between the two highest—between Burr and Jefferson—was up to the House of Representatives, with the delegation from each state casting a single vote.

Since the Federalists controlled a majority of the states' votes in the existing Congress, they had the privilege of deciding which of their opponents was to be the next president, though the Republicans, in making their nominations, had clearly intended Jefferson to have the first place on their ticket. Some of the more extreme of the Federalists now hoped to postpone or prevent any breaking of the tie and, instead, to make new arrangements for the presidential succession so that the highest office in the land would still fall to a Federalist. Others, fearing chaos and possible civil war if no election were made, thought it would be better to come to an understanding with Burr and elect him. Hamilton disapproved of both proposals. Though he had little love for Jefferson, he had even less for Burr, his bitter rival in law and politics in New York. Burr himself remained strangely silent, neither campaigning for himself nor refusing to accept office.

During the winter of 1800–1801 the House balloted again and again without mustering a majority for either candidate. Finally, only a few weeks before inauguration day, some of the Federalist die-hards gave in, the tie was broken, and Jefferson was named president, Burr vice president. Afterward one of the Federalists claimed that he had given in because Jefferson's friends had assured him that Jefferson would appoint him to a government job and would preserve the main Federalist policies with respect to commerce, the navy, and the public debt, while making no wholesale removals of Federalists from the lower offices of the government.

In addition to winning a majority of the presidential electors in 1800, the Republicans also won a majority of the seats in both houses of the next Congress. The only branch of the government left in Federalist hands was the judiciary, and Adams and his fellow partisans during his last months in office took steps to make their hold on the courts secure.

By the Judiciary Act of 1801, the Federalists succeeded in reducing the number of Supreme Court justiceships by one but at the same time greatly increasing the number of federal judgeships as a whole. The act created a separate system of circuit courts of appeal, standing between the federal district courts and the Supreme Court. Formerly (in accordance with the Judiciary Act of 1789) a district judge had sat with two Supreme Court justices to hear appeals on the circuit. The new law also provided for ten additional district judgeships.

To these newly created positions Adams proceeded to appoint deserving Federalists. It was said that he stayed up until midnight on his last day in office, March 3, 1801, in order to complete the signing of the judges' commissions, and so these officeholders were known as his "midnight appointments." Since federal judges held office for life, Jefferson as the incoming president would be powerless to remove Adams's appointees. Or so the Federalists assumed.

Despite these last Federalist efforts, the Republicans viewed their victory as almost complete. The nation had, they believed, been saved from tyranny. A new era could now begin, one in which the true principles on which America had been founded would once again govern the land. The exuberance with which the victors viewed the future—and the importance they ascribed to the defeat of the Federalists—were clearly revealed by the phrase Jefferson himself later used to describe his election. He called it the "Revolution of 1800." It remained to be seen how revolutionary it would really be.

SUGGESTED READINGS

The fullest account of the Constitutional Convention is the records of the meetings themselves, available in Max Farrand (ed.), *Records of the Federal Convention of 1787*, 4 vols. (1911–1937). Farrand is also the author of one of the best accounts of the convention, *The Framing of the Constitution of the United States* (1913). One of the most influential and controversial works of American history is Charles A. Beard, *An Economic Interpretation of the Constitution of the United States* (1913), which argues that the Constitution was the product of conservative economic interests attempting to protect their investment in the national government. Harshly critical of the Beard argument is Forrest McDonald, *We the People: The Economic Origins of the Constitution* (1958) and *E Pluribus Unum: The Formation of the American Republic, 1776–1790* (1965). Also critical of Beard is Robert E. Brown, *Charles Beard and the Constitution* (1956). Clinton Rossiter, *1787: The Grand Convention* (1965), is a careful account of the Constitutional Convention. See also Douglas Adair, *Fame and the Founding Fathers* (1974).

Opposition to the Constitution is examined in Jackson Turner Main, *The Anti-Federalists* (1961), and in Alpheus T. Mason, *The State Rights Debate* (1964). The best source for examining the argument for the Constitution is *The Federalist*, the most complete edition being that edited by J. E. Cooke (1961). Garry Wills, *Explaining America* (1981), is a study of *The Federalist Papers* emphasizing the influence of the Scottish philosopher David Hume on the Founding Fathers. Linda G. DePauw, *The Eleventh Pillar: New York State and the Federal Constitution* (1966), studies the debate in a single state. Gerald Stourzh, *Alexander Hamilton and the Idea of Republican Government* (1970), is an intellectual portrait of one of the Constitution's chief defenders. See also Robert A. Rutland, *The Ordeal of the Constitution* (1966).

A general history of American government during the Federalist period (the 1790s) is John C. Miller, *The Federalist Era, 1789–1801* (1960). Leonard D. White, *The Federalists* (1948), is a valuable history of the process of setting up the administrative structure of the new government. The first administration under the Constitution is examined in Forrest McDonald, *The Presidency of George Washington* (1974). The second is discussed in Ralph Adams Brown, *The Presidency of John Adams* (1975); Stephen Kurtz, *The Presidency of John Adams* (1957); John R. Howe, *The Changing Political Thought of John Adams* (1966); and Manning Dauer, *The Adams Federalists* (1953). More specialized studies of the period include Richard Kohn, *Eagle and Sword: The Federalists and the Creation of the Military Establishment in America, 1783–1802* (1975); and Carl E. Prince, *The Federalists and the Origins of the U.S. Civil Service* (1978).

Leonard Levy, *Legacy of Suppression: Freedom of Speech and Press in Early American History* (1960), discusses some of the controversies over civil liberties of the 1790s, as does James M. Smith, *Freedom's Fet-*ters: *The Alien and Sedition Laws and American Civil Liberties* (1956). Leland D. Baldwin, *The Whiskey Rebels* (1939), examines the most prominent challenge to the new government. Irving Brant, *The Bill of Rights* (1965), examines early protections of civil liberties; while John C. Miller, *Crisis in Freedom* (1951), discusses early infringements.

Charles A. Beard, *The Economic Origins of the Jeffersonian Opposition* (1915), is a classic study of the subject and, like his work on the Constitution, highly controversial. Joseph Charles, *The Origins of the American Party System* (1956), challenges Beard's contention that the Jeffersonian opposition was a continuation of the antifederalism of small farmers in the 1780s. Noble Cunningham, *The Jeffersonian Republicans* (1957), is a good general account of the rise of opposition; while Merrill D. Peterson, *Thomas Jefferson and the New Nation* (1970), is a biography of the opposition leader. The most authoritative biography of Jefferson is Dumas Malone, *Jefferson and His Time*, 6 vols. (1948–1981), of which volume 3, *Jefferson and the Ordeal of Liberty*, examines the 1790s and the election of 1800. The emergence of party competition is examined in Richard Hofstadter, *The Idea of a Party System* (1970); Norman K. Risjord, *Chesapeake Politics, 1781–1800* (1978); Alfred F. Young, *The Democratic-Republicans of New York* (1967); and William N. Chambers, *Political Parties in a New Nation* (1963). Patricia Watlington, *The Partisan Spirit* (1972), examines the ideology of partisan conflict in Kentucky and its relation to national politics. John Zvesper, *Political Philosophy and Rhetoric: A Study of the Origins of American Party Politics* (1977), is a broader study. See also Richard W. Buel, Jr., *Securing the Revolution: Ideology in American Politics, 1789–1815* (1972).

Federalist diplomacy is examined in Felix Gilbert, *To the Farewell Address* (1961). Samuel F. Bemis, *Jay's Treaty* (1923) and *Pinckney's Treaty* (1926, rev. 1960), examine two of the leading diplomatic episodes of the era. American relations with France are the subject of several important books: Alexander DeConde, *Entangling Alliance* (1958) and *The Quasi-War* (1966); Lawrence S. Kaplan, *Jefferson and France* (1967); Harry Ammon, *The Genêt Mission* (1973); and Louis M. Sears, *George Washington and the French Revolution* (1960). Bradford Perkins, *The First Rapprochement: England and the United States* (1967), and Charles Ritcheson, *Aftermath of Revolution: British Policy Toward the United States, 1783–1795*, examine Anglo-American relations. Paul A. Varg, *Foreign Policies of the Founding Fathers* (1963), is an overview.

An unusual number of fine biographies of the major public figures of this period are available. In addition to the Malone biography of Jefferson mentioned above and the Freeman biography of Washington mentioned in the readings for Chapter 5, see Irving Brant, *James Madison* (1950); James T. Flexner, *George Washington*, 4 vols. (1965–1972); Page Smith, *John Adams* (1962); and John C. Miller, *Alexander Hamilton* (1959).

The Jeffersonian Era 7

Thomas Jefferson
Thomas Jefferson posed for this portrait, by Rembrandt Peale, in the White House in 1805. It conveys some of the "democratic simplicity" that Jefferson tried to convey in his personal manner: decidedly inelegant clothing, slightly disheveled hair, and an expression of quiet amusement rather than solemnity or arrogance. (The Bettmann Archive)

Thomas Jefferson and his followers assumed control of the national government in 1801 as the champions of a distinctive vision of America. They envisioned a society of sturdy, independent farmers, happily free from the workshops, the industrial towns, and the city mobs of Europe. They favored a system of universal education that would introduce all Americans to the scientific rationalism of the Enlightenment. They promoted a cultural outlook that emphasized localism and republican simplicity. And above all, they proposed a federal government of sharply limited power, with most authority remaining at the level of the states.

Almost nothing worked out as they had planned, for during their years in power the young republic was developing in ways that made much of their vision obsolete. The American economy in the period of Republican ascendancy became steadily more diversified and complex. Growing cities, expanding commerce, and nascent industrialism made the ideal of a simple, agrarian society impossible to maintain. The quest for universal education foundered, and the nation's institutions of learning remained largely the preserve of privileged elites. American cultural life, far from reflecting localism and simplicity, was dominated by a vigorous and ambitious nationalism reminiscent of (and often encouraged by) the Federalists. And although American religion began, as the Jeffersonians had hoped, to confront and adjust to the spread of Enlightenment rationalism, the new skepticism did not survive unchallenged. A great wave of revivalism, beginning early in the century, ultimately almost submerged the new rational philosophy.

The Republicans did manage to translate some of their political ideals into reality. Jefferson dismantled much of the Federalist power structure that had been erected in the 1790s, and he helped to ensure that in many respects the federal government would remain a relatively unimportant force in American life. Yet at the same time, he frequently encountered situations that required him to exercise strong national authority. On occasion, he used his power more forcefully and arbitrarily than his Federalist predecessors.

The Republicans did not always like these nationalizing and modernizing trends, and on occasion they resisted them. For the most part, however, they had the sense to recognize what could not be changed. And in adjusting to the new realities, they themselves began to become agents of the very transformation of American life they had once strenuously resisted.

THE RISING GLORY OF AMERICA

In many respects, American cultural life in the early eighteenth century seemed to reflect the Republican vision of the nation's future. Opportunities for education increased; the nation's literary and artistic life began to free itself from European influences; and American religion began to confront and adjust to the spread of Enlightenment rationalism. In other respects, however, the United States was developing a culture that challenged Republican ideals.

Education and Professionalism

Central to the Republican vision of America was the concept of a virtuous and enlightened citizenry. An ignorant electorate, the Jeffersonians believed, could not be trusted to preserve democracy; education, therefore, was essential. Jefferson himself, for one, called emphatically for a national "crusade against ignorance." Republicans believed, therefore, in the creation of a nationwide system of public schools, in which all citizens would receive free educations.

Such hopes were not fulfilled. Although some states endorsed the principle of public education for all, none actually created a working system of free schools. A Massachusetts law of 1789 reaffirmed the colonial laws by which each town was obliged to support a school, but enforcement was so lax as to make it almost meaningless. Even in Boston, there were only seven public schools in 1790, most of them poorly housed. In Virginia, Jefferson had as wartime governor proposed a plan by which elementary education would be provided for all, and higher education for the gifted. Neither during nor after the war did the state legislature enact the proposal into law. As late as 1815—after more than a decade of Republican ascendancy in the nation's politics—not a single state had a comprehensive public school system.

Instead, schooling became primarily the responsibility of private institutions, most of which were open only to those who could afford to pay for them. In the South and in the Middle Atlantic states, where most schools were run by religious groups, almost every institution required tuition from the parents of prospective students. Poor farmers and workers, therefore, were usually excluded. In New England (and to a lesser extent elsewhere), there were a growing number of private academies available to the children of the relatively prosperous, but few schools for the less favored. Many of the new academies were modeled on those founded by the Phillips family: at Andover, Massachusetts, in 1778, and at Exeter, New Hampshire, three years later. By 1815, there were thirty such private secondary schools in Massachusetts, thirty-seven in New York, and several dozen more scattered throughout the country. Many were frankly aristocratic in outlook, training their students to become members of the nation's elite. Most of them admitted only boys, although a few seminaries and academies—such as the Salem Female Academy, founded in 1772 by the Moravian church in North Carolina—were established for girls as well.

There were some efforts to provide the poor with access to this system of private education or with separate schools of their own. Religious schools and private academies occasionally waived tuition for some who could not afford to pay it. In New York, the Free School Society provided a special institution for the poor. But such efforts fell far short of fulfilling Jefferson's vision of equal and universal education. The institutions available to the poor were not nearly numerous enough to accommodate everyone; and the education they offered was often clearly inferior to that provided more prosperous students. The New York Free School, for example, economized by adopting the so-called Lancastrian method from England, by which teachers taught only a few bright student "monitors," who then drilled their fellow pupils in what they had learned.

There was a similar gap between the Republican ideal and the early eighteenth-century reality in the nature of American higher education. On the one hand, the nation experienced a dramatic increase in the number of colleges and universities in its midst. At the outbreak of the Revolution there had been a total of nine colleges in all the colonies. By 1800, there were twenty-two, and the number continued to increase steadily thereafter. A majority of those founded in the first decades of independence, moreover, were nonsectarian; and five were state institutions—the universities founded in Georgia in 1785, North Carolina in 1789, Vermont in 1791, Ohio in 1804, and South Carolina in 1805. Yet none of the new schools was truly public. Because state legislatures were reluctant to appropriate funds for the universities, most relied on private contributions and on tuition fees to survive. Scarcely more than one man in a thousand (and no women at all) had access to any college education; and those few who did attend universities were almost without exception members of prosperous, propertied families.

Unequal access was only one of the problems facing American universities. Another was their inability to provide adequate training in the liberal arts or the professions. Jefferson, Adams, and others hoped for a time to establish a great national university in Washington to rival the eminent institutions

A School in Session, About 1800
In such a one-room school, children of practically all ages were brought together. While one group recited, the rest learned their lessons—or were supposed to. Paper and ink were scarce; a slate and a slate pencil were commonly used instead. There was little in the way of furnishings except for backless benches and a few desks, usually placed under the windows, where the light was best. The teacher had to look out for the fire and perform the other chores of a janitor. Often a teacher was a college student, earning money during the long winter vacation from his own studies, or he was a recent college graduate supporting himself while he prepared for the law and politics. Daniel Webster and Thaddeus Stevens once taught school, and so did many another young man who afterward became prominent in public life. (Library of Congress)

of Europe, but nothing came of their plans. And the provincial colleges continued to offer exceedingly limited curricula. There were a few institutions that attempted to provide advanced professional training to their students. Under Jefferson's prodding, the College of William and Mary in Virginia added professorships in law, medicine, and modern languages; and George Wythe, the first law professor at the college, trained a number of students who later became distinguished lawyers and statesmen. The University of Pennsylvania and Columbia College both instituted law programs before 1800; and Judge Tapping Reeve established a private law school in Litchfield, Connecticut.

However, most lawyers in America entered the profession without benefit of university training. They simply apprenticed themselves to a practicing attorney and "read law" in his office.

Medical education remained similarly crude. There were a few medical schools in operation by the early 1800s, the oldest of them at the University of Pennsylvania under the leadership of the distinguished physician Benjamin Rush. Most doctors, however, studied medicine by working with an established practitioner. And those such as Rush who believed in applying new scientific methods to medicine continued to struggle against age-old prejudices and superstitions.

Efforts to teach anatomy, for example, encountered strong public hostility because of the dissection of cadavers that the study required. Medical knowledge remained so limited that cities were virtually helpless when faced with epidemics; only slowly did urban officials respond to the warnings of Rush and others that lack of adequate sanitation programs were to blame for disease. Individual patients often had more to fear from doctors than from the illnesses themselves. George Washington's death in 1799 was probably less a result of the minor throat infection that had afflicted him than of the efforts of his physicians to cure the disease by bleeding and "purging" him.

Education and professional training in the early republic thus fell far short of the Jeffersonian vision. Indeed, efforts to promote education often had the effect of strengthening existing elites rather than eroding them. Nevertheless, the ideal of equal educational opportunity survived, and in later decades it would become a vital force behind universal public education.

Cultural Nationalism

Jeffersonian Americans may have repudiated the belief of the Federalists in political and economic centralization. But they embraced another form of nationalism with great fervor. Having won political independence from Europe, they aspired now to a form of cultural independence. And in the process, they raised a vision of American literary and artistic life that would rival the greatest achievements of Europe. As a "Poem on the Rising Glory of America" had foretold as early as 1772, Americans believed that their "happy land" was destined to become the "seat of empire" and the "final stage" of civilization, with "glorious works of high invention and of wond'rous art." The United States, one eighteenth-century writer proclaimed, would serve as "the last and greatest theatre for the improvement of mankind."

Such nationalism found expression, among other places, in early American schoolbooks. The Massachusetts geographer Jedidiah Morse, author of *Geography Made Easy* (1784), said the country must have its own textbooks so that the people would not be infected with the aristocratic ideas of England. The Connecticut schoolmaster and lawyer Noah Webster likewise contended that the American schoolboy should be educated as a patriot, his mind filled with nationalistic, American thoughts. "As soon as he opens his lips," Webster wrote, "he should rehearse the history of his own country; he should lisp the praise of liberty, and of those illustrious heroes and statesmen who have wrought a revolution in her favor."

Further to encourage a distinctive American culture and help unify the new nation, Webster insisted on a simplified and Americanized system of spelling—"honor" instead of "honour," for example. His *American Spelling Book*, first published in 1783 and commonly known as the "blue-backed speller," eventually sold over 100 million copies, to become the best-selling book (except for the Bible) in the entire history of American publishing. Webster also wrote grammars and other schoolbooks. His school dictionary, issued in 1806, was republished in many editions and was eventually enlarged to become *An American Dictionary of the English Language* (1828). His speller and his dictionary established a national standard of words and usages. Although Webster's Federalist political views fell into disfavor in the early nineteenth century, his cultural nationalism remained popular and influential.

Those Americans who aspired to create a more elevated national literary life faced a number of obstacles. There was, to be sure, a large potential audience for a national literature—a reading public developed in large part by the wide circulation of newspapers and political pamphlets during the Revolution. But there were few opportunities for a would-be American author to get his work before the public. Printers preferred to publish popular works by English writers (for which they had to pay no royalties); magazine publishers filled their pages largely with items clipped from British periodicals. Only those American writers willing to pay the cost and bear the risk of publishing their own works could compete for public attention.

Yet a growing number of American au-

thors strove to create a strong native literature so that, as the poet Joel Barlow wrote,
"true ideas of glory may be implanted in the
minds of men here, to take the place of the
false and destructive ones that have degraded
the species in other countries." Barlow himself, one of a group of Connecticut writers
known as the "Hartford Wits," published an
epic poem, *The Columbiad*, in 1807, in an effort to convey the special character of American civilization. The acclaim it received
helped to encourage other native writers.

Among the most ambitious was the Philadelphia writer Charles Brockden Brown. Like
many Americans, he was attracted to the new
literary form of the novel, which had become
popular in England in the late eighteenth
century and had been successfully imported
to America. But Brown sought to do more
than simply imitate the English forms; he
tried to use his novels to give voice to distinctively American themes, to convey the
"soaring passions and intellectual energy" of
the new nation. His obsession with original-
ity led him to produce a body of work characterized by a fascination with horror and
deviant behavior—novels that failed to develop a large popular following.

Far more successful was Washington Irving, a resident of New York who won wide
acclaim for his satirical histories of early
American life and his powerful fables of society in the New World. His popular folk
tales, recounting the adventures of such
American rustics as Ichabod Crane and Rip
Van Winkle, made him the widely acknowledged leader of American literary life in the
early eighteenth century and one of the few
writers of that era whose works would continue to be read by later generations.

Perhaps the most influential works by
American authors in the early republic were
not poems, novels, or stories, but works of
history that glorified the nation's past. Mercy
Otis Warren, the influential pamphleteer and
agitator during the 1770s, continued her literary efforts with a three-volume *History of the
Revolution*, published in 1805 and emphasizing the heroism of the American struggle.
Mason Weems, an Anglican clergyman,
published a eulogistic *Life of Washington* in
1806, which became one of the best-selling

books of the era. Weems had little interest in
historical accuracy. He portrayed the aristocratic former president as a homespun man
possessing simple republican virtues. (He
also invented the story of Washington cutting down the cherry tree.) History, like literature, was serving as a vehicle for instilling a
sense of nationalism in the American people.

Religion and Revivalism

The American Revolution had had a disastrous impact on traditional forms of religious
practice. Not only had the Anglicans suffered
for their alleged British sympathies and the
Quakers for their pacifism, but the positions
of almost all churches had in some ways declined. The detachment of religion from government in the years following independence
weakened some established religions—notably Congregationalism in New England. The
ideology of individual liberty and reason
weakened others. By the 1790s, although
most Americans continued to hold strong religious beliefs, only a small proportion (perhaps as few as 10 percent) were members of
formal churches. And the evangelical fervor
aroused by the Great Awakening of the
1730s had almost entirely vanished. There
were ample reasons for the frequent complaints of ministers during the Revolutionary
era about the "decay of vital piety" and the
luxurious growth of "vice."

Among the most disturbing challenges to
religious traditionalists was the emergence of
new, "rational" religious doctrines—theolo-
gies that attempted to reconcile modern, scientific attitudes with Christian faith. They
offered an approach to religion that sharply
de-emphasized the role of God in the world
and challenged much of conventional Christian orthodoxy. Some Americans—including
Jefferson and Franklin—embraced "deism,"
which had originated among Enlightenment
philosophers in France. Deists accepted the
existence of God, but they considered Him a
remote being who, after having created the
universe, had withdrawn from direct involvement with the human race and its sins. Such
views remained confined to a small group of
highly educated people at first, but by 1800

deist ideas were reaching a much wider audience. Books and articles attacking religious "superstitions" were widely read and much discussed. Among the most influential was *The Age of Reason* (1794–1796) of Thomas Paine, who once declared that Christianity was the "strangest religion ever set up," for "it committed a murder upon Jesus in order to redeem mankind from the sin of eating an apple."

Religious skepticism also produced the philosophies of "universalism" and "unitarianism," which emerged at first as dissenting views within the New England Congregational church. Disciples of these new ideas rejected the traditional Calvinist belief in predestination, arguing that salvation was available to all. They rejected, too, the idea of the Trinity. Jesus was only a great religious teacher, they claimed, not the son of God. So wide was the gulf between these dissenters and the Congregationalist establishment, that a permanent schism finally occurred. The Universalist church was founded as a separate denomination in Gloucester, Massachusetts, in 1779, and the Unitarian church was established in Boston three years later.

Yet although many Americans believed that the spread of rationalism foretold the end of traditional, evangelistic religion in the new nation, nothing could have been further from the truth. Deism, universalism, and unitarianism all seemed more powerful than they actually were, in part because those who clung to more traditional faiths were for a time confused and disorganized, unable to react effectively. Beginning in 1801, however, traditional religion staged a dramatic comeback in the form of a wave of revivalism known as the Second Great Awakening.

The origins of the awakening lay in the efforts of conservative theologians of the 1790s to fight the spread of religious rationalism. Presbyterians strengthened their organization and expanded their efforts on the frontier, with conservatives in the church becoming increasingly militant in response to so-called New Light dissenters. Methodism, founded in England by John Wesley, spread to America in the 1770s and established itself as a formal church in 1784 under the leadership of Francis Asbury. Authoritarian and hierarchical in structure, the Methodists sent itinerant preachers throughout the nation to win recruits for the new church, which soon became the fastest-growing denomination in America. Almost as successful were the Baptists, who were themselves relatively new to America; they found an especially fervent following in the South.

By 1800, the revivalist energies of all these congregations were combining to create the greatest surge of evangelical fervor since the first Great Awakening sixty years before. Beginning among Presbyterians in several Eastern colleges (most notably at Yale, under the leadership of President Timothy Dwight), the new awakening soon spread throughout the country, reaching its greatest heights in the Western regions. In only a few years, a large proportion of the American people were mobilized by the movement; and membership in those churches embracing the revival—most prominently the Methodists, the Baptists, and the Presbyterians—was mushrooming. At Cane Ridge, Kentucky, in the summer of 1801, a group of evangelical ministers presided over the nation's first "camp meeting"—an extraordinary revival that lasted several days and impressed all who saw it with its fervor. Such events became common in subsequent years, as the Methodists in particular came to rely on them as a way to "harvest" new members. The Methodist circuit-riding preacher Peter Cartwright won national fame as he traveled from region to region exhorting his listeners to embrace the church. Even Cartwright, however, was often unprepared for the results of his efforts—a religious frenzy that manifested itself at times in convulsions, fits, rolling in the dirt, and the twitching "holy jerks."

The message of the Second Great Awakening was not entirely uniform, but its basic thrust was clear. Individuals must readmit God and Christ into their daily lives, must embrace a fervent, active piety, and must reject the skeptical rationalism that threatened traditional beliefs. Yet the wave of revivalism did not serve to restore the religion of the past. Few denominations any longer accepted the idea of predestination; and the belief that a person could affect his or her own destiny,

A Camp Meeting
Originating in 1800, the camp meeting soon became a popular American religious institution in rural areas, especially in the South and West. By 1820, about 1,000 meetings a year were held. The painting reproduced here was made in the 1830s. A typical camp meeting (in Maryland, in 1806) was described by a participant who wrote of the tents, the wagons, the plank seats, the covered stand for the preacher, and the daily schedule. "At day break the trumpets were blown round the camp for the people to rise 20 minutes afterward for family prayer at the door of every tent—if fair weather—at sunrise they blew at the stand for public prayer, and then breakfasted. At 10 oclock they blew for preaching—by 2 ocl. dinner was to be over in every tent. At 3 ocl. preaching again, and again at night." After several days of this, "hundreds were prostrate upon the earth before the Lord. . . . Will I ever see anything more like the day of Judgment on this side of eternity—to see the people running, yes, running, from every direction to the stand, weeping, shouting, and shouting for joy. Prayer was then made—and every Brother fell upon the neck of his Brother, and the Sisters did likewise. Then we parted. O! glorious day they went home singing and shouting." (Courtesy of the New-York Historical Society, New York City)

rather than encouraging irreligion as many had feared, added intensity to the individual's search for salvation. Nor did the awakening work to reestablish old institutional forms of religion. Instead, it reinforced the spread of different sects and denominations and helped to create a general public acceptance of the idea that men and women could belong to different Protestant churches and still be committed to essentially the same Christian faith. Finally, the new evangelicalism—by spreading religious fervor into virtually every area of the nation, including remote regions where no formal church had

ever existed—provided a vehicle for establishing a sense of order and social stability in communities still searching for an identity.

The rational "freethinkers," whose skeptical philosophies had done so much to produce the awakening, did not disappear after 1800, but their influence rapidly declined; and for many years to come they remained a distinct and defensive minority within American Christianity. Instead, the dominant religious characteristic of the new nation would be a fervent revivalism, which would survive well into the mid-nineteenth century.

The new religious enthusiasm meshed

with the cultural and political optimism of the early republic. Many Americans were coming to believe that their nation had a special destiny: that its political system would serve as a model to the world, that its culture would become a beacon to mankind. Now there were voices arguing that the United States had a religious mission as well, that American revivalism would lead to the salvation of the entire globe. This expansive, at times even arrogant assumption that Americans had been anointed to lead the world into a new era became one of the most powerful forces in the nation's outlook.

STIRRINGS OF INDUSTRIALISM

It was not only culturally and religiously that the nation was developing in ways unforeseen by Jefferson and his followers. Economically, the United States was taking the first, tentative steps toward a transformation that would ultimately shatter forever the vision of a simple, agrarian republic.

The Industrial Revolution in England

While Americans were engaged in a revolution to win their independence, an even more important revolution was in progress in England: the emergence of modern industrialism. Historians differ over precisely when the Industrial Revolution began, but it is clear that by the end of the eighteenth century it was well under way. Its essence was relatively simple: power-driven machines were taking the place of hand-operated tools and were permitting manufacturing to become more rapid and extensive. But however simple the causes, the social and economic consequences of the transformation were complex and profound.

The factory system in England took root first in the manufacture of cotton thread and cloth. There, one invention followed another in quick succession. Improvements in weaving made necessary improvements in spinning; and these changes required new devices for carding (combing and straightening the fibers for the spinner). Water, wind, and animal power continued to be important in the textile industry, but far more important was the emergence of steam power—which began to proliferate after the appearance of James Watt's advanced steam engine (patented in 1769). Cumbersome and inefficient by modern standards, Watt's engine was nevertheless a major improvement over the earlier "atmospheric" engine of Thomas Newcomen. England's textile industry quickly became the most profitable in the world, and it helped encourage comparable advances in other fields of manufacturing as well.

At the same time, England's social system was undergoing a wrenching change. Hundreds of thousands of men and women were moving from rural areas into cities to work in factories; and there they experienced both the benefits and the costs of industrialization. The standard of living of the new working class, when objectively quantified, was significantly higher than that of the rural poor. Most of those who moved from farm to factory, in other words, experienced some improvement in their material circumstances. But the psychological costs of being suddenly uprooted from one way of life and thrust into another, fundamentally different one often outweighed the economic gains. There was little in the prior experience of most workers to prepare them for the nature of industrial labor: disciplined, routinized work on a fixed schedule, which stood in sharp contrast to the varying, seasonal work pattern of the rural economy. Nor were the factory workers often prepared for life in the new industrial towns and expanding cities where they were obliged to live. They experienced, too, a fundamental change in their relationship with their employers. Unlike the landlords and local aristocrats of rural England, factory owners and managers—the new class of industrial capitalists, many of them accumulating unprecedented wealth—were usually remote and inaccessible figures. They dealt with their workers impersonally, and the result was a growing schism between the two classes—each lacking access to or understanding of the other.

As a result, English life was being transformed at every level. The middle class was expanding and coming to dominate the economy, although not yet the culture or the nation's politics. Working class men and women were beginning to think of themselves as a distinct class, with common goals and interests. And their simultaneous efforts to adjust to their new way of life and to resist its most damaging aspects made the late eighteenth and early nineteenth centuries a time of continuing social turbulence.

Not since the agrarian revolution thousands of years earlier, when man had turned from hunting to farming for sustenance, had there been an economic change of a magnitude comparable to the Industrial Revolution. Centuries of traditions, of social patterns, of cultural and religious assumptions, were challenged and often shattered. Almost nothing would ever again be quite the same.

Technology in America

Nothing even remotely comparable to the English Industrial Revolution occurred in America in the first decade of the nineteenth century. Indeed, it was opposition to the kind of economic growth occurring in England that had helped the Republicans defeat the Federalists in 1800; and Americans continued to view British industrialization with deep ambivalence. Yet even while they warned of the dangers of rapid economic change, Americans of the age of Jefferson were welcoming a series of technological advances that would ultimately help ensure that the United States too would be transformed.

Some of these technological advances were imported from England. The British government attempted to protect the nation's manufacturing preeminence by preventing the export of textile machinery or the emigration of skilled mechanics. But despite such efforts, a number of immigrants arrived in the United States with advanced knowledge of English technology, eager to introduce the new machines to America. Samuel

Slater, for example, used knowledge he had acquired before leaving England to build a spinning mill in Pawtucket, Rhode Island, for the Quaker merchant Moses Brown in 1790. It was generally recognized as the first modern factory in America.

More important than imported technology, however, was that of purely domestic origin. America in the early nineteenth century produced several important inventors of its own. Among them was Oliver Evans, of Delaware, who devised a number of ingenious new machines: an automated flour mill, a card-making machine, and others. He worked several important improvements in the steam engine, and he even published America's first textbook of mechanical engineering: *The Young Mill-Wright's and Miller's Guide* (1795). In his own flour mill, which went into operation in 1787 (the same year the Constitutional Convention first met), virtually all operations were mechanized. Only two men were required to operate the mill: one of them emptying a bag of wheat into the machinery, another putting the lid on the barrels of flour and rolling them away.

Even more influential for the future of the nation were the inventions of the Massachusetts-born, Yale-educated Eli Whitney, who revolutionized both cotton production and weapons manufacturing. The growth of the textile industry in England had created an enormous demand for cotton, a demand that planters in the American South were finding impossible to meet. Their greatest obstacle was the difficulty of separating the seeds from the cotton fiber—a process that was essential before the cotton could be sold. There was one variety of cotton with smooth black seeds and long fibers that was easily cleaned; but this "long-staple" or "sea-island" variety could be grown successfully only along the coast or on the offshore islands of Georgia and South Carolina. There was not nearly enough of it to satisfy the demand. Another variety, short-staple cotton, could be grown almost anywhere in the South; but its sticky green seeds were extremely difficult to remove, and a skilled worker could clean no more than a few pounds a day by hand. Then, in 1793, Whitney, who was working at the time as a tutor on the Georgia plantation

Slater Mill
Samuel Slater left England in the disguise of a farm boy, since English law prohibited the emigration of mechanics with a knowledge of textile machinery. At Pawtucket, Rhode Island, in 1790, he designed what became the first successful cotton-spinning mill in the United States. In 1815, he added facilities for weaving woolen cloth. This watercolor-and-ink drawing represents the Pawtucket bridge, falls, and mill as they were sometime between 1810 and 1819.
(The Rhode Island Historical Society)

of General Nathanael Greene's widow, invented a machine that performed the arduous task quickly and efficiently. It was dubbed the cotton gin ("gin" being a derivative of "engine"); and it would soon transform the life of the South.

Mechanically, the gin was very simple. A toothed roller caught the fibers of the cotton boll and pulled them between the wires of a grating. The grating caught the seeds, and a revolving brush removed the lint from the roller's teeth. With the device, a single operator could clean as much cotton in a few hours as a whole group of workers had once been able to do in a day. The results were profound. Soon cotton growing spread into the upland South, and within a decade, the total

crop increased eightfold. Negro slavery, which with the decline of tobacco production had seemed for a time to be a dwindling institution, was now restored to importance, expanded, and firmly fixed upon the South.

The cotton gin not only changed the economy of the South. It also helped transform the North. The large supply of domestically produced fiber served as a strong incentive to entrepreneurs in New England and elsewhere to develop a native textile industry. Few Northern states could hope to thrive on the basis of agriculture alone; by learning to process cotton, they could become industrially prosperous instead. The manufacturing preeminence of the North, which emerged with the development of the textile industry in the 1820s and 1830s, helped drive a wedge between the nation's two most populous regions and ultimately contributed to the coming of the Civil War. It also helped ensure the eventual Union victory.

Whitney's contribution to industrialization and warfare went beyond the indirect effects of the cotton gin. He helped as well to produce modern weaponry and, in the process, to introduce modern industrial techniques. During the undeclared war with France (1798–1800), Americans were deeply troubled by their lack of sufficient armaments for the expected hostilities. Production of muskets—each carefully handcrafted by a skilled gunsmith—was distressingly slow. Whitney responded by devising a machine to make each of the parts of a gun according to an exact pattern. Tasks could thus be divided among several workmen, and one laborer could assemble a rifle out of parts made by several other workers. Before long, the same system was being applied to sewing machines, clocks, and many other complicated products.

The new technological advances were relatively isolated phenomena during the early years of the nineteenth century. Not until at least 1820 did the nation begin to develop a true manufacturing economy. But the inventions of this period were crucial in making the eventual transformation possible.

Trade and Transportation

One of the prerequisites for industrialization is a transportation system that allows the efficient conveyance of raw materials to factories and of finished goods to markets. The United States had no such system in the early years of the republic, and thus it had no domestic market extensive enough to justify large-scale production. Yet even then efforts were under way that would ultimately remove the transportation obstacle.

There were several ways to solve the problem of the small American market. One was to develop markets overseas; and American merchants continued to do that with alacrity. One of the first acts of the new Congress when it met in 1789 was to pass two

acts giving preference in tariff rates and port duties to American ships, helping to stimulate an expansion of shipping. Also helpful was the outbreak of war in Europe in the 1790s, allowing Yankee merchant vessels to take over most of the carrying trade between Europe and the Western Hemisphere. As early as 1793, the young republic had a merchant marine and a foreign trade larger than those of any country except England. In proportion to its population, the United States had more ships and international commerce than any country in the world. And the shipping business was growing fast. Between 1789 and 1810, the total tonnage of American vessels engaged in overseas traffic rose from less than 125,000 to nearly 1 million. Whereas only 30 percent of the country's exports had been carried in American ships in 1789, over 90 percent was being so carried by 1810. The figures for imports increased even more dramatically, from 17.5 percent to 90 percent in the same period.

Another solution to the problem of limited markets was to develop new markets at home, by improving transportation between the states and into the interior. Progress was slower here than in international shipping, but some improvements were occurring nevertheless. In river transportation, a new era began with the development of the steamboat. Oliver Evans's high-pressure engine, lighter and more efficient than James Watt's, made steam more feasible for powering boats as well as mill machinery and, eventually, the locomotive. Even before the high-pressure engine was available, a number of inventors experimented with steam-powered craft, and John Fitch exhibited to some of the delegates at the Constitutional Convention a forty-five-foot vessel with paddles operated by steam. The perfecting of the steamboat was chiefly the work of the inventor Robert Fulton and the promoter Robert R. Livingston. Their *Clermont*, equipped with paddle wheels and an English-built engine, sailed up the Hudson in the summer of 1807, demonstrating the practicability of steam navigation (even though it took the ship thirty hours to go 150 miles). In 1811, a partner of Livingston's, Nicholas J. Roosevelt, introduced the steamboat to the West by sending the *New*

Orleans from Pittsburgh down the Ohio and Mississippi. The next year, this vessel entered on a profitable career of service between New Orleans and Natchez.

Meanwhile, in land transportation, what was to become known as the turnpike era had begun. In 1792, a corporation constructed a toll road running the sixty miles from Philadelphia to Lancaster, with a hard-packed surface of crushed rock. This venture proved so successful that similar turnpikes (so named from the kind of tollgate frequently used) were laid out from other cities to neighboring towns. Since the turnpikes were built and operated for private profit, construction costs had to be low enough and the prospective traffic heavy enough to ensure an early and ample return. Therefore these roads, radiating from Eastern cities, ran for comparatively short distances and through thickly settled areas. If similar highways were to be extended over the mountains, the state governments or the federal government would have to finance the construction, at least in part.

Country and City

Despite all the changes and all the advances, America remained in the early nineteenth century an overwhelmingly rural and agrarian nation. Only three people in a hundred lived in towns of more than 8,000 at the time of the second census in 1800. Ten in a hundred lived west of the Appalachian Mountains, far from what urban centers there were. Much of the country remained a wilderness. Even the nation's largest cities could not begin to compare, either in size or in cultural sophistication, with such European capitals as London and Paris.

Yet here too there were signs that the future might be different from the Jeffersonian vision of rural simplicity. The leading American cities might not yet have become world capitals, but they were large and complex enough to rival the important secondary cities of Europe. Philadelphia, with 70,000 residents, and New York, with 60,000, were becoming major centers of commerce, of learning, and of a distinctively urban culture.

Brooklyn, New York, in the Early 1800s
Settled by the Dutch, Brooklyn was not incorporated as a city until almost two centuries later, in 1834. It became a part of New York City in 1898. During the early 1800s, Brooklyn, on the western tip of Long Island, retained a village atmosphere, though separated only by the East River from the bustling city of New York on Manhattan Island. Note the village pump—the water supply of the surrounding householders. From "Winter Scene in Brooklyn," a contemporary painting by Francis Guy. (The Brooklyn Museum, Gift of the Brooklyn Institute of Arts and Sciences)

So too were the next largest cities of the new nation: Baltimore (26,000 in 1800), Boston (24,000), and Charleston (20,000).

Much remained to be done before this small and still half-formed nation would become a complex modern society. It was still possible in the early nineteenth century to believe that those changes might not ever occur. But forces were already at work that, in time, would lastingly transform the United States. And Thomas Jefferson, for all his commitment to the agrarian ideal, found himself as president obliged to confront and accommodate them.

JEFFERSON THE PRESIDENT

Privately, Thomas Jefferson may well have considered his victory over John Adams in 1800 to be what he later termed it: a revolution "as real . . . as that of 1776." Publicly, however, he was at the time restrained and conciliatory, attempting to minimize the differences between the two parties and calm the passions that the bitter campaign had aroused. "We are all Republicans, we are all Federalists," he said in his inaugural address. And during his eight years in office, he did much to prove his words correct. There was no complete repudiation of Federalist policies, no true "revolution." Indeed, at times Jefferson seemed to outdo the Federalists at their own work—most notably in overseeing a remarkable expansion of the territory of the United States.

In other respects, however, the Jefferson presidency did indeed represent a fundamental change in the direction of the federal government. The new administration oversaw a drastic reduction in the powers of some national institutions, and it forestalled the development of new powers in areas where the Federalists would certainly have attempted to expand them. Neither the executive nor the legislative branch of government was either willing or able to exercise decisive authority in most areas of national life. Only the courts continued trying to assert federal power in the ways the Federalists had envisioned.

The Federal City

The relative unimportance of the federal government during the era of Jefferson was symbolized by the character of the newly

---

Jefferson's First Inaugural [1801]

We are all Republicans, we are all Federalists. If there be any among us who would wish to dissolve this Union or to change its republican form, let them stand undisturbed as monuments of the safety with which error of opinion may be tolerated where reason is left free to combat it. I know, indeed, that some honest men fear that a republican government can not be strong, that this Government is not strong enough; but would the honest patriot, in the full tide of successful experiment, abandon a government which has so far kept us free and firm on the theoretic and visionary fear that this Government, the world's best hope, may by possibility want energy to preserve itself? I trust not. I believe this, on the contrary, the strongest Government on earth. I believe it the only one where every man, at the call of the law, would fly to the standard of the law, and would meet invasions of the public order as his own personal concern. Sometimes it is said that man can not be trusted with the government of himself. Can he, then, be trusted with the government of others? Or have we found angels in the forms of kings to govern him? Let history answer this question.

Washington in 1800
Even this somewhat idealized view of Washington (as seen looking west from Capitol Hill) reveals how small and crude a village the new "city" actually was in 1800. So dismal were the surroundings that few employees of the federal government—and even fewer elected officials—lived in Washington any longer than was strictly necessary. Even the president regularly fled the hot, steamy city during the long summer months. The unattractiveness of the federal city symbolized the dominant political idea of the early nineteenth century: the Jeffersonian view that the federal government should be as small and insignificant a force as possible in the new nation. (Library of Congress)

founded national capital, the city of Washington. John Adams had moved to the new seat of government during the last year of his administration. And there were many at that time who envisioned that the raw, uncompleted town would soon emerge as a great and majestic city, a focus for the growing nationalism that the Federalists were promoting. The French architect Pierre L'Enfant had designed the capital on a grand scale, with broad avenues radiating from the uncompleted Capitol building, which was to adorn one of the area's highest hills. Washington was, many Americans believed, to become the Paris of the United States.

In actuality, throughout Jefferson's presidency—indeed throughout most of the nineteenth century—Washington remained little more than a straggling, provincial village. Although the population increased steadily from the 3,200 counted in the 1800 census, it never rivaled that of New York, Philadelphia, and the other major cities of the nation. One problem was the climate: wet and cold in winter, hot and almost unbearably humid in summer, reflecting the marshy character of the site. Another problem, however, was that those in the federal government responsible for the development of the city did little to further its growth. The Republican administrations of the early nineteenth century oversaw the completion of several sections of the present-day Capitol, of the White House, and of a few other government buildings.

Otherwise, they allowed the city to remain a raw, inhospitable community, one whose muddy streets were at times almost impassable, one in which the Capitol and the White House were often cut off from one another by rising creeks and washed-away bridges.

Members of Congress viewed the city not as a home but as a place to visit briefly during sessions of the legislature and leave as quickly as possible. Few owned houses in Washington. Most lived in a cluster of simple boardinghouses in the vicinity of the Capitol. It was not unusual for a member of Congress to resign his seat in the midst of a session to return home if he had an opportunity to accept the more prestigious post of member of his state legislature. During the summers, the entire government in effect packed up and left town. The president, the cabinet, the Congress, and most other federal employees spent the hot summer months far from the uncomfortable capital.

President and Party Leader

From the outset, Jefferson acted in a spirit of democratic simplicity in keeping with the frontierlike character of the unfinished federal city. Although a wealthy and aristocratic planter by background, the owner of more than a hundred slaves, and a man of rare cultivation and cultural sophistication, he conveyed to the public an image of plain, almost crude disdain for pretension. He walked like an ordinary citizen to and from his inauguration at the Capitol, instead of riding in a coach at the head of a procession. In the presidential mansion, which had not yet acquired the name the White House, he disregarded the courtly etiquette of his predecessors (in part, no doubt, because as a widower he had no first lady to take charge of social affairs). At state dinners, he let his guests scramble pell-mell for places at the table. He did not always bother to dress up, prompting the fastidious British ambassador to complain on one occasion of being received by the president in coat and pantaloons that were "indicative of utter slovenliness and indifference to appearances." Even when carefully dressed, the tall, freckle-faced, sandy-haired Jefferson did not offer an impressive physical appear-

ance. He was shy. His posture was awkward. He walked with a shambling gait. And he was an ineffective public speaker.

Yet Jefferson managed nevertheless to impress most of those who knew him. He was a brilliant and charming conversationalist, a writer endowed with literary skills unmatched by any president before or since (with the possible exception of Lincoln), and undoubtedly one of the nation's most intelligent and creative men, with a wider range of interests and accomplishments than any public figure in our history. In addition to politics and diplomacy, he was an active architect, educator, inventor, scientific farmer, and philosopher-scientist. He diverted himself with such pastimes as sorting the bones of prehistoric animals or collecting volumes for one of the nation's greatest private libraries (which later became the basis of the original Library of Congress). Many years later, President John Kennedy referred to a White House dinner for Nobel Prize laureates as the greatest collection of genius ever gathered in the building except for those nights when "Thomas Jefferson dined alone."

Jefferson was, above all, a shrewd and practical politician, equaled in that regard perhaps only by Lincoln and Franklin D. Roosevelt. On the one hand, he went to great lengths to eliminate the aura of majesty surrounding the presidency that he believed his predecessors had created. He decided, for example, to submit his messages to Congress not by delivering them in person, as Washington and Adams had done, but by sending them in writing, thus avoiding even the semblance of attempting to dictate to the legislature. (The precedent he established survived for more than a century, until the administration of Woodrow Wilson.) At the same time, however, Jefferson worked hard to exert influence as the leader of his party, giving direction to Republicans in Congress by quiet and sometimes even devious means.

To his cabinet he appointed members of his own party who shared his philosophy. His secretary of state was James Madison, a long-time friend and neighbor whose collaboration with the president throughout Jefferson's administration was so close that it was often difficult to tell who was more responsible for government policy. Secretary of the treasury was Albert Gallatin, a Swiss-born politician with a French accent who, despite a financial expertise that made him the rival of Hamilton, was a staunch opponent of Federalist policies. He had, for example, once acted as the lawyer defending the tax-resisting western Pennsylvania farmers who were engaged in the Whiskey Rebellion.

Although the Republicans had objected strenuously to the efforts of their Federalist predecessors to build up a network of influence through patronage, Jefferson too used his powers of appointment as an effective political weapon. Like Washington before him, he believed that federal offices should be filled with men loyal to the principles and policies of the administration. True, he did not attempt a sudden and drastic removal of Federalist officeholders, possibly because of assurances to the contrary that had been given in his name when Federalist votes in Congress were needed to break the tie with Burr. Yet at every convenient opportunity he replaced the holdovers from the Adams administration with his own trusted followers. By the end of his first term about half the government jobs, and by the end of his second term practically all of them, were held by good Republicans The president punished Burr and the Burrites by withholding patronage from them; he never forgave the man whom he believed guilty of plotting to frustrate the intentions of the party and the ambitions of its rightful candidate.

A tie vote between the presidential and vice-presidential candidates of the same party could not occur again. The Twelfth Amendment, added to the Constitution in 1804 before the election of that year, by implication recognized the function of political parties; it stipulated that the electors should vote for president and vice president as separate and distinct candidates. Burr had no chance to run on the ticket with Jefferson a second time. In place of Burr, the congressional caucus of Republicans nominated his New York factional foe, George Clinton. The Federalist nominee, C. C. Pinckney, made a poor showing against the popular Jefferson, who carried even the New England states ex-

cept Connecticut and was reelected by the overwhelming electoral majority of 162 to 14. The Republican membership of both houses of Congress increased.

During his second term Jefferson lost some of his popularity, and he had to deal with a revolt within the party ranks. His brilliant but erratic relative John Randolph of Roanoke, the House leader, turned against him, accusing him of acting like a Federalist instead of a states' rights Republican. Randolph mustered a handful of anti-Jefferson factionalists who called themselves "Quids." Randolph became particularly excited on the subject of the Yazoo land claims. These claims arose from the action of the Georgia legislature, which, before ceding its territorial rights to the federal government, had made and then canceled a grant of millions of acres along the Mississippi to the Yazoo Land Companies. Jefferson favored a compromise settlement that would have satisfied both the state of Georgia and the Yazoo investors, many of whom were Northern Republicans whose support he needed. But Randolph, insisting that the claims were fradulent, charged the president with complicity in corruption. A number of members of Congress were investors in the land companies or supporters of their claims, and time and again the tall, skinny Virginian would point his bony finger at one or another of these men and shriek contemptuously, "Yazoo!" He prevented the government from making any settlement of the question until both he and Jefferson were out of office.

Randolph had a special antipathy toward Madison, whom he considered as one of the worst of the Yazoo men. He did all he could, which was not enough, to prevent Madison's nomination for the presidency in 1808. Jefferson refused to consider a third term for himself, for he was opposed to it in principle, unlike Washington, who had declined to run again in 1796 only because he was weary of public office. Jefferson's refusal established a tradition against a third term for any president, a tradition that remained unbroken until 1940. Although unwilling himself to be a candidate in 1808, Jefferson was determined that his alter ego, Madison, should succeed him and carry on his policies.

Dollars and Ships

Despite Jefferson's use of forceful political methods, his administration did move far toward dismantling the federal power structure that the Federalists had attempted to erect. Under Washington and Adams, the Republicans believed, the government had been needlessly extravagant. Yearly expenditures had risen so much that in 1800 they were almost three times as high as they had been in 1793. The public debt had also risen, as Hamilton had intended. And an extensive system of internal taxation, including the hated whiskey excise tax, had been erected.

The Jefferson administration moved deliberately to reverse the trend. In 1802, it persuaded Congress to abolish all internal taxes, leaving customs duties and the sale of Western lands as the only source of revenue for the government. At the same time, Secretary of the Treasury Gallatin carried out a plan for drastic retrenchment in government spending, scrimping as much as possible on expenditures for the normal operations of government, cutting the already small staffs of the executive departments to minuscule levels. Although Jefferson was unable entirely to retire the national debt as he had hoped, he did cut it almost in half (from $83 million to $45 million).

Jefferson also effected a "chaste reformation" of the armed forces. The tiny army of 4,000 men he reduced to 2,500. The navy he pared down from twenty-five ships in commission to seven, cutting the number of officers and sailors accordingly. Anything but the smallest of standing armies, he argued, might menace civil liberties and civilian control of government. And a large navy, he feared, might be misused to promote overseas commerce, which Jefferson believed should remain secondary to agriculture.

Yet despite his claims that "Peace is our passion," Jefferson was not a pacifist. At the same time that he was reducing the size of the army and navy, he was helping to establish the United States Military Academy at West Point, founded in 1802. And when trouble began to brew overseas, he began again to build up the fleet.

For years the Barbary states of North Africa—Morocco, Algiers, Tunis, and Tripoli—had made piracy a national enterprise. They demanded protection money from all nations whose ships sailed the Mediterranean. Even the ruler of the seas, Great Britain, gave regular contributions (England did not in fact particularly desire to eliminate a racket that hurt its naval rivals and maritime competitors more seriously than itself). During the 1780s and 1790s the United States agreed to treaties providing for annual tribute to Morocco and the rest, and from time to time the Adams administration ransomed American sailors who had been captured and were being held as slaves. Jefferson doubted the wisdom of continuing appeasement. "Tribute or war is the usual alternative of these Barbary pirates," he said. "Why not build a navy and decide on war?"

The decision was not left to Jefferson. In 1801, the pasha of Tripoli, dissatisfied with the American response to his extortionate demands, had the flagpole of the American consulate chopped down—his way of declaring war. Jefferson concluded that, as president, he had a constitutional right to defend the United States without a war declaration by Congress; and he sent a squadron to the relief of the ships already at the scene. Not until 1803, however, was the fleet strong enough to take effective action, under commodores Edward Preble and Samuel Barron. In 1805, the pasha, by threatening to kill captive Americans, compelled Barron to agree to a peace that ended the payment of tribute but exacted a large ransom ($60,000) for the release of the prisoners. It was hardly a resounding victory for the United States.

Conflict with the Courts

Having won control of the executive and legislative branches of government, the Republicans looked with suspicion on the judiciary, which remained largely in the hands of Federalist judges. Soon after Jefferson's first inauguration, his followers in Congress launched an attack on this last preserve of the opposition. First, the legislators repealed the Judiciary Act of 1801, thus abolishing the new circuit courts and arranging instead for

Marbury v. Madison [1803]

Chief Justice Marshall:

It is emphatically the province and duty of the judicial department to say what the law is. Those who apply the rule to particular cases must of necessity expound and interpret that rule. If two laws conflict with each other, the courts must decide on the operation of each.

So if a law be in opposition to the constitution; if both the law and the constitution apply to a particular case, so that the court must either decide that case conformably to the law, disregarding the constitution, or conformably to the constitution, disregarding the law, the court must determine which of these conflicting rules governs the case. This is of the very essence of judicial duty.

If, then, the courts are to regard the constitution, and the constitution is superior to any ordinary act of the legislature, the constitution, and not such ordinary act, must govern the case to which they both apply.

---

each of the Supreme Court justices to sit with a district judge on circuit duty. With their energies stretched thin, the Republicans believed, the jurists would be unable to become active or influential foes. Since Jefferson lacked authority to remove Adams's "midnight appointees" from their newly created jobs, Congress had achieved the same object by pulling their benches out from under them, despite Federalist protests that the repeal violated the constitutional provision that judges should hold office for life.

The debate over the Judiciary Act of 1801 led to one of the most important judicial decisions in the history of the nation. Federalists had long maintained that the Supreme Court had the authority to review acts of Congress and to nullify those that were in conflict with the Constitution. Hamilton had argued for such a power in *The Federalist Papers* (although the Constitution said nothing specifically to support him), and the Court itself had actually exercised the review power in 1796 when it upheld the validity of a law passed by the legislature. But the Court's authority would not be secure, it was clear, until it actually declared a congressional act unconstitutional.

In 1803, in the case of *Marbury* v. *Madison*, it did so. William Marbury, one of Adams's "midnight appointments," had been named a justice of the peace in the District of Columbia. But his commission, though duly signed and sealed, had not been delivered to him before Adams left office. Madison, who as Jefferson's secretary of state was responsible for transmitting appointments, then refused to hand over the commission. Marbury applied to the Supreme Court for an order (a writ of mandamus) directing Madison to perform his official duty. In a historic ruling, the Court found that Marbury had a right to his commission but that the Court had no authority to order Madison to deliver it. On the surface, therefore, the decision was a victory for the administration. But of far greater importance than the relatively insignificant matter of Marbury's commission was the Court's reasoning in the decision.

The original Judiciary Act of 1789 had given the Court the power to compel executive officials to act in such matters, and it was on that basis that Marbury had filed his suit. But the Court ruled that Congress had exceeded its authority, that the Constitution had defined the powers of the judiciary and that the legislature had no right to expand them. The relevant section of the 1789 act was, therefore, void. In seeming to deny its own authority, the Court was in fact radically enlarging it. The justices had repudiated a relatively minor power—the power to force the delivery of a commission—by asserting a vastly greater one—the power to nullify an act of Congress. The administration, recognizing the significance of the ruling, was alarmed. But since the Court had shrewdly encased this assertion of its power within a ruling favorable to the government, there was no way for the Republicans to respond.

The chief justice of the United States at the time of the ruling was (as he would remain until 1835) John Marshall, one of the towering figures in the history of American law. A leading Federalist and prominent Virginia lawyer, he had served John Adams as secretary of state. (It had been Marshall, ironically, who had neglected to deliver Marbury's commission in the closing hours of the administration.) In 1801, just before leaving office, Adams had appointed him chief justice; and almost immediately Marshall established himself as the dominant figure on the Court, shaping virtually all its most important rulings, including of course *Marbury* v. *Madison*. Marshall had served with George Washington's army at Valley Forge during the Revolution, and he retained from the experience a vivid impression of a weak, divided, and inefficient government. Through a succession of Republican presidents, he battled to give the federal government unity and strength. And in so doing, he established the judiciary as a coequal branch of government with the executive and the legislature—a position that the founders of the republic had never clearly indicated it should occupy.

Jefferson recognized the threat that an assertive judiciary could pose to his policies, and even while the Marbury case was still pending he was preparing for a renewed assault on the last Federalist stronghold. If he could not remove the judges he considered obnoxious directly, perhaps he could do so indirectly through the process of impeachment. According to the Constitution, the House of Representatives was empowered to bring impeachment charges against any civil officer for "high crimes and misdemeanors," and the Senate sitting as a court was authorized to try the officer on the charges. Jefferson sent evidence to the House to show that one of the district judges, John Pickering of New Hampshire (who was suffering from severe mental illness), was unfit for his posi-

tion. The House accordingly impeached him, and the Senate found him guilty of high crimes and misdemeanors. He was removed.

Later the Republicans went after bigger game, a justice of the Supreme Court itself. Justice Samuel Chase, a rabidly partisan Federalist, had applied the Sedition Act with seeming brutality and had delivered political speeches from the bench, insulting President Jefferson and denouncing the Jeffersonian doctrine of equal liberty and equal rights. In doing so, Chase was guilty of no high crime or misdemeanor in the constitutional sense, and he was only saying what thousands of Federalists believed. Some Republicans concluded, however, that impeachment should not be viewed merely as a criminal proceeding, and that a judge could properly be impeached for political reasons—for obstructing the other branches of the government and disregarding the will of the people.

At Jefferson's own suggestion, the House of Representatives set up a committee to investigate Chase's conduct. Impeached on the basis of the committee's findings, the justice was brought to trial before the Senate early in 1805. Jefferson did his best to secure a conviction, even temporarily cultivating the friendship of Aaron Burr, who as vice president presided over the trial. But Burr performed his duties with aloof impartiality, and John Randolph as the impeachment manager bungled the prosecution. A majority of the senators finally voted for conviction, but not the necessary two-thirds majority. Chase was acquitted.

In one sense, the effort to impeach Chase was helpful to the Republicans despite the failure, for it pressured federal judges as a whole to be more discreet and less partisan in statements from the bench. Federalist jurists had reason to fear that were they to antagonize the Republicans and the public too greatly, future impeachment efforts might succeed. But in a larger sense, the Republican assault on the judiciary was a failure. Marshall remained secure in his position as chief justice. The duel between the Court and the president continued. And the judiciary survived as a powerful force within the government—more often than not on behalf of the centralizing, expansionary policies that the Republicans had been trying to reverse.

DOUBLING THE NATIONAL DOMAIN

In the year that Jefferson was elected president of the United States, Napoleon made himself ruler of France with the title of first consul, and in the year that Jefferson was reelected, Napoleon assumed the name and authority of emperor. These two men, the democrat and the dictator, had little in common. Yet for a time they were good friends in international politics—until Napoleon's ambitions leaped from Europe to America and brought about an estrangement.

Jefferson and Napoleon

Napoleon failed in a grandiose plan to seize India from the British Empire, although he succeeded in the conquest of Italy. Then he was reminded that France at one time had possessed a vast empire in North America. In 1763, French possessions east of the Mississippi had gone to Great Britain, and those west of it to Spain. The former were lost for good, but the latter might be recovered. In 1800 (on the very day after the signing of the French peace settlement with the United States) Napoleon arranged for Spain to cede these North American possessions to him in the secret treaty of San Ildefonso. Thus he got title to Louisiana, which included roughly the whole of the Mississippi Valley to the west of the river, plus New Orleans to the east of the river near its mouth. He intended Louisiana to form the continental heartland of his proposed empire.

Other essential parts of his empire-to-be were the sugar-rich and strategically valuable West Indian islands that still belonged to France—Guadeloupe, Martinique, and above all Santo Domingo. Unfortunately for his plans, the slaves on Santo Domingo had been inspired by the French Revolution to rise in revolt and create a republic of their own, under the remarkable black leader, Toussaint L'Ouverture. Taking advantage of a truce in his war with England, Napoleon sent to the West Indies an army led by his brother-in-law, Charles Leclerc, to put down the insurrection and restore French authority.

Meanwhile, unaware of Napoleon's imperial aims, Jefferson pursued the kind of foreign policy that was to be expected of such a well-known friend of France. He appointed as the American minister to Paris the ardently pro-French Robert R. Livingston. Continuing and hastening the peace policy of Adams, he carried through the ratification of the Franco-American settlement of 1800 and put it into effect even before it was ratified. With respect to Santo Domingo, however, he did not continue the policy of Adams, who had cooperated with the British in recognizing and supporting the rebel regime of Toussaint. Jefferson assured the French minister in Washington that the American people, especially those of the slave-holding states, did not approve of the black revolutionary, who was setting a bad example for their own slaves. He even led the French minister to believe that the United States would join with France in putting down the rebellion.

Jefferson began to reappraise the whole subject of American relations with France when he heard rumors of the secret retrocession of Louisiana. "It completely reverses all the political relations of the U.S.," he wrote to Minister Livingston on April 18, 1802. Always before, we had looked to France as our "natural friend." But there was on the earth "one single spot" the possessor of which was "our natural and habitual enemy." That spot was New Orleans, the outlet through which the produce of the fast-growing West was shipped to the markets of the world. If France should actually take and hold New Orleans, Jefferson said, then "we must marry ourselves to the British fleet and nation."

Jefferson was even more alarmed when, in the fall of 1802, he learned that the Spanish intendant in charge at New Orleans had prohibited Americans from continuing to deposit their goods at that port for transshipment from river craft to oceangoing vessels. By the Pinckney Treaty (of 1795) Spain had guaranteed to Americans the right to deposit goods either at New Orleans or at some other suitable place. Without such a right, Spain's permission to use the lower Mississippi was of little value to the United States.

Westerners suspected, as did Jefferson himself, that Napoleon had procured the closing of the river for sinister purposes of his own. They demanded that something be done to reopen the river, and some of the more extreme among them clamored for war with France. The Federalists of the Northeast, though they had no real concern for the welfare of the West, played on the discontent of the frontiersmen and encouraged the war cry for political reasons. The more the Federalists could arouse the West, the more they could embarrass the Jefferson administration. The president faced a dilemma. If he yielded to the frontier clamor and sought satisfaction through force, he would run the risk of renewed war with France. If, on the other hand, he disregarded the clamor, he would stand to lose the political support of the West.

There was possibly a way out of the dilemma, and that was to purchase from Napoleon the port so indispensable to the United States. Jefferson did not think of trying to buy any part of Louisiana to the west of the Mississippi; he was content, for the time being, to let that river form the boundary between the French Empire and the United States. Soon after hearing rumors of the Louisiana retrocession, he instructed Livingston in Paris to negotiate for the purchase of New Orleans, and Livingston on his own authority proceeded to suggest to the French that they might be glad to be rid of the upper part of Louisiana as well.

Jefferson also induced Congress to provide an army and a river fleet, and he allowed the impression to emerge that American forces, despite his own desire for peace, might soon descend on New Orleans. Then he sent a special envoy to work with Livingston in persuading the French to sell. For this extraordinary mission he chose an ideally suited man, James Monroe, who was well remembered in France and who, at the same time, had the confidence of the American frontiersmen; his appointment would reassure them that the president was looking after their interests. Jefferson told Monroe that if he and Livingston could not satisfy even the minimum needs of the United States—the use of the Mississippi or some other river emptying into the Gulf—they were to cross the Channel and discuss some kind of understanding with the British government. Whether Jefferson, in his hints at an

attack on New Orleans and an alliance with Great Britain, merely meant to bluff the French, he had no chance to show. While Monroe was still on his way to Paris, Napoleon suddenly decided to dispose of the entire Louisiana Territory.

Startling though this decision seemed to some of his advisers, Napoleon had good reasons for it. His plans for an American empire had gone awry, partly because of certain mischances, which might be summarized in two words—*mosquitoes* and *ice*. The mosquitoes brought yellow fever and death to General Leclerc and to thousands of the soldiers whom Napoleon had sent to reconquer Santo Domingo. The ice, forming earlier than expected in a Dutch harbor as winter came in 1802, delayed the departure of an expeditionary force that Napoleon was readying to reinforce Leclerc's army and also to take possession of Louisiana. By the spring of 1803 it was too late. Napoleon then was expecting a renewal of the European war, and he feared that he would not be able to hold Louisiana if the British, with their superior naval power, should attempt to take it. He also realized that, quite apart from the British threat, there was danger from the United States: he could not prevent the Americans, who were pushing steadily into the Mississippi Valley, from sooner or later overrunning Louisiana.

The Louisiana Purchase

Napoleon left the negotiations over Louisiana to his finance minister, Barbé-Marbois, rather than his foreign minister, Talleyrand, since Talleyrand was remembered for the XYZ Affair and was distrusted by Americans. Barbé-Marbois had their respect, having lived for some time in the United States and having married an American woman. Livingston and Monroe, after the latter's arrival in Paris, had to decide first of all whether they should even consider making a treaty for the purchase of the entire Louisiana Territory, since they had not been authorized by their government to do so. They dared not wait until they could get new instructions from home, for Napoleon might change his mind as suddenly as he had made it up. They decided to go ahead, realizing that Jefferson could reject their treaty if he disapproved of what they had done. After a little haggling over the price—Barbé-Marbois asked and got somewhat more than Napoleon's minimum—Livingston and Monroe put their signatures to the treaty on April 30, 1803.

By the terms of the purchase arrangement, the United States was to pay 60 million francs directly to the French government and up to 20 million more to American citizens who held claims against France for ship seizures in the past—the sum totaled approximately $15 million. The United States was also to give France certain commercial privileges in the port of New Orleans, privileges not extended to other countries. Moreover, the United States was to incorporate the people of Louisiana into the Union and grant them as soon as possible the same rights and privileges as other citizens. This seemed to imply that the Louisiana inhabitants were to have the benefits of statehood in the near future. The boundaries were not defined, Louisiana being transferred to the United States simply with the "same extent" as when owned by France and earlier by Spain. When Livingston and Monroe appealed to Talleyrand for his opinion about the boundary, he merely replied: "You have made a noble bargain for yourselves, and I suppose you will make the most of it."

In Washington, the president was both pleased and embarrassed when he received the treaty. He was glad to get such a "noble bargain," but, according to his often-repeated views on the Constitution, the United States lacked the constitutional power to accept the bargain. In the past he had always insisted that the federal government could rightfully exercise only those powers assigned to it in so many words, and nowhere did the Constitution say anything about the acquisition of new territory. But his advisers assured him that he already possessed all the constitutional power he needed: the president with the consent of the Senate obviously could make treaties, and the treaty-making power would justify the purchase of Louisiana. Years afterward (in 1828) the Supreme Court upheld this view, but Jefferson—strict

constructionist that he had been—continued to have doubts about it. Finally he gave in, trusting, as he said, "that the good sense of our country will correct the evil of loose construction when it shall produce ill effects." Thus, by implication, he left the question of constitutional interpretation to public opinion, and he cut the ground from under his doctrine of states' rights.

When Jefferson called Congress into special session, a few of the die-hard Federalists of New England raised constitutional and other objections to the treaty, but the Senate promptly gave its consent and the House soon passed the necessary appropriation bill.

Though Madison and Jefferson had a good case for the American title to Louisiana itself, they had considerably less justification when, taking advantage of the vagueness of the boundaries, they also claimed part of West Florida as American by virtue of the treaty with France. The Spaniards denied that any of Florida was included in Louisiana. To persuade the Spaniards to give up Florida, Jefferson tried both promises of money and threats of force. Despite John Randolph's outraged opposition, the president obtained from Congress an appropriation for secret purposes, one of which was to bribe France to put pressure on Spain. It was no use. All of Florida remained in Spanish hands until after Jefferson left the presidency.

When the United States concluded the purchase treaty with France, Spain was still administering Louisiana, the French never having taken actual possession. France did not finally take possession until late in 1803, and then only long enough to turn the territory over to General James Wilkinson, the commissioner of the United States and the commander of a small occupation force. In New Orleans, beneath a bright December sun, the recently raised French tricolor was brought down and the Stars and Stripes run up. For the time being, Louisiana Territory was given a semimilitary government with officials appointed by the president; later it was organized on the general pattern of the Northwest Territory, with the assumption that it would be divided into states. The first of these was admitted to the union as the state of Louisiana in 1812.

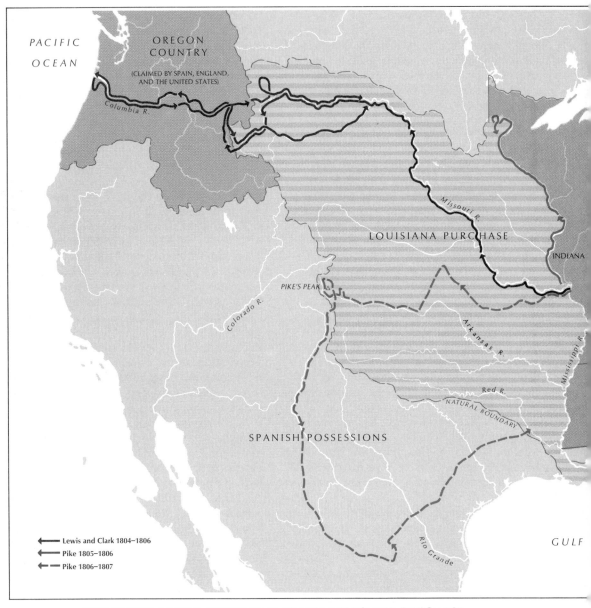

PACIFIC

OCEAN

OREGON
COUNTRY

(CLAIMED BY SPAIN, ENGLAND,
AND THE UNITED STATES)

Columbia R.

LOUISIANA PURCHASE

Missouri R.

INDIANA

PIKE'S PEAK

Colorado R.

Arkansas R.

Mississippi R.

Red R.

NATURAL BOUNDARY

SPANISH POSSESSIONS

Rio Grande

GULF

◄——— Lewis and Clark 1804–1806
◄——— Pike 1805–1806
◄— — Pike 1806–1807

THE UNITED STATES AT THE TIME OF THE LOUISIANA PURCHASE

Exploring the West

Meanwhile, the geography of the far-flung new territory was revealed by a series of explorations. Even before he became president, Jefferson had as a scientist been interested in finding out all he could about the nature and extent of the North American continent, and he had encouraged explorers interested in the Far West. After becoming president he renewed his efforts. In 1803, before Napoleon's offer to sell Louisiana, Jefferson planned an expedition that was to cross all the way to the Pacific Ocean and gather not only geographical facts but also information about the prospects for Indian trade. Congress having secretly provided the necessary funds, Jefferson named as leader of the

of four dozen hardy men, set up winter quarters in St. Louis at about the time the United States took formal possession of Louisiana. In the spring of 1804, they started up the Missouri River, and with the Shoshoni woman Sacajawea as their guide, her baby on her back, they eventually crossed the Rocky Mountains, descended the Snake and the Columbia rivers, and in the late autumn of 1805 camped on the Pacific coast. In September 1806, they were back in St. Louis with carefully kept records of what they had observed along the way. No longer was the Far West a completely unknown country.

While Lewis and Clark were on their epic journey, Jefferson sent out other explorers to fill in the picture of the Louisiana Territory. The most important of these was Lieutenant Zebulon Montgomery Pike. In the fall of 1805, then only twenty-six, Pike led an expedition from St. Louis up the Mississippi River in search of its source, and though he did not find it, he learned a good deal about the upper Mississippi Valley. In the summer of 1806 Pike was sent out again, this time by Wilkinson, to proceed up the valley of the Arkansas. He discovered, but failed in his attempt to climb, the peak that now bears his name. Then he turned southward into Mexico and ran into a Spanish army; he was compelled to surrender his maps and papers and return to the United States. His account of his Western travels left the impression that the land between the Missouri and the Rockies was a desert that American farmers could never cultivate and that ought to be left forever to the nomadic Indian tribes.

The Burr Conspiracy

In the long run, the Louisiana Purchase prepared the way for the growth of the United States as a great continental power. Immediately, however, the purchase provoked reactions that threatened or seemed to threaten the very existence of the Union. From both the Northeast and the Southwest there soon arose rumors of secession plots.

Most of the American people heartily approved the acquisition of the new territory, as they indicated by their presidential votes

expedition his private secretary and Virginia neighbor, the thirty-two-year-old Meriwether Lewis, who as a veteran of Indian wars was skilled in wilderness ways. Lewis chose as a colleague the twenty-eight-year-old William Clark, who—like George Rogers Clark, his older brother—was an experienced frontiersman and Indian fighter.

Lewis and Clark, with a chosen company

The Lewis and Clark Expedition, 1804–1806
Patrick Gass, one of the men who accompanied Lewis and Clark, wrote *A Journal of the Voyages and Travels of a Corps of Discovery* (1811), which was the first account of the expedition to be published. The book was illustrated with crude drawings. The one here reproduced was captioned "Captain Lewis & Clark holding a Council with the Indians."

in 1804, but some of the New England Federalists raged against it. Both their party and their section stood to lose in importance with the growth of the West, for they would soon be outnumbered in national politics with the creation of new states. A group of the most extreme Federalists, known as the Essex Junto, concluded that the only recourse for New England was to secede from the Union and form a separate "Northern Confederacy." They justified such action by means of states' rights arguments similar to those Jefferson had used only about five years earlier in opposition to the Alien and Sedition Acts.

If a Northern Confederacy were to have any hope for lasting success as a separate nation, it would have to include New York as well as New England, or so the prospective seceders believed. But the prominent New York Federalist Alexander Hamilton had no sympathy with the secessionist scheme. He wrote: "Dismemberment of our empire will be a clear sacrifice of great positive advantages without any counterbalancing good, administering no relief to our real disease, which is *democracy*." He feared that disorders like those of the French Revolution were about to sweep over the United States. Then, he thought, the country would need a military dictator, a sort of American Napoleon, to bring order out of chaos—perhaps Hamilton himself, who by now clearly had no future in electoral politics.

His New York Republican rival, Aaron Burr, was another politician without prospects, at least within the party of the vengeful Jefferson. When some of the Federalists approached Burr, he agreed to run with their support for governor in 1804. Rumor had it that he was implicated in the disunion plot and that, if elected, he would lead the state into secession along with New England, but the rumor lacked proof and the plot itself was fantastic, an impossible dream. Nevertheless, Hamilton accused Burr of plotting treason and cast slurs on his personal character. Burr lost the election, then challenged Hamilton to a duel. Hamilton dared not refuse; if he did, he would sacrifice his reputation for honor and manliness, a reputation that would be indispensable to the career supposedly awaiting him as the savior of his country. And so the two men with their seconds met at Weehawken, New Jersey, across the Hudson River from New York City, on a July morning in 1804. Hamilton was mortally wounded; he died the next day.

Burr, indicted for murder in both New Jersey and New York, presided over the United States Senate the following winter and then, at the end of his term as vice president, faced a political outlook more hopeless than ever. He was ambitious and resourceful, with almost magical powers of attracting people to him. What could he do? During the next year he busied himself with mysterious affairs in the Southwest. He talked and corresponded with prominent men of the region, especially with General James Wilkinson, now governor of the Louisiana Territory. Some people believed (and some historians still believe) that Burr (in partnership with Wilkinson) intended to separate the Southwest from the Union and rule it as an empire of his own. In fact, his ultimate aim was probably the conquest of Spanish territory beyond the boundaries of Louisiana rather than the division of the United States.

In the fall of 1806, the armed followers of Burr started by boat down the Ohio River, Burr joining them after they were well under way. Wilkinson, suddenly turning against Burr, sent a messenger to tell Jefferson that treason was afoot and that an attack on New Orleans was expected. Jefferson issued a proclamation calling for the arrest of Burr and his men as traitors. Eventually Burr was tracked down and brought to Richmond for trial.

Jefferson, not present in Richmond but managing the prosecution by remote control from Washington, was determined to convict his one-time running mate. The prosecution relied hopefully on its star witness, General Wilkinson—a despicable character who had accepted pay as a spy for the Spaniards and had demanded extra money from them on the grounds that in heading off the Burr expedition, he had saved their territory from attack. Despite the administration's efforts to influence the trial, Chief Justice Marshall, presiding over the case on circuit duty, had political as well as judicial reasons for insisting that Burr be given a fair hearing.

At the trial (1807–1808) Marshall applied literally the constitutional provision that no one shall be convicted of treason except on the testimony of at least two witnesses to the same "overt act." He excluded all evidence not bearing directly on such an act. Thus the jury had little choice but to acquit Burr, since not even one witness had actually seen him waging war against the United States or giving aid and comfort to its enemies.

Although he was now freed, Burr gained lasting notoriety as a traitor; after exiling himself abroad for a few years, he returned and lived long enough to hail the Texas revolution (1836) as the fruition of the same sort of movement that he had hoped to start. The trial had given the chief justice another chance to frustrate the president. It had set a precedent that made it almost impossible to convict anyone of treason against the United States.

Above all, the Burr conspiracy stood as a symbol of the perils still facing the new nation. With a central government that remained deliberately weak, with vast tracts of land only nominally controlled by the United States, with ambitious political leaders willing, if necessary, to circumvent normal channels in their search for power, the United States remained an imperfectly realized nation; the legitimacy of its government was yet to be fully asserted. Although nothing quite like the affair of Aaron Burr was to occur again, Americans would continue in the coming years to experience serious challenges to the survival of their union.

SUGGESTED READINGS

The cultural life of the young republic is surveyed in Joseph J. Ellis, *After the Revolution: Profiles of Early American Culture* (1979); Russel B. Nye, *The Cultural Life of the New Nation* (1960); and Kenneth Silverman, *A Cultural History of the American Revolution* (1976). On education, see Lawrence A. Cremin, *American Education: The National Experience* (1981); Carl F. Kaestle, *The Evolution of an Urban School System* (1973); and Harry Warfel, *Noah Webster, Schoolmaster to America* (1936). There are several important studies of religion and revivalism in the young republic. The standard work has long been William W. Sweet, *Revivalism in America* (1944). A more recent study of importance is William G. McLoughlin, *Revivals, Awakenings, and Reform* (1978). Sydney Ahlstrom, *A Religious History of the American People* (1972), is a valuable overview. Whitney R. Cross, *The Burned Over District* (1950), discusses revivalism in upstate New York; and John Boles, *The Great Revival in the South* (1972), examines its influence on that region.

Stuart Bruchey, *The Roots of American Economic Growth* (1965), is a useful introduction to the emergence of industrialization. Douglas C. North, *The Economic Growth of the United States, 1790–1860* (1961), provides a valuable interpretation; while W. Elliot Brownlee, *Dynamics of Ascent* (1979), is a survey of American economic history. Nathan Rosenberg, *Technology and American Economic Growth* (1972), is a broad view of the role technology played in spurring early economic development; while Merritt Roe Smith, *Harpers Ferry Armory and the New Technology* (1977), provides a skillful local study. Anthony F. C. Wallace, *Rockdale* (1978), is a perceptive examination of the impact of industrialization on a Pennsylvania town. Arthur H. Cole, *The American Wool Manufacture*, 2 vols. (1926), and C. F. Ware, *Early New England Cotton Manufacture* (1931), examine the birth of the textile industry. C. M. Green, *Eli Whitney and the Birth of American Technology* (1956), studies the inventor of the cotton gin. George R. Taylor, *The Transportation Revolution* (1951), examines the economic impact of the growth of the American transportation network. See also P. D. Jordan, *The National Road* (1948), and J. A. Durrenburger, *Turnpikes* (1931).

General histories of the Jeffersonian era in politics include the classic study by Henry Adams, *History of the United States of America During the Administrations of Thomas Jefferson and of James Madison*, 9 vols. (1889–1891), which is also available in a two-volume abridged edition edited by Herbert Agar (1947). More recent surveys of the period are Marcus Cunliffe, *The Nation Takes Shape* (1959); Charles M. Wiltse, *The New Nation* (1961); and Marshall Smelser, *The Democratic Republic* (1968). Morton Borden, *Parties and Politics in the Early Republic* (1967), is a useful study of political rivalries, as is Noble Cunningham, *The Jeffersonian Republicans in Power* (1963). James S. Young, *The Washington Community* (1966), is an excellent study of life in the nation's capital during the Jeffersonian era. The Federalist opposition is considered in David Hackett Fischer, *The Revolution of American Conservatism* (1965); Linda Kerber, *Federalists in Dissent* (1970); and James M. Banner, *To the Hartford Convention* (1967). The workings of the Jefferson administration are examined in Noble Cunningham, *The Process of Government Under Jefferson* (1978); Leonard White, *The Jeffersonians* (1951); Alexander Balinky, *Albert Gallatin: Fiscal Theories and Policy* (1958); and Robert M. Johnstone, Jr., *Jefferson and the Presidency* (1978). Two volumes of the great Dumas Malone biography of Jefferson: *Jefferson the President: First Term* (1970) and *Jefferson the President: Second Term* (1974) study the president himself.

On Jeffersonian thought, see, in addition to the various biographies of leading figures, Adrienne Koch, *The Philosophy of Thomas Jefferson* (1943); Charles M. Wiltse, *The Jeffersonian Tradition in American Democracy* (1935); Merrill Peterson, *The Jeffersonian Image in the American Mind* (1960); and Leonard W. Levy, *Jefferson and Civil Liberties: The Darker Side* (1963), a critical study. On Jefferson's conflict with the courts, see Richard Ellis, *The Jeffersonian Crisis* (1971); and Leonard Baker, *John Marshall: A Life in Law* (1974).

The foreign policy of the Jefferson administration is recounted in Irving Brant, *James Madison: Secretary of State* (1953). On the Louisiana Purchase, consult Alexander DeConde, *The Affair of Louisiana* (1976); and Arthur P. Whitaker, *The Mississippi Question* (1934). George Dangerfield, *Chancellor Robert R. Livingston of New York* (1960), and Harry Ammon, *James Monroe and the Quest for National Identity* (1971), are also useful sources for the diplomacy of the era. Bernard deVoto, *Course of Empire* (1952), examines the travels of Lewis and Clark, as does his edition of *The Journals of Lewis and Clark* (1953). On the Burr conspiracy, see Nathan Schachner, *Aaron Burr* (1937), for a sympathetic biography, and Thomas P. Abernethy, *The Burr Conspiracy* (1954), for an unfriendly account. B. W. Sheehan, *Seeds of Extinction* (1973), discusses Jeffersonian views of the American Indian. Francis S. Philbrick, *The Rise of the New West* (1965), and Ray Allen Billington, *Westward Expansion* (1967), are overviews of territorial growth.

Free Seas and Fresh Lands

8

The Burning of Washington, 1812 Flames engulf one of the two wings of the still unfinished Capitol in this illustration of the British attack on Washington in the summer of 1812. The invaders also set fire to the White House and other major public buildings. (The Bettmann Archive)

After years of mounting tension, in 1803, the great powers of Europe once again became engaged in war, a conflict that would last for more than a decade. Although the fighting did not at first involve the United States directly, its indirect effects were profound. On the one hand, the war benefited the new nation by enabling Americans to develop a profitable trade with belligerents on both sides and even at times to play the warring nations against one another to American advantage. Both Pinckney's Treaty with Spain and the Louisiana Purchase agreement with France were the result in large part of the wartime pressures on Europe. On the other hand, however, the conflict posed great dangers to the United States. The tensions with France in 1798 had almost drawn America into war. By the early years of the nineteenth century, new controversies involving Great Britain once again challenged the nation's neutrality. The result, ultimately, was the War of 1812.

The war itself was far from a glorious experience for the United States. It provoked wide domestic opposition, largely from those whose economic fortunes were endangered by it. It produced several humiliating defeats (including the British capture and burning of Washington) and only a few decisive American victories. It ended with a treaty that fell far short of guaranteeing the nation's war aims. At best, the conflict was a draw.

Yet the war had other important consequences for the growth of the nation that many Americans later would enthusiastically applaud. It gave military leaders an opportunity to crush some of the powerful Indian tribes on the Northwestern and Southwestern frontiers, thus opening the way for the expansion of white settlement. It heightened American nationalism and encouraged a spirit of unity between the sections. Perhaps most important of all, it stimulated manufacturing and accelerated progress toward industrialization. Although it was a Republican administration that presided over the War of 1812, the conflict ultimately became another factor in consigning to oblivion the Jeffersonian vision of a small, decentralized, agrarian nation.

CAUSES OF CONFLICT

Politicians at the time disagreed sharply over the causes of the War of 1812. Historians have continued to disagree over them ever since. Some have argued that the question of frontier lands lay at the heart of the conflict. Others claim that the real issue was freedom of the seas. In fact, the two matters were closely related to one another, and the war cannot be understood without considering both.

Neutral Rights

In the early nineteenth century, the warring nations of Europe found it impossible to take care of their own shipping needs. The merchant ships of France and Spain seldom ventured far on the ocean, dominated as it was by the sea power of Great Britain; and the merchant marine of Britain itself was too busy in the waters of Europe and Asia to devote much attention to those of America. To some degree or other, all the belligerents had to depend on the neutrals of the world for cargoes essential to effective war making, and in the size and activity of its merchant marine the United States was the most important of the neutrals. American shipowners prospered as, year after year, they engrossed a larger and larger proportion of the carrying trade between Europe and the West Indies. Farmers shared in the prosperity, for exports from the United States to the West Indies and Europe also increased prodigiously.

In the Battle of Trafalgar (1805) a British fleet practically destroyed what was left of the French navy. Thereafter the supremacy of Great Britain on the seas was unchallenged, while Napoleon proceeded to extend his domination over the continent of Europe. Powerless to invade the British Isles, Napoleon devised a scheme, known as the Continental System, which he hoped would bring the enemy to terms. The British, he reasoned, were a nation of shopkeepers who depended for their existence on buying and selling in the rest of the world, especially in Europe. If he could close the Continent to their trade, he thought, they ultimately would have to give in. So, in a series of decrees beginning with those of Berlin (1806) and Milan (1807), he proclaimed that British ships and neutral ships touching at British ports were not to land their cargoes at any European port controlled by France or its allies.

The British government replied to Napoleon's decrees with a succession of orders-in-council. These announced an unusual kind of blockade of the European coast. The blockade was intended not to keep goods out of Napoleon's Europe but only to see that the goods were carried either in British vessels or in neutral vessels stopping at a British port and paying for a special license. Thus, while frustrating the Continental System, Britain would compel the neutrals to contribute toward financing its war effort and would limit the growth of its maritime rivals, above all the United States.

Caught between Napoleon's decrees and Britain's orders, American vessels sailing directly for Europe took the chance of capture by the British, and those going by way of a British port ran the risk of seizure by the French. Both of the warring powers disregarded American rights and sensibilities, yet to most Americans the British seemed like the worse offender of the two. Possessing effective sea power, they pounced on Yankee merchantmen all over the wide ocean; the French could do so only in European ports. True, Napoleon's officials sometimes impris-

oned and brutally mistreated the crews of confiscated ships. But the British navy far more often infringed on personal liberty and national sovereignty; they stopped American ships on the high seas and took sailors off the decks, making them victims of impressment.

Impressment

The British navy—with its floggings, its low pay, and its dirty and dangerous conditions on shipboard—was a "floating hell" to its sailors. They had to be impressed (forced) into the service, and at every good opportunity they deserted, many of them joining the merchant marine of the United States and even its navy. To check this loss of vital manpower, the British claimed the right to stop and search American merchantmen (although not naval vessels) and reimpress deserters. They did not claim the right to take native-born Americans, but they did seize naturalized Americans born on British soil; for according to the laws of England, a true-born subject could never give up his allegiance to the king. In actual practice, the British often impressed native as well as naturalized Americans, and thousands upon thousands of sailors claiming the protection of the Stars and Stripes were thus kidnapped. To these hapless men, impressment was little better than slavery. To their American shipowning employers, it was at least a serious nuisance. And to millions of proud and patriotic Americans, even those living far from the ocean, it was an intolerable affront to the national honor.

In the summer of 1807, in the *Chesapeake-Leopard* incident, the British went to more outrageous extremes than ever. The *Chesapeake* was a frigate of the United States Navy, not an ordinary merchantman. Sailing from Norfolk, with several alleged deserters from the British navy among the crew, the *Chesapeake* was hailed by His Majesty's Ship *Leopard*, which had been lying in wait off Cape Henry, at the entrance to the Chesapeake Bay. Commodore James Barron refused to allow the *Chesapeake* to be searched, and so the *Leopard* opened fire and compelled him,

United States of America.

No. 3160

I William R. Lee, Collector for the District of Salem and Beverly, do hereby certify, that John Wallis an American Seaman, aged Nineteen years or thereabouts, of the height of Five feet two½ inches, and of a Dark complexion, Was born in Salem in the State of Massachusetts has this day produced to me proof, in the manner directed in the Act entitled, "An Act for the Relief and Protection of American Seamen," and pursuant to the said Act, I do hereby Certify, that the said John Wallis is a **Citizen of the United States of America.**

In Witness Whereof, I have hereunto set my Hand and Seal of Office, this Nineteenth day of January in the year of our Lord one thousand eight hundred and Eleven

William Lee   Collector.

Seaman's Protection Paper
To protect American sailors from British impressment, Congress authorized the issuance of certificates of American citizenship, which came to be known as "protection" papers. These papers were not always respected by British naval officers. To them a certificate of naturalization was meaningless, for the British government claimed the allegiance of all British subjects for life. A certificate of American birth was not dependable, for it could be obtained by fraud. Some Americans made a business of selling forged documents. One woman, it is said, had an oversized cradle built for British deserters to climb into, so that she could honestly swear that she had known them from the cradle. (Essex Institute, Salem, Massachusetts)

unprepared for action as he was, to surrender. A boarding party from the *Leopard* dragged four men off the American frigate.

When news of the outrage reached America, a loud cry arose for a war of revenge. Not since the days of Lexington and Concord had Americans been so strongly aroused. Even the "most temperate people and those most attached to England," the British minister reported home, "say that they are bound as a people and that they must assert their honor on the first attack upon it." If Congress had been in session, or if President Jefferson had called a special session, as he was urged to do, the country might have stampeded into war. But, as the French minister in Washington informed Talleyrand, "the president does not want war," and "Mr. Madison dreads it now still more."

Instead of assembling Congress and demanding a war declaration, Jefferson made a determined effort to maintain the peace. First, he issued an order expelling all British warships from American waters, so as to lessen the likelihood of future incidents. Then he sent instructions to his minister in England, James Monroe, to get satisfaction from the British government and to insist again on the complete renunciation of impressment. On the whole, the British government was conciliatory enough. It disavowed the action of Admiral Berkeley, the officer primarily responsible for the *Chesapeake-Leopard* affair, recalled him, and offered to indemnify the wounded and the families of the killed and to return the captured sailors (only three were left; one had been hanged). But the British cabinet refused to concede anything to Jefferson's main point; instead, the cabinet issued a proclamation reasserting the right of search to recover deserting seamen.

Thus the impressment issue prevented a compromise that might have led away from war. Although by 1812 the British had made a financial settlement, the *Chesapeake* outrage meanwhile remained an open sore in Anglo-American relations. This incident, together with the impressment issue involved in it, was probably the most important single cause of the War of 1812, even though its final effect was delayed for five years.

"Peaceable Coercion"

Even at the height of the excitement over the *Chesapeake*, Jefferson made no preparations for a possible war. He and Madison believed that, if worse came to worst, the United States could bring Great Britain to terms—and, if necessary, France as well—through the use of economic pressure instead of military or naval force. Dependent as both nations were on the Yankee carrying trade, they presumably would mend their ways if completely deprived of it.

Hence when Congress met for its regular session, Jefferson hastily drafted a drastic measure. Madison revised it, and both the House and the Senate promptly enacted it into law. It was known as the Embargo, and it became one of the most controversial political issues of its time. The Embargo prohibited American ships from leaving the United States for any port in the world (if it had specified only British and French ports, Jefferson reasoned, it could have been evaded by means of false clearance papers). Congress also passed a "force act" to give the government power to enforce the Embargo.

Though the law was nevertheless evaded in various ways, it was effective enough to be felt in France, more in Great Britain, and still more in the United States itself. Throughout the United States—except in the frontier areas of Vermont and New York, which soon doubled their overland exports to Canada—the Embargo brought on a serious depression. The planters of the South and the farmers of the West, though deprived of foreign markets for their crops, were willing to suffer in comparative silence, devoted Jeffersonian Republicans that most of them were. But the Federalist merchants and shipowners of the Northeast, still harder hit by the depression, made no secret of their rabid discontent.

Although the Northeastern merchants disliked impressment, the orders-in-council, and Napoleon's decrees, they hated Jefferson's Embargo much more. Previously, in spite of risks, they had kept up their business with excellent returns; now they lost money every day their ships idled at the wharves.

Again, as at the time of the Louisiana Purchase, they concluded that Jefferson had violated the Constitution (as indeed he had—if judged by the principles he had advocated before becoming president).

In the midst of the Embargo-induced depression came the election of 1808. The Federalists, with C. C. Pinckney again their candidate, made the most of the Embargo's unpopularity and won a far larger proportion of the popular and electoral votes than in 1804. Nevertheless, Madison was safely elected as Jefferson's successor. The Federalists also gained a number of seats in the House and the Senate, although the Republicans continued to hold a majority in both houses. To Jefferson and Madison the returns indicated plainly enough that the Embargo was a growing liability in politics. A few days before leaving office, Jefferson approved a bill terminating his experiment with what he called "peaceable coercion." But Madison's assumption of the presidency meant no basic change in policy, and other experiments with measures short of war were soon to be tried.

By the time he entered the White House, James Madison already had a career behind him that would assure him immortality in his nation's history. He was not only experienced in affairs of government; he was also a profound and original thinker. Unfortunately for his reputation, he was not an impressive figure of a man, for he was small and wizened, with a scholarly frown. Nor was he equipped with the personal charm or politician's skill needed for strong presidential leadership. What he lacked in personality, his wife more than supplied. Dolly Madison, North Carolina–born, was as energetic and gracious a first lady as ever inhabited the White House.

Just before Madison's inauguration, Congress passed a modified embargo bill known as the Nonintercourse Act. The Nonintercourse Act was soon replaced by another expedient, commonly called Macon's Bill No. 2 (1810). This measure permitted free commercial relations with the whole world, including Great Britain and France, but authorized the president to prohibit intercourse with either belligerent if it should continue

its violations after the other had stopped. Napoleon had every incentive to induce the United States to reimpose the Embargo against his enemy. He succeeded in doing so by means of a trick, the Cadore letter, which pretended to revoke the Berlin and Milan decrees as far as they interfered with American commerce. Madison accepted the Cadore letter as evidence of Napoleon's change of policy, even though the French continued to confiscate American ships. He announced that early in 1811, an embargo against Great Britain alone would automatically go into effect, in accordance with Macon's Bill, unless Britain meanwhile rescinded its orders-in-council.

In time, the new embargo, although less well enforced than the earlier, all-inclusive one had been, hurt the economy of England enough to cause influential Englishmen to petition their government for repeal of the orders-in-council. Eventually the orders were repealed—too late to prevent war, even if they had been the only grievance of the United States. But there were other grievances—namely, impressment and a border conflict between the British Empire and the expanding American frontier.

Conflicts on the Frontier

Given the ruthlessness with which white settlers had dislodged Indian tribes to make room for expanding settlement, it was hardly surprising that most Indians had since the Revolution continued to look to England—which had historically attempted to limit Western expansion—for protection. The British in Canada, for their part, had relied on Indian friendship to keep up their fur trade, even within the territory of the United States, and to maintain potentially useful allies. At one time, in 1794, America nearly went to war with Great Britain because of its Indian policy, but Anthony Wayne's victory over the tribes at Fallen Timbers and the conclusion of Jay's Treaty dispelled the war danger and brought on a period of comparative peace. Then, in 1807, the border quiet was disturbed by an event occurring far away—the British assault on the *Chesapeake*.

The ensuing war crisis would greatly aggravate the frontier conflict between tribesmen and settlers. Much of this conflict between red men and white was personified in the two opposing leaders, Tecumseh and William Henry Harrison.

The Virginia-born Harrison, already a veteran Indian fighter at twenty-six, went to Washington as the congressional delegate from the Northwest Territory in 1799. He was largely responsible for the passage of the Harrison Land Law (1800), which enabled settlers to acquire farms from the public domain on much easier terms than before. Land in the Northwest Territory soon was selling fast. The growth of population led to a division of the area into the state of Ohio and the territories of Indiana, Michigan, and Illinois. By 1812, Ohio contained 250,000 people and was beginning to look like an Eastern state, as paths widened into roads, villages sprang up and in some cases grew into cities, and the forests receded before the spreading cornfields. By 1812, Michigan had few settlers; but Illinois contained a scattered population of about 13,000, and Indiana 25,000.

Receiving from Jefferson an appointment as governor of Indiana Territory, Harrison devoted himself to carrying out Jefferson's policy of Indian removal. According to the Jeffersonian program, the Indians must give up their claims to tribal lands and either convert themselves into settled farmers or migrate to the west of the Mississippi. Playing off one tribe against another, and using whatever tactics suited the occasion—threats, bribes, trickery—Harrison made treaty after treaty with the separate tribes of the Northwest. By 1807, the United States claimed treaty rights to eastern Michigan, southern Indiana, and most of Illinois. Meanwhile, in the Southwest, millions of acres were taken from other tribes in the states of Georgia and Tennessee and in Mississippi Territory. Having been forced off their traditional hunting grounds, the Indians throughout the Mississippi Valley seethed with discontent. But the separate tribes, helpless by themselves against the power of the United States, might have accepted their fate if two complicating factors had not arisen.

One complication was the policy of the British authorities in Canada. For years they had neglected their Indian friends across the border to the south. Then came the *Chesapeake* incident and the surge of anti-British feeling throughout the United States. Now the Canadian authorities, expecting war and an attempted invasion of Canada, began to take desperate measures for their own defense. "Are the Indians to be employed in case of a rupture with the United States?" asked the lieutenant governor of Upper Canada in a letter of December 1, 1807, to Sir James Craig, governor general of the entire province. The governor replied: "If we do not employ them, there cannot exist a moment's doubt that they will be employed against us." Craig at once took steps to renew friendship with the Indians and provide them with increased supplies. Thus the trouble on the sea over the question of impressment intensified the border conflict hundreds of miles inland.

The second factor intensifying this conflict was the rise of a remarkable native leader, one of the most heroic in Indian history. Tecumseh, "The Shooting Star," chief of the Shawnees, aimed to unite all the tribes of the Mississippi Valley, resist the advance of white settlement, and recover the whole Northwest, making the Ohio River the boundary between the United States and the Indian country. He maintained that Harrison and others, by negotiating with individual tribes, had obtained no real title to land in the various treaties, since the land belonged to all the tribes and none of them could rightfully cede any of it without the consent of the rest. "The Great Spirit gave this great island to his red children. He placed the whites on the other side of the big water," Tecumseh told Harrison. "They were not contented with their own, but came to take ours from us. They have driven us from the sea to the lakes—we can go no farther."

In his plans for a united front, Tecumseh was aided by his brother, a one-eyed, epileptic medicine man known as the Prophet. The Prophet, visiting the Great Spirit from time to time in trances, inspired a religious revival that spread through numerous tribes and helped unite them. Few Indians doubted his supernatural powers after, having secretly learned from Canadian traders of a forthcoming eclipse, he commanded the sun to be dark on the appointed day. The Prophet's town, at the confluence of Tippecanoe Creek and the Wabash River, became the sacred place of the new religion as well as the headquarters of Tecumseh's confederacy. Leaving his brother there after instructing him to avoid war for the time being, Tecumseh journeyed down the Mississippi in 1811 to bring the Indians of the South into his alliance. At that time a great earthquake, with its center at New Madrid, Missouri, rumbled up and down the Mississippi Valley, causing much of the river to change its course. To many of the Indians, this phenomenon seemed another sign that a new era was at hand.

During Tecumseh's absence, Governor Harrison saw a chance to destroy the growing influence of the two Indian leaders. With 1,000 soldiers he camped near the Prophet's town and provoked an attack (November 7, 1811). Although he suffered losses as heavy as those of the enemy, Harrison succeeded in driving off the Indians and burning the town. This, the Battle of Tippecanoe, disillusioned many of the Prophet's followers, for they had been led to believe that his magic would protect them from the white man's bullets. Tecumseh returned to find his confederacy shattered. Yet there were still plenty of warriors eager for combat, and by the spring of 1812 they were busy all along the frontier, from Michigan to Mississippi.

Westerners blamed Great Britain for the bloodshed along the border. Britain's agents in Canada encouraged Tecumseh (used the Prophet as a "vile instrument," as Harrison put it) and provided the guns and supplies that enabled the Indians to attack. To Harrison and to most of the frontiersmen, there seemed only one way to make the West safe for Americans. That was to drive the British out of Canada and annex that province to the United States.

While frontiersmen in the North demanded the conquest of Canada, those in the South looked to the acquisition of Florida. In Spanish hands, that territory was a perpetual nuisance, with slaves escaping across the line in one direction and Indians raiding across it in the other. Through Florida ran such rivers as the Alabama, the Apalachicola, and others

that, in American possession, would give access to the Gulf of Mexico and the markets of the world. In 1810, American settlers in West Florida took matters into their own hands, fell upon the Spanish fort at Baton Rouge, and requested that the territory be annexed to the United States. President Madison unhesitatingly proclaimed its annexation, then schemed to get the rest of Florida too. With Madison's connivance, the former Georgia governor George Mathews attempted to foment a revolt in East Florida (1811). Spain protested, and Madison backed down; but the desire of Southern frontiersmen for all of Florida did not abate.

Thus the war fever was raging on both the Northern and the Southern frontiers by 1812. The denizens of these outlying regions were not numerous as compared with the population of the country as a whole, and for the most part they were not directly represented in Congress, except by a few territorial delegates. Nevertheless, they were ably represented at the national capital by a group of determined young congressmen who soon gained the name of "war hawks."

The War Hawks

Three days before the Battle of Tippecanoe, a new Congress met in Washington for the session of 1811–1812. In the congressional elections of 1810, most of the voters had indicated their disgust with such expedients as Macon's Bill No. 2 by defeating large numbers of Republican advocates of measures short of war, as well as Federalist advocates of continued peace. Of the newly elected congressmen and senators, the great majority were warlike Republicans; and after the news of Tippecanoe they became more eager than ever for a showdown with the power that seemed to threaten both the security of the frontier and the freedom of the seas.

A new generation had arrived on the political scene, a group of daring young men of whom the most influential came from the new states in the West or from the back country of the old states in the South. Two of the natural leaders, both recently elected to the House of Representatives, were Henry Clay and John C. Calhoun, whose careers were to provide much of the drama of American politics for the next four decades. The tall, magnetic Clay, barely thirty-four, was a Virginian by birth but had made Kentucky his home. Already he had served briefly in the United States Senate (1806–1807). As handsome as Clay if less appealing personally, the twenty-nine-year-old Calhoun was the son of Scotch-Irish pioneers in the South Carolina hills.

When Congress organized in 1811, the war faction of young Republicans got control of both the House and the Senate. On his election in 1811 as Speaker of the House, Clay held a position of influence then second only to that of the president. Clay filled the committees with the friends of force, appointing Calhoun to the crucial Committee on Foreign Affairs, and launched a drive toward war for the conquest of Canada.

THE ELECTION OF 1812

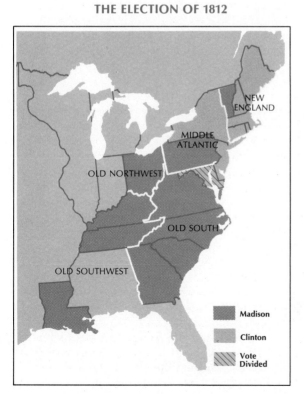

Madison

Clinton

Vote Divided

The Federalists in Congress, representing the commercial interests of the Northeast, denounced the clamor for Canada and war. But they were powerless to stem the drive toward hostilities, even with the aid of such dissident Republicans as the eccentric John Randolph of Roanoke. Dubbing the Clay men "war hawks," Randolph ridiculed their cry as being like that of the whippoorwill, "one eternal monotonous tone—Canada! Canada! Canada!"

While Congress debated, President Madison moved reluctantly toward the conclusion that war was necessary. In May, the war faction took the lead in the caucus of Republican congressmen who renominated him for the presidency; and on June 1, he sent a war message to Congress.

In his message, the president maintained that Great Britain—by impressing American citizens, interfering with American trade, and inciting the Indians along the frontier—was already waging a war against the United States. He recommended that Congress declare war in return. Congress responded with a declaration of hostilities on June 18, two days after a new ministry had announced in Parliament that the orders-in-council were to be suspended, but before the news could reach Washington. The close vote on the declaration, 19 to 13 in the Senate and 79 to 49 in the House, showed how badly the American people were divided.

The division of public opinion was again revealed in the election of 1812. Opposing Madison and the war, a peace faction of the Republicans nominated a rival candidate, De Witt Clinton of New York, and the Federalists gave their support to him. Most of the electors in the Northeast voted for Clinton and peace, but all of those in the South and the West sustained Madison and war. The president was reelected, 128 to 89.

With the people thus divided, the country as a whole was not psychologically ready for war. Nor was it financially or militarily prepared. Congress had adjourned without increasing the army and navy, voting war taxes, or renewing the charter of the Bank of the United States, which expired in 1811. The war hawks, however, continued to agitate for open conflict.

THE WAR OF 1812

At first, Great Britain, preoccupied with its mighty struggle against Napoleon, paid little attention to the American war and saw it as a mere annoyance. Then, in the fall of 1812, Napoleon launched the Russian campaign that, before the winter was over, was to bring him disaster and prepare the way for his ultimate defeat. As the months passed, Britain was able to divert more and more of its military and naval power to America.

The Course of Battle

The conquest of Canada, supposedly a "mere matter of marching," as Thomas Jefferson put it, soon proved to be an exercise in frustration. A three-pronged invasion was planned to strike into Canada by way of Detroit, the Niagara River, and Lake Champlain, with the greatest concentration of force at Detroit. But after marching into Canada, the elderly General William Hull, governor of Michigan Territory, retreated to Detroit and surrendered the fort (August 1812). The other invasion efforts also failed and Fort Dearborn (Chicago) fell before an Indian attack.

During the year of disaster and defeat on land, the Madison administration and its supporters took what consolation they could in the news of successes on the sea. American frigates engaged British warships in a series of duels and won some spectacular victories, one of the most renowned being the victory of the *Constitution* over the *Guerrière*. American privateers destroyed or captured one British merchant ship after another, occasionally braving the coastal waters of the British Isles and burning vessels within sight of the shore. After that first year, however, the score was evened by the British navy, which not only drove the American frigates to cover but also instituted a close blockade of the United States.

While British sea power dominated the ocean, American fleets arose to control the Great Lakes. First, the Americans took command of Lake Ontario, enabling troops to cross over to York (Toronto), the capital of Canada. At York (April 27, 1813), the invaders ran upon a cunningly contrived land mine, the explosion of which killed more than fifty, including General Zebulon M. Pike. Some of the enraged survivors, without authorization, set fire to the capital's public buildings, which burned to the ground. After destroying some ships and military stores, the Americans returned across the lake.

Next, Lake Erie was redeemed for American use, mainly through the work of the youthful Oliver Hazard Perry. Having constructed a fleet at Presque Isle (Erie, Pennsylvania), Perry took up a position at Put-in Bay, near a group of islands off the mouth of the Maumee River. With the banner "Don't Give Up the Ship" flying on his flagship, he awaited the British fleet, whose intentions he had learned from a spy. He smashed the fleet on its arrival (September 10, 1813) and established American control of the lake.

This made possible, at last, an invasion of Canada by way of Detroit. The post had been hard to reach overland, for supply wagons either had to struggle through the almost impassable Black Swamp of the Maumee Valley or had to make a long detour around it. After Perry's victory at Put-in Bay, supplies as well as men could be quickly and easily transported by water. William Henry Harrison, who had replaced Hull in the Western command, now pushed up the river Thames into Upper Canada and won a victory (October 5, 1813) that was chiefly notable for the death of Tecumseh, who had been commissioned a brigadier general in the British army. The Battle of the Thames resulted in no lasting occupation of Canada, but it disheartened the Indians of the Northwest and eliminated the worst of their threat to the frontier.

While Harrison was harrying the tribes of the Northwest, another Indian fighter was striking an even harder blow at the Creeks in the Southwest. The Creeks, aroused by Tecumseh on his Southern visit, were supplied by the Spaniards in Florida. These Indians had fallen upon Fort Mims, on the Alabama River just north of the Florida border, and had massacred the frontier families taking

Victory at Sea
As of 1812, the British in the course of the Napoleonic Wars had fought 200 naval battles and won 200 victories, in engagements between individual ships or whole fleets. Great Britain seemed invincible on the ocean. Then the United States frigate *Constitution* met and defeated three British vessels in a row. The third victim, off the coast of Brazil on December 19, 1812, was the *Java*, which was blown up after surrender and the removal of her crew, as shown in this sketch by an American naval lieutenant. (The Mariners Museum, Newport News, Virginia)

shelter within its stockade. Andrew Jackson, Tennessee planter and militia general, turned from his plans for invading Florida and tracked down the Creeks. In the Battle of Horseshoe Bend (March 27, 1814), Jackson's men took frightful vengeance, slaughtering women and children along with warriors. Then Jackson went into Florida and seized the Spanish fort at Pensacola.

After the Battles of the Thames and Horseshoe Bend, the Indians were of little use to the British. But with the surrender of Napoleon in Europe, the British could send their veterans of the European war to dispose

of the "dirty shirts," the unkempt Americans. In 1814, the British prepared to invade the United States by three approaches—the Chesapeake Bay, Lake Champlain (the historic route of Burgoyne), and the mouth of the Mississippi.

An armada under Admiral Sir George Cockburn sailed up the Patuxent River from the Chesapeake Bay and landed an army that marched a short distance overland to Bladensburg, on the outskirts of the District of Columbia. Hastily drawn up to oppose this army was a much more numerous force of poorly trained militiamen. When the firing

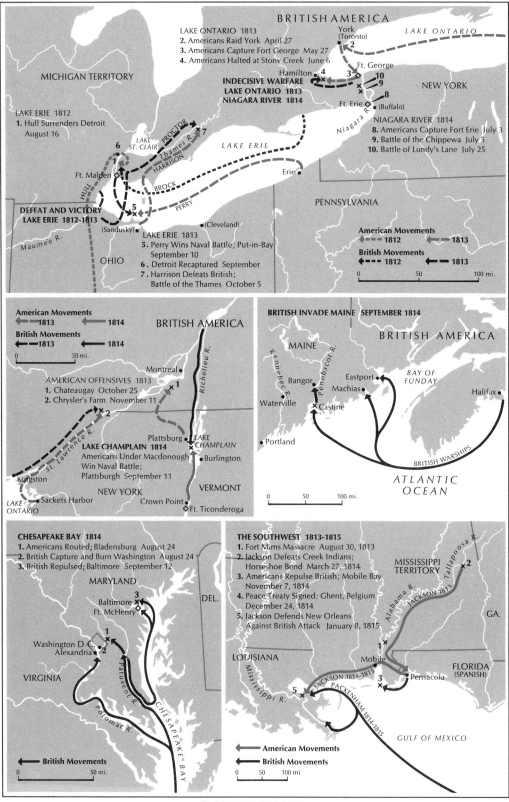

THE WAR OF 1812

LAKE ONTARIO 1813
2. Americans Raid York April 27
3. Americans Capture Fort George May 27
4. Americans Halted at Stony Creek June 6

**INDECISIVE WARFARE
LAKE ONTARIO 1813
NIAGARA RIVER 1814**

LAKE ERIE 1812
1. Hull Surrenders Detroit August 16

NIAGARA RIVER 1814
8. Americans Capture Fort Erie July 3
9. Battle of the Chippewa July 5
10. Battle of Lundy's Lane July 25

**DEFEAT AND VICTORY
LAKE ERIE 1812-1813**

LAKE ERIE 1813
5. Perry Wins Naval Battle; Put-in-Bay September 10
6. Detroit Recaptured September
7. Harrison Defeats British; Battle of the Thames October 5

American Movements
1812   1813
British Movements
1812   1813
0   50   100 mi.

BRITISH AMERICA
LAKE ONTARIO
York (Toronto)
Ft. George
Hamilton
NEW YORK
Ft. Erie
(Buffalo)
Niagara R.
MICHIGAN TERRITORY
LAKE ST. CLAIR
PROCTOR
Thames R.
HARRISON
LAKE ERIE
Ft. Malden
HULL
BROCK
PERRY
Erie
PENNSYLVANIA
(Sandusky)
(Cleveland)
Maumee R.
OHIO

American Movements
1813   1814
British Movements
1813   1814
0   50 mi.

BRITISH AMERICA

AMERICAN OFFENSIVES 1813
1. Chateaugay October 25
2. Chrysler's Farm November 11

LAKE CHAMPLAIN 1814
Americans Under Macdonough Win Naval Battle; Plattsburgh September 11

Montreal
Richelieu R.
St. Lawrence R.
Plattsburg
LAKE CHAMPLAIN
Burlington
Kingston
NEW YORK
VERMONT
LAKE ONTARIO
Sackets Harbor
Crown Point
Ft. Ticonderoga

BRITISH INVADE MAINE   SEPTEMBER 1814

BRITISH AMERICA
MAINE
Kennebec R.
Penobscot R.
Bangor
Eastport
Machias
BAY OF FUNDY
Halifax
Waterville
Castine
Portland
BRITISH WARSHIPS
ATLANTIC OCEAN
0   50   100 mi.

CHESAPEAKE BAY 1814
1. Americans Routed; Bladensburg August 24
2. British Capture and Burn Washington August 24
3. British Repulsed; Baltimore September 12

MARYLAND
DEL.
Baltimore
Ft. McHenry
Washington D.C.
Alexandria
VIRGINIA
Patuxent R.
Potomac R.
CHESAPEAKE BAY

British Movements
0   50 mi.

THE SOUTHWEST 1813-1815
1. Fort Mims Massacre August 30, 1813
2. Jackson Defeats Creek Indians; Horseshoe Bend March 27, 1814
3. Americans Repulse British; Mobile Bay November 7, 1814
4. Peace Treaty Signed; Ghent, Belgium December 24, 1814
5. Jackson Defends New Orleans Against British Attack January 8, 1815

MISSISSIPPI TERRITORY
Tallapoosa R.
JACKSON 1813
Alabama R.
GA.
Mobile
FLORIDA (SPANISH)
Pensacola
LOUISIANA
Mississippi R.
JACKSON 1814-1815
PACKENHAM 1814-1815
GULF OF MEXICO

American Movements
British Movements
0   50   100 mi

started they gave more than they received, but they were unnerved by the repeated assaults of the well-disciplined redcoats and finally broke formation and ran. The British marched on into Washington (August 24, 1814), putting the government to flight. Then they deliberately burned the public buildings, including the White House, in retaliation for the earlier unauthorized incendiarism at York. The sack of Washington marked the low point of American fortunes in the war.

Leaving Washington in partial ruins, the invading army reembarked and proceeded up the bay toward Baltimore. But Baltimore, guarded by Fort McHenry, was ready. To block the river approach, the garrison had stretched a chain across the Patapsco and had sunk several boats in the river. From a distance, the British bombarded the fort. Through the night an American, Francis Scott Key, watched from one of the enemy ships where he had gone to secure the release of a prisoner. The next morning (September 14, 1814), "by the dawn's early light," as Key wrote in a poem inspired by the moment, he could see the flag on the fort still flying "o'er the land of the free and the home of the brave." The British withdrew, and Key's words, set to the tune of an old English drinking song, became an enduring American favorite (and in 1931 the official national anthem).

Meanwhile, another invasion force was descending on northern New York. On Lake Champlain, the British had mustered a fleet about the size of the American fleet drawn up to oppose it, and nearby they had an army three times as large as the mixed force of regulars and militia facing it. Yet, in the Battle of Plattsburgh (September 11, 1814), the defenders destroyed the invading fleet, and the invading army then retreated to Canada. The northern border was safe.

Far to the south, the most serious threat of all soon materialized. In December 1814, a formidable array of battle-hardened veterans, fresh from the Duke of Wellington's peninsular campaign against the French in Spain, landed below New Orleans. On Christmas Day, Wellington's brother-in-law Sir Edward Pakenham arrived to take command. Neither he nor anyone else in America knew that a treaty of peace between the British and American governments had been signed in faraway Belgium the day before. Awaiting Pakenham's advance up the Mississippi was Andrew Jackson with a motley collection of Tennesseans, Kentuckians, Creoles, blacks, and pirates drawn up behind breastworks. For all their drill and bravery, the redcoats advancing through the open (January 8, 1815) were no match for Jackson's well-protected men. Making good use of artillery as well as rifles, the Americans held their fire as each wave of attackers approached, then sent out deadly volleys at close range. Finally the British retreated while an American band struck up "Hail, Columbia!" Left behind were 700 dead, including Pakenham himself, 1,400 wounded, and 500 other prisoners. Jackson's losses: 8 killed, 13 wounded.

New Englanders Object

With notable exceptions, such as the Battle of New Orleans, the military operations of the United States, 1812–1815, were rather badly bungled. This should cause little surprise. What is surprising is the fact that American arms succeeded as well as they did. After all, the government was woefully unprepared for the war at the outset and faced increasing popular opposition as the contest dragged on. The opposition centered in New England, and it went to remarkable extremes. Some of the Federalists there celebrated British victories, sabotaged their own country's war effort, and even plotted disunion and a separate peace.

Until 1814 the enemy blockade did not extend north of Newport, Rhode Island. The British government was deliberately cultivating the New England trade. Goods carried in Yankee ships helped to feed British troops in Canada as well as in Spain, and for a time many a shipowner grew rich by trading with the enemy while denouncing Madison and the war (although eventually the business of the shipowners as a whole fell far below the level of the prosperous prewar years).

Although most of the money in the nation was concentrated in New England, only a small part of the government's war bonds could be sold there. One of the Treasury loans, desperately needed to keep soldiers in the field, almost fell through because of the refusal of the New England banks to lend. Secretary of the Treasury Gallatin had to turn to his friend John Jacob Astor of New York and two foreign-born bankers of Philadelphia for the necessary funds. On several occasions, the governors of New England states refused to allow the state militia to take orders from the president or to fight outside the country.

In Congress, the Republicans had continual trouble with the Federalist opposition. The leadership of the administration party fell to Calhoun, who devoted himself to justifying the war and raising men and money with which to fight it. At every step he ran against the obstructionists, foremost among them the young congressman from New Hampshire, Daniel Webster. Introducing resolution after resolution to embarrass the administration, Webster demanded to know reasons for the war and intimated (correctly) that Napoleon had tricked the president into antagonizing England. Every measure to finance the fighting—by loans, taxes, tariffs, or a national bank—Webster and his Federalist allies vehemently denounced. At a time when volunteering lagged and the army was seriously undermanned, he opposed a bill to encourage enlistments. In its extremity, the administration proposed a draft of men into the regular army from the state militias. Helping to defeat the conscription bill, Webster warned that no such law could be enforced in his part of the country.

As new states in the South and West, strongly Republican, were added to the Union, the Federalists had become more and more hopelessly a minority party in the country as a whole. But they were still the majority in New England. If that section were to become a separate nation, they could control its destinies and escape the dictation of slave holders and backwoodsmen. The talk of secession, heard before at the time of the Louisiana Purchase and again at the time of Jefferson's Embargo, was revived during the war and reached a climax in the winter of

1814–1815, when the republic appeared to be on the verge of ruin.

On December 15, 1814, while the British were beginning their invasion by way of New Orleans, delegates from the New England states met in Hartford, Connecticut, to consider the grievances of their section against the Madison administration. The would-be seceders were overruled by the comparatively moderate men, who were in the overwhelming majority at the Hartford Convention. The convention's report reasserted the right of nullification but only hinted at secession, observing that "the severance of the Union by one or more States, against the will of the rest, and especially in time of war, can be justified only by absolute necessity." But the report proposed seven essential amendments of the Constitution, presumably as the condition of New England's remaining in the Union. These amendments were intended to protect New England from the growing influence of the South and the West.

The Federalists, apparently in a strong bargaining position, assumed that the Republicans would have to give in to the Hartford Convention terms, since the government was in such dire extremity. Soon after the convention adjourned, however, the news of Jackson's smashing victory at New Orleans reached the cities of the Northeast. While most Americans rejoiced, the Federalists were plunged into gloom. A day or two later came tidings from abroad concerning the conclusion of a treaty of peace. The treaty, of course, had been signed before the Battle of New Orleans, but the people heard of the battle first. They got the impression that the United States had won the war. "Peace is signed in the arms of victory!" the magazine *Niles's Register* exclaimed. The Hartford Convention and the Federalist party were discredited as both treasonable and futile.

The Peace Settlement

During the War of 1812, peace talks began even before the first battles were fought. President Madison, reluctant to ask for a declaration of war and "regretting the necessity that had produced it," looked hopefully toward an early end to hostilities. Soon after the declaration, the British government, wishing to liquidate a minor war and concentrate upon the major one, against Napoleon, sent an admiral to Washington with armistice proposals, but negotiations failed to develop because of Madison's continued insistence on the renunciation of impressment. Britain's ally Russia, eager to get supplies from America as well as unhampered military aid from England, twice offered to mediate, the first time on the day before Napoleon's invading forces entered Moscow (September 13, 1812). The British politely declined both of the czar's offers but finally agreed to meet the Americans in direct negotiations on neutral ground. After prolonged delays the peacemakers got together in Ghent, Belgium, on August 8, 1814.

The American peace delegation at Ghent was composed of men of exceptional ability, men who were more than a match for their opposite numbers around the peace table. The delegation included men of both parties and all sections. At the head of it was John Quincy Adams, a former Federalist who had broken with his party to support Jefferson's Embargo, and a diplomat of varied experience who recently had been minister to Russia. One of his colleagues was Henry Clay, once a war hawk, now a peace dove. Another was the secretary of the treasury in both Jefferson's and Madison's administrations, Albert Gallatin. A natural diplomat, Gallatin held the delegation together by moderating the disputes between Adams and Clay.

At Ghent, the two sets of peacemakers at first presented fantastically extreme demands, then gradually backed down and finally agreed to a compromise. The Americans, in accordance with their instructions, originally demanded the renunciation of impressment as a necessary condition to peace, and they also asked for all or part of Canada and for British aid in acquiring Florida from Spain. The English, contrary to their instructions, presented an ultimatum requiring the United States to cede territory in the Northwest for the formation of an Indian buffer state. Then, when their home government refused to sustain them in the ultimatum,

they withdrew it and proposed that peace be made on the principle of *uti possidetis*. This meant that each of the belligerents should keep the territory it actually held whenever the fighting stopped. Expecting large territorial gains from the invasion of America, the English at Ghent tried to delay negotiations so as to maximize the gains. But the government in London, becoming more and more alarmed by developments in Europe, decided to hasten the settlement with the United States and recommended peace on the basis of the *status quo ante bellum*, which meant a return to things as they had been before the war began. Already President Madison had advised his delegation that they need no longer make an issue of impressment. A treaty providing for the status quo, hastily drawn up, was signed on Christmas Eve 1814.

According to the Treaty of Ghent, the war was to end when the document had been ratified and proclaimed on both sides. Each of the belligerents was to restore its wartime conquests to the other. Four commissions composed of both Americans and Britons were to be appointed to agree on disputed or undetermined segments of the boundary between Canada and the United States.

The Treaty of Ghent was followed by other settlements that contributed to the improvement of Anglo-American relations. A separate commercial treaty (1815) gave Americans the right to trade freely with England and the British Empire except for the West Indies. A fisheries convention (1818) renewed the privileges of Americans to catch and dry fish at specified places along the shores of British North America. The Rush-Bagot agreement (1817) provided for mutual disarmament on the Great Lakes. Gradually disarmament was extended to the land, and eventually (although not until 1872) the Canadian-American boundary became the longest "unguarded frontier" in the world.

Though the British had not renounced impressment in principle, they ceased to apply it in practice after 1815. With the final end of the Napoleonic wars after the Battle of Waterloo, the nations of Europe entered upon a century of comparative peace, broken only by wars of limited scale. So the British no longer had occasion to violate American sovereignty on the high seas, and the government and people of the United States could afford to devote their energies primarily to affairs at home.

Free Seas Again

No sooner had peace come in 1815 than Congress declared war again, this time against Algiers, which had taken advantage of the War of 1812 to loose its pirates once more against American shipping in the Mediterranean. Two American squadrons now proceeded to North African waters. One of the two, under the command of Stephen Decatur, a naval hero of the late war with England, captured a number of corsair ships, blockaded the coast of Algiers, and forced the dey (the Algerian ruler) to accept a treaty that not only ended the payment of tribute by the United States but required the dey to pay reparations to America. Going on to Tunis and Tripoli, Decatur collected additional indemnities in both of those places. This naval action in the Mediterranean brought a more clear-cut victory for the freedom of the seas than had the War of 1812 itself. Of course, the victory was made possible by the growth in naval strength and national spirit that the war with England had occasioned. After 1816, when the dey of Algiers began to make trouble again, only to have his entire fleet destroyed by combined British and Dutch forces, the United States had no further difficulties with the Barbary pirates.

POSTWAR EXPANSION

With the international conflict settled, Americans could turn their full attention to their internal affairs. And the aftermath of the war made clear how far the nation had already moved from its simple, agrarian origins. Commerce, which had become central to the American economy, revived and expanded. Industry, which had made a few tentative beginnings in the first years of the century, advanced rapidly. Westward expansion, deterred for a time by the conflicts with the Indians and the British, now accelerated dramatically. The period following the war, in short, was one of rapid growth and progress—too rapid, as it turned out, for the boom was followed in 1819 by a disastrous bust. The collapse proved to be only a temporary obstacle to economic expansion, but it revealed clearly that the United States continued to lack some of the basic institutions necessary to sustain long-term growth.

Banks, Tariffs, Roads

The War of 1812 may have stimulated the growth of manufactures. But it also produced chaos in shipping and banking; and it exposed dramatically the inadequacy of the existing transportation system. Hence arose the postwar issues of reestablishing the Bank of the United States (the first Bank's charter having been allowed to expire in 1811), protecting the new industries, and providing a nationwide network of roads and waterways. On these issues, the former war hawks Clay and Calhoun became the leading advocates of the national, as opposed to the local or sectional, point of view. The party of Jefferson now sponsored measures of a kind once championed by the party of Hamilton. In regard to the Bank and the tariff, the new nationalists were fully successful; in regard to internal improvements, only partly so.

The wartime experience seemed to make necessary another national bank. After the expiration of the Bank's charter, a large number of state banks sprang up. These banks issued vast quantities of banknotes (promises to pay, which then served much the same purpose as bank checks were later to do) and did not always bother to keep a large enough reserve of gold or silver to redeem the notes on demand. The notes passed from hand to hand more or less as money; but their actual value depended on the reputation of the bank that issued them, and the variety of issues was so confusing as to make honest business difficult and counterfeiting easy. This bank money was not legal tender, and it was not issued directly by the state governments; yet its issuance hardly conformed with the clause of the Constitution giving Congress the exclusive power to regulate the currency and forbidding the states to emit bills of credit.

Congress struck at the currency evil not by prohibiting state banknotes but by chartering a second Bank of the United States in 1816. Except that it was allowed a larger capital, this institution was essentially the same as the one founded under Hamilton's leadership in 1791. In return for the charter, the Bank had to pay a "bonus" of $1.5 million to the government. Although its potential was not fully realized during the first few years of its existence, this national bank possessed the power of controlling the state banks by presenting their notes from time to time and demanding payment either in cash or in its own notes, which were as good as gold. Once the Bank of the United States began to exercise its power, the state banks had to stay on a specie-paying basis or risk being forced out of business.

The war had a disastrous effect on American shipping, especially after the British blockade was extended to include the New England coast. Between 1811 and 1814 exports dropped from $61 million to $7 million, and imports from $53 million to $13 million. The total tonnage of American vessels engaged in foreign trade declined from about 950,000 to fewer than 60,000 tons. Some ships managed to escape the blockade, but others were caught and confiscated—altogether about 1,300 of them.

Farmers, unable to get their produce out to the markets of the world, suffered from the ruin of the carrying trade, but manufacturers prospered, as foreign competition almost disappeared in consequence of the embargoes and the blockade. Much of the capital and labor formerly employed in commerce and shipbuilding was diverted to manufacturing. Goods were so scarce that, even with comparatively unskilled labor and poor management, new factories could be started with an assurance of quick profits.

The American textile industry had grown rather slowly until English imports were checked by Jefferson's Embargo of 1807 and then by the War of 1812. The first census of manufacturing, in 1810, counted 269 cotton and 24 woolen mills in the country. From 1807 to 1815, the total number of cotton spindles increased from 8,000 to 130,000. Most of the factories were located in New England. Until 1814, they produced only yarn and thread: the weaving of cloth was left to families operating hand looms at home. Then the Boston merchant Francis C. Lowell, after examining textile machinery in England, perfected a power loom that was an improvement on its English counterpart. Lowell organized the Boston Manufacturing Company and founded at Waltham, Massachusetts, the first mill in America to carry on the processes of spinning and weaving under a single roof.

As the war came to an end, the manufacturing prospects of the United States were suddenly dimmed. British ships swarmed alongside American wharves and began to unload their cargoes of manufactured goods at cut prices, even selling below cost. As Lord Brougham explained to Parliament, it was "well worth while to incur a loss upon the first exportation, in order, by the glut, to stifle in the cradle those rising manufactures in the United States, which war had forced into existence, contrary to the natural course of things."

The "infant industries" needed protection if they were to survive and grow strong enough to stand on their own feet against foreign competition. So the friends of industry maintained, reviving the old arguments of Hamilton. In 1816, the protectionists brought about the passage of a tariff law with rates high enough to be definitely protective, especially on cotton cloth.

The war had delayed the extension of steamboat lines on both eastern and western waters. Not until 1816 did a river steamer, the *Washington*, make a successful voyage upstream as far as Louisville, at the falls of the Ohio. Within a few years steamboats were carrying far more cargo on the Mississippi than all the flatboats, barges, and other primitive craft combined.

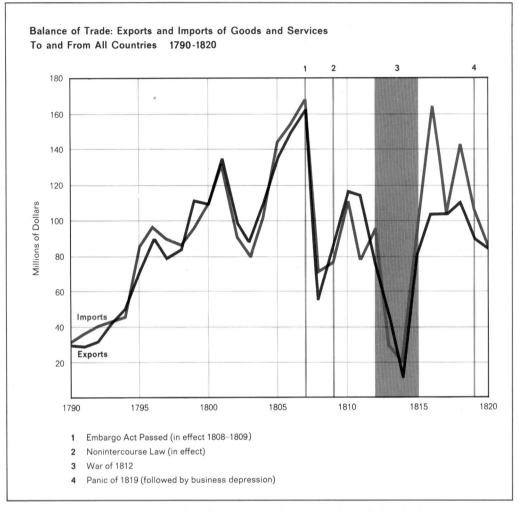

Balance of Trade: Exports and Imports of Goods and Services
To and From All Countries   1790-1820

1   Embargo Act Passed (in effect 1808–1809)
2   Nonintercourse Law (in effect)
3   War of 1812
4   Panic of 1819 (followed by business depression)

The Embargo Act (1807) reduced trade in 1808 and 1809 to about half of what it had been in the years immediately preceding, when it was stimulated by the war in Europe. The War of 1812 caused trade to shrink still further in 1813 and 1814. During the postwar recovery, imports considerably exceeded exports, creating an "unfavorable balance of trade" and provoking demands for increased tariff protection.

When Ohio was admitted as a state (1803), the federal government agreed that part of the proceeds from the sale of public lands there should be used for building roads. In 1807, Jefferson's secretary of the treasury, Albert Gallatin, proposed that a national road, financed partly by Ohio land sales, be built from the Potomac to the Ohio, and both Congress and the president approved. The next year, Gallatin presented a comprehensive plan of internal improvements requiring an appropriation of $20 million. But Jefferson doubted the constitutionality of such an expenditure, and the plan was shelved. Finally, in 1811, construction of the National Road began, at Cumberland, Maryland, on the Potomac. By 1818, this highway, with a crushed stone surface and massive stone bridges, was completed to Wheeling, Virginia, on the Ohio. Meanwhile, the state of Pennsylvania gave $100,000 to a private company that extended the Lancaster pike westward to Pittsburgh.

Over both of these roads moved a heavy traffic of stagecoaches, Conestoga wagons, private carriages, and other vehicles, as well as droves of cattle. Despite the high tolls, freight rates across the mountains now were lower than ever before. They were not low enough to permit the long-distance hauling of such bulky loads as wheat or flour. But commodities with a high value in proportion to their weight, especially manufactures, moved from the Atlantic seaboard to the Ohio Valley in unprecedented quantities.

Despite the progress being made with steamboats and turnpikes, there remained serious gaps in the transportation network of the country, as experience during the War of 1812 had shown. Once coastwise shipping had been cut off by the British blockade, the coastal roads became choked by the unaccustomed volume of north-south traffic. At the river ferries, long lines of wagons waited for a chance to cross. Oxcarts, pressed into emergency service, took six or seven weeks to go from Philadelphia to Charleston. In various localities there appeared serious shortages of goods normally carried by sea, and prices rose to new heights, rice costing three times as much in New York as in Charleston,

flour three times as much in Boston as in Richmond. On the Northern and Western frontiers, the military campaigns of the United States were frustrated partly by the absence of good roads.

With this wartime experience in mind, President Madison in 1815 called the attention of Congress to the "great importance of establishing throughout our country the roads and canals which can be best executed under the national authority," and he suggested that a constitutional amendment would resolve any doubts about the authority of Congress to provide for the construction of canals and roads. Representative Calhoun promptly espoused a bill by which the moneys due the government from the Bank of the United States—both the "bonus" and the government's share of the annual profits—would be devoted to internal improvements. "Let us, then, bind the republic together with a perfect system of roads and canals," Calhoun urged. "Let us conquer space."

Congress passed the bonus bill, but President Madison, on his last day in office (March 3, 1817), returned it with his veto. While he approved its purpose, he still believed that a constitutional amendment was necessary. And so, with some exceptions, the tremendous task of internal improvements

THE NATIONAL ROAD

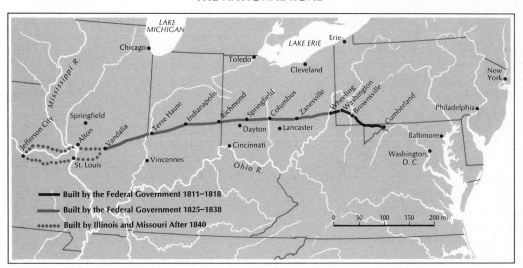

was left to the state governments and to private enterprise.

The "Era of Good Feelings"

Ever since 1800, the presidency seemed to have been the special possession of Virginians, who passed it from one to another in unvarying sequence. After two terms in office Jefferson named his secretary of state, James Madison, to succeed him; and after two more terms, Madison secured the nomination of *his* secretary of state, James Monroe. Many in the North already were muttering against this succession of Virginians, the so-called Virginia Dynasty, yet the Republicans had no difficulty in electing their candidate in the remarkably listless campaign of 1816. Monroe received 183 ballots in the electoral college; his opponent, Rufus King of New York, only 34, from the states of Massachusetts, Connecticut, and Delaware.

At the time he became president, Monroe was sixty-one years old. Tall and dignified, he wore the old-fashioned garb of his youthful days, including knee-length pantaloons and white-topped boots. He had reached the peak of a long and varied career as Revolution soldier, diplomat, and cabinet officer. Although when young he had been regarded as impulsive and changeable, he now was noted for his caution and patience. He was neither so subtle nor so original as his gifted predecessors from Virginia, Jefferson and Madison, but he had a mind of his own, and he was the master of his administration, even though he picked a group of exceptionally strong men for his advisers.

In choosing his cabinet, Monroe intended to recognize and harmonize the major interests of the country. For the first and most important position, that of secretary of state, he selected the New Englander and former Federalist John Quincy Adams. This choice was significant in view of the well-established custom that made the State Department a stepping stone to the presidency: Monroe appeared to be announcing that he would be the last of the Virginia Dynasty and that the next president would be a Massachusetts

James Monroe
When James Monroe was governor of Virginia (1799–1802) an acquaintance said of him: "To be plain, there is often in his manner an inartificial and even an awkward simplicity, which, while it provokes the smile of a more polished person, forces him to the opinion that Mr. Monroe is a man of most sincere and artless soul." In 1825, when Monroe was in his last year as president, a Virginia lady gave her impression of him after attending a New Year's reception at the White House: "From the frank, honest expression of his eye . . . I think he well deserves the encomium passed upon him by the great Jefferson, who said, 'Monroe is so honest that if you turned his soul inside out there would not be a spot on it.' " The portrait here reproduced was done by Gilbert Stuart, who painted portraits of all the men who served as president during his lifetime— Washington, Adams, Jefferson, Madison, Monroe, and John Quincy Adams.
(The Pennsylvania Academy of the Fine Arts)

man. For secretary of war, Monroe chose the forceful South Carolinian John C. Calhoun, after Henry Clay had declined the office, preferring to continue as Speaker of the House.

Soon after his inauguration, Monroe did what no other president since Washington had done: he made a goodwill tour through the country, eastward to New England, westward as far as Detroit. In New England, so recently the scene of rabid Federalist discontent, he was greeted everywhere with enthusiastic demonstrations. The *Columbian Centinel*, a Federalist newspaper of Boston, commenting on the "Presidential Jubilee" in that city, observed that an "era of good feelings" had arrived. This phrase soon became popular; it spread throughout the country, and eventually it came to be almost synonymous with the presidency of Monroe.

There was a good deal of hidden irony in this phrase of 1817, for the "good feelings" did not last long. The period over which Monroe presided turned into one of very bad feelings indeed. Yet he was reelected in 1820 with the nearest thing to a unanimous electoral vote that any presidential candidate, with the exception of George Washington, has ever had. Indeed, all but one of the electors cast their ballots for Monroe. The lone dissenter, an elector from New Hampshire with no love for Monroe, voted for John Quincy Adams so that Washington would remain the only unanimously elected president. The Federalists had not even bothered to put up an opposing candidate. For all practical purposes, the opposition party had now ceased to exist.

Florida and the Far West

The first big problem facing John Quincy Adams as secretary of state was Florida. Already the United States had annexed West Florida; but Spain still claimed the whole of the province, East and West, and actually held most of it, although with a grasp too feeble to stop the abuses against which Americans long had complained—the escape of slaves across the border in one direction, the marauding of Indians across it in the other. In 1817, Adams began negotiations with the Spanish minister, Luis de Onís, for acquiring all of Florida (or rather for acquiring that part of it which the United States did not already claim). Talks between the cantankerous puritan and the wily don progressed haltingly, then were broken off when the hot-headed Andrew Jackson took matters forcefully into his own hands.

Jackson, in command of American troops along the Florida frontier, had orders from Secretary of War Calhoun to "adopt the necessary measures" to end the border troubles. Jackson also had an unofficial hint—or so he afterward claimed—that the administration would not mind if he undertook a punitive expedition into Spanish territory. At any rate, he invaded Florida, seized the Spanish forts at St. Marks and Pensacola, and ordered the hanging of two British subjects on the charge of supplying the Indians and inciting them to hostilities. News of these events provoked a sharp discussion behind the scenes in Monroe's cabinet. Calhoun and others insisted that the general should be punished or at least reprimanded for exceeding his authority, but Adams defended Jackson so ably as to prevent any action against him.

Instead of blaming Jackson or disavowing the raid, Adams wished the government to assume complete responsibility for it, for he saw in it a chance to further his Florida diplomacy. Rejecting a Spanish protest, he demanded reparations from Spain to pay the cost of the expedition, although he did not press this demand. He pointed out that Spain had promised in Pinckney's Treaty to restrain the Indians in Spanish territory but had failed to live up to its treaty obligations. The United States, he argued, was justified by international law in taking drastic measures for self-defense. He implied that the nation would be justified in going even further than it had done.

Jackson's raid demonstrated that the United States, if it tried, could easily take Florida by force, unless Spain could get aid from some other power. The only power to which it could look was Great Britain. Unable to obtain British support, Spain had little choice but to come to terms with the United States, although the resourceful Onís made the most of a bad situation for his country. In the treaty of 1819, it was agreed that the king of Spain should cede "all the territories which belong to him situated to the eastward of the Mississippi and known by the name of East and West Florida." This ambiguous wording was used so as to evade the troublesome question of whether Spain was ceding both East and West Florida or whether West

Florida already belonged to the United States. In return, the United States assumed the claims of its citizens against the Spanish government to the amount of $5 million. This money was to be paid to American citizens, not to the Spanish government; the government thus did not "purchase" Florida, as is sometimes said. The United States also gave up its claims to Texas, and Spain its claims to territory north of the 42nd parallel from the Rockies to the Pacific. Thus a line was drawn from the Gulf of Mexico northwestward across the continent delimiting the Spanish Empire and transferring to the United States the Spanish title to the West Coast north of California. Adams and Onís had concluded something more than a Florida agreement: it was a "transcontinental treaty."

President Monroe, with the approval of the Senate, promptly ratified the treaty, but the coming of a revolution delayed ratification by Spain. The treaty finally went into ef-

fect in 1821. Thereafter the whole of Florida, was, without question, territory belonging to the United States. And for the first time the area of the Louisiana Purchase had a definite southwestern boundary.

At the time of his negotiations with Onís, Adams showed much more interest in the Far West than did most of his fellow countrymen. Except for New Englanders engaged in Pacific whaling or in the China trade, few Americans were familiar with the Oregon coast. Only the fur traders and trappers knew intimately any of the land between the Missouri and the Pacific. Before the War of 1812, John Jacob Astor's American Fur Company had established Astoria as a trading post at the mouth of the Columbia River. When war came, Astor sold his interests to the Northwestern Fur Company, a British concern operating from Canada; and after the war he centered his own operations in the Great Lakes area, from which he eventually ex-

BOUNDARY SETTLEMENTS, 1818–1819

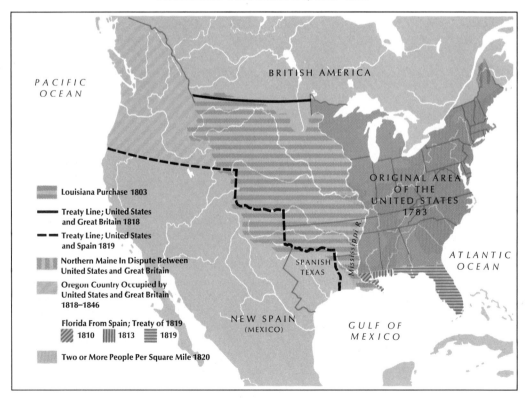

tended them westward to the Rockies. Manuel Lisa's Missouri Fur Company, founded in 1809, with headquarters in St. Louis, sent traders and supplies up the Missouri and its tributaries and brought back peltries obtained from the Indians. The Rocky Mountain Fur Company, which Andrew Henry and William Henry Ashley organized in 1822, pushed the trade farther north and west and revolutionized the business by sending out white trappers who procured their furs directly and brought them to an annual "rendezvous" in the mountains to be sold to the company's agents.

The trappers or "mountain men," notably Jedediah S. Smith, explored the Far West and gained an intimate knowledge of it, but they did not write books. General information about the region increased as a result of the explorations of Major Stephen H. Long. In 1819 and 1820, with instructions from the War Department to find the sources of the Red River, Long with nineteen soldiers ascended the Platte and South Platte rivers, discovered the peak named for him, and returned eastward by way of the Arkansas River; but they failed to find the headwaters of the Red. "In regard to this extensive section of country between the Missouri River and the Rocky Mountains," Long said in his report, "we do not hesitate in giving the opinion that it is almost wholly unfit for cultivation, and of course uninhabitable by a people depending upon agriculture for their subsistence." On the published map of his expedition, the Great Plains were marked as the "Great American Desert." Thus Long gave increased currency to the idea earlier put forth by Pike that the farming frontier would run against a great natural barrier beyond the Missouri. Meanwhile the vacant lands to the east, between the Appalachians and the Mississippi, were rapidly being converted into plantations and farms.

The Great Migration

One of the central themes of American history, for nearly three centuries after the founding of Jamestown, was the movement of population from the Atlantic coast to the interior and ultimately across the continent.

This was no steady march, uniform along a broad front. It proceeded in irregular waves, following the lines of greatest attraction and least resistance, and accelerating in times of prosperity and peace. A sudden surge, greater than any preceding it, swept westward during the boom years that followed the War of 1812.

Weakened though it had been, the Indian threat still had to be taken into account. In a series of treaties forced on the tribes after 1815, the federal government resumed the policy of compelling the Indians to choose between settling down as farmers and migrating beyond the Mississippi. Along the Great Lakes and the upper Mississippi, a chain of stockaded forts was erected to protect the frontier. A "factory" system, by which government factors or agents traded with the Indians, supplying them with goods at cost, was instituted in an effort to drive out of business the Canadian traders who persisted in carrying on their activities on American soil. After several years the government factories were abandoned because of the opposition of American fur companies, which objected to government competition with private enterprise. By that time the Canadian traders had retreated across the border, and foreign influence over the American tribes finally came to an end.

The land abandoned by the Indians in the so-called Old Northwest (generally known today as part of the Midwest) had been richly favored by nature, although its qualities were not entirely recognized by the early pioneers. Over most of the Northwest extended the great primeval forest, but in central Illinois the forest gave way to a grand prairie billowing with wild grass as tall as six feet. The first settlers avoided this treeless stretch, for they saw unfamiliar problems in its tough sod and scarcity of wood. They were largely unaware of the productivity of its black loam.

"Old America seems to be breaking up and moving westward," remarked an Englishman who joined the throng. Some of the migrants were Kentucky and Tennessee frontiersmen, restless spirits who had begun to feel crowded as their states became increasingly populous. Others were small farmers from the back country of Virginia

From Forest to Farm

First (*top left*), a clearing is begun and a rude cabin is built. The stream remains un-
bridged and has to be forded. Second (*bottom left*), the cabin is fenced in (note the
"worm" fence), more trees are cut, stumps are burned, a small crop is put in, and the
stream is spanned by a log bridge. Third (*top right*), the cabin is enlarged, a barn is built,

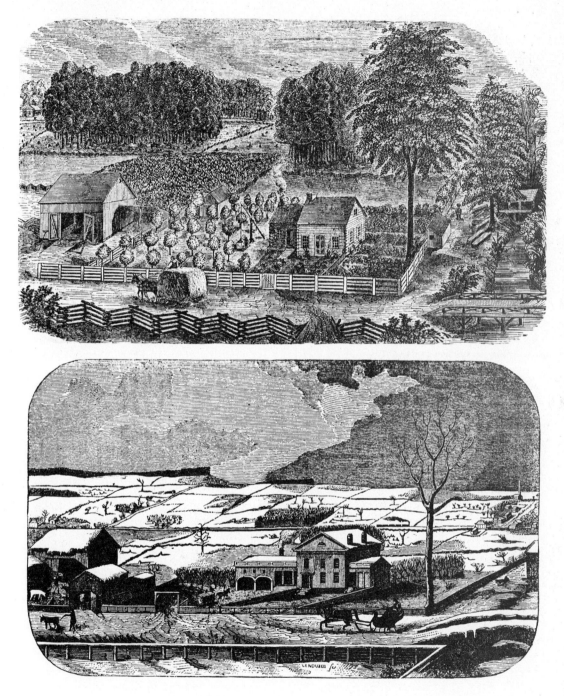

the fencing is improved, fields are widened, and a bridge is erected. Finally (*bottom right*), all trace of the wilderness is gone, an imposing house has replaced the cabin, a village has grown up nearby, and an arched stone bridge has been built. These illustrations are from O. Turner, *Pioneer History of the Holland Land Purchase of Western New York* (1850).

and the Carolinas who fled the encroachment of slavery and the plantation system. Still others came from the middle states, New England, and foreign countries. But the great majority were Southerners. Whatever the starting point, the Ohio River was for most of the migrants the main route, the "grand track," until the completion of the Erie Canal in 1825. They took the turnpike to Pittsburgh or the National Road to Wheeling and thus reached the river, or they took one of its tributaries such as the Kanawha, the Cumberland, or the Tennessee. Downstream they floated on flatboats bearing all their worldly goods. Then, leaving the Ohio at Cincinnati or at some place farther down, they pressed on overland with wagons, handcarts, packhorses, cattle, and hogs.

Once having arrived at his destination, preferably in the spring or early summer, the settler built a lean-to or cabin for his family, then hewed a clearing out of the forest and put in a crop of corn to supplement the wild game he caught and the domestic animals he had brought with him. These frontier folk knew loneliness and poverty and dirt, and suffered much from forest fevers and from malnutrition. As a result, they commonly had a lean and sallow look. Yet they were on the whole remarkably proud, bold, and independent—"half wild and wholly free," as some said admiringly.

To the Southwest moved people from Kentucky, from Tennessee, and from as far away as New England. Most numerous among the settlers on the Southern frontier, however, were farmers and planters from the South Atlantic states, especially from the piedmont of Georgia and the Carolinas. Their motive for migrating was, in a word, cotton. With the spread of cotton cultivation throughout the uplands of the older South, the soil there had lost much of its natural fertility from repeated croppings or had been washed away as torrential rains gullied the hillsides. Seeking fresh soil with a climate suitable for cotton, the planters naturally looked to the Southwest, around the end of the Appalachian range, where there stretched a broad zone within which cotton could thrive. Included in this zone was what was to become known as the Black Belt of central Alabama and Mississippi, a prairie with a productive soil of rotted limestone.

The advance of the Southern frontier meant the spread of cotton and slavery. Usually the first arrivals were ordinary frontiersmen like those farther north, small farmers who made rough clearings in the forest. Then came wealthier planters, who bought up the cleared or partially cleared land, while the original settlers moved on west and started over again. As a rule, the planters made the westward journey in a style quite different from that of the other pioneers. Over the alternately dusty and muddy roads came great caravans consisting of herds of livestock, wagonloads of household goods, long lines of slaves, and bringing up the rear, the planter and his family riding in carriages. Soon the clearings expanded into vast fields white with cotton, and the cabins of the pioneers gave way to more sumptuous log dwellings and ultimately to imposing mansions that demonstrated the rise of a newly rich class.

Although by 1819 settlers already were pushing beyond the Mississippi, much of the area to the east of the river, around the Great Lakes and along the Gulf of Mexico, was yet to be occupied. Despite the gaps in settlement, the population of the Mississippi Valley had increased far more rapidly than that of the nation as a whole. The census of 1810 indicated that only one American in seven lived to the west of the Appalachian Mountains; the census of 1820, almost one in four. During the immediate postwar years, four new states were created in this region—Indiana (1816), Mississippi (1817), Illinois (1818), and Alabama (1819). Meanwhile Missouri had grown populous enough for statehood, and the struggle over its admission would indicate how important, politically and otherwise, the West was becoming to the rest of the nation. For the time being, however, the westward movement was slowed by a depression following the Panic of 1819.

The Panic of 1819

In part, the Panic of 1819 was a delayed reaction to the War of 1812 and to the preceding years of warfare in Europe. Since 1793, the continual fighting had drawn manpower from European fields, disrupted business as well as agriculture, and created an abnormal demand for the produce of American plantations and farms. The whole period was one of exceptionally high prices for American producers, and although some prices fell with the decline of trade in 1814, they recovered with the resumption of exports to Europe after the war.

Rising prices for farm products stimulated a land boom in the United States, particularly in the West. After the war, the government land offices did a bigger business than ever before; not for twenty years were they to do as good a business again. In 1815, sales totaled about a million acres; in 1819, more than 5 million. Many settlers bought on credit; under the land laws of 1800 and 1804 they could pay as little as $80 down, and then, they hoped, raise the remaining three installments within four years from the proceeds of their farming. Speculators bought large tracts of choice land, hoping to resell it at a profit to incoming settlers. At the land-office auctions, bidding became so spirited that much of the public land sold for prices far above the minimum of $2 an acre, some in the Black Belt of Alabama and Mississippi going for $100 and more. Still higher prices were sometimes paid by optimistic real estate promoters who laid out town sites, even in swamps, and expected to make fortunes through the sale of city lots. Until 1817, neither the settlers nor the speculators needed hard cash to buy government land: they could borrow from the state banks and pay the government with bank notes.

Even after the refounding of the Bank of the United States in 1817, wildcat banks continued to provide easy credit for a few years. Indeed, the United States Bank itself at first offered easy loans. Then in 1819, concerned about the potential for instability in excessive credit, a new management suddenly began to tighten up. It called in loans and foreclosed mortgages, acquiring thousands of acres of mortgaged land in the West. It gathered up state bank notes and presented them to the state banks for payment in cash. Having little money on hand, many of these banks closed their doors. Most of the rest soon had to follow suit, for they were beset by depositors with notes to be cashed. The panic was on. And many Americans, particularly those in the West, blamed the Bank for the crisis.

Six years of depression followed. Prices fell rapidly. With the prices of farm products so low, those settlers buying land on credit could not hope to keep up their payments. Some stood to lose everything—their land, their improvements on it, their homes. They demanded relief, and Congress responded with the land law of 1820 and the relief act of 1821. The new land law abolished the credit system but lowered the minimum price of land from $2.00 to $1.25 an acre and the minimum tract from 160 to 80 acres. Thereafter, a purchaser would have to buy his farm outright, but he could get one for as little as $100. The relief act allowed a previous buyer to pay off his debt at the reduced price, to accept the reduced acreage and apply the payments to it, and to have more time to meet his installments.

The Panic of 1819 and the widespread distress that followed seemed to some Americans to confirm fears that rapid economic growth and territorial expansion would destabilize the nation and threaten the survival of the republic. But to far more Americans, the crisis suggested the need for a more advanced set of institutions to support national progress. Those who continued to embrace the Jeffersonian vision of a simple, agrarian republic had become a tiny minority, even within the Republican party. Instead, Americans would, after 1820, embark on a heady period of growth; and public debate would revolve less around the question of whether such growth was good or bad, and more around the question of how it should be encouraged and controlled.

SUGGESTED READINGS

Julius W. Pratt, *Expansionists of 1812* (1925), is a standard account of the causes of the conflict, which should be supplemented with Reginald Horsman, *The Causes of the War of 1812* (1962); Bradford Perkins, *Prologue to War: England and the United States, 1805–1812* (1961); and A. L. Burt, *The United States, Great Britain, and British North America* (1940). Roger H. Brown, *The Republic in Peril: 1812* (1964), examines the outbreak of hostilities. For the war itself, see four books, all entitled *The War of 1812*, by the following authors: Harry L. Coles (1965), Reginald Horsman (1969), F. F. Beirne (1949), and J. K. Mahon (1975). William Wood, *The War with the United States* (1915), examines the Canadian viewpoint. Irving Brant, *James Madison: Commander-in-Chief* (1961), is a sympathetic study of the president's role in the conflict; while Robert V. Remini, *Andrew Jackson and the Course of American Empire* (1977), is a study of one of the nation's leading generals. Alfred T. Mahan, *Sea Power in Its Relation to the War of 1812*, 2 vols. (1905), is a classic military study. Samuel F. Bemis, *John Quincy Adams and the Foundations of American Foreign Policy* (1949), and Bradford Perkins, *Castlereagh and Adams* (1964), examine the peace negotiations.

The general subject of American nationalism and expansion in the postwar era is well told in George Dangerfield, *The Awakening of American Nationalism* (1965) and *The Era of Good Feelings* (1952). Shaw Livermore, Jr., *The Twilight of Federalism* (1962), is a useful study of the ideas behind nationalism. Bray Hammond, *Banks and Politics in America from the Revolution to the Civil War* (1957), examines economic policy. Frederick Jackson Turner, *The Rise of the New West* (1906), emphasizes the importance of the West in the early nineteenth century. Francis S. Philbrick, *The Rise of the West, 1745–1830* (1965), challenges many of Turner's views. Thomas P. Abernethy, *The South in the New Nation* (1961), examines the influence of expansionism on the slave states. The classic work on the influence of the West in American history is Frederick Jackson Turner, *The Frontier in American History* (1920). On the westward migration, see Ray Billington, *The Far Western Frontier* (1965) and *Westward Expansion* (1974); John A. Hawgood, *America's Western Frontier* (1967); David J. Wishart, *The Fur Trade of the American West* (1979); Frederick Merk, *History of the Westward Movement* (1978); and Dale Van Every, *The Final Challenge* (1964). Murray N. Rothbard, *The Panic of 1819* (1962), examines the economic crisis.

PART THREE

Expansion and Disunion, 1820-1860

Rapid growth and rapid change have been constant features of American history. But in perhaps no era of national life were growth and change more sudden or profound than in the years from 1820 to 1860. During those four decades, the United States experienced a remarkable expansion of the size of its population, of the area of its settlement, and of the extent and complexity of its economy. Together, these changes transformed American life. And together, they helped produce a great national crisis that threatened to destroy the Union forever.

The American population had already, in 1820, nearly tripled in size since the end of the Revolution. Over the next forty years it more than tripled again—from just under 10 million to just over 31 million. And the population fanned out during those years to inhabit an expanse of territory that would make the United States one of the largest countries in the world. Americans were not only pouring into the regions that the nation had acquired in the first years of the century—the vast Louisiana Purchase, the great Florida accession. They were also pressuring their government to acquire, and on one occasion to go to war for, still more land—Texas, Oregon, the Southwest, and more. It was the nation's destiny, many Americans argued, to span the North American continent. And some continued to dream of adding Canada and Mexico to the national realm as well.

Of equal importance, the American economy transformed itself in those years. Agriculture—in the North, in the South, and in the newly settled regions of the West—grew dramatically in both extent and productivity. Commerce—domestic and international—expanded steadily. And industry, which had made its first, tentative beginnings as early as the eighteenth century, emerged as a major force in the national economy—not yet the dominant force it would eventually become, but one strong enough to re-shape the social, economic, and political lives of millions of men and women.

Much of this growth was a result of the energy and resourcefulness of the American people, who displayed in the mid-nineteenth century courage, vision, and remarkable entrepreneurial and technological talents. Indeed, the United States became in these years one of the marvels of the world, a society that served as a model for many Western nations. But American growth was a result, too, of ruthless exploitation: of land, of resources, and of people.

Americans exploited their land and their natural resources with a reckless abandon, always aware that a vast, largely untouched continent still awaited them. They farmed fertile lands until the lands were exhausted and then casually abandoned them. They stripped forests bare to provide lumber and fuel for their homes and factories. They fished streams empty, hunted forests until certain breeds of animals were virtually extinct. Americans viewed themselves as masters of their land; and with so much of it available to them, they saw little reason for restraint in its use.

In much the same spirit, the growing nation exploited people. Indians were ruthlessly driven from their ancestral lands, as they had been since the first years of European and African settlement in the seventeenth century. Then they were driven from the Western preserves into which many of the tribes had retreated. Between 1820 and 1860, white men drove virtually the whole of the Indian population west of the Mississippi—killing many of the natives in the process, relegating those few who stayed behind to permanent poverty and subjugation. The relentless march of civilization, white Americans almost universally believed, could not be allowed to falter because of the opposition of "savages."

In one region of the country, American growth rested on the exploitation of another group of people: black slaves. Southern agriculture, which experienced a booming prosperity through much of the mid-nineteenth century as a result of the expanding world market for cotton, was based almost entirely on slave labor. Thus, while in some other nations the institution of slavery was in decline during these years, in the United States it was growing stronger; and the black population of America, as well as becoming more numerous, was developing a distinctive culture and society that reflected the conditions of bondage.

And in the North, economic growth rested in large part on the exploitation of white men and women—the new labor force that developed in response to the needs of industrial capitalism. White factory workers were not formally in bondage; indeed, many of them found in industrial labor an avenue to economic advancement. But the rise of the factory system did require a large number of people—some of them native-born Americans; a growing number of them, as the century progressed, immigrants from Europe—to adapt to a new way of life in which individuals exercised far less control than in the past over their livelihoods or the conditions of their labor. It was a harsh adjustment—so harsh that some critics of the factory system likened it to the condition of Southern blacks and called it "wage slavery."

With changes so sudden and so vast, political and social tensions were inevitable. And that these changes were occurring within a nation still only a few decades old, a nation still in many ways only half-formed, meant that the tensions could become a threat to American unity. At first, the political struggles of the mid-nineteenth century involved issues that largely transcended regional differences. In the 1820s and 1830s, much of the nation's political energy was devoted to defining the position of elites—to debating how to balance the need for stability and order with the desire for expanding individual opportunity. Slowly, however, another set of concerns—related to the first, but different in impact—rose to the fore. Most prominent among them was the issue of slavery. As territorial expansion forced the nation time and again to confront the question of whether new areas of settlement were to be slave or free, as the power of the South in national politics began slowly to decline, as residents of both North and South began to see in the social structure of the other a threat to their own way of life, the conflict between sections grew to menacing proportions. For a time, the forces of nationalism were strong enough to counterbalance the divisive issues of sectionalism. By the 1850s, however, those unifying forces were in decline; and the pressures for disunion, no longer contained, were leading inexorably to the greatest domestic crisis in American history.

A Resurgence of Nationalism

9

Opening the Erie Canal, 1825
Nothing better symbolized the optimism and the material growth of the United States in the first decades of the nineteenth century than the construction of the Erie Canal, which connected the lake ports of upstate New York to the Hudson River and therefore to the seaport of New York City. To celebrate the completion of the new canal, Governor De Witt Clinton and other dignitaries sailed from Buffalo to New York City. Upon their arrival, Clinton poured a bucket of Lake Erie water into the Atlantic Ocean. (Culver Pictures)

Like a "fire bell in the night," as Thomas Jefferson put it, the issue of slavery arose only five years after the end of the War of 1812 to threaten the unity of the nation. The specific question was whether the territory of Missouri should be admitted to the Union as a free or as a slaveholding state. But the larger issue, one that would arise again to plague the republic, was the question of whether the vast new Western regions of the United States would ultimately be controlled by the North or by the South.

Yet the Missouri crisis, which was settled by a compromise in 1820, was significant at the time not only because it augured the sectional crises to come but because it stood in such sharp contrast to the rising American nationalism of the 1820s. Whatever forces might be working to pull the nation apart, far stronger ones were acting to hold it together. The American economy was experiencing revolutionary growth. And while ultimately the industrialization of the North would contribute to sectional tensions, economic progress—which brought with it new systems of transportation and communication—seemed likelier for the moment to link the nation more closely together. The federal government, in the meantime, was acting in both domestic and foreign policy to assert a vigorous nationalism— through the judicial decisions of John Marshall's Supreme Court; through congressional legislation encouraging economic growth; and through the foreign policy of the Monroe administration, which attempted to assert the nation's rising stature in the world.

Above all, the United States was held together in the 1820s by a set of shared sentiments and ideals, the "mystic bonds of union," as they were occasionally described. The memory of the Revolution, the veneration of the framers and the Constitution, the widely held sense that America had a special destiny in the world—all combined to obscure sectional differences and arouse a vibrant, even romantic, patriotism. Every year, Fourth of July celebrations reminded Americans of their common struggle for independence, as fife and drum corps and flamboyant orators appealed to patriotism and nationalism. When the Marquis de Lafayette, the French general who had aided the United States during the Revolution, revisited the country in 1824, the glorious past was revived as never before. Everywhere Lafayette traveled, crowds without distinction of section or party cheered him in frenzied celebration.

And on July 4, 1826—the fiftieth anniversary of the adoption of the Declaration of Independence—there occurred an event which seemed to many to confirm that the United States was a nation specially chosen by God. On that special day, Americans were to learn, two of the greatest of the country's founders—Thomas Jefferson, author of the Declaration, and John Adams, "its ablest advocate and defender" (as Jefferson had said)—had died within hours of each other.

Events would prove that the forces of nationalism were not, in the end, strong enough to overcome the emerging sectional differences. For the time being, however, they permitted the republic to enter an era of unprecedented growth confident and united.

AMERICA'S ECONOMIC REVOLUTION

There had been signs for many years that the United States was poised for a period of dramatic economic growth. In the 1820s and 1830s, that period finally began. Improvements in transportation and the expanding range of business activity created, for the first time, a national market economy. Each area of the country could concentrate on the production of a certain type of goods, relying on other areas to buy its surplus production and to supply it with those things it no longer produced itself. This regional specialization enabled the South, for example, to concentrate on growing its most lucrative crop: cotton. And it enabled the North to develop a new factory system—to begin an industrial revolution that would, in time, become even greater than the one that had begun in England some forty years before. By the mid-1820s, the nation's economy was growing more rapidly than its population.

Many factors combined to produce this dramatic transformation. The American people were becoming more numerous and were spreading across a far greater expanse of territory, providing both a labor supply for the production of goods and a market for the sale of them. A "transportation revolution"—based on the construction of roads, canals, and eventually railroads—was giving merchants and manufacturers access to new markets and raw materials. New entrepreneurial techniques were making a rapid business expansion possible. And technological advances were helping to spur industry to new levels of activity. Equally important, perhaps, Americans in the 1820s adopted an ethic of growth that was based on a commitment to hard work, individual initiative, thrift, and ambition. The results of their efforts seemed, to many people at least, to confirm the value of such a commitment.

The Population, 1820–1840

During the 1820s and 1830s, as during the whole of American history, three trends of population were clear: rapid increase, migration to the West, and movement to towns and cities.

Americans continued to multiply almost as fast as in the colonial period, the population still doubling every twenty-five years or so. The total figure, below 4 million in 1790, approached 10 million by 1820 and rose to nearly 13 million in 1830 and to about 17 million in 1840. The United States was growing much more rapidly in population than the British Isles or Europe. By 1860 it had gone ahead of the United Kingdom and had nearly overtaken Germany and France.

The black population increased more slowly than the white. After 1808, when the importation of slaves was made illegal, the proportion of blacks to whites in the nation as a whole steadily declined. In 1820, there was one black to every four whites; in 1840, one to every five. The slower increase of the black population was a result of its comparatively high death rate, not of a low birth rate. Slave mothers had large families, but life was shorter for both slaves and free blacks than for whites.

The mortality rate for whites slowly declined. Epidemics continued to take their periodic toll, among them a cholera plague that swept the country in 1832; but public health efforts gradually improved and reduced the number and ferocity of such outbreaks. On the average, people lived somewhat longer than in earlier generations. The population increase, however, was a result less of lengthened life than of the maintenance of a high birth rate, which more than offset the death rate.

Immigration accounted for little of the population growth before the 1840s. The long years of war in Europe, from 1793 to 1815, had kept the number of newcomers to America down to not more than a few thousand a year, and then the Panic of 1819 checked the immigrant tide that had risen after the restoration of peace. During the 1820s, arrivals from abroad averaged about 14,000 annually. Of the total population of nearly 13 million in 1830, the foreign-born numbered fewer than 500,000, most of them naturalized citizens. Soon, however, immigration began to grow, reaching a total of 60,000 for 1832 and nearly 80,000 for 1837.

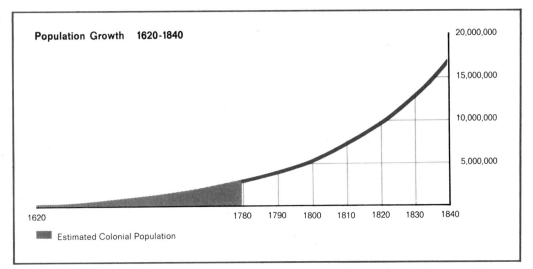

Population Growth   1620-1840

Estimated Colonial Population

The United States was the first country to undertake a complete and periodic population count, beginning with the census of 1790. From 1790 to 1840 the American population grew, by actual count, from a little less than 4 million to a little more than 17 million. Meanwhile the world population grew, according to estimate, from about 700 million to more than 1 billion. During this period the population of the United States was increasing by about 3 percent a year, that of the United Kingdom less than 1 percent, and that of France less than one-half of 1 percent.

Since the United States exported more goods than it imported, returning ships often had vacant space and took on immigrants to fill it. Competition among shipping lines reduced fares so that, by the 1830s, immigrants could get passage across the Atlantic for as little as $20 or $30. No longer did they need to sell their services to a temporary master in America in order to pay for the voyage. And so the system of indentured servitude, which had dwindled steadily after the Revolution, disappeared entirely after the Panic of 1819.

Until the 1830s, most of the new arrivals came from the same sources as had the bulk of the colonial population—from England and the northern (predominantly Protestant) counties of Ireland. In the 1830s, however, the number arriving from the southern (Catholic) counties of Ireland began to grow, anticipating the tremendous influx of the Irish that was to occur in the next two decades. Generally the newcomers—the Irish as well as others—were welcomed in the United States. They were needed to provide labor for building canals and railroads, manning

ships and docks, and performing other heavy work essential to the expanding economic system. But the Irish, as Roman Catholics, excited Protestant prejudices in some communities. In 1834, an anti-Catholic mob set fire to a convent in Charlestown, Massachusetts. The next year, Samuel F. B. Morse (who is better remembered as a portrait painter and as the inventor of the telegraph) published his *Foreign Conspiracy*, which served thereafter as a textbook for nativists crusading against what they imagined was a popish plot to gain control of the United States.

The West (including both Northwest and Southwest) continued to grow much more rapidly than the rest of the country. By 1830, more than a fourth of the American people lived to the west of the Appalachians; by 1850, nearly half. Some of the seaboard states suffered serious losses of human resources, as well as of the material goods that departing migrants took with them. Year after year the Carolinas, for example, gave up nearly as much through migration as they gained by natural increase, so that their populations remained almost stationary. The same was true of Vermont and New Hampshire. Many a village in these two states was completely depopulated, its houses and barns left to rot, as its people scattered over the country in search of a better life than the granite hills afforded.

Not all the migrating villagers and farmers sought the unsettled frontier: some moved instead to increasingly crowded population centers. Cities (defined as communities of 8,000 or more) grew faster than the nation as a whole. In 1820 there were more than twice as many cities, and in 1840 more than seven times as many, as there had been in 1790. While the vast majority of Americans continued to reside in the open country or in small towns, the number of city dwellers increased remarkably. In 1790, one person in thirty lived in a community of 8,000 or more; in 1820, one in twenty; and in 1840, one in twelve.

The rise of New York City was phenomenal. By 1810 it had surpassed Philadelphia, which earlier had replaced Boston as the largest city in America. New York steadily increased its lead in both population and trade. Its growth was based on the possession of a superior natural harbor and on several historical developments after the War of 1812. After the war, the British chose New York as the chief place to "dump" their manufactured goods and thus helped make it

New York Port, 1828
A view of South Street, from the intersection with Maiden Lane, which got its name from the fact that Dutch washermaidens in New Amsterdam used to come here to do their laundry in a brook outside of town. The East River docks lined South Street; there were other docks along the Hudson River on the opposite side of Manhattan Island. Below Maiden Lane, the city by 1828 was almost solidly built up. Above the lane, there were gardens around the houses, and there were vacant lots which in some cases ran out into open fields. In summer, boys swam nude in the East River. The population of the city was approaching 150,000. From a contemporary print. (Courtesy of the New York Public Library, Stokes Collection)

an import center. State laws, which were liberal with regard to auction sales, encouraged inland merchants to do their buying in New York. The first packet line, with regularly scheduled monthly sailings between England and the United States, made New York its American terminus (1816) and hence a more important center of overseas commerce than ever. And the Erie Canal (completed in 1825) gave the city unrivaled access to the interior.

The Canal Age

The so-called turnpike era, which lasted from 1790 to about 1830, saw the construction of an important network of roads that did much to link the nation together and to open access to new markets and sources of materials. Roads alone, however, were not sufficient to provide the system of transportation necessary for a modern, industrial society. And so, in the 1820s and 1830s, Americans began to construct other means of transport as well. As in colonial times, they looked first to water routes.

The larger rivers, especially the Mississippi and the Ohio, became increasingly useful as steamboats grew in number and improved in design. A special kind of steamboat evolved to meet the problems of navigation on the Mississippi and its tributaries. These waters were shallow, with strong and difficult currents, shifting bars of sand and mud, and submerged logs and trees. So the boat needed a flat bottom, paddle wheels rather than screw propellers, and a powerful, high-pressure—and thus dangerously explosive—engine. To accommodate as much cargo and as many passengers as possible, the boat was triple-decked, its superstructure rising high in the air.

River boats carried to New Orleans the corn and other crops of Northwestern farmers and the cotton and tobacco of Southwestern planters. From New Orleans, ships took the cargoes on to Eastern ports. Neither the farmers of the West nor the merchants of the East were completely satisfied with this pattern of trade. Farmers could get better prices for their crops if the alternative existed of sending them directly eastward to market,

and merchants could sell larger quantities of their manufactured goods if they could be transported more directly and more economically to the West.

The highways across the mountains, such as the Philadelphia-Pittsburgh turnpike and the National Road, provided a partial solution to the problem. But the costs of hauling goods overland, though lower than before these roads were built, were too high for anything except the most compact and valuable merchandise. New waterways were needed in addition to highways. It was calculated that four horses could pull a wagon weight of one ton twelve miles a day over an ordinary road and one and a half tons eighteen miles a day over a turnpike. On the other hand, four horses could draw a boatload of a hundred tons twenty-four miles a day on a canal.

Sectional jealousies and constitutional scruples stood in the way of action by the federal government, and necessary expenditures were too great for private enterprise. If extensive canals were to be dug, the job would be up to the various states.

New York was the first to act. It had the natural advantage of a comparatively level route between the Hudson River and Lake Erie, through the only break in the Appalachian chain. Yet the engineering tasks were imposing. The distance was more than 350 miles, several times as long as any of the existing canals in America, and there were ridges to cross and a wilderness of woods and swamps to penetrate. For many years, New Yorkers debated whether the scheme was practical. The canal advocates finally won the debate after De Witt Clinton, a late but ardent convert to the cause, was elected governor. Digging began on July 4, 1817.

This, the Erie Canal, was by far the greatest construction job that Americans ever had undertaken, and it was the work of self-made engineers. One of them made a careful study of English canals, but he and his associates did more than merely copy what he saw abroad. They devised ingenious arrangements of cables, pulleys, and gears for bringing down trees and uprooting stumps. Instead of the usual shovels and wheelbarrows, they used specially designed plows and

The Erie Canal
Canal boats, loaded with migrants on their way to the West, arrive at the landing at Little Falls, New York. Note the tandem team of horses on the towpath. The boats moved so slowly that passengers could lighten their tedium from time to time by getting off and walking alongside. From a contemporary pencil sketch. (Courtesy of the New-York Historical Society, New York City)

scrapers for moving earth. To make water-tight locks they produced cement from native limestone. The canal itself was of simple design: basically a ditch, forty feet wide and four feet deep, with towpaths along the banks for the horses or mules that were to draw the canal boats. (Steamboats were not to be used: the churning of a paddle wheel or propeller would cave in the earthen banks.) Cuts and fills, some of them enormous, enabled the canal to pass through hills and over valleys; stone aqueducts carried it across streams; and eighty-eight locks, of heavy masonry, with great wooden gates, took care of the necessary ascents and descents.

Not only was the Erie Canal an engineering triumph; it quickly proved a finan-cial success as well. It was opened for through traffic in October 1825, with fitting ceremonies. Governor Clinton at the head of a parade of canal boats made the trip from Buffalo to the Hudson and then downriver to New York City, where he emptied a keg of Erie water into the Atlantic to symbolize the wedding of the lake and the ocean. Soon traffic was so heavy that, within about seven years, the tolls brought in enough to repay the whole construction cost. The prosperity of the Erie encouraged the state to enlarge its canal system by building several branches. An important part of the system was the Champlain Canal, begun at about the same time as the Erie and completed in 1822, which connected Lake Champlain with the

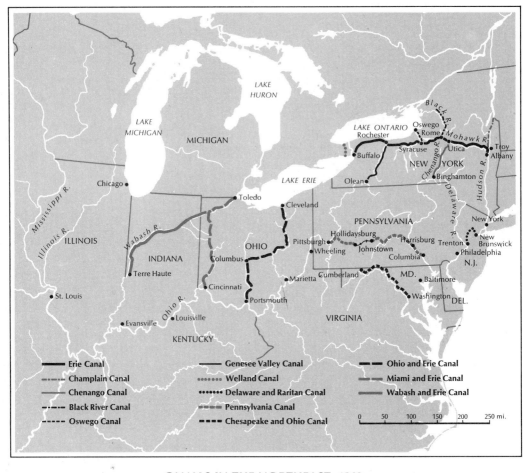

CANALS IN THE NORTHEAST, 1840

Hudson River. Although some of the branches did not pay for themselves, they provided useful water connections between New York City and the larger towns of the state. The main line, giving access to Lake Erie as it did, led beyond the state's borders, to the West.

The range of the New York canal system was still further extended when the states of Ohio and Indiana, inspired by the success of the Erie Canal, provided water connections between Lake Erie and the Ohio River. In 1825, Ohio began the building of two canals, one between Portsmouth and Cleveland and the other between Cincinnati and Toledo, both of which were in use by 1833. In 1832, Indiana started the construction of a canal to connect Evansville with the Cincinnati-To-

ledo route. These canals made it possible to ship or to travel by inland waterways all the way from New York to New Orleans, though several changes among canal, lake, and river craft would be necessary. By way of the Great Lakes, it was possible to go by water from New York to Chicago. After the opening of the Erie Canal, shipping on the Great Lakes by sail and steam rapidly increased.

The consequences of the development of this transportation network were far-reaching. One of the immediate results was the stimulation of the settlement of the Northwest, not only because it had become easier for migrants to make the westward journey but also, and more important, because it had become easier for them, after taking up their farms, to ship their produce to markets.

Towns boomed along the Erie and other canals, New York City benefiting the most of all. Although much of the Western produce, especially corn, continued to go downriver to New Orleans, an increasing proportion of it and most of the wheat of the Northwest went toward New York. And manufactured goods now went in growing volume from New York by the comparatively direct and economical new routes to the West.

Rival cities along the Atlantic seaboard took alarm at the prospect of New York's acquiring so vast a hinterland, largely at their expense. If they were to hold their own, they too must find ways of tapping the Western market. Boston, remote from the West, its way to the Hudson River impeded by the Berkshire Hills, seemed out of the running, at least so far as a canal was concerned. Philadelphia and Baltimore, although they had the still more formidable Allegheny Mountains to contend with, did not give up without an effort at canal building. Beginning in 1834, the commonwealth of Pennsylvania invested in a complicated and costly system of waterways and railways—with an arrangement of "inclined planes," stationary engines, and cable cars to take canal boats over the mountains—intending thus to connect Philadelphia with Pittsburgh. This "Pennsylvania system" proved a failure, financially and otherwise. From Baltimore a canal was projected to ascend the Potomac Valley and tunnel through the mountains, thus achieving essentially the same object as George Washington once had hoped to accomplish. The digging of this grandly conceived Chesapeake and Ohio Canal began in 1828, but it never got farther west than Cumberland, Maryland. In the South, Richmond and Charleston also aspired to reach the Ohio Valley; Richmond, planning at first to join the James and Kanawha rivers, eventually saw a canal built as far as Lynchburg.

For none of these rivals of New York did canals provide a satisfactory way to the West. Some cities, however, saw their opportunity in a different and newer means of transportation. Before the canal age had reached its height, the era of the railroad was already beginning.

The Early Railroads

Through most of the 1820s and 1830s, railroads played a relatively secondary role in the nation's transportation system. But the emergence of these first rail lines was of inestimable importance to the future of the American economy. The tentative beginnings of these early years led, by the time of the Civil War, to a great surge of railroad building, linking the nation together as no previous system of transportation had ever done. The railroads were to become the primary means of transport for the United States and were to remain so until the creation of the interstate highway system in the mid-twentieth century.

It is difficult to identify the precise date of the invention of the railroad. It emerged from a combination of elements, each of which had its own history. One of these elements was the use of rails, wooden or iron, laid on a prepared roadbed to make a fairly straight and level track. Another was the employment of steam-powered locomotives. A third was the operation of trains as public carriers of passengers and freight. For nearly 200 years before the nineteenth century opened, railways with cars pulled by men (and women) or by animals had been used to haul coal from English mines; and in the early 1800s similar railways had appeared in the United States. By 1804, both English and American inventors had experimented with steam engines for propelling land vehicles as well as boats. In 1820, John Stevens ran a locomotive and cars around a circular track on his New Jersey estate. Finally, in 1825, the Stockton and Darlington Railroad in England began to operate with steam power over a short length of track and to carry general traffic.

This news quickly aroused the interest of American businessmen, especially in those seaboard cities that sought better communications with the West. First to organize a railroad company was a group of New Yorkers, who in 1826 obtained a charter for the Mohawk and Hudson and five years later began running the trains the sixteen miles between Schenectady and Albany. First to begin actual operations was the Baltimore and Ohio; the only living signer of the Declaration of Independence, Charles Carroll of Carrollton, dug a spadeful of earth in the ceremonies to start the work on July 4, 1828; and a thirteen-mile stretch opened for business in 1830. Not only the seaboard but also the Mississippi Valley became the scene of railroad building. By 1836, a total of more than 1,000 miles of track had been laid in eleven states.

There did not yet exist what could properly be called a railroad system. Even the longest of the lines was comparatively short in the 1830s, and most of them served to connect water routes and otherwise to supplement water transportation. Even when two lines did connect with one another, the tracks of different companies might differ in gauge (width), so that the cars from one line often could not fit onto the tracks of another. Schedules were erratic, and since roadbeds and bridges were often of shoddy construction, wrecks were frequent.

In response to these deficiencies, railroad pioneers produced a series of important technological developments in the 1830s. Roadbeds were improved through the introduction of heavier iron rails attached to wooden ties resting on crushed rock—a system that enabled tracks to withstand the shock of use far better than the earlier methods. American manufacturers began to produce steam locomotives more flexible and powerful than the engines of the past, which had usually been imported from Europe. Passenger cars, originally mere stagecoaches, were redesigned after 1840 as elongated boxes with two rows of reversible seats and a center aisle—thus making room for more passengers.

From the outset, railroads and canals were bitter competitors. For a time, the Chesapeake and Ohio Canal Company blocked the advance of the Baltimore and Ohio Railroad through the narrow gorge of the upper Potomac, and the state of New York prohibited railroads from hauling freight in competition with the Erie Canal and its branches. But railroads had the advantages of speed and year-round operation (canals closed down for the winter freeze) and could be located almost anywhere, regardless of terrain and the availability of water. Where free competition existed, railroads took most of the passenger traffic and the light freight.

The future, in fact, belonged to the towns and cities along the path of the "iron horse," not to those that continued to depend exclusively on waterways.

Traveling by Railroad [1835]

In her widely read work, Society in America *(1836), the scholarly Englishwoman Harriet Martineau recalled railroad trips she had taken in South Carolina and Pennsylvania:*

My journeys on the Charleston and Augusta railroad were by far the most fatiguing of any I underwent in the country. The motion and the noise are distracting. Whether this is owing to its being on piles in many places, whether the fault is in the ground or the construction, I do not know. Almost all the railroad traveling in America is very fatiguing and noisy. . . .

One great inconvenience of the American railroads is that, from wood being used for fuel, there is an incessant shower of large sparks, destructive to dress and comfort, unless all the windows are shut, which is impossible in warm weather. Some serious accidents from fire have happened in this way; and during my last trip on the Columbia and Philadelphia railroad, a lady in the car had a shawl burned to destruction on her shoulders; and I found that my own gown had thirteen holes in it; and my veil, with which I saved my eyes, more than could be counted.

The Expansion of Business

The rapid expansion of business activity in the 1820s and 1830s was in part a result of the growth in population and improvements in the means of transportation. It was also, however, the result of daring and imagination on the part of new generations of businessmen and their employees. Two industries, one old and one new, illustrate the capacities of Yankee enterprise. One was the whaling industry, which was reaching its heyday in the 1830s. From New Bedford and other New England ports, bold skippers and their crews, having driven most of the whales from the Atlantic, voyaged far into the Pacific in their hazardous tracking of the source of spermaceti for candles, whale oil for lamps, and whalebone for corset stays and other uses. Another example of Yankee enterprise was the ice industry. For years, Northeastern farmers had harvested winter ice from ponds and stored it for the summer; but the large-scale transportation and sale of ice as a commodity began in the 1830s. The New England ice harvest then found a ready market in Northern cities, on Southern plantations, and around the world in India, where it was carried in fast-sailing ships; a voyage was considered highly successful if no more than half the cargo melted on the way.

The distribution of goods, whether of foreign or of domestic origin, although somewhat haphazard by later standards, was becoming more systematic. Stores specializing in groceries, dry goods, hardware, and other lines appeared in the larger cities, but smaller towns and villages depended on the general store. The storekeeper did much of his business by barter, taking country eggs and other produce in exchange for such things as pins and needles, sugar and coffee. Many customers, living remote from any store, welcomed the occasional visits of the peddler, who came afoot or by horse.

The organization of business was undergoing a gradual change. Most business continued to be operated by individuals or partnerships operating on a limited scale. The dominating figure was the great merchant capitalist, who owned and directed much of the big business of the time. He owned his own ships, and he organized certain industries—for example, that of shoe manufacturing—on the putting-out system, according to which he provided the materials, directed the work, and sold the finished product. In the larger enterprises, however, the individual merchant capitalist was giving way before the advance of the corporation. Corporations had the advantage of combining the resources of a large number of shareholders, but their development was long held back by handicapping laws. A corporation had to have a charter, granted by a special act of the state legislature. By the 1830s, the states were beginning to pass general corporation laws according to which a group could secure a charter merely by paying a fee. Moreover, the laws began to grant the privilege of limited liability, which meant that the individual stockholder was liable only to the extent of losing the value of his stock if the corporation should fail.

Corporations made possible the accumulation of larger and larger amounts of capital for manufacturing enterprises as well as for banks, turnpikes, and railroad companies. Some of this capital came from the profits of wealthy merchants who turned from shipping to newer ventures, some from the savings of men of only moderate means, and some from tax collections, since state governments often bought shares in turnpike, canal, and railroad companies. A considerable part was supplied by foreign, especially English, investors. But these sources provided too little capital to meet the demands of the ambitious schemes of some promoters. Hence the banks, instead of confining their long-term lending to the limit of their deposits, often were induced to issue excessive amounts of bank notes as a means of providing capital for expanding business ventures. As a result of this practice, bank failures were not uncommon and bank deposits often insecure.

The Rise of the Factory

All of these changes—increasing population, improved transportation, and the expansion of business activity—contributed to perhaps the most profound economic development in mid-nineteenth-century America: the rise of factory manufacturing. Although it was in the 1840s that industry experienced its most spectacular surge of growth in the antebellum period, it was in the 1820s and 1830s that the factory system established itself as an integral part of the national economy.

Before the War of 1812, most of what manufacturing there was in the United States took place within households or in small, individually operated workshops. Most goods were produced by hand; most were sold in local markets. Gradually, however, improved technology and increased opportunities for commerce stimulated a fundamental change. It came first in the New England textile industry. There, even before the war and the Embargo, some farsighted entrepreneurs were beginning to make use of the region's extensive waterpower and of the new machines (some imported from England, some developed at home) to bring textile operations together under a single roof. This factory system, as it was to be called, spread rapidly in the 1820s, gradually reducing—although not yet entirely eliminating—the practice of spinning and weaving in the home. In the shoe industry as well, mass production through the specialization of tasks was by the 1830s beginning to dominate the industry. Although most of the work on shoes continued to be done by hand, manufacturing was increasingly divided among men and women who, in a careful division of labor, specialized in one or another of the various tasks involved in production and worked not in their homes but in factories. Private cobblers continued to produce shoes for individual customers; but the future of the industry was more clearly suggested by the production of large numbers of identical shoes in ungraded sizes and without distinction as to rights and lefts. As with textiles, the new shoe factories emerged first in eastern Massachusetts. By the 1830s, factory production was spreading from textiles and shoes into other industries as well; and manufacturing was moving beyond Massachusetts and New England to become an important force throughout the American Northeast.

From the beginning, American industry relied heavily on technology for its growth. Because labor was, at least in comparison to other industrializing countries, relatively scarce, there was great incentive for entrepreneurs to improve the efficiency of their productive enterprises by introducing new labor-saving devices. In no country in the world did machine technology advance as rapidly as in the United States in the mid-nineteenth century. Change was so rapid, in fact, that some manufacturers built their new machinery out of wood; by the time the wood wore out, they reasoned, improved technology would have made the machine obsolete. By the end of the 1830s, so advanced had American technology—particularly in textile manufacturing—become that industrialists in Britain and Europe were beginning to travel to the United States to learn new techniques, instead of the other way around.

Yet however advanced their technology, manufacturers still needed a supply of labor. In later years, much of that supply would come from great waves of immigration from abroad. In the 1820s and 1830s, however, labor had to come primarily from the native population. Recruitment was not an easy task. Ninety percent of the American people still lived and worked on farms early in the nineteenth century. City residents were relatively few, and the potential workers among them even fewer. Many urban laborers were skilled artisans who owned and managed their own shops—small businessmen, not employees. The available unskilled workers were not numerous enough to form a reservoir of manpower from which the new industries could draw.

What did produce the beginnings of an industrial labor supply was the transformation of American agriculture in the nineteenth century. The opening of vast, fertile new farmlands in the Midwest; the improvement of transportation systems; the development of new farm machinery: all combined to increase food production dramatically. No longer did each region have to feed itself entirely from its own farms; it could import food from other regions. Thus in the Northeast, and especially in New England, where poor land had always placed harsh limits on farm productivity, the agricultural economy began slowly to decline, freeing up rural people to work in the factories.

Two systems of recruitment emerged to bring this new labor supply to the expanding textile mills. One, common in the mid-Atlantic states and in parts of New England, brought whole families from the farm to the mill. Parents and children, even some who were no more than four or five years old, worked together tending the looms. The second system, common in Massachusetts, enlisted young women—mostly the daughters of farmers—in their late teens and early twenties. It was known as the Lowell or Waltham system, after the factory towns in which it first emerged. Most of these women worked for several years in the factories, saved their wages, and ultimately returned home to marry and raise children. They did not form a permanent working class.

Labor conditions in these early years of the factory system were significantly better than those in English industry, better too than they would ultimately become in the United States. The employment of young children entailed undeniable hardships. But the evils were fewer than in Europe; for working children in American factories remained under the supervision of their parents. In England, by contrast, asylum authorities often hired out orphans to factory employers who showed little solicitude for their welfare.

Even more distinctive from the European labor system was the lot of working women in the mills in Lowell and factory towns like it. In England, as a parliamentary investigation revealed, woman workers were employed in coal mines in unimaginably wretched conditions. Some of these workers had to crawl on their hands and knees, naked and filthy, through cramped, narrow tunnels, pulling heavy coal carts behind them. It was

Girls in Cotton Mills

In cotton mills, such as this one in Lowell, Massachusetts, about 1850, most of the employees were farm girls from the surrounding countryside who worked for a few years as factory hands and then returned to their homes to marry and settle down. Of Lowell, it was said: "Visitors will be agreeably surprised by the neat and respectable appearance of the operatives of this industrious city; and equally so with their moral condition." (Prints Division, The New York Public Library, Astor, Lenox and Tilden Foundations)

little wonder, then, that English visitors to America considered the Lowell mills a female paradise by contrast. The Lowell workers lived in clean boardinghouses and dormitories maintained for them by the factory owners. They were well fed and carefully supervised. Because many New Englanders considered the employment of women to be vaguely immoral, the factory owners placed great emphasis on maintaining an upright environment for their employees, enforcing strict curfews and requiring regular church attendance. Factory girls suspected of immoral conduct were quickly dismissed. Wages for the Lowell workers, modest as they were, were nevertheless generous by the standards of the time. The women even found time to write and publish a monthly magazine, the *Lowell Offering.*

Yet even these relatively privileged workers often found the transition from farm life to factory work difficult, even traumatic. Uprooted from everything familiar, forced to live among strangers in a regimented environment, many women suffered greatly from loneliness and disorientation. Still more had difficulty adjusting to the nature of factory work—to the repetition of fixed tasks hour after hour, day after day. That the women had to labor from sunrise to sunset was not in itself always a burden; many of them had worked similarly long days on the farm. But that they now had to spend those days performing tedious, unvarying chores, and that their schedules did not change from week to week or season to season, made the adjustment to factory work a painful one.

For other workers, conditions were far worse. Construction gangs performed the heavy, unskilled work on turnpikes, canals, and railroads under often intolerable conditions. A growing number of such men were Irish immigrants; and in part because they had no marketable skills, in part because of native prejudice against the Irish, they received wages so low—and received them so intermittently, since the work was seasonal and uncertain—that they generally did not earn enough to support their families in even minimal comfort. Many of them lived in flimsy, unhealthful shanties. By the 1840s,

Irish men and women began to find employment as well in the expanding textile mills, gradually displacing the native farm girls who had worked there originally. The result was a rapid breakdown of the paternalistic factory system. There was far less social pressure on owners to provide a decent environment for Irish workers than for native women. As a result, working conditions soon deteriorated. Employers paid piece rates rather than a daily wage and employed other devices to speed up production and exploit the labor force more efficiently. By the mid-1840s, the town of Lowell—once a model for foreign visitors of enlightened industrial development—had become a squalid slum. Similarly miserable working-class neighborhoods were emerging in other Northeastern cities.

It was not only the unskilled workers who suffered from the transition to the modern factory system. It was the skilled artisans whose trades the factories were displacing. Threatened with obsolescence, faced with increasing competition from industrial capitalists, craftsmen began early in the nineteenth century to form organizations—the first American labor unions—to protect their endangered position. As early as the 1790s, printers and cordwainers took the lead. The cordwainers—makers of high-quality boots and shoes—suffered from the competition of merchant capitalists. These artisans sensed a loss of security and status with the development of mass-production methods, and so did members of other skilled trades: carpenters, joiners, masons, plasterers, hatters, and shipbuilders. In such cities as Philadelphia, Baltimore, Boston, and New York, the skilled workers of each craft formed societies for mutual aid. During the 1820s and 1830s, the craft societies began to combine on a city-wide basis and set up central organizations known as trade unions. Since, with the widening of the market, workers of one city competed with those at a distance, the next step was to federate the trade unions or to establish craft unions of national scope. In 1834, delegates from six cities founded the National Trades' Union; and in 1836, the printers and the cordwainers set up their own national craft unions.

This labor movement soon collapsed. Labor leaders struggled against the handicap of hostile laws and hostile courts. By the common law, as interpreted by judges in the industrial states, a combination among workers was viewed as, in itself, an illegal conspiracy. But adverse court decisions did not halt, although they handicapped, the rising unions. The death blow came from the Panic of 1837 and the ensuing depression.

SECTIONALISM AND NATIONALISM

For a brief but alarming moment, the increasing differences between the nation's two leading sections threatened in 1819 and 1820 to damage the unity of the United States. But once a sectional crisis was averted with the Missouri Compromise, the forces of nationalism continued to assert themselves; and the federal government began to assume the role of promoter of economic growth.

The Missouri Compromise

When Missouri applied for admission as a state in 1819, slavery was already well established there. The French and Spanish inhabitants of the Louisiana Territory (including what became Missouri) had owned slaves, and in the Louisiana Purchase treaty of 1803 the American government promised to maintain and protect the inhabitants in the free enjoyment of their property as well as their liberty and religion. By 1819, approximately 60,000 people resided in Missouri Territory, of whom about 10,000 were slaves. In that year, while Missouri's application for statehood was being considered in Congress, Representative James Tallmadge, Jr., of New York, moved to amend the enabling bill so as to prohibit the further introduction of slaves into Missouri and to provide for the gradual emancipation of those already there. This Tallmadge Amendment provoked a controversy that was to rage for the next two years.

Although the issue arose suddenly, the sectional jealousies that produced it had long been accumulating. Already the concept of a balance of power between the Northern and Southern states was well developed. From the beginning, partly by chance and partly by design, new states had come into the Union more or less in pairs, one from the North, another from the South. With the admission of Alabama in 1819, the Union contained an equal number of free and slave states, eleven of each. If Missouri should be admitted as a slave state, not only would the existing sectional balance be upset but a precedent would be established that, in the future, would still further increase the political power of the South.

In the North, the most active opponents of slavery were well-to-do philanthropists and reformers who generally supported the Federalist party. They opposed the extension of slavery on both humanitarian and political grounds. On the eve of the dispute over Missouri, the Manumission Society of New York was busy with attempts to rescue runaway slaves, and the Quakers were conducting a campaign to strengthen the laws against the African slave trade and to protect free blacks from kidnappers who sold them into slavery. (In the South, there were still a large number of critics of slavery and its abuses; but here the humanitarian impulse was not reinforced by political interest as it was in the North.)

Once the Missouri controversy had arisen, it provided the opportunity, which Federalist leaders such as Rufus King had awaited, to attempt a revival and reinvigoration of their party. By appealing to the Northern people on the issue of slavery extension, the Federalists could hope to win many of the Northern Republicans away from their allegiance to the Republican party's Southern leadership. In New York, the De Witt Clinton faction of the Republicans, who had joined with the Federalists in opposition to the War of 1812 and were outspoken in their hostility to "Virginia influence" and "Southern rule," were more than willing to cooperate with the Federalists again. The cry against slavery in Missouri,

Thomas Jefferson wrote, was "a mere party trick." He explained: "King is ready to risk the union for any chance of restoring his party to power and wriggling himself to the head of it, nor is Clinton without his hopes nor scrupulous as to the means of fulfilling them."

The Missouri question soon was complicated by the application of Maine for admission as a state. Massachusetts had earlier consented to the separation of this northern part of the commonwealth, but only on the condition that Maine be granted statehood before March 4, 1820. The Speaker of the House, Henry Clay, informed Northerners that if they refused to consent to Missouri's becoming a slave state, Southerners would deny the application of Maine. In the House, the Northern majority nevertheless insisted on the principle of the Tallmadge Amendment; but in the Senate, a few of the Northerners sided with the Southerners and prevented its passage.

A way out of the impasse opened when the Senate combined the Maine and Missouri bills, without prohibiting slavery in Missouri. Then, to make the package more acceptable to the House, Senator Jesse B. Thomas of Illinois proposed an amendment prohibiting slavery in all the rest of the Louisiana Purchase territory north of the southern boundary of Missouri (latitude 36°30'). The Senate adopted the Thomas Amendment, and Speaker Clay guided the amended Maine-Missouri bill through the House. A group of Northern Republicans, some of them suspecting the political designs of the Federalists, voted with the Southerners to make the compromise possible.

The first Missouri Compromise (1820) did not end the dispute; a second compromise was necessary. In 1820, Maine was actually admitted as a state, but Missouri was authorized only to form a constitution and a government. When the Missouri constitution was completed, it contained a clause forbidding free blacks or mulattoes to enter the state. Several of the existing states already had similar laws. But other states, among them New York, recognized nonwhites as citizens. According to the federal Constitution, "The citizens of each State shall be en-titled to all privileges and immunities of citizens in the several States." This meant that a citizen of a state such as New York, white or black, was entitled to all the privileges of a citizen of Missouri, including of course the privilege of traveling or residing in the state. The antiblack clause was clearly unconstitutional, and a majority in the House of Representatives threatened to exclude Missouri until the clause was eliminated. Finally, Clay offered a resolution that the clause should never be construed in such a way as to deny to any citizen the privileges and immunities to which he was entitled under the Constitution. The resolution was meaningless; but Clay secured its passage and enhanced his reputation as the "Great Pacificator," a reputation he was again and again to confirm during his long career. Clay's resolution made possible the admission of Missouri as a state in 1821.

Although the Missouri controversy did not unite the North, as some of the Federalists hoped it would, it made at least a beginning toward the creation of a solid South. At that time the most disaffected of the Southern states was Virginia, not, as later, South Carolina. The Carolinian Calhoun hailed the compromise as a means of preserving the Union. The Virginian Jefferson looked to the fateful day when the South might have to defend itself in a civil war.

In this perspective the subject of education, always one of Jefferson's chief concerns, became even more crucial. He was afraid that Southern youths attending Northern colleges might be indoctrinated with "lessons of anti-Missourianism." Already the University of Virginia, the favorite project of his old age, was under construction. He hoped that this university, devoting itself to sound Southern doctrines, would attract from Virginia and other Southern states a large number of students who otherwise would have pursued their studies in the North.

Marshall and the Court

John Marshall remained as chief justice for almost thirty-five years, from 1801 to 1835. During these years Republican presidents

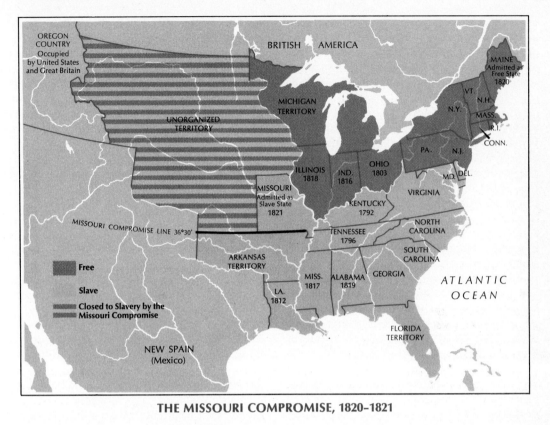

THE MISSOURI COMPROMISE, 1820–1821

filled vacancies with Republican justices, one after another, and yet Marshall continued to carry a majority with him in most of the Court's decisions. He was a man of practical and penetrating mind, of persuasive and winning personality, and of strong will. The members of the Court boarded together, without their families, during the winter months when the Court was in session, and Marshall had abundant opportunity to bring his talents to bear upon his younger associates. He not only influenced their ways of thinking; he also molded the development of the Constitution itself. The net effect of the hundreds of opinions delivered by the Marshall Court was to strengthen the judicial branch at the expense of the other two branches of the government; increase the power of the United States and lessen that of the states themselves; and advance the interests of the propertied classes, especially those engaged in commerce.

No state, the Constitution says, shall pass any law "impairing the obligation of contracts." The first Supreme Court case involving this provision was that of *Fletcher v. Peck* (1810), which arose out of the notorious Yazoo Land frauds. The Court had to decide whether the Georgia legislature of 1796 could rightfully repeal the act of the previous legislature granting lands under shady circumstances to the Yazoo Land Companies. In the unanimous decision, Marshall held that a land grant was a contract and therefore, regardless of any corruption involved, the repeal was invalid. This was the first time the Supreme Court had voided a state law on the ground that it conflicted with a provision of the United States Constitution, though the Court previously had declared state laws unconstitutional because they were inconsistent with federal laws or treaties.

Dartmouth College v. *Woodward* (1819) expanded further the meaning of the contract clause. The case had originated in a quarrel between the trustees and the president of the college, and it became a major political issue in New Hampshire when the Republicans championed the president and the Federalists took the side of the trustees. Having gained control of the state government, the Republicans undertook to revise Dartmouth's charter (granted by King George III in 1769) so as to convert the private college into a state university. Daniel Webster, a Dartmouth graduate, represented the trustees in opposing the charter revision when the case came before the Supreme Court in Washington. The Court, he reminded the judges, had decided in *Fletcher* v. *Peck* that "a *grant* is a contract." The Dartmouth charter, he went on, "is embraced within the very terms of that decision," since "a grant of corporate powers and privileges is as much a *contract* as a grant of land." Then, according to a later story, he brought tears to the eyes of the justices with an irrelevant peroration concluding: "It is, sir, as I have said, a small college. And yet there are those who love it." A year later, the Court gave its decision in favor of Webster and the trustees. The ruling had a significant bearing on the development of business corporations. It proclaimed that corporation charters were contracts, and contracts were inviolable; thereafter the states had to contend against this doctrine in their efforts to control corporate activity.

Did the Supreme Court rightfully have the power to hear appeals from the state courts, as in the *Dartmouth College* case? The Judiciary Act of 1789 provided that whenever the highest state court decided against a person claiming rights under the federal Constitution, laws, or treaties, the judgment could be reviewed and possibly reversed by the Supreme Court. But Virginia states'-rightists denied the constitutionality of the Judiciary Act. They insisted that the federal government, of which the Supreme Court was a branch, could not be the final judge of its own powers. In the case of *Cohens* v. *Virginia* (1821) Marshall gave the Court's reply to the dissident Virginians. A Virginia court had convicted the Cohens of selling lottery tickets in violation of a state law, and the Cohens had appealed their case under the disputed provision of the Judiciary Act. Although Marshall decided against the Cohens, he did

not satisfy the state of Virginia. He affirmed the constitutionality of the Judiciary Act, explaining that the states no longer were sovereign in all respects, since they had given up part of their sovereignty in ratifying the Constitution. The state courts, he insisted, must submit to federal jurisdiction; otherwise the government would be prostrated "at the feet of every state in the Union."

Meanwhile, in *McCulloch* v. *Maryland* (1819), Marshall had confirmed the "implied powers" of Congress by upholding the constitutionality of the Bank of the United States. The Bank, with headquarters in Philadelphia and branches in various cities throughout the country, became so unpopular in the South and the West that several of the states tried to drive the branches out of business by outright prohibition or by prohibitory taxes. Maryland, for one, laid a heavy tax on the Baltimore branch of the Bank. This case presented two constitutional questions to the Supreme Court: Could Congress charter a bank, and if so, could one of the states thus tax it? As one of the Bank's attorneys, Webster first repeated the arguments used originally by Hamilton to prove that the establishment of such an institution came within the "necessary and proper" clause. Then, to dispose of the tax issue, Webster added an ingenious argument of his own. The power to tax, he said, involved a "power to destroy," and if the states could tax the Bank at all, they could tax it to death. Since the Bank with its branches was an agency of the federal government, the power to tax it was the power to destroy the United States itself. Marshall adopted Webster's words in deciding for the Bank.

The case of *Gibbons* v. *Ogden* (1824) brought up the question of the powers of Congress, as against the powers of the states, in regulating interstate commerce. The state of New York had granted Robert Fulton and Robert Livingston's steamboat company the exclusive right to carry passengers on the Hudson River to New York City. From this monopoly, Aaron Ogden obtained the business of navigation across the river between New York and New Jersey. Thomas Gibbons, with a license granted under an act of Congress, went into competition with

McCulloch v. Maryland [1819]

Chief Justice Marshall used the following argument in his decision that a state, such as Maryland, could not constitutionally tax a branch of the United States Bank:

That the power to tax involves the power to destroy; that the power to destroy may defeat and render useless the power to create; that there is a plain repugnance in conferring on one government a power to control the constitutional measures of another, which other, with respect to those very measures, is declared to be supreme over that which exerts the control, are propositions not to be denied. . . .

If the States may tax one instrument, employed by the [federal] government in the execution of its powers, they may tax any and every other instrument. They may tax the mail; they may tax the mint; they may tax patent rights; they may tax the papers of the customhouse; they may tax judicial processes; they may tax all the means employed by the government, to an excess which would defeat all the ends of government. This was not intended by the American people. They did not design to make their government dependent on the States.

Ogden, who brought suit against him and was sustained by the New York courts. When Gibbons appealed to the Supreme Court, the justices faced the twofold question whether "commerce" included navigation and whether Congress alone or Congress and the states together could regulate interstate commerce. Marshall replied that "commerce" was a broad term embracing navigation as well as the buying and selling of goods. Although he did not say that the states had no authority whatever regarding interstate commerce, he asserted that the power of Congress in regard thereto was "complete in itself" and might be "exercised to its utmost extent." He concluded that the state-granted monopoly was void.

The decision, the last of Marshall's great pronouncements, was the first conspicuous one in which the Marshall Court appeared to be on the popular side. Most people, then as always, hated monopolies, and he had declared a monopoly unconstitutional. The lasting significance of *Gibbons* v. *Ogden* was that it freed internal transportation from restraints by the states, and thus prepared the way for the unfettered economic development of the nation. More immediately, it had the effect of helping to head off a movement

that was under way to hamstring the Supreme Court.

For some time, such Virginia Republicans as Thomas Jefferson, Spencer Roane, and John Taylor had protested against the views of their fellow Virginian John Marshall. In *Construction Construed and Constitutions Vindicated* (1820), Taylor argued that Marshall and his colleagues were not merely interpreting but were actually changing the nature of the Constitution, which should properly be changed only by the amending process. In Congress some critics of the Court, mostly from the South and the West, proposed various means of curbing what they called judicial tyranny. A Kentucky senator suggested making the Senate, not the Court, the agency to decide the constitutionality of state laws and to settle interstate disputes. Other senators and congressmen introduced bills to increase the membership of the Court (from seven to ten) and to require more than a mere majority to declare a state law unconstitutional.

Still others argued for "codification," that is, for making legislative statutes the basis of the law, rather than the common law precedents that judges used. Such a reform, codifiers argued, would limit the power of the judiciary and prevent "judge-made" law. The Court reformers did not succeed, however, in passing any of their various panaceas; and after the *Gibbons* v. *Ogden* decision, the hostility to the judicial branch of the government gradually died down.

The Latin American Revolution

Just as the Supreme Court was asserting American nationalism in the shaping of the country's economic life, so the Monroe administration was expressing nationalism in the shaping of foreign policy. As in earlier and later years, the central concern of the United States was its position in relation to Europe. But in defining that position, Americans were forced in the 1820s to develop a policy toward Latin America, which was suddenly winning its independence.

To most citizens of the United States, South and Central America had long seemed to constitute a "dark continent." After the War of 1812, however, they suddenly emerged into the light, and Americans looking southward beheld a gigantic spectacle: the Spanish Empire struggling in its death throes, a whole continent in revolt, new nations in the making with a future no one could foresee.

Already a profitable trade had developed between the ports of the United States and those of the Río de la Plata (Argentina), Chile, and above all Cuba, with flour and other staples being exported in return for sugar and coins. This trade was smaller than that of Great Britain. But the American trade was growing steadily, and during the depression that followed after 1819 it held up better than business in general did. Presumably the trade would increase much faster once the United States had established regular diplomatic and commercial relations with the countries in revolt.

In 1815, the United States proclaimed its neutrality in the wars between Spain and its rebellious colonies. This neutrality was in itself advantageous to the rebels, since it implied a partial recognition of their status as nations. It meant, for example, that their warships would be treated as bona-fide bel-

ligerent vessels, not as pirate ships. Moreover, even though the neutrality law was revised and strengthened in 1817 and 1818, it still permitted the revolutionists to obtain unarmed ships and supplies from the United States. In short, the United States was not a strict and impartial neutral but a nonbelligerent whose policy, though cautious, was intended to help the insurgents and actually did.

Secretary Adams and President Monroe hesitated to take the risky step of recognition unless Great Britain would agree to do so at the same time. In 1818 and 1819, the United States made two bids for British cooperation, and both were rejected. Finally, in 1822, President Monroe informed Congress that five nations—La Plata, Chile, Peru, Colombia, and Mexico—were ready for recognition, and he requested an appropriation to send ministers to them. The United States was going ahead alone as the first country to recognize the new governments, in defiance of the rest of the world.

The Monroe Doctrine

In 1823, President Monroe stood forth as an even bolder champion of America against Europe. Presenting to Congress his annual message on the state of the Union, he announced a policy that afterward—though not for thirty years—was to be known as the "Monroe Doctrine." One part of this policy had to do with the role of Europe in America. "The American continents," Monroe declared, ". . . are henceforth not to be considered as subjects for future colonization by any European powers." Furthermore, "we should consider any attempt on their part to extend their system to any portion of this hemisphere as dangerous to our peace and safety." And the United States would consider any "interposition" against the sovereignty of existing American nations as an unfriendly act. A second aspect of the pronouncement had to do with the role of the United States in Europe. "Our policy in regard to Europe," said Monroe, ". . . is not to interfere in the internal concerns of any of its powers."

How did the president happen to make these statements at the time he did? What specific dangers, if any, did he have in mind? Against what powers in particular was his warning directed? To answer these questions, it may be well to consider first the relations of the United States with the European powers as of 1823, and then the main steps in the decision of the Monroe administration to make an announcement to Congress and the world.

After Napoleon's defeat, the powers of Europe combined in a "concert" to uphold the principle of "legitimacy" in government and to prevent the overthrow of existing regimes from within or without. When Great Britain withdrew from the concert, it became a quadruple alliance, with Russia and France as the strongest of its four members. In 1823, after assisting in the suppression of other revolts in Europe, the European allies authorized France to intervene in Spain to restore the Bourbon dynasty that revolutionists had overthrown. Some observers in England and the Americas wondered whether the allies next would back France in an attempt to retake by force the lost Spanish Empire in America.

Actually, France was still a relatively weak power, not yet recovered from the long and exhausting Napoleonic wars. The French endeavored to bring about the establishment of friendly kingdoms in Latin America by means of intrigue, but it dared not challenge British sea power with an expedition to subvert the new governments by force.

In the minds of most Americans, certainly in the mind of their secretary of state, Great Britain seemed an even more serious threat to American interests. Adams was much concerned about supposed British designs on Cuba. Like Jefferson and others before him, Adams opposed the transfer of Cuba from a weak power such as Spain, its owner, to a strong power such as Great Britain. He thought Cuba eventually should belong to the United States, for the "Pearl of the Antilles" had great economic and strategic value and, because of its location, was virtually a part of the American coastline. Adams did not desire to seize the island; he wanted only to keep it in Spanish hands until, by a kind of political gravitation, it should fall naturally to the United States. Despite his worries over the supposed British threat to Cuba, he and other American leaders were pleased to see the rift between Great Britain and the concert of Europe. He was willing to cooperate with Britain, but only to the extent that its policies and his own coincided.

These policies did not exactly coincide, however, as was shown by the British rejection of the American overtures for joint rec-

The Monroe Doctrine [1823]

... The American continents, by the free and independent condition which they have assumed and maintain, are henceforth not to be considered as subjects for further colonization by any European powers. ...

In the wars of the European powers in matters relating to themselves we have never taken any part, nor does it comport with our policy to do so. ... We should consider any attempt on their part to extend their system to any portion of this hemisphere as dangerous to our peace and safety. With the existing colonies or dependencies of the European powers we have not interfered and shall not interfere. But with the Governments who have declared their independence and maintained it, and whose independence we have, on great consideration and on just principles, acknowledged, we could not view any interposition for the purpose of oppressing them, or controlling in any other manner their destiny, by any European power, in any other light than as the manifestation of an unfriendly disposition toward the United States.

ognition of Latin American independence in 1818 and 1819, and as was shown again by the American reaction to a British proposal for a joint statement in 1823. That summer, the British secretary for foreign affairs, George Canning, suggested to the American minister in London, Richard Rush, that Great Britain and the United States should combine in announcing to the world their opposition to any European movement against Latin America. But Canning's refusal to join the United States in recognizing the Latin American nations forestalled agreement. And in the fall, after receiving assurances from France that it had no plans to intervene militarily in Latin America, the British abandoned the proposal altogether.

Even before Canning changed his mind about cooperation with the United States, Monroe and Adams were developing grave reservations about a joint pronouncement. Adams, in particular, argued that the American government should act alone instead of following along like a "cock-boat in the wake of a British man-of-war." Canning's loss of interest, therefore, only strengthened an already growing inclination within the administration to make its own pronouncement.

Although Canning's overture led to Monroe's announcement, the message was directed against all the powers of Europe, including Great Britain, which seemed at least as likely as Russia to undertake further colonizing ventures in America. The message aimed to rally the people of Latin America to look to their own security. It also aimed to stir the people of the United States. In issuing his challenge to Europe, Monroe had in mind the domestic situation as well as the international scene. At home, the people were bogged down in a business depression, divided by sectional politics, and apathetic toward the rather lackluster administration of Monroe. In the rumors of European aggression against the Western Hemisphere lay a chance for him to arouse and unite the people with an appeal to national pride.

THE REVIVAL OF OPPOSITION

For a time during the "era of good feelings," it seemed that the dream of the founders of the republic—of a nation free of party strife—had been realized. After 1816, the Federalist party offered no presidential candidate. Soon it ceased to exist as a national political force. Presidential politics was now conducted wholly within the Republican party, which considered itself not a party at all but an organization representing the whole of the population.

Yet the policies of the federal government during and after the War of 1812, and particularly the nationalizing policies of the 1820s, continued to spark opposition. At first, criticism remained contained within the existing one-party structure. But by the late 1820s, partisan divisions were emerging once again. In some respects, the division mirrored the schism that had produced the first party system in the 1790s. The Republicans had in many ways come to resemble the early Federalist regimes in their promotion of economic growth and centralization. And the opposition, like the opposition in the 1790s, stood opposed to the federal government's expanding role in the economy. There was, however, a crucial difference. At the beginning of the century, the opponents of centralization had also been opponents of economic growth. Now, in the 1820s, the controversy involved not whether but how the nation should continue to expand.

"Corrupt Bargain!"

From 1796 to 1816, presidential candidates had been nominated by caucuses of the members of each of the two parties in Congress. In 1820, when the Federalists declined to oppose his candidacy, Monroe ran unopposed as the Republican nominee without the necessity of a caucus nomination. If the caucus system were revived and followed in 1824, this would mean that the nominee of the Republicans in Congress would also run unopposed. Several men aspired to the presidency, however, and they and their followers were unwilling to let a small group of congressmen and senators determine which one was to win the prize.

In 1824, therefore, "King Caucus" was overthrown. Fewer than a third of the Republicans in Congress bothered to attend the gathering that went through the motions of nominating a candidate (William H. Crawford of Georgia), and he found the caucus nomination as much a handicap as a help in the campaign. Other candidates received nominations from state legislatures and endorsements from irregular mass meetings throughout the country.

John Quincy Adams, secretary of state for two terms, had made a distinguished record in the conduct of foreign affairs, and he held the office that had become traditionally the stepping stone to the presidency. But as he himself ruefully realized, he was a man of cold and forbidding manners, not a candidate with strong popular appeal. Contending against Adams was the secretary of the treasury, William H. Crawford, an impressive giant of a man who had the backing not only of the congressional caucus, but also of the extreme states'-rights faction of the Republican party. In midcampaign, however, he was stricken by a paralyzing illness.

Challenging the cabinet contenders was Henry Clay, the Speaker of the House. The tall, black-haired, genial Kentuckian had a personality that gained him a devoted following. He also stood for a definite and coherent program, which he called the "American System." His plan, attractive to citizens just recovering from a business depression, was to create a great home market for factory and farm producers by raising the tariff to stimulate industry, maintaining the national bank to facilitate credit and exchange, and spending federal funds on internal improvements to provide transportation between the cities and the farms.

Andrew Jackson offered no such clear-cut program. Although Jackson had served briefly as a representative in Congress and was a member of the United States Senate, he had no legislative record. Nevertheless, he had the inestimable advantages of a military hero's reputation and a campaign shrewdly managed by the Tennessee politician friends who had put him forward as a candidate. To some of his contemporaries he seemed a crude, hot-tempered frontiersman and Indian fighter. Actually, although he had arisen from a humble background as an orphan in the Carolinas, he had become a well-to-do planter who lived in an elegant mansion ("The Hermitage") near Nashville.

Once the returns were counted, there was no doubt that the next vice president was to be John C. Calhoun, of South Carolina, who ran on both the Adams and the Jackson tickets. But there was considerable doubt as to who the next president would be. Jackson received a plurality, although not a majority of the popular vote. In the electoral college too he came out ahead, with 99 votes to Adams's 84, Crawford's 41, and Clay's 37. Again, however, he lacked the necessary majority. So, in accordance with the Twelfth

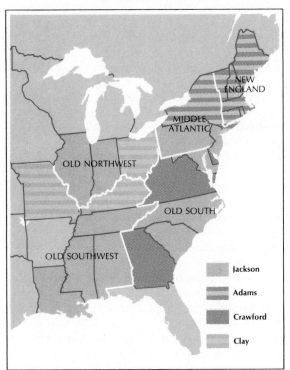

THE ELECTION OF 1824

Jackson

Adams

Crawford

Clay

Amendment, the final decision was left to the House of Representatives, which was to choose among the three candidates with the highest electoral vote. Clay, for all his charm, was out of the running.

If Clay, in 1825, could not be president, he could at least be president maker. As Speaker, he was in a strategic position to influence the decision of the House of Representatives. In deciding among the three leading candidates, the House was to vote by states, the delegation from each state casting one vote. Clay, as the winner of the recent election in Kentucky, Ohio, and Missouri, could swing the congressional delegations of those three states at least.

Before Congress made its decision, the friends of Jackson, Crawford, and Adams approached Clay on behalf of their respective candidates. Jackson's followers insisted that Jackson, with his popular and electoral pluralities, was really the people's choice and that Congress had no rightful alternative but to ratify the people's will. But Jackson was Clay's most dangerous rival for the political affections of the West, and he could not be depended on to champion Clay's legislative program. Crawford was out of the question, for he was now a paralytic, incapable of discharging the duties of the presidency. Only Adams was left. Personally, he was no friend of Clay and had clashed with him repeatedly when both were peace delegates at Ghent and afterward. Politically, however, Adams was similar to Clay in cherishing nationalistic principles such as those of the "American System." Finally Clay gave his support to Adams, and the House elected him.

The Jacksonians were angry enough at this, but they became far angrier when the new president made known his appointments. Clay was to be the secretary of state. The State Department being the well-established route to the presidency, Adams thus appeared to be naming Clay as his own successor. The two must have agreed to make each other president—Adams now, Clay next—or so the Jacksonians claimed; and they pretended to be horrified by this "corrupt bargain." Very likely there had been some sort of understanding; and though

there was nothing improper in it, it proved to be politically unwise for both Adams and Clay.

Soon after Adams's inauguration as president, Jackson resigned from the Senate to accept a renomination for the presidency from the Tennessee legislature and to begin a three-year campaign for election in 1828. Politics now overshadowed all else. Throughout his term in the White House, Adams and his policies were to be thoroughly frustrated by the political bitterness arising from the "corrupt bargain."

The Second President Adams

The career of John Quincy Adams divides naturally into three parts. In the first part, as befitted the son of John Adams, he was a brilliant diplomat, serving as the American minister in one foreign capital after another and then as one of the most successful of all secretaries of state. In the second phase of his career, as president (1825–1829), he endured four ineffectual years that amounted to a mere interlude between the periods of his greatness. In the third, as a congressman from Massachusetts, he served with high distinction, gaining fame as "Old Man Eloquent," the foremost congressional champion of free speech. His frustration in the White House shows that the presidency demands more than exceptional ability and high-mindedness, for John Quincy Adams possessed both. The presidency also requires political skill and political luck, and these he did not have.

In his inaugural address and in his first message to Congress, Adams boldly stated a broad conception of the powers and duties of the federal government. He recommended "laws promoting the improvement of agriculture, commerce, and manufactures, the cultivation of the mechanic and of the elegant arts, the advancement of literature, and the progress of the sciences, ornamental and profound." He had no chance of getting an appropriation from Congress for most of these goals. All he could get was a few million dollars to improve rivers and harbors and to extend the National Road westward

John Quincy Adams
When this photograph was taken, shortly before Adams's death in 1848, he was more than eighty years old and a congressman from Massachusetts. He had left the presidency almost twenty years earlier. During his White House days, as always, he was a hard, conscientious worker. He rose at four in the morning and built a fire before the servants were up. Then he made a long entry in his diary for the previous day. He wrote so much that his right hand sometimes became paralyzed with writer's cramp, so he taught himself to use his left hand also. (Brown Brothers)

from Wheeling. This was more than Congress had appropriated for internal improvements under all his predecessors together, but it was far less than he had hoped for.

Even in the field of diplomacy, where Adams had more experience than any other president before or since, he failed in the major efforts of his administration. Yielding to Secretary of State Clay's wish for cooperation with the Latin American governments, Adams appointed two delegates to attend an international conference that the Venezuelan liberator, Simón Bolívar, had called to meet at Panama in 1826. Objections arose in Congress for two reasons. One was that Southerners hated to think of white Americans mingling in Panama with black delegates from Haiti, a country whose independence the United States refused to recognize. The other reason for obstruction was simply politics—the determination of Jacksonians to discredit the administration. They charged that Adams aimed to sacrifice American interests and involve the nation in an entangling alliance. While the Jacksonians filibustered, Congress delayed the Panama mission so long that it became futile. One of the American delegates died on the way to the conference and the other arrived after it was over. The United States had accomplished nothing to offset British influence, which prevailed in Latin America.

Adams was also worsted in a contest with the state of Georgia. That state attempted to remove the remaining Creek and Cherokee Indians so as to gain additional soil for cotton planters. The Creeks, however, had a treaty with the United States (1791) that guaranteed them possession of the land they occupied. A new treaty (1825) ceded the land to the state, but Adams refused to enforce this treaty, believing that it had been obtained by fraud. The Georgia governor defied the president and went ahead with plans for Indian removal. At last the Creeks agreed to still another treaty (1827), in which they yielded their claims. Adams's stand had been honorable but unpopular.

Southerners again denounced the administration and its supporters because of the tariff of 1828. This measure originated in the demands of Massachusetts and Rhode Island woolen manufacturers, who complained that the British were dumping woolens on the American market at prices with which the domestic mill owners could not compete. Frustrated at first by Southern opposition in Congress, the protectionists of New England combined with those of the middle and Western states to create political pressures that could not be resisted.

The bill of 1828 that resulted from these efforts contained high duties not only on woolens but also on a number of other items, such as flax, hemp, iron, lead, molasses, and raw wool. Thus it distressed New England manufacturers, for it would raise the cost of their raw materials as well as the price of their manufactured goods. A story arose that the bill had taken its shape from a Jacksonian plot to embarrass New Englanders and discredit Adams. The bill related to "manufactures of no sort or kind but the manufacture of a president of the United States," John Randolph said. Supposedly it was intended to put Adams in a dilemma that would lose him friends whether he signed or vetoed it. While some politicians did see the measure as an electioneering device, others intended it seriously as a means of benefiting the farmers and manufacturers of the middle states and the West.

When Congress considered the bill item by item, Southerners voted against reductions in the hope that some of its outrageous duties would so antagonize New Englanders that they would help defeat it. But when it came to a final test, Daniel Webster voted for it despite its duties on raw materials, and he carried with him enough New England votes to enable it to pass. Adams signed it. The Southerners, whose tactics had backfired, cursed it as the "tariff of abominations."

THE ELECTION OF 1828

Jackson Triumphant

By 1828, the schism within the Republican party was complete. Once again, as in 1800, two parties offered candidates in the presidential election. On one side stood the supporters of John Quincy Adams, who called themselves the National Republicans. They supported the economic nationalism of the preceding years. Opposing them were the followers of Andrew Jackson, who took the name Democratic Republicans. They argued for a dispersal of public authority, an assault on privilege, and a widening of opportunity. Adams attracted the support of most of the remaining Federalists (among whose number he had once counted himself); Jackson appealed to a broad coalition that stood opposed to the economic "aristocracy."

Issues figured little in the campaign of 1828, though much was said about the "cor-

rupt bargain" and something was said about the West Indian trade and the "tariff of abominations." Regarding the tariff, Adams was on record, having signed the abominations bill, but nobody knew where Jackson stood. Again, as in 1824, more was made of personalities than of policies. Indeed, the tone of the campaign was such as to suggest that two criminals were running for the highest office in the land.

As for Adams, the Jacksonians charged that as president he had been guilty of gross waste and extravagance, using public funds to buy gambling devices (a chess set and a billiard table) for the White House. But that was not the worst of Adams's alleged crimes. Once, as minister to Russia, he had, the Jacksonians falsely claimed, tried to procure a beautiful American girl for the sinful pleasures of the czar.

As for Jackson, the Adamsites had accusations even worse. He was a murderer and an adulterer, according to the speeches, handbills, and pamphlets of his foes. A "coffin handbill" listed within coffin-shaped outlines the names of militiamen whom Jackson was said to have shot in cold blood during the War of 1812. (The men had been deserters who were executed after due sentence by a court-martial.) It was also rumored that Jackson knowingly had lived in sin with the wife of another man. Actually, he had married the woman, his beloved Rachel, at a time when the pair apparently believed her first husband had divorced her.

Jackson's victory was decisive, if sectional. He won 56 percent of the popular vote and an electoral majority of 178 votes to Adams's 83. But the Jacksonians made few inroads into the National Republican strongholds of the Northeast. Adams swept virtually all of New England, and he showed significant strength in the mid-Atlantic region. Nevertheless, the Jacksonians considered their victory complete, and they hailed it as an event as important as the victory of Jefferson in 1800. Once again, the forces of privilege had been ejected from Washington. Once again, a champion of democracy would occupy the White House and restore liberty to the society and the economy. America had entered, many claimed, the "era of the common man." And Andrew Jackson, the people's champion, departed for Washington determined to transform the federal government.

SUGGESTED READINGS

Many of the books cited in the readings for Chapter 7 as sources for American economic and technological growth are useful as well for the period described in this chapter. In addition, see W. Elliot Brownlee, *Dynamics of Ascent* (1974), and Stuart Bruchey, *The Growth of the Modern American Economy* (1975), which are useful overviews. George R. Taylor, *The Transportation Revolution* (1951), is a valuable source for the construction of roads, canals, and railroads; while Nathan Miller, *The Enterprise of a Free People* (1962), examines New York during the Canal Age, as does R. E. Shaw, *Erie Water West* (1966). Harry N. Scheiber, *Ohio Canal Era* (1969), examines the government's role in transportation and in the economy in general in the mid-nineteenth century. Albert Fishlow, *American Railroads and the Transformation of the Ante-Bellum Economy* (1965), examines early railroad building. E. P. Douglas, *The Coming of Age of American Business* (1971), examines early entrepreneurs, as does Thomas C. Cochran and William Miller, *The Age of Enterprise* (1942). Thomas C. Cochran, *Business in American Life* (1972), is an overview of the subject; and Richard D. Brown, *Modernization: The Transformation of American Life, 1600–1865* (1976), examines business development in a much larger context. Diane Lindstrom, *Economic Development in the Philadelphia Region, 1810–1850* (1978), is a useful study of that growth in a particular area.

The early factory system is examined in Arthur H. Cole, *The American Wool Manufacture*, 2 vols. (1926), a classic study; and in Caroline Ware, *The Early New England Cotton Manufacture* (1931). H. J. Habbakuk, *American and British Technology in the Nine-teenth Century* (1962), discusses some of the technological developments that made the growth of the factory system possible. Thomas Dublin, *Women at Work (1979)*, is an important study of industrialization and labor in Lowell. Alan Dawley, *Class and Community* (1977), examines the shoe industry and its workers in Lynn, Massachusetts.

Two good overviews of the political life of the era following the War of 1812 are by George Dangerfield: *The Awakening of American Nationalism* (1965) and *The Era of Good Feelings* (1952). Glover Moore, *The Missouri Compromise* (1953), is a basic work on the sectional crisis of 1819–1820. Paul C. Nagle, *One Nation Indivisible: The Union in American Thought, 1815–1828* (1965), discusses the intellectual background of postwar nationalism. Biographies of leading nationalists of the era also shed light on the phenomenon. See particularly Glyndon Van Deusen, *The Life of Henry Clay* (1937), a study of the architect of the Missouri Compromise; Harry Ammon, *James Monroe: The Quest for National Identity* (1971); and Charles M. Wiltse, *John C. Calhoun: American Nationalist* (1944). Wesley Frank Craven, *The Legend of the Founding Fathers* (1956), discusses the influence of the past on nationalism in the nineteenth century. Shaw Livermore, *The Twilight of Federalism* (1962), is a valuable study of the decline of the Federalists after the War of 1812.

Albert J. Beveridge, *The Life of John Marshall*, 4 vols. (1916–1919), is the classic study of the Supreme Court in the early national period. Leonard Baker, *John Marshall: A Life in Law* (1974), is a more recent study. Richard E. Ellis, *The Jeffersonian Crisis: Courts*

and Politics in the Young Republic (1971), R. Kent New-
myer, *The Supreme Court Under Marshall and Taney*
(1968), Charles G. Haines, *The Role of the Supreme
Court in American Government and Politics, 1789–1835*
(1970), and D. O. Dewey, *Marshall Versus Jefferson:
The Political Background of* Marbury *v.* Madison (1970),
are likewise useful. Alexander M. Bickel, *Justice Joseph Story and the Rise of the Supreme Court* (1971), and
James McClellan, *Joseph Story and the American Constitution* (1971), examine one of the most influential of
Marshall's judicial contemporaries.

Arthur P. Whitaker, *The United States and the Independence of Latin America* (1941), examines the background of the Monroe Doctrine. The standard study
of the shaping of the doctrine itself is Dexter Perkins,
The Monroe Doctrine (1927); a later study by Perkins,
Hands Off: A History of the Monroe Doctrine (1941),
summarizes his earlier, larger work. Ernest R. May,
The Making of the Monroe Doctrine (1975), is a provocative reexamination of the subject. Samuel F. Bemis,
*John Quincy Adams and the Foundations of American For-
eign Policy* (1949), is a biography of the architect of the
Monroe Doctrine. See also Bradford Perkins, *Castlereagh and Adams: England and the United States,
1812–1823* (1964), and Frank Thistlethwaite, *The
Anglo-American Connection in the Early Nineteenth Century* (1959).

Samuel F. Bemis, *John Quincy Adams and the Union*
(1956), recounts the troubled administration of the
second President Adams. Robert V. Remini, *The Election of Andrew Jackson* (1963), examines the revival of
partisan opposition and the eventual triumph of it.
See also Norman K. Risjord, *The Old Republicans:
Southern Conservatism in the Age of Jefferson* (1965).

The Age of Jackson

The Inaugural Levee, 1829
Even in the relatively rustic days of the early republic, presidential inaugurations often took on an almost monarchical grandeur. When Andrew Jackson entered office in 1829, having won election as the champion of democratic simplicity, he avoided the formal receptions that had become tradition and threw the White House open to the public. Since frontiersmen and common people of all kinds had flocked to Washington to witness the inauguration of their hero, the result was an invasion of the mansion by an enormous and, in the view of more conservative observers, cretinous horde. Jackson's opponents viewed the inaugural levee as evidence of the triumph of "King Mob."
(Library of Congress)

When the French aristocrat Alexis de Tocqueville visited the United States in 1831, one feature of American society struck him as "fundamental": the "general equality of condition among the people." Unlike older societies, in which privilege and wealth were passed from generation to generation within an entrenched upper class, America had no rigid distinctions of rank. "The government of democracy," he wrote in his brilliant study *Democracy in America* (1835–1840), "brings the notion of political rights to the level of the humblest citizens, just as the dissemination of wealth brings the notion of property within the reach of all the members of the community."

Yet Tocqueville also wondered how long the fluidity of American society could survive in the face of the growth of manufacturing and the rise of the factory system. Industrialism, he feared, would create a large class of dependent workers and a small group of new aristocrats. For, as he explained it, "at the very moment at which the science of manufactures lowers the class of workmen, it raises the class of masters."

Americans, too, pondered the future of their democracy in these years of economic and territorial expansion. Some feared that the nation's rapid growth would produce social chaos and insisted that the country's first priority must be to establish order and a clear system of authority. Others argued that the greatest danger facing the nation was privilege, and that society's goal should be to eliminate the favored status of powerful elites and make opportunity more widely available. The advocates of this latter vision seized control of the federal government in 1829 with the inauguration of Andrew Jackson.

Jackson and his followers were not egalitarians. They did nothing to challenge the existence of slavery; they supervised one of the most vicious assaults on American Indians in the nation's history; and they accepted the necessity of economic inequality and social gradation. Jackson himself was a frontier aristocrat, and most of those who served him were themselves people of wealth and standing. They were not usually aristocrats by birth, however; they had risen to prominence on the basis of their own talents and energies, and their goal in public life was to ensure that others like themselves would have the opportunity to do the same. The "democratization" of government over which Andrew Jackson presided was permeated with the rhetoric of equality and aroused the excitement of working people. Its real intent, however, was less to aid the farmers and laborers who were Jackson's greatest champions than to challenge the power of Eastern elites for the sake of the rising entrepreneurs of the South and the West.

THE ADVENT OF MASS POLITICS

On March 4, 1829, an unprecedented throng—thousands of Americans from all regions of the country: farmers, laborers, and others of humble rank—crowded before the Capitol in Washington, D.C., to witness the inauguration of Andrew Jackson. After the ceremonies, the boisterous crowd poured down Pennsylvania Avenue, following their hero to the White House. And there, at a public reception open to all, they filled the state rooms to overflowing, trampling one another, soiling the carpets, ruining the elegantly upholstered sofas and chairs in their eagerness to shake the new president's hand.

"It was a proud day for the people," wrote Amos Kendall, one of Jackson's closest political associates. "General Jackson is *their own* President." To other observers, however, the scene was less appealing. Justice of the Supreme Court Joseph Story, a friend and colleague of John Marshall, looked on the inaugural levee, as it was called, and remarked with disgust: "The reign of King 'Mob' seems triumphant."

In a sense, both Kendall and Story were correct. For if the age of Jackson did not mark the elevation of all Americans to prosperity and equality, it did mark a transformation of American politics that extended power widely to new groups. Formerly the preserve of a relatively small group of property owners, politics now became the province of virtually all the nation's citizens (that is, all its white males; for few Jacksonians were willing to contemplate the participation of women or blacks in the electoral process). In a political sense at least, the era well earned its title of the age of the common man.

President of the Common Man

Unlike Thomas Jefferson, Jackson was no democratic philosopher. Nevertheless, in his own plain, straightforward way, he too expressed a distinct theory of democracy. Government, he insisted, should offer "equal protection and equal benefits" to all the people. It should provide special favors to no one. And once in office, he set about to dismantle those institutions and policies that he believed worked to protect special privileges and restrict opportunity.

His first target was the personnel procedures of the federal government. For a generation, ever since the downfall of the Federalists in 1800, there had been no change of party in the national administration. Officeholders in Washington, therefore, had stayed on year after year, many of them growing gray and some of them growing corrupt. "Office is considered as a species of property," Jackson told Congress in a bitter denunciation of the entrenched "class" of permanent officeholders, "and government rather as a means of promoting individual in-

terests than as an instrument created solely for the service of the people." Official duties, he believed, could be made "so plain and simple that men of intelligence may readily qualify themselves for their performance." According to him, offices belonged to the people, not to the entrenched officeholders. Or, as one of his henchmen, William L. Marcy of New York, more cynically put it, "To the victors belong the spoils."

In actual practice, Jackson did not make such drastic removals as his partisan critics then and afterward asserted. During the entire eight years of his presidency he removed a total of no more than one-fifth of the federal officeholders, and many of these he removed for cause, such as misuse of government funds. Proportionally, Jackson dismissed no more of the jobholders than Jefferson had done. The fact remains, nevertheless, that the Jackson administration, adapting the spoils system from some of the states, fixed it firmly upon national politics.

Eventually the Jacksonians adopted another instrument of democratic politics: the national nominating convention. Jackson supporters had long resented the process by which presidential candidates were selected by congressional caucus, a process that they believed was designed to restrict access to the office to those favored by entrenched elites. Jackson himself had achieved office without resort to the caucus; and in 1832, to renominate him for the presidency, his followers staged the first national convention of a major party. Although in later generations, the party convention would be seen by many as the source of corruption and political exclusivity, in the 1830s it was viewed as a great triumph of the people. Power in the party would, through the convention, arise directly from the populace, circumventing established political institutions.

In fact, the acceptance of the "spoils" system and the creation of the political convention exposed not only the extent but the limits of Jacksonian political democracy. Both served to limit the power of entrenched elites—permanent officeholders and the exclusive party caucus. Yet neither really transferred power to the common people. Appointments to office almost always went to

Andrew Jackson
One of the few photographs of Andrew Jackson, taken late in his life. Jackson's military achievements, his forceful, uncompromising personality, and his adherence to his own version of democracy made him one of the most beloved (and, among his foes, the most despised) figures of his era. He was one of the first American politicians to rise to power by mobilizing mass popular support. Earlier leaders had relied instead upon the loyalties of congressional and local party elites. (Culver Pictures)

prominent political allies of the president and his associates. Delegates to national conventions were less often common men than members of local party elites. Political opportunity within the party was expanding, but within narrow limits.

The Expanding Electorate

In other ways, however, Jacksonian politics did indeed transfer power to the population at large. For it was in this era that a true mass electorate emerged. The expansion of the franchise began in Ohio and other new states of the West, which, on joining the Union, adopted constitutions that guaranteed all adult white males the right to vote and permitted all voters the right to hold public office. Older states, concerned about the loss of their population to the West, began slowly and haltingly to grant additional political rights to their people so as to encourage them to stay. Even before the War of 1812 a few of the Eastern states permitted white men to vote whether or not they owned property or paid a tax. Eventually, all the states (some of them not until after the Civil War) changed their constitutions in the direction of increased democracy.

Change was resisted, and at times the democratic trend was stopped short of the aims of the more radical reformers, as when Massachusetts held its constitutional convention in 1820. The reform-minded delegates complained that in the Massachusetts government the rich were better represented than the poor, both because of the restrictions on voting and officeholding and because of the peculiar system of property representation in the state senate. Daniel Webster, one of the conservative delegates, opposed democratic changes on the grounds that "power *naturally* and *necessarily* follows property" and that "property as such should have its weight and influence in political arrangement." Webster and the rest of the conservatives could not prevent the reform of senate representation, nor could they prevent elimination of the property requirement for voting. But, to the dismay of the radicals, the new constitution required that every voter be a taxpayer and that the governor be the owner of considerable real estate.

In the New York convention of 1821, the conservatives, led by Chancellor James Kent, insisted that a taxpaying requirement for suffrage was not enough and that, at least in the election of state senators, the property qualification should be retained. Kent argued that society "is an association for the protection of property as well as of life" and that "the individual who contributes only one cent to the common stock ought not to have the same power and influence in directing the property concerns of the partnership as he who contributes his thousands." The reformers, appealing to the Declaration of Independence, maintained that life, liberty, and the pursuit of happiness, not property, were the main concerns of society and government. The property qualification was abolished.

Other states proceeded more slowly in the broadening of democracy. Progress was peaceful, except in Rhode Island. There the constitution was the old colonial charter, little changed, and it disqualified as voters more than half of the adult males of the state. Thomas L. Dorr and his suffragist followers, despairing of reform by legal processes, held a convention of their own, drew up a new constitution, and tried to set up an administration with Dorr as governor. When the existing state government began to imprison his followers he led a band of his men in an attack on the Providence arsenal (1842). The Dorr Rebellion was quickly put down, yet it hastened the reforms that came afterward in Rhode Island.

In the South, reformers criticized the overrepresentation of the tidewater areas and the underrepresentation of the back country in the legislatures. When the Virginia constitutional convention met, in 1829, the delegates from the western counties gained some slight concessions but not enough to satisfy them. Elsewhere in the Southeast the planters and politicians of the older counties continued to dominate the state governments.

With few exceptions, free blacks could not vote anywhere in the South, nor could they vote in most of the Northern states. Pennsylvania at one time allowed black suffrage but eventually (1838) amended the constitution to prohibit it. In North and South, women continued to be denied the vote, regardless of the amount of property they might own. Everywhere the ballot was

---

An Argument Against Universal Suffrage [1821]

According to the original constitution of New York, the state senate was elected by owners of land worth at least $250 and the assembly by owners of land worth at least $50. At the constitutional convention of 1821 the radicals proposed to abolish all property qualifications for voting. A conservative delegate, James Kent, objected. Then chancellor of the state chancery court, Kent was one of the nation's foremost legal authorities. Later he wrote a classic four-volume work entitled Commentaries on American Law *(1826–1830). In 1821, he was willing to abolish the property qualification for assembly elections, but he wished to "preserve our Senate as the representative of the landed interest." He told his fellow delegates:*

By the report before us, we propose to annihilate, at one stroke, all those property distinctions and to bow before the idol of universal suffrage. That extreme democratic principle, when applied to the legislative and executive departments of the government, has been regarded with terror, by the wise men of every age, because in every European republic, ancient and modern, in which it has been tried, it has terminated disastrously, and been productive of corruption, injustice, violence, and tyranny. . . .

The apprehended danger from the experiment of universal suffrage applied to the whole legislative department, is no dream of the imagination. It is too mighty an excitement for the moral constitution of men to endure. The tendency of universal suffrage is to jeopardize the rights of property and the principles of liberty. There is a constant tendency . . . in the poor to covet a share in the plunder of the rich; in the debtor to relax or avoid the obligation of contracts; in the majority to tyrannize over the minority, and trample down their rights; in the indolent and profligate to cast the whole burthens of society upon the industrious and the virtuous; and there is a tendency in ambitious and wicked men to inflame these combustible materials.

open, not secret, and often it was cast as a spoken vote rather than a written one. The lack of secrecy meant that voters could be, and sometimes were, bribed or intimidated.

In most of the states, there was at first no popular vote for president. As late as 1800, the legislature chose presidential electors in ten of the states, and the people in only six. The trend was toward popular election, however, and after 1828 the legislature made the choice only in South Carolina. There the people had no chance to vote in presidential elections until after the Civil War.

Despite the persisting limitations, the number of voters increased far more rapidly than did the population as a whole. In the presidential election of 1824 fewer than 27 in 100 adult white males voted. In the election of 1828 the proportion rose to about 55 in 100—more than twice the figure for 1824—and in the elections of 1832 and 1836 the proportion remained approximately the same as in 1828. Then, in 1840, people flocked to the polls as never before, 78 in 100 white men casting their ballots. The multiplication of voters was only in part the result of a widening of the electorate. It was in greater measure the result of a heightening of interest in politics and a strengthening of party organization. Citizens now were aroused and brought out to vote who in former times had seldom bothered with elections.

The Legitimation of Party

At the same time that the electorate was expanding and the number of elective offices was increasing, another, equally profound political development was in progress: the establishment of the idea of party as a legitimate part of American public life. Even at the peak of the first party system in 1800, virtually no one had been willing to accept the *idea* of a party system. There was wide agreement that parties were evils to be avoided, that the nation should strive for a broad consensus in which permanent factional lines would not exist. But in the 1820s and 1830s, those assumptions gave way to a new view: that permanent, institutionalized parties were a desirable part of the political process, that indeed they were essential to democracy.

Like so many other American political developments, the elevation of the idea of party occurred first at the state level, most prominently in New York. There a dissident political faction under the leadership of Martin Van Buren (known as the "Bucktails" or the "Albany Regency") began, in the years after the War of 1812, to challenge the political oligarchy—led by the New York aristocrat De Witt Clinton—that had been dominating the state for years. In itself, the challenge was nothing new; factional rivalries occurred in virtually every state. What was new was the way in which Van Buren and his followers posed their challenge. Refuting the traditional view of a political party as undemocratic, they argued that only an institutionalized party, based in the populace at large, could ensure genuine democracy. The alternative was the sort of oligarchy that Clinton had created. In this new kind of party, ideological commitments would be less important than loyalty to the party itself. Preservation of the party as an institution—through the use of favors, rewards, and patronage—would be the principal goal of the leadership. Above all, for a party to survive, it must have a permanent opposition. The existence of two competing parties would give each political faction a sense of purpose and would force politicians to remain continually attuned to the will of the people. The opposing parties would check and balance one another in much the same way that the different branches of government checked and balanced one another.

By the late 1820s, this new idea of party was emerging in other states beyond New York—in Pennsylvania, for example, where the spoils system was introduced well before it was transplanted to the federal government. The election of Jackson in 1828, the result of a popular movement apparently removed from the usual political elites, seemed further to legitimize the idea of party. And finally, in the 1830s, a fully formed two-party system began to operate at the national level, with each party committed to its own existence as an institution and willing to accept the legitimacy of its opposition. "Parties of some sort must exist," said a New York newspaper. " 'Tis in the nature and genius of our government."

True to the new concept of party, Andrew Jackson had won election on the basis of no clearly articulated program. His followers—who were soon calling themselves simply Democrats, thus giving a permanent name to what would become the nation's oldest political party—had interests so diverse that a statement of precise aims would have alienated many of them at the outset. Yet Jackson entered office with certain strong convictions about the purposes of government and about the nature of the presidency. He believed that the federal government should work on behalf of the common man, eliminating the privileges of established elites. In general, that meant reducing the functions of government, since a concentration of power in Washington would, he believed, almost inevitably produce a restriction of opportunity to those favored few with political connections. But Jackson believed, too, in forceful presidential leadership. And although he spoke frequently of the importance of states' rights, he was strongly committed to the preservation of the Union. Thus at the same time that Jackson was contemplating an economic program to reduce the power of the national government, he was forced to assert the supremacy of the Union in the face of a potent challenge. For he had no sooner entered office, than his own vice president—John C. Calhoun—began to assert a dangerous new constitutional theory: what became known as nullification.

Calhoun and Nullification

At the age of forty-six (in 1828) Calhoun had a promising future as well as a distinguished past. A congressional leader during the War of 1812, afterward head of the War Department for eight years (making a record that entitles him to rank as one of the few truly great secretaries of war), then vice president in John Quincy Adams's administration, he now was running as the vice-presidential candidate on the Jackson ticket. And he could look forward to the presidency itself after a term or two for Jackson.

But the tariff question placed Calhoun in a dilemma. Once he had been a forthright protectionist, coming out strongly for the tariff of 1816. But since that time many South Carolinians had changed their minds on the subject. Carolina cotton planters were disturbed because their plantations were less profitable than they thought they should be. The whole state appeared to be stagnating, its population remaining almost stationary, its countryside showing signs of ruin and decay. One reason was the exhaustion of the South Carolina soil, which could not well compete with the newly opened fertile lands of the Southwest. But the Carolinians blamed their trouble on another cause—the "tariff of abominations" of 1828. They reasoned that protective duties raised the prices of the things they had to buy, whether they bought them at home or from abroad, and lowered the price of the cotton they sold, most of which was exported. They had a point: in order to export, a nation has to import, and to the extent that the tariff kept foreign goods out of the United States it also reduced the foreign market for American cotton. Some exasperated Carolinians were ready to seek escape from the hated law through revolution—that is, through secession. Here was a challenge Calhoun had to meet in order to maintain his leadership in the state and make a future for himself in national politics.

Quietly he worked out a theory to justify state action in resisting the tariff law. He intended this action to be strictly legal and constitutional, not revolutionary. So he had to find a basis for his plan in the Constitution itself. Calhoun believed that he was following the lines laid down by Madison and Jefferson in their Virginia and Kentucky resolutions of 1798–1799. Indeed, his reasoning was quite similar to theirs; but he carried it further and provided a definite procedure for state action.

Calhoun started his reasoning with the assumption that sovereignty, the ultimate source of power, lay in the states considered as separate political communities. These separate peoples had created the federal government, through their conventions that had rat-

John C. Calhoun
Calhoun was one of the most brilliant of all the leaders of the early republic, and for a time he was one of the most effective in promoting the cause of American nationalism. But as the years passed, bringing an increase in sectional tensions and an erosion of Calhoun's own political prospects, he became one of the leading forces in articulating a vision of Southern autonomy. Partly because of his influence, his native South Carolina became the most militantly independent of all the states of the future Confederacy. Calhoun served six years in the United States House of Representatives (1811–1817); eight years as secretary of war (1817–1825); seven years as vice president (under both John Quincy Adams and Andrew Jackson, 1825–1832); and as a member of the United States Senate from South Carolina from 1832 to 1850 (with the exception of a two-year term as secretary of state in 1844–1845). (Library of Congress)

ified the Constitution in the 1780s. Putting this in legal terminology, he described the states (meaning their peoples, not their governments) as the "principals," the federal government as their "agent," and the Constitution as a "compact" containing instructions within which the agent was to operate.

From these assumptions, the rest of his theory followed more or less logically. The Supreme Court was not competent to judge whether acts of Congress were constitutional, since the Court, like the Congress, was only a branch of an agency created by the states. The principals must decide, each for itself, whether their instructions were violated. If Congress enacted a law of doubtful constitutionality—say, a protective tariff—a state could "interpose" to frustrate the law. That is, the people of the state could hold a convention, and if (through their elected delegates) they decided that Congress had gone too far, they could declare the federal law null and void within their state. In that state, the law would remain· inoperative until three-fourths of the whole number of states should ratify an amendment to the Consti-

tution specifically assigning Congress the power in question. The nullifying state would then submit—or it could secede.

The legislature of South Carolina published Calhoun's first statement of his theory, anonymously, in a document entitled *The South Carolina Exposition and Protest* (1828). This paper condemned the recent tariff as unconstitutional, unfair, and unendurable—a law fit to be nullified. Calhoun had good reason for not wishing to be identified publicly as the author of the document. It was bound to arouse opposition in parts of the country, and of course he hoped to be reelected vice president and later to be elected president.

After the Jackson-Calhoun ticket had won its victory at the polls, Calhoun was no more eager than before to see nullification put into effect. He waited, hoping that Jackson as president would persuade Congress to make drastic reductions in tariff rates and thus mollify the outraged Carolina planters. It remained to be seen what stature Calhoun would have within the administration. As soon as the major appointments had been made, he gained an inkling of his importance, or unimportance, in the new administration. He then realized he had a powerful rival for Jackson's favor in the person of Martin Van Buren.

The Rise of Van Buren

Van Buren, about the same age as Calhoun and equally ambitious, was quite different in background and personality. Born of Dutch ancestry in the village of Kinderhook, near Albany, New York, he advanced himself through skillful maneuvering to the position of United States senator (1820–1828). He also made himself the party boss of his state by organizing and leading the Albany Regency, the Democratic machine of New York. Though he supported Crawford for president in 1824, he afterward became one of the most ardent of Jacksonians, doing much to carry his state for Jackson in 1828 while getting himself elected governor. By this time he had a reputation as a political wizard. Short and slight, with reddish-gold sideburns and a quiet manner, he gained a variety of revealing nicknames, such as "the Sage of Kinderhook," "the Little Magician," and "the Red Fox." Never giving or taking offense, he was in temperament just the opposite of the choleric Jackson, yet the two were about to become the closest of friends. Van Buren promptly resigned the governorship and went to Washington when Jackson called him to head the new cabinet as secretary of state.

Except for Van Buren, this cabinet contained no one of more than ordinary talent. It was intended to represent and harmonize the sectional and factional interests within the party. No Virginian was included (for the first time since 1789). Friends of both Van Buren and Calhoun were given places. This cabinet was not intended to form a council of advisers: Jackson did not even call cabinet meetings.

Instead, he relied on an unofficial circle of political allies who came to be known as the "Kitchen Cabinet." Noteworthy in this group were several newspaper editors, among them Isaac Hill, from New Hampshire, and Amos Kendall and Francis P. Blair, from Kentucky. After 1830, Blair edited the administration's official organ, the Washington *Globe*. The closed-mouthed, asthmatic, "invisible" Kendall was said to be the genius who, behind the scenes, really ran the administration. While doubtless influential, he was no more so than several others, especially Jackson's old Tennessee friend and political manager William B. Lewis, who lived at the White House and had ready access to the president. Soon to be the most important of all was Van Buren, a member of both the official and the unofficial cabinets.

Martin Van Buren
As the leader of the so-called Albany Regency in New York in the 1820s, Van Buren helped to create one of the first modern party organizations in the United States. Later, as Andrew Jackson's secretary of state and, after 1832, vice president, he helped to bring party politics to the national level. Elected to the presidency in 1836 as Jackson's hand-picked successor, he encountered both economic troubles and rising sectional tensions during his four years in the White House. In 1840, he lost the presidency to William Henry Harrison, whose Whig party made effective use of many of the techniques of mass politics that Van Buren had helped to pioneer.
(The Granger Collection)

Vice President Calhoun, to his dismay, saw signs of Van Buren's growing influence when he viewed the division of the spoils. Not only did Van Buren get cabinet places for himself and his friends; he also secured the appointment of his followers to most of the lesser offices. Already, beneath the surface, there was the beginning of a rift between the vice president and the president. Then Calhoun and Jackson were further estranged, and Jackson and Van Buren were brought closer together, through a curious quarrel over a woman and etiquette.

Peggy O'Neil, the bright-eyed, vivacious daughter of a Washington tavern keeper, was the kind of woman whom men admire and women dislike. Jackson's Tennessee friend Senator John H. Eaton took the young widow as his wife, with Jackson's blessing. Washington gossips told and retold scandalous stories about her relationship with Eaton while her former husband had still been alive. All the talk would have amounted to little if Jackson had not appointed Eaton as his secretary of war and thus made Mrs. Eaton a cabinet wife. The rest of the administration wives, led by Mrs. Calhoun, snubbed Mrs. Eaton. Jackson was furious. His own wife, Rachel, now dead, had been slandered by his political enemies; and he was confident that Peggy too was an innocent victim of dirty politics. He not only defended her virtue; he demanded that his secretaries and associates concede it and treat her with respect. But Calhoun, bowing to his wife's demands, refused, thus taking sides against Mrs. Eaton's champion, Jackson. Van Buren, a widower, befriended the Eatons and thus ingratiated himself with the president. By 1831, Jackson had settled on Van Buren as his choice to succeed him in the White House. Calhoun's dreams of the presidency had all but vanished.

The Webster-Hayne Debate

If there had been only personal differences between Jackson and Calhoun, their parting would have been less significant. But there were also differences of principle. At the height of the Eaton affair, the opposing views of the two men were dramatically revealed as a result of a great debate on the nature of the Constitution.

The Webster-Hayne debate, in January 1830, grew out of a Senate discussion of public lands, a discussion provoked when a senator from Connecticut suggested that all land sales and surveys be discontinued for the time being. This suggestion immediately aroused Senator Thomas Hart Benton of Missouri, the Jacksonian leader in the Senate and a sturdy defender of the West. Always suspicious of New England, he charged that the proposal to stop land sales was intended to keep New England workers from going West and thus to choke off the growth and prosperity of the frontier.

A young, debonair senator from South Carolina, Robert Y. Hayne, took up the argument after Benton. Hayne and other Southerners hoped to get Western support for their drive to lower the tariff, and at the moment they were willing to grant abundant and cheap lands to the Westerners in exchange for such support. He hinted that the South and the West might well combine in self-defense against the Northeast.

Daniel Webster, now a senator from Massachusetts, once had been a states'-rights and antitariff man; but like Calhoun in reverse, he had changed his position with the changing interests of his section. The day after Hayne's speech, Webster took the floor. Ignoring Benton, he directed his remarks to Hayne and, through him, to Calhoun in the vice president's chair. He reviewed much of the history of the republic, with occasional disregard for historical facts, to prove that New England always had been the friend of the West. Referring to the tariff of 1816, he said that New England was not responsible for the protectionist policy but had accepted it after other sections had fixed it upon the nation. Then, changing the subject, he spoke gravely of disunionists and disunionism in South Carolina.

Thus Webster challenged Hayne to debate him not on the original grounds of the public lands and the tariff but on the issue of states' rights versus national power, an issue that could be made to seem one of treason versus patriotism. And in due time Hayne, coached by Calhoun, came back with a defense of the nullification theory. It took Webster two afternoons to deliver his remarkable and long-revered second reply to Hayne. "I go for the Constitution as it is, and for the Union as it is," he declaimed, as he turned to an exposition of the "true principles" of the Constitution. "It is, Sir, the people's Constitution, the people's government, made for the people, made by the people, and answerable to the people." He concluded with the ringing appeal: "Liberty *and* Union, now and for ever, one and inseparable!"

Calhoun's followers were sure that Hayne had the better of the argument. The important question at the moment, however, was what President Jackson thought and what side, if any, he would take.

The answer soon became clear at a Democratic banquet to honor Thomas Jefferson as the founder of the party. As was customary at such affairs, the guests settled down after dinner to an evening of toasts. The president, forewarned by Van Buren, was ready with a toast of his own, which he had written down, underscoring certain words. When his turn came, he stood up and proclaimed: "Our *Federal* Union—*It must be preserved.*" While he spoke he looked sternly at Calhoun. Van Buren, who stood on his chair to see better from the far end of the table, thought he saw Calhoun's hand shake and a trickle of wine run down the outside of his glass. Calhoun responded to Jackson's toast with his own: "The Union—next to our liberty most dear. May we always remember that it can only be preserved by distributing evenly the benefits and the burthens of the Union."

The Nullification Crisis

For more than two years, the sectional tensions aroused by the Webster-Hayne debate and the nullification doctrine continued without producing a direct confrontation between the federal government and the South. In 1832, however, the state of South Carolina precipitated a crisis. Having waited four

years for Congress to repeal the "tariff of abominations," South Carolinians watched with horror the enactment of a new tariff that offered them virtually no relief. And beyond the immediate economic issue involved was another concern. If the federal government could wield enough power to foist a hated tariff on the South, what was to prevent it from passing laws interfering with the institution of slavery?

Some of the more militant South Carolinians were now ready for revolt. Had it not been for Calhoun, they might have attempted to withdraw the state from the Union. Instead, the vice president soon established himself as the leader of his state's discontent. Having lost the confidence of Jackson, Calhoun was now an open advocate of nullification; and in the aftermath of the 1832 tariff, he persuaded extremists in South Carolina to adopt that doctrine—not secession—as their remedy. The question of whether to nullify the tariff act was the leading issue in the state elections of 1832, and the result was a ringing victory for the nullifiers (although opponents of nullification—the Unionists—constituted a sizable minority; a referendum question on the issue passed 23,000 to 17,000).

Without delay, the newly elected legislature called for the election of delegates to a state convention. And the convention, once assembled, voted to declare null and void the tariffs of 1828 and 1832 and to forbid the collection of duties within the state. The legislature then passed laws to enforce the ordinance and make preparations for military defense. Needing strong leaders to take command at home and to present the South Carolina case ably in Washington, the nullifiers arranged for Hayne to become governor and for Calhoun to replace Hayne as senator. So Calhoun resigned as vice president.

Privately, the president threatened to hang Calhoun. Officially, he proclaimed that nullification was treason and its adherents traitors. Cooperating closely with the Unionists of South Carolina, he took steps to strengthen the federal forts in the state, ordering General Winfield Scott and a warship and several revenue cutters to Charleston. When Congress met, the president asked for specific authority with which to handle the crisis. His followers introduced a "force bill" authorizing him to use the army and navy to see that acts of Congress were obeyed. The force bill, like Jackson's proclamation, further antagonized the South Carolina extremists. Violence seemed a real possibility early in 1833, as Calhoun took his place in the Senate to defend his theory and its practice. He introduced a set of resolutions on the "constitutional compact" and then made a speech against the force bill.

Webster's reply to Calhoun (February 16, 1833), if less colorful than his reply to Hayne three years earlier, dealt more fully and more cogently with the constitutional issues at stake. The Constitution, Webster argued, was no mere compact among sovereign states. It was an "executed contract," an agreement to set up a permanent government, supreme within its allotted sphere and acting directly upon the people as a whole. Webster dismissed secession as a revolutionary but not a constitutional right, then denounced nullification as no right at all. The nullifiers, he said, rejected "the first great principle of all republican liberty; that is, that the majority must govern." They pretended to be concerned about minority rights, but did they practice what they preached? "Look to South Carolina, at the present moment. How far are the rights of minorities there respected?" Obviously the nullificationist majority was proceeding with a "relentless disregard" for the rights of the Unionist minority—"a minority embracing, as the gentleman himself will admit, a large portion of the worth and respectability of the state."

At the moment Calhoun was in a predicament. South Carolina, standing alone (not a single state had come to its support), itself divided, could not hope to prevail if a showdown with the federal government should come. If the nullifiers meekly yielded, however, they would lose face and their leader would be politically ruined. Calhoun was saved by the timely intervention of the Great Pacificator, Henry Clay. Newly elected to the Senate, Clay in consultation with Calhoun devised a compromise scheme by which the tariff would be lowered year after year, reaching in 1842 approximately the same

level as in 1816. Finally Clay's compromise and the force bill were passed on the same day (March 1, 1833). Webster consistently opposed any concessions to the nullifiers, but Jackson was satisifed. He signed the new tariff measure as well as the force bill.

In South Carolina the convention reassembled and repealed its ordinance of nullification as applied to the tariffs of 1828 and 1832. Then, as if to have the last word, the convention adopted a new ordinance nullifying the force act. This proceeding meant little, since the force act would not go into effect anyhow, the original ordinance (against which it was directed) having been withdrawn. Although Calhoun and his followers, having brought about tariff reduction, claimed a victory for nullification, the system had not worked out in the way its sponsors had intended. Calhoun had learned a lesson: no state could assert and maintain its rights by independent action. Thereafter, while continuing to talk of states' rights and nullification, he devoted himself to building up a sense of Southern solidarity so that, when another trial should come, the whole section might be prepared to act as a unit in resisting federal authority.

Jackson and States' Rights

Despite his ringing defense of the authority of the federal government in the nullification crisis, Andrew Jackson was not an opponent of the rights of the states. On the contrary, some of his most important decisions as president reflected his view that, as he had declared in his inaugural address, none but "constitutional" undertakings should be pursued by the federal government. Thus, throughout his administration, he frequently vetoed laws that he considered to exceed the powers originally granted to Congress by the states.

The Maysville Road Bill (1830) brought on the most significant of Jackson's vetoes. This bill, by authorizing the government to buy stock in a private company, would have given a federal subsidy for the construction of a turnpike from Maysville to Lexington, within the state of Kentucky. The Maysville pike was a segment of a projected highway that was to form a great southwestern branch of the National Road. Nevertheless, since the pike itself was an intrastate and not an interstate project, Jackson doubted whether Congress constitutionally could give aid to it. Earlier (in 1822) President Monroe, vetoing the Cumberland Road Bill, had declared that the federal government should support only those improvements that were of general rather than local importance. Now, with Van Buren's assistance, Jackson prepared a veto message based on similar grounds. He also urged economy, denounced the selfish "scramble for appropriations," and stressed the desirability of paying off the national debt. Although Jackson also refused to sign other appropriation bills, he did not object to every proposal for federal spending to build roads or improve rivers and harbors. During his two terms such expenditures continued to mount, far exceeding even those of the John Quincy Adams administration.

The Maysville veto was not popular in the West, where better transportation was a never-ending demand. Others of Jackson's policies, however, met with wholehearted approval in both the South and the West—most prominently, his use of federal powers to remove all Indian tribes from the areas of white settlement.

The Removal of the Indians

As an old Indian fighter, Jackson was no lover of the red man, and he desired to continue and expedite the program, which Jefferson had begun, of removing all the eastern tribes to the west of the Mississippi. The land between the Missouri and the Rockies, according to such explorers as Lewis and Clark and Stephen H. Long, was supposed to be a vast desert, unfit for white habitation. Why not leave that land for the Indians? By the Indian Removal Act of 1830, Congress proposed to exchange tribal lands within the states for new homes in the West, and by the Indian Intercourse Act of 1834, Congress marked off an Indian country and provided for a string of forts to keep the Indians inside it and the whites outside. Meanwhile the president saw that treaties, nearly a hundred

in all, were negotiated with the various tribes and that reluctant tribesmen along with their women and children were moved west, with the prodding of the army.

In the process of Indian removal there was much tragedy and a certain amount of violence. When (in 1832) Chief Black Hawk, with a thousand of his hungry Sac and Fox followers—men, women, and children—recrossed the Mississippi into Illinois to grow corn, the frontiersmen feared an invasion. Militiamen and regular troops soon drove the unfortunate Indians into Wisconsin and then slaughtered most of them as they tried to escape. Such was the Black Hawk War, in which Abraham Lincoln was a captain of militia (he saw no action) and Jefferson Davis a lieutenant in the regular army.

More troublesome to the government was the Seminole War. It began when Chief Osceola led an uprising of his tribesmen (including runaway blacks), who refused to move west in accordance with a treaty of 1833. The fighting lasted off and on for several years. Jackson sent troops to Florida, but the Seminoles with their black associates were masters of guerrilla warfare in the jungly Everglades. Even after Osceola had been treacherously captured under a flag of truce and had died in prison, the red and black rebels continued to resist.

Unlike the Sacs and Foxes or the Seminoles, the Cherokees in Georgia had a written language of their own (invented by the half-breed Sequoyah in 1821) and a settled way of life as farmers. Yet the state of Georgia, after getting rid of most of the Creeks, was eager to remove the Cherokees also and open their millions of acres to white occupation. In 1827, these Indians adopted a constitution and declared their independence as the Cherokee Nation. Promptly, the Georgia legislature extended its laws over them and directed the seizure of their territory. Hiring a prominent lawyer, the Cherokees appealed to the Supreme Court. In the case of *Cherokee Nation* v. *Georgia* (1831) Chief Justice Marshall gave the majority opinion that the Indians were "domestic dependent nations" and had a right to the land they occupied until they voluntarily ceded it to the United States. In another case, *Worcester* v. *Georgia*

(1832), Marshall and the Court held that the Cherokee Nation was a definite political community over which the laws of Georgia had no force and into which Georgians could not enter without permission.

Jackson did not sympathize with the Cherokees as Adams had done with the Creeks. Vigorously supporting Georgia's position, Jackson did nothing to see that the rulings of the Supreme Court were carried out. The chief justice had implied that it was the president's duty to uphold the rights of the Indians. Jackson's attitude is well expressed in the comment attributed to him: "John Marshall has made his decision; now let him enforce it." The decision was never enforced.

In 1835, a few of the Cherokees, none of them a chosen representative of the Cherokee Nation, were induced to sign a treaty giving up the nation's Georgia land in return for $5 million and a reservation in Indian Territory (Oklahoma). The great majority of the 17,000 Cherokees were unwilling to leave their homes, so Jackson sent an army of 7,000 under General Winfield Scott to drive them westward at bayonet point. About 1,000 fled across the state line to North Carolina, where eventually the federal government provided a reservation for them.

Most of the rest—along with others of the "Five Civilized Tribes": Choctaws, Chickasaws, Creeks, and Seminoles—made the long, forced trek to the West, beginning in midwinter 1838. Along the way a Kentuckian observed: "Even aged females, apparently

The Trail of Tears

By 1838, the Indian tribes in the eastern sections of the United States had been all but totally subdued by the expanding new nation. And in that year, the five major tribes of the East were forcibly moved over the "Trail of Tears" to a specially established Indian Territory in Oklahoma (where in later years they would encounter more challenges from the spread of white civilization). This painting by Robert Lindneux depicts the removal of the Cherokees, one of the "Five Civilized Nations" to be evacuated to the West. (The Granger Collection)

nearly ready to drop in the grave, were trav-
elling with heavy burdens attached to their
backs, sometimes on frozen ground and
sometimes on muddy streets, with no covering for their feet." Several thousand perished

before reaching their undesired destination.
In Indian Territory the survivors were never
to forget the hard journey. They called their
route "The Trail Where They Cried," the
Trail of Tears.

JACKSON AND THE BANK WAR

How far Jackson was willing to go to destroy
the power of institutions of centralized elite
power was clearly revealed in one of the
most celebrated episodes of his presidency:
the war against the Bank of the United States.
Jackson harbored no doubts in this case as to
the identity of his opponents: they were the
same Eastern aristocrats he had battled
throughout his political career.

The Bank of the United States was a private corporation with a charter from the federal government, which owned one-fifth of
the stock. It was a monopoly, having an exclusive right to hold the government's deposits. With its headquarters in Philadelphia
and its branches in twenty-nine other cities,
it also did a tremendous business in general
banking, totaling about $70 million a year. Its
services were important to the national economy because of the credit it provided for
profit-making enterprises; because of its
bank notes, which circulated throughout the
country as a dependable medium of exchange; and because of the restraining effect
that its policies had on the less well-managed
banks chartered by the various states. Nevertheless, Andrew Jackson was determined to
destroy it.

Biddle's Institution

Nicholas Biddle, president of the Bank from
1823 on, had done much to put the company
on a sound and prosperous basis. A member
of an aristocratic Philadelphia family, Biddle
was educated at the University of Pennsylvania and thereafter devoted himself to a number of intellectual interests, including poetry.
He personally owned a large proportion of
the Bank's stock, so much of it that together
with two other large stockholders he con-

trolled the Bank. He could and did choose
the officials of the branches, decide what
loans were to be made, and set the interest
rates. For several years after he took charge,
he made these decisions according to financial considerations. A banker, not a politician, he had no desire to mix in politics. But
he finally concluded it was necessary to do so
in self-defense when, with the encouragement of Jackson, popular opposition to the
Bank rose to a threatening pitch.

Opposition came from two very different
groups, the "soft-money" and the "hard-
money" men. The former, consisting largely
of state bankers and their friends, objected to
the Bank of the United States because it restrained the state banks from issuing notes as
freely as some of them would have liked. The
Philadelphia bank inhibited the issue of such
notes by collecting them and presenting
them for payment in cash. The other set of
critics, the hard-money people, had the opposite complaint. Believing in coin as the
only safe currency, these people condemned
all banks of issue—that is, all banks issuing
bank notes—whether chartered by the states,
as all but one of them were, or by the federal
government, as the Bank alone was.

Jackson himself was a hard-money man.
At one time in his life he had dealt in grandiose land and mercantile speculations based
on paper credit. Then a financial panic (1797)
had ruined his business and put him deeply
into debt. Thereafter he was suspicious of all
banks. After he became president, he raised
the question whether the charter of the Bank
of the United States should be renewed. Unless renewed, it would expire in 1836.

To preserve the institution, Biddle began
to grant banking favors to influential men in
the hope of winning them to his side. At first
he sought to cultivate Jackson's friends, with

some success in a few instances. Then he turned more and more to Jackson's opponents. He extended loans on easy terms to several prominent newspaper editors, to a number of important state politicians, and to more than fifty congressmen and senators. In particular, he relied on Senators Clay and Webster, the latter of whom was connected with the Bank in various ways—as legal counsel, director of the Boston branch, frequent and heavy borrower, and Biddle's personal friend.

Clay, Webster, and other advisers persuaded Biddle to apply to Congress for a recharter bill in 1832, four years ahead of the expiration date. After investigating the Bank and its business, Congress passed the recharter bill. At once Jackson vetoed it, sending it back to Congress with a stirring message in which he denounced the Bank as unconstitutional, undemocratic, and un-American. The veto stood, for the Bank's friends in Congress failed to obtain the two-thirds majority necessary to override it. And so the Bank question emerged as the paramount issue of the coming election, just as Clay had fondly hoped it would.

In 1832, Clay ran as the unanimous choice of the National Republicans, who had held a nominating convention in Baltimore late in the previous year. Jackson, with Van Buren as his running mate, sought reelection as the candidate of the Democratic Republicans, or Democrats. Still another candidate was in the field, representing a third party for the first time in American history. He was William Wirt, a prominent Baltimore lawyer and man of letters, the nominee of the Anti-Masonic party. Although he preferred Clay to Jackson, Wirt drew more votes away from the former than from the latter, though he did not draw a great many from any source, carrying only the state of Vermont. The legislature of South Carolina gave that state's electoral vote in protest to a man who was not even a candidate, John Floyd, one of Calhoun's Virginia followers. Of the remaining electoral votes, Jackson received more than five times as many as Clay.

The "Monster" Destroyed

Jackson took his decisive reelection as a sign that the people endorsed his views on the Bank of the United States. As soon as the nullification crisis had been disposed of, he determined to strike a blow at the banking "monster." He could not put an end to the Bank before the expiration of its charter, but at least he could lessen its power by seeing to the removal of the government's deposits. By the law establishing the Bank, the secretary of the treasury had to give the actual order to remove them. When the incumbent secretary refused to give the order, Jackson appointed a new one; and when this man procrastinated, Jackson named a third, Roger B. Taney, previously the attorney general and a member of the Kitchen Cabinet. Taney was more than willing to cooperate.

With Taney at the head of the Treasury Department, the process of removing the government's deposits began immediately. The government stopped putting new funds in the Bank but continued paying its bills by drawing on its existing deposits, which steadily dwindled. Meanwhile the government opened accounts with a number of state banks, depositing its incoming receipts with them. These banks, including one in Baltimore with which Taney himself was associated, were chosen presumably on the basis of their financial soundness but not always without consideration of their political leanings. Jackson's enemies called them his "pet banks." By 1836 there were eighty-nine of them.

The proud and poetic Biddle, "Czar Nicholas" to Jacksonians, was not the man to give in without a fight. "This worthy President," he wrote sarcastically, "thinks that because he has scalped Indians and imprisoned Judges, he is to have his way with the Bank. He is mistaken." Biddle struck back when the Jackson administration began to transfer funds directly from the Bank of the United States to the pet banks. He felt that the loss of government deposits, amounting to several millions, made it necessary for him to call in loans and raise interest rates, since the government deposits had served as the basis for much of the Bank's credit. He realized that by making borrowing more difficult, he was bound to hurt business and cause unemployment; but he consoled himself with the belief that a short depression would help to bring about a recharter of the Bank. "Noth-

"The Downfall of Mother Bank"
This 1832 cartoon shows President Jackson destroying the Bank of the United States and driving away its corrupt supporters by means of his order to withdraw government deposits from the Bank. (Library of Congress)

ing but the evidence of suffering," he told the head of the Boston branch, would "produce any effect in Congress."

During the winter of 1833–1834, with interest high and money scarce, there was suffering indeed, as many businessmen failed and thousands of workers lost their jobs. All over the country, friends of the Bank organized meetings to adopt petitions begging for relief from Congress, petitions that delegates then brought in person to Washington and that pro-Bank senators or representatives introduced with appropriately lugubrious speeches. But Jackson and the Jacksonians denied responsibility. When distressed citizens appealed to the president he answered, "Go to Biddle."

The banker finally carried his contraction of credit too far to suit his own friends among the anti-Jackson businessmen of the Northeast, and some of them did go to Bid-

dle. A group of New York and Boston merchants protested (as one of them reported) that the business community "ought not and would not sustain him in further pressure, which he very well knew was not necessary for the safety of the bank, and in which his whole object was to coerce a charter." To appease the business community he at last reversed himself and began to grant credit in abundance and on reasonable terms.

The "Bank War" was over, and Jackson had won it. But with the passing of the Bank of the United States (in 1836), the country lost an indispensable financial institution. Economic troubles lay ahead.

The Taney Court

The discouraging aftermath of the Bank War did not weaken Jackson's commitment to "democratizing" the nation's political and economic life. On the contrary, he continued to move forcefully against what he perceived to be institutions of aristocratic privilege and excessive federal power. And in 1835, he moved against the most powerful institution of economic nationalism of all: the Supreme Court. When John Marshall died in 1835, the president appointed as the new chief justice his trusted ally in the Bank War, Roger B. Taney—a man fervently committed to Jacksonian democracy.

Taney never dominated the Court in the way Marshall had managed to do; nor did he preside over a sharp break in constitutional interpretation. But there was a marked change in emphasis. Taney and the majority of his colleagues were moderate agrarian liberals, and in general they tended to support the right of the people, acting through state legislatures, to regulate private property rights and the activities of corporations. Although they stopped far short of accepting Calhoun's extreme states'-rights philosophy, the justices were modifying Marshall's vigorous nationalism.

Perhaps the clearest indication of the new judicial mood was the celebrated case of *Charles River Bridge* v. *Warren Bridge* of 1837. The case involved a dispute between two Massachusetts companies over the right to build a bridge across the Charles River between Boston and Cambridge. One company had a longstanding charter from the state to operate a toll bridge for a specified number of years, a charter that guaranteed them, they claimed, a monopoly of the bridge traffic. The second company had applied to the legislature for authorization to construct a second, competing bridge that would—since it

would be toll-free—greatly reduce the value of the first company's charter. The first company contended that in granting the second charter the legislature was engaging in a breach of contract.

The Marshall Court, in the *Dartmouth College* case and other decisions, had ruled clearly that states had no right to abrogate contracts. But now Taney, speaking for the Democratic majority on the Court, supported the right of Massachusetts to award the second charter. Although he advanced elaborate legal precedents to support the decision, the ruling reflected less the influence of the law than the influence of Jacksonian social theory. The object of government, Taney maintained, was to promote the general happiness, an object that took precedence over the rights of property. A state, therefore, had the right to amend or abrogate a contract if such action was necessary to advance the well-being of the community. In the *Charles River Bridge* case, he maintained, such abrogation had been clearly necessary. The original bridge company, by exercising a monopoly, was benefiting from unjustifiable privilege. (It did not help the first company that its members were largely Boston aristocrats, and that it was closely associated with elite Harvard College; the challenging company, by contrast, was composed largely of newer, aspiring entrepreneurs—the sort of people with whom Jackson and his allies instinctively identified.) The decision was another indication of one of the cornerstones of Jacksonian philosophy. The key to democracy was an expansion of economic opportunity, which would not occur if older corporations could maintain monopolies and choke off competition from newer companies.

THE EMERGENCE OF WHIGGERY

Jackson's forceful—some claimed tyrannical—tactics in crushing first the nullification movement and then the Bank of the United States helped galvanize a growing opposition coalition that by the mid-1830s was ready to assert itself in national politics. It began as a gathering of national political leaders op-

posed to Jackson's use of power. Denouncing the president as "King Andrew I," they began to refer to themselves as Whigs, after the party in England that traditionally worked to limit the power of the king. As the new party began to develop as a national organization with constituencies in every state, its appeal became more diffuse. Nevertheless, both in philosophy and in the character of its adherents, the Whig party offered a discernible contrast to the party of Jackson.

Party Philosophies

Even before the election of Jackson in 1828, those who would ultimately form the Democratic party had stood for a certain general approach to government and society; and during the years of the Jackson administration, that approach began to take the form of something approaching a philosophy. To the Democrats, America's future was to be one of steadily expanding opportunities. To that end, the federal government should be limited in power, the rights of states should be protected, and the nation should work to eliminate all social and economic arrangements that served to entrench privilege and stifle the common man. Jacksonians tended to romanticize the "honest workmen," the "simple farmers," and the forthright businessmen who stood, they believed, in sharp contrast to the corrupt, monopolistic, aristocratic forces of established wealth. As Jackson himself said in his farewell address, the society of America should be one in which "the planter, the farmer, the mechanic, and the laborer, all know that their success depends on their own industry and economy," in which no man's opportunity would be stifled by artificial privilege.

There was no necessary connection between this philosophy of a fluid, open society and an opposition to economic development; and indeed, many Jacksonians believed wholeheartedly in the necessity of material progress. Yet in practice, Democrats were far more likely than others to look with suspicion on proposals for stimulating modern commercial and industrial growth. They tended to associate such growth with the creation of menacing institutions of power—the Bank of the United States, for example; and they often spoke yearningly of a simpler era in which no such concentrations of privilege had existed. This vague opposition to economic progress found reflection in the political behavior of many Democrats. Both in Washington and in state governments, Democratic legislators, much more often than their Whig counterparts, opposed such modernizing institutions as chartered banks and corporations, state-supported internal improvements, even public schools. Rather than economic development and consolidation, Democrats favored territorial expansion, which would, they believed, widen opportunities for aspiring Americans. And among the most radical members of the party—the so-called Locofocos, mainly workingmen and small businessmen and professionals in the Northeast—sentiment was strong for a vigorous, ultimately perhaps even violent, assault on monopoly and privilege far in advance of anything Jackson himself ever contemplated.

The political philosophy that became known as Whiggery, by contrast, looked far more favorably on expanding the power of the federal government, encouraging industrial and commercial development, and knitting the country together into a consolidated economic system. While Democrats often looked with suspicion on such technological advances as railroads, telegraphs, and manufacturing machinery, Whigs embraced such material progress enthusiastically. And where Democrats advocated rapid geographic expansion, Whigs urged a more prudent, cautious movement into the West, fearful that too rapid territorial growth would produce instability. Their vision of America was of a nation embracing the industrial future, of a nation rising to world greatness as a commercial and manufacturing power. And although Whigs insisted that their vision would result in increasing opportunities for all Americans, they tended to attribute particular value to the enterprising, modernizing forces in their society—the entrepreneurs and institutions that most effectively promoted economic growth. Thus while Democrats were inclined to oppose legislation establishing banks, corporations, and other modernizing institutions, Whigs generally favored such measures.

Party Constituencies

To some extent, the constituencies of the two major parties were reflections of these dif-

Jacksonian Democracy

Andrew Jackson was one of the central political figures of the nineteenth century; and historians have, therefore, taken a particular interest in his legacy. Time and again, their views of Jackson have reflected the political climate of their own day. In the late nineteenth century, when the historical profession was dominated by aristocratic Easterners with Whiggish political views, studies of Jackson were largely hostile. Conservative biographers such as James Parton (*Life of Andrew Jackson*, 1860) denounced the Jacksonians as "barbarians" who had turned government over to the "rabble." By embracing the spoils system, such historians argued, Jackson had paved the way for the rampant corruption in government of later years. By destroying the Bank of the United States, he had struck a heavy blow against American financial stability.

By the early twentieth century, the writing of history, and with it the historical view of the Jacksonians, had begun to experience an important transformation. Under the influence of Frederick Jackson Turner, historians began to emphasize the role of the West in American life and to see in the frontier a healthy, democratic influence on the nation. Turner and his disciples, most of them Westerners or Southerners themselves, rejected the view of Whiggish historians that the Jacksonians had been ill-bred rabble. Instead, they argued, the Democrats of Jackson's time had been the freedom-loving frontiersmen of the West, challenging the conservative aristocracy of the East, which was attempting to restrict opportunity. Jackson himself, they claimed, was much like the progressives of their own time: a true democrat who strove to make government responsive to the will of the people rather than to the desires of special interests. Dissenters such as Thomas P.

Abernethy (*From Frontier Plantation in Tennessee*, 1932) argued that Jackson had himself been a frontier aristocrat and had opposed the democratic trend in his own state. For the most part, however, the view of Jacksonianism as "frontier democracy" (as Turner had argued in his famous essay "The Significance of the Frontier in American History," 1893) prevailed through the first half of the twentieth century.

A new era in Jacksonian scholarship began in 1945 with the publication of the celebrated study by Arthur M. Schlesinger, Jr., *The Age of Jackson*. Like Turner and others, Schlesinger admired Jackson for bringing a healthy democratic influence to American politics and saw the Jacksonian era as one of steadily expanding political opportunity. He did not, however, share the view of earlier historians that the roots of Jacksonianism lay in the West. Instead, Schlesinger claimed, the conflict between Democrats and Whigs was a conflict "not of sections, but of classes." Jacksonian Democracy was an effort "to control the power of the capitalistic groups, mainly Eastern, for the benefit of noncapitalist groups, farmers and laboring men, East, West, and South." Emphasizing the role of the urban working classes in the Jacksonian coalition, he saw in the 1830s an early version of modern reform efforts to "restrain the power of the business community."

Other historians have accepted Schlesinger's view that classes were more important than sections, but they have disagreed with him about which class Jackson represented. Richard Hofstadter's influential essay in *The American Political Tradition* (1948) portrayed Jackson as the spokesman of rising entrepreneurs—aspiring businessmen who saw the road to opportunity blocked by the monopolistic power of the Eastern aristoc-

fuse philosophies. The Whigs were strongest among the more substantial merchants and manufacturers of the Northeast, the wealthier planters of the South (those who favored commercial development and the strengthening of ties with the North), and the ambitious farmers and rising commercial class of the West—usually migrants from the North-

east—who advocated internal improvements, expanding trade, and rapid economic progress. The Democrats drew more support from the smaller merchants and the workingmen of the Northeast, from those Southern planters who looked with some suspicion on Northern industrial growth, and from those Westerners—usually with Southern racy. Thus the Jacksonians were opposed to special privileges only to the extent that those privileges blocked their own road to success. They were less sympathetic to the aspirations of those below them—workers and small farmers. Bray Hammond, in *Banks and Politics in America from the Revolution to the Civil War* (1957), argued similarly that the Jacksonian cause was "one of enterprise against capitalist, of banker against regulation, and of Wall Street against Chestnut"—that is, of the rising bankers of New York City against the established bankers of the Philadelphia-based Bank of the United States.

Still another view of Jacksonianism emerged in the 1950s from historians concerned with the ideological origins of the movement. Marvin Meyers, in *The Jacksonian Persuasion* (1957), emphasized the appeal of the Jeffersonian heritage to the Jacksonians. Jackson and his followers looked with mistrust on the new industrial society emerging around them and yearned instead for a restoration of the agrarian, republican virtues of an earlier time. In destroying the Bank, limiting federal economic activities, and emphasizing states' rights, they were attempting to restore a simpler, more decentralized world. Ironically, their actions contributed instead to the expansion of unregulated capitalism.

Lee Benson, in *The Concept of Jacksonian Democracy* (1961), a study of political parties in New York, used new quantitative techniques to challenge virtually all previous interpretations of Jacksonianism. There was no consistent difference—in class, occupation, or region—between the Jacksonians and anti-Jacksonians, Benson argued. Both parties contained big as well as small businessmen, farmers, and city workers. Nor were there any significant ideological differences. Both parties used the same "agrarian" rhetoric; both

were in favor of greater equality of opportunity and greater political democracy. Local and cultural factors—religion and ethnicity, for example—were the crucial determinants of party divisions, not economic interests or ideology. Because the movement toward democracy was much broader than the Democratic party, he suggested, the "Age of Jackson" should be renamed the "Age of Egalitarianism."

More recent historians have continued Benson's de-emphasis of party divisions in the Jacksonian period and have cited instead social and economic developments that transcended partisan concerns. Edward T. Pessen, in *Jacksonian America* (1969), portrayed the mid-nineteenth century as a time of widespread and increasing social and economic inequality and suggested that party divisions did not reflect the broader stratification of American society. Richard McCormick (1966) and Glyndon Van Deusen (1963) similarly emphasized the pragmatism of Jackson and the Democrats and de-emphasized clear ideological or social divisions between the parties.

The new image of Jackson as an opportunistic politician and of party rivalries and government policies as essentially irrelevant to the broader social and economic concerns of the day reflects the political climate of modern America. In an era in which political figures and public institutions have fallen into low regard, historians have begun to question how important or effective such leaders or institutions were in the past. Thus the prevailing contemporary view of the Jacksonian era is that it was indeed a time of expanding political (although not economic) democracy; but that Jackson himself and the Democratic party were at best secondary to that expansion.

roots—who favored a predominantly agrarian economy and opposed the development of powerful economic institutions in their region. Whigs, in short, tended to be wealthier than Democrats, tended to have more aristocratic backgrounds, and tended to be more commercially ambitious.

But party divisions were not always so

simple. For one thing, although Democrats tended to be people of more modest means than the Whigs, they did not include those men and women most conspicuously excluded from economic opportunity. Some of the poorest residents of the Northeast—unskilled laborers, recent Protestant immigrants, and others—gravitated toward the

Whigs. To them, the Democrats, often representatives of the lower middle class that stood one rung above them on the social ladder, were often more menacing and hostile than the Whigs.

Furthermore, Whigs and Democrats alike were more interested in winning elections than in maintaining philosophical purity. And both parties made adjustments from region to region in order to attract the largest possible number of voters, so that often the original ideology of the party appeared to be almost lost. In New York, for example, the Whigs—under the leadership of party boss Thurlow Weed—developed a large popular following by turning the Democrats' own tactics against their opponents. Their vehicle was a movement known as Anti-Masonry. The so-called Anti-Masonic party had emerged in the 1820s in response to widespread resentment against the secret and exclusive, hence supposedly undemocratic, Society of Freemasons. Such resentments rose to new heights when, in 1826, a former Mason, William Morgan, mysteriously disappeared from his home in Batavia, New York, shortly before he was scheduled to publish a book purporting to expose the secrets of Freemasonry. The assumption was widespread that Morgan had been abducted and murdered by the vengeful Masons. Weed and other opponents of Jackson seized on the Anti-Masonic frenzy to launch spirited attacks on Jackson and Van Buren (both members of the Masonic order), implying that the Democrats were connected with the antidemocratic conspiracy. (The excitement soon spread to other states—most notably Pennsylvania; and in 1831, Anti-Masons held a national convention in Harrisburg to nominate a presidential candidate for the next year's campaign.)

By embracing Anti-Masonry, Whigs discovered a vehicle that permitted them to portray themselves to the public as opponents of aristocracy and exclusivity. They were, in other words, attacking the Democrats with the Democrats' own issues. Both parties, therefore, were adopting the rhetoric of democracy and equality; and the specific legislative issues that divided them in their legislative battles were often obscured in actual campaigns.

Religious and ethnic divisions also tended to play an important role in determining the constituencies of the two parties. Irish Catholics, one of the largest of the recent immigrant groups, tended to support the Democrats, who appeared to reflect their own vague cultural aversion to commercial development and entrepreneurial progress. Catholics resented such Whiggish reform movements as temperance and public education, seeing them as attempts to impose Protestant moral standards on them. Evangelical Protestants, by contrast, embraced a religious and cultural outlook that encouraged constant development and improvement; and they tended to look more favorably on the Whigs. In many communities, these and other local ethnic, religious, and cultural tensions were far more influential in determining party alignments than any concrete political or economic proposals.

Party Leadership

If presidential politics were indicative of popular favor, it would be fair to say that the Whigs, in the more than twenty years of their existence as a party, enjoyed relatively little public support. Only in 1840 and 1848 were Whig candidates able to capture the White House, and in each of those elections the winning contestant was a popular military hero. Yet when elections at every level—congressional, state, and local, as well as presidential—are considered, the balance between the two parties appears much more even.

Where the Democrats maintained a consistent edge over the Whig opponents was at the level of national leadership. Throughout the 1830s, the Democratic party was the party of Andrew Jackson—beloved war hero, champion of the people, a political figure of such magnetism that no opponent could hope to match him. The Whigs, on the other hand, rallied behind three national leaders—each a powerful and charismatic figure in his own right, but each, too, a man with significant political limitations. Henry Clay, Daniel Webster, and John C. Calhoun all brought their own formidable constituencies into the Whig coalition. (They all brought, too, their own overweening ambitions for the presidency.) But none was ever able to forge a

Daniel Webster
"The great god Webster," as he was occasionally known, was the most passionately admired public figure of his age. An orator without peer, he sometimes attracted crowds as large as 100,000 people—most of whom, in an age before amplification, presumably could not even hear him. Yet Webster inspired contempt as well as admiration. To many Americans, his shady connections with influential businessmen tarnished his reputation. To others, his unquenchable, unseemly (and ultimately unfulfilled) ambition for the presidency seemed to overshadow all else. To still others, his affection for brandy (and, as a result, his frequent drunkenness) made him a man unfit for higher office. Webster served for eight years in the United States House of Representatives (as a delegate first from New Hampshire and later from Massachusetts); as United States senator from 1827 to 1841 and from 1845 to 1850; and as secretary of state (where, according to many scholars, he attained his greatest distinction) from 1841 to 1843 and from 1850 to 1852. (Library of Congress)

truly national constituency capable of winning a presidential election.

The glamorous Clay, "Harry of the West," won many friends throughout the country through his support for internal improvements and economic development—the so-called American System. But his image as a devious political operator and his regional identification with the West proved an insuperable liability. He ran for president three times and never won. Daniel Webster, the greatest orator of his era, gained fame and respect for his passionate speeches in defense of the Constitution and the Union. Some of his admirers, of whom an inordinate number were wealthy businessmen, considered him a greater man than any president. But Webster's close connection with the Bank of the United States and the protective tariff, his reliance on rich men for financial support, and his unfortunate and often embarrassing affinity for brandy—all prevented him from developing enough of a national constituency to win him the office he so desperately wanted.

John C. Calhoun, the third member of what became known as the Great Triumvirate, was equally controversial. He never considered himself a true Whig, and his

identification with the nullification controversy in effect disqualified him from national leadership in any case. Yet he sided with Clay and Webster on the issue of the national bank. And he shared with them an abiding animosity toward Andrew Jackson. Calhoun did not embrace the belief of most Southern Whigs in the importance of commercial development. He did, however, produce reasons of his own for advocating an alliance between the upper classes of the two regions. In his *South Carolina Exposition and Protest* (1828) and later writings, he presented a critique of modern capitalism that in its frank predictions of class struggle augured much of what Karl Marx and Friedrich Engels would say in later decades. Capitalist society would, he predicted, inevitably become divided into two classes: "capitalists" and "operatives." The former, he argued, would expropriate and impoverish the latter; and unless steps were taken to prevent it, a revolutionary struggle would ensue. "There is and always has been in an advanced stage of wealth and civilization," he insisted in 1837, "a conflict between labor and capital." Northern businessmen had a common interest with Southern planters, therefore, in working to prevent the revolutionary danger by protecting their positions against threats from below. (Such views found scant sympathy among Northern Whigs. Webster, for example, admitted that "in the old countries of Europe there is a clear and well-defined line between capital and labor," but he declared that there was no line so "broad, marked, and visible" in the United States.)

The Whigs, in other words, were able to marshal an imposing array of national leaders, each with his own powerful constituency. For many years, however, they were unable to find a way to merge those constituencies into a single winning combination. The result was that the Democrats for a time, as in the election of 1836, appeared far more dominant than they actually were.

The Crowded Campaign of 1836

The importance of incumbency in the age of party politics became abundantly clear in 1836. Despite the growing power of the Whigs, Jackson and the Democrats continued to control federal appointments and contracts; and they made liberal use of their patronage powers to bolster the fortunes of their candidates. The party also benefited from Jackson's continuing popularity and from its elaborate party organization. With little debate, the party convention nominated Jackson's personal favorite, Martin Van Buren, as its candidate for president.

The Whigs in 1836 could boast no such unity and discipline. Indeed, they could not even agree on a single candidate. Their strategy, masterminded by Biddle, was to run several candidates, each of them supposedly strong in part of the country. Webster was the man for New England, and Hugh Lawson White of Tennessee was to seek the votes of the South. The former Indian fighter and hero of the War of 1812 from Ohio, William Henry Harrison, was counted on in the middle states and in the West. As Biddle advised: "This disease is to be treated as a local disorder—apply local remedies—if General Harrison will run better than anybody else in Pennsylvania, by all means unite upon him." None of the three candidates could expect to get a majority in the electoral college, but

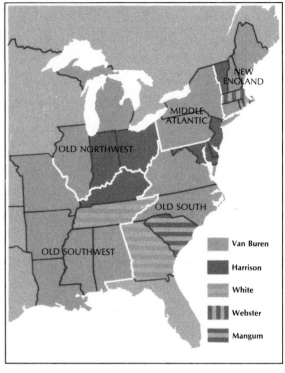

Van Buren

Harrison

White

Webster

Mangum

THE ELECTION OF 1836

separately they might draw enough votes from Van Buren to prevent his getting a majority. The election would then devolve, as in 1824–1825, upon the House of Representatives, where conceivably the Whigs might be able to elect one of their men. But the three Whigs proved to be no match for the one Democrat. When the returns were in, Van Buren had 170 electoral votes to 124 for all his opponents.

Economic Dilemmas

At the time of the election of 1836, a nationwide boom was reaching its height. Canal enterprisers and railroad builders were at a peak of activity. Prices were rising as people indulged in an orgy of spending and speculating. Money was plentiful—most of it manufactured by the banks, which multiplied their loans and notes with little regard to their reserves of cash. By 1837 bank loans outstanding amounted to five times as much as in 1830. Never had the nation seemed so prosperous.

Land as usual was a favorite target of speculation, especially the land sold by the federal government. After the act of 1821 had abolished installment buying and set the minimum price at $1.25 an acre, sales of public lands reached an average of 300,000 to 400,000 acres a year in the late 1820s and early 1830s. Then the business suddenly boomed. Between 1835 and 1837 nearly 40 million acres were disposed of, and the expression "doing a land-office business" came into use to describe fast selling of any kind. Nearly three-fourths of the land being sold went to speculators—men acquiring large tracts in the hope of reselling at a profit—and only about a fourth of it to actual settlers. Speculators generally borrowed from the banks to make payment at the land offices.

For the time being the government profited. Receipts from land sales, which had averaged less than $2.4 million annually for the ten years preceding 1835, rose to more than $24 million in 1836. Land sales were the government's largest source of revenue, but customs duties under the compromise tariff of 1833 added considerably to total income. The government received more money than it paid out. Steadily the national debt was reduced, as Jackson insisted it should be, and finally, from 1835 to 1837, the government for the first and only time in its history was out of debt. Not only that; there was also a large and growing surplus in the treasury.

The question for Congress and the administration was how to get rid of the treasury surplus. Tampering with the tariff was not to be considered, since the recent compromise had put to rest that touchy subject, and few wanted to reopen it.

Why not give the federal surplus to the states? This would be an effective way of getting rid of it, and the idea appealed to Congress. In 1836, Congress passed and Jackson signed a distribution act providing that the surplus accumulated by the end of the year (estimated at $40 million) be paid to the states in four quarterly installments as a loan

without security or interest; each state getting a share proportional to its representation in Congress. No one seriously expected the "loan" to be repaid. As the states began to receive their shares, they promptly spent the money, mainly to encourage the construction of highways, railroads, and canals. The distribution of the surplus thus gave further stimulus to the economic boom. At the same time the withdrawal of federal funds strained the "pet banks," for they had to call in a large part of their own loans in order to make the transfer of funds to the state governments.

Congress did nothing to check the speculative fever, with which many congressmen themselves were badly infected, Webster for one buying up thousands of acres in the West. But the president was much concerned. Though money continued to pour into the treasury from the land offices, most of it was money of dubious value. The government was selling good land and was receiving in return a miscellaneous collection of state bank notes, none of them worth any more than the credit of the issuing bank. Jackson finally decided to act. He issued his Specie Circular (1836), announcing that in the future only hard money or the notes of specie-paying banks would be accepted in payment for public lands.

Van Buren had been president less than three months when panic struck. The banks of New York, followed by those of the rest of the country, suddenly suspended specie payments (that is, they stopped paying cash on demand for their bank notes and other obligations). During the next few years, hundreds of banks failed, and so did hundreds of other business firms. As unemployment grew, bread riots occurred in some of the larger cities. Prices fell, especially the price of land. Webster was only one of a great many who all at once found themselves "land-poor." Many railroad and canal schemes were abandoned; several of the debt-burdened state governments ceased to pay interest on their bonds, and a few repudiated their debts, at least temporarily. The depression, the worst the American people had ever experienced, lasted for five years.

The Whigs blamed Jackson for the depression. It had come, they said, because of his destruction of the national bank and his mismanagement of public finance. But they were also in part to blame. The distribution of the treasury surplus was a Whig measure, though Jackson signed it. (With the onset of the panic, the distribution was halted before the entire surplus had been transferred to the states.) This step, by weakening the pet banks, helped to bring on the crash. So did Jackson's Specie Circular, which started a general run on the banks as land buyers rushed to get cash in return for bank notes to make land-office payments. Distribution of the surplus and the Specie Circular only precipitated the depression, however; they did not cause it.

While the Bank of the United States, if continued, could have lessened the overexpansion of credit, a period of financial stringency doubtless would have come sooner or later. For the depression was international, affecting England and Western Europe as well. As English investors faced a financial crisis at home, they began to withdraw funds from America, thus accounting for part of the strain on American banks. A succession of crop failures on American farms not only reduced the purchasing power of farmers but also necessitated imports of foodstuffs; to pay for these imports, additional money was drawn out of the country.

Besides its economic consequences, the Panic of 1837 had other significant results. Hard times increased social, sectional, and economic tensions. Want in the cities heightened the feeling that there existed even in America a real and dangerous class conflict. Heavy losses suffered by Southern planters confirmed them in their conviction that national policies worked to their disadvantage, while the decline of business profits in the North intensified the belief of manufacturers that the compromise of 1833 must be undone and the tariff raised. Defaults on interest payments and outright repudiation of state bonds, many of them held by Englishmen, added to difficulties in the relations between the United States and Great Britain. Distress among the people was turned into dissatisfaction with the administration, so that the predominance of the Democrats was brought temporarily to an end after Van Buren had served but a single term.

The Van Buren Program

The modern concept that government can successfully fight depressions, and has an obligation to do so, did not exist in Van Buren's time. The only tradition of government intervention in economic matters was the Federalist-National Republican-Whig program of aid to business, to which Democrats were fiercely opposed. Consequently, Van Buren recommended but few direct antidepression measures. He advised Congress to authorize the borrowing of $10 million to meet expenses during the emergency, and Congress did so. He also urged that the government accept only specie for taxes and other due payments, a policy that would not raise either prices or confidence in the banking system.

In formulating a program of permanent legislation, the administration clearly reflected the wishes of the dominant farmer-labor segment of the party. The president urged Congress to reduce the price of public lands, and he recommended passage of a general preemption bill giving settlers the right to buy 160 acres at a set minimum price before land in any particular area was opened for public sale. A bill graduating land prices downward passed the Senate three times but was blocked in the House. A similar fate befell the preemption bill. Stymied by legislative opposition, Van Buren resorted to executive action to please his urban followers. By presidential order he established a ten-hour work day on all federal works. For the first time in the nation's history the government thus took direct action to aid the rising labor class.

The most important measure in the president's program, and the most controversial, was his proposal for a new fiscal system. With the Bank of the United States destroyed and with Jackson's expedient of "pet banks" discredited, some kind of new system was urgently needed. Van Buren's fiscal ideas demonstrated both his mental ingenuity and his commitment to Democratic principles. The plan he suggested, known as the "Independent Treasury" or "Subtreasury" system, was simplicity itself. Government funds would be placed in an independent treasury at Washington and in subtreasuries in specified cities throughout the country. Whenever the government had to pay out money, its own agents would handle the funds. No bank or banks would have the government's money or name to use as a basis for speculation. The government and the banks would be "divorced."

Van Buren placed the Independent Treasury proposal before Congress in a special session he called in 1837. It encountered the immediate and bitter opposition of most Whigs and of many conservative Democrats. Twice a bill to establish an independent treasury passed the Senate only to fail in the House. Not until 1840, the last year of Van Buren's presidency, did the administration succeed in driving the measure through both houses of Congress.

The Log Cabin Campaign

As the campaign of 1840 approached, the Whigs scented victory. The effects of the depression still gripped the country, and the Democrats, the party in power, were thus vulnerable to attack. The Whigs, who now realized that a party representing the upper-income groups must, if it expected to win, pose as a party of the people.

The Whigs also realized that they would have to achieve more unity and a stronger organization than they had demonstrated in 1836. They would have to settle on one candidate who could appeal to all segments of the party and to all sections of the country. Obviously the easiest way to coordinate the party was through the new mechanism of the national nominating convention, already used by the Democrats. Accordingly the Whigs held their first convention in Harrisburg, Pennsylvania, in December 1839. Their

veteran leader, Henry Clay, "Mr. Whig," expected the nomination, but the party bosses decided otherwise. Clay had too definite a record; he had been defeated too many times; he had too many enemies. Passing him over, the convention nominated William Henry Harrison of Ohio, and for vice president, John Tyler of Virginia.

William Henry Harrison was a descendant of the Virginia aristocracy, but he had spent all his adult life in the Northwest, where he first went as a young army officer in General Wayne's campaign against the Indians. Although he had little governmental experience, he was a renowned Indian fighter (like Jackson) and a popular national figure.

The Democrats, meeting in national convention at Baltimore, nominated Van Buren, pointed proudly to their record, especially the Independent Treasury, and condemned all the works of the Whigs, especially the Bank of the United States. Demonstrating that their party was, in some respects, no more united than the Whigs, the Democrats failed to nominate a vice-presidential candidate, declaring vaguely that they would leave the choice of that office to the wisdom of the voters.

The campaign of 1840 displayed in full the effects of an established party system on American politics and, in so doing, established a new pattern for presidential contests. The Whigs—who had emerged as a party largely because of their opposition to Andrew Jackson's common-man democracy, who in most regions represented the more substantial elements of the population, who stood for government policies that would aid businessmen—were in the 1840 campaign almost indistinguishable from their opponents. Democrats and Whigs used the same techniques of mass voter appeal; the same evocation of simple, rustic values; the same identification with the common people. What mattered now was not the philosophical purity of the party but its ability to win votes.

Thus it was that the eager Whigs depicted themselves as the party of the people, the party able to save the nation from depression; and thus it was that they turned on Martin Van Buren the same tactics that the

Whig Broadside of 1840
This Whig campaign document depicts the principal episodes in the career of General Harrison—from his humble log-cabin beginnings to fame as soldier and statesman.
(Library of Congress)

Democrats had so often turned on them: accusing the president of being an aloof aristocrat who used cologne, drank champagne, ate off gold plates, and otherwise engaged in undemocratic and un-American practices. In retaliation, a Democratic newspaper unwisely sneered that Harrison was a simple soul who would be glad to retire to a log cabin if provided with a pension and plenty of hard cider. In a country where many people lived or had lived in log cabins, this was an unwise line of attack; and the Whigs took full advantage. Yes, their candidate was a simple man of the people, they proclaimed, and he loved log cabins and cider. (Actually he was a man of substance and lived in a large and well-appointed house).

Thereafter the log cabin was an established symbol at every Whig meeting, and hard cider an established beverage. Against such techniques and the lingering effects of the depression the Democrats could not avail. When the votes were counted in November, Harrison had 234 electoral votes to 60 for Van Buren. But the Whig victory was not so sweeping as it seemed; of the popular vote, Harrison had 1,275,000 to Van Buren's 1,129,000, a majority of less than 150,000.

The Frustration of the Whigs

Despite their decisive victory, the Whigs were to find the next four years frustrating and divisive ones. In large part, that was because their appealing new president, "Old Tippecanoe," William Henry Harrison, never had a chance to demonstrate what sort of leader he might become. Sixty-eight years old in 1841, he had appeared to be in good health. But the strain of the campaign, of the inauguration (after which he rode bareheaded through the streets of Washington to the White House in bitter cold), and of the pressing demands of grasping job seekers apparently became too much for him. Shortly after taking office, he contracted a cold. It soon turned into pneumonia; and Harrison died on April 4, 1841, exactly one month after he had been inaugurated.

Harrison was the first president to die in office, and there was momentary uncertainty as to what should happen next. The Constitution clearly stated that the "Powers and Duties" of the highest office would "devolve on the Vice President" in the event of a president's death. But there were some who believed that the "Powers and Duties" were not the same thing as the office, that the vice president could only become an "acting president," that his authority might in some way be compromised. This potentially critical constitutional problem was resolved by Vice President Tyler, who calmly took the oath of office as president and left no doubt that he considered himself a legitimate chief executive. The question of the status of a vice president who succeeded to the presidency was never raised again.

More troubling to the leaders of the Whig party than such constitutional questions was that with Harrison gone, control of government had fallen to a man with whom they had much weaker ties. Harrison in his brief weeks in office had generally deferred to Henry Clay and Daniel Webster, confirming the predictions of those who had foretold that the Whig chieftains would be the real powers in government. Webster had become secretary of state. Four of Clay's friends had taken other positions in the cabinet. Under Tyler, things were to change.

Tyler was a member of an aristocratic Virginia family. Originally a Democrat, he had left the party in reaction to what he considered Jackson's excessively egalitarian program and his imperious methods. One reason the Whigs had included him on their ticket was to attract the votes of similarly disenchanted conservative Democrats. But while Tyler had certain attitudes in common with the Whig leadership, there were still signs of his Democratic past in his approach to public policy. Clay apparently had the impression that the new president would support the restoration of a national bank and other Whig projects, but Tyler soon indicated otherwise. A break occurred between the president and Clay that was never to heal.

There were, to be sure, some elements of Clay's ambitious program that Tyler was willing to accept. He signed a bill abolishing the Independent Treasury system. He agreed to a raising of tariff rates to nearly the same level as 1832 (although he displayed little enthusiasm for the proposal). And he approved a measure—the Preemption Act of 1841—designed to increase the appeal of the Whigs to Western settlers and farmers. The bill made it possible for settlers to claim up to 160 acres of undeveloped land before the land was officially offered for sale by the government, and to pay for this acreage later at $1.25 an acre. This "log cabin bill," as the Whigs called it, was promoted as a measure to relieve the suffering of the depression and to prove the party's devotion to the welfare of the common man.

But the heart of the Whig program—the creation of a national financial system similar to the Bank of the United States—met a different fate. Tyler favored a national bank, but one very different from that proposed by Clay. His was to be a "states'-rights national bank," one that would confine its operations to the District of Columbia and establish branches in the states only with the consent of those states. Twice he vetoed bills that would have set up what the Whigs tried to disguise as a "fiscal corporation."

Lacking a sufficient majority to override the veto, the Whigs fumed with rage at the president, who added to their anger by vetoing a number of internal improvement bills. In an unprecedented action, a conference of congressional Whigs read Tyler out of the party. All the cabinet members resigned except Webster. To fill their places, the president appointed five men of his own stripe—former Democrats.

A portentous new political alignment was taking shape. Tyler and a small band of conservative Southern Whigs who followed him were getting ready to rejoin the Democrats. When the office of secretary of state became vacant in 1844, Tyler appointed John C. Calhoun, who had left the Democratic party in the 1830s and had since rejoined it. Into the common man's party of Jackson and Van Buren came a group of men who had aristocratic ideas about government, who thought that government had an obligation to protect and even expand the institution of slavery, and who believed in states' rights with a single-minded, almost fanatical devotion.

Webster's Diplomacy

Starting in the late 1830s, a series of incidents brought Great Britain and the United States to the brink of war. In 1837, rebellion broke out in the eastern provinces of Canada, and many Americans applauded the rebels and furnished them with material aid. The rebels chartered a small American steamship, the *Caroline*, to carry supplies across the Niagara River from New York. One night while the ship was moored at a wharf on the American side, the Canadian authorities sent over a force that took possession of the *Caroline* and burned it; in the melee one American was killed. Excitement flared on both sides of the border. President Van Buren issued a proclamation asking Americans to abide by the neutrality laws, and he sent General Winfield Scott to the border to act as a pacifier. The State Department demanded an apology and reparations from Great Britain, but the British government neither disavowed the attack nor offered compensation for it.

While the *Caroline* affair simmered, the troublesome issue of the Maine boundary arose. As defined by the Treaty of 1783, this line was impossible to locate. Previous attempts to fix it by mutual agreement and by arbitration had failed. In 1838, Americans and Canadians, mostly lumberjacks, began to move into the Aroostook River region in the disputed area. A head-smashing brawl between the two parties—the "Aroostook War"—threatened more trouble between England and America.

Soon a Canadian named Alexander McLeod was arrested in New York and charged with the murder of the American who had died in the *Caroline* incident. The British government reacted with majestic rage, contending that McLeod could not be accused of murder because he had acted under official orders. The foreign secretary, the bellicose Lord Palmerston, demanded McLeod's release and threatened that his execution would bring "immediate and frightful" war. Webster as secretary of state did not think McLeod was worth a war but could do nothing to release him. The prisoner was under New York jurisdiction and had to be tried in the state courts, a peculiarity of American jurisprudence that the British did not seem to understand. Fortunately for the cause of peace—and for himself—McLeod was acquitted.

Festering points of disagreement still remained. In an attempt to stamp out the African slave trade, Great Britain was asking for the right to search American merchant ships suspected of carrying black cargoes. Since the American government, sensitive on the matter of search, had always refused the British request, slavers of other nations frequently sought to avoid capture by hoisting the American flag. Complicating the issue was the domestic slave trade, in which slaves were carried by sea from one American port to another. Sometimes the ships in this trade were blown off their course to the British West Indies, where the authorities, acting under English law, freed the slaves. In 1841, an American brig, the *Creole*, sailed from Virginia for New Orleans with more than a hundred slaves aboard. En route the slaves mutinied, took possession of the ship, and took it to the Bahamas. Here British officials declared the bondsmen free. Although Webster protested, England refused to return the slaves. Many Americans, especially Southerners, were infuriated.

At this critical juncture a new government came to power in Great Britain, one that was more disposed to conciliate the United States and to settle the outstanding differences between the two countries. The new ministry sent to America an emissary, Lord Ashburton, to negotiate an agreement on the Maine boundary and other matters. Ashburton liked Americans, and Webster admired the English. To avoid war, both were willing to compromise. The result of their deliberations was the Webster-Ashburton Treaty of August 9, 1842.

By the terms of this arrangement, the United States received about seven-twelfths of the disputed area. Minor rectifications were made in other areas, and the boundary was now established as far west as the Rocky Mountains. It was agreed that both Great Britain and the United States would maintain naval squadrons off the African coast, the American ships being charged with chasing slavers using the American flag.

Through exchanges of notes that were not part of the treaty, Webster and Ashburton also eased the memory of the *Caroline* and *Creole* affairs. Ashburton expressed "regret" for the raid on the *Caroline*, and he pledged that in the future there would be no "officious interference" with American ships forced by "violence or accident" to enter British ports.

Webster used secret funds to inspire newspaper propaganda favorable to his arrangements with Ashburton, and the treaty proved quite popular. War talk was forgotten for a time, as Anglo-American relations suddenly looked better than they had for many years.

During the Tyler administration, the United States established diplomatic relations with China. In 1842, Britain forced China to open certain ports to foreign trade. Eager to share the new privileges, American mercantile interests persuaded Tyler and Congress to send a commissioner to China to negotiate a trade treaty. Webster wrote the instructions for the first commissioner, Caleb Cushing. In the Treaty of Wanghia, concluded in 1844, Cushing secured most-favored-nation provisions giving Americans the same privileges as Englishmen. In the next ten years American trade with China steadily increased.

In their diplomatic efforts, at least, the Whigs were able to secure some important successes. But by the end of the Tyler administration, the party could look back on few other victories. Having elected a president in 1840, they had watched as the administration moved steadily toward the Democrats. And in 1844, they lost even nominal control of the White House. They were to win only one more national election in their history—in 1848—before a great sectional crisis arose that would shatter their party and, for a time, the Union.

SUGGESTED READINGS

Alexis de Tocqueville provided the finest analysis of the social and political climate in Jacksonian America, and one of the greatest of all analyses of American life, in *Democracy in America,* 2 vols. (1835), initially published in French, but available in many later, English editions. Moisie Ostrogorskii, *Democracy and the Organization of Political Parties,* 2 vols. (1902), is another classic study of Democratic trends in the era. Chilton Williamson, *American Suffrage from Property to Democracy, 1760–1860* (1960), is an important study of the expansion of the franchise; while Louis Hartz, *The Liberal Tradition in America* (1955), includes observations about the intellectual climate of the time. Marvin E. Gettleman, *The Dorr Rebellion* (1973), and Patrick T. Conley, *Democracy in Decline* (1977), offer contrasting views of democratic controversies in Rhode Island. Edward Pessen, *Riches, Class, and Power Before the Civil War* (1973), offers observations about the distribution of wealth and power in the Jacksonian period. Douglas T. Miller, *Jacksonian Aristocracy* (1967), is a case study of social stratification in New York. Lee Benson, *The Concept of Jacksonian Democracy* (1961), also examines New York, using quantitative methods to reveal the nature of political alignments in the state.

Surveys of the Jacksonian era emphasizing political developments include Glyndon Van Deusen, *The Jacksonian Era* (1959); Charles M. Wiltse, *The New Nation* (1961); James C. Curtis, *Andrew Jackson and the Search for Vindication* (1976); and Edward Pessen, *Jacksonian America,* rev. ed. (1979). Important works attempting to explain the meaning of "Jacksonian Democracy" abound. One of the most influential is Arthur M. Schlesinger, Jr., *The Age of Jackson* (1945). Marvin Meyers, *The Jacksonian Persuasion* (1960), stresses ideology. Richard Hofstadter's important essay on Jackson in *The American Political Tradition* (1948) was especially influential in shaping later views of Jacksonianism, as was John William Ward, *Andrew Jackson: Symbol for an Age* (1955).

The leading modern biographer of Jackson is Robert V. Remini, author of *Andrew Jackson and the Course of American Empire: 1767–1821* (1977), and *Andrew Jackson and the Course of American Freedom: 1822–1832* (1981). Remini has also written a briefer study, *Andrew Jackson* (1966). Marquis James, *Andrew Jackson,* 2 vols. (1933–1937), is an earlier major biography, which in turn succeeded James Parton, *Life of Andrew Jackson,* 3 vols. (1860), the first major study. More specialized studies of the Jackson administration include Leonard White, *The Jacksonians: A Study in Administrative History* (1954), and Richard B. Latner, *The Presidency of Andrew Jackson: White House Politics, 1829–1837* (1979). Party politics in the Jacksonian era is the subject of Richard B. McCormick, *The Second American Party System: Party Formation in the Jacksonian Era* (1966), and Ronald P. Formisano, *The*

Birth of Mass Political Parties: Michigan, 1827–1861 (1971).

The nullification crisis is vividly recounted by William V. Freehling in *Prelude to Civil War: The Nullification Controversy in South Carolina* (1966). A broader study is Charles S. Sydnor, *The Development of Southern Sectionalism 1819–1848* (1948). The Indian policies of the Jackson years are examined in R. N. Satz, *American Indian Policy in the Jacksonian Era* (1975). A controversial analysis of Jackson's attitudes and behavior toward Indians, using psychohistorical methods, is Michael Rogin, *Fathers and Children: Andrew Jackson and the Destruction of American Indians* (1975). Angie Debo, *A History of the Indians of the United States* (1970), and Wilcomb E. Washburn, *The Indian in America* (1975), are general studies containing observations about the Jackson years, as is William Brandon, *The Last Americans* (1974). B. W. Sheehan, *Seeds of Extinction: Jeffersonian Philanthropy and the American Indian* (1973), provides background for later Indian policies; while F. P. Prucha, *American Indian Policy in the Formative Years* (1962), examines the policies themselves. Two additional works by Angie Debo—*The Road to Disappearance: A History of the Creek Indians* (1941) and *And Still the Waters Run: The Betrayal of the Five Civilized Tribes* (1973)—provide detailed analyses of the effects of white policies on Indians. Cecil Elby, "*That Disgraceful Affair*" (1973), is a history of the Black Hawk War.

Robert V. Remini, *Andrew Jackson and the Bank War* (1967), is a good account of the political aspects of the controversy over the Bank of the United States; while Bray Hammond, *Banks and Politics in America from the Revolution to the Civil War* (1957), is an important study of some of the economic aspects. Peter Temin, *The Jacksonian Economy* (1969), and J. M. McFaul, *The Politics of Jacksonian Finance* (1972), provide background to the controversy. William G. Shade, *Banks or No Banks: The Money Issue in Western Politics, 1832–1865* (1972), provides a regional perspective. J. A. Wilburn, *Biddle's Bank* (1967), examines public support for the Bank of the United States; and T. P. Govan, *Nicholas Biddle; Nationalist and Public Banker* (1959), makes a case for its subject. Reginald C. McGrane, *The Panic of 1837* (1924), studies the aftermath of the "Bank War"; and J. R. Sharp, *The Jacksonians Versus the Banks* (1970), looks at state banks after the panic. C. B. Swisher, *Roger B. Taney* (1936), is a good biography of Jackson's secretary of the treasury and, later, chief justice of the Supreme Court. Morton Horwitz, *The Transformation of American Law, 1780–1860* (1977), is an important study of the role of courts and the legal process in nineteenth-century America, with particular emphasis on the Jackson period and the period immediately following it. Two useful works on Van Buren and his administration are Robert V. Remini, *Martin Van*

Buren and the Making of the Democratic Party (1959), and James C. Curtis, *The Fox at Bay; Martin Van Buren and the Presidency* (1970).

In addition to the works by McCormick and Van Deusen cited above, there are several works that give specific attention to the rise of the Whig party. Still the most thorough account is E. M. Carroll, *Origins of the Whig Party* (1925). Daniel Walker Howe, *The Political Culture of the American Whigs* (1979), examines party ideology. Daniel Webster has been the subject of several major biographies: Claude M. Fuess, *Daniel Webster*, 2 vols. (1930); Richard N. Current, *Daniel Webster and the Rise of National Conservatism* (1955); and Irving Bartlett, *Daniel Webster* (1978). Other studies of Webster include Norman D. Brown, *Daniel Webster and the Politics of Availability* (1969); Sydney Nathans, *Daniel Webster and Jacksonian Democracy* (1973); and Robert Dalzell, *Daniel Webster and the Trial of American Nationalism* (1973). On Henry Clay, in addition to the Van Deusen biography mentioned above, see Clement Eaton, *Henry Clay and the Art of American Politics* (1957); and George R. Poage, *Henry Clay and the Whig Party* (1936). Thomas H. O'Connor, *Lords of the Loom: The Cotton Whigs and the Coming of the Civil War* (1968), follows the party into its last days. Oscar D. Lambert, *Presidential Politics in the United States, 1841–1844* (1936), examines the Tyler administration, R. G. Gunderson, *The Log Cabin Campaign* (1957), is a study of the contest that put the Whigs in power. Oliver P. Chitwood, *John Tyler: Champion of the Old South* (1939), examines Tyler himself. On Whig foreign policy, see Howard Jones, *To the Webster-Ashburton Treaty* (1977); A. B. Corey, *The Crisis of 1830–1842 in Canadian–American Relations* (1941); and John B. Brebner, *North Atlantic Triangle* (1945).

North and South: Diverging Ways

11

A Cotton Plantation on the Mississippi
This 1883 print (by the famous nineteenth-century printmakers Currier and Ives) depicts a scene that was representative of the economy of much of the antebellum South. The great cotton plantations, manned by crews of black slaves and serviced by Mississippi River boats, were the backbone of the Southern economy. And because the cotton they produced was the raw material for Northern textile mills, they contributed to the economy of the rest of the nation as well.
(Culver Pictures)

Americans in the mid-nineteenth century liked to believe that theirs was a nation specially ordained by God, that their Union represented a beacon of liberty and stability that would serve as a model to the rest of the world. In fact, however, the United States in these years was in many respects not truly a nation at all—at least not in the way nations would be defined in later times. It was, rather, a highly decentralized confederation of states, many of which had little in common with one another. And those states remained together in part because the union was so loose, and the central authority of the nation so weak, that the differences among them did not often have to be confronted.

When the United States began to move in the direction of greater national unity, as it did in the 1840s, it encountered a series of major obstacles. And one obstacle, in particular, became so powerful that it soon threatened to tear the nation apart: sectionalism. The rivalry of one part of the country with another was not, of course, new to the mid-nineteenth century. There had been sectional differences as early as the seventeenth century among the colonies of the South, the mid-Atlantic, and New England. By the 1840s and 1850s, however, sectionalism had changed both in its nature and in its intensity. In one sense, there were now three distinct regions: the Northeast, the Northwest, and the South, each with its own economy and its own social system. But in other senses, there were only two: the North and the South, developing in markedly different ways and finding themselves increasingly in conflict.

The most obvious aspect of this division was a basic difference in the labor systems of the sections. The South was not only maintaining but, as its plantation economy expanded into new areas of the Southwest, intensifying its commitment to slavery as its primary source of labor. The Northeast and the Northwest were committed to a free-labor economy. But slavery was only a part of a much larger difference between the sections. In the North was developing a modern, diversified economy, with an important manufacturing sector, a flourishing commercial life, and an expanding range of urban services and activities. Between the North and the Northwest, moreover, were developing close economic and cultural ties. And the South, as a result, was becoming—or at least sensed itself becoming—isolated, left behind. Increasingly dependent on the North for manufactured goods, for commercial services, for many of the most basic necessities of life; increasingly cut off from the flourishing agricultural regions of the Northwest; increasingly committed to a way of life that much of the rest of the nation considered obsolete, the South was coming to seem a colonial appendage of the powerful regions to the north. In the 1840s and 1850s, this schism between Northern and Southern societies would produce tensions and conflicts that would contribute, finally, to the disruption of the Union.

THE DEVELOPING NORTH

The most conspicuous change in American life in the 1840s and 1850s was the rapid development of the economy and society of the North. Industrialization, which had begun slowly in the years immediately following the War of 1812 and had gathered force in the 1820s and 1830s, now burst forth as a major factor in the Northern economy.

Urban centers, in the past relatively few and relatively small, now grew rapidly. Class divisions—between the new industrial capitalists and financiers on the one hand and the new industrial work force on the other—became more pronounced. The North, and with it in many ways its new economic ally the Northwest, was developing a complex, modern society, one that would greatly increase the differences that had always existed between that region and the South.

Northeastern Industry

Between 1840 and 1860, American industry experienced a steady and, in some fields, a spectacular growth. In 1840, the total value of manufactured goods produced in the United States stood at $483 million; ten years later the figure had climbed to over $1 billion; and in 1860 it reached close to $2 billion. For the first time, the value of manufactured goods was approximately equal to that of agricultural products.

Industrial growth was greatest in the states of the Northeast. Most conspicuous in this part of the country were the change from domestic or household manufactures to the factory system, the shift of economic power from merchant capitalism to industrial capitalism, the spread of the corporate organization in business, and other innovations that heralded the coming of modern America. Of the approximately 140,000 manufacturing establishments in the country in 1860, 74,000 were located in the Northeast; they represented well over half the total national investment in manufactures, and the annual value of their products was two-thirds of the national figure. Of the 1,311,000 workers in the entire country, about 938,000 were employed in the mills and factories of New England and the middle states.

But even the most highly developed industries still showed qualities of immaturity and were far from the production levels they would attain after 1865. The cotton manufacturers, for example, concentrated on producing goods of coarse grade, making little attempt to turn out fine items, which continued to be imported from England. A similar situation existed in the woolens industry, which because of a short American supply of raw wool could not meet even the domestic demand for coarse goods. As yet, American industry, which exported little, was unable to satisfy fully the wants of American consumers.

Technology and industrial ingenuity were, however, preparing the way for future American industrial supremacy. The machine tools used in the factories of the Northeast, such as the turret lathe, the grinding machine, and the universal milling machine, were better than those in European factories. The principle of interchangeable parts, applied earlier in gun factories by Eli Whitney and Simeon North, was being introduced into other lines of manufacturing. Coal was replacing wood as an industrial fuel, particularly in the smelting of iron. Coal was also being used in increasing amounts to generate power in the steam engines that were replacing the water power that had driven most of the factory machinery in the Northeast. The production of coal, most of it mined in the Pittsburgh area of western Pennsylvania, leaped from 50,000 tons in 1820 to 14 million tons in 1860.

The great technical advances in American industry owed much to American inventors. The patent records reveal the growth of Yankee ingenuity. In 1830, the number of inventions patented was 544; in 1850, the figure rose to 993; and in 1860, it stood at 4,778. In 1839, Charles Goodyear, a New England hardware merchant, discovered a method of vulcanizing rubber; his process had been put to 500 uses by 1860, and the rubber industry was firmly established. In 1846, Elias Howe of Massachusetts constructed a sewing machine. Improvements on it were made by Isaac Singer; and the Howe-Singer machine was soon employed in the manufacture of ready-to-wear clothing. A little later, during the Civil War, it would supply the Northern troops with uniforms.

In an earlier period, the dominant economic figure in the Northeast had been the merchant capitalist—the man who engaged in foreign or domestic trade, who invested his surplus capital in banks, and who sometimes financed small-scale domestic manu-

The Clipper Ship *Three Brothers*
The 328-foot, 2,972-ton clipper *Three Brothers* was the largest sailing ship in the world when it was built. But it was only one of many of these swift, spectacular vessels, which enabled American trade to expand into the far corners of the world in the mid-nineteenth century. The clipper ships not only made traditional trade routes to Europe more attractive; they made it possible for American traders to begin to penetrate the Orient. (Library of Congress)

facturers. And in the 1840s, the merchant capitalists remained figures of importance. In such cities as New York, Philadelphia, and Boston, there were important and influential mercantile groups that operated shipping lines to Southern ports—carrying away cotton, rice, and sugar—or dispatched fleets of trading vessels to the ports of Europe and the Orient. Many of these vessels were the famous clippers, the most beautiful and fastest sailing ships afloat. In their heyday in the late forties and early fifties, the clippers were capable of averaging 300 miles a day, which compared favorably with the best time then being made by steamships. Nevertheless, merchant capitalism was entering a state of decline by the middle of the century. Although the value of American exports, almost entirely agricultural in nature, increased from $124 million in 1840 to $334

million in 1860, American merchants in the 1850s saw much of their carrying trade fall into the hands of British competitors, who enjoyed the advantages of steam-driven iron ships and government subsidies.

It was not foreign rivalry, however, that caused the decline of the merchant capitalist, but rather the rise of the factory system in the United States. The merchants saw greater opportunities for profit in manufactures than in trade. They shifted their capital from mercantile investments to industry, becoming owners and operators of factories or placing their money in companies operated by others. Indeed, one reason that industries developed soonest in the East was that the merchant class had the money and the will to finance them.

Many business concerns were owned by one man, by a family, or by partners. But, particularly in the textile industry, the corporate form of organization spread rapidly. In their overseas ventures the merchants had been accustomed to diversifying their risks by buying shares in a number of vessels and voyages. They employed the same device when they moved their capital from trade to manufacturing, purchasing shares in several textile companies.

Regardless of the forms of business organization, the industrial capitalists became the ruling class, the aristocrats of the Northeast. As they had sought and secured economic dominance, they reached for and grasped political influence. In politics, local or national, they liked to be represented by highly literate lawyers who could articulate their prejudices and philosophy. Their ideal of a representative was Daniel Webster of Massachusetts, whom the businessmen of the section, at considerable financial cost to themselves, supported for years in the United States Senate.

Northeastern Agriculture

The story of agriculture in the Northeast after 1840 is largely one of economic deterioration. The reason for the worsening situation is simple: the farmers of this section could not produce crops in competition with the new and richer soil of the Northwest. Eastern farmers turned, therefore, to a system of production that aimed at a rude self-sufficiency or to the cultivation of products that would not suffer from Western competition. Many went West and took up new farms or moved to mill towns and became laborers. As a result, the rural population in many parts of the Northeast continued to decline.

The centers of production shifted westward for wheat, corn, grapes, cattle, sheep, and hogs. In 1840, the leading wheat-growing states were New York, Pennsylvania, Ohio, and Virginia; in 1860, they were Illinois, Indiana, Wisconsin, Ohio, and Michigan. In the case of corn, Illinois, Ohio, and Missouri supplanted New York, Pennsylvania, and Virginia. In 1840, the most important cattle-raising areas in the country were New York,

Pennsylvania, and New England; but by the 1850s, the leading cattle states were Illinois, Indiana, Ohio, and Iowa, in the West, and Texas in the South.

In some lines of agriculture the Northeast held its own or even surpassed the Northwest. As the Eastern urban centers increased in population, many farmers turned profitably to the task of supplying foods to the city masses, engaging in truck gardening (vegetables) or fruit raising. New York led all other states in apple production. Also stimulated by the rise of cities was dairy farming. The profits to be derived from supplying milk, butter, and cheese to local markets attracted many farmers in central New York, southeastern Pennsylvania, and various parts of New England. Approximately half of the dairy products of the country were produced in the East; the other half came from the West, with Ohio being the dairy center of that section. Partly because of the expansion of the dairy industry, the Northeast led other sections in the production of hay. New York was the leading hay state in the nation, and large crops were grown in Pennsylvania and New England. The Northeast also exceeded other areas in producing potatoes.

Migration and Immigration

One of the most profound changes in the nature of Northeastern society in the antebellum period was in the character and distribution of the population, above all the growing size of cities. Between 1840 and 1860, the population of New York, for example, rose from 312,000 to 805,000. (New York's population numbered 1.2 million in 1860 if Brooklyn, which was then a separate municipality, is included.) Philadelphia's population grew over the same twenty-year period from 220,000 to 565,000; Boston's from 93,000 to 177,000. By 1860, 26 percent of the population of the free states was living in towns or cities (places of 2,500 people or more), up from 14 percent in 1840; that percentage was even higher for the industrializing states of the Northeast. In the South, by contrast, the percentage of urban residents increased from 6 percent in 1840 to only 10 percent in 1860.

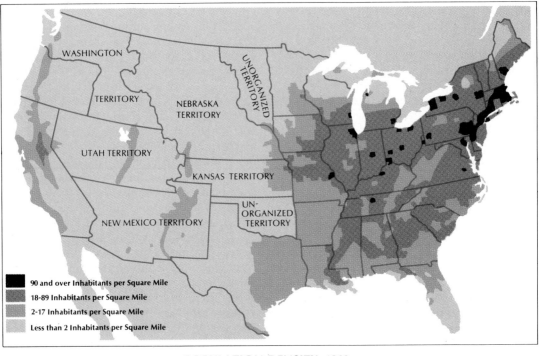

POPULATION DENSITY, 1860

The new urban population was in part simply a reflection of the growth of the national population as a whole, which rose by more than a third—from 23 million to over 31 million—in the decade of the 1850s alone. But it was also a result of the flow of people into the cities from two sources in particular. The first and for a time larger source was the native farming classes of the Northeast, whose members were being forced off their lands by Western competition. The second and ultimately at least equally important source was immigration from Europe. Between 1830 and 1840, only a relatively small number of foreigners had moved to the United States, about 500,000 in all. Beginning in 1840, however, the floodgates opened. The number of immigrants arriving in 1840—84,000—was the highest for any year in all the preceding decades. But in the ensuing years, even that number would come to seem insignificant. Between 1840 and 1850, more than 1.5 million Europeans moved to America; in the last years of the decade, the average number arriving yearly was almost

300,000. Of the 23 million people in the United States in 1850, 2,210,000 were foreign-born; of these almost 1 million were Irish and more than 500,000 were German. Special reasons accounted for the prevalence of immigrants from Ireland and Germany: widespread poverty caused by the economic dislocations of the Industrial Revolution; famines resulting from the failure of the potato and other crops; dislike of English rule by the Irish; and the collapse of the liberal revolutions of 1848 in Germany. The great majority of the Irish settled in the Eastern cities, where they swelled the ranks of unskilled labor. Most of the Germans, having a little more money than the Irish, who had practically none, moved on to the Northwest, where they became farmers or went into business in the Western towns.

The number of immigrants who came in the fifties exceeded even that of the previous decade, reaching an estimated aggregate of over 2.5 million. As before, the overwhelming majority of the newcomers hailed from Ireland and Germany. By 1860, more than 1.5

million Irishmen and approximately 1 million Germans had migrated to the United States. Other nationalities represented in the immigrant tide were Englishmen, Frenchmen, Italians, Scandinavians, Poles, and Hollanders. Most of the foreigners collected in the urban centers of the Northern states. Almost half of the population of New York City consisted of aliens, and in St. Louis, Chicago, and Milwaukee the foreign-born outnumbered those of native birth. Few immigrants settled in the South. Only 500,000 lived in the slave states in 1860, and a third of these were concentrated in Missouri.

Ethnicity and Politics

The new foreign population almost immediately became a major factor in American political life. In some parts of the country, indeed, the immigrants quickly proved to be of pivotal political importance. Wisconsin, from the moment of its admission to the Union in 1848, permitted aliens to become voters as soon as they had declared their intention of seeking citizenship and had resided in the state for a year. Other states followed Wisconsin's lead in liberalizing voting laws, and in most places the polling officials were even more generous than the law allowed. Politicians saw in the immigrant population, therefore, a source of important potential support; and they eagerly courted the new arrivals for their ballots.

On the whole, the Democrats succeeded in attracting a larger number of immigrant voters, whether alien or naturalized, than did the Whigs. The Democrats won over almost all the Roman Catholics among the Germans and the Irish, while the Whigs gained adherents from the less numerous Protestant arrivals. Whig politicians accused the Democrats of shameless, large-scale vote buying; but this was not the real reason for the Democrats' success with foreign-born Catholics. The real reason was the Democrats' willingness to respect and protect the cultural values of those immigrants. Generally, the Whigs demonstrated no such willingness; they remained under the constraints of the old Yankee culture. Thus in state and local politics,

they often endorsed such puritanical reforms as laws to limit or prevent the sale of alcoholic beverages and to require a quiet, joyless Sunday. Such laws were abhorrent to most of the Germans and Irish, and so they were opposed by Democratic politicians.

The presence of huge numbers of aliens occasioned the first important organized nativist movement in American history. Critics contended that many of the immigrants were mentally and physically defective, that they created slums, and that they corrupted politics by selling their votes. Native laborers complained that the aliens, willing to work for low wages, were stealing their jobs. Protestants, impressed by the aptitude that the Catholic Irish demonstrated for politics claimed that the Church of Rome was attaining an undue power in American government. Whig politicians were outraged because so many of the newcomers voted Democratic. Many Americans of older stock were concerned that the immigrants would not assimilate into national life or would inject new and radical philosophies into national thought.

Out of these tensions and prejudices emerged a number of secret societies to combat the "alien menace." Originating in the East and later spreading to the West and South, these groups combined in 1850 to form the Supreme Order of the Star-Spangled Banner. Included in the official program of the order were opposition to the holding of public office by Catholics or aliens and support of stricter naturalization laws and literacy tests for voting. When members were asked to define their platform, they replied, because of the secrecy rule, "I know nothing" and hence were dubbed "Know-Nothings."

Soon the leaders, deciding to seek their objectives by political methods, formed what they called the Native American party. In the East, the new organization scored an immediate and astonishing success in the elections of 1854, casting a large vote in Pennsylvania and New York and winning control of the state government in Massachusetts. Elsewhere, the progress of the Know-Nothings was more modest. Western members of the party, because of the presence of many German voters in the area, found it expedient to proclaim that they were not opposed to naturalized Protestants.

Labor in the Northeast

In the early years of industrial growth, the work force of the Northeastern factories had remained both small and impermanent. Because mills had been relatively few, manufacturers had made do with a relatively modest, largely female labor supply—for example, the mill girls of Waltham and Lowell, who generally worked only temporarily in the factories before returning home. By the 1840s, however, the need for factory workers was such that a large, permanent laboring class was beginning to emerge, drawn from the new urban population of migrating native farmers and European immigrants.

It had also been possible in the early years for mill owners to treat their workers with a paternal solicitude that often softened the conditions of living and working in a new and alien environment. But with the expansion of industry, such niceties were quickly forgotten. No longer did workers live in neat boardinghouses or dormitories carefully maintained and patrolled by their employers. Instead, they were left to their own devices, to find whatever accommodations they could in the cheerless, ugly factory towns that were rapidly growing up. No longer were the conditions of factory labor monitored so as to reduce the hardship of the workers. Instead, factories were becoming large, noisy, unsanitary, and often dangerous places to work; the average workday was extending to twelve, often fourteen hours; and wages were declining, so that even skilled workers could hope to earn only from $4 to $10 per week, while women, children, and unskilled laborers were likely to earn only about $1 to $6 per week. Conditions were still not as bad as in most factory towns in England and Europe; but neither were they any longer models of cleanliness, efficiency, and human concern, as many people had once believed them to be.

Workers faced with the arduous conditions of the new factory complexes made a number of efforts to improve their lot. They tried, with little success, to persuade state legislatures to pass laws setting a maximum workday. Two states—New Hampshire in 1847 and Pennsylvania in 1848—actually passed such laws, limiting the workday to ten hours unless the workers agreed to an "express contract" calling for more time on the job. Such measures were virtually without impact, however, because employers could simply require prospective employees to sign the "express contract" as a condition of hiring. Three states—Massachusetts, New Hampshire, and Pennsylvania—passed laws regulating child labor. But again, the results were minimal. The laws simply limited the workday to ten hours for children unless their parents agreed to something longer; employers had little difficulty compelling parents to consent to additional hours.

Perhaps the greatest legal victory of industrial workers came in Massachusetts in 1842, when the supreme court of the state, in *Commonwealth* v. *Hunt*, declared that unions were lawful organizations and that the strike was a lawful weapon. Other state courts gradually accepted the principles of the Massachusetts decision. But the union movement of the 1840s and 1850s remained generally feeble and ineffective. Partly because many workers were reluctant to think of themselves as members of a permanent laboring force, resistance to organization remained strong. And those unions that did manage to establish a foothold in industry were usually not strong enough to stage strikes, and even less frequently strong enough to win them.

What organization there was among workers usually occurred at the local level and among limited groups of skilled workers. These early unions often had more in common with preindustrial guilds than with modern labor organizations. Their primary purpose was in most cases to protect the favored position of their members in the labor force by restricting admission to the skilled trades. By the early 1850s, some of these local craft unions were beginning to associate with one another to form national organizations. The first was the National Typographical Union, founded in 1852, followed by the Stone Cutters (1853), the Hat Finishers (1854), the Molders (1859), and the Machinists (also 1859).

Despite these modest efforts at organization and protest, what was most notable about the American working class in the 1840s and 1850s was its relative passivity. In England, workers were becoming a powerful, united, and often even violent economic and political force, creating widespread social turmoil and helping to transform the nation's political structure. In America, nothing of the sort happened. Many factors combined to inhibit the growth of effective labor resistance. Among the most important was the flood of immigrant laborers into the country. The newcomers were usually willing to work for lower wages than native workers; and because they were so numerous, manufacturers had little difficulty replacing disgruntled or striking workers with eager immigrants. Ethnic divisions and tensions—both between natives and immigrants, and among the varying immigrant groups themselves—often caused working-class resentments to be channeled into internal bickering rather than against employers. There was, too, the sheer strength of the industrial capitalists, who had not only economic but political and social power and could usually triumph over even the most militant challenges. But a full understanding of the nature of the working-class response to industrialism requires an examination of the emerging social and economic structure of antebellum America.

Wealth and Mobility

The commercial and industrial growth of the United States greatly increased national wealth in the 1840s and 1850s. It elevated, too, the average income of the American people. But what evidence there is—and it is admittedly sketchy—suggests that this increasing wealth was not being widely or equitably distributed. Some groups of the population, of course, shared virtually not at all in the economic growth: slaves, Indians, landless farmers, and many of the unskilled workers on the fringes of the manufacturing system. And among the population at large, disparities of income were becoming so marked as to be impossible to ignore. Wealth had always been unequally distributed in the United States, to be sure. Even in the era of the Revolution, according to some estimates, 45 percent of the wealth was concentrated in the hands of about 10 percent of the population. But by the mid-nineteenth century, that concentration had become far more pronounced. In Boston in 1845, for example, 4 percent of the citizens are estimated to have owned more than 65 percent of the wealth; in Philadelphia in 1860, 1 percent of the population possessed more than half the wealth. Among the American people at large in 1860, 5 percent of the families possessed more than 50 percent of the wealth.

On the surface, such figures would seem likely to have encouraged a far greater level of class conflict than actually occurred. But a number of inhibiting factors operated to quell resentments. There was, first, the fact that however much the *relative* economic position of American workers may have been declining, the *absolute* living standards of most laborers was improving. Life, in material terms at least, was usually better for factory workers than it had been on the farms or in the European societies from which they had migrated. They ate better; they were often better clothed and housed; and they had greater access to consumer goods.

There was also a significant amount of mobility within the working class, which helped to limit discontent. Opportunities for *social* mobility, for working one's way up the economic ladder, were strictly limited. But they were not impossible. Some workers did manage to move from poverty to riches by dint of work, ingenuity, and luck—a very small number, but enough to support the dreams of those who watched them. And a large number of workers managed to move at least one notch up the ladder—for example, perhaps becoming in the course of a lifetime a skilled, rather than unskilled, laborer. Such people could envision their children and grandchildren moving up even further.

More important than social mobility was geographical mobility. Unlike European nations, America had a huge expanse of unsettled land in the West, much of it being opened for settlement for the first time in the 1840s and 1850s. To some workingmen, the dream of saving money to move out to the frontier became a reality—thus creating what the historian Frederick Jackson Turner called a "safety valve" for discontent. But for most workers, the expense and expertise required for a movement to the frontier made such a step impossible. Far more frequent was the movement of laborers from one industrial town to another. Restless, always questing, these "people in motion," as some scholars have described them, were often the victims of layoffs, looking for better opportunities elsewhere. Their search may seldom have led to a marked improvement in their circumstances; but the rootlessness of this large segment of the work force—perhaps the most distressed segment—made effective organization and protest far more difficult.

There was, finally, another "safety valve" for working-class discontent: politics. Economic opportunity may not have greatly expanded in the nineteenth century, but opportunities to participate in politics did. And to many working people, access to the ballot seemed to offer a way to help guide their society and to feel a part of their communities.

The Old Northwest

Life was different in the states of what was known as the Northwest—and what is now known as the Midwest—in the mid-nineteenth century. There was some industry in this region, more than in the South; and in the two decades before the Civil War, the section experienced steady industrial growth. By 1860, it had 36,785 manufacturing establishments employing 209,909 workers. Along the southern shore of Lake Erie was a flourishing industrial and commercial area of which Cleveland was the center. Another manufacturing locality was in the Ohio River Valley, with the meat-packing city of Cincinnati as its nucleus. Farther west, the rising city of Chicago, destined to be the great metropolis of the section, was emerging as the national center of the agricultural machinery and meat-packing industries. The most important industrial products of the West were farm machines, flour, meats, distilled whiskey, and leather and wooden goods.

On the whole, however, industry was far less important in the Northwest than in the Northeast. The Northwest remained primarily an agricultural region. Its rich and plentiful lands made farming there a lucrative and expanding activity, in contrast to the Northeast, where agriculture was in decline. Thus the typical citizen of the Northwest was not the industrial worker or poor, marginal farmer, but the owner of a reasonably prosperous family farm. The average size of Western farms was 200 acres, the great majority of them owned by the people who worked them.

In concentrating on corn, wheat, cattle, sheep, and hogs, the Western farmer was motivated by sound economic reasons. As the Northeast became more industrial and urban, it enlarged the domestic market for farm goods. At the same time, England and certain European nations, undergoing the same process, started to import larger amounts of food. This increasing world-wide demand for farm products resulted in steadily rising farm prices. For the farmers, the forties and early fifties were years of prosperity.

The expansion of agricultural markets had profound effects on sectional alignments in the United States. Of the Northwest's total output, by far the greatest part was disposed of in the Northeast; only the surplus remaining after domestic needs were satisfied was exported abroad. The new well-being of Western farmers, then, was in part sustained by Eastern purchasing power. Eastern industry, in turn, found an important market for its products in the prospering West. Between the two sections there was being forged a fundamental economic relationship that was profitable to both—and that was increasing the isolation of the South within the Union.

To meet the increasing demands for its products, the Northwest had to enlarge its productive capacities. The presence of large blocks of still unoccupied land made it possible to enlarge the area under cultivation during the 1840s. By 1850, the growing Western population had settled the prairie regions east of the Mississippi and was pushing beyond the river. Stimulated to greater production by rising prices and conscious of the richness of his soil, the average Western

St. Louis in the 1850s
As the West grew in population and expanded its economy, its cities became larger. They began to assume the form and to exercise the functions of metropolitan centers in the East. This print shows one of the principal Western cities, St. Louis, as it appeared in the 1850s. Of the three major cities of the West, St. Louis and Cincinnati were older than Chicago and for years were more populous. But by 1860, the Lake Michigan city, experiencing a spectacular growth, was hard on their heels, and after the Civil War it would emerge as the leading metropolis of the section. (Courtesy, Chicago Historical Society)

farmer engaged in wasteful, exploitive methods of farming that often resulted in rapid soil exhaustion.

Some improvements in farming methods did, however, find their way into use. New varieties of seed, notably Mediterranean wheat, which was hardier than the native type, were introduced in some areas; better breeds of animals, such as hogs and sheep from England and Spain, were imported to take the place of native stock.

Of greater importance were the improvements that Americans continued to introduce in farm machines and tools. During the forties, more efficient grain drills, harrows, mowers, and hay rakes were placed in wide use. The cast-iron plow, devised earlier, continued to be popular because its parts could be replaced when broken. An even better implement appeared in 1847, when John Deere established at Moline, Illinois, a fac-

tory to manufacture plows with steel moldboards, which were more durable than those made of iron.

Two new machines heralded a coming revolution in grain production. The most important was the automatic reaper, invented by Cyrus H. McCormick of Virginia. The reaper, taking the place of sickle, cradle, and hand labor, enabled a crew of six or seven men to harvest in a day as much wheat (or any other small grain) as fifteen men could harvest using the older methods. McCormick, who had patented his device in 1834, established in 1847 a factory at Chicago, in the heart of the grain belt. By 1850, he was turning out 3,000 reapers a year; by 1860, more than 100,000 were in use on Western farms. Almost as helpful an aid to the grain grower was the thresher, which appeared in large numbers after 1840. Before that time, grain was flailed by hand (seven bushels a

Cyrus McCormick's Reaper
In 1831, Cyrus McCormick demonstrated the first successful mechanical reaper near the town of Steele's Tavern, Virginia. Two men were required to operate the machine, one to ride the horse and the other to rake the grain stalks off the platform. Other workers followed to bind the grain. (Library of Congress)

day was a good average) or trodden by farm animals (twenty bushels a day on the average). The threshing machines could thresh twenty-five bushels or more in an hour. Most of the threshers were manufactured at the Jerome I. Case factory in Racine, Wisconsin.

The Northwest was the most democratic of the three sections, in the sense that the farmers, the majority, were the dominant economic class and generally had their way in politics. It was a conservative brand of democracy—capitalistic, property-conscious, middle-class. Abraham Lincoln, an Illinois Whig, voiced the economic opinions of many of the people of his section. "I take it that it is best for all to leave each man free to acquire property as fast as he can," said Lincoln. "Some will get wealthy. I don't believe in a law to prevent a man from getting rich; it would do more harm than good. . . . When one starts poor, as most do in the race of life, free society is such that he knows he can better his condition; he knows that there is no fixed condition of labor for his whole life."

Railroads and Telegraphs

The swelling domestic trade between East and West could not have developed without an adequate transportation system. In the 1830s, most of the goods exchanged between the two sections were carried on the Erie Canal. After 1840, railroads gradually supplanted canals and all other modes of transport. In 1840, the total railroad trackage of the country was only 2,818 miles; by the end of the decade, the trackage figure had risen to 9,021 miles. The railroads enabled the Western farmers to ship their products cheaply and quickly to Eastern markets and thus helped to force many Eastern farmers out of business.

An outburst of railroad construction without previous parallel occurred in the fifties. The amount of trackage tripled between 1850 and 1860. The Northeast had the most efficient system, with twice as much trackage per square mile as the West and four times as much as the South. Railroads were reaching even west of the Mississippi, which at several points was spanned by iron bridges. One line ran from Hannibal to St. Joseph on the Missouri River, and another was being built from St. Louis to Kansas City. As for the South, many of its lines were short ones, and there were few through lines. Nevertheless, such towns as Charleston, Atlanta, Savannah, and Norfolk had direct connections with Memphis, and thus with the Northwest; and Richmond was connected, via the Virginia Central, with the Memphis and Charleston railroad. In addition, several independent lines furnished a continuous connection between the Ohio River and New Orleans.

A new feature in railroad development—

A Railroad Train in the 1850s
By the 1850s, locomotives in this country had become standardized according to what was known as the "American type." This had a cowcatcher, a four-wheel leading truck, two pairs of drive wheels, and a funnel-shaped smokestack with a screen to check the escape of sparks from the wood-burning boiler. Note the wood stacked in the tender. Posing on the locomotive are artists taking an excursion from Baltimore to Wheeling in June 1858. (Baltimore and Ohio Railroad Company)

and one that would profoundly affect the nature of sectional alignments—was the trend toward the consolidation of short lines into trunk lines. By 1853, four roads had surmounted the Appalachian barrier to connect the Northeast with the Northwest. Two, the New York Central and the New York and Erie, gave New York City access to the Lake Erie ports. The Pennsylvania road linked Philadelphia and Pittsburgh, and the Baltimore and Ohio connected Baltimore with the Ohio River at Wheeling. From the terminals of these lines, other railroads into the interior touched the Mississippi River at eight points. Chicago became the rail center of the West, served by fifteen lines and more than a hundred daily trains. The appearance of the great trunk lines tended to divert traffic from the water routes—the Erie Canal and the Mississippi River. By lessening the dependence of the West on the Mississippi, the railroads helped to weaken further the connection between the Northwest and the South.

Capital to finance the railroad boom came from various sources. Part of it was provided by American investors, and large sums were borrowed abroad. Substantial aid was provided by local governmental units—states, cities, towns, counties—eager to have a road to serve their needs. This support took the form of loans, stock subscriptions, subsidies, and donations of land for rights of way. The railroads also obtained assistance from the federal government in the shape of public land grants. In 1850, Senator Stephen A. Douglas and other railroad-minded politicians persuaded Congress to grant federal lands to the state of Illinois to aid the Illinois Central, then building toward the Gulf of Mexico; Illinois was to transfer the land to

THE GROWTH OF RAILROADS, 1850–1860

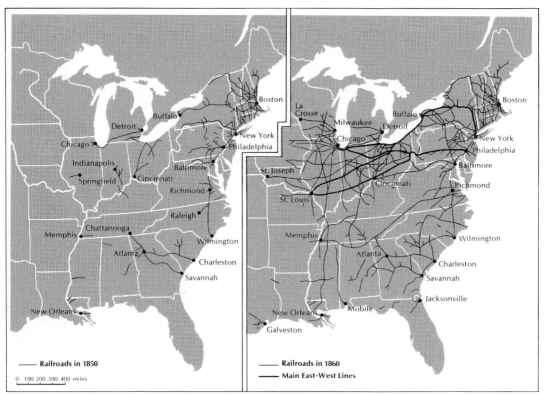

the Central. Other states and their railroad promoters demanded the same privileges; and by 1860, Congress had allotted over 30 million acres to eleven states.

Facilitating the operation of the railroads was another important technological innovation: the magnetic telegraph. Its lines extended along the tracks, connecting one station with another, and aiding the scheduling and routing of the trains. But the telegraph had an importance to the nation's economic development all its own. It permitted instant communication between distant cities, tying the nation together as never before. And yet, ironically, it also helped reinforce the schism between the two sections. As with railroads, telegraph lines were far more extensive in the North than in the South; and they helped similarly to link the North more closely to the Northwest (and thus to separate that region further from the South).

The telegraph had burst into American life in 1844, when Samuel F. B. Morse, after several years of experimentation, succeeded in transmitting from Baltimore to Washington the news of James K. Polk's nomination for the presidency. The Morse telegraph seemed, because of the relatively low cost of constructing wire systems, the ideal answer to the problems of long-distance communication. By 1860, more than 50,000 miles of wire connected most parts of the country; and a year later, the Pacific telegraph, with 3,595 miles of wire, was open between New York and San Francisco. Nearly all of the independent lines had been absorbed into one organization, the Western Union Telegraph Company.

The New Journalism

In 1846, Richard Hoe invented the steam cylinder rotary press, making it possible to print newspapers rapidly and cheaply. The development of the telegraph, together with the introduction of the rotary press, made possible much speedier collection and distribution of news than ever before. In 1846, the Associated Press was organized for the purpose of cooperative news gathering by wire; no longer did publishers have to depend on an exchange of newspapers for out-of-town reports.

Other changes in journalism also occurred. Originally, Washington had been the national news center, and the papers published there had been government or party organs that filled their columns with documents and speeches. With the advent of the telegraph and the railroad, and with the government's assumption of the function of public printing, the center of news transmission shifted to New York. A new type of newspaper appeared, one that was more attuned to the spirit and the needs of the new America. Although newspapers continued to concentrate on politics, they also reported human interest stories and recorded the most recent news, which they could not have done before the telegraph.

Most of the metropolitan journals were owned in whole or in part by their editors, who were also in many cases their founders; unlike modern newspapers they bore the imprint of a single personality. The leading Northern papers were Horace Greeley's *Tribune,* James Gordon Bennett's *Herald,* and Henry J. Raymond's *Times,* all of New York. The *Herald* specialized in scandal and crime, the *Tribune* in self-improvement and social uplift. With a separate weekly edition, the *Tribune* served as a national or at least a sectional paper, having mail subscribers scattered throughout the Northeast and Northwest. Southern papers, with smaller budgets, tended to follow the older pattern of reporting mainly stale political news. The combined circulation of the New York *Tribune* and the New York *Herald* exceeded that of all the daily newspapers published in the South. In the country as a whole, there were more than 3,000 newspapers being published by 1860.

During the 1850s, Americans experienced the impact of a new kind of magazine journalism. In increasing numbers the upper and middle classes were reading monthly magazines that featured fiction and news articles by some of the country's outstanding writers. Easily the leader in this field was *Harper's New Monthly Magazine,* with 170,000 subscribers; but competition was furnished by *Putnam's Magazine* and the *Atlantic Monthly,* both founded in the 1850s. For the edification of the masses, there appeared pictorial weeklies, lavishly illustrated with drawings by America's best popular artists. The pioneer among the picture journals was the *National Police Gazette,* established in 1845 by George Wilkes. It was also the most sensational, reporting "horrid murders, outrageous robberies, bold forgeries, astounding burglaries, hideous rapes, vulgar seductions." Other picture magazines reaching huge audiences were *Leslie's Illustrated Newspaper* (1855) and *Harper's Weekly* (1857).

In the long run, the new journalism would become an important unifying factor in American life. In the 1840s and 1850s, however, the rise of the new journalism helped to feed the fires of sectional discord. Most of the major magazines and newspapers were in the North, reinforcing the South's sense of subjugation. And the rapid reporting of detailed information regarding differences between the sections prompted people to anger more quickly and more often than might otherwise have been the case. Above all, the news revolution—along with the revolutions in systems of transportation and communications that accompanied it—contributed to a growing awareness within each section of how the other section lived, an awareness of the deep and ultimately seemingly irreconcilable differences that had grown up between the North and the South.

THE EXPANDING SOUTH

In contrast to the North, the South possessed in the middle years of the nineteenth century a relatively static economy. To be sure, the Southern way of life—the agricultural economy based on a plantation system and slave labor—expanded dramatically as new and fertile lands in the Southwest were opened to settlement. And Southern society was, it is true, becoming more diversified as it expanded; there were great differences—in climate, in soil, and in the conditions of life—between the original South of the Atlantic coast and the newer, more rugged South of Alabama, Mississippi, Louisiana, and other states. But neither the expansion nor the diversification altered a basic fact. The South remained a fundamentally rural and agricultural region, with little industry or commerce of its own. As one historian has written, "the Southern economy *grew,* but it did not *develop.*" And as a result, the South remained a far more homogeneous region than the North, and a region far more sensitive to threats to its distinctive way of life.

Elements of Southernism

The qualities that gave the South its distinctive flavor are not easy to define. Generally, the climate is warm and mild; on the lower Gulf coast, it is subtropical. The growing seasons are longer than in the North, varying from six months in the upper South to nine months in the Gulf states. The economy, predominantly agricultural, was characterized by the presence of the large plantation as well as the small farm. Farming was largely commercial, concentrating on producing certain staple crops—cotton, tobacco, sugar, and rice—for sale to outside areas. Unlike the West, the South disposed of the bulk of its products in England and Europe rather than on the domestic market; it felt closer economic ties with England than with the Northeast. The South had far fewer cities, towns, and villages than did the Northern states, and its population was more diffused (about thirteen persons per square mile in 1860 as compared with twenty in the North). The great majority of Southern whites were Anglo-Saxon in origin and Protestant in religion.

The South was the only area in the United States (indeed, in all the Western world except for Brazil and Cuba) where slavery still existed. It was the only section that contained vast numbers of a race other than white. Southerners might differ among themselves on political and economic ques-

A Sugar Plantation
This scene, from a newspaper illustration of 1852, is located along the Mississippi River in Louisiana. At the right is the mansion, overhung by Spanish moss. To the left is the sugar mill, conveniently accessible to river shipping. In the foreground is a raft of the kind that some northern farmers used for transporting their crops to New Orleans. Raftsmen and boatmen, as shown here, had to contend with floating logs, branches, and other debris. (Granger Collection)

tions, but by the 1850s they had closed ranks on the issue of race. They were determined to keep the South a white man's country, and they viewed slavery as the best means to that end. Thus slavery was more than a labor system. It was also a white-supremacy device, and as such it finally enlisted the support of the Southern white masses, including the great majority who did not own slaves. Race consciousness, then, helped to account for the oneness of the South.

Thoughtful Southerners realized that slavery isolated them from most of the rest of mankind. Said William Harper of South Carolina:

The judgment is made up. We can have no hearing before the tribunal of the civilized world. Yet, on this very account, it is more important that we, the inhabitants of the slave-holding States, insulated as we are by this institution, and cut off, in some degree, from the communion and sympathies of the world by which we are surrounded, . . . and exposed continually to their animadversions and attacks, should thoroughly understand this subject, and our strength and weakness in relation to it.

Was slavery profitable? On the whole, the planters themselves believed they were making very satisfactory profits. At the same time, there can be no doubt that the slave system, or rather the economic system of which slavery was a part, retarded Southern development and posed some grave problems for the section. Because of the concentration on agriculture, the South had to purchase its finished goods from the outside. Perceptive Southerners recognized the economic subordination of their region. "From the rattle with which the nurse tickles the ear of the child born in the South to the shroud that covers the cold form of the dead, everything comes to us from the North," exclaimed Albert Pike. Said a writer in *De Bow's Review:* "I think it would be safe to estimate the amount which is lost to us annually by our vassalage to the North at $100,000,000. Great God!" The antebellum South had a colonial economy.

The white Southerners' sense of being exploited by the North, together with their race consciousness and their minority status in the nation and in the world, intensified their feeling of sectional unity.

Gradations of Southern White Society

Only a minority of Southern whites owned slaves. In 1850, when the total white population of the South was over 6 million, the number of slaveholders was 347,525. In 1860, when the white population was just above 8 million (the slave population was 3,950,513), the number of slaveholders had risen to only 383,637. These figures by themselves are somewhat misleading, for each slaveholder was normally the head of a family averaging five members. But even if all members of slaveowning families are included in the figures, those owning slaves still amount to perhaps no more than one-quarter of the white population. And of the minority of whites holding slaves, only a small proportion owned them in substantial numbers.

How, then, has Southern society come to be characterized as one dominated by great plantations and wealthy landowning planters? In large part, it is because the planter aristocracy—the cotton magnates, the sugar, rice, and tobacco nabobs, the whites who owned at least forty or fifty slaves and 800 or more acres—exercised power and influence far in excess of their numbers. They stood at the apex of society, determining the political, economic, and even social life of their region. Below them stood the small and medium planters, with ten to forty slaves apiece, who did not so much challenge the aristocracy as emulate and aspire to it. Then came the mod-

est farmers with from one to nine slaves; and then the largest white group of all, those farmers who owned no slaves at all. And finally, of course, occupying a special sphere of their own, were the millions of blacks, the vast majority of them slaves.

The large planters represented the social ideal of the South. Enriched by vast annual incomes, dwelling in palatial homes, surrounded by broad acres and many black servants, they were the class to which all others paid a certain deference. Enabled by their wealth to practice the leisured arts, they cultivated gracious living, good manners, learning, and politics. Their social pattern determined to a considerable degree the tone of all Southern society.

The Southern planters constituted the closest approach to an aristocracy to be found in the United States. They enjoyed in their section a higher social position, a greater political power, a more unquestioned leadership than did the factory owners of the Northeast.

Class distinctions were more sharply drawn in the South than in other sections. Some Southerners spoke scornfully of democracy. Yet, particularly in the newer states, an ambitious person could move from one class to another. Farmers nursed the hope of becoming small slaveholders, and small planters aimed to become large ones. Many achieved their goal. In fact, the great majority of the cotton lords of the Mississippi Valley states had come from the ranks of the obscure and the ordinary.

The farmers, those who owned a few slaves and the greater number who owned none, devoted more attention to subsistence farming than did the planters. Most of them owned their land. During the 1850s, the number of nonslaveholding landowners increased much faster than the number of slaveholding landowners. This large group of nonslaveowning whites—what historians have often called the "plain folk" of the Old South—present an important question. Why did they not oppose the aristocratic social system in which they shared so little? Why did they not resent the system of slavery, from which they did not benefit? There is no single answer to such questions.

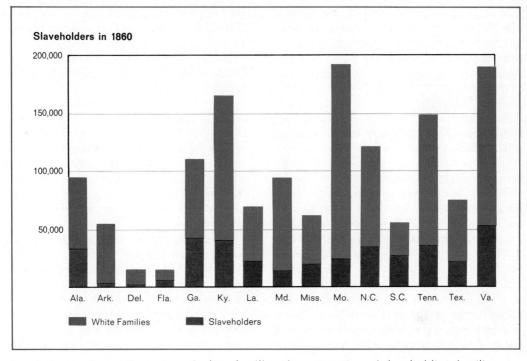

Slaveholders in 1860

White Families   Slaveholders

In relation to the total number of white families, the proportion of slaveholding families tended to be higher in the cotton states of the Deep South than in the border states. For example, although the number of slaveholders in Georgia and Kentucky was about the same, they constituted almost half of the white population in Georgia but less than one-third in Kentucky.

Some nonslaveowning whites did oppose the slaveholding oligarchy, but for the most part in limited ways and in a relatively few, isolated areas. These were the Southern highlanders, the "hill people," who lived in the Appalachian ranges east of the Mississippi and in the Ozarks to the west of the river. Of all Southern whites, they were the most set apart from the mainstream of the region's life. They practiced a crude form of subsistence agriculture, owned practically no slaves, and had a proud sense of seclusion. They held to old ways and old ideals, which included the ideal of loyalty to the nation as a whole. Such whites frequently expressed animosity toward the planter aristocracy of the other regions of the South and misgivings about (although seldom moral objections to) the system of slavery. The mountain region was the only part of the South to defy the trend toward sectional conformity; and it was the only part to resist the movement toward secession when it finally developed. Even during the Civil War itself, many refused to support the Confederacy; some went so far as to fight for the Union.

Far greater in number, however, were the nonslaveowning whites who lived in the midst of the plantation system. Many, perhaps most of them accepted that system because they were tied to it in important ways. Small farmers depended on the local plantation aristocracy for many things: for access to cotton gins, for markets for their modest crops and their livestock, for financial assistance in time of need. In many areas, there were also extensive networks of kinship linking lower- and upper-class whites. The poorest resident of a county might easily be a cousin of the richest aristocrat. These extensive mutual ties—a system of almost paternal relationships—helped to mute what might otherwise have been pronounced class tensions.

But there were other white Southerners who did not share in the plantation economy in even these limited ways and yet continued to accept its premises. These were the members of that tragic and degraded class—numbering perhaps a half million in 1850—known variously as "crackers," "sand hillers," or "poor white trash." Occupying the infertile lands of the pine barrens, the red hills, and the swamps, they lived in miserable cabins surrounded by almost unbelievable squalor. Their degradation resulted partly from dietary deficiencies and disease. These poor whites resorted at times to eating clay; and they were afflicted by pellagra, hookworm, and malaria. Held in contempt by both the planters and the small farmers of the South, they formed a true underclass. In many ways, their plight was worse than that of the black slaves (who themselves often looked down on the poor whites).

Even among these Southerners—the true outcasts of white society in the region—there was no real opposition to the plantation system or slavery. In part, undoubtedly, their acquiescence resulted from these men and women being so benumbed by poverty that they had little strength to protest. But it resulted also from perhaps the single greatest unifying factor among the Southern white population—the one force that was most responsible for reducing tensions among the various classes. That force was race. However poor and miserable a white Southerner might be, he could still consider himself a member of a ruling race; he could still look down on the black population of the region and feel a bond with his fellow whites born of a determination to maintain their racial supremacy. As Frederick Law Olmsted, a Northerner who visited the South and chronicled Southern society in the 1850s, wrote: "From childhood, the one thing in their condition which has made life valuable to the mass of whites has been that the niggers are yet their inferiors."

Southern Trade and Industry

The business classes of the South—the manufacturers and merchants—were small in number but not without importance. Flour milling and textile and iron manufacturing were the main Southern industries, concentrated largely in Virginia, the Carolinas, and Georgia. The Tredegar Iron Works in Richmond compared favorably with the best iron mills in the Northeast. The value of Southern textile goods increased from $1.5 million in 1840 to $4.5 million in 1860. Despite some promising beginnings, however, Southern industry before 1860 remained largely in a formative stage. Most Southerners showed a distaste for industrialism, and those with surplus capital usually preferred to invest it in slaves and land.

More important than the budding manufacturers were the merchants, particularly the brokers or factors who marketed the planters' crops. These individuals, in such towns as New Orleans, Charleston, Mobile, and Savannah, acted as selling agents for the planters, and sometimes also as purchasing agents. Frequently the broker became a banker to the planter, furnishing money or goods on credit. In such cases the planter might be in debt to his factor for a long period, during which time he would have to consign his entire crop to the factor. The merchant-broker, dominating as he did the credit facilities of the rural South, was in a position to exert great economic pressure on the planter.

Closely linked economically with the planters were the professional classes—lawyers, editors, doctors, and others. Because their well-being largely depended on planter prosperity, the professional groups usually agreed with and voiced the ideals of the dominant class.

But however important these manufacturers, merchants, and professionals might have been to Southern society, they were relatively unimportant in comparison with the manufacturers, merchants, and professionals of the North, on whom Southerners were coming more and more (and increasingly unhappily) to depend. Again, a question arises. Why did the South not make more serious efforts to remedy its "colonial" dependency on the North? Why did it not develop a larger industrial and commercial economy of its own?

In part, Southern dependency resulted from the profitability of the region's agricultural system, particularly of cotton. In part, it resulted from the fact that wealthy Southerners had so much capital invested in their slaves, they had little left for other investments. And in part, some historians have gone so far as to suggest, it resulted from Southern work habits; Southerners appeared—at least to such Northern observers as Olmsted—simply not to work very hard, to lack the strong work ethic that fueled Northern economic development.

But the Southern failure to create a flourishing commercial or industrial economy was also in part a result of a set of values distinctive to the South that discouraged the growth of cities and industry. White Southerners liked to think of themselves as representatives of a special way of life: one based on traditional values of chivalry, leisure, and elegance. Southerners were, they argued, "cavaliers"—people happily free from the base, acquisitive instincts of the Northerners, people more concerned with a refined and gracious way of life than with rapid growth and development.

The "cavalier" image was in many ways a myth. Southern planters were for the most part no less businessmen than Northern industrialists; they were no less interested in profit, no less ambitious to improve their lot, often no less ruthless in their dealings with competitors. Nevertheless, the image survived. And with it survived a powerful resistance to commercial and industrial development.

King Cotton

The Southern agricultural system was organized around the great staples: tobacco, rice, sugar, and above all cotton. These were the section's money crops, but they did not constitute by any means its only forms of agricultural effort. What might be termed general or diversified farming was carried on in many areas, notably in the Shenandoah Valley of Virginia and the bluegrass region of central Kentucky. Most planters aimed to produce on the plantation the foodstuffs needed by the family and the slaves. On some large plantations, more acres were planted in corn than in cotton, and in 1850 half the corn crop of the country was raised in the South. Despite the planters' efforts to achieve self-sufficiency, they could not supply all the needs of their slaves, and large amounts of corn and pork had to be imported annually from the Northwest.

But the staples dominated the economic life of the section and absorbed the attention of the majority of the people. Climatic and geographical conditions dictated the areas where each was produced. Tobacco, which needed only a fairly short growing season (six months), was grown in tidewater Maryland west of the Chesapeake, in piedmont Virginia and adjacent North Carolina, in northern and western Kentucky, in northwestern Tennessee, and in the Missouri River Valley of Missouri. Rice demanded irrigation and a growing season of nine months, and hence was restricted to the coastal region of South Carolina and Georgia. Sugar, with a similar period necessary for maturation, was concentrated in southern Louisiana and a small area in eastern Texas (around Galveston). Cotton, which required a growing season of seven to nine months and could be produced in a variety of soil formations, occupied the largest zone of production. The Cotton Kingdom stretched from North Carolina to Texas.

From the sale of the great staples the South derived its chief revenue. Into the markets of the world in the 1850s the section poured annually more than 400,000 pounds of tobacco, more than 360,000 hogsheads (casks) of sugar, and more than 240,000 pounds of rice. But the big money crop was cotton. From 1 million bales in 1830, Southern production of cotton steadily increased until it reached 4 million bales in 1860. In that year, Southern cotton brought $191 million in the European markets and constituted almost two-thirds of the total export trade of the United States. (By way of contrast, the annual value of the rice crop was $2 million.) No wonder that Southerners said smugly, "Cotton is king."

As cotton culture expanded, the centers of production moved westward into the

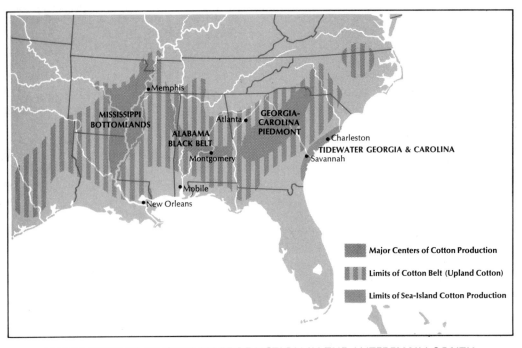

MAJOR CENTERS OF COTTON PRODUCTION IN THE ANTEBELLUM SOUTH

fresher lands of Alabama, Mississippi, Arkansas, Louisiana, and Texas. The extension of the Cotton Kingdom into this area bore certain resemblances to the rush of gold seekers into a new frontier. The prospect of tremendous profits quickly drew settlers by the thousands. Some who came were wealthy planters from the older states who transferred their assets and slaves to a cotton plantation. Most were small slaveholders or slaveless farmers who intended to become planters.

A similar shift occurred in the slave population. The number of slaves in Alabama leaped from 41,000 in 1820 to 435,000 in 1860, and in Mississippi from 32,000 to 436,000. In the same period in Virginia, the increase was only from 425,000 to 490,000. It has been estimated that between 1840 and 1860, 410,000 slaves were moved from the upper South to the cotton states.

Like the farmers of the Northwest, those of the South employed methods that exhausted the soil. They gave little attention to crop rotation, the use of fertilizers, or deep plowing. Like other Americans, they consid-

ered it easier to migrate to new lands than to restore old ones. Still, there were agricultural societies and journals in the South, as in the other sections, and there were dedicated individuals who labored to improve farm techniques. Such a man was the famous Edmund Ruffin of Virginia, advocate of fertilization, rotation, and deep plowing. The founder of the *Farmers' Register*, Ruffin was one of the best agricultural experts in the country during the 1850s. Through his efforts and those of others, some progress in checking soil depletion was made in the older states.

The Mind of the South

Just as with manufactured goods and commercial services, so with literary and artistic life: Southerners were to a great extent dependent on the North. Planters bought books in large numbers, almost all of them the works of English or Northern writers. Newspapers and magazines circulated throughout the South, but they were largely publications originating in the North. When native

Southerners attempted to publish books or magazines of their own, they faced great difficulties. There were few printers or publishers available to them in their own region; and there was little interest in their work from the majority of literate Southerners. Of the one hundred magazines founded in the South in the antebellum period, only nine survived for any length of time.

Nevertheless, there did emerge, on however modest a scale, a Southern literary and journalistic life—one that reflected the increasing distinctiveness of Southern culture. Southern novelists of the 1830s, some of them writers of great talent, many of them residents of Richmond, produced historical romances or romantic eulogies of the plantation system of the upper South. Among them were Beverly Tucker, author of *The Partisan Leader* (1836), William Alexander Caruthers, who wrote *The Cavaliers of Virginia* (1834–35), and John Pendleton Kennedy, author of, among many other novels, *Horse-Shoe Robinson* (1835). Later, in the 1840s, the Southern literary capital moved to Charleston, where lived and wrote the most distinguished of the region's many distinguished men of letters: William Gilmore Simms. Although also a poet and essayist, Simms was known during his lifetime primarily for his fiction, of which he wrote more than thirty volumes. Many of his books (such as *The Yemassee*, published in 1835) were novels glorifying Charleston and South Carolina. Others were historical romances of the American Revolution. For a time, his work expressed a broad nationalism that transcended his regional background; but by the 1840s he had developed into a strong defender of Southern institutions—especially slavery—against the encroachments of the North. There was, he believed, a distinctive quality to Southern life that it was the duty of intellectuals to defend. Simms's best work displayed his talent for earthy descriptions of common folk, but he always made it clear that he supported the survival of the Southern plantation system.

Among Southern journalists, one of the most influential was James B. D. De Bow, a resident of New Orleans. He published a magazine advocating Southern commercial and agricultural expansion: *De Bow's Review*, which survived from its founding in 1846 until 1880. De Bow was a tireless advocate of Southern economic independence from the North, warning constantly of the dangers of the "colonial" relationship between the sections. Yet his own magazine was clear evidence of that dependency. It was printed in New York, because no New Orleans printer had facilities adequate to the task; it was filled with advertisements from Northern manufacturing firms; and its circulation was always modest in comparison with those of Northern publications. In Charleston, for example, it sold an average of 173 copies per issue, while *Harper's Magazine* of New York regularly sold 1,500 copies to Carolinians.

One group of Southern writers, however, produced works that were more distinctively American and less committed to a glorification of the peculiarities of Southern life. These were the writers of the frontier, who depicted the society of the backwoods rural areas. They focused not on aristocratic cavaliers, but on ordinary people and poor whites. Instead of romanticizing their subjects, they were deliberately and sometimes painfully realistic. And they seasoned their sketches with a robust, vulgar humor that was something new in American literature. The leading frontier writer was Augustus B. Longstreet of Georgia (*Georgia Scenes*). Others who wrote in the same vein were Joseph G. Baldwin (*Flush Times of Alabama and Mississippi*) and Johnson J. Hooper (*Some Adventures of Captain Simon Suggs*). Together, these Southern realists established a tradition of humor that was uniquely American and that was ultimately to find a supreme exponent in Mark Twain.

It has been said that in the South there were more people who could read Latin and fewer who could read English than in any other part of the country. The educational system of the section reflected the aristocratic ideals of the plantation regime. In 1860 there were 260 Southern colleges and universities, public and private, with 25,000 students enrolled in them, or more than half the total number of students in the United States. The lower South had 11,000 students in its institutions of higher learning, while New England, with approximately the same population, could boast of only 3,748. Below the college level, however, the schools of the South were not only fewer but also inferior to those of the East, but about as good as those of the West. The South had more than 500,000 white illiterates, or over half of the country's total.

Among the reasons for the relative backwardness of the South was the rural character of the region. There were few cities, and not one that, like New York or Boston, could act as a focal point of culture. The high illiteracy rate among white adults decreased the potential reading audience. The planters, the class that might have patronized a Southern literature, considered oratory and statesman-ship to be much more significant activities. At a time when writing was becoming a recognized and respected profession in the North, Southern authors, as so many of them bitterly testified, were regarded as amusing fellows who had little to offer their society.

Furthermore, after 1830 much of the creative energy of the South was channeled into the defense of slavery. Under criticism from the outside, the section felt a compulsion to glorify its image of itself and to enforce conformity to that image. Freedom of thought, which was largely accepted in the North and which Jefferson and other former Southern leaders had said was necessary in a good society, was stifled in the South.

THE "PECULIAR" INSTITUTION

White Southerners often referred to slavery in their region as the "peculiar institution." By that, they meant not that the institution was odd but that it was distinctive, special. The description was an apt one, for American slavery was indeed distinctive. It differed significantly from the slave systems of other countries—even from its closest counterparts in the Caribbean and Latin America. And, of course, it differed fundamentally from the labor system of the North and became perhaps the most important factor in driving a wedge between the sections.

Within the South itself, the institution of slavery had paradoxical results. On the one hand, it isolated blacks from whites, drawing a sharp and inviolable line between the races. As a result, blacks under slavery began to develop a society and culture of their own, one that was in many ways unrelated to the white civilization around them. On the other hand, slavery created a unique bond between blacks and whites—masters and slaves—in the South. The two races may have maintained separate spheres, but each sphere was deeply influenced by, indeed dependent on, the other.

The Conditions of Slavery

Slavery was an institution established by law and regulated in detail by law. The slave codes of the Southern states forbade a slave to hold property, to leave his master's premises without permission, to be out after dark, to congregate with other slaves except at church, to carry firearms, to strike a white man even in self-defense. The codes prohibited teaching a slave to read or write, and denied the right of a slave to testify in court against a white person. They contained no provisions to legalize slave marriages or divorces. Any person showing a strain of African ancestry was presumed to be a slave unless he could prove otherwise. If an owner killed a slave while punishing him, the act was not considered a crime.

These and dozens of other restrictions and impositions indicate that the slaves lived under a harsh and dismal regime, which would have been unrelieved had the laws been drastically enforced. In fact, they were applied unevenly. Sometimes slaves did acquire property, were taught to read and write, and did assemble with other slaves, the laws to the contrary notwithstanding. Most slave offenses were tried by the master, who might inflict punishments ranging from some mild disciplinary action to flogging or branding for running away. Major offenses, including crimes, were generally referred to the courts. Slaves faced the death penalty for killing or even resisting a white person and for inciting to revolt.

Slave Workers on a Sugar Plantation
Although the growing of cotton employed
the greatest number of black slaves by the
mid-nineteenth century, the production of
sugar cane continued to require a large labor
force as well. This wood engraving, clearly
the work of an opponent of slavery, shows
black laborers engaged in the arduous work
of sugar cultivation, while an arrogant white
overseer saunters by, holding a whip. In the
background, another overseer can be seen
beating an unfortunate slave.
(The Granger Collection)

The routine of plantation life was governed by a system of rules created by custom
and the planters. A small planter directly supervised the work on his place. A medium or
large planter hired an overseer and perhaps
an assistant overseer to represent him. The
"head driver," a trusted and responsible
slave, acted under the overseer as a kind of
foreman. Under him might be several sub-
drivers. Two methods or systems of assigning slave labor were employed. One was the
task system, most widely used in rice culture.

Here a slave was allotted a particular task in
the morning, say to hoe one acre; when he
completed the job he was free for the rest of
the day. The other was the gang system, employed on the cotton, sugar, and tobacco
plantations. Here the slaves were simply divided into groups, each of which was
directed by a driver, and were worked for as
many hours as the overseer considered a reasonable workday.

Slaves were provided with at least enough
necessities to enable them to live and work.
They were furnished with an adequate if
rough diet, consisting mainly of corn meal,
salt pork, and molasses. Many were allowed
to raise gardens for their own use and were
issued fresh meat on special occasions. They
received issues of cheap clothes and shoes.
They lived in rude cabins, called slave quarters. Medical care was provided by the plantation mistress or a doctor retained by the
owner. The slave worked hard, beginning
with light tasks as a child; and his workday
was longest at harvest time. He sometimes
had time off to hunt and fish, and he attended
the church services and some of the social
festivities of his white family.

Some historians have argued that the material conditions of slavery were, in fact, superior to those of Northern industrial workers. Whether or not that is true (and the
evidence for this conclusion is at best debat-
able), the conditions of American slavery
were undoubtedly less arduous than those of
slavery in the Caribbean and South America.
There, the slave supply was constantly re-
plenished well into the nineteenth century by
the African slave trade, giving owners less
incentive to protect their existing laborers.
Working and living conditions there were
arduous, and masters at times literally
worked their slaves to death. In the United
States, by contrast, there were strong economic incentives to maintain a healthy slave
population. One result of this was that
America became the only country in the
world where a slave population actually increased through natural reproduction.

One example of the solicitude with which
masters often treated their slaves was the
frequent practice of using hired labor, when
available, for the most unhealthful or dangerous tasks. A traveler in Louisiana noted, for

example, that Irishmen were employed to clear malarial swamps and to handle cotton bales at the bottom of chutes extending from the river bluff down to a boat landing. If an Irishman died of disease or was killed in an accident, the master could hire another for a dollar a day or less. But he would lose perhaps $1,000 or more if he lost a prime field hand. Still, a cruel master might forget his pocketbook in the heat of momentary anger. And slaves were often left to the discipline of an overseer, who had no pecuniary stake in their well-being; he was paid in proportion to the amount of work he could get out of them.

Household servants had a somewhat easier life than did field hands. On a small plantation the same persons might serve in both capacities; but on a large one there would be a separate staff of nursemaids, housemaids, cooks, butlers, coachmen, and the like. These people lived close to the master and his family, eating the leftovers from the family table, and in some cases even sleeping in the "big house." Between the blacks and whites of such a household, there might develop an affectionate, almost familial relationship.

Slavery in the cities differed significantly from slavery in the country. On the more or less isolated plantation the slaves were kept apart from free blacks and lower-class whites. The master, his family, and his overseers maintained a fairly direct and effective control. A deep and unbridgeable chasm yawned between slavery and freedom. In the city, however, the master often could not supervise his slaves closely and at the same time use them profitably. Even if they slept at night in carefully watched backyard barracks, they went about by day on errands of various kinds. Others were hired out, and after hours they fended for themselves, neither the owner nor the employer caring to look after them. Thus the urban slaves gained numerous opportunities to mingle with free blacks and with whites, including fair-complexioned prostitutes. A line between slavery and freedom remained, but it became less and less distinct.

Indeed, slavery was basically incompatible with city life; and as Southern cities grew, the number of slaves in them dropped, relatively if not absolutely. The reasons were social rather than economic. Fearing conspiracies and insurrections, urban slaveowners sold off much of their male property to the countryside. The cities were left with an excess of black women while continuing to have an excess of white men (a circumstance that helped to account for the birth of many mulattoes). While slavery in the cities declined, segregation of blacks both free and slave increased. Segregation was a means of social control intended to make up for the loosening of the discipline of slavery itself.

The Continuing Slave Trade

The transfer of slaves from one part of the South to another (when the slaves were not carried by their migrating owners) was accomplished through the medium of professional slave traders. In long-distance traffic, the slaves were moved on trains or on river or ocean steamers. Or they were moved on foot, trudging in coffles of hundreds along the dusty highways. Eventually they arrived at some central market such as Natchez, New Orleans, Mobile, or Galveston, where purchasers collected to bid for them. At the auction, the bidders checked the slaves like livestock, watching them as they were made to walk or trot, inspecting their teeth, feeling their arms and legs, looking for signs of infirmity or age. It paid to be careful, for traders were known to deceive buyers by blacking gray hair, oiling withered skin, and concealing physical defects in other ways. A sound young field hand would fetch a price that, during the 1840s and 1850s, varied from $500 to $1,700, depending mainly on fluctuations in the price of cotton. The average figure was about $800. An attractive woman, desirable as a concubine, might bring several times that much.

The domestic slave trade was essential to the growth and prosperity of the whole system. It was also one of the least defensible aspects of it. Not only did the trade dehumanize all who were involved in it; it also separated children from parents, and parents from one another. Even in the case of a kindly master who had kept families together, they might be broken up in the division of his estate after his death. Planters condoned the trade and eased their consciences by holding the traders in contempt and assigning them a low social position.

The foreign slave trade was as bad or worse. Though federal law had prohibited the importation of slaves from 1808 on, they continued to be smuggled in as late as the 1850s. The numbers can only be guessed at. They were not large enough to satisfy all planters, and the Southern commercial conventions, which met annually to consider means of making the South economically independent, began to discuss the legal reopening of the trade. "If it is right to buy slaves in Virginia and carry them to New Orleans," William L. Yancey of Alabama asked his fellow delegates at the 1858 meeting, "why is it not right to buy them in Cuba, Brazil, or Africa and carry them there?" The convention that year voted to recommend the repeal of all laws against slave imports. Only the delegates from the states of the upper South, which profited from the domestic trade, opposed the foreign competition.

The Slaves' Response

Few issues have sparked as much debate among historians as the effects of slavery on the blacks themselves. (See "Where Historians Disagree," pp. 344–345.) The slaveowners, and many white Americans for generations to come, liked to argue that the slaves were generally content, "happy with their lot." That may well have been true in certain individual cases, particularly among favored domestic servants, some of whom came to identify with their masters and to view themselves as somehow above their fellow slaves. But it is clear that the vast majority of Southern blacks were not content with being slaves, that they yearned for freedom even though most realized there was little they could do to secure it. Evidence for that conclusion comes, if from nowhere else, from the reaction of slaves when emancipation finally came. Virtually all Southern blacks reacted to freedom with joy and celebration; relatively few chose to remain in the service of the whites who had owned them before the Civil War (although most blacks, of course, remained for many years subservient to whites in one way or another).

Rather than contented acceptance, the dominant response of blacks to slavery was a complex one: a combination of adaptation and resistance. At the extremes, slavery could produce two opposite reactions—each of which served as the basis for a powerful stereotype in white society. One extreme was what became known as the "Sambo"—the shuffling, grinning, head-scratching, deferential slave who acted out the role that he recognized the white expected of him. More often than not, the "Sambo" pattern of behavior was a charade, a façade assumed in the presence of whites. In some cases, however, it might have represented more than that—the tragic distortion of personality that the rigors of slavery inflicted on its victims. The other extreme was the slave rebel—the black who could not bring himself (or herself) to either acceptance or accommodation but harbored an unquenchable spirit of rebelliousness. Here, too, there may at times have been personality disorders at work (as is suggested by newspaper advertisements for runaways who were described as having stutters or other behavioral quirks). It was, after all, not an entirely normal act to rise up in rebellion against odds so overwhelming that there existed virtually no chance of success. Yet to attribute slave rebellions to mental disorder is to accept a largely white point of view. It is also possible to see in the rebellious slave signs of a strength and courage far greater than most white Southerners were disposed to admit a black man could possess.

Actual slave revolts were extremely rare, but the knowledge that they were possible struck terror into the hearts of white Southerners everywhere. In 1800, Gabriel Prosser gathered 1,000 rebellious slaves outside Richmond, but two blacks gave the plot away, and the Virginia militia was called out in time to head it off. Prosser and thirty-five others were executed. In 1822, the Charleston free black Denmark Vesey and his followers—rumored to total 9,000—made preparations for revolt; but again the word leaked out, and retribution followed. In 1831, Nat Turner, a slave preacher, led a band of blacks who armed themselves with guns and axes and, on a summer night, went from house to house in Southampton County, Virginia. They slaughtered sixty white men, women,

The Nature of Plantation Slavery

Few subjects have produced so rich a historical literature in recent years as the nature of American slavery. And in that literature is lodged one of the liveliest of all scholarly debates. Even more vividly than other historical controversies, the argument over slavery illustrates the extent to which historians are influenced by the times in which they write. From one era to the next, prevailing popular attitudes about race have found reflection in historical examinations of slavery. Never has that been more true than in the past two decades.

The first accounts of slavery, written before the Civil War by contemporaries of the institution, were usually stark expressions of the political beliefs of their authors. Southern chroniclers emphasized the benevolent features of the system, the paternalism with which masters cared for their slaves (a stark contrast, they implied, to the brutal impersonality of Northern factory owners and their "wage slaves"), and the carefree, happy demeanor of the slaves themselves. From Northern writers (many of them abolitionists) came a picture of slavery as a brutal, savage institution that dehumanized all who were touched by it. Theodore Dwight Weld's *American Slavery as It Is* (1839), for many years a widely cited book, depicted a system so horrible in its impact that it was little wonder the book inspired many of its readers to political action.

By the end of the nineteenth century, however, the political climate had changed. White Americans were now eager to foster a spirit of sectional reconciliation; and in both North and South, there was emerging—in popular literature, in folktales and myths, and increasingly in scholarship—a romantic vision of the Old South as a graceful and serene civilization. It was a receptive climate for the publication in 1918 of the most influential study of slavery of the time (and for many years thereafter): Ulrich B. Phillips's *American Negro Slavery*. Phillips portrayed slavery as an essentially benign institution, in which kindly masters looked after submissive, childlike, and generally contented blacks. Black people, he suggested, were for the most part lazy and irresponsible; and the occasional harshness of the slave system was simply a necessary part of supervising a backward labor force. The book was, in effect, an apology for the Southern slaveowner; and for nearly thirty years, it remained the authoritative work on the subject.

Beginning in the 1940s, when the nation began finally to confront the issue of racial injustice in a more forthright way, new approaches to slavery started to emerge. As early as 1941, Melville J. Herskovits was challenging one of Phillips's assumptions: that slaves had retained little if any of their African cultural inheritance. In fact, Herskovits argued, many Africanisms survived in slave culture for generations. Two years later, Herbert Aptheker attacked another of Phillips's claims: that slaves were submissive and content. "Discontent and rebelliousness," he wrote in *American Negro Slave Revolts*, "were not only exceedingly common, but, indeed, characteristic of American Negro slaves."

But for the time, at least, the more influential challenge to Phillips came from those who claimed that he had neglected the brutality of the system and the damage it did to those who lived under it. Kenneth Stampp's *The Peculiar Institution* (1956), the first comprehensive study of slavery since Phillips, emphasized the harshness of the system—not only its physical brutality but its psychological impact on men and women kept in a virtual prison, with little room to develop their own social and cultural patterns. An even more devastating portrait of slavery came from Stanley Elkins, whose *Slavery* (1959) argued that many slaves had, indeed, displayed childlike, submissive,

and children before being overpowered by state and federal troops. More than a hundred blacks were put to death in the aftermath. Nat Turner's was the only actual slave insurrection in the nineteenth-century South, but slave conspiracies and threats of renewed violence continued throughout the section as long as slavery lasted.

For the most part, however, resistance to slavery took other, less drastic forms. In some cases, slaves worked "within the system" to free themselves from it—earning

"Sambo" personalities, as Phillips had suggested. But to Elkins, such personalities were evidence of the terrible damage the institution had inflicted on them. Comparing the slave system to Nazi concentration camps in World War II, he cited the effects on the individual of enforced "adjustment to absolute power" and the tragic distortions of character that resulted.

Stampp and Elkins reflected the general belief of white liberals in the 1950s and early 1960s that their society bore a large measure of guilt for the injustices it had inflicted on blacks, that whites must work to undo the damage they had done in the past. By the early 1970s, however, racial attitudes had changed again, with the emergence of the "black power" ideology and the widespread belief among blacks and some whites that blacks themselves should determine their own future. The new emphasis on black pride and achievement, therefore, helped produce a new view of the black past, emphasizing the cultural and social accomplishments of blacks under slavery. John Blassingame, in *The Slave Community* (1973), echoed many of the findings of Herskovits and Aptheker thirty years before in arguing that "the most remarkable aspect of the whole process of enslavement is the extent to which the American-born slaves were able to retain their ancestors' culture." Herbert Gutman, in *The Black Family in Slavery and Freedom, 1750–1925* (1976), provided voluminous evidence to support his claim that the black family, far from being weakened and destroyed by the slave system, survived with remarkable strength—although with some differences from the prevailing form of the white family. The slave community, Gutman claimed, was so successful in preserving and developing its own culture that the master class was unable, despite its great legal power, to affect it in any significant way.

This emphasis on the ability of blacks to maintain their own culture and society under slavery, and on their remarkable achievements within the system, formed the basis of two studies in 1974 that claimed to present comprehensive new portraits of the entire system. *Time on the Cross*, by Robert Fogel and Stanley Engerman, used quantitative methods to show not only that slaves were skilled and efficient workers, not only that the black family was strong and healthy, but that the institution of slavery was a prosperous one that benefited masters and slaves alike. Slave workers, Fogel and Engerman claimed, were generally better off than Northern industrial workers. Slaves often rose to managerial positions on plantations. Whippings were few, and families were rarely broken up. The findings of *Time on the Cross* soon came under devastating attack—both from those who were offended by what they considered an apology for slavery, and more important, from historians who exposed crucial flaws in Fogel and Engerman's methods. Far more influential in the long run was Eugene Genovese's *Roll, Jordan, Roll: The World the Slaves Made*. Genovese revived the idea of "paternalism" as the central element of the slave system. But in his view, paternalism was not an expression of white generosity; it was a powerful instrument of control. And it worked in two directions, enabling blacks to make demands of whites as well as the other way around. Moreover, within this paternal system, Genovese claimed, blacks retained a large cultural "space" of their own within which they developed their own family life, traditions, social patterns, and above all religion. Indeed, slaves had by the mid-nineteenth century developed a sense of themselves as part of a separate black "nation"—a nation tied to white society in important ways, but nevertheless powerful and distinct.

money with which they managed to buy their own and their families' freedom. Some had the good luck to be set free by their master's will after his death—for example, the more than 400 slaves belonging to John Randolph of Roanoke (1833). From the 1830s on, however, state laws made it more and more difficult, and in some cases practically impossible, for an owner to manumit his slaves. The laws, when permitting manumission, often required the removal of the freed slaves from the state. The masters objected to the very presence of free blacks, who by their existence set a disturbing example for the slaves.

By 1860, there nevertheless were about 250,000 free blacks in the slaveholding states, more than half of them in Virginia and Maryland. A few, as in the North, attained wealth and prominence. A few themselves owned slaves, usually relatives whom they had bought in order to ensure their ultimate emancipation. Most, however, lived in abject poverty, even worse than in the North. Law or custom closed many occupations to them, forbade them to assemble without white supervision, and placed numerous other restraints on them. They were only quasi-free, and yet they had all the burdens of freedom, including the obligation of paying taxes. Yet great as were the hardships of freedom, blacks usually preferred them to slavery.

Some blacks attempted to resist slavery by escaping from it, by running away. A small number managed to escape to the North or to Canada, especially after sympathetic whites began organizing the so-called underground railroad to assist them in flight. But the odds against a successful escape, particularly from the Deep South, were almost impossibly great. The hazards of distance and the slaves' ignorance of geography were serious obstacles. So were the white "slave patrols," which stopped wandering blacks on sight throughout the South demanding to see travel permits. Without such a permit, slaves were presumed to be runaways and were taken captive. For blacks who attempted to escape through the woods, slave patrols often employed bloodhounds. Despite all the obstacles to success, however, blacks continued to run away from their masters in large numbers. Some did so repeatedly, undeterred by the whippings and other penalties inflicted on them when captured.

The Underground Railroad

The abolitionist efforts to aid slaves to escape from their masters were never as organized or successful as the term "underground railroad" suggests. But there was a network of sorts that helped smuggle slaves to freedom, guiding them from one hiding place to another en route to the North or to Canada. This illustration depicts slaves arriving at the home of Levi Coffin in Newport, Indiana, one of the first stops on their passage to freedom. (Culver Pictures)

But perhaps the most important method of resistance was simply a pattern of everyday behavior by which blacks defied their masters. That whites so often considered blacks to be lazy and "shiftless" suggests one means of resistance: refusal to work hard. Slaves might also steal from their masters or from neighboring whites. They might perform isolated acts of sabotage: losing or breaking tools (Southern planters gradually began to buy unusually heavy hoes because so many of the lighter ones got broken) or performing tasks improperly. In extreme cases, blacks might make themselves useless by cutting off their fingers or even committing suicide. Or, despite the terrible consequences, they might on occasion turn on their masters and kill them. The extremes, however, were rare. For the most part, blacks resisted by building into their normal patterns of behavior subtle methods of rebellion.

But resistance was only part of the slave response to slavery. The other was an elaborate process of accommodation—a process that did not imply contentment with bondage, but a recognition that there was no realistic alternative and that some adaptation was necessary. One of the ways blacks adapted was by developing a rich and complex culture, one that enabled them to retain a sense of racial pride and unity. In many areas, they retained a language of their own, sometimes incorporating African speech patterns into English. They developed a distinctive music, establishing in the process what was perhaps the most impressive of all American musical traditions. The most important features of black culture, however, were the development of two powerful institutions: religion and the family.

A separate slave religion was not supposed to exist. Almost all blacks were Christians, and their masters expected them to worship under the supervision of white ministers—often in the same chapels as whites. Indeed, autonomous black churches were banned by law. Nevertheless, blacks throughout the South developed their own version of Christianity, at times incorporating such African practices as voodoo, but more often simply bending religion to the special circumstances of bondage. Natural leaders emerging within the slave community rose to the rank of preacher; and when necessary blacks would hold services in secret. Sermons and hymns alike expressed a vague but deep longing for freedom.

The slave family also had certain restrictions placed on it by whites—most notably the lack of legal marriage. Nevertheless, the nuclear family consistently emerged as the dominant kinship pattern among blacks. Up to a third of all black families were broken up by the slave trade; but networks of kinship—which grew to include not only spouses and parents, but aunts, uncles, grandparents, even distant cousins—remained strong and important. One of the most frequent causes of escape from the plantation was a slave's desire to find a husband, wife, or child who had been sent elsewhere.

It was not only by breaking up families through sale that whites intruded on black family life. Masters, overseers, and sons of masters often enticed or compelled slave women to become their mistresses. And black women often bore the children of whites—children whom the whites seldom recognized as their own and who were consigned to slavery from birth.

In addition to establishing social and cultural institutions of their own, slaves adapted themselves to slavery by forming complex relationships with their masters. However much blacks resented their lack of freedom, they often found it difficult to maintain an entirely hostile attitude toward their owners. Not only were they dependent on whites for the material means of existence—food, clothing, and shelter; they also often derived from their masters a sense of security and protection. There was, in short, a paternal relationship between slave and master—sometimes harsh, sometimes kindly, but almost invariably important. It was in many ways an insidious relationship; for paternalism is, in the end, a form of social control. By creating a sense of mutual dependence between masters and slaves, whites helped to reduce resistance to an institution that, in essence, was designed solely for the benefit of the ruling race.

SUGGESTED READINGS

Most of the books on economic development cited in the readings for Chapters 7 and 9 are relevant for the changes described in this chapter as well. In particular, see the works by Brownlee, Bruchey, and North for useful overviews. For the expansion of agriculture, see Paul W. Gates, *The Farmer's Age* (1960). Peter Temin, *Iron and Steel in Nineteenth-Century America* (1964), examines one of the growing industries of the antebellum period. Alfred D. Chandler, Jr., *The Visible Hand: The Managerial Revolution in American Business* (1977), is an important study of the origins of modern business management, beginning in the 1850s. James Norris, *R. G. Dun & Co., 1841–1900* (1978), is a study of the growth of a single company; and Joseph E. Walker, *Hopewell: A Social and Economic History of an Ironmaking Community* (1966), is an examination of a single town. On the growth of railroads, see, in addition to the books cited in the readings for Chapter 9, Robert W. Fogel, *Railroads and American Economic Growth* (1964), a controversial quantitative study that questions the centrality of railroads to American economic growth. Carter Goodrich, *Government Promotion of Canals and Railroads, 1800–1890* (1960), examines the role of the state in building transportation systems. See also two works by John F. Stover: *The Life and Decline of the American Railroad* (1970), a broadly focused work; and *Iron Road to the West: American Railroads in the 1850s* (1978), which is more narrow in scope. R. L. Thompson, *Wiring a Continent* (1947), studies the early growth of the telegraph system.

Marcus Hansen, *The Immigrant in American History* (1940) and *The Atlantic Migration, 1607–1860* (1940), are valuable surveys, along with Maldwyn A. Jones, *American Immigration* (1960). Several studies examine the experiences of immigrants on their arrival in the United States: Oscar Handlin, *The Uprooted* (1951, rev. 1973); Charlotte Erickson, *Invisible Immigrants* (1972); Philip Taylor, *The Distant Magnet* (1971); Robert Ernst, *Immigrant Life in New York City, 1825–1863* (1949); and Kathleen N. Conzen, *Immigrant Milwaukee: 1836–1860* (1976). Carl Wittke, *We Who Built America*, rev. ed. (1964) is also useful. On particular immigrant groups, see Oscar Handlin, *Boston's Immigrants* (1941), which focuses largely on the Irish; Harold Runblom and Hans Norman, *From Sweden to America* (1976); Carl Wittke, *Refugees of Revolution: The German Forty-Eighters in America* (1952) and *The Irish in America* (1956); Theodore C. Blegen, *Norwegian Migration to America*, 2 vols. (1931–1940); Stuart C. Miller, *The Unwelcome Immigrant* (1969), on the Chinese; and Rowland T. Berthoff, *British Immigrants in Industrial America, 1790–1950* (1953). Jay P. Dolan, *The Immigrant Church: New York's Irish and German Catholics* (1975), examines immigrant religion. On mid-nineteenth-century nativism, see Ray Billington, *The Protestant Crusade, 1800–1860* (1938), a valuable

study of anti-Catholicism. I. M. Leonard and R. D. Parmet, *American Nativism, 1830–1860* (1971), is a more general view, as is T. J. Curran, *Xenophopia and Immigration* (1975). Allan Nevins, *The Ordeal of the Union*, 2 vols. (1947), contains a good analysis of antebellum nativism.

In addition to works cited in the readings for Chapter 9, useful studies of antebellum labor include Susan E. Hirsch, *Roots of the American Working Class: The Industrialization of Crafts in Newark, 1800–1860* (1978); Bruce Laurie, *Working People of Philadelphia* (1980); Norman Ware, *The Industrial Worker, 1840–1860* (1924), a pioneering work that remains valuable; Henry Pelling, *American Labor* (1960), a concise survey; and Hannah Josephson, *The Golden Threads* (1949), a study of mill girls and their employers in New England.

A host of community studies shed important light on society and culture in industrializing America, as well as on the conditions of labor and immigrants. Among the most valuable are Alan Dawley, *Class and Community: The Industrial Revolution in Lynn* (1977); Michael Frisch, *Town into City: Springfield, Massachusetts, and the Meaning of Community, 1840–1880* (1972); Peter Knights, *The Plain People of Boston, 1830–1860* (1971); Don Doyle, *The Social Order of a Frontier Community: Jacksonville, Illinois, 1825–1870* (1978); and Stuart Blumin, *The Urban Threshold: Growth and Change in a Nineteenth-Century Community* (1976). Sam Bass Warner, Jr., *The Urban Wilderness* (1972), examines urban growth, as does Richard C. Wade, *The Urban Frontier, 1790–1830* (1957). Raymond A. Mohl, *Poverty in New York, 1783–1825* (1971), and Edward Pessen, *Riches, Classes, and Power Before the Civil War* (1973), explore economic stratification and poverty. Stephan Thernstrom, *Poverty and Progress* (1964), is an important study of social mobility in nineteenth-century Newburyport, Massachusetts. A good introduction to the skimpy literature on the history of journalism is Frank Luther Mott, *American Journalism* (1950). Glyndon Van Deusen, *Horace Greeley* (1953), examines a leading nineteenth-century editor.

The question of what distinguished the South from the rest of the nation has produced a large literature and a wide range of viewpoints. A classic analysis, one that has been the source of much later theorizing and has spawned great controversy, is W. J. Cash, *The Mind of the South* (1941). Avery Craven, *The Growth of Southern Nationalism* (1953), emphasizes political developments but includes discussion of social and cultural factors. John McCardell, *The Idea of a Southern Nation* (1979), considers the social and intellectual roots of Southern nationalism; while Charles S. Sydnor, *The Development of Southern Sectionalism, 1819–1848* (1948), examines an earlier period. Two works by Clement Eaton—*Freedom of*

Thought in the Old South (1940) and The Growth of Southern Nationalism, 1848–1861 (1961)—discuss the intellectual history of the region. William R. Taylor, Cavalier and Yankee: The Old South and American National Character (1961), is an important study of Southern culture, viewed largely through its literary products. Rollin G. Osterweis, Romanticism and Nationalism in the Old South (1949), and John Hope Franklin, The Militant South (1956), take contrasting views of the Southern outlook. See also Drew Faust, A Sacred Circle: The Dilemma of the Intellectual in the Old South (1977).

The economy of the plantation South is examined in Gavin Wright, The Political Economy of the Cotton South: Households, Markets, and Wealth in the Nineteenth Century (1978). Earlier studies of importance include Lewis C. Gray, History of Agriculture in the Southern United States to 1860, 2 vols. (1933); Ulrich B. Phillips, Life and Labor in the Old South (1929); and R. R. Russel, Economic Aspects of Southern Sectionalism, 1840–1861 (1924). Frank L. Owsley, Plain Folk of the Old South (1949), is the most important of a relatively few studies examining the nonplantation economy and society of the South. A contemporary view of the South through Northern, antislavery eyes is Frederick Law Olmsted, The Cotton Kingdom (1953; ed. by Arthur M. Schlesinger, Sr.). Several collections of letters and diaries by Southerners themselves offer particularly vivid portraits of life in the Old South. See especially Robert Manson Myers (ed.), The Children of Pride (1972); Mary D. Robertson (ed.), Lucy Breckinridge of Grove Hill (1979); Carol Bleser, The Hammonds of Redcliffe (1981); and Frances Ann Kemble, Journal of a Residence on a Georgian Plantation in 1838–1839 (1863). Anne Firor Scott, The Southern Lady (1970), is an important study of the position of women in antebellum Southern society; and Mary Boykin Chesnut, A Diary from Dixie (1981, ed. by C. Vann Woodward), is an eloquent record of the views of a prominent Southern woman as her society began to crumble. On Southern religion, see Donald G. Mathews, Religion in the Old South (1977). Frank Freidel, Francis Lieber (1947), is a biography of a prominent antebellum Southern educator and reformer.

The nature of American slavery is the subject of a vast literature. Long the most influential study of the subject was Ulrich B. Phillips, American Negro Slavery (1918), an important work of scholarship flawed by the proslavery bias of its author. Kenneth Stampp, The Peculiar Institution (1955), and Stanley Elkins,

Slavery (1959), are more hostile studies written from the perspective of liberals in the 1950s. Studies emphasizing black culture and achievement, as well as resistance to slavery, began to emerge in the 1940s with Herbert Aptheker, American Negro Slave Revolts (1943), and Melville J. Herskovits, The Myth of the Negro Past (1941). Such studies proliferated in the 1970s, beginning with John Blassingame, The Slave Community (1973). Eugene Genovese, Roll, Jordan, Roll: The World the Slaves Made (1974), is perhaps the finest achievement of historians examining the roots of black culture. Herbert Gutman, The Black Family in Slavery and Freedom (1976), is a masterful study of one of the most important elements of slave culture. More specialized studies include Judith Chase, Afro-American Art and Craft (1971), which emphasizes black artistic achievement; and Dena Epstein, Sinful Tunes and Spirituals (1977), and Lawrence W. Levine, Black Culture and Black Consciousness: Afro-American Folk Thought from Slavery to Freedom (1977), which emphasize music and folk culture. G. P. Rawick, From Sundown to Sunup: The Making of the Black Community (1973), examines plantation life. Leslie Howard Owens, This Species of Property (1976), is a useful survey employing recent scholarship. A controversial quantitative study of the slave economy is Robert Fogel and Stanley Engerman, Time on the Cross, 2 vols. (1974), which has been roundly and effectively attacked by, among others, Herbert Gutman, Slavery and the Numbers Game (1975), and P. A. David et al., Reckoning with Slavery (1976). Robert Starobin, Industrial Slavery in the Old South (1970), and Richard C. Wade, Slavery in the Cities (1964), examine the institution away from the plantation. The world of the slaveowners themselves is examined in Eugene Genovese, The Political Economy of Slavery (1965) and The World the Slaveholders Made (1969); and James Oakes, The Ruling Race: A History of American Slaveholders (1982). Stephen B. Oates, The Fires of Jubilee (1974), examines the Nat Turner uprising; and Robert Starobin, Denmark Vesey (1970), discusses the Vesey conspiracy. Carl Degler, Neither Black nor White (1971), is a comparative study of race relations in Brazil and the United States. Joel Williamson, New People: Miscegenation and Mulattoes in the United States (1980), is a study of the sensitive subject of race mixture. Ira Berlin, Slaves Without Masters (1974), considers free blacks in the antebellum South; while Leon Litwack, North of Slavery (1961), examines free blacks in the North.

Freedom's Ferment 12

A Boston School, 1850
The rapid expansion of education, both public and private, was one of the major accomplishments of the energetic burst of reform in mid-nineteenth-century America. This photograph of a schoolroom in Boston depicts a class of young women, who not many years before had been considered unfit subjects for education. Earlier in the century, Ralph Waldo Emerson had attended this same school. (Culver Pictures)

The American people in the mid-nineteenth century lived in a society in transition. Their nation was growing rapidly in geographical extent, in the size and diversity of its population, and in the dimensions and complexity of its economy. And like any people faced with such rapid and fundamental alterations in their surroundings, Americans reacted with ambiguity. On the one hand, they were excited by the new possibilities that economic growth was providing. On the other hand, they were painfully aware of the dislocations that it was creating: the challenges to traditional values and institutions, the social instability, the uncertainty about the future.

The result of these conflicting attitudes was the emergence of a bewildering array of movements to adapt society to its new realities, to "reform" the nation. These reform efforts took so many different shapes that generalizations about them are difficult, but in general they reflected one of two basic impulses, and at times elements of both. Many of these movements rested on an optimistic faith in human nature, a belief that within every individual resided a spirit that was basically good and that society should attempt to unleash. This assumption—which spawned in both Europe and America a movement known, in its artistic aspects at least, as romanticism—stood in marked contrast to the traditional Calvinist assumption that man's impulses and instincts were evil and needed to be repressed. In-

stead, reformers now argued, individuals should strive to give full expression to the inner spirit, should work to unleash their capacity to experience joy and to do good.

A second impulse, which appeared directly to contradict the first but in practice often existed alongside it, was a desire for order and control. With their society changing so rapidly, with their traditional values and institutions being challenged and eroded, many Americans yearned above all for a restoration of stability and discipline to their nation. Often, this impulse embodied a conservative nostalgia for better, simpler times. But it also inspired efforts to create new institutions of social control, suited to the realities of the new age.

The reforms that flowed from these two impulses came in many guises and embraced many different groups within the population. But the heart of reform activity remained always the Northeast, in particular New England; and in the course of the 1840s, the focus of this core group of reformers began to shift to one issue that came to overshadow all others: slavery. Not all Northern reformers agreed on how precisely to deal with the existence of slavery in their nation, but virtually all came to believe that the institution was an evil that must ultimately be eliminated. And in taking this position, they added another powerful force to the many that were driving a wedge between America's two major sections.

CULTURE AND LIBERATION

"In the four quarters of the globe," wrote the English wit Sydney Smith in 1820, "who reads an American book? or goes to an American play? or looks at an American picture or statue?" The answer, he assumed, was obvious—no one.

American intellectuals were painfully aware of the low regard in which their culture was held by Europeans; and they continued in the middle decades of the century to work for a liberation of their nation's culture—for the creation of an American artistic life independent of Europe, one that would express their own nation's special virtues. At the same time, however, the nation's cultural leaders were beginning to strive for another kind of liberation, one that would gradually come almost to overshadow their self-conscious nationalism. That impulse, which was—ironically—largely an import from Europe, was the spirit of romanticism. In literature, in philosophy, in art, even in politics and economics, American intellectuals were committing themselves to the liberation of the human spirit.

A Literary Flowering

The effort to create a distinctively American literature, which Washington Irving and others had advanced in the first decades of the century, bore important fruit in the 1820s with the emergence of the first great American novelist: James Fenimore Cooper. The author of over thirty novels in the space of three decades, Cooper was known to his contemporaries as a master of adventure and suspense. What most distinguished his work, however, was its evocation of the American frontier. Cooper had grown up in western New York, at a time when the wilderness was not far away; and he retained throughout his life a fascination with man's relationship to nature and with the challenges (and dangers) of America's expansion westward. His most important novels—the "Leatherstocking Tales," among them *The Last of the Mohicans* (1826) and *The Deerslayer* (1841)—explored the American frontiersman's experience with Indians, pioneers, violence, and the law.

Cooper's novels were a continuation, in many ways a culmination, of the early-nineteenth-century effort to produce a truly American literature. But they also served as a link to the concerns of later intellectuals. For in the "Leatherstocking Tales" could be seen not only a celebration of the American spirit and landscape but an evocation, through the character of Natty Bumppo, of the ideal of the independent individual, with a natural inner goodness. There was also evidence of the second impulse that would motivate American reform: the fear of disorder. In

Walt Whitman
This picture of the youthful, jaunty, bearded poet appeared as the frontispiece in the first edition of *Leaves of Grass* (1855). It is an engraving made from a painting by Francis B. Carpenter. Born in Homer, New York, and largely self-taught, Carpenter became one of the most successful portrait painters of the second half of the nineteenth century. He lived in the White House from February to July 1864 while doing a canvas of Lincoln reading his emancipation proclamation to the cabinet. He afterward wrote *Six Months at the White House* (1866), giving an inside view of Lincoln at home. (New York Public Library)

portraying other characters, who exemplified the vicious, grasping nature of some of the nation's Western settlers, Cooper was suggesting a need for social discipline even in the wilderness.

Emerging on the heels of Cooper was another group of important American writers who displayed even more clearly the grip of romanticism on the nation's intellectual life. Walt Whitman, the self-proclaimed poet of American democracy, was the son of a Long Island carpenter and lived for many years roaming the country doing odd jobs. Finally, in 1855, he hired a printer and published a first, thin volume of work, *Leaves of Grass*. His poems were an unrestrained celebration of democracy, of the liberation of the individual, and of the pleasures of the flesh as well as of the spirit. Identifying himself with the American people, he wrote:

I celebrate myself, and sing myself,
And what I assume you shall assume,
For every atom belonging to me as good as
    belongs to you.

In these poems, as well as in a large body of other work spanning nearly forty more years until his death in 1892, Whitman not only helped liberate verse from traditional, restrictive conventions but helped express the questing spirit of individualism that characterized his age.

But the new literary concern with the unleashing of human emotions did not always produce optimistic and exuberant works. Herman Melville is a case in point. Born in New York in 1819, Melville ran away to sea as a youth and spent years sailing the world (including the South Seas) before returning home to become the greatest American writer of his era. The most important of his novels, indeed one of the most important novels ever written in the English language, was *Moby Dick*, published in 1851. Through his portrayal of Ahab, the powerful, driven captain of a whaling vessel, Melville exposed the power of the human spirit when unleashed from traditional social constraints. Yet the story of Ahab was not simply a story of courage and will, but a tragedy of pride and revenge. Ahab's maniacal search for the great white whale, Moby Dick, who had maimed him, became symbolic of a search for the deepest meanings of life and for the final triumph over evil. The result, however, was the annihilation of Ahab himself—evidence of the power of the human spirit not only to liberate but to destroy.

Similarly bleak were the works of one of the few Southern writers of the time to embrace the search for the essence of the human spirit: Edgar Allan Poe. In the course of his short and unhappy life (he died in 1849 at the age of forty), Poe produced stories and poems that were primarily sad and macabre.

His first book, *Tamerlane and Other Poems* (1827), received little recognition. But later works, including his most famous poem, "The Raven" (1845), established him as a major, if controversial, literary figure. Through it all, Poe evoked images of man rising above the narrow confines of his intellect and exploring the deeper world of the spirit and the emotions. Yet that world, he seemed to say, was one of pain and horror. Other American writers were contemptuous of Poe's work and his message, but he was ultimately to have a profound effect on such European poets as Baudelaire.

The Transcendentalists

The outstanding expression of the romantic impulse in America came from a group of New England writers and philosophers known as the transcendentalists. Borrowing heavily from German philosophers such as Kant, Hegel, and Schelling, and from the English writers Coleridge and Carlyle, the transcendentalists embraced a theory of the individual that rested on a distinction (first suggested by Kant) between what they called "reason" and "understanding." Reason, as they defined it, was man's highest faculty; it was the individual's innate capacity to grasp beauty and truth by giving full expression to the instincts and emotions. Understanding, by contrast, was the use of intellect in the narrow, artificial ways imposed by society; it involved the repression of instinct and the victory of externally imposed categories. Man's goal, therefore, should be to free himself from the confines of "understanding" and to cultivate his "reason." Each individual should strive to "transcend" the limits of the intellect and allow the emotions, the "soul" to create an "original relation to the Universe."

Transcendentalist philosophy emerged first among a small group of intellectuals centered in Concord, Massachusetts. Their leader and most eloquent voice was Ralph Waldo Emerson. A Unitarian minister in his youth, Emerson left the church in 1832 to devote himself entirely to writing and teaching the elements of transcendentalism. He produced a significant body of poetry, but he was most renowned for his essays and lectures. In "Nature" (1836), one of his best-known essays, Emerson wrote that in the quest for self-fulfillment, man should work for a communion with the natural world: "in the woods, we return to reason and faith. . . . Standing on the bare ground,—my head bathed by the blithe air, and uplifted into infinite space,—all mean egotism vanishes. . . . I am part and particle of God." In other essays, he was even more explicit in advocating a commitment of the individual to the full exploration of his own inner capacities. "Nothing is at last sacred," he wrote in "Self-Reliance" (1841), perhaps his most famous essay, "but the integrity of your own mind." In seeking self-reliance, he explained, man was searching for communion with the unity of the universe, the wholeness of God, the great spiritual force that he described as the "Oversoul." Each person's innate capacity to become, through his or her private efforts, a part of this essence was perhaps the classic expression of the romantic belief in the "divinity" of the individual.

Almost as influential as Emerson was another leading Concord transcendentalist, Henry David Thoreau. Thoreau went even further than his friend Emerson in repudiating the repressive forces of society, which produced, he said, "lives of quiet desperation." Man should work for self-realization by breaking all ties with organized civilization, by attempting to create a private world in which the individual communed only with nature. Thoreau's own effort to create such a world—immortalized in his most famous book, *Walden* (1854)—led him to build an isolated cabin in the Concord woods on the edge of Walden Pond, where he lived for two years as simply as he could. "I went to the woods," he explained, "because I wished to live deliberately, to front only the essential facts of life, and see if I could not learn what it had to teach, and not, when I came to die, discover that I had not lived." Thoreau's rejection of what he considered the artificial constraints of society extended as well to his relationship with government. In 1846, he went to jail (briefly) rather than agree to pay a poll tax. He would not, he insisted, give fi-

Ralph Waldo Emerson
Emerson was the most influential American intellectual of his generation and one of the leading forces in introducing nineteenth-century European (particularly German) ideas to the United States. Trained for the ministry but soon disillusioned by traditional religious forms, Emerson spent several years in Europe, absorbing the philosophies of such thinkers as Carlyle, Wordsworth, Coleridge, and the German idealists. Convinced that the key to human fulfillment lay in the cultivation of the individual, Emerson advocated that each person develop "an original relationship with the visible universe"; and he himself attempted to do so by spending a part of each day in solitary communion with nature. For many years a resident of Concord, Massachusetts, Emerson became the center of a large circle of New England writers and intellectuals known collectively as the transcendentalists. (Library of Congress)

nancial support to a government that permitted the existence of slavery. In his 1849 essay "Resistance to Civil Government," he explained his refusal by claiming that the individual's personal morality had the first claim on his actions, that a government which required him to violate that morality had no legitimate authority. The proper response was "civil disobedience," or "passive resistance"—a public refusal to obey unjust laws.

Visions of Utopia

Although transcendentalism was above all an individualistic philosophy, it helped to spawn the most famous of all nineteenth-century experiments in communal living: Brook Farm. The dream of the Boston transcendentalist George Ripley, Brook Farm was established as an experimental community in West Roxbury, Massachusetts, in 1841. There, according to Ripley, individuals would gather to create a new form of social organization, one that would permit every member of the community full opportunity for self-realization. All residents would share equally in the labor of the community so that all could share too in the leisure; for it was leisure that was the first necessity for cultivation of the self. (Ripley was one of the first Americans to attribute positive connotations to the idea of leisure; most of his contemporaries equated it with laziness and sloth.) But participation in manual labor served another purpose as well: it helped the individual bridge the gap between the world of the intellect and the world of the flesh, thus aiding him to become a whole person. The obvious tension between the ideal of individual freedom and the demands of a communal society took their toll on Brook Farm. Increasingly, individualism gave way to a form of socialism. Many residents became disenchanted and left; when a fire destroyed the central building of the community in 1847, the experiment dissolved.

Among the original residents of Brook Farm was the writer Nathaniel Hawthorne, who expressed his disillusionment with the experiment and, to some extent, with transcendentalism itself in a series of notable novels. In *The Blithedale Romance* (1852), he wrote scathingly of Brook Farm itself, portraying the disastrous consequences of the experiment on the individuals who submitted to it. In other novels—most notably *The Scarlet Letter* (1850) and *The House of Seven Gables* (1851)—he wrote equally passionately about the price the individual pays for cutting himself off from society. Egotism, he claimed (in an indirect challenge to the transcendentalist faith in the self), was the "serpent" that lay at the heart of human misery.

The failure of Brook Farm did not, however, discourage the formation of other experimental communities. Some borrowed, as Ripley had done, from the ideas of the French philosopher Charles Fourier, whose ideas of socialist communities organized as cooperative "phalanxes" received wide attention in America. Others drew from the ideas of the Scottish industrialist and philanthropist Robert Owen. Owen himself founded an experimental community in Indiana in 1825, which he named New Harmony. It was to be a "Village of Cooperation," in which every resident worked and lived in total equality. The community was an economic failure, but the vision that had inspired it continued to enchant Americans. Dozens of other "Owenite" experiments began in other locations in the ensuing years.

Among the most enduring of the Utopian colonies was the Oneida Community, established in 1848 in upstate New York by John Humphrey Noyes. The Oneida "Perfectionists," as residents of the community called themselves, embraced communalism so completely that they rejected even traditional notions of family. Every resident was to be free to engage in sexual activity with any consenting partner; there were to be no permanent conjugal ties. The only constraints on individual freedom were to be the collective needs of the community; no artificial moral barriers need be maintained.

The Mormons

Brook Farm, New Harmony, and other experimental communities were intended to maximize the freedom of individual residents (although in practice, precisely the opposite at times occurred). Other experimental communities emphasized a different impulse. They attempted to create new societies, apart from the mainstream of American life, in order to protect their members from the

The Oneida Community
Members of the Oneida Community, in upstate New York, believed in "complex marriage,"
according to which all the men were considered married to all the women. Women enjoyed
the same rights as men, and the whole community took care of the children. The members
looked upon all kinds of work as honorable. Here, on the lawn at Oneida, some of them are
taking part in a "working bee," in which (like many other Americans of the time) they
combined labor with conversation and merrymaking. (Library of Congress)

chaos and disorder of the rest of the nation.
More than personal freedom, such communities stressed social discipline. In general,
these were religious communities founded
by relatively small, dissenting sects. The
Shakers, for example, practiced a form of
tightly disciplined socialism in more than
twenty communities throughout the Northeast and Northwest in the 1840s. Their goal
was to provide a means of realizing a truly
Christian life. (They derived their name from
a unique religious ritual—a sort of dance, in
which members of a congregation would
"shake" themselves free of sin while performing a loud chant.) The Amana Community, founded by German immigrants in 1843
and moved to Iowa in 1855, was a similar ef-

fort to realize Christian ideals by creating a
socialist society.

But the most important of all efforts to
create a new society within the old was that
of the Church of Jesus Christ of Latter Day
Saints—the Mormons. Mormonism began in
upstate New York as a result of the efforts of
Joseph Smith, a young, energetic, but economically unsuccessful man, who had spent
most of his twenty-four years moving
restlessly through New England and the
Northeast. Then in 1830, he published
a remarkable document—The Book of
Mormon—which was, he claimed, a transla-
tion of a set of golden plates he had found in
the hills of New York, revealed to him by an
angel of God. The Book of Mormon told the

story of an ancient civilization of Christians in America, whose now vanished kingdom could become a model for a new holy community in the United States. Gathering a small group of believers around him, Smith began in 1831 an effort to find a sanctuary for his new community of saints, an effort that would continue, unhappily, for more than twenty years. Time and again, the Mormons attempted to establish their "New Jerusalem." Time and again, they met with persecution from surrounding communities suspicious of the radical religious doctrines—which included polygamy, a rigid form of social organization, and most damaging of all, an intense secrecy, which gave rise to wild rumors of conspiracy and depravity.

Driven from their original settlements in Independence, Missouri, and Kirkland, Ohio, the Mormons moved on to the new town of Nauvoo, Illinois, which in the early 1840s became an imposing and economically successful community. In 1844, however, Jo-

seph Smith was arrested, charged with treason (for conspiring against the government to win foreign support for a new Mormon colony in the Southwest), and imprisoned in Carthage, Illinois. There an angry mob attacked the jail, forced Smith from his cell, and shot and killed him. The Mormons now abandoned Nauvoo and, under the leadership of Smith's successor, Brigham Young, traveled across the desert—a society of 12,000 people, one of the largest group migrations in American history—and established a new community in Utah, the present Salt Lake City. There, at last, the Mormons were able to create a permanent settlement. And although they were not always to remain as completely isolated from the rest of American society as they were at the beginning, never again were they to be dislodged.

Like other experiments in social organization of the era, Mormonism reflected a belief in human perfectibility. God had once been a man, the church taught; and thus every man

Brigham Young
Brigham Young was born in Vermont and grew up in western New York in an area known, because of the fiery religious revivals that swept across it, as the "burnt-over district." Here the Mormon faith originated, and here Young was converted to it. He quickly became a leader in the church and became its president on Joseph Smith's death in 1844. He led his people to Utah, and on seeing the grim and forbidding Great Salt Lake basin, he exclaimed: "This is the place!" (Library of Congress)

or woman could aspire to become—as Joseph Smith had done—a god. But unlike other new communities, the Mormons did not embrace the doctrine of individual liberty. Instead, they created a highly organized, centrally directed, even militarized social structure, a refuge against the disorder and uncertainty of the secular world. The original Mormons were, for the most part, men and women who felt displaced in their rapidly changing society—economically marginal people left behind by the material growth and social progress of their era. In the new religion, they found security and order.

REMAKING SOCIETY

The simultaneous efforts to liberate the individual and impose order on a changing world helped to create a wide range of new movements to remake society. By the 1830s, such movements had taken the form of organized reform societies. "In no country in the world," Tocqueville had observed, "has the principle of association been more successfully used, or more unsparingly applied to a multitude of different objects, than in America. . . . for there is no end which the human will, seconded by the collective exertions of individuals, despairs of attaining." The new organizations did indeed work on behalf of a wide range of goals: temperance, education, peace, the care of the poor, the handicapped, and the mentally ill, the treatment of criminals, the rights of women, and many more. Few eras in American history have witnessed as wide a range of reform efforts. And few eras have exposed more clearly the simultaneous attraction of Americans to the ideas of personal liberty and social order.

Revivalism, Morality, and Order

The dislocations and social ills of the new industrial economy, combined with the promise of abundance that this growth created, provided a context for reform efforts. But the actual philosophy of reform arose from two distinct sources. One was the optimistic vision of those who, like the transcendentalists, rejected Calvinist doctrines and preached the divinity of the individual. These included not only Emerson, Thoreau, and their followers, but a much larger group of Americans who embraced the doctrines of Unitarianism and Universalism and absorbed European romanticism.

The second, and in many respects more important, source was Protestant revivalism—the movement that had begun with the Second Great Awakening early in the century and had, by the 1820s, evolved into a powerful force for social reform. Although the "New Light" revivalists were theologically far removed from the transcendentalists and Unitarians, they had come to share the optimistic belief that every individual was capable of salvation. According to Charles Grandison Finney, a Presbyterian minister who became the most influential revival evangelist of the 1820s and 1830s, traditional Calvinist doctrines of predestination and individual human helplessness were both obsolete and destructive. Each person, he preached, contained within himself or herself the capacity to experience spiritual rebirth and achieve salvation. A revival need not depend on a miracle from God; it could be created by individual effort.

Finney enjoyed particular success in upstate New York, where he helped launch a series of passionate revivals in towns along the Erie Canal—a region so prone to religious awakenings that it was known as the "burned-over district." It was no coincidence that the new revivalism should prove so powerful there, for this region of New York was experiencing—largely as a result of the construction of the canal—a major economic transformation. And with that transformation had come changes in the social fabric so profound that many men and women felt baffled and disoriented. (It was in roughly this same area of New York that Joseph Smith first organized the Mormon church.)

"The Drunkard's Progress"
From the first casual glass, the young man rises step by step to the summit of drunken jollification and then declines to desperation and suicide, while his wife and child mourn. This lithograph was published in 1846 by Nathaniel Currier, who later joined with James M. Ives to form the most famous American firm of lithographers. Currier and Ives turned out thousands of color prints of artwork reflecting manners, movements, and events in the days before photographs could be accurately reproduced by means of halftone engravings. (Library of Congress)

Finney's doctrine of personal regeneration appealed strongly to those who felt threatened by change. In Rochester, New York, the site of his greatest success, he staged a series of emotionally wrenching religious meetings that aroused a large segment of the community—particularly the relatively prosperous citizens who were enjoying the economic benefits of the new commercial growth but were also uneasy about the introduction into their community of a new, undisciplined pool of transient laborers. For them, revivalism became not only a means of personal salvation but a mandate for the reform (and control) of the larger society. In particular, Finney's revivalism became a call for a crusade against personal immorality. "The church," he maintained, "must take right ground on the subject of Temperance, and Moral Reform, and all the subjects of practical morality which come up for decision from time to time."

Evangelical Protestantism added major strength, therefore, to one of the most influential reform movements of the era: the crusade against drunkenness. No social vice, some reformers (including, for example, many of Finney's converts in cities such as Rochester) argued, was more responsible for crime, disorder, and poverty than the excessive use of alcohol. Although advocates of temperance had been active since the late eighteenth century, the new reformers gave the movement an energy and influence it had never known. In 1826, the American Society for the Promotion of Temperance emerged as a coordinating agency among various groups; it attempted to use many of the techniques of revivalism in preaching abstinence. Then, in 1840, six reformed drunkards in Baltimore organized the Washington Temperance Society and began to draw large crowds to hear their impassioned and intriguing confessions of past sins. By then, temperance advocates had grown dramatically in numbers; more than a million people had signed a formal pledge to forgo hard liquor.

As the movement gained in strength, it also became divided in purpose. Some temperance advocates now urged that abstinence include not only liquor but beer and wine; not everyone agreed. Others began to demand state legislation to restrict the sale and consumption of alcohol (Maine passed such a law in 1851); but others insisted that temperance must rely on the conscience of the individual. Whatever their disagreements, however, most temperance advocates shared similar motives. By promoting abstinence, reformers were attempting to promote individual, moral self-improvement; but they were also trying to impose discipline on society. The latter impulse was reflected particularly clearly in the battle over prohibition laws, which pitted established Protestants against new Catholic immigrants. The arrival of the immigrants was profoundly disturbing to established residents of many communities; and the restriction of alcohol seemed to them a way to curb the disorder that they believed the new population was creating.

Education and Rehabilitation

One of the outstanding reform movements of the mid-nineteenth century was the effort to produce a system of universal public education. As of 1830, no state could yet boast such a system, although some—such as Massachusetts—had supported a limited version for many years. Now, however, interest in public education grew rapidly—a reflection of the new belief in the innate capacity of every person and of society's obligation to

tap that capacity; but a reflection, too, of the desire to expose students to stable social values as a way to resist instability.

The greatest of the educational reformers was Horace Mann, the first secretary of the Massachusetts Board of Education, which was established in 1837. To Mann and his followers, education was the only way to "counterwork this tendency to the domination of capital and the servility of labor." It was also the only way to protect democracy, for an educated electorate was essential to the workings of a free political system. Mann reorganized the Massachusetts school system, lengthened the academic year (to six months), doubled teachers' salaries, enriched the curriculum, and introduced new methods of professional training for teachers. Other states experienced similar expansion and development: building new schools, creating teachers' colleges, and offering vast new groups of children access to education. Henry Barnard helped produce a new educational system in Connecticut and Rhode Island. Pennsylvania passed a law in 1835 appropriating state funds for the support of universal education. Governor William Seward of New York extended public support of schools throughout the state in the early 1840s. By the 1850s the principle of tax-supported elementary schools had been accepted in all the states; all, despite continuing opposition from certain groups, were making at least a start toward putting the principle into practice.

Yet the quality of the new education continued to vary widely. In some places—Massachusetts, for example, where Mann established the first American state-supported teachers' college in 1839, and the first professional association of teachers was created in 1845—educators were usually capable men and women, often highly trained, and with an emerging sense of themselves as career professionals. In other areas, however, teachers were often barely literate and funding for education was so limited as to restrict opportunities severely. In the newly settled regions of the West, where the population was highly dispersed, many children had no access to schools at all. In the South, the entire black population was barred from education (although approximately 10 percent of the slaves managed to achieve literacy anyway); and only about a third of all white children of school age were actually enrolled in schools in 1860. In the North, the percentage was 72 percent; but even there, many students attended classes only briefly and casually. Despite all the limitations and inequities, however, the achievements of the school reformers were impressive by any standard. By the beginning of the Civil War, the United States had the highest literacy rate of any nation of the world: 94 percent of the population of the North and 83 percent of the white population of the South (58 percent of the total population).

The conflicting impulses that underlay the movement for school reform were visible in some of the different institutions that emerged. In New England, for example, the transcendentalist Bronson Alcott established an experimental school in Concord that reflected his strong belief in the importance of complete self-realization. He urged children to learn from their own inner wisdom, not from the imposition of values by the larger society. Children were to teach themselves, rather than relying on teachers. A similar emphasis on the potential of the individual sparked the creation of new institutions to help the handicapped, institutions that formed part of a great network of charitable activities known as the Benevolent Empire. Among them was the Perkins School for the Blind in Boston, the first such school in America. Nothing better exemplified the romantic impulse of the era than the belief of those who founded Perkins that even society's least-favored members—the blind and otherwise handicapped—could be helped to discover an inner strength and wisdom. One teacher at the school expressed such attitudes when he described to the visiting English writer Charles Dickens the case of a blind, deaf, and speechless young woman who had been taught to communicate with the world. Although the "darkness and the silence of the tomb were around her," the teacher explained, "the immortal spirit which had been implanted within her could not die, nor be maimed nor mutilated." Gradually, she had learned to deal with the world around her, even to sew and knit, and most importantly, to speak through sign language. No longer was she a "dog or parrot." She was "an immortal spirit, eagerly seizing upon a new link of union with other spirits!"

Far more typical of educational reform, however, were efforts to use schools to impose a set of social values on children—the values that reformers believed were appropriate for their new, industrializing society. These values included thrift, order, discipline, punctuality, and respect for authority. Horace Mann, for example, spoke frequently of the role of public schools in extending democracy and expanding individual opportunity. But he spoke, too, of their role in creating social order. "The unrestrained passions of men are not only homicidal, but suicidal," he said in words that directly contradicted the emphasis of Alcott and other transcendentalists on instinct and emotion. "Train up a child in the way he should go, and when he is old he will not depart from it."

Similar impulses helped create another powerful movement of reform: the creation of "asylums," as they were now called for the first time, for criminals and for the mentally ill. On the one hand, in advocating prison and hospital reform, Americans were reacting against one of society's most glaring ills. Criminals of all kinds, debtors unable to pay their debts, the mentally ill, even senile paupers—all were crowded together indiscriminately into prisons and jails, which in some cases were literally holes; one jail in Connecticut was an abandoned mine shaft. Beginning in the 1820s, numerous states replaced these antiquated facilities with new penitentiaries and mental institutions designed to provide a proper environment for inmates. New York built the first penitentiary at Auburn in 1821; in Massachusetts, the reformer Dorothea Dix began a national movement for new methods of treating the mentally ill. Imprisonment of debtors and paupers was gradually eliminated, as were such traditional practices as public hangings.

But the creation of "asylums" for social deviants was not simply an effort to curb the abuses of the old system. It was also an attempt to reform and rehabilitate the inmates. New forms of rigid prison discipline were

Dorothea Dix
Dorothea Dix
(1802–1887) was born
in Maine and brought
up in Massachusetts.
She taught school and
wrote books for chil-
dren before starting
her campaign to es-
tablish public hospi-
tals for the mentally
ill (and also to make
prisons less inhu-
mane). Until she was
eighty she continued
to travel the United
States and Europe in
furtherance of this
cause. (Library of Con-
gress)

designed to rid criminals of the "laxness" that had presumably led them astray. Solitary confinement and the imposition of silence on work crews (both instituted in Pennsylvania and New York in the 1820s) were meant to give the prisoner an opportunity to meditate on his wrongdoing. Some reformers argued that the discipline of the asylum could serve as a model for other potentially disordered environments—for example, factories and schools. But penitentiaries and even many mental hospitals soon fell victim to overcrowding, and the original reform ideal was gradually lost. Most prisons ultimately degenerated into little more than warehouses for criminals, with scant emphasis on rehabilitation. The idea, in its early stages, had envisioned far more.

The Rise of Feminism

The reform ferment of the antebellum period had a particular meaning for American women. They played central roles in a wide range of reform movements, and a particularly important role in the movement on behalf of the abolition of slavery. In the process, they developed an awareness of the problems that women themselves faced in a male-dominated society. The result was the creation of the first important American feminist movement, one that laid the groundwork for more than a century of agitation for women's rights.

The rise of feminism reflected not only the participation of women in social crusades but a more basic change in the nature of the family. The modern commercial-industrial economy of the Northeast had changed the economic basis of the household. Increasingly, work was performed and income produced not in the home but in the factory or mill or office. Families worked together less frequently; it was not uncommon for the male head of the household to be the only income producer, and the importance of children as an economic asset declined. The result was, among other things, a declining family size. Another result was a redefinition of the role of women within the family. Wives and mothers were now seen as providing a particular form of emotional nurture to their husbands and children. Their major function was the maintenance of the household and the care of the young. If the family was now seen as a purely domestic unit, with no direct relationship to the marketplace, then woman was seen as being the center of that domestic sphere.

In one sense, this gradual change elevated the position of women, placing a positive value on their special role as mother and homemaker. But in another sense it accentuated women's inferiority by clearly defining and limiting their own, separate sphere. Women remained legally subordinate to their husbands, who retained almost absolute authority over their wives' property and persons. In case of divorce, he was far more likely than she to get custody of the children. Women had virtually no access to professional careers. They were forbidden by custom to speak in public to a mixed audience. Although they were encouraged to attend school at the elementary levels, they were strongly discouraged—and in most cases effectively barred—from pursuing higher education. Oberlin in Ohio became the first college in America to accept woman students; it permitted four to enroll in 1837, despite criti-

cism that coeducation would become a rash experiment approximating free love. Oberlin authorities were confident that "the mutual influence of the sexes upon each other is decidedly happy in the cultivation of both mind & manners." But few other institutions shared their views. Coeducation remained extraordinarily rare until long after the Civil War; and only a very few women's colleges—such as Mount Holyoke, founded in Massachusetts by Mary Lyon in 1837—emerged.

Those women who began to involve themselves in reform movements in the 1820s and 1830s came to look on such restrictions with rising resentment. Some began to defy them. Sarah and Angelina Grimké, sisters born in South Carolina who had become active and outspoken abolitionists, ignored attacks by men who claimed that their activities were inappropriate for their sex. "Men and women were CREATED EQUAL," they argued. "They are both moral and accountable beings, and whatever is right for man to do, is right for women to do." Other reformers—Catharine Beecher, Harriet Beecher Stowe (her sister), Lucretia Mott, Elizabeth Cady Stanton, and Dorothea Dix—similarly pressed at the boundaries of "acceptable" female behavior, chafing at the restrictions placed on them by men. Finally, in 1840, the patience of several women snapped. A group of American female delegates arrived at a world antislavery convention in London, only to be turned away by the men who controlled the proceedings. Angered at the rejection, several of the delegates—notably Lucretia Mott and Elizabeth Cady Stanton—became convinced that their first duty as reformers should now be to elevate the status of women. Over the next several years, Mott, Stanton, and others began drawing pointed parallels between the plight of women and the plight of slaves; and in 1848, they organized in Seneca Falls, New York, a convention to discuss the question of women's rights. Out of the meeting emerged a "Declaration of Sentiments and Resolutions" (patterned on the Declaration of Independence), which stated that "all men and women are created equal," that women no less than men

Equal Rights for Women [1848]

*After declaring that "all men and women are created equal" and list-
ing the "injuries and usurpations on the part of man toward
woman," the Seneca Falls women's rights convention adopted a series of resolutions for constructive action, among them the following:*

Resolved, That the same amount of virtue,
delicacy, and refinement of behavior that
is required of woman in the social state,
should also be required of man, and the
same transgressions should be visited with
equal severity on both man and woman.

Resolved, That the objection of indelicacy
and impropriety, which is so often brought
against women when she addresses
a public audience, comes with a very ill
grace from those who encourage, by their
attendance, her appearance on the stage,
in the concert, or in feats of the circus.

Resolved, That it is the duty of the
women of this country to secure to themselves their sacred right to the elective
franchise.

Resolved, That the equality of human
rights results necessarily from the fact of
the identity of the race in capabilities and
responsibilities.

Resolved, That the speedy success of our
cause depends upon the zealous and un-
tiring efforts of both men and women, for
the overthrow of the monopoly of the
pulpit, and for the securing to women an
equal participation in the various trades,
professions, and commerce.

---

are endowed with certain inalienable rights.
Their most prominent demand was for the
right to vote, thus launching a movement for
woman suffrage that would survive until the
battle was finally won in 1920. But the document was in many ways more important
for its rejection of the whole notion that men
and women should be assigned separate
"spheres" in society.

Progress toward these feminist goals was
limited in the antebellum years, but certain
individual women did manage to break the
social barriers to advancement. Elizabeth
Blackwell, born in England, gained acceptance and fame as a physician. Her sister-in-
law Antoinette Brown Blackwell became the
first ordained woman minister in the United
States; and another sister-in-law, Lucy Stone,
took the revolutionary step of retaining her
maiden name after marriage. She became a
successful and influential lecturer on
women's rights. Emma Willard, founder of
the Troy Female Seminary in 1821, and
Catharine Beecher, who founded the Hartford Female Seminary in 1823, worked on
behalf of women's education. Some women
expressed their feminist sentiments even in
their choice of costume—by wearing a distinctive style of dress (introduced in the
1850s) that combined a short skirt with full
length pantalettes—an outfit that allowed
freedom of movement without loss of mod-
esty. Introduced by the famous actress Fanny
Kemble, it came to be called the "bloomer"
costume, after one of its advocates, Amelia
Bloomer. (It provoked so much controversy
that feminists finally abandoned it, believing
that the furor was drawing attention away
from their more important demands.)

Yet there was an irony in this rise of interest in the rights of women. Feminists benefited greatly from their association with
other reform movements, most notably abolitionism; but at the same time, they suffered
as a result. For the demands of women were
always assigned—even by many women
themselves—a secondary position to the far
greater issue of the rights of slaves.

THE CRUSADE AGAINST SLAVERY

The antislavery movement was not new to the mid-nineteenth century. There had been efforts even before the Revolution to limit, and even eliminate, the institution, efforts that had helped remove slavery from most of the North by the end of the eighteenth century. There were powerful antislavery movements in England and Europe that cried out forcefully against human bondage. But American antislavery sentiment remained relatively muted in the first decades after independence. Not until 1830 did it begin to gather the force that would ultimately enable it to overshadow virtually all other efforts at social reform.

Early Opposition to Slavery

In the early years of the nineteenth century, those who opposed slavery were, for the most part, a calm and genteel lot, expressing moral disapproval but engaging in few overt activities. To the extent that there was an organized antislavery movement, it centered around the concept of colonization—an effort to encourage the resettlement of American blacks in Africa or the Caribbean. In 1817, a group of prominent white Virginians organized the American Colonization Society, which worked carefully to challenge slavery without challenging property rights or Southern sensibilities. The ACS proposed a gradual manumission of slaves, with masters receiving compensation (through funds raised by private charity or appropriated by state legislatures). The liberated blacks would then be transported out of the country and helped to establish a new society of their own. The ACS was not without impact. It received some funding from private donors, some from Congress, some from the legislatures of Virginia and Maryland. And it arranged the shipment of several groups of blacks out of the country, some of them to the west coast of Africa, where in 1830 they established the nation of Liberia (which became an independent black republic in 1846, with its capital, Monrovia, named for the American president who had presided over

the initial settlement). But the ACS was in the end a negligible force. Neither private nor public funding was nearly enough to carry out the vast projects its supporters envisioned. In the space of a decade, they managed to "colonize" fewer slaves than were born in the United States in a month. And they met resistance from blacks themselves, many of whom were now three or more generations removed from Africa and had no wish to move to an alien land. (The Massachusetts free black Paul Cuffe had met similar resistance from members of his race in the early 1800s when he proposed a colonization scheme of his own.)

By 1830, in other words, the early antislavery movement was rapidly losing strength. Colonization was proving not to be a viable method of attacking the institution, particularly since the cotton boom in the Deep South was increasing the commitment of planters to their "peculiar" labor system. Those opposed to slavery had reached what appeared to be a dead end.

Garrison and Abolitionism

It was at this crucial juncture, with the antislavery movement seemingly on the verge of collapse, that a new figure emerged to transform it into a dramatically different phenomenon. He was William Lloyd Garrison. Born in Massachusetts in 1805, Garrison was in the 1820s an assistant to the New Jersey Quaker Benjamin Lundy, who published the leading antislavery newspaper of the time—the *Genius of Universal Emancipation*—in Baltimore. Garrison shared Lundy's abhorrence of slavery, but he soon grew impatient with his employer's moderate tone and mild proposals for reform. In 1831, therefore, he returned to Boston to found his own weekly newspaper, the *Liberator*.

Garrison's philosophy was so simple as to be genuinely revolutionary. Opponents of slavery, he said, should view the institution from the point of view of the black man, not the white slaveowner. They should not, as earlier reformers had done, talk about the

William Lloyd Garrison
Founder and editor of *The Liberator*, Garrison was for many years, beginning in 1831, the most forceful and outspoken white abolitionist in America. He was the first to call for "immediate and complete emancipation" of black slaves; and he remained a bitter and outspoken enemy of the institution of slavery for three decades. On July 4, 1854, he publicly burned a copy of the United States Constitution, explaining, "So perish all compromises with tyranny." After the Civil War and the abolition of slavery, Garrison turned his attention to other issues and paid little attention to the plight of the emancipated blacks. In his last years (he lived until 1879), he became involved with such matters as woman suffrage, prohibition of alcohol, and the rights of Indians. (Library of Congress)

strengthen slavery by ridding the country of those blacks who were already free. The true aim of foes of slavery, he insisted, must be to extend to blacks all the rights of American citizenship. As startling as the drastic nature of his proposals was the relentless, uncompromising tone with which he promoted them. "I am aware," he wrote in the very first issue of the *Liberator*, "that many object to the severity of my language; but is there not cause for severity? I *will* be as harsh as truth, and as uncompromising as justice. . . . I am in earnest—I will not equivocate—I will not excuse—I will not retreat a single inch—AND I WILL BE HEARD."

Garrison soon attracted a large group of followers throughout the North, enough to enable him to found the New England Antislavery Society in 1832 and, a year later, after a convention in Philadelphia, the American Antislavery Society. Membership in the new organizations mushroomed. By 1835, there were more than 400 societies; by 1838, there were 1,350, with more than 250,000 members. Antislavery sentiment was developing a strength and assertiveness greater than at any point in the nation's history.

This success was in part a result of the similarity between abolitionism and other reform movements of the era. Like reformers in other areas, abolitionists were calling for an unleashing of the individual human spirit, the elimination of artificial social barriers to fulfillment. Who, after all, was more in need of assistance in realizing individual potential than the enslaved blacks? Theodore Dwight Weld, a prominent abolitionist (and husband of Angelina Grimké), expressed this belief in an 1833 letter to Garrison. Slavery was a sin, Weld wrote, because "no condition of birth, no shade of color, no mere misfortune of circumstances can annul the birthright charter, which God has bequeathed to every being upon whom he has stamped his own image, by making him a *free moral agent.*"

Black Abolitionists

Abolitionism had a particular appeal, needless to say, to the free black population of the North, which in 1850 numbered about

evil influence of slavery on white society; they should talk about the damage the system did to blacks. And they should, therefore, reject "gradualism" and demand the immediate, unconditional, universal abolition of slavery. Garrison spoke with particular scorn about the advocates of colonization. They were not emancipationists, he argued; on the contrary, their real aim was to

250,000, mostly concentrated in cities. These free blacks lived in conditions of poverty and oppression often far worse than their slave counterparts in the South. An English traveler who had visited both sections of the country wrote in 1854 that he was "utterly at a loss to imagine the source of that prejudice which subsists against [the black man] in the Northern states, a prejudice unknown in the South, where the relations between the Africans and the European [white American] are so much more intimate." This confirmed an earlier observation by Tocqueville that "the prejudice which repels the Negroes seems to increase in proportion as they are emancipated." Northern blacks were often victimized by mob violence; they had virtually no access to education; they could vote only in a few states; and they were barred from all but the most menial of occupations. Most worked either as domestic servants or as sailors in the American merchant marine, and their wages were such that they lived, for the most part, in squalor. Some were kidnapped by whites and forced back into slavery.

For all their problems, however, Northern blacks were aware of, and fiercely proud of, their freedom. And they remained acutely sensitive to the plight of those members of their race who remained in bondage, aware that their own position in society would remain precarious as long as slavery existed. Many in the 1830s came to support Garrison. But there were black leaders as well who expressed the aspirations of their race. One of the most militant was David Walker, a resident of Boston, who in 1829 published a harsh pamphlet: *Walker's Appeal . . . to the Colored Citizens.* In it he declared: "America is more our country than it is the whites'—we have enriched it with our *blood and tears.*" He warned: "The whites want slaves, and want us for their slaves, but some of them will curse the day they ever saw us." Slaves should, he declared, cut their masters' throats, should "kill, or be killed!"

Most black critics of slavery, however, were less violent in their rhetoric. The greatest of them all—one of the most electrifying orators of his time, black or white—was Frederick Douglass. Born a slave in Maryland, Douglass escaped to Massachusetts in

Frederick Douglass
The most prominent black American of the pre–Civil War era, and indeed of the nineteenth century, was Frederick Douglass. He was born in Maryland of an unknown white father and a slave mother. In 1838, he escaped from slavery and went to the Northeast. There, he soon became a leader in the abolitionist movement, appearing on the lecture platform, editing a newspaper, the *North Star,* and publishing his autobiography, *Narrative of the Life of Frederick Douglass* (1845). Douglass demanded not only emancipation for his race but also social and economic equality. (United Press International)

1838, became an outspoken leader of antislavery sentiment, and spent two years lecturing in England, where he was lionized by members of that country's vigorous antislavery movement. On his return to the United States in 1847, Douglass purchased his freedom from his Maryland owner and founded an antislavery newspaper, the *North Star,* in Rochester, New York. He achieved wide renown as well for his autobiography, *Narrative of the Life of Frederick Douglass* (1845), in which he presented a damning picture of slavery. Douglass demanded for blacks not only freedom but full social and economic equality as well. Black abolitionists had been active for years; they had held their first national convention in 1830. But with Douglass's leadership, they became a far more influential force; and they began, too, to forge alliances with white antislavery leaders such as Garrison.

Anti-Abolitionism

The rise of abolitionism was a powerful force, but it provoked a powerful opposition as well. Almost all white Southerners, of course, looked on the movement with fear and loathing. But so too did many Northern whites. To its critics, the abolitionist crusade was a dangerous and frightening threat to the existing social system. It would, some whites (including many substantial businessmen) warned, produce a destructive war between the sections. It might, others feared, lead to a great influx of free blacks into the North. But whatever its long-range consequences might be, the emergence of this strident, outspoken movement served as another reminder of the disorienting social changes that Northern society was experiencing. It was yet another threat to stability and order.

The result was an escalating wave of violence directed against abolitionists in the 1830s. When Prudence Crandall attempted to admit several black girls to her private school in Connecticut, local citizens had her arrested, threw filth into her well, and forced her to close down the school. A mob in Philadelphia attacked the abolitionist headquarters, the "Temple of Liberty," in 1834, burned it to the ground, and began a bloody race riot. Another mob seized Garrison on the streets of Boston in 1835 and threatened to hang him. He was saved from death only by being locked in jail. Elijah Lovejoy, the editor of an abolitionist newspaper in Alton, Illinois, was victimized repeatedly by mob violence. Three times angry whites invaded his offices and smashed his presses. Three times Lovejoy installed new machines and began publishing again. When a mob attacked his office a fourth time, he tried to defend his press. The attackers set fire to the building and, as Lovejoy fled, shot and killed him.

That so many men and women continued to embrace abolitionism in the face of such vicious opposition from within their own communities suggests much about the nature of the movement. Abolitionists were not people who made their political commitments lightly or casually. They were strong-willed, passionate crusaders, displaying enormous courage and moral strength, and displaying too at times a level of fervency that many of their contemporaries (and some historians) found disturbing. Abolitionists were widely attacked, even by some who shared their aversion to slavery, as wild-eyed fanatics bent on social revolution. The anti-abolitionist mobs, in other words, were only the most violent expression of a sentiment that many other white Americans shared.

Abolitionism Divided

By the mid-1830s, the abolitionist crusade had gained such influence that it was impossible to ignore. It had also begun to experience serious internal strains and divisions. One reason was the violence of the anti-abolitionists, which persuaded some members of the movement that a more moderate approach was necessary. Another reason was the growing radicalism of William Lloyd Garrison, who shocked even many of his own allies (including Frederick Douglass) by attacking not only slavery but the government itself. The Constitution, he said, was "a covenant with death and an agreement with hell." The nation's churches, he claimed, were bulwarks of slavery. In 1840, finally, Garrison precipitated a formal division within the American Antislavery Society by insisting that women be permitted to participate in the movement on terms of full equality. He continued after 1840 to arouse controversy with new and even more radical stands: an extreme pacifism that rejected even defensive wars; opposition to all forms of coercion—not just slavery but prisons and asylums; and finally, in 1843, a call for Northern disunion from the South. The nation could, he suggested, purge itself of the sin of slavery by expelling the slave states from the Union.

From 1840 on, therefore, abolitionism moved in many channels and spoke with many different voices. The Garrisonians remained influential, with their uncompromising moral stance. Others operated in more moderate ways, arguing that abolition could be accomplished only as the result of a long, patient, peaceful struggle, "immediate abolition gradually accomplished," as they called it. At first, they depended on "moral suasion." They would appeal to the conscience of the slaveholders and convince them that their institution was sinful. When that produced no results, they turned to political action, seeking to induce the Northern states and the federal government to aid the cause wherever possible. They helped runaway slaves find refuge in the North or in Canada through the so-called underground railroad (although their efforts were never as highly organized as the term suggests). After the Supreme Court (in *Prigg* v. *Pennsylvania*, 1842) ruled that states need not aid in enforcing the 1793 law requiring the return of fugitive slaves to their owners, abolitionists secured the passage of "personal liberty laws" in several Northern states. These laws forbade state officials to assist in the capture and return of runaways. Above all, the antislavery societies petitioned Congress to abolish slavery in places where the federal government had jurisdiction—in the territories and in the District of Columbia—and to prohibit the interstate slave trade. But political abolitionism had severe limits. Few members of the movement believed that Congress could constitutionally interfere with a "domestic" institution such as slavery within the individual states themselves.

While the abolitionists engaged in pressure politics, they never formed a political party with an abolition platform. Antislavery sentiment underlay the formation in 1840 of the Liberty party, which offered the Kentucky antislavery leader James G. Birney as its presidential candidate. But this party, and its successors, never campaigned for outright abolition. They stood instead for "free soil," for keeping slavery out of the territories. Some free-soilers were concerned about the welfare of blacks; others were racists who cared nothing about slavery but simply wanted to keep the West a white man's country. Garrison dismissed free-soilism as "white-manism."

The frustrations of political abolitionism drove some critics of slavery to embrace more drastic measures. A few began to advocate violence; it was a group of prominent abolitionists in New England, for example, who funneled money and arms to John Brown for his bloody uprisings in Kansas and Virginia (see Chapter 13). Others attempted to arouse widespread public anger through propaganda. Abolitionist descriptions of slavery (for example, Theodore Dwight Weld and Angelina Grimké's *American Slavery as It Is: Testimony of a Thousand Witnesses* of 1839) presented what the authors claimed were careful, factual pictures of slavery, but what were in fact highly polemical, often wildly distorted images. The most powerful of all abolitionist propaganda, however, was a work of fiction: Harriet Beecher Stowe's *Uncle Tom's Cabin*. It appeared first, in 1851–1852, as a serial in an antislavery weekly. Then, in 1852, it was published as a book. It rocked the nation. It sold more than 300,000 copies within a year of publication and was later reissued again and again to become one of the most remarkable best sellers in American history. And it succeeded, as a result, in bringing the message of abolitionism to an enormous new audience—not only those who read the book, but those who watched dramatizations of its story by countless theater companies throughout the nation. The novel's emotional portrayal of good, kindly blacks victimized by a cruel system, of the loyal, trusting Uncle Tom, of the vicious overseer Simon Legree (described as a New Englander so as to prevent the book from seeming to be an attack on Southern whites), of the escape of the beautiful Eliza, of the heart-rending death of Little Eva: all became a part of American popular legend. Reviled throughout the South, Stowe became a hero to many in the North. And in both regions, her novel helped to inflame sectional tensions to a new level of passion. Few books in American history have had so great an impact on the course of public events.

Even divided, therefore, abolitionism remained a powerful influence on the life of the nation. Only a relatively small number of people before the Civil War ever accepted the abolitionist position that slavery must be entirely eliminated in a single stroke. But the crusade that Garrison had launched, and that thousands of committed men and women

kept alive for three decades, was a constant, visible reminder of how deeply the institution of slavery was dividing America.

SUGGESTED READINGS

The literary flowering of the antebellum period is examined in the stimulating, if partially discredited, work of Vernon L. Parrington, *The Romantic Revolution in America, 1800–1860* (1927). More durable has been the remarkable work of F. O. Matthiessen, *American Renaissance* (1941). Leo Marx, *The Machine and the Garden* (1964), considers the tension between the pastoral tradition and the growth of a modern economy. Henry F. May, *The Enlightenment in America* (1976), is a good overview of cultural trends; while Van Wyck Brooks, *The Flowering of New England, 1815–1865* (1936), examines the region that produced much of the most important literature of the period. Neil Harris, *Humbug: The Art of P. T. Barnum* (1973), is revealing of trends in popular culture. On the transcendentalists, see—in addition to the works by Brooks and Matthiessen cited above—P. F. Boller, Jr., *American Transcendentalism, 1830–1860: An Intellectual Inquiry* (1974). Biographies of individual transcendentalists include Gay Wilson Allen, *Waldo Emerson* (1981); Arthur M. Schlesinger, Jr., *Orestes A. Brownson: A Pilgrim's Progress* (1939); Henry Steele Commager, *Theodore Parker* (1936); and Richard Lebeaux, *Young Man Thoreau* (1977). Perry Miller considers the transcendentalists in a collection of their writings, *The Transcendentalists* (1950), as well as in relevant sections of *The Life of the Mind in America: From the Revolution to the Civil War* (1966). Arthur Bestor, *Backwoods Utopias: The Sectarian and Owenite Phases of Communitarian Socialism in America, 1663–1829* (1950), M. L. Carden, *Oneida: Utopian Community to Modern Corporation* (1971), Raymond Muncy, *Sex and Marriage in Utopian Communities* (1973), and R. D. Thomas, *The Man Who Would Be Perfect: John Humphrey Noyes and the Utopian Impulse* (1977), consider several antebellum utopian experiments. Fawn Brodie, *No Man Knows My Name* (1945), is a valuable biography of Mormon founder Joseph Smith. Klaus J. Hansen, *Quest for Empire* (1967), examines Mormon theology and politics. Wallace Stegner, *The Gathering of Zion* (1964), is a vivid account of the Mormon trek westward.

The standard overview of the reform agitation of the mid-nineteenth century is Alice Felt Tyler, *Freedom's Ferment* (1944); although a more recent survey, better attuned to current scholarship, is Ronald G. Walter, *American Reformers, 1815–1860* (1978). William G. McLoughlin, *Revivals, Awakenings, and Reform* (1978), is a valuable study of the relationship between reform and religious revivals. Whitney R. Cross, *The Burned-Over District* (1950), examines the

revival-prone region of upstate New York; while Paul Johnson, *A Shopkeeper's Millennium* (1978), is a fine study of the relationship between revivalism and socioeconomic forces in the community of Rochester, New York. Timothy L. Smith, *Revivalism and Social Reform in Mid-Nineteenth Century America* (1957), and William W. Sweet, *Revivalism in America* (1949), are general studies. Charles A. Johnson, *The Frontier Camp Meeting* (1955), is more specialized. C. C. Cole, Jr., *The Social Ideas of the Northern Evangelists, 1826–1860* (1954), links revivalism and reform. W. J. Rorabaugh, *The Alcoholic Republic* (1979), discusses American drinking habits, and Ian R. Tyrrell, *Sobering Up: From Temperance to Prohibition in Antebellum America, 1800–1860* (1979), examines efforts to curb alcohol consumption.

Michael Katz, *The Irony of Early School Reform* (1968), is a provocative and iconoclastic view of the most widely praised of the antebellum reform movements. Lawrence A. Cremin's sweeping study *American Education: The National Experience* (1980), includes valuable information about school reform; while Stanley K. Schultz, *The Culture Factory: Boston's Public Schools, 1789–1860* (1973), examines a particular community. Paul Monroe, *The Founding of the American Public School System* (1949), and Carl Bode, *The American Lyceum* (1956), are earlier studies. Jonathan Messerli, *Horace Mann* (1972), is a biography of the leading exponent of educational reform. David Rothman, *The Discovery of the Asylum* (1971), is an examination of prison and hospital reform that reveals much about the broader reform spirit. On antebellum feminism, see Barbara Berg, *The Remembered Gate: Origins of American Feminism. The Woman and the City* (1977); Ellen Du Bois, *Feminism and Suffrage: The Emergence of an Independent Woman's Movement in America, 1848–1860* (1978); Nancy Cott, *The Bonds of Womanhood: "Woman's Sphere" in New England, 1780–1835* (1977); Ann Douglas, *The Feminization of American Culture* (1977), a provocative literary and cultural study; Lois Banner, *Elizabeth Cady Stanton* (1980); William L. O'Neill, *Everyone Was Brave: The Rise and Fall of Feminism in the United States* (1970); and Eleanor Flexner, *Century of Struggle*, rev. ed. (1975), a standard study of the women's rights movement. Carl Degler, *At Odds: Women and the Family in America from the Revolution to the Present* (1980), is a valuable social history of the role of women in American life.

Surveys of the antislavery movement and abolitionism include Louis Filler, *The Crusade Against Slavery* (1960); and Gerald Sorin, *Abolitionism* (1972). See also M. L. Dillon, *The Abolitionists* (1974); and J. B. Stewart, *Holy Warriors* (1976). Aileen Kraditor, *Means and Ends in American Abolitionism: Garrison and His Critics on Strategy and Tactics, 1834–1850* (1967), is a valuable study of the first important abolitionist. G. H. Barnes, *The Antislavery Impulse* (1933), stresses the role of Theodore Dwight Weld in the movement. Gerda Lerner, *The Grimké Sisters of South Carolina: Rebels Against Slavery* (1967), is a good study of two of the leading feminist abolitionists. John L. Thomas, *The Liberator* (1963), is a standard biography of Garrison, while Bertram Wyatt-Brown, *Lewis Tappan and the Evangelical War Against Slavery* (1969), examines another antislavery leader. Robert Abzug, *Theodore Dwight Weld* (1980), Irving Bartlett, *Wendell Phillips* (1962), and Betty Fladelan, *James Gillespie Birney*

(1955), are other biographies of abolitionist figures. Martin Duberman (ed.), *The Anti-Slavery Vanguard* (1965), is a collection of admiring essays about the abolitionists. Benjamin Quarles, *Black Abolitionists* (1969), and William H. Pease and Jane H. Pease, *They Would Be Free* (1974), consider the contributions of blacks themselves to the struggle. Arna Bontemps, *Free at Last: The Life of Frederick Douglass* (1971), and Nathan Huggins, *Slave and Citizen* (1980), are biographies of the leading black antislavery spokesman. Leonard Richards, *Gentlemen of Property and Standing* (1970), examines anti-abolition mobs; while George Fredrickson, *The Black Image in the White Mind: The Debate on Afro-American Character and Destiny, 1817–1914* (1971), considers American racial attitudes.

The Impending Crisis

13

Migrants Crossing the Missouri
Migrants, their covered wagons loaded with their possessions, crossed the Missouri River en route to the West. Two major trails crossed the Missouri between Council Bluffs, Iowa, and Omaha, Nebraska: the Mormon Trail and one branch of the Oregon Trail. So heavy was the ferry traffic along the river that ferry companies became instrumental in establishing new towns (among them Omaha). This 1855 illustration is from James Linforth's travel book, *Route from Liverpool to the Great Salt Lake Valley*. (Library of Congress)

Until the 1840s, the sectional tensions between North and South had remained relatively contained. On two occasions, serious crises had emerged that had threatened the Union; but neither had been permitted to develop very far. The first was resolved in 1819 by the Missouri Compromise. The second, the nullification crisis of the 1830s, was not so much resolved as allowed quietly to die. Throughout these early decades, the nation avoided confronting its sectional differences. This was in part because the Union was so loose and the federal government so weak and unobtrusive that open conflicts seldom arose; and in part because people of all sections had certain shared sentiments—memories of the Revolutionary past, respect for the Constitution, dreams of national glory—and certain common institutions—the vigorous two-party system, an increasingly interdependent economy—that held them together. Had no new sectional issues arisen, it is possible that the United States would have avoided a civil war, that the two sections might have resolved their differences peaceably over time.

But new issues did arise, and almost without exception they centered around the question of slavery. From the North came the strident and increasingly powerful abolitionist movement, which kept the matter alive in the public mind and greatly increased sectional animosities.

And from the West, more important, came a series of controversies that would ultimately destroy the fragile Union. For, ironically, the vigorous nationalism that was in some ways helping to keep the United States together was also producing a desire for territorial expansion that would tear the nation apart. As America annexed extensive new lands—Texas, the Southwest, California, the Oregon Country, and more—the question continually arose: what would be the status of slavery in the territories? Only the most fervent abolitionists believed that anything could be done to eliminate slavery in the states where it already existed; but a powerful coalition of Northerners began to insist that slavery be banned from new acquisitions. White Southerners, in the meantime, began to argue that slavery extension was essential to protect the future status of their region in the nation. Unless the Southern economic system expanded, they came to believe, it would be consigned to a helpless minority position.

By the late 1840s, these differences had grown to create a dangerous and enduring crisis. Twice—first in 1850 and again in 1854—national leaders attempted to settle the issue by means of a great compromise. But after each such effort, the sectional question arose again in more virulent form, until finally, in 1861, the American people took up arms against one another.

EXPANSION AND WAR

In the course of the 1840s, more than a million square miles of new territory came under the control of the United States—the greatest wave of expansion since the Louisiana Purchase nearly forty years before. By the end of the decade, the nation possessed nearly all the territory of the present-day United States—everything except Alaska, Hawaii, and a few relatively small areas acquired later through border adjustments.

What accounted for this great new wave of expansion after a lull of nearly four decades? In part, it was a result of simple growth—growth of population and growth in the economy—which created pressures to extend the borders westward. In part, too, it was a result of American fears that European nations might somehow extend their influence into the Western lands. But neither of these factors was alone sufficient to explain the new thrust westward. America had not yet even approached developing all the lands it already held; and the threat of European intervention on the continent was limited to a few areas. What gave the decisive push to the nation's quest for new territory was a set of ideas—an ideology that acquired the name "Manifest Destiny."

Manifest Destiny

Manifest Destiny emerged out of a combination of the vigorous nationalism of the 1830s and the reform sentiment of the same era, for it reflected both national pride and an idealistic vision of social perfection. It was the idea that America was destined by God to expand its boundaries over a vast area—an area not clearly defined but certainly including much of the continent of North America. The motive for this expansion, advocates of Manifest Destiny maintained, was not a selfish desire for economic gain but an altruistic attempt to extend American liberty to new realms. John L. O'Sullivan, the influential Democratic editor who gave the movement its name, wrote in 1845 that the American claim to new territory

. . . is by the right of our manifest destiny to overspread and to possess the whole of the continent which Providence has given us for the development of the great experiment of liberty and federative self government entrusted to us. It is a right such as that of the tree to the space of air and earth suitable for the full expansion of its principle and destiny of growth.

By the 1840s, the idea of Manifest Destiny had spread throughout the nation, publicized by the new "penny press," which had made newspapers available to a far greater proportion of the population than ever before, and fanned by the rhetoric of nationalist politicians. The sentiment was strongest in the North and West, but there were advocates as well in the South.

Devotees of Manifest Destiny disagreed among themselves, however, as to how far and by what means the nation should expand. Some had relatively limited territorial goals; others envisioned a vast new American "empire of liberty" extending north into Canada and south into Mexico, and including islands in the Caribbean and in the Pacific. A few visionaries dreamed of the United States becoming a federation of much of the entire world. There was disagreement too over whether the nation could be justified in using force to achieve its goals. Democratic politicians such as O'Sullivan implied that it could. Others, especially among the Whigs, believed that only peaceful methods should be used to acquire new territory. Daniel Webster, for example, said: "I have always wished that this country should exhibit to the nations of the earth the example of a great, rich, and powerful republic which is not possessed by a spirit of aggrandizement." America should, in other words, encourage other areas to join the nation through the strength of her example, not through force.

And there were other politicians—men such as Henry Clay—who were hesitant about any further expansion at all. They feared, correctly as it turned out, that the acquisition of new territories would reopen the painful controversy over slavery and threaten the stability of the Union. Their voices, however, were all but drowned out in the enthusiasm over expansion in the 1840s, which began with the issues of Texas and Oregon.

The Question of Texas

Southwest of the United States stretched the northern provinces of Mexico—Texas, New Mexico, and Upper California—once parts of Spain's colonial empire in North America but, since 1822, states in the independent republic of Mexico. Under Spanish rule, the provinces had been subject to only the lightest supervision from the government of the viceroyalty in Mexico, and only a few thousand white men had settled in them. The same conditions prevailed under the republic, which lacked the power and the population to govern and settle such distant areas. The United States had once advanced a claim to Texas as a part of the Louisiana Purchase; but it had renounced the claim in 1819. Twice thereafter, however, in the presidencies of John Quincy Adams and Jackson, the United States had offered to buy Texas, only to meet with indignant Mexican refusals.

But the Mexican government itself soon invited difficulties in Texas. In the early 1820s it encouraged American immigration by offering land grants to Stephen Austin and other men who promised to colonize the land. Probably the motive of the government was to build up the economy of Texas, and hence its tax revenues, by increasing the population with foreigners. But the experiment was to result in the loss of Texas to the United States. Thousands of Americans, attracted by reports of the rich soil in Texas, took advantage of Mexico's welcome. The great majority came from the Southern states, sometimes bringing slaves with them. By 1835, approximately 35,000 Americans were living in Texas.

Almost from the beginning, there was friction between the settlers and the Mexicans. Finally the Mexican government, realizing that its power over Texas was being challenged by the settlers, moved to exert control. A new law reduced the powers of the various states of the republic, a measure that the Texans took to be aimed specifically at them. In 1836, the Texans defiantly proclaimed their independence.

The Mexican dictator, Antonio de Santa Anna, advanced into Texas with a large army. Even with the aid of volunteers, money, and supplies from private groups in the United States, the Texans were having difficulty in organizing a resistance. Their garrison at the Alamo mission in San Antonio was exterminated; another at Goliad suffered substantially the same fate when the Mexicans murdered most of the force after it had surrendered. But General Sam Houston, emerging as the national hero of Texas, kept a small army together, and at the Battle of San Jacinto (April 23, 1836, near present-day Houston) he defeated the Mexican army and took Santa Anna prisoner. Although the Mexican government later refused to recog-

nize officially the captured dictator's vague promises to withdraw Mexican authority from Texas, it made no further attempt to subdue the province. Texas had won its independence.

The new republic desired to join the United States and through its president, Sam Houston, asked for recognition, to be followed by annexation. Although President Andrew Jackson favored annexation, he proceeded cautiously.

Many Northerners opposed the annexation of a large new slave territory. Others were opposed to incorporating a region that would add to Southern votes in Congress and in the electoral college. Jackson feared that annexation might cause an ugly sectional controversy and even lead to a war with Mexico. He did not, therefore, propose annexation and did not even extend recognition to Texas until just before he left office in 1837. His successor, Van Buren, also refrained, for similar reasons, from pressing the issue.

Spurned by the United States, Texas sought recognition, support, and money in Europe. Texan leaders talked about creating a vast southwestern nation, stretching to the Pacific, which would be a rival to the United States. It was the kind of talk that Europe, particularly England, was charmed to hear. An independent Texas would be a counterbalance to the United States and a barrier to further American expansion; it would supply cotton for European industry and provide a market for European exports. England and France hastened to recognize and conclude trade treaties with Texas. Observing all this, and also eager to increase Southern power, President Tyler persuaded Texas to apply again, and Secretary of State Calhoun submitted an annexation treaty to the Senate in April 1844. Unfortunately for Texas, Calhoun presented annexation as if its only purpose were to extend and protect slavery. The treaty was soundly defeated.

By now, however, the issue of Texas had become one of the major concerns of advocates of Manifest Destiny. And the rejection of the treaty of annexation only spurred them to greater efforts toward their goal. The Texas question would soon become the central issue in the election of 1844.

The Question of Oregon

American interest in what was known as the Oregon Country had, like the interest in Texas, a long history. And like Texas, Oregon became in the 1840s a major political issue. The ownership of the territory had long been in dispute, but its boundaries were clearly defined—on the north the latitude line of 54°40′, on the east the crest of the Rocky Mountains, on the south the 42nd parallel, and on the west the Pacific. Its half-million square miles included the present states of Oregon, Washington, and Idaho, parts of Montana and Wyoming, and half of British Columbia.

At various times in the past, the Oregon Country had been claimed by Spain, Russia, France, England, and the United States. By the 1820s, the former three had withdrawn

AMERICAN EXPANSION IN OREGON

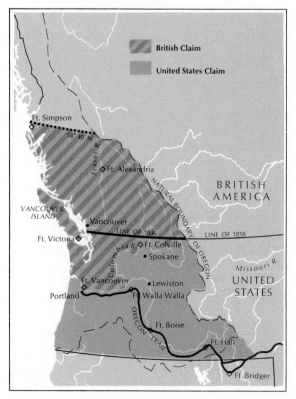

and surrendered their rights to Britain or to the United States or to both. Each nation could assert title on the basis of the activities of its explorers, maritime traders, and fur traders. The English had one solid advantage: they were in actual possession of a part of the area. In 1821, the powerful British fur trading organization, the Hudson's Bay Company, under the leadership of its factor, John McLoughlin, established a post at Fort Vancouver, north of the Columbia River.

Several times the English government proposed the Columbia as a suitable line of division. The United States, also showing a desire to compromise, countered by suggesting the 49th parallel. This difference in official views prevented a settlement of the Oregon question in the treaty of 1818, which ended the War of 1812. Unable to agree on a demarcation line, the diplomats of the two powers provided in the treaty that citizens of each were to have equal access to Oregon for ten years. This arrangement, called joint occupation, was renewed in 1827 for an indefinite period, with either nation empowered to end it on a year's notice.

The first real American interest in Oregon came as a result of the activities of missionaries, notably Jason Lee, Marcus Whitman, and Father Pierre Jean de Smet. All the missionaries located their posts east or south of the Columbia River, mostly in the fertile Willamette Valley. They described their work in reports and letters that were published in the United States in influential religious journals and widely reprinted in secular newspapers. These reports dwelt as much on the rich soil and lovely climate of Oregon as on the spiritual condition of the Indians.

Beginning in 1841, thousands of American pioneers set out for Oregon in a display of what became known as "Oregon fever." Two thousand miles in length, the Oregon Trail penetrated Indian country and crossed mountains and semidesert regions. To the emigrants, traveling in caravans of covered wagons and accompanied by huge herds of cattle, it presented enormous problems in transportation. The average period required for the journey was from May to November. Some never lived to complete it. But the great majority got through. By 1845, 5,000 Americans were living south of the Columbia—and demanding that their government take possession of Oregon. Their cries were echoed by the supporters of Manifest Destiny within the United States.

Polk and Expansion

The election of 1844 was widely expected to be a contest between two old foes: Henry Clay, the anticipated presidential candidate of the Whigs, and former president Martin Van Buren, assumed to be the favorite for the Democratic nomination. Both men wished to avoid taking a stand on the heated issue of the annexation of Texas, because whatever stand they took was certain to lose them some votes. Consequently, they issued separate statements on the question so similar in tone as to suggest that they had consulted with one another in advance: both favored annexation, but only with the consent of Mexico. Since such consent was unlikely at best, the statements had little or no meaning.

Sentiment for expansion was relatively mild within the Whig party, and Clay had no difficulty securing the nomination despite his noncommittal position. The Whig platform discreetly omitted any reference to Texas. Among the Democrats, however, sentiment for annexation had grown to major proportions, particularly among party members in the South. They were enraged by Van Buren's equivocal stand on Texas, and their opposition destroyed the former president's chance of regaining the White House. Instead, the Democratic convention nominated James K. Polk.

Polk's supporters had skillfully exploited their candidate's support for the annexation of Texas to generate support for him at the convention. And in doing so, they won a victory for the first "dark horse" to win the presidential nomination of his party. Polk was not as obscure as his Whig critics suggested when they asked sarcastically during the campaign, "Who is James K. Polk?" Neither, however, was he a genuinely major figure within his party. Born in North Carolina, he had in his mid-twenties moved to Tennessee (following the pattern of the man who

would become his political mentor, Andrew Jackson). For fourteen years, beginning in 1825, he had served in the U.S. House of Representatives, four of them as its Speaker. Most recently, he had been governor of Tennessee. But in 1844, he had been out of public office—and for the most part out of the public mind—for three years. Hence his nomination was unexpected.

The sentiment that had made his victory possible could be seen in the key resolution of the Democratic platform: "that the re-occupation of Oregon and the re-annexation of Texas at the earliest practicable period are great American measures." The words *"re-occupation"* and *"re-annexation"* were intended to imply that in taking Oregon and Texas, the United States would only be confirming its claim to territories that had already belonged to it. By combining Oregon and Texas, the Democrats hoped to appeal to both Northern and Southern expansionists.

Too late, Clay realized that he had mishandled the expansion issue. In midcampaign he announced that under certain circumstances he might be for the acquisition of Texas. His tardy straddling probably cost him more votes than it gained. Polk carried the election by 170 electoral votes to 105, although his popular majority was less than 40,000. The Liberty party, running James G. Birney a second time, polled 62,000 votes (as compared with 7,000 in 1840), mainly antislavery Whigs who had turned against Clay.

The new president was an ordinary-looking man: short, thin, and grim of expression, with public manners that comported with his appearance. But Polk was both intelligent and energetic, and he entered office with a clear idea of what he wished to accomplish and a firm grasp of the means necessary to attain it. Perhaps no president in American history was as successful in fulfilling his stated goals as James K. Polk.

One of those goals was achieved for him even before he took office. John Tyler, who remained in the White House until March 1845, interpreted the election returns as a mandate for annexation of Texas. He proposed to Congress that the territory be accepted into the Union by a joint resolution of both houses, a device that would eliminate

James K. Polk
Polk was not really as obscure a figure as many claimed when he became the first "dark horse" candidate to win the presidency in 1844. He had spent fourteen years in the United States House of Representatives, four of them (1835–1839) as its speaker. And he had been elected to a term as governor of Tennessee as well. But by the time of the 1844 election, he had been out of public life for more than three years; and thus his nomination and election came as something of a surprise. He entered office with a clear set of goals: "a reduction of the tariff," "the independent treasury," "the settlement of the Oregon boundary question," and "the acquisition of California." He achieved all four, and in the process led the United States into a successful but controversial war with Mexico, which led to the acquisition of still more territory. (Library of Congress)

the necessity of obtaining a two-thirds majority in the Senate for a treaty. In February 1845, Congress complied. There were conditions. Texas could be subdivided into no more than four additional states (in fact, it was never subdivided at all); it would retain responsibility for paying the debts that it had acquired as an independent nation (although it was permitted to retain its public lands as well, rather than ceding them to the federal

government); and it had to submit to the United States any boundary disputes in which it became involved. After the inauguration of Polk, Texas accepted the conditions; and in December 1845, it became a state.

Polk himself resolved the perplexing question of Oregon, although not without difficulty and not to the thorough satisfaction of his supporters. In his inaugural address, the new president seemed to reassert American title to all of the Oregon Country. In reality, however, he was willing to compromise—to effect a division on the line of the 49th parallel. The British minister in Washington was less conciliatory. He rejected Polk's offer without even referring it to London.

Abruptly, Polk took a more militant attitude. Saying America should look John Bull "straight in the eye" and hinting at war, he asserted again the American claim to all of Oregon. In his annual message to Congress in December 1845, he asked for approval to give notice to England that joint occupation was to end in a year. Citing the Monroe Doctrine (which had been largely forgotten during the previous twenty years), he insisted that the United States would permit no further European colonization. Congress, despite the dissent of some Whigs, complied with the president's request.

There was loose talk of war on both sides of the Atlantic—talk that in the United States often took the form of the bellicose slogan "Fifty-four forty or fight!" Neither nation, however, genuinely wished to resort to force. Finally, the British government offered to divide Oregon at the 49th parallel—that is, to accept Polk's original proposal. The president pretended to believe that the offer should be rejected, but with little resistance he allowed himself to be persuaded by the cabinet to submit the proposal to the Senate for advice. The result was that responsibility for the decision now shifted, no doubt to the president's great relief, from the White House to the Capitol. The Senate accepted the proposed agreement, and on June 15, 1846, a treaty was signed fixing the boundary at the 49th parallel, where it remains today. The United States had secured the larger and better part of the Oregon Country. It had certainly obtained all that it could reasonably have expected to get without war.

The Southwest and California

One of the reasons the Senate and the president had agreed so readily to the British proposal for settling the Oregon question was that new tensions were emerging in the Southwest—tensions that threatened to lead (and ultimately did lead) to a war with Mexico. The moment the United States admitted Texas to statehood in 1845, the Mexican government broke diplomatic relations with Washington. To make matters worse, a dispute now developed over the boundary between Texas and Mexico (which was now, of course, the southern boundary of the United States). The Texans claimed that the Rio Grande constituted the western and southern border, an assertion that included much of what is now New Mexico within Texas. Mexico, still refusing formally to concede the loss of Texas, nevertheless argued that the border had always been the Nueces River, well to the north of the Rio Grande. Polk recognized the Texas claim, and in the summer of 1845 he sent a small army under General Zachary Taylor to the Nueces line—to protect Texas, he claimed, against a possible Mexican invasion.

The semiprimitive economy of New Mexico, part of the area in dispute, supported a scanty population. The trade center of the region was the small metropolis of Santa Fe, 300 miles from the nearest settlements to the south and more than 1,000 miles from Mexico City and Vera Cruz, the economic centers on which New Mexico had relied during Spanish rule. This geographical isolation from Mexico helped produce a social and cultural isolation as well; for after Mexico had won its independence, the new government did in New Mexico much the same thing it did in Texas: it invited American traders into the region. The Mexicans hoped that the new trade with the United States would enhance the development of their province. It did. But it also, although on a more limited scale than in Texas, started a

process by which New Mexico began to become more American than Mexican.

Soon a flourishing commerce—inaugurated in 1821 by William Becknell—developed between Santa Fe and Independence, Missouri, with long caravans moving back and forth along the Santa Fe Trail, carrying manufactured goods west and bringing back gold, silver, furs, and mules. The Santa Fe trade, as it was called, increased the American presence in New Mexico, and it signaled to advocates of expansion another direction for their efforts.

Americans were similarly increasing their interest in an even more distant province of Mexico: California. In this vast region lived perhaps 7,000 Mexicans, descendants of Spanish colonists, who engaged in agricultural pursuits, chiefly ranching, and carried on a skimpy trade with the outside world. Gradually, however, Americans began to arrive: first maritime traders and captains of Pacific whaling ships, who stopped to barter goods or buy supplies; then merchants, who established stores, imported merchandise, and developed a profitable trade with the Mexicans and Indians. Some of these new settlers began to dream of bringing California into the United States. Thomas O. Larkin, for example, set up a business in Monterey in 1832, quickly became a leading citizen of the region, and in 1844 accepted an appointment as American consul, with instructions to arouse sentiment among the Californians for annexation.

As reports spread of the rich soil and mild climate, immigrants began to enter California from the east by land. These were pioneering farmers, men of the type that were penetrating Texas and Oregon in search of greener pastures. By 1845, there were 700 Americans in California, most of them concentrated in the valley of the Sacramento River. The overlord of this region was John A. Sutter, once of Germany and Switzerland, who had moved to California in 1839 and had become a Mexican citizen. His headquarters at Sutter's Fort was the center of a magnificent domain where the owner ranched thousands of cattle and horses and maintained a network of small manufacturing shops to supply his armed retainers.

President Polk feared that Great Britain wanted to acquire or dominate California as well as Texas—a suspicion that was given credence by the activities of British diplomatic agents in the province. His dreams of expansion thus began to extend beyond the Democratic platform. He was determined to acquire for his country New Mexico and California and possibly other parts of northern Mexico.

At the same time that he sent Taylor to the Nueces, Polk also sent secret instructions to the commander of the Pacific naval squadron to seize the California ports if he heard that Mexico had declared war. A little later, Consul Larkin was informed that, if the people wanted to revolt and join the United States, they would be received as brethren. Still later, an exploring expedition led by Captain John C. Frémont, of the army's corps of topographical engineers, entered California. The Mexican authorities, alarmed by the size of the party and its military aspects, ordered Frémont to leave. He complied, but moved only over the Oregon border.

After seemingly preparing for war, Polk resolved on a last effort to achieve his objectives by diplomacy. He dispatched to Mexico a special minister, John Slidell, a Louisiana politician, with instructions to settle with American money all the questions in dispute between the two nations. If Mexico would acknowledge the Rio Grande boundary for Texas, the United States would assume the damage claims, amounting to several millions, which Americans held against Mexico. If Mexico would cede New Mexico, the United States would pay $5 million. And for California, the United States would pay up to $25 million. Slidell soon notified his government that his mission had failed. Immediately after receiving Slidell's report, on January 13, 1846, Polk ordered Taylor's army to move across the Nueces to the Rio Grande.

If Polk was hoping for trouble, he was disappointed for months. Finally, in May, he decided to ask Congress to declare war on the grounds that Mexico had refused to honor its financial obligations and had insulted the United States by rejecting the Slidell mission. While Polk was working on a war message, the news arrived from Taylor that Mexican troops had crossed the Rio Grande and attacked a unit of American soldiers. Polk now revised his message. He declared: "Mexico has passed the boundary of the United States . . . and shed American blood upon the American soil. . . . War exists by the act of Mexico herself." Congress accepted Polk's interpretation of events and on May 13, 1846, declared war by votes of 40 to 2 in the Senate and 174 to 14 in the House.

The Mexican War

The war was never popular in the United States. Whig critics charged from the beginning that Polk had deliberately maneuvered the country into the conflict, that the border incident that had precipitated the declaration had been staged. Many argued that the hostilities with Mexico were draining resources and attention away from the far more important issue of Oregon; when the United States finally reached its agreement with Britain, opponents claimed that Polk had settled for less than he should have because he was preoccupied with Mexico. This opposition, limited at first to a relatively few Whigs in Congress, increased and intensified as the war continued and as the public became aware of the level of casualties and of the expense. Whigs in Congress generally supported military appropriation bills, not wishing to face accusations of obstructing the war effort. But they became ever bolder and more bitter in denouncing "Mr. Polk's war" as an aggressive and unnecessary conflict.

The president himself, in the meantime, was finding it more difficult than he had thought to achieve his goals. Although American forces were generally successful in their campaigns against the Mexicans, final victory did not come nearly as quickly as Polk had hoped. In the opening phases of the war, the president assumed the planning of grand strategy, a practice that he continued almost to the end of the war. His basic idea was to seize key areas on the Mexican frontier and then force the Mexicans to make peace on American terms. Accordingly, he ordered Taylor to cross the Rio Grande and occupy northeastern Mexico, taking as his first objective the city of Monterrey. Polk seems to have had a vague idea that from Monterrey Taylor could advance southward, if necessary, and menace Mexico City. Taylor, "Old Rough and Ready," beloved by his soldiers for his courage and easy informality but ignorant of many technical aspects of war, attacked Monterrey in September 1846. After a hard fight he captured it, but at the price of agreeing to let the garrison evacuate without pursuit. Although the country hailed Taylor as a hero, Polk concluded that he did not possess the ability to lead an offensive against Mexico City. Also, Polk began to re-

THE MEXICAN WAR, 1846–1848

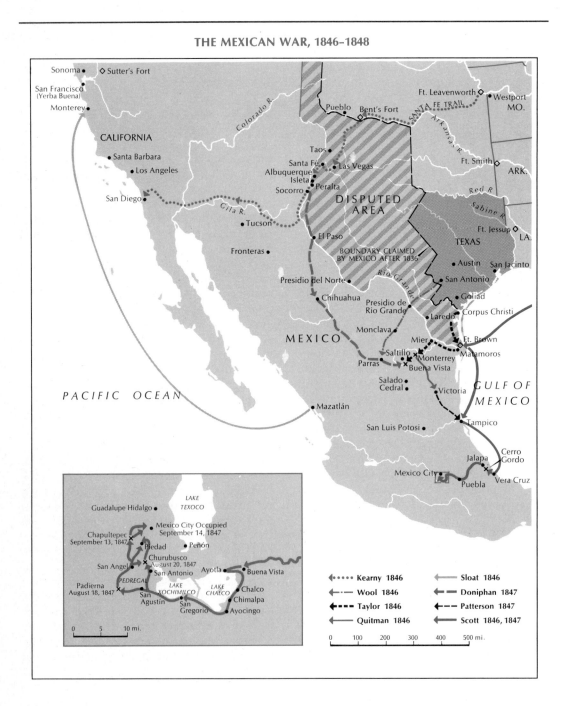

◄····· **Kearny 1846**		◄──── **Sloat 1846**	
◄─·─ **Wool 1846**		◄══ **Doniphan 1847**	
◄═══ **Taylor 1846**		◄─── **Patterson 1847**	
◄─── **Quitman 1846**		◄━━━ **Scott 1846, 1847**	

0   100   200   300   400   500 mi.

alize that an advance south through the mountains would involve impossible problems of supply.

Two other offensives planned by Polk were aimed at New Mexico and California. In the summer of 1846, a small army under Colonel Stephen W. Kearny made the long march to Santa Fe and occupied the town with no opposition. Kearny sent part of his army (Missouri volunteers under Colonel A. W. Doniphan) south to join Taylor, and disposed other parts to garrison the province. Then, acting under instructions from Polk, Kearny proceeded with a few hundred troopers to California to take charge of operations there. In California a combined revolt and war was being staged by the settlers, Frémont's exploring party, and the American navy. The settlers had proclaimed California an independent state in the "Bear Flag Revolution." Frémont had returned from Oregon to lead the rebels, and the navy had landed forces and annexed California to the United States. When Kearny arrived, the Americans were fighting under the direction of Commodore R. F. Stockton of the navy. With some difficulty, Kearny brought the disparate American elements under his command, and by the autumn of 1846 completed the conquest of California.

In addition to northeastern Mexico, the United States now had possession of the two provinces for which it had gone to war. In a sense, the original objectives of the war had been achieved. Mexico, however, refused to recognize realities and would not agree to a peace or cede the conquered territory. At this point, Polk turned to General Winfield Scott, the commanding general of the army and its finest soldier, for help. Together, the two men devised a plan to force peace on the Mexicans—and, perhaps, gain even more new territory for the United States. Scott was to assemble an army at Tampico made up partly of troops from Taylor's army and partly of other forces. The navy would transport this new army down the coast to Vera Cruz, which the Americans would seize and make into a base. From Vera Cruz, Scott would move west along the National Highway to Mexico City. Late in 1846, Scott went to Mexico to organize his forces. Taylor, who

lost about half of his army to Scott, was instructed to stand on the defensive.

While Scott was assembling his army off the coast, General Santa Anna, the Mexican dictator, decided to take advantage of the division of American forces by marching northward, crushing Taylor, and then returning to deal with Scott. With an army much larger than Taylor's, Santa Anna attacked the Americans at Buena Vista (February 1847). But he could not break the American line and had to return to defend Mexico City.

In the meantime, Scott had taken Vera Cruz by siege and was moving inland, in one of the most brilliant campaigns in American military annals. With an army that never numbered more than 14,000, he advanced 260 miles into enemy territory, conserved the lives of his soldiers by using flanking movements instead of frontal assaults, and finally achieved his objective without losing a battle. At Cerro Gordo, in the mountains, he inflicted a smashing reverse on the Mexicans. He met no further resistance until he was within a few miles of Mexico City. After capturing the fortress of Chapultepec in a hard fight, the Americans occupied the enemy capital. A new Mexican government came into power, one that recognized defeat and was willing to make a peace treaty.

President Polk was now growing thoroughly unclear about his objectives. He continued to encourage those who demanded that the United States annex much of Mexico itself. At the same time, concerned about the approaching presidential election, he was growing anxious to get the war finished quickly. Along with the invading army, Polk had sent a special presidential agent authorized to negotiate a settlement with Mexico. The agent—Nicholas Trist, one of those obscure figures who occasionally have a major impact on history—concluded a treaty with the new Mexican government on February 2, 1848: the Treaty of Guadalupe Hidalgo. Mexico agreed to cede California and New Mexico to the United States and acknowledge the Rio Grande as the boundary of Texas. In return, the United States contracted to assume the claims of its citizens against Mexico and pay to the Mexicans $15 million.

Entrance of Scott's Army into Mexico City
This print of the American army taking possession of the Mexican capital in 1847 appeared in a history of the war written by George W. Kendall of the New Orleans *Picayune*. Kendall was one of the first war correspondents ever to accompany an army on its campaigns. (Library of Congress)

When the treaty reached Washington, Polk faced a dilemma. Trist had obtained for the United States most of Polk's original demands; but he had stopped far short of the expansive dreams the president had come to harbor of acquiring some more territory in Mexico. Polk angrily claimed that Trist had violated his instructions, but he soon realized he had no choice but to accept the treaty. Some ardent expanionists were demanding that he hold out for annexation of—in a phrase widely bandied about at the time— "All Mexico!" Antislavery leaders, in the meantime, were charging that Southern

slaveholders were controlling the government for their own ends, that the demands for acquisition of Mexico were part of a Southern scheme to extend slavery to new realms (although other antislavery people, convinced that slavery could never be established in Mexico, were among those arguing for taking the whole country). To silence this bitter and potentially destructive debate, Polk submitted the Trist treaty to the Senate, which approved it by a vote of 38 to 14. The war was over, and America had gained a vast new territory. But it had also acquired a new set of troubling and divisive issues.

A NEW SECTIONAL CRISIS

James Polk tried during his presidency to be a leader whose policies transcended sectional issues. Thus, he responded to the expansion-

ist demands of Northerners and Southerners both. And he pursued economic policies designed similarly to strengthen the Democratic party as an organization with strong national support. He persuaded Congress, for example, to reestablish the Independent Treasury system—the Van Buren plan of 1840 to stabilize the nation's banks without resorting to another Bank of the United States. The Tyler administration had dismantled the system two years earlier, and Polk now delighted Democrats throughout the country by restoring it. He also delighted the South by fulfilling his campaign pledge to lower tariff rates—through the tariff of 1846, which achieved support as well from Northwestern Democrats.

Yet Polk was not to find it so easy to conciliate the sections. Although he acquired territory both in the Northwest and in the Southwest, Northerners continued to accuse him of having made Oregon a second prior-

ity so as to favor the expansionists of the South. The tariff bill, moreover, not only alienated manufacturers and merchants in the Northeast. It encouraged those Northwesterners who had supported it to believe that the president should, in return for their backing, now support internal improvements in their region. When Polk vetoed two bills providing federal funds for construction of roads and other improvements in the West, arguing that the national government had no authority to fund such projects, Westerners charged again that the administration was sacrificing their interests to those of the South.

The Sectional Debate

Sectional tensions were already rising, therefore, when a much more dangerous issue

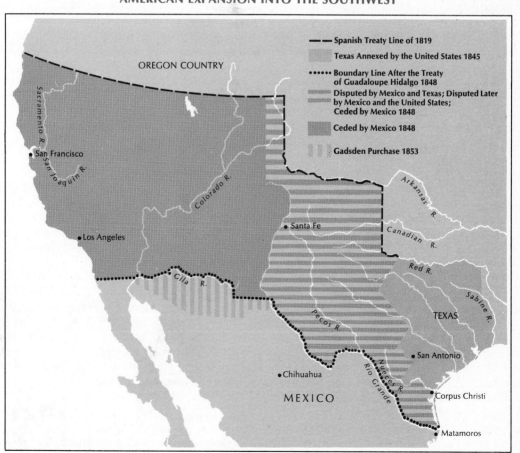

AMERICAN EXPANSION INTO THE SOUTHWEST

Legend:
- — — Spanish Treaty Line of 1819
- Texas Annexed by the United States 1845
- ●●●●● Boundary Line After the Treaty of Guadaloupe Hidalgo 1848
- Disputed by Mexico and Texas; Disputed Later by Mexico and the United States; Ceded by Mexico 1848
- Ceded by Mexico 1848
- Gadsden Purchase 1853

OREGON COUNTRY

Sacramento R.
San Joaquin R.
San Francisco
Colorado R.
Los Angeles
Gila R.
Santa Fe
Arkansas R.
Canadian R.
Red R.
Pecos R.
Sabine R.
TEXAS
San Antonio
Chihuahua
Nueces R.
Rio Grande
Corpus Christi
MEXICO
Matamoros

emerged. In August 1846, while the war was still in progress, Polk had asked Congress to provide him with $2 million that he could use to purchase peace with Mexico. When the appropriation was introduced in the House, David Wilmot of Pennsylvania, an antislavery Democrat from a high-tariff state, moved an amendment that slavery should be prohibited in any territory secured from Mexico. The so-called Wilmot Proviso passed the House but failed in the Senate. It would be called up again and be debated and voted on for years.

Diametrically opposed to the Wilmot Proviso was the formula of the Southern extremists. They contended that the states jointly owned the territories and that the citizens of each state possessed equal rights in them, including the right to move to them with their property, particularly slave property. According to this view, Congress had no power to prohibit the movement of slavery into the public domain or to regulate it in any way except by extending protection. Neither could a territorial legislature, which was a creature of Congress, take any action to ban slavery.

Two compromise plans were presented. One, which numbered President Polk among its advocates, proposed to run the Missouri Compromise line of 36°30' through the new territories to the Pacific coast, banning slavery north of the line and permitting it south. The other, first prominently espoused by Lewis Cass, Democratic senator from Michigan, was originally called "squatter sovereignty." Some years later, when taken up by Stephen A. Douglas, an Illinois senator of the same party, it was given the more dignified title of "popular sovereignty." According to this formula, the question of slavery in each territory should be left to the people there, acting through the medium of their territorial legislature.

Congress and the country debated the various formulas, but at the end of Polk's administration a decision had still not been reached. No territorial government had been provided for California or New Mexico (New Mexico included most of present New Mexico and Arizona, all of Utah and Nevada, and parts of Colorado and Wyoming). Even the organization of Oregon, so far north that slavery obviously would never enter it, was held up by the controversy. Southern members of Congress, hoping to gain some advantage in the regions farther south, blocked a territorial bill for Oregon until August 1848, when a free-soil government was finally authorized.

The debate was partially stilled by the presidential campaign of 1848. Both the Democrats and the Whigs tried to avoid provocative references to the slavery question. When Polk declined to run for a second term, the Democrats nominated as their candidate Lewis Cass of Michigan, an elderly, honest, dull wheel horse of the party—and, according to most accounts (and portraits), a man of stunning physical unattractiveness. Although the platform was purposely vague, it could be interpreted as an endorsement of squatter sovereignty. The Whigs adopted no platform and presented as their candidate a military hero with no political record, General Zachary Taylor of Louisiana.

Ardent abolitionists and even moderates who merely opposed the expansion of slavery found it difficult to swallow either Cass or Taylor. The situation was ripe for the appearance of a powerful third party. The potential sources for such a group were the existing Liberty party and the antislavery Whigs and Democrats. Late in the campaign, third-party promoters held a national convention, adopted a platform endorsing the Wilmot Proviso, free homesteads, and a higher tariff, and nominated former president Van Buren for the presidency. Thus was launched the Free Soil party—a major step toward what would ultimately be a dissolution of the existing party system and its replacement with another.

Taylor won a narrow victory. Although Van Buren failed to carry a single state, he polled an impressive 291,000 votes (10 percent of the total), and the Free-Soilers elected ten members to Congress. It is probable that Van Buren pulled enough Democratic votes away from Cass, particularly in New York, to throw the election to Taylor.

Taylor and the Territories

Zachary Taylor was the first man to be elected president with no previous political training or experience. He was also the first professional soldier to occupy the White House (although not, of course, the first general—Washington, Jackson, and Harrison all having attained that rank during their military service). Taylor was a Southerner and a slaveholder, but from his long years in the army he had acquired a national outlook.

Almost immediately, the new president encountered problems connected with the territories recently acquired from Mexico. Congress had failed to provide a civil government for the new possessions, and the regions were being administered by military officials responsible to the president. There was particular pressure to establish a new government in California, for that territory was experiencing a remarkable boom. In January 1848, gold was accidentally discovered in the Sacramento Valley. As word of the strike spread, inhabitants of California and the whole Far West, fired by hopes of becoming immediate millionaires, stampeded

to the area to stake out claims. By the end of summer the news had reached the Eastern states and Europe. Then the gold rush really started. From the United States and all the world, thousands of "forty-niners" poured into California. Those who left from the older states could choose among three routes of travel: overland by covered wagon, inexpensive but involving a long journey over the Great Plains and across the Rockies; by ship around Cape Horn, quicker but more expensive; or the dangerous, difficult shortcut across the Isthmus of Panama. By all three routes, disdaining hunger, thirst, disease, and even death, the seekers after gold came— more than 80,000 of them in 1849. By the end of that year, California had a population of approximately 100,000, more than enough to entitle it to statehood.

President Taylor believed that statehood would serve as the solution not only to the inadequacy of the military government in California but to the whole issue of slavery in

Washing for Gold

These miners in a Western gold camp are engaging in placer mining. The gold found in the first strikes was located in the form of particles along stream beds. Prospectors separated the gold from sand or gravel by washing the deposit in a swirl of water. Washing was done in pans or boxes. From Samuel Bowles, *Our New West*.

the territories. Let California and New Mexico both frame state constitutions and apply for admission to the Union, he declared. Once they had become states, no one could deny their right to dispose of slavery as they wished. So Taylor directed military officials in the territories to expedite statehood movements.

California promptly ratified a constitution in which slavery was prohibited. When Congress assembled in December 1849, Taylor rather proudly described his efforts. He recommended that California be admitted as a free state and that New Mexico, when it was ready, be permitted to come in with complete freedom to decide the status of slavery as it wished. But Congress was not about to accept the president's program.

Complicating the situation was the emergence of side issues generated by the conflict over slavery in the territories. One such issue concerned slavery in the District of Columbia. Antislavery people, charging that human servitude in the capital was a national disgrace, demanded that it be abolished there. Southerners angrily replied that the institution could not be touched without the consent of Maryland, which had originally donated the land.

Another disturbing question concerned the question of fugitive slaves. Northern "personal liberty laws," forbidding courts and police officers to assist in the return of runaways, provoked Southerners to call for a new, more stringent *national* fugitive slave law.

A third issue related to the boundary between Texas and New Mexico. Texas claimed the portion of New Mexico east of the Rio Grande, although the federal government during the Mexican War had assigned this region to New Mexico. To Texans, it seemed that Washington was trying to steal part of their territory. They also resented the government's refusal to assume the Texas war debt. Southern extremists supported the pretensions of Texas, while Northerners, eager to cut down the size of a slave state, upheld New Mexico.

But the biggest obstacle in the way of the president's program was the South—angered and frightened by the possibility that two new free states would be added to the Northern majority. Only in the Senate did the South still maintain equality. The number of free and slave states was equal in 1849—fifteen of each. But now the admission of California would upset the balance, with New Mexico, Oregon, and Utah still to come.

Responsible Southern leaders declared that if California was to be admitted, and if slavery was to be prohibited in the territories, the time had come for the South to secede from the Union. At the suggestion of Mississippi, a call went out for a Southern-rights convention to meet in June 1850 at Nashville, Tennessee, to consider whether the South should resort to the ultimate act of secession. In the North excitement ran equally high. Every Northern state legislature but one adopted resolutions demanding that slavery be barred from the territories. Public meetings all through the free states called for the passage of the Wilmot Proviso and the abolition of slavery in the District of Columbia. Such was the crisis that confronted Congress and the country as the tense year of 1850 opened.

The Compromise of 1850

Moderates and lovers of the Union turned their thoughts, during the winter of 1849–1850, to the framing of a great congressional compromise that would satisfy both sections and restore tranquillity. The venerable statesman from Kentucky, Henry Clay, headed the forces of conciliation. In Clay's view, no compromise would have any lasting effect unless it settled all the issues in dispute between the sections. Accordingly, he took a number of separate measures, which had been proposed before, combined them into one set of resolutions, and on January 29, 1850, presented them to the Senate. He recommended (1) that California be admitted as a free state; (2) that, in the rest of the Mexican cession, territorial governments be formed without restrictions as to slavery; (3) that Texas yield in its boundary dispute with New Mexico and be compensated by the federal government's taking over its public debt;

Henry Clay
Like his contemporaries Webster and Calhoun, Henry Clay spent many years yearning to become president of the United States (and ran, unsuccessfully, for the office three times). Also like Webster and Calhoun, he remained a far better known and often far more powerful figure than many of the men who actually served in the White House. He was best known during his lifetime for his successes in producing compromises to settle sectional controversies: the Missouri Compromise of 1820, the compromises of 1833 to settle the nullification crisis, and—most prominently—the Compromise of 1850, which helped to postpone, but which ultimately did not prevent, the Civil War. Yet Clay was at least equally important as an advocate of a particular vision of America's future. The "American System" he promoted called for active federal efforts to promote economic development. Clay spent nearly thirty years in Congress, many of them as Speaker of the House of Representatives. He also served as secretary of state from 1825 to 1829. (Library of Congress)

(4) that the slave trade, but not slavery itself, be abolished in the District of Columbia; and (5) that a new and more effective fugitive slave law be passed. These resolutions launched a debate that raged for seven months—both in Congress and throughout the nation. It occurred in two phases, the differences between which revealed much about how American politics was changing in the 1850s.

In the first phase of the debate, the dominant voices in Congress were those of old men, national leaders who still remembered Jefferson, Adams, and other founders, who argued for or against the Compromise on the basis of broad ideals. Clay himself, seventy-three years old in 1850, was the most prominent of these spokesmen. He opened the oratorical tournament with a defense of his measures and a broad plea to both North and South to be mutually conciliatory. It was the Union, he claimed, and the shared sentiments of nationalism that had emerged from America's glorious past, that should be the primary concern of the lawmakers.

Early in March, another of the older leaders—John C. Calhoun, sixty-eight years old and so ill that he had to sit grimly in his seat while a colleague read his speech for him—made his contribution to the debate. Almost ignoring Clay's proposals, he devoted his argument to what to him was the larger, in fact the only subject—the minority status of the South—and he asked more for his section than any realistic observer believed could be given. Like Clay, however, Calhoun spoke emotionally of the bonds holding the nation together. Because of Northern aggressions, the cords that bound the Union were snapping. What could save the Union? The North, he insisted, must admit that the South possessed equal rights in the territories, must agree to observe the laws concerning fugitive slaves, must cease attacking slavery, and must accept an amendment to the Constitution guaranteeing a balance of power between the sections. The amendment would provide for the election of dual presidents, one from the North and one from the South, each possessing a veto power. In short, nothing would satisfy Calhoun but a comprehensive, permanent solution to the sectional problem. His proposal, however, would have required an abject surrender by the North.

After Calhoun came the third of the elder statesmen, the sixty-eight-year-old Daniel Webster. His "Seventh of March Address" was probably the greatest forensic effort of his long oratorical career. Still nourishing White House ambitions, he now sought to calm angry passions and to rally Northern moderates to support Clay's compromise.

After six months of debate, however—six months dominated by ringing appeals to the memory of the founders, to nationalism, to idealism—the effort to win approval of the compromise failed. In July, Congress defeated the Clay proposal. And with that, the controversy moved into its second phase, in which a very different cast of characters would predominate. Clay, ill and tired, left Washington to spend the summer resting in the mountains. He would return, but never with his old vigor; he died in 1852. Calhoun had died even before the vote in July. And Webster in the course of the summer accepted a new appointment as secretary of state, thus removing himself from the Senate and from the debate.

In place of these leaders, a new, younger group now emerged as the dominant voices. There was William H. Seward of New York, forty-nine years old, a wily political operator who staunchly opposed the proposed compromise. The ideals of Union were to him clearly less important than the issue of eliminating slavery. Emerging as the new voice of the South was Jefferson Davis of Mississippi, forty-two years old, a representative not of the old aristocratic South of Calhoun but of the new, cotton South—a hard, frontierlike country that was growing and prospering rapidly. To him, and to those he represented, the slavery issue was less one of principles and ideals than one of economic self-interest.

Most important of all, there was Stephen A. Douglas, the thirty-seven-year-old senator from Illinois. More than any of the others, Douglas represented the new generation of politicians coming to dominate national life. A Westerner from a rapidly growing frontier state, a man unpolished in manner, he was an open spokesman for the economic needs of his section—and especially for the new railroads. His was a career devoted not to any broad national goals, as Clay's, Webster's, and even Calhoun's had often been, but one devoted frankly to sectional gain and personal self-promotion.

The new leaders of the Senate were able, where the old leaders were not, to arrive at a compromise in 1850. In part, they were aided by a shift in popular sentiment. The country was entering a period of prosperity—the re-

sult of an expanding foreign trade, the flow of gold from California, and a boom in railroad construction—reminiscent of the flush days of the 1830s. Conservative economic interests everywhere wanted to end the sectional dispute and concentrate on internal expansion. Even in the South, excitement seemed to be abating. The Nashville convention met in June, adopted a few tame resolutions, and then quietly adjourned to await final action by Congress.

Progress toward the Compromise was also furthered by the removal of the most powerful obstacle to it: the president. Zachary Taylor had been unyielding in his stand that the admission of California and possibly New Mexico must come first, that only then could other measures be discussed. Taylor had threatened not only to veto any measure that diverged from this proposal but to use force against the South (even to lead the troops in person) if they attempted to secede. But on July 9, Taylor suddenly died—the victim of a violent stomach disorder following an attack of heat prostration. He was succeeded by his vice president, Millard Fillmore of New York—a handsome and dignified man of no particular ability, but one who understood the political importance of flexibility. He ranged himself on the side of the Compromise and used his powers of persuasion to swing Northern Whigs into line.

But the new leaders were also aided by their own, pragmatic tactics. Douglas's first step, after the departure of Clay, was to break up the "omnibus bill" that Clay had envisioned as a great, organic solution to the sectional crisis and introduce instead a series of separate measures to be voted on one by one. Thus representatives of different sections could support those elements of the Compromise favorable to them and abstain from voting on or vote against those they opposed. Douglas also gained support by avoiding the grand appeals to patriotism of Clay and Webster and resorting instead to complicated backroom maneuverings and deals—linking the Compromise to such nonideological matters as the sale of government bonds and the construction of railroads. As a result of his efforts, by mid-September all the components of the Compromise had been

A Southern View on Compromise in 1850

In his last speech Calhoun insisted that the North should either agree to everything that the South demanded as its rights or permit the minority section to depart the Union.

It is time, Senators, that there should be an open and manly avowal on all sides, as to what is intended to be done. If the question is not now settled, it is uncertain whether it ever can hereafter be; and we, as the representatives of the States of this Union, regarded as governments, should come to a distinct understanding as to our respective views, in order to ascertain whether the great questions at issue can be settled or not. If you, who represent the stronger portion, cannot agree to settle them on the broad principle of justice and duty, say so; and let the States we both represent agree to separate and part in peace, tell us so; and we shall know what to do, when you reduce the question to submission or resistance. If you remain silent, you will compel us to infer by your acts what you intend.

A Northern View on Compromise in 1850

William H. Seward, senator from New York, expressed the feelings of those Northerners who refused to make any further concessions to the South in 1850.

I AM OPPOSED TO ANY SUCH COMPROMISE, IN ANY AND ALL THE FORMS IN WHICH IT HAS BEEN PROPOSED. Because, while admitting the purity and the patriotism of all from whom it is my misfortune to differ, I think all legislative compromises radically wrong and essentially vicious. They involve the surrender of the exercise of judgment and conscience on distinct and separate questions, at distinct and separate times, with the indispensable advantages it affords for ascertaining truth. They involve a relinquishment of the right to reconsider in future the decisions of the present, on questions prematurely anticipated. And they are a usurpation as to future questions of the province of future legislators.

enacted by both houses of Congress and signed by the president. The outcome was a great victory for Douglas and the forces of conciliation; but it was a clouded victory. For the passage of the Compromise of 1850, unlike the creation of the Missouri Compromise thirty years before, had not resulted from any widespread agreement on common national ideals. It was, rather, a victory largely of self-interest that had not resolved the underlying problems. Nevertheless, leaders in Congress hailed the event as a great triumph; and Millard Fillmore, signing the measure, called it a just settlement of the sectional problem, "in its character final and irrevocable."

It was one thing to pass the Compromise through Congress and another to persuade the country to accept it. In the North, the most objectionable of the measures was the Fugitive Slave Act. By this law, a black accused of being a runaway was denied trial by jury and the right to testify in his own behalf. His status was to be decided by a federal judge or by a special commissioner appointed by the federal circuit courts. He could be remanded to slavery simply on the evidence of an affidavit presented by the man who claimed to be his owner.

But the Fugitive Slave Act was the only part of the Compromise that most Southerners could approve. The Nashville convention met again in November 1850 (with only about a third of the original delegates present) and condemned the Compromise. Eventually the South brought itself to accept

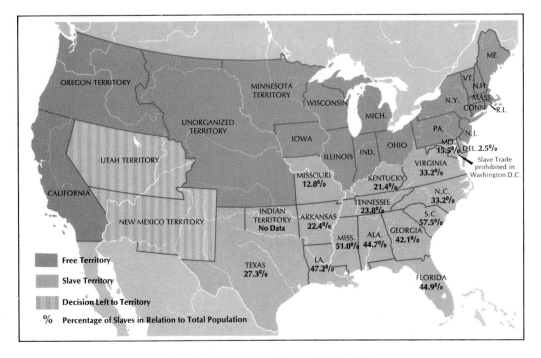

SLAVE AND FREE TERRITORIES, 1850

the settlement, but only after much agonizing, and then only conditionally. Epitomizing such feelings was the "Georgia Platform," which declared that Georgia would acquiesce in the Compromise—but if the North disregarded the Fugitive Slave Act, or attempted to abolish slavery in the District of Columbia, or denied admission to a state because it wished to have slavery, then Georgia would consider the compact broken and would protect its rights even to the point of seceding from the union.

THE CRISES OF THE 1850s

For a few years after the Compromise of 1850, the sectional conflict seemed briefly to be forgotten, and much of the nation concentrated on enjoying prosperity and growth. But the tensions between North and South remained, and the crisis continued to smolder until—in 1854—it once more burst into flames.

The Uneasy Truce

How difficult it would be for the nation to put aside its sectional differences became clear almost immediately. For while the major parties attempted to display an unswerving devotion to the Compromise of 1850, events in the nation began to make their efforts seem unrealistic and even irrelevant.

Both major parties endorsed the Compromise in their platforms in 1852—the Democrats pledging fervently to avoid all attempts in any "shape or color" or renew agitation over slavery, the Whigs making the same promise in somewhat milder language. Both parties, similarly, nominated presidential candidates who were moderates on the sectional issue and were unlikely to arouse passionate opposition in either North or

South. The Democrats chose the obscure New Hampshire politician Franklin Pierce (although not until after wrangling through forty-nine ballots, with the convention deadlocked among the three leading contenders—Lewis Cass, Stephen Douglas, and James Buchanan of Pennsylvania). The Whigs chose as their nominee the military hero General Winfield Scott, a man whose political views were so undefined that no one even knew whether he approved of the Compromise of 1850 or not.

Yet the gingerliness with which party leaders dealt with the sectional question could not prevent its divisive influence from intruding on the election. The Whigs, in particular, suffered from their attempts to straddle the issue. Already plagued by the defections of those antislavery Northerners who had formed the Free Soil party in 1846, they alienated still more party members—the "Conscience" Whigs—by refusing to take an open stand against slavery now. Partly as a result of these divisions, Scott was the last presidential candidate the Whigs were ever to nominate. In the meantime, the Free Soil party was gaining in numbers and influence in the North; its presidential candidate, John P. Hale, repudiated the Compromise of 1850.

The divisions among the Whigs, and the vagueness of the party's support of the Compromise, helped produce a victory for the Democrats in 1852. The new president, Franklin Pierce, was forty-nine years old when inaugurated the following March—the youngest man to serve in the office to that date. A charming, amiable man of no great distinction, he attempted to maintain party—and national—harmony by avoiding divisive issues. But those issues arose despite him.

Partly, they arose because there remained active political forces in the North—most notably the abolitionist organizations—who had never supported the Compromise of 1850 and continued to work actively for the elimination of slavery. Partly, too, they arose because of the presence of eloquent and combative antislavery leaders in Congress—Senator Charles Sumner of Massachusetts, elected in 1850; Congressman Joshua R. Giddings of Ohio; and others. Their denunciations of the South and its institution re-

sounded from a national forum. Most of all, however, the sectional tensions continued because of Northern response to the Fugitive Slave Act. Always strong, that opposition intensified after 1850 when Southerners began appearing in Northern states to pursue fugitives or to claim as slaves blacks who had been living for years in Northern communities. So fervently did many opponents of slavery resent such efforts that mobs formed in city after city to prevent enforcement of the law. In 1851, a crowd in Boston took a runaway named Shadrach from a federal marshal and sent him on his way to Canada; in Syracuse, New York, later in the same year, another crowd rescued a slave named Jerry McHenry. In 1854, a Boston mob led by respectable and prominent citizens attempted, unsuccessfully, to seize the escaped slave Anthony Burns from federal officers.

Northern states attempted to undermine the Fugitive Slave Act through legal means as well. Several states passed new personal liberty laws, designed to interpose state authority between the accused fugitive and the federal government. In Wisconsin and Massachusetts, such laws directed state courts to grant all fugitives a judicial hearing (heavily weighted in the fugitives' favor) before they could be deported from the state. The supreme court of Wisconsin, in *Ableman* v. *Booth* (1857), went so far as to declare the federal Fugitive Slave Act void and to ignore the U.S. Supreme Court when it overruled the Wisconsin ruling.

White Southerners watched all this with growing anger and alarm. The Fugitive Slave Act had been the one element of the Compromise of 1850 they had considered a victory. Now they had to watch while the North, through the extralegal device of mobs, and ghrough legal efforts of dubious constitutionality, made that victory meaningless.

"Young America"

The Pierce administration tried to avoid taking a position on most domestic issues likely to produce controversy. And in foreign policy as well, the Democrats tried to revive a sense of cross-sectional nationalism. Here, too, however, their efforts created more problems than they resolved.

Spearheading the revival of nationalist diplomacy was a group of Democrats who organized what they called the Young America movement. Aware of the great liberal and nationalist revolutions of 1848 in Europe, these adventurous Democrats were stirred by the vision of a republican Europe with governments based on the model of the United States. They continued to dream as well of expanding American commerce in the Pacific and of extending the sweep of Manifest Destiny with new acquisitions in the Western Hemisphere. The sentiments they aroused had a profound effect on the nation's foreign policy.

Those sentiments were first felt in the second half of the Whig administration, under the new president, Millard Fillmore, and his new secretary of state, Daniel Webster. Webster, for example, defied the powerful government of Austria by supporting the effort of Hungary to win its independence. The Fillmore administration sponsored an expedition into the Pacific under Commodore Matthew C. Perry, who began efforts to open Japan—for nearly two centuries all but totally closed to the West—to American trade. Perry's efforts resulted in 1854 in a treaty giving Americans access to two Japanese ports.

Few Americans in either section objected to these displays of nationalism. But efforts by both the Fillmore and Pierce administrations to extend the nation's domain in its own hemisphere produced new problems. First Fillmore and then Pierce sanctioned a series of ill-considered and ultimately unsuccessful attempts to wrest Cuba from the Spanish Empire. Frustrated in efforts to acquire the island through open diplomacy, Pierce turned to more devious means—authorizing his minister to Spain, the impetuous Pierre Soulé, to try to "detach" Cuba from the empire by subterfuge. Soulé's clumsy efforts only deepened the gap between Spain and the United States, particularly when he collaborated with several other American diplomats in Europe (John Y. Mason, minister to France, and James Buchanan, minister to Great Britain) to produce a preposterous document, the so-called Ostend Manifesto. In it, Soulé and the others declared that all parties—Spain, Cuba, and the United States—would benefit from the annexation of Cuba by America. What was more, if disturbances there became a threat to American security, the United States would be justified "by every law human and divine" in "wresting" the island from Spain. The document was meant to be confidential, but its contents soon became public, enraging many antislavery Northerners, who charged the administration with conspiring to bring a new slave state into the Union even at the risk of war.

The South, for its part, opposed all efforts to acquire new territory that would not support a slave system. The kingdom of Hawaii agreed to join the United States in 1854, but the treaty had no chance in the Senate because it contained a clause prohibiting slavery in the islands. A powerful movement to annex Canada to the United States—a movement that had the support of many Canadians eager for access to American markets—similarly foundered, at least in part because of slavery. Southerners eager to prevent the addition of free territory to the Union supported an 1854 treaty providing trade reciprocity between the two nations—a treaty that undercut pressures for annexation.

The Kansas-Nebraska Controversy

Controversy over the return of fugitive slaves and the efforts to extend American dominion abroad kept sectional tensions alive in the early 1850s. But what fully revived the crisis between North and South was the same issue that had produced it in the first place: slavery in the territories. By the 1850s, the line of frontier settlement had moved west to the great bend of the Missouri River. Beyond the boundaries of Minnesota, Iowa, and Missouri stretched a great expanse of plains, which most Americans had always believed was unfit for cultivation (it was widely known as the Great American Desert) and which the nation had thus assigned to the Indian tribes it had dislodged from the more fertile lands to the east. Now it was becoming apparent that large sections of this region were, in fact, suitable for farming. In the states of the Old Northwest, therefore, pressure began to build for efforts to extend settlement westward once again. Prospective settlers urged the government to open the area to them, provide territorial government, and—despite the solemn assurance the United States had earlier given the Indians of the sanctity of their reservations—to dislodge the tribes so as to make room for the white man. The interest in further settlement, however, raised two divisive issues, which gradually became entwined with one another: railroads and slavery.

As the nation expanded westward, the problem of communication between the older states and the so-called trans-Mississippi West (those areas west of the Mississippi River) became more and more critical. As a result, the idea of building a transcontinental railroad gradually gained favor both in and out of Congress. The problem, however, was where to place it—in particular, where to locate the railroad's eastern terminus. Northerners favored Chicago, the growing capital of the free states of the Northwest. Southerners supported St. Louis, Memphis, or New Orleans—all located in slave states. The transcontinental railroad, in other words, was—like nearly everything else in the 1850s—becoming entangled in sectionalism. It had become a prize that both North and South were struggling to secure.

One argument against a southern route had been removed through the foresight of Pierce's secretary of war, Jefferson Davis, a Mississippian. Surveys had indicated that a road with a southern terminus would probably have to pass through an area south of the Gila River, in Mexican territory. At Davis's suggestion, Pierce appointed James Gadsden, a Southern railroad builder, to negotiate with Mexico for the sale of this region. Gadsden persuaded the Mexican government to dispose of a strip of land that today comprises a part of Arizona and New Mexico, the so-called Gadsden Purchase (1853), which cost the United States $10 million.

Particularly interested in a transcontinental railroad was Senator Stephen A. Douglas, and his interest influenced him to introduce in Congress a fateful legislative act, one that accomplished the final destruction of the Compromise of 1850. As a senator from Illinois, a resident of Chicago, and, above all, the acknowledged leader of the Northwestern Democrats, Douglas naturally wanted the transcontinental railroad for his own city and section. He realized too the potency of the principal argument urged against the northern route: that west of the Mississippi it would run largely through unsettled Indian country. In January 1854, as chairman of the Committee on Territories, he acted to forestall this argument. He introduced a bill to organize a huge new territory, to be known as Nebraska, west of Iowa and Missouri.

Douglas seemed to realize that this bill would encounter the opposition of the South, partly because it would prepare the way for a new free state, the proposed territory being in the Louisiana Purchase area north of the 36°30' line of the Missouri Compromise and hence closed to slavery. In an effort to make the measure acceptable to Southerners, Douglas inserted a provision that the status of slavery in the territory would be determined by the territorial legislature, that is, according to popular sovereignty. Theoretically, at least, this would open the region to slavery. The concession was not enough to satisfy extreme Southern Democrats, particularly those from Missouri, who feared that their state would be surrounded by free territory. They demanded more, and Douglas had to give more to get their support. He agreed to two additions to his bill: a clause specifically repealing the antislavery provision of the Missouri Compromise, and another creating two territories, Nebraska and Kansas, instead of one. Presumably Kansas would become a slave state. In its final form the measure was known as the Kansas-Nebraska Act.

Douglas induced President Pierce to endorse his bill, and so it became an official Democratic measure. But even with the backing of the administration, it encountered stiff opposition and did not become a law until May 1854. Nearly all the Southern members of Congress, whether Whigs or Democrats, supported the bill, and nearly all the Northern Whigs opposed it. The Northern Democrats in the House split evenly.

Of greater importance than the opposition to the Kansas-Nebraska Act in Congress was the reaction against it in the Northern states. The effort to repeal the Missouri Compromise—a measure that many Northerners believed had a special sanctity, almost as if it were a part of the Constitution—was particularly alarming. The whole North seemed to blaze with fury at this latest demonstration of the power of the slavocracy, and much of the fury was directed at Douglas, who, in the eyes of many Northerners, had acted as a tool of the slaveholders. No other piece of legislation in congressional history produced so many immediate, sweeping, and ominous changes as the Kansas-Nebraska Act. It destroyed the Whig party in the South except in the border states. At the same time, as many Southern Whigs became Democrats, it increased Southern influence in the Democratic party. It destroyed the popular basis of Whiggery in the North, with the result that by 1856 the national Whig party had disappeared and a conservative, nationalistic influence in American politics had been removed. It divided the Northern Democrats and drove many of them from the party. Most important of all, it called into being a new party that was frankly sectional in composition and creed.

Men in both the major parties who opposed Douglas's bill began to call themselves Anti-Nebraska Democrats and Anti-Nebraska Whigs. In 1854, these men formed a new party and began to call themselves "Republicans." Originating in a series of spontaneous popular meetings throughout the Northwest, the Republican movement soon spread to the East. In the elections of 1854, the Republicans, often cooperating with the Know-Nothings, elected a majority to the U.S. House of Representatives and won control of a number of Northern state governments.

At the start the Republican party was a one-idea organization: it simply opposed the expansion of slavery into the territories. Its original members were mostly the former Whigs and Free-Soilers but also included a substantial number of former Democrats. In part it represented the democratic idealism of the North. But it also represented the agricultural and business interests of that section. Soon the party gained additional support from advocates of federal aid to economic activity—advocates of high tariffs, homesteads, and internal improvements—who blamed the South for blocking such aid and thus hindering Northern development. When the Know-Nothing organization broke up, the Republicans absorbed most of its members. Thus the new party inherited the odor of nativism that once had clung to the Whigs. Like the Whigs, the Republicans repelled the Roman Catholics among the German, Irish, and other foreign-born groups. Yet the Republicans succeeded in attracting Protestants among German and Scandinavian, as well as British, immigrants.

"Bleeding Kansas"

The pulsing popular excitement aroused in the North by the Kansas-Nebraska Act was sustained by events during the next two years in Kansas. Almost immediately, settlers moved into this territory. Those from the North were encouraged by press and pulpit and the powerful organs of abolitionist propaganda. Often they received financial help from such organizations as the New England Emigrant Aid Company. Those from the South often received financial contributions from the communities they left.

In the spring of 1855, elections were held for a territorial legislature. Thousands of Missourians, some traveling in armed bands, moved into Kansas and voted. Although there were probably only some 1,500 legal votes in the territory, more than 6,000 votes were counted. With such conditions prevailing, the proslavery forces elected a majority to the legislature, which proceeded immediately to enact a series of laws legalizing slavery. The outraged free-staters, convinced that they could not get fair treatment from the Pierce administration, resolved on extralegal action. Without asking permission from Congress or the territorial governor, they elected delegates to a constitutional convention that met at Topeka and adopted a constitution excluding slavery. They then chose a governor and legislature and petitioned

FREE STATE
CONVENTION!

All persons who are favorable to a union of effort, and a permanent organization of all the Free State elements of Kansas Territory, and who wish to secure upon the broadest platform the co-operation of all who agree upon this point, are requested to meet at their several places of holding elections, in their respective districts on the 25th of August, instant, at one o'clock, P. M., and appoint five delegates to each representative to which they were entitled in the Legislative Assembly, who shall meet in general Convention at

Big Springs, Wednesday, Sept. 5th '55,

at 10 o'clock A. M., for the purpose of adopting a Platform upon which all may act harmoniously who prefer Freedom to Slavery.

The nomination of a Delegate to Congress, will also come up before the General Convention.

Let no sectional or party issues distract or prevent the perfect co-operation of Free State men. Union and harmony are absolutely necessary to success. The pro-slavery party are fully and effectually organized. No jars nor minor issues divide them. And to contend against them successfully, we also must be united.— Without prudence and harmony of action we are certain to fail. Let every man then do his duty and we are certain of victory.

All Free State men, without distinction, are earnestly requested to take immediate and effective steps to insure a full and correct representation for every District in the Territory. "United we stand; divided we fall."

By order of the Executive Committee of the Free State Party of the Territory of Kansas, as per resolution of the Mass Convention in session at Lawrence, Aug 15th and 16th, 1855.

J. K. GOODIN, Sec'y.

C. ROBINSON, Chairman.

Herald of Freedom, Print.

Free-Soilers Organize in Kansas
After the Kansas proslavery elements, with the aid of "border ruffians" from Missouri, had elected a proslavery legislature, the Free-Soilers called a convention and prepared to organize their own, antislavery government. A broadside was widely posted to announce the call. (The Kansas State Historical Society, Topeka)

Congress for statehood. Pierce stigmatized their movement as unlawful and akin to treason. The full weight of the government, he announced, would be thrown behind the proslavery territorial legislature.

A few months later a proslavery federal marshal assembled a huge posse, consisting mostly of Missourians, to arrest the free-state leaders in Lawrence. The posse not only made the arrests but sacked the town. Several free-staters died in the melee. Retribution came immediately. Among the more extreme antislavery men was a fierce, fanatical man named John Brown, who considered himself an instrument of God's will to destroy slavery. Estimating that five antislavery men had been murdered, he decided that it was his sacred duty to take revenge. He gathered six followers, and in one night murdered five proslavery settlers, leaving their

mutilated bodies to discourage other supporters of slavery from entering Kansas. The episode was known as the Pottawatomie Massacre; and its result was more civil strife in Kansas—irregular, guerrilla warfare conducted by armed bands, some of them more interested in land claims or loot than in ideologies.

In both North and South, the belief was widespread that the aggressive designs of the other section were epitomized by (and responsible for) what was happening in Kansas. Whether or not such beliefs were entirely correct is less important than that they became passionately held articles of faith in both sections. Thus "Bleeding Kansas" became a symbol of the sectional controversy.

Another symbol soon appeared, in the United States Senate. In May 1856, Charles Sumner of Massachusetts rose to discuss the

problems of the strife-torn territory. He entitled his speech "The Crime Against Kansas."
Handsome, humorless, eloquent, and passionately doctrinaire, Sumner embodied the
most extreme element of the political antislavery movement. And in his speech, entitled
"Bleeding Kansas" and delivered with the
righteous eloquence for which he was becoming famous, he fiercely denounced the
Pierce administration, the South, and the institution of slavery. He singled out for particular attention his colleague in the Senate Andrew P. Butler of South Carolina, an
outspoken defender of slavery. It was an age
in which orators were accustomed to indulg-
ing in personal invective; but in his discussion of Butler, Sumner far exceeded the normal bounds. The South Carolinian was,
Sumner claimed, the "Don Quixote" of slavery, having "chosen a mistress ... who,
though ugly to others, is always lovely to
him, though polluted in the sight of the
world, is chaste in his sight ... the harlot
slavery." The pointedly sexual references
and the general viciousness of the speech
enraged Butler's nephew, Preston Brooks, a
member of the United States House of Representatives from South Carolina. Brooks resolved to punish Sumner for his insults by a
method approved by the Southern gentleman's code—a public, physical chastisement.
Several days after the speech, Brooks approached Sumner at his desk in the Senate
chamber during a recess, raised a heavy cane,
and began beating him repeatedly on the
head and shoulders. Sumner, trapped behind
his desk, rose in agony with such strength
that he tore the table from the bolts holding it
to the floor, then collapsed, bleeding and unconscious. So severe were his injuries that he
was unable to return to the Senate for four
years, during which time his state refused to
elect a successor. He became a potent symbol
throughout the North—a martyr to the bar-
barism of the South.

Preston Brooks became a symbol too.
Censured by the House, he resigned his seat,
returned to South Carolina, and stood for reelection. He won the virtually unanimous
support of his state. Brooks's assault had
made him a Southern hero. And as a result,
he, like Sumner, served as evidence of how
deep the antagonism between North and
South had become.

The Free-Soil Ideology

What had happened to produce such deep
hostility between the two sections? There

The Martyred Sumner
Senator Charles Sumner
of Massachusetts lies
bleeding on the Senate
floor, as Representative
Preston Brooks of South
Carolina pummels him
with a cane. The sensa-
tional 1856 incident made
Sumner and Brooks
heroes to their respective
sections. This obviously
Northern cartoon depicts
a saintly Sumner with a
frail pen as his only de-
fense. In his left hand he
holds a scroll labeled
"Kansas," the issue that
had aroused the alterca-
tion. (From Nevins and Weiten-
kampf, *A Century of Political
Cartoons*, Charles Scribner's
Sons, 1944)

were, obviously, important differences between the North and the South; but many of
these differences had always existed. There
were real issues—above all the question of
slavery in the territories—dividing them; but
these issues alone are not a sufficient explanation. Despite the passions generated by the
conflict in Kansas, neither the North nor the
South really seemed to believe that there was
ever a genuine prospect of slavery becoming
established there. At the height of the struggle between pro- and antislavery forces in
the territory, there were almost no blacks in
Kansas at all. Similarly, few of the remaining
territories seemed likely ever to support
flourishing slave systems.

Slavery and other issues attained such destructive importance largely because they
served as symbols for a set of larger concerns
on both sides. As the nation expanded and
political power grew more dispersed, the
North and the South each became concerned
with ensuring that its vision of America's future would be the dominant one. And those
visions were becoming—partly as a result of
internal developments within the sections
themselves, partly because of each region's
conceptions (and misconceptions) of what
was happening outside it—more and more
distinct and more and more rigid.

In the North, assumptions about the
proper structure of society came to center
around the belief in "free soil" and "free
labor." The abolitionists generated some
support for their argument that slavery was a
moral evil and must be eliminated. Theirs,
however, was never the dominant voice of
the North. Instead, an increasing number of
Northerners, gradually becoming a majority,
came to believe that the existence of slavery
was dangerous not because of what it did to
blacks but because of what it threatened to
do to whites. At the heart of American democracy, they believed, was the right of
every individual to own property, to control
his own labor, and to have access to opportunities for advancement. The ideal society, in
other words, was one of small-scale capitalism, with every man entitled to a stake for
himself and his family, and with the chance
of upward mobility available to all.

According to this vision, the South was

the antithesis of democracy. It was a closed,
static society, in which the slave system preserved an entrenched aristocracy and where
the common white man had no opportunity
to improve himself. More than that, the
South was a backward society—decadent,
lazy, dilapidated. While the North was growing and prospering, displaying thrift, industry, and a commitment to progress, the South
was stagnating, rejecting the Northern values
of individualism and growth. The South was,
Northern free-laborites further maintained,
engaged in a conspiracy to extend slavery
throughout the nation and thus to destroy the
openness of Northern capitalism and replace
it with the closed, aristocratic system of the
South. This "slave power conspiracy," as it
came to be known, threatened the future of
every white laborer and property owner in
the North. The only solution was to fight the
spread of slavery and work for the day when
the nation's democratic (i.e., free-labor)
ideals extended to all sections of the country—the day of the victory of what Northerners called "Freedom National."

This was the ideology that lay at the heart
of the new Republican party. There were abolitionists and others in the organization who
sincerely believed in the rights of blacks to
freedom and citizenship. Far more important,
however, were those who cared less about
blacks than about the threat that slavery
posed to white labor and to individual opportunity. This ideology also strengthened the
commitment of Republicans to the Union.
Since the idea of continued growth and
progress was central to the free-labor vision,
the prospect of dismemberment of the nation—a diminution of America's size and
economic power—was unthinkable.

The Proslavery Argument

In the South, in the meantime, a very different ideology was emerging—one that was
entirely incompatible with the vision of
America's future being promoted by the
free-labor defenders of the North. As late as
the early 1830s, there had been a substantial
number of white Southerners who harbored
deep reservations about slavery. Between

1829 and 1832, for example, a Virginia constitutional convention, and then the state legislature, responding to demands from non-slaveholders in the western part of the state, had seriously considered ending slavery through compensated emancipation. They chose not to do so in large part because of the tremendous expense it would have entailed. There were, moreover, many antislavery societies in the South—in 1827, more than there were in the North, most of them in the border states. And there were prominent Southern politicians who spoke openly in opposition to slavery—among them Cassius M. Clay of Kentucky.

By the mid-1830s, however, this ambivalence about slavery was beginning to be replaced by a militant defense of the system. In part, the change was a result of events within the South itself. The Nat Turner uprising terrified whites throughout the region. They had always been uneasy, always mindful of the horrors of the successful slave uprising in Santo Domingo in the 1790s. Now they were reminded again of their insecurity, and they were especially horrified because there had been long-trusted house servants among Turner's followers who, ax in hand, had suddenly turned on their masters' sleeping families. Many slaveowners blamed Garrison and the abolitionists for the slaves' defection, and they grew more determined than ever to make slavery secure against all dangers. There was, too, an economic incentive to defend the system. With the expansion of the cotton economy into the Deep South, slavery—which had begun to seem unprofitable in many areas of the original South—now suddenly became lucrative once again.

But the change was also a result of events in the North, and particularly of the growth of the abolitionist movement, with its strident attacks on Southern society. Harriet Beecher Stowe's *Uncle Tom's Cabin* (1851–1852) was perhaps the most glaring example of such an attack, a book that enraged the South and increased its resentment of the North. But other abolitionist writings had been antagonizing white Southerners for years.

In response to these pressures, a growing number of white Southerners began to elaborate an intellectual defense of slavery. It began as early as 1832, when Professor Thomas R. Dew of the College of William and Mary published a pamphlet outlining the slavery case. In subsequent years, many others added their contributions to the cause; and in 1852, the defense was summed up in an anthology that gave the philosophy its name: *The Pro-Slavery Argument.*

The essence of the argument, as John C. Calhoun boasted in 1837, was that Southerners should cease apologizing for slavery as a necessary evil and defend it as "a good—a positive good." It was, according to such theorists, good for the slave because he was an inferior creature. He needed the guidance of a master, and he was better off—better fed, clothed, and housed, and more secure—than Northern factory workers. It was good for Southern society because it was the only way the two races could live together in peace. It was good for the country as a whole because the Southern economy, dependent on slavery, was the key to the prosperity of the nation. And it was good in itself because it was sanctioned by the Bible—did not the Hebrews of the Old Testament own bondsmen, and did not the New Testament apostle Paul advise, "Servants, obey your masters"?

Above all, Southern apologists argued, slavery was good because it served as the basis for the Southern way of life—a way of life superior to any other in the United States, perhaps in the world. White Southerners looking at the North saw a society that they believed was losing touch with traditional American values and replacing them with a spirit of greed, debauchery, and destructiveness. "The masses of the North are venal, corrupt, covetous, mean and selfish," wrote one Southerner. Others wrote with horror of the exploitation of the factory system, the growth of crowded, pestilential cities filled with unruly immigrants. The South, in contrast, was a stable, orderly society, operating at a slow and human pace. It had a labor system that avoided the feuds between capital and labor that plagued the North, a system that protected the welfare of its workers, a system that allowed the aristocracy to enjoy a refined and accomplished cultural life. It was, in short, as nearly perfect

Calhoun on Slavery [1837]

I hold that in the present state of civilization, where two races of different origin, and distinguished by color, and other physical differences, as well as intellectual, are brought together, the relation now existing in the slaveholding States between the two is, instead of an evil, a good—a positive good. I feel myself called upon to speak freely upon the subject where the honor and interests of those I represent are involved. I hold then, that there never has yet existed a wealthy and civilized society in which one portion of the community did not, in point of fact, live on the labor of the other. . . . I may say with truth that in few countries so much is left to the share of the laborer, and so little exacted from him, or where there is more kind attention paid to him in sickness or infirmities of age. Compare his condition with the tenants of the poor houses in the more civilized portions of Europe—look at the sick and the old and infirm slave, on one hand, in the midst of his family and friends, under the kind superintending care of his master and mistress, and compare it with the forlorn and wretched condition of the pauper in the poor house.

as any human civilization could become, an ideal social order in which all elements of the population were secure and content. Proslavery theoreticians—and the vast number of white Southerners, slaveowners, and nonslaveowners alike, who were coming to accept their arguments—were creating a dream world as a defense against the growing criticism from the North. It was, as one historian has described it, an "affirmation of Southern perfection."

Some proslavery propagandists went so far as to argue that slavery was such a good thing that it should be extended to include white workers in the North as well as black laborers in the South. George Fitzhugh of Virginia—in *Sociology for the South, or the Failure of Free Society* (1854), *Cannibals All* (1857), and other writings—claimed that all society lived on forced labor, and that in the South masters at least acknowledged responsibility for those whose labor they were exploiting. Slavery, therefore, was the only workable form of socialism—a system that all societies should adopt as the sole cure for class conflict and the other ills of competitive society. (Such arguments fueled the fears of those Northern free-labor advocates who argued that the South was plotting to extend slavery everywhere, even into the factory system.)

Southern leaders had, by the 1850s, not only committed themselves to a militant proslavery ideology. They had also become convinced that they should silence advocates of freedom. Southern critics of slavery found it healthful to leave the region, among them Hinton Rowan Helper, whose *Impending Crisis of the South* (1857) contended that slavery hurt the welfare of the nonslaveholder and made the whole region backward. Beginning in 1835 (when a Charleston mob destroyed sacks containing abolitionist literature in the city post office), Southern postmasters generally refused to deliver antislavery mail. Southern state legislatures passed resolutions demanding that Northern states suppress the "incendiary" agitation of the abolitionists. Southern representatives even managed for a time to force Congress to honor a "gag rule" (adopted in 1836), according to which all antislavery petitions would be tabled without being read. Only the spirited protests of such Northerners as John Quincy Adams led to the repeal of the gag rule in 1844. Southern defenders of slavery, in other words, were not only becoming more militant about its virtues; they were becoming less tolerant of criticism of it—further encouraging those Northerners who warned of the "slave power conspiracy" against their liberties.

Buchanan and Depression

It was in this unpromising climate—with the country convulsed by the Brooks assault and the continuing violence in Kansas, and with each section becoming increasingly militant in support of its own ideology—that the presidential campaign of 1856 began. The Democrats adopted a platform that endorsed the Kansas-Nebraska Act and defended popular sovereignty. The leaders wanted a candidate who had not made many enemies and who was not closely associated with the explosive question of "Bleeding Kansas." So the nomination went to James Buchanan of Pennsylvania, a reliable party stalwart who as minister to England had been safely out of the country during the recent troubles, although he was a signer of the highly controversial Ostend Manifesto.

The Republicans, engaging in their first presidential contest, faced the campaign with confidence. They denounced the Kansas-Nebraska Act and the expansion of slavery but also approved a program of internal improvements, thus combining the idealism of antislavery with the economic aspirations of the North. Just as eager as the Democrats to present a safe candidate, the Republicans nominated John C. Frémont, who had made a national reputation as an explorer of the Far West and who had no political record.

The Native American, or Know-Nothing, party was beginning to break apart on the inevitable rock of sectionalism. At its convention, many Northern delegates withdrew because the platform was not sufficiently firm in opposing the expansion of slavery. The remaining delegates nominated former president Millard Fillmore. His candidacy was endorsed by the sad remnant of another party, the few remaining Whigs who could not bring themselves to support either Buchanan or Frémont.

The campaign was the most exciting since 1840. Its frenzied enthusiasm was largely a result of the fervor of the Republicans, who shouted for "Free Soil, Free Speech, Free Men, and Frémont," depicted "Bleeding Kansas" as a sacrifice to the evil ambitions of the slavocracy, and charged that the South,

using Northern dupes such as Buchanan as its tools, was plotting to extend slavery into every part of the country.

The returns seemed to indicate that the prevailing mood of the country was still relatively conservative. Buchanan, the winning candidate, polled 1,838,000 popular votes to 1,341,000 for Frémont and 874,000 for Fillmore. A slight shift of votes in Pennsylvania and Illinois, however, would have thrown those states into the Republican column and elected Frémont.

The election of Buchanan was a disaster for the nation. He had been in public life for more than forty years at the time of his inauguration, and he was at age sixty-five the oldest president, except for William Henry Harrison, ever to have taken office. Whether because of his age and physical infirmities or because of a more fundamental weakness of character, he became a painfully timid and indecisive president in a time when the nation cried out as perhaps never before for strong, effective leadership.

In the year Buchanan took over, a financial panic struck the country, followed by several years of stringent depression. Europe had shown an unusual demand for American food during the Crimean War (1854–1856). When that demand fell off, agricultural prices declined. The depression sharpened sectional differences. The South was not hit as hard as the North, and Southern leaders thus found what they believed was confirmation for their claim that their economic system was superior to that of the free states. Smarting under previous Northern criticisms of Southern society, they loudly boasted of their superiority to the North.

In the North, the depression strengthened the Republican party. Distressed economic groups—manufacturers and farmers—came to believe that the hard times had been caused by unsound policies of Southern-controlled Democratic administrations. These groups thought that prosperity could be restored by a high tariff (the tariff was lowered again in 1857), a homestead act, and internal improvements—all measures to which the South was opposed. In short, the frustrated economic interests of the North were being drawn into an alliance with the antislavery elements and thus into the Republican party.

The Dred Scott Decision

The Supreme Court of the United States now projected itself into the sectional controversy with one of the most controversial decisions in its history—its ruling in the case of *Dred Scott* v. *Sanford,* handed down two days after Buchanan was inaugurated.

Dred Scott was a Missouri slave, once the property of an army surgeon who on his military pilgrimages had carried him to Illinois, a free state, and to Minnesota Territory, where slavery was forbidden by the Missouri Compromise. Scott was persuaded by some abolitionists to bring suit in the Missouri courts for his freedom on the ground that residence in a free territory had made him a free man. The state supreme court decided against him. Meanwhile, the surgeon having died and his widow having married an abolitionist, ownership of Scott was transferred to her brother, J. F. A. Sanford, who lived in New York. Now Scott's lawyers could get the case into the federal courts on the ground that the suit lay between citizens of different states. Regardless of the final decision, Scott would be freed; his abolitionist owners would not keep him a slave. The case was intended less to determine Scott's future than to secure a federal decision on the status of slavery in the territories.

Of the nine justices, seven were Democrats (five of them from the South), one was a

Roger B. Taney and Dred Scott

A former Maryland slaveowner, Taney (*left*) was one of the greatest of all chief justices of the United States, but his reputation in the North was badly damaged by his proslavery, antiblack decision in the Dred Scott case. After the decision, Scott (*right*) was freed by his owner and was employed as a hotel porter in St. Louis. A year later, in 1858, he died of tuberculosis. (National Archives)

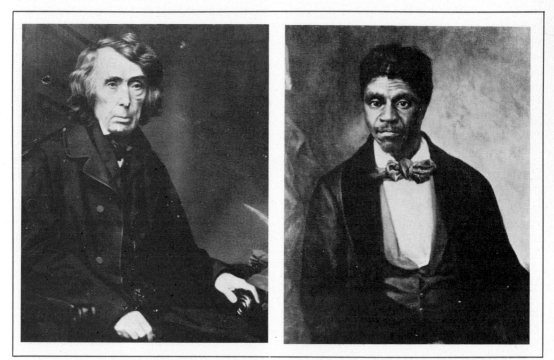

Whig, and one was a Republican. Chief Justice Taney, in the majority opinion, declared that Scott was not a citizen of Missouri and hence could not bring a suit in the federal courts. According to Taney, no black could qualify as a citizen. So far as the Constitution was concerned, he added, blacks had no rights that white men were bound to respect. Having said this, Taney could simply have declined jurisdiction over the case. Instead, he went on to argue that Scott's sojourn in Minnesota had not affected his status as a slave. Slaves were property, said Taney, and the Fifth Amendment prohibited Congress from taking property without "due process of law." Consequently, Congress possessed no authority to pass a law depriving persons of their slave property in the territories. The Missouri Compromise, therefore, had always been null and void.

The ruling did nothing to challenge the right of an individual state to prohibit slavery within its borders, but the statement that the federal government was powerless to act on the issue was a drastic and startling one. Few judicial opinions have stirred as much popular excitement. Southern whites were elated: the highest tribunal in the land had invested with legal sanction the extreme Southern argument. On behalf of abolitionists, black and white, Frederick Douglass declared: "This very attempt to blot out forever the hopes of an enslaved people may be one necessary link in the chain of events preparatory to the complete overthrow of the whole slave system." Republicans claimed that the decision deserved as much consideration as any pronouncement by a group of political hacks "in any Washington bar room." They threatened that when they secured control of the national government, they would reverse the decision—by altering the personnel of the Court and "packing" it with new members.

Deadlock over Kansas

Endorsing the decision, President Buchanan concluded that the best solution for the Kansas troubles was to force the admission of that territory as a slave state. The existing proslavery territorial legislature called an election for delegates to a constitutional convention. The free-state people refused to participate. As a result, the proslavery forces won control of the convention, which met in 1857 at Lecompton and framed a constitution establishing slavery. When an election for a new territorial legislature was called, the antislavery groups turned out to vote and won a majority. Promptly the legislature moved to submit the Lecompton constitution to the voters. The document was rejected by more than 10,000 votes.

Although both sides had resorted to fraud and violence, the Kansas picture was clear enough. The majority of the people in the territory did not want to see slavery established. Buchanan, however, ignored the evidence. He urged Congress to admit Kansas under the Lecompton constitution, and he tried to force the party to back his proposal. Stephen A. Douglas and other Western Democrats refused to accept this perversion of popular sovereignty. Openly breaking with the administration, Douglas denounced the Lecompton proposition. And although Buchanan's plan passed the Senate, Western Democrats helped to block it in the House. Partly to avert further division in the party, a compromise measure, the English bill, was now offered (1858) and passed. It provided that the Lecompton constitution should be submitted to the people of Kansas for the third time. If the document was approved, Kansas was to be admitted and given a federal land grant; if it was disapproved, statehood would be postponed until the population reached 93,600, the legal ratio for a representative in Congress. Again, and for the last time, the Kansas voters decisively rejected the Lecompton constitution. Not until the closing months of Buchanan's administration in 1861, when a number of Southern states had withdrawn from the Union, would Kansas enter the Union—as a free state.

The Emergence of Lincoln

The congressional elections of 1858 were of greater interest and importance than most midterm contests. Not only did they have an immediate and powerful influence on the course of the sectional controversy but they projected into the national spotlight the man who was to be the dominating figure in the tragic years just ahead.

The widest public attention was directed toward the senatorial election in Illinois. There Stephen A. Douglas, the most prominent Northern Democrat, was a candidate for reelection; and he was fighting for his political life. Since Douglas, or his successor, would be chosen by a legislature that was yet to be elected, the control of that body became a matter of paramount importance. To punish Douglas for his resistance to the Lecompton constitution, the Buchanan administration entered Democratic candidates opposed to him in many legislative districts. But Douglas's greatest worry was that he faced Abraham Lincoln, the ablest campaigner in the Republican party.

Lincoln had been the leading Whig in Illinois. He was now the leading Republican in the state, although hardly a national figure, for his reputation still could not compare with that of the famous Douglas. Lincoln challenged the senator to a series of seven debates. Douglas accepted, and the two candidates argued their cases before huge crowds. The Lincoln-Douglas debates were widely reported by the nation's press, and before their termination the Republican who had dared to challenge the "Little Giant" of Democracy was a man of national prominence.

Douglas, while defending popular sovereignty, accused the Republicans of promoting a war of sections, of wishing to interfere with slavery in the South, and of advocating social equality of the races. Lincoln denied these charges (properly, since neither he nor his party had ever advocated any of these things). He, in turn, accused the Democrats and Douglas of conspiring to extend slavery into the territories and possibly, by means of another Supreme Court decision, into the free states as well (a charge that was equally unfounded). Lincoln was particularly effective in making it appear that Douglas did not regard slavery as morally wrong. He quoted Douglas as saying he did not care whether slavery was "voted up, or voted down."

Lincoln was opposed to slavery—on moral, political, and economic grounds. He believed that it contradicted the American ideal of democracy. Let the idea be established that blacks were not created with an equal right to earn their bread, he said, and the next step would be to deny the right to certain groups of whites, such as day laborers. Thus, it was his solicitude for the economic well-being of the white masses—his commitment to the ideology of free labor—that impelled Lincoln to oppose the introduction of slavery into the territories. He maintained that the national lands should be preserved as places for poor white people to go to better their condition.

Yet as much as he opposed the extension of slavery, Lincoln did not share the views of the abolitionists. The physical fact of slavery, he believed, must be taken into account. "We have a due regard to the actual presence of it amongst us and the difficulties of getting rid of it in any satisfactory way and all the constitutional obligations thrown about it." He and his party would "arrest the further spread of it," that is, prevent its expansion into the territories; he would not directly challenge it where it already existed. Yet the implications of Lincoln's argument were far greater than this relatively moderate formula suggests, for both he and other Republicans believed that by penning up slavery in the South, they would be consigning it to its "ultimate extinction." As he said in the most famous speech of the campaign:

A house divided against itself cannot stand. I believe this government cannot endure permanently half slave and half free. I do not expect the Union to be dissolved—I do not expect the house to fall—but I do expect it will cease to be divided. It will become all one thing, or all the other.

In the debate at Freeport, Lincoln asked Douglas: Can the people of a territory exclude slavery from its limits prior to the formation of a state constitution? Or in other words, is popular sovereignty still a legal formula despite the Dred Scott decision? The question was a deadly trap, for no matter how Douglas answered it, he would lose something. If he disavowed popular sovereignty he would undoubtedly be defeated for

Lincoln and Douglas in Debate
This is a depiction by a later artist, R. M. Root, of the debate between Lincoln and Douglas at
Charleston. Lincoln, who was beardless until 1861, is speaking, and Douglas sits at his right.
Various dignitaries of both parties are on the platform. The man behind Lincoln and to the left
taking notes is probably a reporter. In the 1850s speeches were frequently recorded by men
known as "stenographic reporters." They used a system of shorthand devised by Isaac Pitman
and described by him in a book published in 1837, *Stenographic Sound Hand*.
(Illinois State Historical Library)

reelection and his political career would be
ended. But if he reaffirmed his formula,
Southern Democrats would be offended, the
party split deepened, and his chances of securing the Democratic nomination in 1860
damaged if not destroyed.

Boldly Douglas met the issue. The people
of a territory, he said, could, by lawful
means, shut out slavery prior to the formation of a state constitution. Slavery could not
exist a day without the support of "local police regulations": territorial laws recognizing
the right of slave ownership. The mere failure of a legislature to enact such laws would
have the practical effect of keeping slaveholders out. Thus despite the Dred Scott decision, a territory could exclude slavery.
Douglas's reply became known as the Freeport Doctrine or, in the South, as the Freeport Heresy. It satisfied his followers sufficiently to win him a return to the Senate, but
throughout the North it aroused little enthusiasm.

Elsewhere, the elections went heavily
against the Democrats, who lost ground in
almost every Northern state. The administration retained control of the Senate but lost its
majority in the House, where the Republicans gained a plurality. In the holdover or
short session of 1858–1859, in which the
Democrats were in the majority, and in the
regular session of 1859 (elected in 1858),
every demand of the Republicans and
Northern Democrats was blocked by Southern votes or by presidential vetoes. These
defeated measures included a tariff increase,
a homestead bill, a Pacific railroad, and federal land grants to states for the endowment
of agricultural colleges. The 1859 session was
also marked by an uproarious struggle over
the election of a Speaker of the House.

The controversies in Congress, however,
were almost entirely overshadowed by another event in the fall of 1859: an event that
enraged and horrified the entire South and
greatly hastened the rush toward disunion.

John Brown's Raid

John Brown, the antislavery zealot whose bloody actions in Kansas had done so much to exaggerate the crisis there, made an even greater contribution to sectional conflict through a grim and spectacular episode that had major national implications. Still convinced that he was God's instrument to de-

John Brown
Even in this formal, posed portrait taken in 1859, the last year of his life, John Brown conveys the fierce sense of righteousness that fueled his extraordinary activities in the fight against slavery. His contemporaries were sharply divided over their assessments of Brown. To a few Northern abolitionists, he appeared an inspiring crusader for justice; and he became, after his execution for the famous raid at Harpers Ferry, a widely admired martyr within antislavery circles. To the majority of more moderate Northerners, Brown was a fanatic and a madman whose actions were to be repudiated and abhorred. And to many Southerners, Brown was even more ominous; to them, he was a symbol of what they considered the real aims of the North, a representative of its "secret will" to destroy slavery by any means necessary.
(Library of Congress)

stroy slavery, he decided to transfer his activities from Kansas to the South itself. With encouragement and financial aid from some Eastern abolitionists, he made plans to seize a mountain fortress in Virginia from which he could make raids to liberate slaves. He would arm the freedmen, set up a black republic, and eventually force the South to concede emancipation. Because he needed guns, he chose Harpers Ferry, where a United States arsenal was located, as his base of operations. In October, at the head of eighteen followers, he descended on the town and captured the arsenal. Almost immediately he was attacked by citizens and local militia companies, who were shortly reinforced by a detachment of United States Marines sent to the scene by the national government. With ten of his men killed, Brown had to surrender. He was promptly tried in a Virginia court for treason against the state, found guilty, and sentenced to death by hanging. Six of his followers met a similar fate.

Probably no other event had so much influence as the Harpers Ferry raid in convincing Southerners that their section was unsafe in the Union. Despite all their eulogies of slavery, one great fear always secretly gnawed at their hearts: the possibility of a general slave insurrection. Southerners now jumped to the conclusion that the Republicans were responsible for Brown's raid. This was, of course, untrue; prominent Republicans such as Lincoln and Seward condemned Brown as a criminal. But Southerners were more impressed by the words of such abolitionists as Wendell Phillips and Ralph Waldo Emerson, who now glorified Brown as a new saint. His execution made him a martyr to thousands of Northerners.

The Election of Lincoln

The election of 1860, judged by its consequences, was the most momentous in American history.

As the Democrats gathered in convention at Charleston, South Carolina, in April, most of the Southern delegates came with the determination to adopt a platform providing for federal protection of slavery in the territories: that is, an official endorsement of the principles of the Dred Scott decision. The Western Democrats, arriving with bitter recollections of how Southern influence had blocked their legislative demands in the recent Congress, were angered at the rule-or-ruin attitude of the Southerners. The Westerners hoped, however, to negotiate a face-saving statement on slavery so as to hold the party together. They vaguely endorsed popular sovereignty and proposed that all questions involving slavery in the territories be left up to the Supreme Court. When the convention adopted the Western platform, the delegations from eight lower South states withdrew from the hall. The remaining delegates then proceeded to the selection of a candidate. Stephen A. Douglas led on every ballot, but he could not muster the two-thirds majority (of the original number of delegates) required by party rules. Finally the managers adjourned the convention to meet again in Baltimore in June. At the Baltimore session, most of the Southerners reappeared, only to walk out again. Other Southerners, meanwhile, had assembled at Richmond. The rump convention at Baltimore nominated Douglas. The Southern bolters at Baltimore joined the men in Richmond to nominate John C. Breckinridge of Kentucky. Sectionalism had at last divided the Democratic party.

The Republicans held their convention in Chicago in May. Although the divisions developing in the Democratic ranks seemed to spell a Republican triumph, the party managers were taking no chances. They were determined that the party, in both its platform and its candidate, should appear to the voters to represent conservatism, stability, and moderation rather than radical idealism. No longer was the Republican party a one-idea organization composed of crusaders against slavery. It now embraced, or hoped to embrace, every major interest group in the North that believed the South, the champion of slavery, was blocking its legitimate economic aspirations.

The platform endorsed such measures as a high tariff, internal improvements, a homestead bill, and a Pacific railroad to be built with federal financial assistance. On the slav-

ery issue, the platform affirmed the right of each state to control its own institutions. That was the Republicans' way of saying they did not intend to interfere with slavery in the South. But they also denied the authority of Congress or of a territorial legislature to legalize slavery in the territories. This was equivalent to saying that they would still oppose the expansion of slavery.

The leading contender for the nomination was William H. Seward, who faced the competition of a number of favorite-son candidates. But Seward's prominence and his long, controversial political record damaged his chances. Passing him and other aspirants over, the convention nominated on the third ballot Abraham Lincoln, who was prominent enough to be respectable but obscure enough to have few foes, and who was radical enough to please the antislavery faction in the party but conservative enough to satisfy the ex-Whigs. The vice-presidential nomination went to Hannibal Hamlin of Maine, a former Democrat.

As if three parties were not enough, a fourth entered the lists—the Constitutional Union party. Although posing as a new organization, it was really the last surviving remnant of the oldest conservative tradition in the country; its leaders were elder statesmen and most of its members were former Whigs. Meeting in Baltimore in May, this party nominated John Bell of Tennessee and Edward Everett of Massachusetts. Its platform favored the Constitution, the Union, and enforcement of the laws.

In the North, the Republicans conducted a campaign reminiscent of the exciting Harrison–Van Buren contest of 1840, with parades, symbols, and mass meetings. For the most part, they stressed the economic promises in their platform and subordinated the slavery issue. Lincoln, following the customary practice of candidates, made no speeches, leaving this work to lesser party luminaries. Unlike previous candidates, he refused to issue any written statements of his views, claiming that anything he said would be seized on by Southerners and misrepresented.

In the November election, Lincoln won a majority of the electoral votes and the presi-

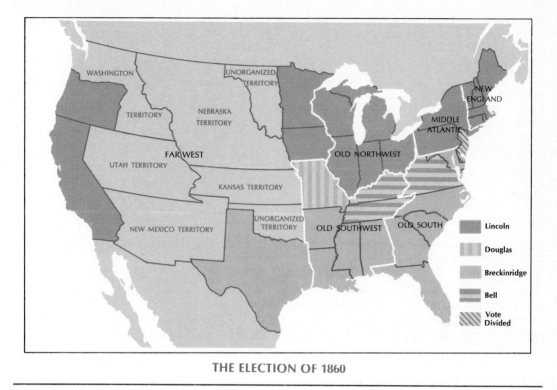

THE ELECTION OF 1860

dency, but only about two-fifths of the popular votes. The Republicans had elected a president, but they had failed to secure a majority in Congress; and of course they did not control the Supreme Court.

Nevertheless, the election of Lincoln served as the final signal to many Southerners that their position in the Union was hopeless. Throughout the campaign, various Southern leaders had warned that if the Re-

publicans should win, they would secede from the Union. Within a few weeks of Lincoln's victory, this process of disunion began—a process that would quickly lead to a prolonged and bloody war between two groups of Americans, both heirs of more than a century of struggling toward nationhood, each now convinced that with the other there could be no lasting accommodation.

SUGGESTED READINGS

Several good surveys of westward expansion are available, of which two of the most prominent are Frederick Merk, *History of the Westward Movement* (1978), and Ray Allen Billington, *Westward Expansion*, rev. ed. (1974). John D. Unruh, *The Plains Across: The Overland Emigrants and the Trans-Mississippi West, 1840–1860* (1979), is an important study of the migrations westward in the antebellum period, revising earlier interpretations. On the expansionist impulse, which became known as Manifest Destiny, see above all Frederick Merk, *Manifest Destiny and Mis-*

sion in American History (1963). Merk is also the author of *The Monroe Doctrine and American Expansionism, 1843–1849* (1966), which examines some of the diplomatic aspects of expansionism. Albert K. Weinberg, *Manifest Destiny* (1935), is an important study that Merk's book revises. William H. Goetzmann, *Exploration and Empire* (1966), examines the roles of explorers and scientists in the expansionist efforts. Henry Nash Smith, *Virgin Land* (1950), examines the image of the West in American literature. Other works of value on Manifest Destiny include Ray

Allen Billington, *The Far Western Frontier, 1830–1860* (1956); Norman A. Graebner, *Empire of the Pacific* (1955); and Frederick Merk, *Fruits of Propaganda in the Tyler Administration* (1971).

The Texas question is considered, again by Frederick Merk, in *Slavery and the Annexation of Texas* (1972). Other standard works include E. C. Barker, *Mexico and Texas, 1821–1835* (1928); and William C. Binkley, *The Texas Revolution* (1952). Francis Parkman, *The Oregon Trail* (1849 and many later editions), is a classic account of the migration to the Far West. R. L. Duffus, *The Santa Fe Trail* (1930), examines expansion into the Southwest. R. G. Cleland, *From Wilderness to Empire: A History of California, 1542–1900* (1944), R. W. Paul, *California Gold* (1947), and J. S. Holliday, *The World Rushed In* (1981), describe the settlement of California. Frederick Merk, *The Oregon Question* (1967), examines some of the political and diplomatic controversies arising from American expansion into the Northwest. O. O. Winther, *The Great Northwest*, rev. ed. (1950), describes the actual settlement of the region.

The role of James K. Polk in the expansionism of the 1840s is examined in Charles G. Sellers, *James K. Polk: Continentalist, 1843–1846* (1966); J. S. Reeves, *American Diplomacy Under Tyler and Polk* (1907); and David M. Pletcher, *The Diplomacy of Annexation* (1973). G. M. Brack, *Mexico Views Manifest Destiny, 1821–1846* (1975), examines the other side of the controversy. On the Mexican War itself, see K. Jack Bauer, *The Mexican-American War, 1846–1848* (1974); John H. Schroeder, *Mr. Polk's War: American Opposition and Dissent* (1973); Otis A. Singletary, *The Mexican War* (1960); and S. V. Conner and O. B. Faulk, *North America Divided* (1971). Holman Hamilton, *Zachary Taylor, Soldier of the Republic* (1941), and C. W. Elliott, *Winfield Scott* (1937), are biographies of two of the military heroes of the war.

General studies of the sectional crises that followed the Mexican War and continued throughout the 1850s include Allan Nevins, *The Ordeal of the Union*, 2 vols. (1947) and *The Emergence of Lincoln*, 2 vols. (1950); Michael Holt, *The Political Crisis of the 1850s* (1978); Roy F. Nichols, *The Disruption of American Democracy* (1948); Avery Craven, *The Coming of the Civil War* (1942); and David Potter, *The Impending Crisis, 1848–1861* (1976), a work of particular importance. James G. Randall and David Donald, *The Civil War and Reconstruction*, rev. ed. (1969), and James M. McPherson, *Ordeal by Fire* (1981), are excellent overviews of the entire era of crisis, war, and reunion.

The Compromise of 1850 is the subject of Holman Hamilton, *Prologue to Conflict: The Crisis and Compromise of 1850* (1964). Chaplain W. Morrison, *Democratic Politics and Sectionalism: The Wilmot Proviso Controversy* (1973), and Kinley J. Brauer, *Cotton Versus*

Conscience: Massachusetts Whig Politics and Southern Expansion, 1843–1848 (1967), examine the immediate background to the 1850 controversy. Biographies of some of the principals in the political debate are also useful sources of information. Among them are Robert W. Johannsen, *Stephen A. Douglas* (1973); Charles M. Wiltse, *John C. Calhoun: Sectionalist, 1840–1850* (1951); Charles B. Going, *David Wilmot, Free-Soiler* (1924); Holman Hamilton, *Zachary Taylor: Soldier in the White House* (1951); Richard N. Current, *Daniel Webster and the Rise of National Conservatism* (1955); and Robert F. Dalzell, Jr., *Daniel Webster and the Trial of American Nationalism, 1843–1852* (1973).

Diplomacy following the Mexican War is examined in Samuel F. Bemis (ed.), *American Secretaries of State*, vols. 5 and 6 (1928); Basil Rauch, *American Interest in Cuba, 1848–1855* (1948); and Robert E. May, *The Southern Dream of a Caribbean Empire, 1854–1861* (1973). Gerald Wolff, *The Kansas-Nebraska Bill* (1977), and James C. Malin, *The Nebraska Question* (1953), examine the crisis of 1854; and Paul W. Gates, *Fifty Million Acres: Conflict over Kansas Land Policy, 1854–1890* (1954), examines its aftermath. On John Brown, see Stephen Oates, *To Purge This Land with Blood* (1970), an excellent biography; and R. O. Boyer, *The Legend of John Brown* (1973). Truman Nelson, *The Old Man: John Brown at Harper's Ferry* (1973), examines the last episode in Brown's career, as does J. C. Furnas, *The Road to Harpers Ferry* (1959). Benjamin Quarles, *Allies for Freedom* (1974), describes black views of Brown.

Eric Foner, *Free Soil, Free Labor, Free Men* (1970), is the outstanding study of Northern free-labor ideology. See also his collection of essays, *Politics and Ideology in the Age of the Civil War* (1980). David Donald, *Charles Sumner and the Coming of the Civil War* (1960), is a brilliant biography of one of the important figures in the early Republican party. On the proslavery ideology, see William Jenkins, *Pro-Slavery Thought in the Old South* (1935); and Harvey Wish, *George Fitzhugh: Propagandist of the Old South* (1943). Don E. Fehrenbacher, *The Dred Scott Case* (1978), is the definitive account of the Supreme Court decision that exacerbated sectional tensions. On the emergence of Lincoln, see the Nevins volumes of that title mentioned above. Other works in the vast literature on Lincoln that are useful for these years are Richard N. Current, *The Lincoln Nobody Knows* (1958); David Donald, *Lincoln Reconsidered* (1956); Don E. Fehrenbacher, *Prelude to Greatness* (1962); and George B. Forgie, *Patricide in the House Divided* (1979), a provocative psychological portrait of Lincoln and his contemporaries. Carl Sandburg, *Abraham Lincoln: The Prairie Years* (1929), a one-volume abridgement of his larger biography, is a romantic and appealing view of the young Lincoln.

PART FOUR

War and Reunion, 1860-1877

To most of the South, and even to much of the North, the election of Abraham Lincoln to the presidency in 1860 marked the ultimate failure of compromise. The nation's highest office was now to be in the possession of a man unanimously opposed by the residents of one of the sections. No longer, apparently, were there leaders or programs capable of appealing across regional lines to a common national interest. Sentiment on both sides had hardened to the point that there no longer seemed any way for North and South to exist together in amicable union. And so the war came.

Yet despite the apparent irreconcilability of the sections, the war came as something of a surprise to both sides. The Southern states, when they began late in 1860 to secede from the Union, assumed at first that the North would not in the end use force to oppose them. The national government in Washington, for its part, believed that secession was a momentary aberration, that the rebellious states could be made to come to their senses and return to their proper relation to the Union. Even after the first shots over Fort Sumter had signaled the beginning of hostilities, both sides expected at most a brief and limited conflict.

As the fighting continued, however, year after murderous year, killing more than 600,000 people, maiming and injuring many more, and devastating large portions of the nation, Americans on both sides were forced finally to confront the real price of their inability to settle their differences. The Civil War was like no conflict in the nation's history, perhaps like no conflict in the history of mankind to that point. Waged on a scale hitherto unknown, employing horrible new technology that made widespread slaughter the new norm of combat, the war did not so much settle the differences between North and South as exhaust both sides. When, at last, General Robert

E. Lee surrendered the last major force of the once great Confederate army to General Ulysses S. Grant in 1865, only one issue was effectively settled. The institution of slavery was to be abolished. Other questions—the future economic relationship between the sections, the distribution of political power, the status of freed blacks in the nation—remained unanswered. The Civil War had determined that the United States would survive as a single nation. It had not, however, determined what kind of a nation it would be.

Nor was the troubled aftermath of the fighting entirely successful in resolving the difficult sectional issues that remained. The spirit of compromise that had died so painfully in the 1850s did not quickly revive; and both North and South remained intransigent in many ways after the war. White Southerners quickly attempted to rebuild a social order that resembled their antebellum society as closely as possible. Above all, they attempted to reduce the now emancipated black population to a level of economic bondage hardly distinguishable from slavery. Northerners, motivated partly by bitterness and desire for revenge, partly by a genuine commitment to protecting the freedmen, responded by imposing their own system of government on the South—a system that greatly restricted the power of the region's traditional ruling class and so deeply embittered the white residents of the section that even a century later they would refer to Reconstruction as an "outrage" and an "abomination." When at last, in 1877, the last Reconstruction governments began to be replaced and white Southerners once again gained control of their region, they rejoiced that the South had been "redeemed," that the long nightmare of Northern tyranny was over.

There were others, however, who looked on the end of Reconstruction with less enthusiasm. Black Americans had viewed the postwar policies in a very different light from their white counterparts. They saw in the actions of the federal government the first systematic effort in the history of their nation to provide them with the elemental rights of citizenship. Only federal protection, they believed, could effectively guard them from the determination of the white population to keep blacks isolated and demeaned. The withdrawal of this federal support, the result of a series of political bargains between the whites of both regions, consigned black Southerners to another century of poverty and discrimination. It had been the issue of race that had helped to produce the Civil War in the first place. Now, after four years of bloodshed and twelve more years of political acrimony, the issue remained unresolved. Instead, white Americans in both regions of the nation had returned to the spirit of compromise that had permitted the Union to survive during the first half of the nineteenth century. And in the 1870s, as in the 1830s and 1840s, compromise meant abandoning the difficult effort to resolve the status of blacks—leaving the question unsettled to confront and frustrate future generations of Americans.

The War of the Rebellion

14

Confederate Volunteers
Young Southern soldiers pose for a photograph in 1861, shortly before the first Battle of Bull Run. The Civil War was one of the first military conflicts in the age of photography, and it served as a subject for many of America's early photographers. (Courtesy, Valentine Museum, Cook Collection)

By the end of 1860, it seemed that virtually all the cords that had once bound the Union together had snapped. The almost mystical veneration of the Constitution and its framers was no longer working to unite the nation; residents of the North and South—particularly after the controversial *Dred Scott* decision—now differed fundamentally over what the Constitution said and what the framers had meant. The romantic vision of America's great national destiny had ceased to be a unifying force; the two sections now defined that destiny in different and apparently irreconcilable terms. The stable two-party system could not dampen sectional conflict any longer; that system had collapsed in the 1850s, to be replaced by a new one that accentuated rather than muted regional controversy. Above all, the federal government was no longer the remote, unthreatening presence it once had been; the necessity of resolving the status of the territories had made it necessary for Washington to deal with sectional issues in a direct and forceful way. And thus, beginning in 1860, the divisive forces that had always existed within the United States were no longer counterbalanced by unifying forces; and the Union began to dissolve.

To the South, the war that ensued was a legitimate struggle for independence, a conflict no less glorious than the American Revolution of nine decades before. Ultimately, they would call it the "War Between the States," as if to imply that it had reflected a constitutional exercise of states' rights. To the North, however, the conflict was nothing more than a criminal insurrection—illegal, unjustifiable, even treasonous. And the Union government, therefore, assigned to the struggle an official name that attributed far less dignity to the Southern cause: the "War of the Rebellion."

Despite the differences in outlook between the sections, however, both sides encountered very similar experiences. Both were forced to mobilize a high proportion of the resources of their societies for victory; both were required to confront problems of production and organization never before encountered in a modern society; and both found themselves, by the end, fighting in markedly similar ways a war that had resulted from supposedly fundamental regional differences.

THE SECESSION CRISIS

Almost as soon as the news of Abraham Lincoln's election reached the South, the militant leaders of the region—the champions of the new concept of Southern "nationalism," men known both to their contemporaries and to history as the "fire-eaters"—began to demand an end to the Union. The Southern states, they argued, should withdraw from the federal system and form a new nation of their own; and their vehicle should be a device that had, they claimed, firm legal grounding in the Constitution: secession.

The Withdrawal of the South

The concept of secession was rooted in the political philosophy that the South had developed over the course of several decades to protect its minority status in the nation. According to this doctrine, the Union was an association of sovereign states. The individual states had once joined the Union; they could, whenever they wished, dissolve their connections with it and resume their status as separate sovereignties. For a state to leave the

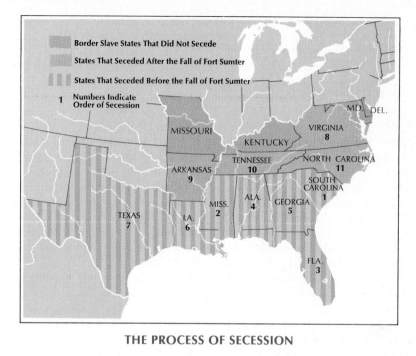

THE PROCESS OF SECESSION

Union was a momentous but lawful act, from the Southern point of view. The governor and the legislature could call an election for a special state convention and this body could pass an ordinance of secession.

South Carolina, long the hotbed of Southern separatism, led off the secession parade, its convention taking the state out of the Union on December 20, 1860, by a unanimous vote. Before Lincoln ever assumed the presidency, six other Southern states—Mississippi (January 9, 1861), Florida (January 10), Alabama (January 11), Georgia (January 19), Louisiana (January 26), Texas (February 1)—had left the Union. Not only that, but in February 1861, representatives of the seceded states met at Montgomery, Alabama, and formed a new, Southern nation—the Confederate States of America.

Something of the indecision in Northern attitudes was reflected by President Buchanan. In his message to Congress of December 1860, he denied the right of a state to secede but openly doubted that the federal government had the power to force a state back into the Union. He intended to avoid a collision of arms and to maintain the symbolic authority of the national government until his successor could take office.

As the various states seceded, they took possession of federal property within their boundaries, but they lacked the strength to seize certain offshore forts, notably Fort Sumter in the harbor of Charleston, South Carolina, and Fort Pickens in the harbor of Pensacola, Florida. South Carolina sent commissioners to Washington to ask for the surrender of Sumter, garrisoned by a small force under Major Robert Anderson. Buchanan, fearful though he was of provoking a clash, refused to yield the fort. In January 1861, he decided to reinforce it. By his direction, an unarmed merchant ship, the *Star of the West*, proceeded to Fort Sumter with troops and supplies. When the vessel attempted to enter the harbor, it encountered the fire of shore batteries and turned back. The first shots between North and South had been fired. But still, neither section was ready to admit that a war had begun. And in Washington, attention turned once again to efforts to resolve the controversy through compromise.

The Failure of Compromise

As the situation in South Carolina deteriorated, President Buchanan urged Congress to try once again to find a peaceful resolution that might hold the Union together. The Senate and the House appointed committees to study various plans of adjustment; and gradually—in the Senate at least—attention began to center on a proposal submitted by Senator John J. Crittenden of Kentucky. The Crittenden Compromise, as it was known, called for a series of constitutional amendments. One would have guaranteed the permanence of slavery in the states; others were designed to satisfy Southern demands on such matters as fugitive slaves and slavery in the District of Columbia. But the heart of Crittenden's plan dealt with slavery in the territories. He proposed to reestablish the Missouri Compromise line of 36°30′ in all the territory that the United States then held or *thereafter acquired.* Slavery was to be prohibited north of the line and permitted south of it. The Southern members of the committee indicated they would accept this territorial division if the Republicans also would. The Republicans, after sounding out President-elect Lincoln in Illinois, voted against the proposal. Lincoln took the position that the restoration of the Missouri Compromise line would encourage the South to embark on imperialist adventures in Latin America. It also, of course, would have represented an abandonment by the Republicans of their most basic position: that slavery could not be allowed to expand.

One notable attempt to effect a compromise was made outside Congress. The legislature of Virginia called for a national peace conference at Washington. Representatives from twenty-one states assembled early in February and spent most of the month framing compromise proposals. The plan of this Peace Convention followed closely the Crittenden scheme. The convention submitted the plan to the Senate, but it received almost no support.

And so nothing had been resolved when Abraham Lincoln arrived in Washington for his inauguration—sneaking into the city in disguise on a train in the dead of night, to avoid assassination as he passed through the slave state of Maryland en route. The country was now divided into two hostile states, waiting for what was coming to seem an inevitable war.

In his eloquent inaugural address, Lincoln laid down several basic principles: the Union was older than the Constitution; no state could of its own volition leave the Union; the ordinances of secession were illegal; and acts of violence to support secession were insurrectionary or revolutionary. He declared that he meant to execute the laws in all the states and to "hold, occupy, and possess" the federal property in the seceded states.

Lincoln soon found an opportunity to apply his policy in the case of Fort Sumter. Major Anderson was running short of supplies; unless he received fresh provisions the fort would have to be evacuated. If Lincoln permitted the loss of Sumter, the South and perhaps the North would never believe that he meant to sustain the Union. After much deliberation he decided to dispatch a naval relief expedition to the fort. Carefully he informed the South Carolina authorities, who, of course, would have to notify the Confederate government, that ships were on the way to bring supplies but not to land troops or munitions unless resistance was offered. His move placed the Confederates in a dilemma. If they permitted the expedition to land, they would be bowing tamely to federal authority; their people would not believe that they meant to sustain secession. But if they fired on the ships or the fort, they would make themselves appear to be the aggressors. After hours of anguished discussion, the government in Montgomery ordered General P. G. T. Beauregard, in charge of Confederate forces at Charleston, to demand Anderson's surrender and, if the demand was refused, to attack the fort. Beauregard made the demand; Anderson rejected it. The Confederates then bombarded the fort for two days, April 12–13, 1861. On April 14, Anderson surrendered.

War had come. Lincoln moved to increase the army and called on the states to furnish troops to restore the Union. Now four more slave states seceded and joined the Confederacy: Virginia (April 17), Arkansas

(May 6), Tennessee (May 7), and North Carolina (May 20). The mountain counties in northwestern Virginia refused to accept the decision of their state, established their own "loyal" government, and in 1863 secured admission to the Union as the new state of West Virginia. The four remaining slave states, Maryland, Delaware, Kentucky, and Missouri, cast their lot with the Union, although not without considerable controversy (and in large part because of heavy pressure from Washington). Lincoln kept a keen watch on their actions, and in two, Maryland and Missouri, helped to ensure their decision by employing military force.

The Question of Inevitability

Was the outbreak of war inevitable? Was there anything that Lincoln (or those before him) could have done to settle the sectional conflicts peaceably? Those questions have preoccupied historians for more than a century without resolution. (See "Where Historians Disagree," pp. 420–421.)

In one sense, the war clearly was not inevitable. If the nation had not acquired new Western lands in the 1840s, if Douglas had not presented the Kansas-Nebraska Act to Congress in 1854, if the Supreme Court had chosen not to rule on the *Dred Scott* case, if John Brown had not raided Harpers Ferry, if Lincoln had acquiesced in the Crittenden Compromise, or if the North had agreed (as some urged) to let the Southern states leave in peace—if any number of things that did happen had not happened, then there might not have been a war. Even after Lincoln's election, even after the secession of the South, it would have been technically possible for the nation to avoid armed conflict.

The real question, however, is not what hypothetical situations might have reversed the trend toward war but whether the preponderance of forces in the nation were acting to hold the nation together or to drive it apart. And by 1861, it seems clear that in both the North and the South, sectional antagonisms—whether justified or not—had risen to such a point that union under the existing terms had become untenable. People in both regions of the country had come to believe that two distinct and incompatible civilizations had developed in the United States, and that those civilizations were incapable of living together in peace. Ralph Waldo Emerson, speaking for much of the North, said at the time: "I do not see how a barbarous community and a civilized community can constitute one state." And a slaveowner, expressing the sentiments of much of the South, said shortly after the election of Lincoln: "These [Northern] people hate us, annoy us, and would have us assassinated by our slaves if they dared. They are a different people from us, whether better or worse, and there is no love between us. Why then continue together?"

That the North and the South had come to believe these things may have made secession and war virtually inevitable. Whether these things were actually true—whether the North and the South were really as different and incompatible as they thought—is another question, one that the preparations for and conduct of the war helped to answer.

The Opposing Sides

A comparison of the combatants on the eve of war reveals that in one crucial area, at least, there were indeed basic differences between the sections. All the great material factors were on the side of the North.

These advantages, important from the beginning, became more significant as the conflict continued and the superior economy of the North became geared for war production. The North had a larger manpower reservoir from which to draw its armed forces. In the North, or the United States, were twenty-three states with a population of approximately 22 million. In the South, or the Confederate States, were eleven states with a population of about 9 million. Of these, approximately 3.5 million were slaves (whom whites were unwilling to use for military purposes), leaving a white population of less than 6 million.

The North's greater economic potential was most formidably apparent in industrial production. Almost any set of comparative

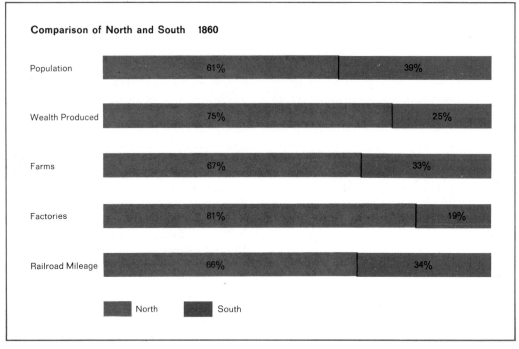

Comparison of North and South   1860

	North	South
Population	61%	39%
Wealth Produced	75%	25%
Farms	67%	33%
Factories	81%	19%
Railroad Mileage	66%	34%

North   South

If the slaves were not included in the South's total population, the North's manpower advantage would appear greater than shown here. And because many of the South's so-called factories were small, the superiority of the North's industrial production was also greater than this chart indicates.

figures can be chosen to illustrate the overwhelming superiority of the North. These statistics, translated into material terms, meant that the Northern armies, once the economic system had been converted to war production, would have more of everything than the Southern forces. This was not true, of course, in the first year of the war, when both sides had to purchase large amounts of supplies, particularly arms, from Europe. After 1862, however, the North was able to manufacture practically all of its war materials; its dependence on Europe ceased. The South, on the other hand, had to rely on Europe throughout the war. It also tried desperately to expand its own industrial facilities. The brilliant Confederate chief of ordnance, Josiah Gorgas, accomplished wonders in building arsenals and in supplying the armies with weapons and munitions. Nevertheless, both the quantity and the quality of Confederate firearms were inferior. The Southern economic system was unable to provide its

soldiers and civilians with the other materiel of modern war: clothes, boots, blankets, stockings, medical supplies, and the like. Its failure in this respect was one reason why Southern morale dropped badly after 1863.

In every respect the transportation system of the North was superior to that of the South. The North had more and better inland water transport (steamboats, barges), more surfaced roads, and more wagons and animals. The North had approximately 20,000 miles of railroads, while the South, containing at least as large a land area, had only 10,000 miles. The trackage figures, however, do not tell the whole story of Southern inferiority. There were important gaps between key points in the South, which meant that supplies had to be detoured long distances or carried between railheads by wagons. As the war wore on, the Confederate railroad system steadily deteriorated, and by the last year and a half of the struggle it had almost collapsed.

When the material factors are considered alone, the impression emerges that the South had absolutely no chance to win the war. Actually, the material strengths of the North were not as decisive as they appear at first glance. The South might have won a decision on the battlefield up to 1863. Southern inferiority in manpower and materials were partially offset by other factors. The South, for the most part, fought on the defensive in its own country and commanded interior lines. The Northern invaders had to maintain long lines of communication, supply themselves in areas where transportation was defective, and garrison occupied regions. Furthermore, the North had to do more than capture the enemy capital or defeat enemy armies. It had to convince the Southern civilian population that the war was hopeless by seizing and holding most of the Confederacy. The South was fighting for something very concrete, very easy for its people to understand. It sim-

ply wanted to be independent, to be let alone; it had no aggressive designs on the North. If the South could have convinced the North that it could not be conquered or that the result would not be worth the sacrifices, it might, even after 1863, have won its independence. Indeed, there were many points during the course of the war when Northern public opinion wavered, when many believed the war should be terminated even at the price of acquiescing in secession. A major Southern victory at one of those points might have shattered the Union's will to persist.

Southerners thought that even if the Southern human resources could not make up for Northern material advantages, there was still an almost certain guarantee of Confederate victory: Europe would intervene in the war on the side of the South. England and France had to have Southern cotton, and they would force the North to recognize the Confederacy.

THE NORTH MOBILIZES

For the North, the war years were a time of political and social discord, of frustration, and of the inevitable suffering that accompanies battle. Yet they were also a period of prosperity and expansion. The war provided a major stimulus to both industry and agriculture. Not only did the rising productivity of the North contribute to its ultimate victory; it also ensured that the region would be more highly developed at the end of the war than at the start.

Economic Measures

A powerful stimulant to the expanding economy was provided by the economic legislation enacted by the Republican party during the war. The Republicans represented Northern industry and agriculture; and now that the war had removed Southern opposition, they proceeded to put into effect the kind of program their supporters expected.

The Homestead Act (1862) and the Morrill Land Grant Act (1862) were measures that

the West had long sought. The first provided that any citizen, or any alien who had declared his intention to become a citizen, could register claim to a quarter section of public land (160 acres) and, after giving proof that he had lived on it for five years, receive title on payment of a small fee. The Morrill Law gave every state 30,000 acres of public land for each of its congressional representatives, the proceeds from the donation to be used for education in agriculture, engineering, and military science. This provided a basis for the development of the so-called land-grant colleges and universities.

Industry scored its first legislative gain a few days before President Buchanan left office. Congress passed the Morrill Tariff Act, which provided a moderate increase in duties, bringing the rates up to approximately what they had been before 1846. Later measures enacted in 1862 and 1864 were frankly protective. By the end of the war, the average of duties was 47 percent, the highest in the nation's history, and more than double the prewar rate.

The Causes of the Civil War

The debate over the causes of the Civil War began even before the war itself. In 1858, Senator William H. Seward of New York took note of the two competing explanations of the sectional tensions that were then inflaming the nation. On one side, he claimed, stood those who believed the sectional hostility to be "accidental, unnecessary, the work of interested or fanatical agitators." Opposing them stood those who believed there to be "an irrepressible conflict between opposing and enduring forces." Although he did not realize it at the time, Seward was drawing the outlines of a debate that would survive among historians for more than a century to come.

The "irrepressible conflict" argument was the first to dominate historical discussion. In the first decades after the fighting, histories of the Civil War generally reflected the views of Northerners who had themselves participated in the conflict. To them, the war appeared to be a stark moral conflict in which the South was clearly to blame. Henry Wilson's *History of the Rise and Fall of the Slave Power* (1872–1877) was (as the title suggests) a particularly vivid version of this moral interpretation of the war, which argued that Northerners had fought to preserve the Union and a system of free labor against the aggressive designs of the "slave power."

A more temperate interpretation, but one that reached generally the same conclusions, emerged in the 1890s, when the first serious histories of the war were written. Preeminent among them was the seven-volume *History of the United States from the Compromise of 1850 . . .* (1893–1900) by James Ford Rhodes. Like Wilson and others, Rhodes identified slavery as the central, indeed virtually the only, cause of the war. "If the Negro had not been brought to America," he wrote, "the Civil War could not have occurred." And because the North and the South had reached positions on the issue of slavery that were both irreconcilable and unalterable, the conflict had become "inevitable."

Although Rhodes placed his greatest emphasis on the moral conflict over slavery, he suggested, too, that the struggle reflected fundamental differences between the Northern and Southern economic systems. Not until the 1920s, however, did the idea of the war as an irrepressible *economic* rather than *moral* conflict receive full expression. As on so many other issues, it was the great historians Charles and Mary Beard who best expressed this viewpoint, in *The Rise of American Civilization* (2 vols., 1927). Slavery, the Beards claimed, was not so much a social or cultural institution as an economic one, a labor system. There were, they insisted, "inherent antagonisms" between Northern industrialists and Southern planters. Each group sought to control the federal government so as to protect its own economic interests. Both groups used arguments over slavery and states' rights only as smoke screens.

The economic determinism of the Beards influenced a generation of historians in important ways; but ultimately most of those who believed the Civil War to have been "irrepressible" returned to an emphasis on social and cultural factors. One of the greatest of all Civil War historians, Allan Nevins, argued as much in *The Ordeal of the Union* (8 vols., 1947–1971). The North and the South, he wrote, "were rapidly becoming separate peoples." At the root of these cultural differences was the "problem of slavery," but "fundamental assumptions, tastes, and cultural aims" of the regions were diverging in other ways as well.

More recent proponents of the "irrepressible conflict" argument have taken more hostile views of the Northern and Southern positions on the conflict but have been equally insistent on the role of culture and ideology in creating them. Eric Foner, in *Free Soil, Free Labor, Free Men* (1970) and other writings, emphasized the importance of the "free-labor ideology" to Northern opponents of slavery. The moral concerns of the abolitionists were not the dominant sentiments in the North, he claimed. Instead, most Northerners (including Abraham Lincoln) opposed slavery largely because they feared it might spread to the North and threaten the position of free white laborers. Convinced that Northern society was superior to that of the South, increasingly persuaded of the

South's intentions to extend the "slave power" beyond its existing borders, Northerners were embracing a viewpoint that made conflict inevitable. Eugene Genovese, writing of Southern slaveholders in *The Political Economy of Slavery* (1965), emphasized their conviction that the slave system provided a far more humane society than industrial labor, that the South had constructed "a special civilization built on the relation of master to slave." Just as Northerners were becoming convinced of a Southern threat to their economic system, so Southerners believed that the North had aggressive and hostile designs on the Southern way of life. Like Foner, therefore, Genovese saw in the cultural outlook of the section the source of an inevitable conflict.

Thus members of this group of historians have disagreed markedly over whether moral, cultural, social, ideological, or economic issues were the primary causes of the Civil War. But they have been in general accord that the conflict between North and South was deeply embedded in the nature of the two societies, that the crisis that ultimately emerged was irrepressible. Other historians, however, have questioned that assumption and have argued that the Civil War could have been avoided, that the differences between North and South were not important enough to have necessitated a war. Like proponents of the "irrepressible conflict" school, advocates of the war as a "repressible conflict" emerged first in the nineteenth century. President James Buchanan, for example, believed that extremist agitators were to blame for the conflict; and many Southerners writing of the war in the late nineteenth century claimed that only the fanaticism of the Republican party could account for the conflict.

But the idea of the war as avoidable did not gain wide recognition among historians until the 1920s and 1930s, when a group known as the "revisionists" began to offer new accounts of the prologue to the conflict. One of the leading revisionists was James G. Randall, who saw in the social and economic systems of the North and the South no differences so fundamental as to require a war.

Slavery, he suggested, was an essentially benign institution; it was, in any case, already "crumbling in the presence of nineteenth century tendencies." Only the political ineptitude of a "blundering generation" of leaders could account for the Civil War, he claimed. Avery Craven, another leading revisionist, placed more emphasis on the issue of slavery than had Randall. But in *The Coming of the Civil War* (1942) he too argued that slave laborers were not much worse off than Northern industrial workers, that the institution was already on the road to "ultimate extinction," and that war could, therefore, have been averted had skillful and responsible leaders worked to produce compromise.

More recent students of the war have kept elements of the revisionist interpretation alive by emphasizing the role of political agitation in the coming of the war. David Herbert Donald, for example, argued in 1960 that the politicians of the 1850s were not unusually inept, but that they were operating in a society in which traditional restraints were being eroded in the face of the rapid extension of democracy. Thus the sober, statesmanlike solution of differences was particularly difficult. Michael Holt, in *The Political Crisis of the 1850s* (1978), similarly emphasized the actions of politicians, rather than the irreconcilable differences between sections, in explaining the conflict, although he avoided placing blame on any one group. "Much of the story of the coming of the Civil War," he wrote, "is the story of the successful efforts of Democratic politicians in the South and Republican politicians in the North to keep the sectional conflict at the center of the political debate."

Like the proponents of the "irrepressible conflict" interpretation, the "revisionist" historians have differed among themselves in important ways. But the explanation of the Civil War has continued, even a century later, to divide roughly into the same two schools of thought that William Seward identified in 1858. And while the idea of the war as inevitable remains, as it has always been, the dominant interpretation, it has yet to establish unchallenged dominance.

Other legislative victories for business were achieved in connection with railroads and immigration. Two laws, passed in 1862 and 1864, created two federal corporations: the Union Pacific Railroad Company, which was to build westward from Omaha, and the Central Pacific, which was to build eastward from California. The government would aid the companies by donating public lands and advancing government loans. Immigration from Europe fell off in the first years of the war, partly because of the unsettled conditions. The decrease, coupled with the military demands for manpower, threatened to cause a labor shortage, and President Lincoln and business leaders asked Congress for governmental encouragement of immigration. In 1864, Congress passed a contract labor law authorizing employers to import laborers and collect the costs of transportation from future wages.

Perhaps the most important measure affecting the business-financial community was the National Bank Act, enacted in 1863 and amended in 1864. The act created the National Banking System, which lasted without serious modification until 1913. Its architects, including Secretary of the Treasury Salmon P. Chase, argued that, both for the military present and the economic future, the country needed a uniform and standard banknote currency. (At the outbreak of the war 1,500 banks chartered by twenty-nine states were empowered to issue notes.) Furthermore, Chase and his supporters claimed, national supervision of the banking system would aid war finance by enabling the government to market bonds more economically.

Under the new law, an existing state bank or a newly formed corporation could secure a federal charter and become a national bank. Each such institution was required to possess a minimum amount of capital and to invest one-third of its capital in government securities. On depositing the securities with the national treasury, it would receive, and could issue as banknotes, United States Treasury notes up to 90 percent of the current value of the bonds. Congress (in 1865) placed a tax on all state banknotes. This measure forced state notes out of existence and induced reluctant state banks to seek federal charters.

The North financed the war from three principal sources: taxation, loans, and paper-money issues. From taxes, including the tariff, the government received approximately $667 million; loans, including Treasury notes, accounted for $2.6 billion; and $450 million worth of paper currency ("greenbacks") was issued.

Since the greenbacks bore no interest, were not supported by a specie reserve, and depended for redemption on the good faith of the government (and its ability to win the war), they fluctuated in value. In 1864, a greenback dollar, in relation to a gold dollar, was worth only 39 cents, and even at the close of the war its value had advanced to but 67 cents.

In America's previous wars, bonds had been sold only to banks and to a few wealthy investors. Through the agency of Jay Cooke, a Philadelphia banker, the Treasury now launched a campaign to persuade ordinary citizens to buy bonds. By high-pressure propaganda techniques, Cooke disposed of $400 million worth of bonds—the first example of mass financing of a war in American history.

Not until 1862, when mounting war expenses forced the country to face realities, did Congress adopt an adequate tax program. Then it passed the Internal Revenue Act, which placed duties on practically all goods and most occupations. For the first time, in 1861, the government levied an income tax: a duty of 3 percent on incomes above $800. Later, the rates were increased to 5 percent on incomes between $600 and $5,000 and 10 percent on incomes above $5,000. Through the medium of the various war taxes, the hand of the government was coming to rest on most individuals in the country. The United States was in the process of acquiring a national internal revenue system—in fact, a national tax system—one of the many nationalizing effects of the war.

Raising the Union Armies

When hostilities started, the regular army of the United States numbered only about 16,000 troops, and many of its units were scattered throughout the West. President

Lincoln, in his first call for troops to repress the "rebellion," summoned 75,000 militiamen for three months, the usual period of service set for state troops by existing militia law. Lincoln soon realized that the war would be of longer duration. Without constitutional sanction, he called for 42,000 volunteers for national service for three years and authorized an increase of 23,000 in the regular army. When Congress met in July 1861, it legalized the president's acts and, at his recommendation, provided for enlisting 500,000 volunteers to serve for three years.

For a time, the volunteering system served to bring out enough men to fill the armies, but not after the first flush of enthusiasm had worn off. Finally, in March 1863, Congress enacted the first national draft law in American history (the South had employed conscription almost a year earlier). Few exemptions were permitted: only high national and state officials, preachers, and men who were the sole support of a dependent family. But a drafted man could escape service by hiring a substitute to go in his place or by paying the government a fee of $300.

The purpose of the law was to spur enlistments by threatening to invoke conscription. Each state was divided into enrollment districts and was assigned a quota of men to be raised. If a state could fill the quota, it would escape the draft completely; if certain districts failed to meet their quotas, a sufficient number of men would be drafted to make up the difference. Although the draft directly inducted only 46,000 men, it stimulated enlistments enormously. These totaled 2.9 million, but that figure includes many who enlisted several times or served short terms. Probably 1.5 million men altogether served in the Union armies (as contrasted with 900,000 in the Confederate forces).

To a people accustomed to a government that had hardly touched their daily lives, conscription seemed a strange and ominous thing. Opposition to the law was widespread, particularly from laborers, immigrants, and Peace Democrats. In places it erupted into violence. Demonstrators against the draft rioted in New York City for four days in July 1863, killed several hundred people, mostly blacks, and burned down the homes and businesses of black people. (Some Northern opponents of the war believed that blacks were responsible for the conflict.) Federal troops had to be brought in to subdue the rioters. Some Democratic governors who supported the war (such as Horatio Seymour of New York) contended that the national government had no constitutional power to conscript, and they openly challenged the Lincoln administration on the issue.

Politics and Emancipation

When Lincoln first took over the presidency, he was widely considered a small-time prairie politician, unfit for his job. He strengthened this impression by his unpretentious air. Actually, he was well aware of his great abilities and of his superiority over other Northern leaders. His supreme confidence in himself was demonstrated by his choice of a cabinet. Representing every faction of the Republican party and every segment of Northern opinion, it was an extraordinary assemblage of advisers and a difficult set of prima donnas to manage. Three of the secretaries, Seward, Chase, and Stanton, were first-rate men. Seward and Chase thought that they were abler than Lincoln and should be in his place. At the very beginning of the administration, Seward made an attempt to dominate Lincoln, failed, and became his loyal supporter. Chase never learned that the president was a bigger man than he.

Lincoln's confidence in his inner strength was revealed by his bold exercise of the war powers of his office. In order to accomplish his purposes, he was ready to violate parts of the Constitution, explaining that he would not lose the whole by being afraid to disregard a part. In this spirit he called for troops to repress the rebellion (an act that was equivalent to a declaration of war), illegally increased the size of the regular army, and proclaimed a naval blockade of the South.

Opposition to the war came from two sources: from Southern sympathizers in the Union slave states and from the peace wing of the Democratic party. War Democrats were willing to support the war and even to accept offices from the administration. Peace Democrats, or, as their enemies called them,

Freedmen in Baltimore, 1865
Most emancipated slaves remained in the rural South during and after the Civil War and
continued to supply the labor force for Southern agriculture. But significant numbers flocked to
urban centers, particularly in the troubled last months of the war and the first months of peace.
Baltimore, located in a former slave state close to the border of the former Confederacy,
received particularly large numbers of freedmen. (Library of Congress)

"Copperheads," feared that agriculture and
the West were being subordinated to industry and the East and that states' rights were
going down before nationalism. These Democrats proposed to call a truce in the fighting,
invite the South to attend a national convention, and amend the Constitution to preserve
both the Union and states' rights. Some advocated the formation of a Western confederacy, and some joined secret societies
(Knights of the Golden Circle, Sons of Liberty), which allegedly conspired to aid the
Southern rebels.

To deal with opponents of the war, Lincoln resorted to military arrests. He suspended the right of habeas corpus, so that an
alleged offender could be arrested and held
without trial or, if tried, had to appear before

a military court. At first, Lincoln denied the
civil process only in specified areas; but in
1862, he proclaimed that all persons who
discouraged enlistments or engaged in dis-
loyal practices would come under martial
law. In all, more than 13,000 persons were
arrested and imprisoned for varying periods.
Among them was a Maryland secessionist
leader whom Lincoln refused to release even
under a writ from Chief Justice Taney (*Ex
parte Merryman*). The most prominent Cop-
perhead in the country, Clement L. Vallan-
digham of Ohio, was seized by military authorities and exiled to the Confederacy.
(After the war, in 1866, the Supreme Court
held, in *Ex parte Milligan*, that military trials
in areas where the civil courts were capable
of functioning were unconstitutional.)

In the Republican as well as in the Democratic party there were factions—the Radicals and the Conservatives. On most questions, including economic matters, the two groups were in fundamental agreement, but they differed violently on slavery. Leaders of the Radicals were Thaddeus Stevens of Pennsylvania, master of the party machine in the House, and Senators Charles Sumner of Massachusetts and Benjamin F. Wade of Ohio. Heading the Conservatives was President Lincoln. The Radicals wanted to seize the opportunity of the war to strike slavery down—abolish it suddenly and violently. The Conservatives, who were also opposed to slavery, wanted to accomplish the same result in a different way—easily and gradually. Lincoln made several notable although unsuccessful attempts to persuade the loyal slave states to agree to a program of compensated gradual emancipation. He feared, at first, that the introduction of abolition as a war aim would divide Northern opinion and alienate the border slave states.

A Confiscation Act, passed in August 1861, declared free all slaves used for "insurrectionary" purposes. Subsequent laws abolished slavery, with compensation to owners, in the District of Columbia (April 1862) and in the western territories (June 1862). In the summer of 1862, the Radicals decided that Northern opinion had reached a point where they could move against slavery in the states. In July they pushed through Congress the second Confiscation Act, which was in essence a bold attempt to accomplish emancipation by legislative action. It declared the property of persons supporting the rebellion subject to forfeiture to the United States government; declared free the slaves of persons aiding and supporting the insurrection; and authorized the president to employ blacks, including freed slaves, as soldiers.

The Republican party was coming under Radical control, and the country was slowly beginning to accept emancipation as an aim of the war. The signs were not lost on the astute master of politics in the White House. To preserve the nation, he had to have the support of his own party, particularly the Radicals, who were the last-ditch Unionists, the men who would never give up the war.

And if a majority of the Northern people wanted slavery destroyed, as seemed the case, he could not afford to divide popular opinion by opposing their will. In July 1862, he decided to take the leadership of the antislavery impulse away from the Radicals by putting himself at the head of it.

On September 22, 1862, after the Battle of Antietam, the president issued his preliminary Emancipation Proclamation; and on the first day of 1863, his final Emancipation Proclamation, which declared forever free the slaves in designated areas of the Confederacy. Exempted from the edict were the state of Tennessee, most of which was under Union control, and western Virginia and southern Louisiana, which were occupied by federal troops. Presumably these areas were omitted because they were not enemy territory and hence were not subject to the president's war powers. For a similar reason, the proclamation did not apply to the border slave states, which had never seceded from the Union.

The proclamation freed immediately only a few slaves. But it indicated that henceforth this was to be a war for the emancipation of the slaves as well as for the preservation of the Union. Eventually, as federal armies occupied much of the South, the proclamation became a practical reality, and hundreds of thousands of slaves were freed by its operation. Equally important in the process of emancipation was the induction of many former slaves into the armed forces of the Union. Some 186,000 served as soldiers, sailors, and laborers, thereby contributing substantially to the freeing of their race. Furthermore, the impulse to abolition that the proclamation symbolized intensified throughout the country, affecting even the border states. Before the end of the war, slavery had been abolished in two Union slave states, Maryland and Missouri, and in three "reconstructed" or occupied Confederate states, Tennessee, Arkansas, and Louisiana. The final and inevitable action was taken early in 1865, when Congress approved the Thirteenth Amendment (ratified by the required number of states several months after the war closed), which freed all slaves everywhere and abolished slavery as an institution.

Early in the war, and particularly after the election of 1862, in which the Republicans suffered heavy losses, party leaders proceeded to form a broad coalition of all groups that supported the war, trying particularly to attract the War Democrats. The new organization, which was composed of a Republican core with a fringe of War Democrats, was known as the Union party. It encountered its major political test in the presidential election of 1864, which was the first national election held in the midst of a great war.

When the Union convention met in June, it nominated Lincoln, with the chilly assent of the Radicals, and, for vice president, Andrew Johnson of Tennessee, a War Democrat who had refused to follow his state into secession. In August, the Democratic convention nominated George B. McClellan, former Union general and an object of hatred to all good Radicals. The peace faction got a plank into the Democratic platform denouncing the war as a failure and calling for a truce to be followed by an invitation to the South to enter a national convention. Although

McClellan repudiated the plank, the Democrats stood before the country as the peace party—ready to profit from the growing war weariness of the nation and from the dismal state of the Union's military position. At this crucial moment, however, several Northern military victories, particularly the capture of Atlanta, Georgia, early in September, rejuvenated Northern morale and gave promise of Republican success in November.

The election was a smashing electoral triumph for Lincoln, who won 212 votes to McClellan's 21 and carried every state except Kentucky, New Jersey, and Delaware. Lincoln's popular majority, however, was uncomfortably small, 2,213,000 to 1,805,000, or an advantage of only 400,000. A slight shift of popular votes in some of the more populous states would have changed the result. Had Union victories not occurred when they did, had Lincoln not made special arrangements to allow Union troops to vote (presumably for him), the Democrats might have won and the future course of the nation might have been altered considerably.

THE SOUTH MOBILIZES

Although the first seven Southern states to secede had left the Union as individual sovereignties, they intended from the first to come together in a common confederation, which they hoped the states of the upper South would eventually join. Accordingly, representatives of the seceded states assembled at Montgomery, Alabama, early in February 1861, to create a Southern nation. When Virginia seceded, the government moved to Richmond, partly out of deference to Virginia, partly because Richmond was one of the few Southern cities large enough to house the government.

Southerners were acutely aware, and boastfully proud, of the differences between their new nation and the nation they had left. Those differences were real. But there were also important similarities between the Union and the Confederacy as they mobilized for war: similarities in their political systems, in the methods they used for financing the war and conscripting troops, even in the way they fought.

The Confederate Government

In the Confederate constitution, state sovereignty was expressly recognized but not the right of secession. A few governmental reforms were introduced, such as the "item veto"—the president's power to veto part of a bill without rejecting the whole thing. Slavery was mentioned by name, and various provisions made its abolition (even by one of the states) practically impossible. In most other respects the constitution of the Confederate States was identical to that of the United States.

Besides framing a constitution and passing temporary laws, the Montgomery convention named a provisional president and a provisional vice president, Jefferson Davis of

Mississippi and Alexander H. Stephens of Georgia. Afterward, in a general election, the same two men were chosen, without opposition, for regular six-year terms. Davis had been a firm but not extreme advocate of Southern rights in the former Union; he was a moderate but not an extreme secessionist. Stephens had been the chief among those who had contended that secession was unnecessary. Indeed the Confederate government, like the Union government, was dominated throughout the war by men of the center. Just as Republican radicals never wielded great power in the Lincoln administration, so in the Confederacy the extremist fire-eaters found themselves generally without influence.

Jefferson Davis embodied the spirit of the nation he had been called to lead. His family, which was of Southern yeoman stock, had moved from Kentucky, where he was born, to the new lush cotton lands of Mississippi,

where they became rich planters almost overnight. Davis was a first-generation aristocrat. So also were most of the members of his government. The Confederacy was run by the cotton nabobs of the newer "Western" South, not by the old aristocracy of the seaboard states.

Whereas Lincoln's task was to preserve a nation, Davis's was to make one. Lincoln succeeded; Davis failed. He spent too much time on routine items, on what one observer called "little trash." A good administrator, he was his own secretary of war; but he rarely rose above the secretarial level to provide genuinely national leadership. Moreover, he proceeded on the assumption that the Confederacy was a legal and permanent organization that could fight a war in the normal fashion of older countries. The situation demanded ruthless efficiency, yet he tried to observe every constitutional punctilio. Lincoln, without clear constitutional sanction,

Jefferson Davis
In the years after the Civil War, Davis became a popular folk hero in the states of the former Confederacy—second only to Robert E. Lee as symbol of the lost, glorious cause. While serving as the Confederate leader, however, Davis was the target of ferocious criticism from all factions within the new nation, who attacked him as a stubborn, ineffectual leader. Many historians have agreed with such assessments. David Potter, one of the greatest scholars of the nineteenth-century South, once wrote, "It hardly seems unrealistic that if the Union and Confederacy had exchanged Presidents with one another, the Confederacy might have won its independence." (Library of Congress)

suspended habeas corpus; Davis asked his Congress to let him suspend it and received only partial permission. One shrewd Confederate official (R. G. H. Kean) wrote: "All the revolutionary vigor is with the enemy. . . . With us timidity—hair splitting."

The Confederate cabinet displayed, at best, only average ability. The personnel changed frequently. There were three secretaries of state, two secretaries of the treasury, four attorneys general, and five secretaries of war. Not one of them ever dared to oppose the will of President Davis.

But outside the administration—in the Congress and among the public at large—opposition and dissent were widespread. Just as in the North, disenchanted citizens throughout the South spoke openly and bitterly about the disappointing progress of the war effort, the incompetence of the president and the government, the problems of the economy. The Confederacy had been established on the ideal of the unity and homogeneity of the South; it was that ideal, in fact, that underlay the decision of the founders that there should be no party system in the new nation, that the public should form a single united group. (A similar impulse supported the effort to create the Union party in the North in 1864.) But the quest for unity was in many ways no more successful in the Confederacy than in the Union. And the absence of a party system meant that disagreements often became far more destructive than they did within the government of the United States.

Money and Men

In contrast to the burgeoning prosperity of the wartime North, the South in the war years underwent shortages, suffering, and sacrifice. The Southern economy, despite a frantic expansion of industrial facilities, was unable to supply the needs of its armies and civilian population.

The men seeking to devise measures to finance the Confederacy's war effort, Secretary of the Treasury Christopher G. Memminger and the congressional leaders, had to reckon with a number of hard facts. A national reve-

nue system had to be created to collect money from a people unaccustomed to bearing large tax burdens. Southern banking houses, except in New Orleans, were fewer and smaller than those of the North. Because excess capital in the South was usually invested in slaves and land, the sum of liquid assets on deposit in banks or in individual hands was relatively small. The only specie possessed by the government was that seized in United States mints located in the South (amounting to about $1 million). In an attempt to secure more specie, the government dispatched an army column into New Mexico, but this force, after some initial success, was repelled.

The Confederate Congress, like its counterpart in the North, showed some reluctance to enact rigorous wartime taxes. In 1861, the legislators provided for a direct tax on property to be levied through the medium of the states. If a state preferred, it could meet its quota by paying as a state. Most of the states, instead of taxing their people, assumed the tax, which they paid by issuing bonds or their own notes. Moving more boldly in 1863, Congress passed a bill that included license levies and an income tax. A unique feature was "the tax in kind." Every farmer and planter had to contribute one-tenth of his produce to the government. Altogether, the revenue from taxation was relatively small—only about 1 percent of total income.

The borrowing record of the Confederacy was little better than its tax program. Eventually the government issued bonds in such large amounts that the people doubted its ability to redeem them. Congress authorized a $100 million loan to be paid in specie, paper money, or produce. The expectation was that the bulk of the proceeds would be in the form of products—the "loan in kind." The loan was subscribed, partly in paper currency and mostly in produce or pledges of produce. But many of the pledges were not redeemed, and often the promised products were destroyed by the enemy. The Confederacy also attempted to borrow money in Europe by pledging cotton stored in the South for future delivery. Its most notable venture in foreign finance was the famous Erlanger loan, which was supposed to net $15 million.

Actually, Erlanger, a French financier, was interested in conducting a huge cotton speculation. The Confederate government received only $2.5 million from the loan.

Since ready revenue was needed and cash was scarce, the Confederate government resorted—like the Union government—to the issuance of paper money and treasury notes in 1861. Once started, the process could not be stopped. By 1864 the staggering total of $1 billion had been issued. In addition, states and cities issued their own notes. The inevitable result was a depreciation of the money—inflation. Prices skyrocketed to astronomical heights. Many people, particularly those who lived in towns or had fixed incomes, could not pay these prices. Such people often lost some of their will to fight.

Like the United States, the Confederate States first raised armies by calling for volunteers. By the latter part of 1861, volunteering had dropped off. As the year 1862 opened, the Confederacy was threatened by a manpower crisis.

The government met the situation boldly. At Davis's recommendation, Congress in April enacted the first Conscription Act, which declared that all able-bodied white males between the ages of eighteen and thirty-five were liable to military service for three years. A man who was drafted could escape his summons if he furnished a substitute to go in his place. The prices for substitutes eventually went as high as $10,000 in Confederate currency. The purpose of the provision was to exempt men in charge of agricultural and industrial production, but to people who could not afford substitutes it seemed like a special privilege to the rich. The provision was repealed late in 1863 after arousing bitter class discontent.

The first draft act and later measures provided for other exemptions, mostly on an occupational basis. The government realized that conscription had to be selective, that some men had to be left on the home front to perform the functions of production. It erred in excusing men who were not doing any vital services and in permitting too many group exemptions. The provision most bitterly criticized was that exempting one white man on each plantation with twenty or more slaves. Angrily denounced as the "twenty-nigger law," it caused ordinary men to say: "It's a rich man's war but a poor man's fight."

In September 1862, Congress adopted a second conscription measure, which raised the upper age limit to forty-five. At the end of the year, an estimated 500,000 soldiers were in the Confederate armies. Thereafter conscription provided fewer and fewer men, and the armed forces steadily decreased in size. Federal armies seized large areas in the South, depriving the Confederacy of manpower in the occupied regions. Military reverses in the summer of 1863 convinced many Southerners that the war was lost, causing a kind of passive resistance to the draft as men sought to avoid it by hiding in the hills and woods, and desertions began to increase.

As 1864 opened, the situation was critical. In a desperate move, Congress lowered the age limit for drafted men to seventeen and raised it to fifty, reaching out, it was said, toward the cradle and the grave. Few men were obtained. War weariness and the certainty of defeat were making their influence felt. In 1864–1865 there were 100,000 desertions. An observant Confederate diarist, Mary Boykin Chestnut, wrote in her journal in March 1865: "I am sure our army is silently dispersing. Men are moving the wrong way, all the time. They slip by with no songs and no shouts now. They have given the thing up." In a frantic final attempt to raise men, Congress in 1865 authorized the drafting of 300,000 slaves. The war ended before this incongruous experiment could be tried out.

Like the North, the South had attempted to recruit an army through forced conscription; and like the North, it had encountered resistance and, for the most part, frustration.

States' Rights in the Confederacy

Despite widespread criticism of the Davis administration and opposition to the draft, the Southern people were ready in overwhelming numbers to support the war for Southern independence. The only important organized opposition came from the inhabitants of the mountain areas, whose population was less than 10 percent of the Southern total. (See above, pp. 334–335.) Here supporters of the national cause carried on a kind of guerrilla warfare against the occupying Confederate forces, until liberated by the Union forces late in 1863.

Although united in their desire to sustain the war, Southerners were bitterly divided on how it should be conducted. The greatest dividing force was, ironically enough, the principle of states' rights—the foundation of Southern political philosophy, for whose conservation and consecration the South had left the old Union. States' rights had become such a cult with Southerners that they reacted against all central controls, even those necessary to win the war. If there was an organized faction of opposition to the government, it was that group of quixotic men who counted Vice President Stephens as their leader. They had one simple, basic idea. They wanted the Confederacy to win its independence, but they would not agree to sacrificing one iota of state sovereignty to

achieve that goal. If victory had to be gained at the expense of states' rights, they preferred defeat. The states'-righters concentrated their criticisms on two powers that the central government sought to exercise: the suspension of habeas corpus and conscription. Such recalcitrant governors as Joseph Brown of Georgia and Zebulon M. Vance of North Carolina, contending that the central government had no right to draft troops, tried in every way to obstruct the enforcement of conscription.

The idea of a negotiated peace fascinated the states'-righters, especially Vice President Stephens. They never made it clear whether they were thinking of reunion or of Southern independence. As early as 1863, they urged a peace based on recognition of state sovereignty and the right of each state to control its domestic institutions—which implied a restored Union. Yet at times they proposed negotiations based on the independence of the Confederacy.

STRATEGY AND DIPLOMACY

In the realm of military planning, the objectives of the Union were positive and those of the Confederacy negative. To achieve a victory, the Union had to conquer the rebels and reduce them to subjection, to obedience to federal law. The Confederacy had only to stave off defeat.

In the realm of diplomacy, the situation was reversed. The objectives of the Confederacy in its dealings with European powers were positive, and those of the Union negative. The Confederacy hoped to persuade foreign governments to step into the war and help make their independence a reality. The Union aimed to prevent foreign recognition and intervention.

The Commanders in Chief

It was the responsibility of the president as commander in chief of the army and navy—of Abraham Lincoln for the Union and Jefferson Davis for the Confederacy—to see to

the making and carrying out of an overall strategy for winning the war. Lincoln, a civilian all his life, had had no military education and no military experience except for a brief militia interlude. Yet he became a great war president and a great commander in chief, superior to Davis, who was a trained soldier. Lincoln made himself a fine strategist, often showing keener insight than his generals. He recognized that numbers and materiel were on his side, and he moved immediately to mobilize the maximum strength of Northern resources. He urged his generals to keep up a constant pressure on the whole defensive line of the Confederacy until a weak spot was found and a breakthrough could be made. At an early date, he realized that the proper objective of his armies was the destruction of the Confederate armies and not the occupation of southern territory.

During the first three years of the war, Lincoln performed many of the functions that in a modern command system would be assumed by the chief of the general staff or the joint chiefs of staff. He formulated policy, devised strategic plans, and even directed tactical movements. Some of his decisions were wise, some wrong, but the general effect of his so-called interfering with the military machine was fortunate for the North.

At the beginning, Lincoln was inclined to take the advice of General Winfield Scott. The old general, however, was unable to adjust his thinking to the requirements of mass war. He retired from service on November 1, 1861, and Lincoln replaced him as general in chief with young George B. McClellan, who was also the commander of the federal field army in the East, the Army of the Potomac. McClellan lacked the abilities needed to formulate strategy for all theaters of the war. The one grand strategic design he submitted was defective because it envisioned operations in only one theater, his own, and because it made places instead of enemy armies his objective. When McClellan took the field in March 1862, Lincoln removed him as general in chief. In July, Lincoln designated General Henry W. Halleck to direct the armies. The foremost American student of the art of war, Halleck had won an undeserved reputation as a successful general in the West. Now he cast himself in the role of an adviser instead of a maker of decisions. Again, Lincoln himself was forced to take up the function of forming and directing strategy, a task that he performed until March 1864, when the nation finally achieved a modern command system.

In the system arrived at in 1864, Ulysses S. Grant, who had emerged as the North's greatest general, was named general in chief. Charged with directing the movements of all Union armies, Grant, because he disliked the political atmosphere of Washington, established his headquarters with the Army of the Potomac but did not technically become commander of that army. As director of the armies, Grant proved to be the man for whom Lincoln had been searching. He possessed in superb degree the ability to think of the war in overall terms and to devise strategy for the war as a whole. Because Lincoln trusted Grant, he gave the general a relatively free hand. Grant, however, always submitted the broad outlines of his plans to the presi-

Ulysses S. Grant
One observer said of Ulysses S. Grant, "He habitually wears an expression as if he had determined to drive his head through a brick wall, and was about to do it." It was an apt metaphor for Grant's military philosophy, which took little account of sophisticated tactical or strategic theories, but relied instead on constant, unrelenting assault. One result was that Grant was willing to fight, and to continue fighting, when other Northern generals held back. Another result was that Grant presided over some of the worst carnage of the Civil War. (Library of Congress)

dent for approval before putting them into action. By the new arrangement, Halleck became "chief of staff," acting as a channel of communication between Lincoln and Grant and between Grant and the departmental commanders.

Lincoln's active command role underlines one of the most important changes occurring with the advent of modern warfare: the emergence of the civilian in strategic planning. As war became more technological and total, strategy became a problem of directing the whole resources of a nation. It was too vast a problem for any one set of leaders, especially for the military.

The most dramatic example of civilian intervention in military affairs was the Committee on the Conduct of the War, a joint investigative committee of both houses of Con-

Robert E. Lee
Lee provided a sharp contrast to his Northern counterpart, Ulysses S. Grant. Grant was slightly built and slouchy in dress and manner. Lee was tall, with a strong and imposing physique, a large head, and wide shoulders. He had an aura of command. Grave and reserved in manner, he sought to emulate his hero, George Washington, in his conduct of the war. And like Washington, he was a Southern aristocrat who lived by a self-imposed code of high conduct. "Duty is the sublimest word in our language," he once wrote. Although he had commanded a losing cause, he remained a national hero—ultimately in both the North and the South—in ensuing decades. (National Archives)

gress and the most powerful agency that the legislative branch has ever created to secure for itself a voice in formulating war policies. Established in December 1861, under the chairmanship of Senator Benjamin F. Wade of Ohio, it became the spearhead of the Radical attack on Lincoln's war program. The Radicals sensed that many of the Northern generals were not animated by a driving, ruthless desire for victory. The generals at first were influenced by the eighteenth-century concept of war as a kind of game—as chessboard maneuvers conducted in leisurely fashion and without heavy casualties. The Radicals ascribed the generals' hesitancy to a secret sympathy for slavery, which the professionals were supposed to have im-

bibed at West Point. The generals whom the committee favored—most of them incompetent amateurs—would have been no improvement, but the spirit represented by the committee helped to infuse a hard, relentless purpose into the conduct of the war.

Southern command arrangements centered on President Davis. The Confederacy failed to achieve a modern command system. Early in 1862, Davis assigned General Robert E. Lee to duty at Richmond, where, "under the direction of the President," he was "charged" with the conduct of the Confederate armies. Despite the fine words, this meant only that Lee, who had a brilliant military mind, was to act as Davis's adviser, furnishing counsel when called on. After serving a few months, Lee went into the field, and Davis did not appoint another adviser until February 1864. Then he selected Braxton Bragg, whom he had been forced to remove from field command after Bragg was defeated in the West. Bragg had real strategic ability, but he understood the weakness of his political position and restricted his function to providing technical advice. In February 1865, the Confederate Congress, in a move directed at Davis, created the position of general in chief, which was intended for Lee. Davis named Lee to the post but took care to announce that legally he himself was still commander in chief. Lee accepted the job on the basis offered by the president: as a loyal subordinate instead of the dictator some people wanted him to be. The war ended before the new command experiment could be fully tested.

Below the level of highest command, the war was conducted—in both North and South—by men of markedly similar backgrounds. Much of the professional military leadership of both of the contenders was a product of the national military academies of the United States—the army academy at West Point and the naval academy at Annapolis, Maryland. Union and Confederate officers, in other words, had been trained along similar lines; many were intimately acquainted, even friendly, with their counterparts on the other side. The amateurs who played an important role in both armies were also in many respects similar. These were the commanders of volunteer regiments—usually the acknowledged economic or social leaders of their communities, who appointed themselves officers and rounded up troops to lead. Although occasionally this system produced officers of real ability, on both sides it more often led to disorganization and frustration.

The Role of Sea Power

The Union had a particular advantage in the area of sea power, where it had an overwhelming preponderance of strength. President Lincoln made the most of it. The Union navy served two main functions. One was to enforce the blockade of the Southern coast that the president proclaimed at the start of the war (April 19, 1861). The other was to assist the Union armies in combined land-and-water operations.

In the Western theater of war—the vast region between the Appalachian Mountains and the Mississippi River—the larger rivers were navigable by vessels of considerable size. The Union navy helped the armies to conquer this area by transporting supplies and troops for them and joining them in attacking Confederate strong points. In defending themselves against the Union gunboats on the rivers, the Confederates had to depend mainly on land fortifications because of their lack of naval power. These fixed defenses proved no match for the mobile land-and-water forces of the Union.

At first, the blockade was too large a task for the Union navy. Even after the navy had grown to its maximum size, it was unable to seal off completely the long shoreline of the Confederacy. Though oceangoing ships were kept away, small blockade runners continued to carry goods into and out of some of the Southern ports. Gradually the federal forces tightened the blockade by occupying stretches of the coast and seizing one port after another, the last remaining important one—Wilmington, North Carolina—early in 1865. Fewer and fewer blockade runners got through, and the blockade increasingly hurt the South.

In bold and ingenious attempts to break the blockade, the Confederates introduced some new weapons, among them an ironclad warship. They constructed this ship by plating with iron a former United States frigate, the *Merrimac*, which the Yankees had scuttled in Norfolk harbor when Virginia seceded. On March 8, 1862, the *Merrimac* steamed out from Norfolk to attack the blockading squadron of wooden ships in Hampton Roads. It destroyed two of the ships and scattered the rest. Jubilation reigned in Richmond and consternation in Washington. But the federal government had already placed orders for the construction of several ironclads of its own, which had been designed by John Ericsson. One of these, the *Monitor*, arrived at Hampton Roads on the night of March 8. When the *Merrimac* emerged on the following day to hunt for more victims, it was met by the *Monitor*, and the first battle between ironclad ships ensued. Neither vessel was able to penetrate the other's armor, but the *Monitor* put an end to the raids of the *Merrimac*.

The Confederates later experimented with other new kinds of craft in the effort to pierce the blockade. One was a torpedo boat, which carried the torpedo (mine) on a long pole projecting in front. Another was a small, cigar-shaped, hand-powered submarine. In 1864, in Charleston harbor, such a submarine, pulling its mine behind it on a cable, dived under a blockading vessel, exploded the mine against the hull, and then was dragged to the bottom by the sinking ship. For the first time in the history of warfare, a submarine had made a successful strike. But such efforts, however ingenious, fell far short of breaking or even weakening the blockade.

After a year or so of these unsuccessful efforts, the South generally ceased trying to break the blockade, using its navy primarily to defend its ports. Nevertheless, attempts to weaken the blockade continued in varying guises. The Confederates decided, for example, to build or buy fast ships to prey on the Northern merchant marine on the high seas. The hope was that the Union would detach ships from the blockade to pursue the commerce raiders. The Confederates also hoped to get from abroad a specially built "ram" with which to smash the wooden blockading

The Ironclad *Atlanta*
In the end, the Confederate navy was unable to break the Union blockade of its rivers and ports. But in the course of the war, the South produced a number of striking naval innovations: crude torpedoes, which scored hits on forty-three Union ships; the first combat submarine; and, most prominently, the famous ironclads, beginning with the *Merrimac*, a damaged conventional vessel that was refitted and renamed the *Virginia* in 1862. The *Atlanta*, pictured above, was a later ironclad, designed to ram Union ships with its pointed, sheathed prow below the waterline. It was typical of a number of such Confederate vessels. The *Atlanta* was ultimately captured by the Union navy on the James River, near Richmond; and this photograph shows Northern sailors standing on its deck. (Library of Congress)

---

ships. As a result of these efforts, the naval war became an important element in the relations of the Union with the Confederacy, on the one hand, and with the powers of Europe on the other.

Europe and the Disunited States

Judah P. Benjamin, who occupied the Confederate foreign office for the greater part of the war, was a clever and intelligent man, but he lacked strong convictions and confined most of his energy to administrative routine. Seward, on the other hand, after some initial blunders, learned his job well and went on to become one of the outstanding American secretaries of state. In the key diplomatic post at London, the North was represented by a distinguished minister, Charles Francis Adams, who seemed to have inherited the diplomatic abilities of his father (John Quincy Adams) and grandfather (John Adams).

In the relationship of Europe to the Civil War, the key nations were Great Britain and France. These two had acted together against Russia in the Crimean War and were united by an entente, one of the understandings of which was that questions concerning the United States fell within the sphere of British influence. Napoleon III, therefore, would not act in American affairs without the concurrence of Britain. Russia, the third major power of Europe, was, like the United States, a rising nation that thought its aspirations were being blocked by England. Feeling a community of interest with democratic America, autocratic Russia openly expressed sympathy for the Northern cause. In 1863, when war threatened to break out between

Russia and England over Poland, Russia, in order to get its navy into position to attack British commerce, dispatched two fleets to American waters. One turned up at New York and the other at San Francisco, thereby creating a legend that they had come to support the United States if England and France should attempt to break the blockade.

At the beginning of the war, the sympathies of the ruling classes of England and France were with the Confederacy. But such English liberals as John Bright and Richard Cobden saw the war as a struggle between free and slave labor, and they presented it in these terms to their followers. The politically conscious but unenfranchised workers in Britain expressed their sympathy for the Northern cause frequently and unmistakably—in mass meetings, in resolutions, and, through the medium of Bright and other leaders, in Parliament itself. After the issuance of the Emancipation Proclamation, these groups intensified their activities on behalf of the Union cause.

In the minds of Southern leaders, cotton was their best diplomatic weapon. Their analysis was founded on the assumption that the textile industry was basic to the economies of England and France, which depended on the South for the bulk of their cotton supply; deprived of Southern cotton, these countries would face economic collapse. Therefore they would have to intervene on the side of the Confederacy.

But this diplomacy based on King Cotton never worked as its champions had envisioned. In 1861, English manufacturers had a surplus of cotton on hand. The immediate effect of the blockade was to enable the textile operators to dispose of their remaining finished goods at high prices. Thereafter, the supply became increasingly short, and many mills were forced to close. Both England and France, however, managed to avoid a complete shutdown of their textile industries by importing supplies from new sources, notably Egypt and India. Most important of all, the workers, the people most seriously affected by the shortage, did not clamor to have the blockade broken. Even the 500,000 English textile workers thrown out of jobs continued to support the North.

The result of all this was that no European nation extended diplomatic recognition to the Confederacy. Although several times England and France considered offering mediation, they never moved to intervene in the war. Neither could afford to do so unless the Confederacy seemed on the point of winning; and the South never attained a prospect of certain victory.

Immediately after the outbreak of hostilities, Great Britain issued a proclamation of neutrality, thus attributing to the Confederacy the status of a belligerent. France and other nations followed suit. Although the Northern government, which officially insisted that the war was not a war but a domestic insurrection, furiously resented England's action, the British government had proceeded in conformity with accepted rules of neutrality and in accordance with the realities of the situation. The United States was fighting a *war*, a fact that Lincoln himself had recognized in his proclamation establishing a blockade. Thereafter three crises or near crises between Great Britain and the United States developed, any one of which could have resulted in war between the two countries.

The first crisis, and the most dangerous one—the so-called *Trent* affair—occurred late in 1861. The Confederate commissioners to England and France, James M. Mason and John Slidell, had slipped through the then ineffective blockade to Havana, Cuba, where they boarded an English steamer, the *Trent*, for England. Hovering in Cuban waters was an American frigate, the *San Jacinto*, commanded by Captain Charles Wilkes, an impetuous officer who knew that the Southern diplomats were on the *Trent*. Acting without authorization from his government, Wilkes stopped the British vessel, arrested the commissioners, and bore them off in triumph to Boston. The British government drafted a demand for the release of the prisoners, reparation, and an apology. Lincoln and Seward, well aware that war with England would be suicidal, spun out the negotiations until American opinion had cooled off, then returned the commissioners with an indirect apology.

The second issue—the case of the Confederate commerce destroyers—generated a long-lasting diplomatic problem. Lacking the resources to construct the vessels, the Confederacy contracted to have them built and equipped in British shipyards. Six cruisers, of which the most famous were the *Alabama,* the *Florida,* and the *Shenandoah,* were sold to the Confederacy. The British government knew what was going on, being regularly and indignantly informed by Minister Adams; but it winked at the practice. The United States protested that this sale of military equipment to a belligerent was in violation of the laws of neutrality. The protests formed the basis, after the war, for damage claims that the United States served on Great Britain. (See below, p. 470.)

The third incident—the affair of the Laird rams—could have developed into a crisis but did not because the British government suddenly decided to mend its ways. In 1863, the Confederacy placed an order with the Laird shipyards in England for two powerful ironclads with pointed prows for ramming and sinking Union vessels and thus breaking the blockade. Adams was instructed to inform the British that if the rams, or any other ships destined for the Confederacy, left port, then there would be danger of war. Even before Adams delivered his message, the British government acted to detain the rams and to prevent the Confederacy from obtaining any other ships.

If Napoleon III had had his way, France and England would have intervened on behalf of the Confederacy at an early date. Unable to persuade Britain to act, he had to content himself with expressing sympathy for the Southern cause and permitting the Confederates to order commerce destroyers from French shipyards. The emperor's primary motive for desiring an independent South was his ambition to establish French colonial power in the Western Hemisphere. A divided America could not block his plans. He seized the opportunity of the war to set up a French-dominated empire in Mexico.

Napoleon's Mexican venture was a clear violation of the Monroe Doctrine, perhaps the most serious one that had ever occurred. The United States viewed it in such a light, but for fear of provoking France into recognizing the Confederacy, it could do no more than register a protest. Only after the Civil War was ended did the United States feel strong enough to put pressure on France to get out of Mexico.

CAMPAIGNS AND BATTLES

In the absence of direct intervention by the European powers, the two contestants in America were left to settle their conflict between themselves. They did so in four long years of bloody combat that produced more carnage than any war in American history, before or since. More than 600,000 Americans died in the course of the Civil War, far more than the 115,000 who perished in World War I or the 318,000 who died in World War II. And in proportion to the total population, the losses suffered in the 1860s were even higher. There were nearly 2,000 deaths for every 100,000 of population during the Civil War; in World War I, the comparable figure was only 109; in World War II, 241.

It was not only battle itself that produced the remarkable death toll. It was disease, to which the miserable conditions in which both armies had to live made soldiers highly vulnerable, and for which only the most primitive medical knowledge or facilities were available. Even minor battle injuries, moreover, could lead to death through infection or other complications because of the inadequate health care. Despite the efforts of such volunteer organizations as the American Sanitary Commission, which provided crucial assistance to the Union armies in nursing and other health needs, military medicine on both sides remained primitive. Not until World War I would scientific knowledge reach the point where disease would claim fewer victims than battle.

And the combat itself in the Civil War was of frightful intensity. After the Battle of Antietam, according to observers, one could have walked all the way across the vast battlefield atop the bodies of the fallen soldiers; the bare ground was almost entirely covered with the dead.

Despite the gruesome cost, the Civil War has become perhaps the most romanticized, the most intently studied, of all American wars. In large part, that is because the conflict produced—in addition to hideous fatalities—a series of military campaigns of classic strategic interest, and a series of military leaders who displayed unusual daring and charisma.

The Opening Clashes, 1861

The year 1861 witnessed several small battles that accomplished large results and one big battle that had no important outcome. The small engagements occurred in Missouri and in western Virginia, the mountainous region that shortly would become the state of West Virginia.

In Missouri, the contending forces were headed on the one hand by Governor Claiborne Jackson and other state officials, who wanted to take the state out of the Union, and on the other by Nathaniel Lyon, commanding a small regular army force at St. Louis. Lyon led his column into southern Missouri, where he was defeated and killed by a superior Confederate force at the Battle of Wilson's Creek (August 10). He had, however,

seriously blunted the striking power of the Confederates, and Union forces were able to hold most of the state.

Into western Virginia came a Union force that had been assembled in Ohio under the command of George B. McClellan. Crossing the Ohio River, McClellan succeeded by the end of the year in "liberating" the mountain people. Although possession of the region placed the Union forces on the flank of Virginia, they could not, because of the transportation obstacles presented by the mountains, use it as a base from which to move eastward. The occupation of western Virginia was, however, an important propaganda victory for the North: a Union-sympathizing area in the Confederacy had been wrenched from Southern control.

The one big battle of the year was fought in Virginia in the area between the two capitals. Just south of Washington was a Union army of over 30,000 under the command of General Irvin McDowell. A Confederate army of over 20,000 under P. G. T. Beauregard was based at Manassas in northern Virginia, about thirty miles southwest of Washington. If McDowell's army could knock out Beauregard's, the war might be ended immediately.

In mid-July McDowell marched his inex-

Union Wounded in Virginia
Much of the treatment of wounded Union soldiers fell to the United States Sanitary Commission, a private organization officially recognized by the War Department in 1861. The Sanitary Commission proved remarkably effective in distributing supplies, staffing hospitals, transporting wounded (through one of the first modern ambulance corps), and raising the standard of medical care for the army and ultimately for the nation. The commission was the major vehicle through which Northern women aided the war effort; thousands served as nurses and volunteers. This photograph shows Union amputees and other wounded at a hospital in Fredericksburg, Virginia. A Sanitary Commission nurse sits in the doorway. (Library of Congress)

perienced troops toward Manassas, his movement well advertised to the Confederates by Northern newspapers and Southern spies. Beauregard retired behind Bull Run, a small stream north of Manassas, and called for reinforcements. They reached him the day before the battle, making the two armies approximately equal in size.

In the Battle of Bull Run, or Manassas (July 21), McDowell's attack almost succeeded. But the Confederates stopped a last strong Union assault, then began a counterattack. A sudden wave of panic struck through the Union troops, wearied after hours of hot, hard fighting. They gave way and crossed Bull Run in a rout. Unable to get them in hand north of the stream, McDowell had to order a retreat to Washington—a chaotic withdrawal complicated by the presence along the route of many civilians, who had ridden down from the capital, picnic baskets in hand, to watch the battle from nearby hills.

The Confederates, as disorganized by victory as the Union forces were by defeat, and lacking supplies and transport, were in no condition to undertake a forward movement. Lincoln replaced McDowell with General McClellan, the victor of the fighting in western Virginia, and took measures to increase the army. Both sides girded themselves for real war.

The Western Theater

The first decisive operations in 1862 were in the Western theater. Here the Union forces were trying to secure control of the Mississippi line by moving on the river itself or parallel to it. Most of their offensives were combined land-and-water operations. To achieve their objective, they advanced on the Mississippi from the north and south, moving down from Kentucky and up from the Gulf of Mexico toward New Orleans.

In April, a Union squadron of ironclads and wooden vessels commanded by David G. Farragut, destined to be the first American admiral, appeared in the Gulf. Smashing past the weak Confederate forts near the mouth of the river, Farragut ran up to New Orleans, defenseless because the Confederate high command had expected the attack to come from the north; Farragut thus forced the civil authorities to surrender the city (April 28–May 1). For the rest of the war Union forces held New Orleans and the southern part of Louisiana. They closed off the mouth of the great river to Confederate trade, grasped the South's largest city and greatest banking center, and secured a base for future operations.

All Confederate troops in the West were under the command of one general, Albert Sidney Johnston. A fatal weakness marked the Confederate line in Kentucky. The center, through which flowed the Tennessee and Cumberland rivers, was located well back (southward) from the flanks, and was defended by two forts, Henry on the Tennessee and Donelson on the Cumberland. The forts had been built when Kentucky was trying to maintain a position of neutrality, and they were located just over the Tennessee line. If the Union forces, with the aid of naval power, could pierce the center, they would be between the two Confederate flanks and in position to destroy either.

This was exactly what the Union forces did in February. Ulysses S. Grant proceeded to attack Fort Henry, whose defenders, awed by the ironclad river boats accompanying the Union army, surrendered with almost no resistance (February 6). Grant then marched to Donelson, while his naval auxiliary moved to the Cumberland River. At Donelson, the Confederates put up a scrap; but eventually the garrison of 20,000 had to capitulate (February 16). Grant, by the simple process of cracking the Confederate center and placing himself astride the river communications, had inflicted a near disaster on the Confederacy. As a result of his movement, the Confederates were forced out of Kentucky and had to yield half of Tennessee.

With about 40,000 men, Grant now advanced up the Tennessee (southward) to get control of railroad lines that were vital to the Confederacy. He debarked his army at Pittsburg Landing. Near there, with a force about equal to his, Albert Sidney Johnston and P. G. T. Beauregard caught him with a surprise attack. In the ensuing Battle of Shiloh (April 6–7), they drove him back to the river in the first day's fighting, which cost Johnston

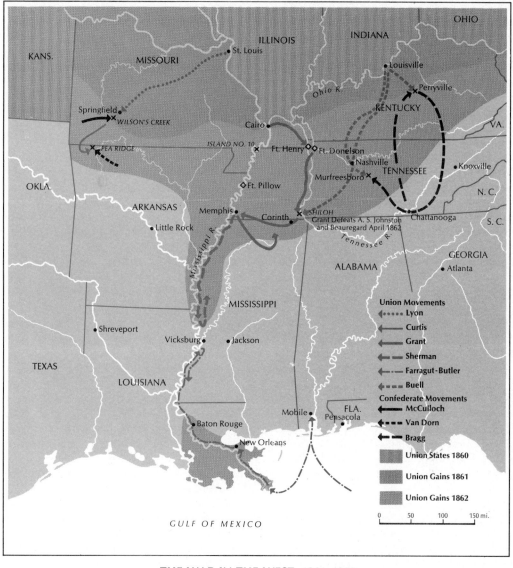

KANS.

MISSOURI

ILLINOIS

INDIANA

OHIO

• St. Louis

• Louisville

Ohio R.

• Perryville

KENTUCKY

VA.

Springfield • ✕ WILSON'S CREEK

Cairo •

✕ PEA RIDGE

ISLAND NO. 10 ✕ Ft. Henry ◇◇ Ft. Donelson

• Nashville

TENNESSEE

• Knoxville

OKLA.

◇ Ft. Pillow

Murfreesboro ✕

N. C.

ARKANSAS

Memphis •

Corinth ✕ SHILOH
Grant Defeats A. S. Johnston
and Beauregard April 1862

Chattanooga

S. C.

• Little Rock

Mississippi R.

Tennessee R.

GEORGIA

ALABAMA

• Atlanta

MISSISSIPPI

Union Movements
◄••••• Lyon
◄—— Curtis
←— Grant
◄=== Sherman
◄-•- Farragut-Butler
◄=== Buell
Confederate Movements
←— McCulloch
◄=== Van Dorn
◄=== Bragg

Shreveport •

Vicksburg •

• Jackson

TEXAS

LOUISIANA

Mobile •

FLA.
Pensacola

Union States 1860

Union Gains 1861

Union Gains 1862

• Baton Rouge

New Orleans •

0   50   100   150 mi.

GULF OF MEXICO

THE WAR IN THE WEST, 1861–1862

his life. The next day, reinforced by 25,000 newly arrived troops, Grant took the offensive and recovered the lost ground. Beauregard then withdrew.

After the narrow victory of the Union forces at Shiloh, they managed to occupy Corinth, Mississippi. Thus they controlled important railroads of which the town was the hub. Furthermore, by dominating a strip parallel with the Mississippi River, they made it impossible for the Confederates to hold their strong points on that river. By

June, Union forces occupied the Mississippi as far south as Memphis.

The Confederate army in Mississippi, now under the command of Braxton Bragg, moved north to Chattanooga, to be in a position to undertake an offensive and win back lost territory. The Confederates still held approximately the eastern half of Tennessee. Bragg's task was to recover the rest of the state and, if possible, to carry the war into Kentucky. Opposing him was an army under Don Carlos Buell, whose assignment was to capture Chattanooga. Bragg, instead of risking an engagement near there, decided to draw Buell away from Tennessee by going north. When the two armies met, in Kentucky, they fought the indecisive Battle of Perryville (October 8). Bragg then turned back to Tennessee, and Buell followed him slowly—so slowly that he was removed from command and replaced by William S. Rosecrans. Bragg and Rosecrans came together in the Battle of Murfreesboro or Stone's River (December 31–January 2). Again Bragg withdrew to the south, his campaign a failure.

In the course of the year, the Union forces had made considerable progress toward the achievement of their objectives in the West. They were having much less success with their land campaigns in the East.

The Virginia Front, 1862

In the Eastern theater in 1862, Union operations were directed by young George B. McClellan, commander of the Army of the Potomac and the most controversial general of the war. McClellan, a superb trainer of men, lacked the fighting instinct to commit his men to decisive battle.

During the winter of 1861–1862, McClellan had concentrated on training his army of 150,000 men near Washington. He finally settled on a plan of operations for the spring campaign. Instead of heading overland directly toward Richmond, he decided on a roundabout route. He would have the navy transport his troops down the Potomac to the Peninsula between the York and the James, and then he would go up the Peninsula and approach the Confederate capital from the east.

McClellan began his Peninsula campaign with about 100,000 men. President Lincoln held back another 30,000—McDowell's corps—to protect the Union capital, although McClellan insisted that Washington would be safe so long as he was threatening Richmond. As he was nearing Richmond he finally persuaded Lincoln to send him the additional men. To keep Lincoln from doing so, a Confederate army under Thomas J. ("Stonewall") Jackson marched rapidly northward in the Shenandoah Valley as if to cross the upper Potomac and attack Wash-

ington from above. Alarmed, Lincoln dispatched McDowell's corps to head off Jackson. In his brilliant Valley campaign (May 4–June 9), Jackson defeated two separate Union armies and slipped away before McDowell could catch him.

Meanwhile, just outside of Richmond, the Confederates under Joseph E. Johnston attacked McClellan's army, but in the Battle of Fair Oaks or Seven Pines (May 31–June 1) could not budge it. Johnston, badly wounded, was replaced by Robert E. Lee, who was to prove a masterly commander in leading the Army of Northern Virginia throughout the rest of the war. Lee recalled Jackson from the Valley and, with a combined force of 85,000 (as compared with McClellan's 100,000), launched a new offensive, which resulted in a series of engagements known as the Battle of the Seven Days (June 25–July 1). Lee intended to cut McClellan off from his base on the York River and then to destroy McClellan's isolated army. Instead, McClellan managed to fight his way across the Peninsula and set up a new base on the James. There, with naval support, the Army of the Potomac was safe. But so was Richmond.

Only twenty-five miles from Richmond, with a secure line of water communications, the Army of the Potomac was in a good position to renew the campaign. McClellan, however, time and again found reasons for delay. And Lincoln, instead of replacing McClellan with a more aggressive commander, decided to remove the army to northern Virginia and combine it with a smaller force under John Pope. Lincoln wished to start a new offensive on the direct Washington-to-Richmond overland route that he himself preferred.

As the Army of the Potomac left the Peninsula by water, Lee moved the Army of Northern Virginia northward to strike Pope before McClellan could join him. Pope, who was as rash as McClellan was cautious, attacked the approaching Confederates without waiting for the arrival of all of McClellan's troops. In the ensuing Battle of Second Manassas or Second Bull Run (August 29–30) Lee threw back the assault and routed Pope's army, which fled to Washington. Removing Pope, Lincoln put McClellan in charge of all the federal forces around the city.

Lee soon went over to the offensive again, heading north through western Maryland. With some misgivings, Lincoln let McClellan go to meet Lee. McClellan had the good luck to discover a copy of Lee's order showing that the Confederate army was divided, a part of it under Jackson having gone to capture Harpers Ferry. McClellan should have attacked quickly, before the Confederates could recombine. Instead, he gave Lee time to pull most of his forces together behind Antietam Creek, near the town of Sharpsburg. Here (September 17) McClellan with 87,000 men repeatedly assaulted Lee, who had 50,000. Late in the day—after appalling casualties on both sides—it seemed that the Confederate line might break, but the rest of Jackson's troops arrived from Harpers Ferry to fill the gap. Even then, McClellan might have won with one more effort. Instead, he allowed Lee to retire to Virginia. In November, Lincoln removed McClellan from command, for good.

McClellan's replacement, Ambrose E. Burnside, proved to be a modest mediocrity. He chose to drive at Richmond by crossing the Rappahannock at Fredericksburg, the strongest defensive point on the river. There (December 13) he flung his army at Lee's defenses in repeated attacks, all bloody, all hopeless. After losing a large part of his army, he withdrew to the north bank of the Rappahannock. Soon he was relieved at his own request.

Year of Decision, 1863

As 1863 opened, Burnside's successor, Joseph Hooker (popularly known as "Fighting Joe"), was at the head of the Army of the Potomac, which, 120,000 strong, still lay north of the Rappahannock, opposite Fredericksburg. With part of the army, Hooker crossed the river farther up and, in a flanking movement, threatened the town and Lee's army. Then he lost his nerve and drew back to a defensive position in a desolate area of brush and scrub trees known as the Wilderness. Here, in the Battle of Chancellorsville (May 1–5), with only half as many men as Hooker had, Lee daringly divided his force. He sent Jackson to hit the Union right while he himself charged the front. Hooker barely managed to extricate his army. Again Lee had won, but not the decisive victory he was

After the Battle of Chancellorsville During the Battle of Chancellorsville, May 1–5, 1863, part of the fighting took place on Marye's Heights, above the town of Fredericksburg, the scene of a bloody battle the previous December. Many Union soldiers were trapped and killed in the Sunken Road on the hill, as shown in this photograph by Mathew B. Brady, the greatest American photographer of the nineteenth century. The cameras of the time used wet plates that required fairly long exposures and had to be developed on the spot, while still wet. It was almost impossible to take action pictures. (Library of Congress)

hoping for. And he had lost his ablest officer, Jackson, who was fatally wounded at the close of the battle.

While the Union forces were suffering repeated frustrations in the East, they continued to do much better in the West. Ulysses S. Grant kept driving at Vicksburg, one of the Confederates' two remaining strongholds on the Mississippi River. Coming downriver with naval support, he struck several unsuccessful blows at the Confederate defenses. The terrain in front of Vicksburg was difficult, with rough country on the north and low, marshy ground on the west. Finally, in May, Grant had the navy run supply boats past the river batteries to a point below Vicksburg. He marched the army safely down the Louisiana side and transported it across the river at the same point. Here the land was good for maneuvering. Moving swiftly to the east, Grant twice defeated Confederates trying to stop him. Then he turned around to the west and approached Vicksburg from the rear. After attempting to take the town by storm, he settled down to a siege. Six weeks later, on July 4, Vicksburg surrendered. Almost immediately, the other Confederate strong point on the river, Port Hudson (Louisiana), also surrendered—to a Union force that had come up from New Orleans.

At last the Union had achieved one of its basic military aims: it had gained control of the whole length of the Mississippi. As a result, the Confederacy was split, and the trans-Mississippi portion was cut off from the main part. The war had reached a great turning point.

Earlier, at the beginning of the siege of Vicksburg, the Confederate government had considered various plans for relieving the town. Lee proposed an invasion of Pennsylvania. If he could win a victory on Northern soil, he said, England and France would probably come to the Confederacy's aid, and the Union might even quit the war. Certainly the pressure on Vicksburg and other places would let up.

Lee started the campaign in June, going west to the Valley and then north through Maryland and into Pennsylvania. Hooker moved back to parallel the Confederates' movement and keep between them and Washington—until, in mid-campaign, he was replaced by George C. Meade, a solid if unimaginative soldier. Units of Lee's and Meade's armies chanced to come together at Gettysburg. Here (July 1–3) was fought the most celebrated battle of the war.

Meade's army got into a strong, well-protected position on the hills south of the town. Lee, combative by nature and confident of his men, decided to attack even though his army was at a tactical disadvantage and was outnumbered 75,000 to 90,000. His first assault failed to reach the main line of the Union forces on Cemetery Ridge, so, a day later, he ordered a second and larger effort. In what is remembered as Pickett's Charge, a force of 15,000 advanced for almost a mile over open country that was swept by hostile fire. Only about 5,000 made it up the ridge, and this remnant finally had to surrender or retreat. Lee was compelled to withdraw from Gettysburg, having lost nearly a third of his army. Meade failed to prevent the return of the Confederates to Virginia, yet they had been so weakened that Lee never again could undertake a serious invasion of the North. The Confederate retreat from Gettysburg, starting on the same day as the surrender at Vicksburg (July 4), was another great turning point.

Before the end of the year, a third turning point was reached, this one in Tennessee. The Union army under Rosecrans occupied Chattanooga (September 9) after Bragg and the Confederates had evacuated the town. Rosecrans then went unwisely in pursuit of Bragg. Just across the Georgia line, Bragg, with reinforcements from Lee's army, was lying in wait. He fell upon Rosecrans in the Battle of Chickamauga (September 19–20), one of the few battles in which the Confederates enjoyed a numerical superiority (70,000 to 56,000). The Union right broke and ran, though the left, under George H. Thomas, "the Rock of Chickamauga," continued to fight. Then Thomas, along with the rest of the beaten army, sought refuge behind the Chattanooga defenses.

Soon the army in Chattanooga was under siege. Bragg held the heights nearby and controlled the roads and the Tennessee River, thus cutting off almost all fresh supplies. Finally Grant came to the rescue. In the

Battle of Chattanooga (November 23–25), the reinforced Union army drove the Confederates back into Georgia. Northern troops then proceeded to occupy most of eastern Tennessee.

The Union forces had achieved a second important objective, the control of the Tennessee River. At Chattanooga they were in a position to split the Confederacy again—what was left of it. No longer could the Southerners hope to gain their independence by some great military victory. They could hope to win only by holding on and exhausting the Northern will to fight.

THE GETTYSBURG CAMPAIGN, 1863

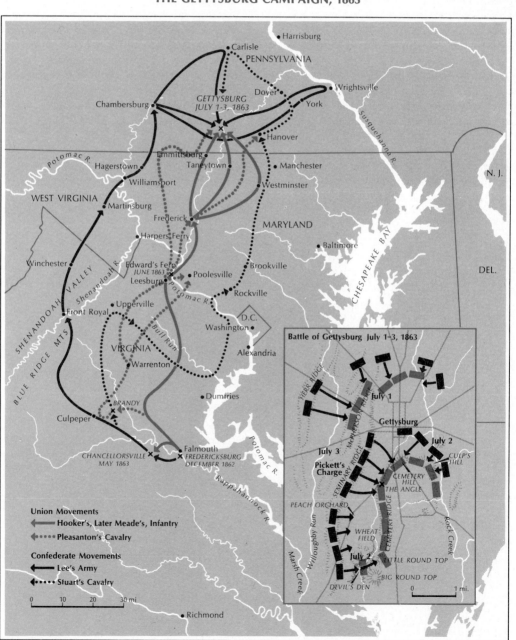

The Ending, 1864–1865

Now general in chief of all the Union armies, Grant planned two grand offensives for 1864. In Virginia, the Army of the Potomac (which Meade continued to command but which Grant accompanied and actually directed) was to advance toward Richmond and bring Lee to decisive battle. In Georgia, the western army, under William T. Sherman, was to advance toward Atlanta and destroy the opposing Confederate force, now under the command of Joseph E. Johnston.

The twofold campaign got under way when the Army of the Potomac, 115,000 strong, crossed the Rappahannock and Rapidan rivers and plunged into the rough, wooded Wilderness area. Lee, with about

75,000 men, was determined to avoid a showdown unless he saw a chance to deal a decisive blow. In the Battle of the Wilderness (May 5–7), Lee stopped Grant, but only for the moment. Instead of withdrawing to rest and reorganize, as his predecessors had done after every battle, Grant resumed his march with a flanking movement to the east and south, still tending in the general direction of Richmond. Lee intercepted him a second time in the Battle of Spotsylvania Court House (May 8–12). Again Grant moved on, curving to the southeast, and Lee continued to keep between him and the Confederate capital. Just a few miles northeast of it, at Cold Harbor (June 1–3), Grant made a desperate attack and was repulsed. In the whole month-long Wilderness campaign Grant had

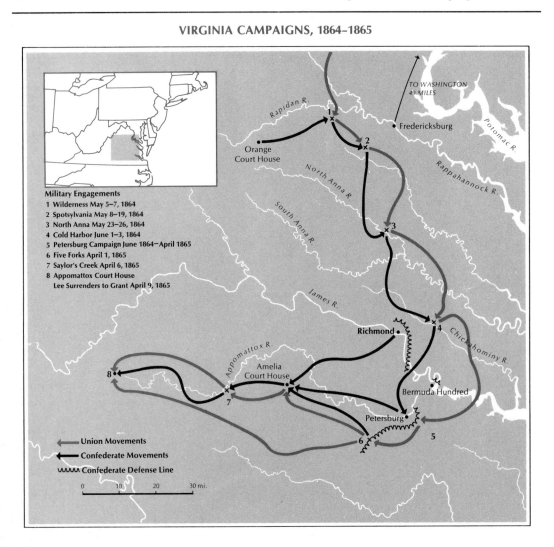

VIRGINIA CAMPAIGNS, 1864–1865

Military Engagements
1 Wilderness May 5–7, 1864
2 Spotsylvania May 8–19, 1864
3 North Anna May 23–26, 1864
4 Cold Harbor June 1–3, 1864
5 Petersburg Campaign June 1864–April 1865
6 Five Forks April 1, 1865
7 Saylor's Creek April 6, 1865
8 Appomattox Court House
  Lee Surrenders to Grant April 9, 1865

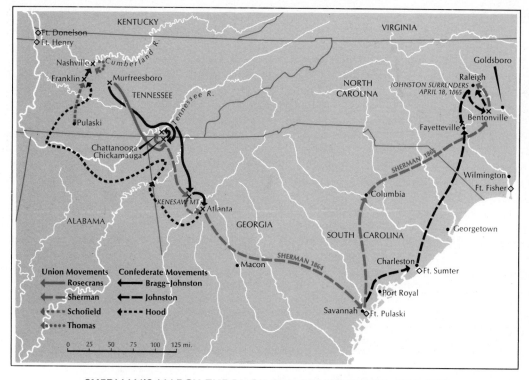

SHERMAN'S MARCH THROUGH THE CONFEDERACY, 1864–1865

lost a total of 55,000 men (killed, wounded, and captured), and Lee 31,000.

"I propose to fight it out on this line if it takes all summer," Grant had declared, but he now tried a different tack. He slipped away with his army, bypassed Richmond, and headed for Petersburg, a railroad center directly south of the capital. If he could seize Petersburg he could cut off the capital's communications and force Lee to fight for them. But Grant failed to take Petersburg by assault. Both sides settled down to a siege, with trenches stretching for miles from Richmond to and around Petersburg. Grant kept trying to extend his left around Lee's right so as to get at the railroads that served as Lee's lifeline. Success was to come only after nine months of struggle.

In Georgia, meanwhile, Sherman had been facing less resistance than Grant in Virginia. Sherman had 90,000 men, Johnston 60,000. As Sherman advanced, Johnston tried to delay him by maneuvering, without risking the destruction of his smaller army. Johnston stopped long enough to fight only one set battle, the Battle of Kennesaw Moun-

tain (June 27). He seemed unable to keep the Union forces from eventually reaching Atlanta, and so, as they neared the city, he was replaced by the combative John B. Hood. Twice Hood daringly attacked; he accomplished nothing except seriously to weaken his own army. Sherman took Atlanta on September 2.

Hood schemed to draw Sherman out of Atlanta by moving back up through Tennessee and threatening an invasion of the North. Sherman refused to follow—he had other plans—but he sent reinforcements under George H. Thomas and again under John M. Schofield to help defend Nashville. Hood caught up with Schofield's force and, in the Battle of Franklin (November 30), further bled his own army by ordering senseless charges against Schofield's well-protected positions. Then, in the Battle of Nashville (December 15–16), Thomas not only put Hood's army to flight but practically drove it to disintegration.

Meanwhile Sherman had started on a march from Atlanta to the sea. Living off the land, destroying supplies it could not use, his army cut a sixty-mile-wide swath of desolation across Georgia. "War is hell," Sherman believed. By that he meant not so much that war was a terrible thing to be avoided as that it should be made as horrible and costly as possible for the opponent. He sought not only to deprive the Confederacy of war materials and railroad communications but also to bring the war home to the Southern people and break their will to fight. By December 20, he was at Savannah, which he offered to President Lincoln as a Christmas gift (and which, almost alone among the areas he conquered, he did not destroy; the city was, he claimed, too beautiful to burn). Early in 1865, Sherman turned northward and carried his destruction through South Carolina. On his entire march, he was virtually unopposed until he was well inside North Carolina, where a small force under Johnston could do no more than cause a brief delay.

In April 1865, Grant's Army of the Potomac finally reached a vital railroad junction southwest of Petersburg. Lee could no longer hold Richmond. With the remnant of his army, now shrunken to about 25,000, he started west with the forlorn hope of turning south and combining forces with Johnston in North Carolina. The pursuing Union army blocked his escape route. Realizing that further bloodshed was futile, Lee met Grant at Appomattox and, on April 9, surrendered what was left of his forces. Nine days later, near Durham, North Carolina, Johnston surrendered to Sherman. Still defiant and unwilling to accept defeat, Jefferson Davis fled to the south and was captured in Georgia. Despite the forlorn efforts of a few Southern diehards, the war was soon over. And well before the last shot was fired, the painful process of trying to reunite the shattered nation had begun.

SUGGESTED READINGS

James M. McPherson, *Ordeal by Fire* (1981), and James G. Randall and David Donald, *The Civil War and Reconstruction*, rev. ed. (1969), are two general studies that offer excellent overviews of the Civil War. Both have superb bibliographies, although McPherson's is more up-to-date.

On the secession crisis and the events surrounding it, see Ralph A. Wooster, *The Secession Conventions of the South* (1962); David Potter, *Lincoln and His Party in the Secession Crisis* (1942); William L. Barney, *The Road to Secession* (1972) and *The Secessionist Impulse: Alabama and Mississippi in 1860* (1974); and Kenneth M. Stampp, *And the War Came* (1950), which describes the crisis in the North. Richard N. Current, *Lincoln and the First Shot* (1963), examines the Sumter decision. See also Steven A. Channing, *Crisis of Fear* (1970). Michael P. Johnson, *Toward a Patriarchal Republic* (1977), and John M. McCardell, Jr., *The Idea of a Southern Nation* (1979), examine the origins of Southern nationhood.

There is no end to the literature on Abraham Lincoln. Two excellent one-volume biographies are Benjamin Thomas, *Abraham Lincoln* (1952), and Stephen B. Oates, *With Malice Toward None* (1979). Classic multivolume works include James G. Randall, *Lincoln the President*, 4 vols. (1945–1955), the final volume completed by Richard N. Current; and Carl Sandburg, *Abraham Lincoln*, 6 vols. (1929–1939), notable more for its literary elegance and its emotional intensity than for its balance. Specialized studies of Lincoln in the war years include T. Harry Williams,

Lincoln and the Radicals (1941) and *Lincoln and His Generals* (1952); William B. Hesseltine, *Lincoln and the War Governors* (1948); Robert V. Bruce, *Lincoln and the Tools of War* (1956); and Harry J. Carman and Reinhard Luthin, *Lincoln and the Patronage* (1943).

Other works useful for an understanding of politics and society in the Northern states during the war include several biographies of leading Union politicians. David Donald, *Charles Sumner and the Rights of Man* (1970), is an excellent study of the leading Republican radical in the Senate. Benjamin P. Thomas and Harold M. Hyman, *Stanton* (1962), examines Lincoln's secretary of war; while Glyndon Van Deusen, *William Henry Seward* (1967), reveals the complex character of Lincoln's secretary of state. Martin Duberman, *Charles Francis Adams* (1961), is a fine portrait of the North's leading diplomat. James G. Randall, *Constitutional Problems Under Lincoln* (1926), is a classic study. Robert P. Sharkey, *Money, Class, and Party* (1959), examines the Union's economic problems. Wood Gray, *The Hidden Civil War* (1942), and Frank Klement, *The Copperheads in the Middle West* (1960), describe political dissent in the Northern states. Allan Nevins, *The War for the Union*, 2 vols. (1960) examines, among other things, Union military mobilization, as does Fred A. Shannon, *Organization and Administration of the Union Army*, 2 vols. (1928).

The background of the Emancipation Proclamation is examined in many of the Lincoln biographies cited above. See also Benjamin Quarles, *Lincoln and the Negro* (1962) and *The Negro in the Civil War* (1953), for a study of the president's racial attitudes. James M. McPherson, *The Struggle for Equality* (1964), examines the role of abolitionists in pressing for emancipation during the war. McPherson is also the author of *The Negro's Civil War* (1965), which uses documents to depict the impact of the war on blacks. Peter Kolchin, *First Freedom* (1972), examines the immediate response of blacks in Alabama to emancipation; while John W. Blassingame, *Black New Orleans* (1973), does the same for that city. Dudley T. Cornish, *The Sable Arm* (1966), considers black soldiers in the Union army. George Fredrickson, *The Inner Civil War* (1965), is an important study of the attitudes of Northern intellectuals toward the conflict. Daniel Aaron, *The Unwritten War* (1973), considers reflections of the war in American literature, as does Edmund Wilson's *Patriotic Gore* (1962), a landmark in literary criticism.

The outstanding study of the South during the war is Emory Thomas, *The Confederate Nation* (1979), which supersedes Clement Eaton, *A History of the Southern Confederacy* (1954), long the standard work. Charles P. Roland, *The Confederacy* (1960), is a brief account. E. Merton Coulter, *The Confederate States of America* (1950), is a useful, if partisan, study. Clement Eaton, *Jefferson Davis* (1978), is the most recent biography of the Confederate president. A more detailed work is Hudson Strode, *Jefferson Davis*, 3 vols. (1955–1964). Thomas B. Alexander and Richard E. Beringer, *The Anatomy of the Confederate Congress* (1972), and W. Buck Yearns, *The Confederate Congress* (1960) consider the Southern legislature. Emory Thomas, *The Confederacy as a Revolutionary Experience* (1971), challenges the conventional view that states' rights survived virtually intact within the Confederacy, a view expressed in Frank L. Owsley, *State Rights in the Confederacy* (1952). Owsley is also the author of an important study of Confederate diplomacy, *King Cotton Diplomacy* (1931). Social histories of the Southern states during the war include the classic studies by Bell I. Wiley, *The Life of Johnny Reb* (1943), companion volume to his study of the Northern soldier, *The Life of Billy Yank* (1952); and *The Plain People of the Confederacy* (1943). See also Paul Escott, *After Secession*

(1978) and *Slavery Remembered* (1979); and James L. Roark, *Masters Without Slaves* (1977). Georgia L. Tatum, *Disloyalty in the Confederacy* (1934), and Ella Lonn, *Desertion During the Civil War* (1928), examine dissent within the Confederacy. Emory Thomas, *The Confederate State of Richmond* (1971), is a local study of the Southern capital.

The classic biography of Robert E. Lee is Douglas Southall Freeman, *Robert E. Lee*, 4 vols. (1934–1935). Thomas L. Connelly, *The Marble Man* (1977), considers the popular image of Lee through the decades. John Carpenter, *Ulysses S. Grant* (1976), is a useful biography; but easily the finest work on the Union commander is William McFeely, *Grant* (1981). Military histories of the Civil War are so numerous as to defy adequate summary. See the bibliography in the study by McPherson and that by Randall and Donald cited above. Bruce Catton has produced a body of literature on the war that has long enjoyed popularity for its eloquence and vividness: *Mr. Lincoln's Army* (1951), *Glory Road* (1952), *A Stillness at Appomattox* (1954), *America Goes to War* (1958), *Banners at Shenandoah* (1965), *Grant Moves South* (1960), and *This Hallowed Ground* (1956), a one-volume overview of the war. A superb three-volume narrative of the military conflict is Shelby Foote, *The Civil War* (1958–1973). Kenneth P. Williams, *Lincoln Finds a General*, 4 vols. (1949–1952), is a lively study of the war from the Union point of view. Richard S. West, Jr., *Mr. Lincoln's Navy* (1957), and C. E. MacCartney, *Mr. Lincoln's Admirals* (1956), examine Union naval operations, as do several more specialized works, including John Niven, *Gideon Welles, Lincoln's Secretary of the Navy* (1973). On the Confederate navy, see two books by William N. Still, Jr.: *Iron Afloat: The Story of the Confederate Armorclads* (1971) and *Confederate Shipbuilding* (1969). T. Harry Williams, *McClellan, Sherman, and Grant* (1962), considers three Union generals; while *P. G. T. Beauregard, Napoleon in Gray* (1955), also by Williams, examines a major Southern general. Burke Davis, *Sherman's March* (1980), depicts the last major offensive of the war. Thomas L. Livermore, *Numbers and Losses in the Civil War in America* (1957), reveals the appalling costs of the conflict.

Reconstructing the Nation

15

Charleston, 1865
Throughout most of the Civil War, the fighting and destruction were restricted largely to isolated battlefields. In the last year or so of the war, however, as Northern armies began to sweep through large areas of the crumbling Confederacy in an effort to cow the seceded states into surrendering, the war came home to the Southern people as a whole. It was not only cities such as Richmond, Atlanta, and Charleston that were ruined by the Northern onslaught, but large areas of agricultural production as well. And the Northern invasion further disrupted Southern society by provoking tens of thousands of former slaves to leave the plantations on which they had lived and follow the Union armies in search of freedom and security. (Library of Congress)

449

Few periods in the history of the United States have produced as much bitterness or created such enduring controversy as the era of Reconstruction—the years following the Civil War during which Americans attempted to reunite their shattered nation. Those who lived through the experience viewed it in sharply different ways. To white Southerners, Reconstruction was a vicious and destructive experience—a period of low, unscrupulous politics, a time when vindictive Northerners inflicted humiliation and revenge on the prostrate South and unnecessarily delayed a genuine reunion of the sections. Northern defenders of Reconstruction, by contrast, argued that their policies were the only way to prevent unrepentant Confederates from restoring Southern society as it had been before the war; without forceful federal intervention, there would be no way to forestall the reemergence of a backward aristocracy and the continued subjugation of blacks—no way, in other words, to prevent the same sectional problems that had produced the Civil War in the first place.

To most black Americans at the time, and to many people of all races since, Reconstruction was notable for other reasons. Not a vicious tyranny, as white Southerners charged, nor a drastic and necessary reform, as many Northerners claimed, it was, rather, an essentially moderate, even conservative program that fell far short of providing the newly freed slaves with the protection they needed. Reconstruction, in other words, was significant less for what it did, than for what it failed to do. And when it came to an end, finally, in 1877—as a result of exhaustion and disillusionment among the white leaders of both sections, and of a series of complex bargains in the aftermath of the election of 1876—black Americans found themselves once again abandoned. Although they had, with the help of federal protection, won some important gains during Reconstruction, those gains were limited; and after 1877 there would be nothing to prevent black people from being consigned to a system of economic peonage and legal subordination. The nation's racial problem, which had done so much to produce the Civil War, was left unresolved—to arise again and again in future generations.

THE PROBLEMS OF PEACEMAKING

In 1865, when the Confederate states finally surrendered to the North, no one knew quite what to do in response. Abraham Lincoln could not negotiate a treaty with the defeated government; he continued to insist that that government had no legal right to exist. Yet neither could he simply readmit the Southern states into the Union as if nothing had happened. The South had been devastated by the war, both socially and economically. And there was now an enormous population of freed slaves, many of them wandering aimless and bewildered through the shattered land. Clearly the federal government had to act.

The Aftermath of War

In the North, the wartime prosperity continued into the postwar years; but Northerners who visited the South were appalled when they gazed on the desolation left in the wake of the war—gutted towns, wrecked plantations, neglected fields, collapsed bridges, and ruined railroads. Much of the personal property of white Southerners had been lost with the lost cause. Confederate bonds and currency were now worthless, and capital that had been invested in them was gone forever. With the emancipation of the slaves, Southern whites were deprived of property worth an estimated $2 billion. And Southern blacks were left with no property at all.

Matching the shattered economy of the South was the disorganization of its social system. In the months that followed the end of the war, when thousands of soldiers were drifting back to their homes—258,000 never returned and other thousands went back wounded or sick—life was seriously deranged. To many people the problem of keeping alive, of securing food and shelter, seemed the only thing that mattered.

If conditions were bad for Southern whites, they were generally worse for Southern blacks—the 4 million who were emerging from the bondage that had held them and their ancestors for two and a half centuries. Many of these people, too, had seen service of one kind or another during the war. Some had served as body servants for Confederate officers or as teamsters and laborers for the Confederate armies. Tens of thousands had fought as combat troops in the Union ranks, and more than 38,000 had given their lives for the Union cause. Countless other blacks, who never wore a uniform or drew army pay, assisted the Union forces as spies or scouts. Still others ran off from the plantations and flocked into the Union lines, often to be put to work for the Union armies.

As the war ended, freedom appeared to be on the way, but the date of its arrival was uncertain. The Thirteenth Amendment, which would make slavery unconstitutional, had yet to be ratified by the requisite number of states (it had passed Congress on February 1, 1865, and was not to be proclaimed in effect until December 18, 1865). On many plantations, blacks were still being detained and forced to work. Most planters agreed with a former Confederate leader who was saying (in June 1865) that slavery had been "the best system of labor that could be devised for the Negro race" and that the wise thing to do now would be to "provide a substitute for it."

To get away from their old masters, thousands of blacks continued to leave the plantations. Old and young, many of them feeble and ill, they trudged to the nearest town or city or they roamed the countryside, camping at night on the bare ground. Few had any possessions except the rags on their backs. Somehow they managed to stay alive.

What blacks wanted was, first of all, to be assured of their freedom—to feel it, to exercise it, and to know it was not going to be taken from them. Next, they needed immediate relief from the threat of starvation. Then, looking ahead, they desired land, farms of their own, a bit of economic independence. The blacks longed also for schooling, for their children if not for themselves. Finally, a number of blacks were beginning to demand political rights. "The only salvation for us besides the power of the Government is in the *possession of the ballot*," a convention of the black people of Virginia resolved in the summer of 1865. "All we ask is an *equal chance*."

The federal government, besides keeping troops (many of them black) in the South to preserve order and protect the freedmen, was doing something to assist them in the transition from slavery to freedom. Congress had set up (in March 1865) the Bureau of Freedmen, Refugees, and Abandoned Lands as an agency of the army. This Freedmen's Bureau was empowered to provide food, transportation, assistance in getting jobs and fair wages, and schools for former slaves, and also to settle them on abandoned or confiscated lands. Under the able direction of General Oliver O. Howard, the bureau undertook to perform its allotted functions and more. Its agents soon distributed 20 million rations in the South, to hungry whites as well as blacks. Cooperating with the bureau, especially in its educational work, were missionaries and teachers who had been sent to the South by Freedmen's Aid Societies and other private and church groups in the North. (The bureau also provided considerable assistance to poor whites—many of whom were left homeless and destitute by the war.)

Nevertheless, the future of the blacks remained in doubt. The Freedmen's Bureau, according to the law creating it, was to last for only one year after the end of the war. Meanwhile, most Southern whites resented the activities of the bureau and its agents. These outsiders stood in the way of the desire to set up a substitute for slavery, a substitute that would serve both as a cheap labor system and as a white-supremacy device.

The Issues of Reconstruction

The word "Reconstruction," as contemporaries used it, referred to the process by which states of the defeated Confederacy were to be brought back to their former places in the Union. One possibility would be to grant easy terms, permitting the states to return promptly and with little internal change except for the elimination of slavery.

Another possibility would be to delay the readmission in such a way as to reduce the power of the rebel leaders.

A quick and easy restoration of the Union would be to the advantage of the former Confederates and the Democratic party, North and South. Ironically, the abolition of slavery would increase the power of the Southern states in national politics. In the past, under the "three-fifths clause" of the Constitution, only three-fifths of the slaves had been counted in determining a state's representation in Congress and its electoral votes in presidential elections. In the future, *all* the former slaves would be counted, whether or not they themselves were given political rights.

Freedmen Receiving Rations
The Freedmen's Bureau, established by Congress in March 1865, was designed to assist the former slaves through their passage from servitude to freedom. As the states of the defeated Confederacy began late in 1865 to pass new Black Codes, whose intent was to restore many of the conditions of slavery to the black population of the South, the bureau attempted to expand its functions to protect its clients from oppression. Although Congress never permitted the bureau to proceed beyond a few tentative first steps with its most ambitious aim— redistribution of land to the freedmen—it continued through Reconstruction to provide desperately needed assistance to the former slaves. Most of all, perhaps, the bureau was responsible for establishing the first important system of schools for blacks. (Library of Congress)

The consequences of any easy peace, by the same token, could be disastrous for the Republican party. The Republicans had gained control of the federal government in 1860–1861 only because of the split in the Democratic party and the secession of the Southern states. Once these states had been restored and the Democratic party had been reunited, the Republicans would face the uncomfortable prospect of being reduced to a minority group once again. The outlook was disturbing also for Northern businessmen who during the war had obtained favors from the federal government—a high tariff, railroad subsidies, the national banking system—which might be ended if the Democrats returned to power.

For the men and women emerging from slavery, a quick restoration of the Southern states would be catastrophic. The master class, which had dominated the state governments before and during the war, would continue to do so. Blacks then could expect to be kept in a position that, at best, would be somewhere between slavery and freedom.

Thus the issues of Reconstruction were very similar to those of the war itself. So far as the Southern leaders were concerned, the war had been fought for the independence of the South and for the preservation of slavery. After the war, these leaders hoped to maintain a considerable degree of Southern autonomy through the assertion of states' rights, and they hoped to retain much of the essence of slavery by finding some substitute for it.

The issues were often obscured and complicated by the emotionalism of the controversy over Reconstruction. In the North there was the memory of sacrifice, suffering, and personal loss; in the South there was the added bitterness of defeat. In the North there was a widespread feeling that Southerners ought to be required to acknowledge their defeat by some gesture of submission, and that at least a few of them ought to be punished. Moreover, there was a general conviction that the former slaves ought to be protected in their freedom and assured of justice. And there was a growing belief that Reconstruction offered a heaven-sent opportunity to recast the South in the image of the North—to take that supposedly backward, feudal, undemocratic section and civilize and modernize it.

Even among the majority in Congress—the Republicans—there was disagreement as to the kind of peace that should be imposed on the South. The same factions of the party (the Conservatives and the Radicals) that had clashed on wartime emancipation now confronted each other on the issue of Reconstruction. The Conservatives advocated a mild peace and the rapid restoration of the defeated states to the Union; beyond insisting that the South accept the abolition of slavery, they would not interfere with race relations or attempt to alter the social system of the South. The Radicals, directed by such leaders as Thaddeus Stevens of Pennsylvania and Charles Sumner of Massachusetts, stood for a harder peace; they urged that the civil and military chieftains of the late Confederacy be subjected to severe punishment, that large numbers of Southern whites be disfranchised, that the legal rights of blacks be protected, and that the property of rich Southerners who had aided the Confederacy be confiscated and distributed among the freedmen. From the first, some Radicals favored granting suffrage to the former slaves, as a matter of right or as a means of creating a Republican electorate in the South. Other Radicals hesitated to state a position for fear of public opinion—few Northern states permitted blacks to vote.

Between the Radicals and the Conservatives stood a faction of uncommitted Republicans, the Moderates. They would go further than the Conservatives in demanding concessions of the South, particularly in regard to rights for blacks, but they rejected the punitive goals of the Radicals.

Lincoln's Plan

The process of Reconstruction began while the war was still going on, under a plan presented by President Lincoln. He believed there were a considerable number of actual or potential Unionists in the South. These people, most of them former Whigs, could possibly be encouraged to rejoin the old Whigs of the North and thus strengthen the

Republican party, once the Union had been restored. More immediately, these men could serve as the nucleus for setting up new and loyal state governments in the South and thereby hastening reunion. Above all, Lincoln wanted to restore the Union as soon as possible. Consequently, he proposed a relatively easy mode of Reconstruction. He would subordinate to his larger goal such questions as punishment of the defeated side or determination of the status of the freedmen. The question of whether the defeated states were in or out of the Union he dismissed as a "merely pernicious abstraction." They were only out of their proper relationship to the Union, he said, and they should be restored to that relationship as soon as possible.

Specifically, Lincoln's plan, which he announced to the public in a proclamation of December 1863, offered a general amnesty to all who would take an oath pledging future loyalty to the government. Temporarily excluded from the right to swear the oath were high civil and military officials of the Confederacy. Whenever in any state 10 percent of the number of voters in 1860 took the oath, those loyal voters could proceed to set up a state government. The oath required acceptance of the wartime acts and proclamations of Congress and the president concerning slavery. Lincoln also urged them to give the ballot to at least a few blacks—to those who were educated, owned property, and had served in the Union army. In three Southern states—Louisiana, Arkansas, and Tennessee—loyal governments were reestablished under the Lincoln formula in 1864.

The Radical Republicans were angered and astonished at the mildness of Lincoln's program, and they were able to induce Congress to repudiate his governments. Representatives from the Lincoln states were not admitted to Congress, and the electoral vote of those states was not counted in the election of 1864. The Radicals could not stop, however, with a rejection of Lincoln's plan. The requirements of politics dictated that they produce a plan of their own. But at the moment the Radicals were not agreed as to how "hard" a peace they should enforce on the South, and they were not certain that

Northern opinion would support the ideas of their more extreme leaders.

Under pressure, they prepared and passed (in July 1864) the Wade-Davis Bill, the first Radical plan of Reconstruction. By its provisions, the president was to appoint for each conquered state a provisional governor who would take a census of all adult white males. If a majority of those enrolled—instead of Lincoln's 10 percent—swore an oath of allegiance, the governor was to call an election for a state constitutional convention. The privilege of voting for delegates to this meeting was limited to those who could swear that they had never borne arms against the United States, the so-called ironclad oath. The convention was required to put provisions into the new constitution abolishing slavery, disfranchising Confederate civil and military leaders, and repudiating war debts. After these conditions had been met, Congress would readmit the state to the Union. The Wade-Davis Bill was more drastic in almost every respect than the Lincoln plan, and it assumed that the seceded states were out of the Union and hence under the dictation of Congress. But the bill, like the president's proposal, left up to the states the question of political rights for blacks.

The Wade-Davis Bill was passed a few days before Congress adjourned, which enabled Lincoln to dispose of it with a pocket veto. His action enraged the authors of the measure, Benjamin F. Wade and Henry Winter Davis, who issued a blistering denunciation of the veto, the Wade-Davis Manifesto, warning the president not to interfere with the powers of Congress to control Reconstruction. Lincoln could not ignore the bitterness and the strength of the Radical opposition. Practical as always, he realized that he would have to accept some of the objections of the Radicals. He began to move toward a new approach to Reconstruction.

What plan he might have produced no one can say. On the night of April 14, 1865, Lincoln and his wife attended a play at Ford's Theater in Washington. As they sat in the presidential box, John Wilkes Booth, an unsuccessful actor obsessed with aiding the Southern cause, shot Lincoln in the head. Then he leaped from the box to the stage

Abraham Lincoln and Tad
This famous photograph of Lincoln in 1864, posing with his son Tad, was the work of Mathew Brady, the most celebrated photographer of the Civil War era. (Library of Congress)

(breaking his leg in the process), shouted "Sic, semper tyrannis!" ("Thus always to tyrants!"), and disappeared into the night. The president was carried unconscious to a house across the street, where early the next morning—surrounded by family, friends, and political associates (including a tearful Charles Sumner)—he died.

The circumstances of Lincoln's death—the heroic war leader, the Great Emancipator, struck down in the hour of victory—earned him immediate martyrdom. It also produced wild fears and antagonisms throughout the North. There were widespread accusations that Booth had acted as part of a great conspiracy—accusations that rested on at least a grain of truth. Booth did indeed have associates, one of whom shot and wounded Secretary of State Seward the night of the assassi-

nation, another of whom set out to murder Vice President Johnson but abandoned the scheme at the last moment. Booth himself escaped on horseback into the Maryland countryside, where, on April 26, he was cornered by Union troops and shot to death in a blazing barn. Eight other conspirators were convicted by a military tribunal of participating in the conspiracy (two of them, at least, on the basis of virtually no evidence). Four were hanged.

To many Northerners, however, the murder of the president seemed evidence of an even greater conspiracy—one masterminded and directed by the unrepentant leaders of the defeated South. (There was never any conclusive evidence to support this—and many other—theory of the assassination; but questions continued to be raised about the event well into the twentieth century.) Militant Republicans exploited such suspicions relentlessly in the ensuing months, ensuring that Lincoln's death would—ironically—help doom his plans for a relatively generous peace.

Johnson and "Restoration"

The conservative leadership in the controversy over Reconstruction fell upon Lincoln's successor, Andrew Johnson. Of all the men who have accidentally inherited the presidency, Johnson was undoubtedly the most unfortunate. A Southerner and former slaveholder, he became president as a bloody war against the South was drawing to a close. A Democrat before he had been placed on the Union ticket with Lincoln in 1864, he became the head of a Republican administration at a time when partisan passions, held in some restraint during the war, were about to rule the government. As if these handicaps of background were not enough, Johnson was intemperate in language and tactless in manner.

Johnson revealed his plan of Reconstruction—or "Restoration," as he preferred to call it—soon after he took office, and he proceeded to execute it during the summer of 1865 when Congress was not in session. He applied it to the seven states of the late Confederacy that had not come under the Lincoln plan; and he recognized as legal organizations the Lincoln governments in Louisiana, Arkansas, Tennessee, and Virginia.

In some ways Johnson's scheme resembled Lincoln's; in others it was similar to the Wade-Davis Bill. Like his predecessor, Johnson assumed that the seceded states were still in the Union; and, also like Lincoln, he announced his design in a proclamation of amnesty that extended pardon for past conduct to all who would take an oath of allegiance. Denied the privilege of taking the oath until they received individual pardons from the president were high-ranking Confederate officials and also men with land worth $20,000 or more: Johnson excluded a larger number of leaders than Lincoln had. (Himself a self-made man, Johnson harbored deep resent-

Andrew Johnson
Born in North Carolina, Johnson moved to Tennessee as a young man and worked as a tailor before going into politics. He had a dark complexion and piercing black eyes. A powerful orator on the stump, he easily lost his temper when heckled and used crude and intemperate language. (Library of Congress)

ments toward the old Southern aristocracy and apparently relished the prospect of these Confederate leaders humbling themselves before him to ask for pardons.) For each state, the president appointed a provisional governor, who was to invite the qualified voters to elect delegates to a constitutional convention. Johnson did not specify that a minimum number of voters had to take the oath, as had the Lincoln and Wade-Davis proposals, but the implication was plain that he would require a majority. As conditions of readmittance, a state had to revoke the ordinance of secession, abolish slavery and ratify the Thirteenth Amendment, and repudiate the Confederate and state war debts—essentially the same stipulations that had been laid down in the Wade-Davis Bill. The final procedure before restoration was for a state to elect a state government and send representatives to Congress.

By the end of 1865, the states affected by

Johnson's plan had complied with its requirements. Indeed, if the Lincoln governments are included, all of the seceded states had been reconstructed and were ready to resume their places in the Union—if Congress chose to recognize them when it met in December 1865. Recognition of the Johnson governments was exactly what the Radicals were determined to prevent. And many people in the North agreed with them that Reconstruction was being rushed too fast and accomplished too easily.

This initial phase of Reconstruction—often known as "presidential Reconstruction"—lasted only until the reconvening of Congress in December 1865. At that point, Republican leaders looked over Andrew Johnson's handiwork and expressed their displeasure. Congress immediately refused to seat the senators and representatives of the states the president had "restored." Instead, Radical leaders insisted, Congress needed to learn more about conditions in the postwar South. There must be assurances that the former Confederates had accepted their defeat and that emancipated blacks and loyal whites would be protected. Accordingly, Congress set up the new Joint Committee on Reconstruction to investigate conditions in the South and to advise Congress in laying down a Reconstruction policy of its own. The period of "congressional" or "Radical" Reconstruction had begun.

Congress Takes Over

During the next few months, the Radicals advanced toward a more severe program than their first plan, the Wade-Davis Bill of 1864, which had left to the states the question of what rights the freed slaves should have. The Radicals gained the support of Moderate Republicans because of Johnson's intransigent attitude. Johnson insisted that Congress had no right even to consider a policy for the South until his own plan had been accepted and the Southern congressmen and senators had been admitted.

Northerners were disturbed by the seeming reluctance of some members of the Southern conventions to abolish slavery and by the refusal of all the conventions to grant suffrage to even a few blacks. They were astounded that states claiming to be "loyal" should elect as state officials and representatives to Congress prominent leaders of the recent Confederacy. Particularly hard to understand was Georgia's choice of Alexander H. Stephens, former vice president of the Confederacy, as a United States senator.

RADICAL RECONSTRUCTION

Thaddeus Stevens
Stern, uncompromising, and severe, Thaddeus Stevens of Pennsylvania was the incarnation of Northern evil in the eyes of many Southerners during Reconstruction. To American blacks, however, he was one of the few white leaders who remained firmly committed to racial equality. He served in the House of Representatives from 1849 to 1853 and again, far more prominently, from 1859 until his death in 1868. He spent much of the last year of his life organizing and managing the impeachment trial of Andrew Johnson.
(Library of Congress)

In the meantime, Northerners were learning more about what was happening in the defeated South; and what they learned persuaded many of them—including most of the important leaders in Congress—that far more drastic measures were necessary than the president had contemplated. For throughout the South in 1865 and early 1866, state legislatures were enacting sets of laws known as the Black Codes. These measures were the white South's solution to the problem of the free black laborer, and they were modeled in many ways on the codes that had regulated free blacks in the prewar South. As such, they created a new set of devices to guarantee white supremacy. Economically, the codes were intended to regulate the labor of a race that, in the opinion of the whites, would not work except under some kind of compulsion. Although there were variations from state to state, all codes authorized local officials to apprehend unemployed blacks, fine them for vagrancy, and hire them out to private employers to satisfy the fine. Some of the codes tried to force blacks to work on the plantations by forbidding them to own or

lease farms or to take other jobs except as domestic servants. Socially, the codes were designed to invest blacks with a legal although subordinate status. To the South, the Black Codes were a realistic approach to a great social problem. To the North, they seemed to herald a return to slavery.

An appropriate agency for offsetting the Black Codes was the Freedmen's Bureau, but its scheduled year of existence was about to end. In February 1866, Congress passed a bill to prolong the life of the bureau and to widen its powers by authorizing special courts for settling labor disputes. Thus the bureau could set aside work agreements that might be forced on freedmen under the Black Codes. Johnson vetoed the bill, denouncing it as unconstitutional. Efforts to override him fell just short of the necessary two-thirds majority.

In April, Congress struck again at the Black Codes by passing the Civil Rights Bill, which made blacks United States citizens and empowered the federal government to intervene in state affairs when necessary to protect the rights of citizens. Johnson vetoed this

---

The Black Code of Louisiana

The sections in the Black Codes regulating black labor angered Northern opinion and turned many people in favor of Radical Reconstruction. The Louisiana Code had this to say:

Sec. 1. Be it enacted by the Senate and House of Representatives of the State of Louisiana in general assembly convened, That all persons employed as laborers in agricultural pursuits shall be required, during the first ten days of the month of January of each year, to make contracts for labor for the then ensuing year, or for the year next ensuing the termination of their present contracts. All contracts for labor for agricultural purposes shall be made in writing, signed by the employer, and shall be made in the presence of a Justice of the Peace and two disinterested

witnesses, in whose presence the contract shall be read to the laborer, and when assented to and signed by the latter, shall be considered as binding for the time prescribed. . . .

Sec. 2. Every laborer shall have full and perfect liberty to choose his employer, but, when once chosen, he shall not be allowed to leave his place of employment until the fulfillment of his contract . . . and if they do so leave, without cause or permission, they shall forfeit all wages earned to the time of abandonment. . . .

bill, too. With Moderates and Radicals acting together, Congress promptly overrode the veto. Then, despite another veto, Congress repassed the Freedmen's Bureau Bill.

Emboldened by their evident support in Congress, the Radicals now struck again. The Joint Committee on Reconstruction submitted to Congress, in April 1866, a proposed amendment to the Constitution, the Fourteenth, which constituted the second Radical plan of Reconstruction. The amendment was adopted by Congress and sent to the states for approval in the early summer.

Section 1 of the amendment declared that all persons born or naturalized in the United States were citizens of the United States and of the state of their residence. This clause, which set up for the first time a national definition of citizenship, was followed by a statement that no state could abridge the rights of citizens of the United States or deprive any person of life, liberty, or property without due process of law or deny to any person within its jurisdiction the equal protection of the laws.

Section 2 provided that if a state denied the suffrage to any of its adult male inhabitants, its representation in the House of Representatives and the electoral college should suffer a proportionate reduction.

Section 3 disqualified from any state or federal office persons who had previously taken an oath to support the Constitution and later had aided the Confederacy—until Congress by a two-thirds vote of each house should remove their disability.

The Southern legislatures knew that if they ratified the amendment their states would be readmitted and Reconstruction probably would be ended. But they could not bring themselves to approve the measure, mainly because of Section 3, which put a stigma on their late leaders. Johnson himself advised Southerners to defeat the amendment. Only Tennessee, of the former Confederate states, ratified it, thus winning readmittance. The other ten, joined by Kentucky and Delaware, voted it down.

The amendment thus failed to receive the required approval of three-fourths of the states and was defeated—but only temporarily. When the time was more propitious, the

Radicals would bring it up again. Meanwhile, its rejection by the South strengthened the Radical cause. To many people in the North, the amendment had seemed to be a reasonable and moderate proposal.

Public acceptance of the Radical program was strikingly manifested in the elections of 1866. This was essentially a contest for popular support between Johnson and the Radicals. The Radicals could point to recent events in the South—bloody race riots in New Orleans and other Southern cities in which blacks were the victims—as further evidence of the inadequacy of Johnson's policy. Johnson harmed his own cause by the intemperate, brawling (and, some believed, drunken) speeches he made on a stumping tour (a "swing around the circle," as it was called) from Washington to Chicago and back. The voters returned to Congress an overwhelming majority of Republicans, most of them Radicals. In the Senate, there were to be 42 Republicans to 11 Democrats; in the House, 143 Republicans to 49 Democrats. Now the Republicans could enact any kind of Reconstruction plan they could themselves agree on. Confidently they looked forward to the struggle with Johnson that would ensue when Congress assembled in December 1866—and to their final victory over the president.

The Congressional Plan

After compromising differences among themselves and with the Moderates, the Radicals formulated their third plan of Reconstruction in three bills that passed Congress in the early months of 1867. All three were vetoed by Johnson and repassed. Together, they constituted a single program.

This plan was based squarely on the principle that the seceded states had lost their political identity. The Lincoln-Johnson governments were declared to have no legal standing, and the ten seceded states (Tennessee was now out of the Reconstruction process) were combined into five military districts. Each district was to be put in the charge of a military commander, supported by troops, who was to prepare his provinces for readmission as states. To this end, he was to institute a registration of voters, which was to include all adult black males and those white males who were not disqualified by participation in rebellion.

After the registration was completed in each province, the commanding general was to call the voters to elect a convention to prepare a new state constitution, which had to provide for black suffrage. If this document were ratified by the voters, elections for a state government could be held. Finally, if Congress approved the constitution, if the state legislature ratified the Fourteenth Amendment, and if this amendment were adopted by the required number of states and became a part of the Constitution—then the state was to be restored to the Union.

By 1868, six of the former Confederate states—Arkansas, North Carolina, South Carolina, Louisiana, Alabama, and Florida—had complied with the process of restoration outlined in the Reconstruction Acts and were readmitted to the Union. Delaying tactics by whites held up the return of Mississippi, Virginia, Georgia, and Texas until 1870. These four laggard states had to meet an additional requirement, which with the existing requirements constituted the fourth and final congressional plan of Reconstruction. They had to ratify another constitutional amendment, the Fifteenth, which forbade the states and the federal government to deny the suffrage to any citizen on account of "race, color, or previous condition of servitude."

Sponsors of the Fifteenth Amendment were motivated by both idealistic and practical considerations. They wished to be consistent in extending to blacks in the North a right they had already given to them elsewhere. The great majority of the Northern states still denied the suffrage to blacks at the time when the Reconstruction Acts granted it to blacks in the Southern states. At the same time they would be putting into the Constitution, where it would be safe from congressional repeal, the basis of Republican strength in the South. They were also concerned with the party's future in the North. A warning of trouble ahead had appeared in the state elections of 1867 in Pennsylvania, Ohio, and Indiana, all of which went Demo-

cratic that year. "We must establish the doctrine of national jurisdiction over all the states in state matters of the franchise," the Radical leader Thaddeus Stevens now concluded. "We must thus bridle Pennsylvania, Ohio, Indiana et cetera, or the South *being in,* we shall drift into Democracy." In several of the Northern states the black vote, though proportionally small, would be large enough to decide close elections in favor of the Republicans.

A number of the Northern and border states refused to approve the Fifteenth Amendment, and it was adopted only with the support of the four Southern states that had to ratify it in order to be readmitted to the Union. In the case of both the Fourteenth and Fifteenth amendments, the Southern states were deemed capable of ratifying even while they were not otherwise recognized as states and had no representation in Congress.

Congressional Supremacy

The Radicals saw themselves as architects of a revolution, and they did not intend to let the executive or the judiciary get in their way. They were prepared, if necessary, to establish a kind of congressional dictatorship.

To curb the president, and also to facilitate Radical administration of the acts of 1867, Congress passed two remarkable laws. One, the Tenure of Office Act (1867), forbade the president to remove civil officials, including members of his cabinet, without the consent of the Senate. Its principal purpose was to protect the job of Secretary of War Edwin M. Stanton, who was cooperating with the Radicals. The other law, the Command of the Army Act (1867), prohibited the president from issuing military orders except through the commanding general of the army (General Grant), whose headquarters were to be in Washington and who could not be relieved or assigned elsewhere without the consent of the Senate.

The Supreme Court, under Chief Justice Salmon P. Chase, declared in *Ex parte Milligan* (1866) that military tribunals were unconstitutional in places where civil courts were functioning. Although the decision was applied to a case originating in the war, it seemed to threaten the system of military government that the Radicals were planning for the South. Radical anger at the Court was instant and intense. In Congress, proposals were made to require a two-thirds majority of the justices to overrule a law of Congress, to deny the Court jurisdiction in Reconstruction cases, to reduce its membership to three, and even to abolish it. The judges apparently took the hint. When the state of Mississippi in 1867 asked for an injunction restraining Johnson from enforcing the Reconstruction Acts, the Court refused to accept jurisdiction (*Mississippi* v. *Johnson*). But the next year, the Court agreed to hear arguments in a case involving military courts in Mississippi (*Ex parte McCardle*) and by implication involving the legality of the Reconstruction Acts. The Radicals rushed through Congress a law denying the Court appellate jurisdiction in cases concerning habeas corpus. The Court bowed by refusing to hear the case.

The Impeachment of the President

The most aggressive move of Congress against another branch of government was the effort of the Radicals to remove Andrew Johnson from office. Although the president had long since ceased to be a serious obstacle to the passage of Radical legislation, he was still the official charged with administering the Reconstruction programs; and as such, the Radicals believed, he was a serious impediment to their plans. Early in 1867, therefore, they began searching for evidence that Johnson had committed crimes or misdemeanors in office, the only legal grounds for impeachment; but they could find nothing on

which to base charges. Then he gave them a plausible reason for action by deliberately violating the Tenure of Office Act. He suspended Secretary of War Stanton, who had worked with the Radicals against Johnson, and named General Grant as his successor. Johnson hoped in this manner to secure a Court test case of the tenure law, which he believed to be unconstitutional. But when the Senate refused to concur in the suspension, Grant relinquished the office to Stanton. Johnson then dismissed Stanton.

In the House of Representatives the elated Radicals presented to the Senate eleven charges against the president. The first nine accusations dealt with the violation of the Tenure of Office Act. The tenth and eleventh charged Johnson with making speeches calculated to bring Congress into disrespect and with not faithfully enforcing the various Reconstruction Acts. In the trial before the Senate (March 25 to May 26, 1868) Johnson's lawyers maintained that he was justified in technically violating a law in order to force a test case and that the measure did not apply to Stanton anyway: it gave tenure to cabinet members for the term of the president by whom they had been appointed, and Stanton had been appointed by Lincoln. The House managers of the impeachment stressed the theme that Johnson had opposed the will of Congress. They implied that in doing so he was guilty of crimes and misdemeanors. They brought terrific pressure on all the Republican senators, but seven Republicans joined the twelve Democrats to vote for acquittal. On three of the charges the vote was identical, 35 to 19, one short of the required two-thirds majority. Thereupon the Radicals called off the proceedings.

THE SOUTH IN RECONSTRUCTION

When white Southerners spoke bitterly in later years of the effects of Reconstruction, they referred most frequently to the governments Congress imposed on them—governments, they claimed, that were both incompetent and corrupt, that saddled the region

with enormous debts, and that trampled on the rights of citizens. When black Southerners and their defenders condemned Reconstruction, by contrast, they spoke of its failure to guarantee to freedmen even the most elemental rights of citizenship—a fail-

Reconstruction

Debate over the nature of Reconstruction—not only among historians, but among the public at large—has created so much controversy over the decades that one scholar, writing in 1959, described the issue as a "dark and bloody ground." Among historians, the passions of the debate have to some extent subsided since then; but in the popular mind, Reconstruction continues to raise "dark and bloody" images.

For many years, a relatively uniform view of Reconstruction prevailed among historians, a reflection of broad currents in popular thought. By the late nineteenth century, most white Americans in both the North and the South had come to believe that few real differences any longer divided the sections, that the nation should strive for a genuine reconciliation. And most white Americans believed as well in the superiority of their race, in the inherent unfitness of blacks for political or social equality. In this spirit was born the first major historical interpretation of Reconstruction, through the work of William A. Dunning. In his *Reconstruction, Political and Economic* (1907), Dunning portrayed Reconstruction as a corrupt outrage perpetrated on the prostrate South by a vicious and vindictive cabal of Northern Republican radicals. Reconstruction governments were based on "bayonet rule." Unscrupulous and self-aggrandizing carpetbaggers flooded the South to profit from the misery of the defeated region. Ignorant, illiterate blacks were thrust into positions of power for which they were entirely unfit. The Reconstruction experiment, a moral abomination from its first moments, survived only because of the determination of the Republican party to keep itself in power. (Some later writers, notably Howard K. Beale, added an economic motive—to protect Northern business interests.) Dunning and his many students (who together formed what became known as the "Dunning school") compiled evidence to show that the legacy of Reconstruction was corruption, ruinous taxation, and astronomical increases in the public debt.

The Dunning school not only shaped the views of several generations of historians. It also reflected and helped to shape the views of much of the public. Popular depictions of Reconstruction for years to come (as the book and movie *Gone with the Wind* suggested) portrayed the era as one of tragic exploitation of the South by the North. Even today, many white Southerners in particular continue to accept the basic premises of the Dunning interpretation. Among historians, however, the old view of Reconstruction has gradually lost its credibility. W. E. B. Du Bois, the great black scholar, was among the first to challenge the Dunning view in a 1910 article and, later, in a 1935 book, *Black Reconstruction*. To him, Reconstruction politics in the Southern states had been an effort on the part of the masses, black and white, to create a true democratic society. The misdeeds of the Reconstruction governments had, he claimed, been greatly exaggerated and their

ure that resulted in a new and cruel system of economic subordination. Controversy has raged for more than a century over which viewpoint is more nearly correct (see "Where Historians Disagree"). Most students of Reconstruction tend now to agree, however, that the complaints of Southern whites, although in some respects accurate, greatly exaggerated the real nature of the postwar governments; while the complaints of blacks, although occasionally overstated, were to a large extent justified.

The Reconstruction Governments

In the ten states of the South that were reorganized under the congressional plan, approximately one-fourth of the white men were at first excluded from voting or holding office. The voter registration of 1867 enrolled a total of 703,000 black and 627,000 white voters. The black voters constituted a majority in half of the states—Alabama, Florida, South Carolina, Mississippi, and Louisiana—although only in the last three of these states achievements overlooked. The governments had been expensive, he insisted, because they had tried to provide public education and other public services on a scale never before attempted in the South. But Du Bois's use of Marxist theory in his work caused many historians who did not share his philosophy to dismiss his argument; and it remained for a group of less radical white historians to shatter the Dunning image of Reconstruction for good.

In the 1940s, historians such as C. Vann Woodward, David Herbert Donald, Thomas B. Alexander, and others began to reexamine the record of the Reconstruction governments in the South and to suggest that their record was not nearly as bad as had previously been assumed. They looked, too, at the Radical Republicans in Congress and suggested that they had not been motivated by vindictiveness and partisanship alone. By the early 1960s, a new view of Reconstruction had emerged from these efforts, summarized finally by John Hope Franklin in *Reconstruction After the Civil War* (1961) and Kenneth Stampp in *The Era of Reconstruction* (1965), which claimed that the postwar Republicans had been engaged in a genuine, if flawed, effort to solve the problem of race in the South by providing much-needed protection to the freedmen. The Reconstruction governments, for all their faults, had been bold experiments in interracial politics; and the congressional Radicals, while far from being saints, had displayed a genuine concern for the rights of

slaves. There had been no such thing as "bayonet rule" or "Negro rule" in the South. Blacks had played only a small part in Reconstruction governments and had acquitted themselves well. Corruption in the South had been no worse than corruption in the North at that time. What was tragic about Reconstruction, the revisionist view claimed, was not what it did to Southern whites but what it did not do for Southern blacks. By stopping short of the reforms necessary to ensure blacks genuine equality, Reconstruction had consigned them to more than a century of injustice and discrimination.

Where historians now tend to disagree is on why Reconstruction fell as short as it did of guaranteeing racial justice. Some scholars claim that conservative obstacles to change were so great that the Radicals, despite their good intentions, simply could not overcome them. Others claim that the Radicals themselves were not sufficiently committed to the principle of racial justice, that they abandoned the cause quickly when it became clear to them that the battle would not easily be won. Still others—for example, Herman Belz, in *A New Birth of Freedom* (1976)—emphasize the positive achievements of Reconstruction. By enacting the Fourteenth and Fifteenth amendments, he argues, the United States took a vital step toward transferring from the states to the federal government the responsibility for protecting the rights of citizenship.

---

did the blacks outnumber the whites in the population as a whole. But once new constitutions had been framed and new governments launched, most of them permitted nearly all whites to vote (although for several years the Fourteenth Amendment continued to keep the leading ex-Confederates from holding office). This meant that in most of the Southern states the Republicans could maintain control only with the support of a great many Southern whites.

These Southern white Republicans,

whom their opponents derisively called "scalawags," consisted in part of former Whigs who, after the breakup of the Whig organization in the 1850s, had acted with the Southern Democrats but had never felt completely at home with them. Some of the scalawag leaders were wealthy (or once wealthy) planters or businessmen. Such men, having long controlled the blacks as slaves, expected to control them also as voters. Many other Southern whites who joined the Republican party were farmers living in areas where slavery had been unimportant or nonexistent. These men, many of whom had been wartime Unionists, favored the Republican program of internal improvements, which would help them get their crops to market.

White men from the North also served as Republican leaders in the South. Opponents of Reconstruction referred to them as "carpetbaggers," thus giving the impression that they were penniless adventurers who had arrived with all their possessions in a carpetbag (a then common kind of valise covered with carpeting material) in order to take advantage of the black vote for their own power and profit. In fact, the majority of the so-called carpetbaggers were veterans of the Union army who had looked on the South as a new frontier, more promising than the West, and at the war's end had settled in it as hopeful planters or business or professional men.

The most numerous Republicans in the South were the freedmen, the vast majority of whom had no formal education and no previous experience in the management of affairs. Among the black leaders, however, were well-educated men, most of whom had never been slaves and many of whom had been brought up in the North or abroad. The blacks quickly became politically self-conscious. In various states they held their own "colored conventions," the one in Alabama announcing (1867): "We claim exactly *the same rights, privileges and immunities as are enjoyed by white men*—we ask nothing more and will be content with nothing less." Blacks were organized, often with the assistance of Freedmen's Bureau agents and other Northern whites, in chapters of the Union League, which had been founded originally as a Republican electioneering agency in the North during the war. Another organization that gave unity and self-confidence to black people was their church. Once they were emancipated, they had begun to withdraw from the white churches and form their own—institutions based on the elaborate religious practices they had developed (occasionally surreptitiously) under slavery. "The colored preachers are *the great power* in controlling and uniting the colored vote," a carpetbagger observed in 1868.

Blacks served as delegates to the conventions that, under the congressional plan, drew up new state constitutions in the South. Then, in the reconstructed states, blacks were elected to public offices of practically every kind. Altogether (between 1869 and 1901) twenty blacks were sent to the House of Representatives in Washington. Two went to the United States Senate, both of them from Mississippi. Hiram R. Revels, an ordained minister and a former North Carolina free black who had been educated at Knox College in Illinois, took in 1870 the Senate seat that Jefferson Davis once had occupied. Blanche K. Bruce, who had escaped from slavery in Virginia and studied in the North, became a senator in 1874.

Hiram R. Revels
Revels was one of the few blacks to attain high office during Reconstruction, acting as United States senator from Mississippi from 1870 to 1871. Born in North Carolina of free parents, Revels became a Methodist minister, and during the Civil War he served as an army chaplain in Mississippi. Returning to the state after the war, he resumed his ministerial duties and entered politics. He was a moderate Republican and, in 1875, joined with the Democrats to overthrow the Republican state regime. For years, he was president of Alcorn College, a black institution. (Library of Congress)

Yet no such thing as "Negro rule" ever existed in any of the states—despite the claims (and complaints) of many Southern whites. No black was elected governor, though Lieutenant Governor P. B. S. Pinchback briefly occupied the governor's chair in Louisiana. Blacks never controlled any of the state legislatures, though for a time they held a majority in the lower house of South Carolina. In the South as a whole the number of black officeholders was less than proportionate to the number of blacks in the population. Nor did the state governments show much if any favoritism toward blacks as a group. Constitutions or statutes prohibited, on paper, discrimination on the basis of color, but segregation remained the common practice.

The record of the Reconstruction governments is many-sided. The financial programs they instituted were a compound of blatant corruption and well-designed, if sometimes impractical, social legislation. The corruption and extravagance are familiar aspects of the Reconstruction story. State budgets expanded to hitherto unknown totals, and state debts soared to previously undreamed-of heights. In South Carolina, for example, the public debt increased from $7 million to $29 million in eight years.

In large measure, the corruption in the South was part of a national phenomenon, with the same social force—an expanding capitalism eager to secure quick results—acting as the corrupting agent in all sections of the country. That much of the alleged corruption was a product of deep forces in contemporary society is demonstrated by the continuance of dishonesty in state government after Republican rule was overthrown.

The state expenditures of the Reconstruction years seem huge only in comparison with the niggardly budgets of the conservative governments of the prewar era; they do not appear large when measured against the sums appropriated by later legislatures. The reconstructed governments represented the poor blacks, who demanded public education, public-works programs, poor relief, and other costly services. Despite theft and foolish spending, there were also positive and permanent accomplishments.

Education

Perhaps the most important of those accomplishments was a dramatic improvement in Southern education—an improvement that benefited both whites and blacks. In the first years of Reconstruction, much of the impetus for educational reform in the South came from outside groups—from the Freedmen's Bureau and from Northern private philanthropic organizations—and from blacks themselves. Over the opposition of many Southern whites, who feared that education would give blacks "false notions of equality," these reformers established a large network of schools for former slaves—4,000 schools by 1870, staffed by 9,000 teachers (half of them black), and teaching 200,000 students (about 12 percent of the total school-age population of the freedmen). In the course of the 1870s, moreover, the Reconstruction governments of the states assumed the initiative and began to build a comprehensive public school system in the South. By 1876, more than half of all white children and about 40 percent of all black children were being educated in Southern schools. A number of black "academies" were also beginning to operate—institutions that were, perhaps, not yet genuine colleges but that were offering more advanced education to freedmen than the public schools provided. Gradually, these academies grew into an important network of black colleges and universities, which would form the basis of black higher education in the South for nearly a century. Among the early institutions, for example, were schools that later became Fisk and Atlanta Universities and Morehouse College.

Already, however, Southern education was becoming divided into two separate systems—one black and one white. Early efforts to integrate the schools of the region were a dismal failure. The Freedmen's Bureau schools, for example, were open to students of all races, but almost no whites attended them. New Orleans set up an integrated school system under the Reconstruction government; again, whites almost universally stayed away. The one federal effort to mandate school integration—the Civil Rights Act

Teachers of the Freedmen
For a few brief years, the Freedmen's Bureau, established by Congress in 1865, served as a visible force for racial equality and for an interracial society in the South. This photograph shows the integrated faculty of a school established by the bureau near Norfolk, Virginia. Hampered by limited funding and local white hostility, the bureau was able to achieve only limited results. But the educational institutions it established helped to create the basis for the important network of black institutes and colleges in the South. (Massachusetts Commandery Military Order of the Loyal Legion and the U.S. Army Military History Institute)

of 1875—had its provisions for educational desegregation removed before it was passed. And as soon as the Republican governments of Reconstruction were replaced, the new Southern Democratic regimes quickly abandoned all efforts to promote integration.

Land Ownership

The most ambitious goal of the Freedmen's Bureau, and of some Republican Radicals in Congress, was to make Reconstruction the occasion for a fundamental reform of land ownership in the South. The effort failed. In the last years of the war and the first years of Reconstruction, the Freedmen's Bureau did oversee the redistribution of substantial amounts of land to freedmen in some areas—notably the Sea Islands off South Carolina and Georgia and areas of Mississippi that had once belonged to the Davis family. By June 1865, the bureau had settled nearly 10,000 black families on their own land—most of it drawn from abandoned plantations. Blacks throughout the South were growing excited at the prospect of achieving a real economic stake in their region—the vision of "forty acres and a mule." By the end of that year, however, the experiment was already collapsing. Southern plantation owners were returning and demanding the restoration of their property. And Andrew Johnson was supporting their demands. Despite the resistance of General Oliver O. Howard and other officials of the Freedmen's Bureau, most of the confiscated land was eventually returned to the original white owners. Congress, moreover, never exhibited much stomach for the idea of land redistribution. Despite the pleas of such Radicals as Thaddeus Stevens, very few Northern Republicans believed that the federal government had the right to confiscate property. Land reform did not become a part of Reconstruction.

Nevertheless, there was a substantial change in the distribution of land ownership in the South in the postwar years—a result of many factors. Among whites, there was a striking decline in ownership of land. Whereas before the war more than 80 percent of Southern whites had lived on their own land, by the end of Reconstruction that proportion had dropped to about 67 percent. Some whites had fallen into debt and been forced to sell; some had fallen victim to increased taxes; some had chosen to leave the marginal lands they had owned to move to more fertile areas, where they rented. Among blacks, during the same period, the proportion who owned land rose from virtually none to more than 20 percent. Black landowners acquired their property through hard work, through luck, and at times through the assistance of such agencies as the Freedman's Bank, established in 1865 by antislavery whites in an effort to promote land ownership among blacks. (The bank failed in 1874, after a combination of internal corruption and a nationwide financial panic had destroyed its reserves.)

Despite these impressive achievements, however, the vast majority of blacks (and a growing minority of whites) did not own their own land during Reconstruction, and some of those who acquired land in the 1860s lost it in the 1890s. These nonlandowners worked for others, through a great variety of systems. Many black agricultural laborers—perhaps 25 percent of the total—simply worked for wages. Most, however, became tenants of white landowners—that is, they acquired control of their own plots of land, working them on their own and paying their landlord either a fixed rent or a share of their crop (hence the term "sharecropping"). The new system represented a breakdown of the traditional plantation system, in which blacks had lived together and worked together under the direction of a master. As tenants and sharecroppers, blacks enjoyed at least a physical independence from their landlords and had the sense of working their own lands, even if in most cases they could never hope to buy them.

Incomes and Credit

The economic effect of Reconstruction on the freedmen, to the extent that it can be calculated, was mixed. In some respects, the postwar years were a period of remarkable economic progress for blacks. If the food, clothing, shelter, and other material benefits they had received under slavery are considered as income, then prewar blacks had earned about a 22 percent share of the profits of the plantation system. By the end of Reconstruction, they were earning 56 percent of the return on investment in Southern agriculture. Measured another way, the per capita income of blacks rose 46 percent between 1857 and 1879, while the per capita income of whites declined 35 percent. This repre-

sented one of the most significant redistributions of income in American history.

Nevertheless, the economic status of blacks did not improve as much as such figures suggest. For one thing, while their share of the profits was increasing, the total profits of Southern agriculture were declining: a result of the dislocations of the war and of a reduction in the world market for cotton. For another thing, while blacks were earning a greater return on their labor than they had under slavery, they were working less. Women and children were less likely to labor in the fields than in the past; and adult men tended to work shorter days. In all, the black labor force worked about one-third fewer hours during Reconstruction than they had under slavery—a reduction that brought their working schedule roughly into accord with that of white farm laborers. The income redistribution of the postwar years raised both the absolute and the relative economic status of blacks in the South substantially. It did not, however, lift many blacks out of poverty. Black per capita income rose quickly after the war, from about one-quarter of white per capita income to about one-half. But after this initial increase, it rose virtually not at all.

For blacks and poor whites alike, whatever gains there might have been as a result of land and income redistribution were often overshadowed by the ravages of another economic burden: the crop lien system. In the postwar South, the traditional credit structure—based on "factors" (see pp. 336–337) and banks—was unable to reassert its former control. In its stead emerged a new system of credit, centered in large part around local country stores—some of them owned by planters, others owned by independent merchants. Blacks and whites, landowners and tenants: all depended on these stores for such necessities as food, clothing, seed, farm implements, and the like. And since the agricultural sector does not enjoy the same steady cash flow as other sectors of the economy, Southern farmers often had to rely on credit from these merchants in order to purchase what they needed. The credit came at high cost. Interest rates were, in effect, as high as 50 or 60 percent. Suppliers held liens (claims) on the crops of debtor farmers as collateral on the loans. If a farmer suffered a few bad years in a row, as often happened in the troubled agricultural markets of the 1870s, he could become trapped in a cycle of debt from which he could never escape.

This burdensome credit system had a number of effects on the South. One was that some blacks who had acquired land during the early years of Reconstruction gradually lost it as they fell into debt. (So, to a lesser extent, did small white landowners.) Another was that Southern farmers became utterly dependent on cash crops—and most of all on cotton—because only such marketable com-

modities seemed to offer any possibility of an escape from debt. Thus Southern agriculture, never sufficiently diversified even in the best of times, became more one-dimensional than ever. Before the war, the South had grown most of its own food. By the end of Reconstruction, the region was importing a large proportion—in some areas more than 50 percent—of what it needed to feed itself. The relentless planting of cotton, moreover, was contributing to an exhaustion of the soil. The crop lien system, in other words, was not only helping to impoverish small farmers; it was also contributing to a general decline in the Southern agricultural economy.

THE GRANT ADMINISTRATION

Exhausted by the political turmoil of the Johnson administration, American voters in 1868 yearned for a strong, stable figure to guide them through the troubled years of Reconstruction. They did not find one. Instead, they turned trustingly to General Ulysses S. Grant, the conquering hero of the war and, by 1868, a widely revered national idol. An inspired general, Grant was a disastrous president. During his two terms in office, he faced problems that would have taxed the abilities of a master of statecraft. Grant, whatever his qualities, was no such leader. He was, rather, a generally dull and unimaginative man with few political skills and little real vision.

The Soldier President

At the end of the war both parties had angled to make Grant their candidate, and he could have had the nomination of either party. As he watched the congressional Radicals triumph over President Johnson, he concluded that the Radical Reconstruction policy expressed the real wishes of the people. He was receptive when the Radical leaders approached him with offers of the Republican nomination, and virtually without opposition, he received the endorsement of the party convention. The Democrats, spurned by Grant, nominated Horace Seymour of New York.

After a bitter campaign revolving around Reconstruction and Seymour's war record as governor of New York (he had been a Peace Democrat), Grant carried twenty-six states and Seymour only eight. But Grant received only 3,012,000 popular votes to Seymour's 2,703,000, a scant majority of 309,000, and this majority was due to black votes in the reconstructed states of the South.

Ulysses S. Grant was the second professional soldier to be elected to the presidency (Zachary Taylor having been the first). After graduating from West Point with no particular distinction, Grant had entered the regular army, from which after years of service he resigned under something of a cloud. In civilian life he undertook several dismal ventures that barely yielded him a living. His career before 1861 could be characterized as forty years of failure. Then came the Civil War, and Grant found at last the one setting, the one vocation for which he was supremely equipped—war.

His political naïveté as president was displayed in many of his appointments. For the important office of secretary of state he chose an old friend, the former Illinois congressman Elihu B. Washburne. By agreement, Washburne was to hold the position only a week before resigning to become minister to France, the purpose being to enable him to brag in Paris that he had headed the foreign office. After offering the appointment to another man, who declined it on the grounds of expense, Grant then named Hamilton Fish of New York.

In choosing his official family, Grant proceeded as if he were creating a military staff. He sent several appointments to the Senate for confirmation without asking the recipients if they would serve; they first heard the news in the papers. Fish, who had been out of politics for twenty years, wired Grant that he could not accept, but his name was already being acted on in the Senate and he was persuaded to let it go through. During his two administrations, Grant named a total of twenty-five men to the cabinet. Most of his later appointments went to men who were, at best, average, and some to men who were incompetent or corrupt or both. Increasingly, in dispensing cabinet and executive patronage, Grant came to rely on the machine leaders in the party—the groups most ardently devoted to the spoils system.

Diplomatic Successes

The Grant administration, like the Johnson administration before it, achieved its greatest success in foreign affairs. These were the accomplishments not of the presidents themselves, who displayed little aptitude for diplomacy, but of two outstanding secretaries of state: William H. Seward, who had served Lincoln during the Civil War and remained in office until 1869; and Hamilton Fish, who served throughout the two terms of the Grant administration.

An ardent expansionist and advocate of a vigorous foreign policy, Seward acted with as much daring as the demands of Reconstruction politics and the Republican hatred of President Johnson would permit. When Russia let it be known that it would like to sell Alaska to the United States, the two nations long having been on friendly terms, Seward readily agreed to pay the asking price of $7.2 million. Only by strenuous efforts was he able to induce the Senate to ratify the treaty and the House to appropriate the money (1867–1868). Critics jeered that the secretary had bought a useless frozen wasteland—

Hamilton Fish
Although he served in an administration best remembered for its corruption and ineptitude, Hamilton Fish earned a reputation as one of the most talented and effective secretaries of state in American history. Faced with a series of extraordinarily difficult diplomatic problems in the aftermath of the Civil War, he managed to resolve most of them with skill and tact. He began his career as a member of Congress from New York, becoming the first of many generations of his family—extending into the 1980s—to serve in the House of Representatives. (The Granger Collection)

"Seward's Icebox" and "Walrussia" were some of the terms employed to describe it—but Alaska, a center for the fishing industry in the North Pacific and potentially rich in such resources as gold (and, as the nation would discover much later, oil), was a bargain. Seward was not content with expansion in continental North America. In 1867, he engineered the annexation of the tiny Midway Islands west of Hawaii.

In contrast with its sometimes shambling course in domestic politics, the performance of the Grant administration in the area of foreign affairs was generally decisive and firm, yet showing a wise moderation. For this, Secretary Fish, to whom President Grant gave almost a free hand, deserves the major credit. A number of delicate and potentially dangerous situations confronted Fish from the beginning, but the most serious one arose out of strained relations with Great Britain.

The United States had a burning grievance against England that had originated during the Civil War. At that time the British government, according to the American interpretation, had violated the laws of neutrality by permitting Confederate cruisers, the *Alabama* and others, to be built and armed in English shipyards and let loose to prey on Northern commerce. American demands that England pay for the damages committed by these vessels became known as the "Alabama claims." Although the British government realized its diplomatic error in condoning construction of the cruisers (in a future war American-built *Alabamas* might operate against Britain), it at first hesitated to submit the issue to arbitration.

Seward tried earnestly to settle the Alabama claims before leaving office. The American minister to England, Reverdy Johnson, negotiated an agreement, the Johnson-Clarendon Convention (1869), providing that all claims on both sides since 1853 be submitted to arbitration. The pact was distasteful to Americans because it embraced so many issues and contained no expression of British regret for the escape of the *Alabama*. Coming before the Senate immediately after Grant took office, it was rejected 54 to 1. The debate featured a speech by Charles Sumner, chairman of the Committee on Foreign Relations, denouncing Britain for its course in the Civil War and arguing that its conduct had prolonged the war by two years. Therefore, said Sumner, England owed the United States for "direct damages" committed by the cruisers and "indirect damages" for the cost of the war for two years—which would have reached the staggering total of some $2 billion.

England naturally would have nothing to do with any arrangement involving indirect claims, and settlement of the problem was temporarily stalled. Secretary Fish, however, continued to work for a solution, and finally, in 1871, the two countries agreed to the Treaty of Washington, one of the great landmarks in international pacification, providing for arbitration of the cruiser issue and other pending controversies. The Alabama claims were to be laid before a five-member tribunal whose members were to be appointed by the governments of the United States, England, Italy, Switzerland, and Brazil. In the covenant, Britain expressed regret for the escape of the *Alabama* and agreed to a set of rules governing neutral obligations that virtually gave the British case away. In effect, this meant that the tribunal would have only to fix the sum to be paid by Britain. Convening at Geneva in Switzerland, the arbitrators awarded $15.5 million to the United States.

The Defection of the Liberals

Through both his foreign and his domestic policies, President Grant antagonized and alienated a number of prominent Republicans, among them the famous Radical Charles Sumner. Senator Sumner's extravagant demand for damages from Great Britain embarrassed Secretary Fish in the latter's diplomacy. Still worse, from the president's point of view, Sumner blocked a treaty for the annexation of Santo Domingo, a project in which Grant took a deep personal interest—indeed, it was a kind of monomania with him. The angry president got revenge by inducing his Senate friends to remove Sumner from the chairmanship of the Committee on Foreign Relations.

Sumner and other Republican leaders joined with civil service reformers to criticize Grant for his use of the spoils system, his reliance on ruthless machine politicians. Such scholarly journalists as E. L. Godkin of *The Nation* and George William Curtis of *Harper's Weekly* were arguing that the government ought to base its appointments not on services to the party but on fitness for office as determined by competitive examinations, as the British government already was doing. Grant yielded to the extent of recommending the establishment of a civil service commission, which Congress authorized in 1871, to devise a system of hiring based on merit. This agency, under the direction of Curtis, proposed a set of rules that seemed to meet with Grant's approval. But Grant was not really much interested in reform, and even if he had been he could not have persuaded his followers to accept a new system that would undermine the very basis of party loyalty— the patronage. Congress, by neglecting to renew the commission's appropriation, soon ended its existence.

Nevertheless, controversy over civil service reform continued, becoming one of the leading political issues of the next three decades of American life. The debate involved more than simply an argument over patronage and corruption. It reflected, too, basic differences of opinion over who was fit to serve in public life. Middle-class reformers were saying, implicitly, that only educated, middle-class people should be permitted access to government office. Those opposing them—not simply party leaders, but immigrant and labor groups, some farmers, and others—argued that the establishment of an elite corps of civil servants would exclude these groups from participation in government and restrict power to the upper classes. The controversy clearly echoed the debate in the Jacksonian era, when the "spoils system" was first introduced and was widely hailed as a "democratic" reform.

Republican critics of the president also denounced him for his support of Radical Reconstruction. He continued to station federal troops in the South, and on many occasions he sent them to support Republican governments that were on the point of collapse. To growing numbers in the North this seemed like dangerous militarism, and they were more and more disgusted by the stories of governmental corruption and extravagance that came up from the South. Some Republicans were beginning to suspect that there was corruption not only in the Southern state governments but also in the federal government. Still others criticized Grant because he had declined to speak out in favor of a reduction of the tariff. The high wartime duties remained substantially unchanged even though the justification for them was past.

Thus, before the end of Grant's first term, members of his own party had begun to oppose him for a variety of reasons—his foreign policies, his use of the patronage, his resort to military force in the South, his

high-tariff stand, and his suspected taint of corruption—all of which added up to what the critics called "Grantism." In 1872, hoping to prevent Grant's reelection, his opponents bolted the party. Referring to themselves as Liberal Republicans, they proceeded to set up their own organization for running presidential and vice-presidential candidates.

They named Horace Greeley, veteran editor and publisher of the New York *Tribune* to head their ticket. The Democratic convention, seeing in his candidacy (and in the alliance with the Liberals it would achieve) the only chance to unseat the Republicans, endorsed him with no great enthusiasm. Despite his recent attacks on Radical Reconstruction, many Southerners, remembering Greeley's own Radical past, prepared to stay at home on Election Day. The Republicans, with Grant as their standard-bearer and a platform justifying Reconstruction and calling for a high tariff, moved into the campaign with confidence. In November, Grant polled 286 electoral votes and 3,597,000 popular votes to Greeley's 62 and 2,834,000. The optimistic editor carried only two Southern and four border states. Three weeks later Greeley, apparently crushed by his defeat, died.

During the campaign the first of a series of political scandals had come to light. Although the wrongdoing had occurred before Grant took office, it involved his party, and the onus for it fell on his administration. This scandal originated with the Crédit Mobilier construction company, which helped build the Union Pacific Railroad. In reality, the Crédit Mobilier was controlled by a few Union Pacific stockholders who awarded huge and fraudulent contracts to the construction company, thus milking the Union Pacific, a company of which they owned a minor share, of money that in part came from government subsidies. To avert a congressional inquiry into the deal, the directors, using Oakes Ames, a Massachusetts representative, as their agent, sold at a discount (in effect gave) Crédit Mobilier stock to key members of Congress. A congressional investigation was held, and it revealed that some high-placed Republicans—including Schuyler Colfax, now Grant's vice president—had accepted stock.

One dreary episode followed another in Grant's second term. Benjamin H. Bristow, Grant's third secretary of the treasury, discovered that some of his officials and a group of distillers operating as a "whiskey ring" were cheating the government out of taxes by means of false reports. Among the prominent Republicans involved was the president's private secretary, Orville E. Babcock. Grant defended Babcock, appointed him to another office, and eased Bristow out of the cabinet. A House investigation revealed that William W. Belknap, secretary of war, had accepted bribes to retain an Indian-post trader in office. Belknap resigned with Grant's blessing before the Senate could act on impeachment charges brought by the House. (In fact, Belknap's actions were not much different from the usual methods of administering Indian reservations. Administrations both before and after Grant's made casual use of these important appointments to satisfy their political backers.) Lesser scandals involved the Navy Department, which was suspected of selling business to contractors, and the Treasury, where John D. Sanborn, a special agent appointed to handle overdue taxes, collected $427,000 and retained a 50 percent commission for himself and the Republican bigwigs who had placed him in the job.

The Greenback Question

Meanwhile, the Grant administration and the nation at large suffered another blow: the Panic of 1873. It began with the failure of a leading investment banking firm, Jay Cooke and Company. Cooke, the "financier of the Civil War," had done well in handling government war bonds, but he had sunk excessive amounts into postwar railroad building. Depressions had come before with almost rhythmic regularity—in 1819, 1837, and 1857—but this was the worst one yet. It lasted four years, during which unemployment rose to 3 million and agricultural prices fell so far that thousands of farmers, unable to meet mortgage payments, went more deeply into debt or lost their farms.

Debtors hoped the government would follow an inflationary easy-money policy, which would have made it easier for them to pay their debts and would have helped to stimulate recovery from the depression. But President Grant and most Republicans preferred what they called a "sound" currency, which was to the advantage of the banks, moneylenders, and other creditors.

The money question had confronted Grant and the Republicans in Congress from the beginning of his administration. The question was twofold: How should interest and principal of the war bonds be paid, and what should be the permanent place of greenbacks in the national currency? Representatives of the debtor interests argued that the bonds had been purchased in greenbacks of depreciated value and should, unless stipulated otherwise by law, by redeemed in the same currency. The president favored payment in gold, and the Republican Congress moved speedily to promise redemption in "coin or its equivalent" and to enact a refunding act providing for long-term refinancing of the debt (1869-1870).

Approximately $450 million in greenbacks had been issued during the Civil War, and $400 million of them were still in circulation at the end of the conflict. During the Johnson administration, Congress had authorized the Treasury to reduce their quantity, but protests by farmers and some business groups had halted further action. When Grant entered the White House, the greenback circulation was some $356 million and the gold value of a greenback dollar was 73 cents.

After the Supreme Court, in *Knox* v. *Lee* (1871), reversed an earlier decision and affirmed the legality of greenbacks, the Treasury moved, in 1873, to increase the amount in circulation in response to the panic. For the same reason Congress, in the following year, voted to raise the total further. Grant, responding to pressures from Eastern financial interests, vetoed the measure—over the loud objections of many members of his own party.

With the greenback issue becoming more and more heated and divisive, and with an election year approaching, Republican leaders in Congress began searching for some way to settle the controversy. Their solu-

The Specter of Inflation
The greenback controversy of the 1870s inspired dire warnings of disaster from both supporters and opponents of paper currency. This cartoon conveys the warnings of the foes of greenbacks of the catastrophic inflation that would result from a failure to return to a "sound" (specie-backed) currency. (Culver Pictures)

AN INFLATION LOOK AHEAD.

BOY. "Mother wants Three Cents' worth of Paregoric."
DRUGGIST. "Where is your money?"
BOY. "In the wheel-barrow, of course. Expect me to carry Three Cents' worth of Greenbacks in my Pocket?"

tion—introduced initially by Senator John Sherman of Ohio—was the Specie Resumption Act of 1875. This law provided that after January 1, 1879, the government would redeem greenback dollars at par with gold; that is, the present greenbacks, whose value constantly fluctuated, could be exchanged for new paper currency, whose value would be firmly pegged to the price of gold. The law served several of its intended purposes. It healed many of the divisions within the Republican Party. It protected the interests of the creditor classes, who had worried that debts would be repaid in debased paper currency and were now assured that debtors would pay them with stable dollars. Other groups, however, were less satisfied. In theory, the new law protected the interests of debtor groups as well; by directing the gov-

ernment to increase its gold reserve, the bill presumably would permit an increase in the amount of specie-backed currency in circulation. In fact, "resumption" did not satisfy those who had been clamoring for an increase in greenbacks, because the gold-based money supply was never able to expand as much as they believed was necessary.

Thus the greenback issue survived after 1875, and the question of the proper composition of the currency now emerged as one of the most controversial and enduring issues in American politics. Creditors and established financial interests continued to insist on a "sound" currency based on gold. Debtor groups—farmers, laborers, and some manufacturers—and debtor regions—the South and the West—continued to clamor for a currency based not on gold reserves but on the productive capacity of the nation. Otherwise, they claimed, they would continue to be strangled by an overvalued dollar circulating in insufficient quantities. But the question of greenbacks, and the many other currency controversies that followed, also became symbols of much deeper concerns. Agrarian dissidents and others came to see in the maintenance of the gold standard a conspiracy by entrenched financiers to keep them in economic bondage. Southerners and Westerners saw in the currency policies evidence of their subordination to the Northeast. Because in accepting the gold standard the United States was following the example of Great Britain and other European nations, many Americans came to view the policy as part of a dire international plot to enslave the American people. The greenbackers, as they were called, expressed their displeasure in 1875 by forming their own political organization: the National Greenback party. Active in the next three presidential elections, it failed to gain widespread support. But it did keep the money issue alive. And in the 1880s, the greenback forces began to merge with another, more powerful group of currency reformers—those who favored silver as the basis of currency—to help produce a political movement that would ultimately attain enormous strength.

THE ABANDONMENT OF RECONSTRUCTION

As the North grew increasingly preoccupied with its own political and economic problems, interest in Reconstruction began to wane. The Grant administration continued to protect Republican governments in the South, but less because of any interest in ensuring the position of freedmen than because of a desire to prevent the reemergence of a strong Democratic party in the region. But even the presence of federal troops was not enough to prevent white Southerners from working to overturn the Republican governments that they believed had been so ruthlessly thrust upon them. In a few states, the Democrats (or Conservatives) returned to power almost as soon as civilian government was restored. In Virginia, North Carolina, and Georgia, Republican rule came to an end in 1870. In other states, the Democrats gradually regained control over several years. Texas was "redeemed," as Southerners liked to call the restoration of Democratic rule, in 1873; Alabama and Arkansas in 1874; and Mississippi in 1875. For three other states— South Carolina, Louisiana, and Florida—the end of Reconstruction had to wait for the withdrawal of the last federal troops in 1877, a withdrawal that was the result of a long process of political bargaining and compromise at the national level.

The Southern States "Redeemed"

In the states where the whites constituted a majority—the upper South states—overthrow of Republican control was a relatively simple matter. The whites had only to organize and win the elections. Their success was facilitated by the early restoration of the suffrage to those whites who had been deprived of it by national or state action. Presidential and congressional pardons returned the privilege to numerous individuals; and in 1872, Congress, responding to public demands to remove penalties imposed on many Southerners after the war, enacted the Amnesty Act, which restored political rights to 150,000 ex-Confederates and left only 500 excluded from political life.

In other states, where blacks were in the majority or the population of the two races was almost equal, the whites resorted to intimidation and violence. Frankly terroristic were the secret societies that appeared in many parts of the South—the Ku Klux Klan, the Knights of the White Camellia, and others—which attempted to frighten or physically prevent blacks from voting. Although the societies were effective, their influence has been exaggerated by writers intrigued by their hooded and robed apparel and their elaborate ritual. Moving quickly to stamp out these societies, Congress passed two bills—termed "force acts" by white Southerners—in 1870 and 1871 and the Ku Klux Klan Act (also in 1871), which authorized the president to use military force and martial law in areas where the orders were active.

More potent than the secret orders were the open semimilitary organizations that operated under such names as rifle clubs, Red Shirts, and White Leagues. After the first such society was founded in Mississippi, the idea spread to other states, and the procedure employed by the clubs was called the Mississippi Plan. Briefly stated, the plan called for the whites in each community to organize and arm, and to be prepared, if necessary, to resort to force to win elections. But the heart of the scheme was in the phrase "drawing the color line." By one method or another, legal or illegal, every white man was to be forced to join the Democratic party or leave the community. By similar methods, every black male was to be excluded from political activity; in a few states blacks were to be permitted to vote—if they voted Democratic.

Perhaps an even stronger influence than the techniques practiced by the armed bands was the simple and unromantic weapon of economic pressure. The war had freed the black man, but he was still a laborer—a hired worker or a tenant—dependent on the whites for his livelihood. The whites readily discovered that this dependence placed blacks in their power. Planters refused to rent land to Republican blacks, storekeepers refused to extend them credit, employers refused to give them work. Economic pressure was a force that the blacks could not fight. If the Radicals, in bringing blacks to political power, had accomplished a revolution, it was a superficial one. They failed to provide black people with economic power, as they might have done by giving them possession of confiscated land. Hence their political rights had no lasting basis.

Certainly the blacks' political position was hopeless without the continued backing of the Republican party and the federal government. But they were losing the support of people in the North, even of many humanitarian reformers who had worked for emancipation and equal rights. After the adoption of the Fifteenth Amendment (1870), most of the reformers convinced themselves that their long campaign in behalf of black people at last was over, that with the vote blacks ought to be able to take care of themselves. Republican disillusionment with the corruption and disorders in the Southern states helped to bring about the party split of 1872, which in turn weakened the Republicans in the South still further. They beheld the discouraging spectacle of such former Radical leaders as Charles Sumner and Horace Greeley now calling themselves Liberals, cooperating with the Democrats, and outdoing even them in denunciations of what they viewed as black-and-carpetbag misgovernment. Most of the white Republicans of the South, including some of those who had come from the North, joined the Liberal movement and went over to the Democrats. Friction between the remaining carpetbaggers and the black Republicans grew because of a well-justified feeling on the part of the blacks that they were not receiving a fair share of the power and the jobs.

When the depression came in 1873, the hard times aggravated political discontent both North and South. In the congressional elections of 1874, the Democrats gained a majority of the seats in the national House of Representatives. After 1875, when the new House met, the Republicans no longer controlled the whole Congress, as they had done since the beginning of the war. And President Grant, in view of the changing temper of the North, no longer was willing to use military force to save from violent overthrow the Republican regimes that were still standing in the South. In 1875, when the Mississippi governor, Adelbert Ames (originally from Maine), appealed to Washington for troops to protect blacks from the terrorism of the Democrats, he received in reply a telegram that quoted Grant as saying: "The whole public are tired out with these annual autumnal outbreaks in the South, and the great majority are now ready to condemn any interference on the part of the government."

After the Democrats had taken Mississippi, only three states were left in the hands of the Republicans—South Carolina, Louisiana, and Florida. In the elections of 1876, again using terrorist tactics, the Democrats claimed victory in all three. But the Republicans maintained that they themselves had won, and they were able to continue holding office because federal troops happened to be on the scene. If the troops should be withdrawn, the last of the Republican regimes would fall. The future was to depend on the settlement of the presidential election of 1876, which was disputed in consequence of the electoral disputes in the South.

The Compromise of 1877

Ulysses S. Grant was eager to run for another term in 1876, and his friends among the Republican bosses tried to secure the nomination for him. But the majority of the Republican leaders ruled Grant out. Impressed by the recent upsurge of Democratic strength, which had delivered the House of Representatives and a number of state governments to the opposition party, and fearful of the third-term issue, they searched for a candidate who was not associated with the scandals of the past eight years and could entice the Liberals back into the fold and unite the party until after the election.

Senator James G. Blaine of Maine offered himself, but he had recently been involved in an allegedly crooked railroad deal. The Republican convention passed over Blaine and other hopefuls and named as the standard-bearer Rutherford B. Hayes, a former Union army officer and congressman, three times governor of Ohio, and a champion of civil service reform.

No personal rivalries divided the Democrats. Only one aspirant commanded serious attention, and with him as their candidate the Democrats were confident of returning to power. The bearer of the party's hopes was Governor Samuel J. Tilden of New York, whose name had become synonymous with governmental reform. A corporation lawyer and a millionaire, Tilden had long been a power in the Democratic organization of his state, but he had not hesitated to turn against the corrupt Tweed Ring of New York City's Tammany Hall and aid in its overthrow. His fight against Tweed brought him national fame and the governorship, in which position he increased his reputation for honest administration.

Despite the fury of the charges flung at each other by the parties in the canvass, there were almost no differences of principle between the candidates. Hayes was on record as favoring withdrawal of troops from the South, he advocated civil service, and his record for probity was equal to Tilden's. Although the New York governor, reflecting Eastern importing interests, was amenable to some kind of tariff reduction, on other economic issues he was at least as conservative as his rival. He was a gold or "sound-money" man, and he believed that government had no business interfering with economic interests. He looked on himself as a modern counterpart of Thomas Jefferson.

The November election revealed an apparent Democratic victory. In addition to the South, Tilden carried several large Northern states, and his popular vote was 4,300,000 to 4,036,000 for Hayes. But the situation was complicated by the disputed returns from Louisiana, South Carolina, and Florida, whose total electoral vote was 19. Both parties claimed to have won these states, and double sets of returns were presented to Congress. Adding to the confusion was a contested vote in Oregon, where one of the three successful Republican electors was declared ineligible because he held a federal office. The Democrats contended that the place should go to the Democratic elector with the highest number of votes, but the Republicans insisted that according to state law the remaining electors were to select someone to fill the vacancy. The dual and disputed returns threw the outcome of the election into doubt. As tension and excitement gripped the country, two clear facts emerged from the welter of conflicting claims. Tilden had for certain 184 electoral votes, only one short of the majority. The 20 votes in controversy would determine who would be president, and Hayes needed all of them to secure the prize.

With surprise and consternation, the nation now learned that no measure or method existed to determine the validity of disputed returns. The Constitution stated: "The President of the Senate shall, in the presence of the Senate and House of Representatives, open all the certificates and the votes shall then be counted." The question was, how and by whom? The Senate was Republican and so, of course, was its president and the House was Democratic. Constitutional ambiguity and congressional division rendered a fair and satisfactory solution of the crisis impossible. If the president of the Senate counted the votes, Hayes would be the victor. If the Senate and House judged the returns separately, they would reach opposite decisions and checkmate each other. And if the houses voted jointly, the Democrats, with a numerical majority, would decide the result. Resort to any one of these lines of action promised to divide the country and possibly result in chaos.

Not until the last days of January 1877 did Congress act to break the deadlock. Then it created a special electoral commission to pass on all the disputed votes. The commission was to be composed of five senators, five representatives, and five justices of the Supreme Court. Because of the party line-up, the congressional delegation would consist of five Republicans and five Democrats. The creating law named four of the judicial commissioners, two Republicans and two Democrats. The four were to select their fifth colleague, and it was understood that they would choose David Davis, an independent Republican, thus ensuring that the deciding vote would be wielded by a relatively unbiased judge. But at this stage Davis was elected to the Senate from Illinois and suddenly resigned his seat. His place on the commission fell to a more partisan Republican. Sitting throughout February, the commission by a straight party vote of 8 to 7 decided every disputed vote for Hayes. Congress accepted the final verdict of the commission on March 2, only two days before the inauguration of the new president.

Ratification of the commission's findings was not accomplished, however, without some complicated compromising among the politicians. Behind the dealing, and partially directing it, were certain powerful economic forces with a stake in the outcome. A decision by the commission was not final until approved by Congress, and the Democrats could have prevented action by filibustering. The success of a filibuster, however, depended on concert between Northern and Southern Democrats, and this the Republicans disrupted by offering the Southerners sufficient inducement to accept the commission's findings. According to the traditional account, certain Republicans and Southern Democrats met at Washington's Wormley Hotel, and the Republicans pledged that Hayes, after becoming president, would withdraw the troops from the South. As withdrawal would mean the downfall of the last carpetbag governments, the Southerners, convinced they were getting as much from Hayes as they could get from Tilden, abandoned the filibuster.

Actually, the story behind the "Compromise of 1877" is somewhat more complex. Hayes was on record before the election as favoring withdrawal of the troops, and in any event the Democrats in the House could have forced withdrawal simply by cutting out appropriations for the army in the Reconstruction process. The real agreement, the one that brought the Southern Democrats over, was reached before the Wormley meeting. As the price for their cooperation, the Southern Democrats (among them some old Whigs) exacted from the Republicans the following pledges: the appointment of at least one Southerner to the Hayes cabinet, control of federal patronage in their sections, generous internal improvements, national aid for the Texas and Pacific Railroad, and, finally, withdrawal of the troops. The Conservatives who were running the redeemed Southern states were primarily interested in economics—in industrializing the South—and they believed that the Republican program of federal aid to business would be more beneficial for their region than the archaic states'-rights policy of the Democrats.

The End of Reconstruction

In his inaugural address, Hayes stressed the Southern problem. While he took care to say that the rights of the blacks must be preserved, he announced that the most pressing need of the South was the restoration of "wise, honest, and peaceful local self-government"—which meant that he was going to withdraw the troops and let the whites take over control of the state governments. Hayes laid down this policy knowing that his action would lend weight to current charges that he was paying off the South for acquiescing in his election and would strengthen those critics who referred to him as "his Fraudulency."

The president hoped to build up a "new Republican" party in the South composed of whatever conservative white groups could be weaned away from the Democrats and committed to some acceptance of black rights. But his efforts, which included a tour of Southern cities and even the decoration of a memorial to the Confederate war dead, failed to produce any positive results. Although many Southern leaders sympathized with the economic credo of the Republicans, they could not advise their people to support the party that had imposed Reconstruction. Nor were Southerners pleased by Hayes's bestowal of federal offices on carpetbaggers or by his vetoes of Democratic attempts to repeal the "force acts." The "solid South," although not yet fully formed, was beginning to take shape. Neither Hayes nor any other Republican could reverse the trend—particularly since no one was willing to use federal power to protect black voting rights, which alone held promise of giving the Republicans lasting strength in the region.

The withdrawal of the troops was a signal that the national government was giving up its attempt to control Southern politics and to determine the place of blacks in Southern society. The surrender, it is to be noted, was made by the Republicans. They could yield with good grace because after 1877 they had no particular need for the support of the reconstructed South. The economic legislation of the war and postwar years was safe from repeal; industry was securely entrenched in the national economy; and Republican domination of national politics could be maintained without Southern votes.

The Tragedy of Reconstruction

The record of the Reconstruction years is not one of complete failure, as many have charged. That slavery would be abolished was clear well before the end of the war; but Reconstruction worked other changes upon Southern society as well. There was a significant redistribution of income, from which blacks benefited. There was a more limited, but not unimportant redistribution of land ownership, which enabled some former slaves to acquire property for the first time. There was both a relative and an absolute improvement in the economic circumstances of most blacks.

Nor was Reconstruction as disastrous an experience for Southern whites as most believed at the time. The region had emerged from a prolonged and bloody war defeated and devastated; and yet within a decade, the South had regained control of its own institutions and, to a great extent, restored its traditional ruling class to power. No harsh punishments were meted out to former Confederate leaders. No drastic program of economic reform was imposed on the region. Few lasting political changes were forced on the South. Not many conquered nations fare as well.

Yet for all that, Americans of the twentieth century cannot but look back on Reconstruction as a tragic era. For in those years the United States made its first serious effort to resolve its oldest and deepest social problem—the problem of race. And it failed in the effort. What was more, the experience so disappointed, disillusioned, and embittered the nation that it would be many years before an attempt would be made again.

Why did this great assault on racial injustice—an assault that had emerged over a period of more than fifty years—end so badly? In part, of course, it was because of the weaknesses and errors of the people who directed it. But in greater part, it was because the resolution of the racial problem required a far more fundamental reform of society than Americans of the time were willing to make. One after another, attempts to produce solutions ran up against conservative obstacles so deeply embedded in the nation's life that they could not be dislodged. Veneration of the Constitution sharply limited the willingness of national leaders to infringe on the rights of states and individuals in creating social change. A profound respect for private property and free enterprise prevented any real assault on economic privilege in the South, ensuring that blacks would not win title to the land and wealth they believed they deserved. Above all, perhaps, a pervasive belief among even the most liberal whites that the black race was inherently inferior served as an obstacle to the full equality of the freedmen. Given the context within which Americans of the 1860s and 1870s were working, what is surprising, perhaps, is not that Reconstruction did so little,

but that it did even as much as it did. The era was tragic not so much because it was a failure—the failure may have been inevitable from the beginning—but because it revealed how great, even insuperable, were the barriers to racial justice in the United States.

Given the odds confronting them, therefore, black Americans had reason for pride in the limited gains they were able to make during Reconstruction. And the nation at large had reason for gratitude that, if nothing else, the postwar era produced two great charters of freedom—the Fourteenth and Fifteenth amendments to the Constitution—which, although largely ignored at the time, would one day serve as the basis for a Second Reconstruction, one that would renew the drive to bring freedom and equality to all Americans.

SUGGESTED READINGS

The studies by McPherson and by Randall and Donald cited in the readings for the previous two chapters are likewise valuable for the Reconstruction period, both for their narratives of the era and for their bibliographies. William A. Dunning, *Reconstruction, Political and Economic, 1865–1977* (1907), long the standard study of Reconstruction, is now widely conceded to be marred by deep prejudices. More recent overviews of the period, better in tune with contemporary values, are Kenneth Stampp, *The Era of Reconstruction* (1965), and John Hope Franklin, *Reconstruction After the Civil War* (1961). W. E. B. Du Bois, *Black Reconstruction* (1935), is an early challenge to the pro-Southern orthodoxy about the period; while E. Merton Coulter, *The South During Reconstruction* (1947), adheres strictly to traditional views of the period as a time of Northern vindictiveness and Southern suffering. Rembert Patrick, *The Reconstruction of the Nation* (1967), is a modern overview that provides more detail than the relatively brief studies by Stampp and Franklin.

Herman Belz, *Reconstructing the Union* (1969), examines the theoretical basis of the Reconstruction problem. William B. Hesseltine, *Lincoln's Plan of Reconstruction* (1960), considers the first presidential plan; and Willie Lee Rose, *Rehearsal for Reconstruction: The Port Royal Experiment* (1964), describes wartime reconstruction policies in an area of South Carolina captured early by the Union. Louis S. Gerteis, *From Contraband to Freedman* (1973), examines federal policy toward blacks during the war itself. There are several valuable studies of the political battles that accompanied the switch from presidential to congressional Reconstruction. William R. Brock, *An American Crisis* (1963), is a particularly judicious work. Howard K. Beale, *The Critical Year: A Study of Andrew Johnson and Reconstruction* (1930), is a traditional approach to the subject; while Eric McKitrick, *Andrew Johnson and Reconstruction* (1960), is far more hostile toward Johnson. Two works by Michael Les Benedict, *A Compromise of Principle: Congressional Republicans and Reconstruction, 1863–1869* and *The Impeachment and Trial of Andrew Johnson* (1973), consider congressional politics and antagonisms toward the president. Hans L. Trefousse, *The Radical Republicans* (1963), and David Donald, *The Politics of Reconstruction* (1965), also examine congressional Radicals. Hans Trefousse is the author of another study of the impeachment proceedings, *The Impeachment of a President* (1975). La Wanda Cox and John H. Cox, *Politics, Principles, and Prejudice, 1865–1867* (1963), is an early work that was important in revising previous views of Reconstruction politics. Also useful for the politics of the era are biographies of leading Reconstruction figures. Richard N. Current, *Old Thad Stevens* (1942), is a hostile view; while Fawn Brodie, *Thaddeus Stevens* (1959), is more sympathetic. David Donald, *Charles Sumner and the Rights of Man* (1970), is also important. Harold Hyman, *A More Perfect Union* (1973), and Stanley Kutler, *The Judicial Power and Reconstruction*

Politics (1968), examine the constitutional problems that Reconstruction posed. Charles Fairman, *Reconstruction and Reunion* (1971), considers the Supreme Court in the postwar years. See also Herman Belz, *A New Birth of Freedom* (1976) and *Emancipation and Equal Rights* (1978). William Gilette, *The Right to Vote* (1965), is a study of the framing of the Fifteenth Amendment.

The South in Reconstruction is the subject of a growing literature. Joel Perman, *Reunion Without Compromise* (1973), is a good study of Southern resistance to Reconstruction policies. Valuable works on individual states include Joel G. Taylor, *Louisiana Reconstructed* (1974); Vernon Wharton, *The Negro in Mississippi, 1865–1890* (1965); Peyton McCrary, *Abraham Lincoln and Reconstruction* (1978), on policies toward Louisiana; Joel Williamson, *After Slavery: The Negro in South Carolina During Reconstruction* (1965); Thomas Holt, *Black over White* (1977), on South Carolina; C. Peter Ripley, *Slaves and Freedmen in Civil War Louisiana* (1976); and William Gilette, *Retreat from Reconstruction* (1980), on the end of Reconstruction. A valuable study of the economic impact of Reconstruction on the South is Roger Ransom and Richard Sutch, *One Kind of Freedom* (1977). Leon Litwack, *Been in the Storm So Long* (1979), is an important examination of the effects of Reconstruction on blacks, which should be supplemented by Robert Higgs, *Competition and Coercion* (1977). Allen Trelease, *White Terror* (1967), discusses the Ku Klux Klan. William S. McFeely portrays the head of the Freedmen's Bureau in *Yankee Stepfather: General O. O.*

Howard and the Freedmen (1968); and George Bentley, *A History of the Freedmen's Bureau* (1955), examines the institution itself. On carpetbaggers, see Otto Olsen, *Carpetbagger's Crusade: Albion Winegar Tourgée* (1965); L. N. Powell, *New Masters: Northern Planters During the Civil War and Reconstruction* (1980); William Harris, *Day of the Carpetbagger* (1979); and Elizabeth Jacoway, *Yankee Missionaries in the South* (1979). Sarah Wiggins, *The Scalawag in Alabama Politics, 1865–1881* (1977), examines Southern "collaborationists." Likewise valuable are Jacqueline Jones, *Soldiers of Light and Love* (1980), and James Sefton, *The United States Army and Reconstruction* (1967).

On the Grant administration, see William McFeely, *Grant* (1981), for a biography of the president. Allan Nevins, *Hamilton Fish* (1936), is a biography of the secretary of state that provides a portrait of the administration as a whole. William B. Hesseltine, *U. S. Grant, Politician* (1935), is another study of the Grant presidency. On the scandals of the era, see David Loth, *Public Plunder* (1938). John G. Sproat, *"The Best Men"* (1968), examines the role of liberal reformers during the period. Specific political controversies of the time are considered in Ari Hoogenboom, *Outlawing the Spoils* (1961), on civil service reform, and Irwin Unger, *The Greenback Era* (1964), on monetary controversies. Two views of the compromise of 1877 are C. Vann Woodward, *Reunion and Reaction* (1951), and K. I. Polakoff, *The Politics of Inertia* (1973). Edwin C. Rozwenc (ed.), *Reconstruction in the South*, rev. ed. (1952), is a valuable collection of essays on the subject.

THE DECLARATION OF INDEPENDENCE

In Congress, July 4, 1776,

THE UNANIMOUS DECLARATION OF THE THIRTEEN
UNITED STATES OF AMERICA

When, in the course of human events, it becomes necessary for one people to dissolve the political bands which have connected them with another, and to assume, among the powers of the earth, the separate and equal station to which the laws of nature and of nature's God entitle them, a decent respect to the opinions of mankind requires that they should declare the causes which impel them to the separation.

We hold these truths to be self-evident, that all men are created equal; that they are endowed by their Creator with certain unalienable rights; that among these, are life, liberty, and the pursuit of happiness. That, to secure these rights, governments are instituted among men, deriving their just powers from the consent of the governed; that, whenever any form of government becomes destructive of these ends, it is the right of the people to alter or to abolish it, and to institute a new government, laying its foundation on such principles, and organizing its powers in such form, as to them shall seem most likely to effect their safety and happiness. Prudence, indeed, will dictate that governments long established, should not be changed for light and transient causes; and, accordingly, all experience hath shown, that mankind are more disposed to suffer, while evils are sufferable, than to right themselves by abolishing the forms to which they are accustomed. But, when a long train of abuses and usurpations, pursuing invariably the same object, evinces a design to reduce them under absolute despotism, it is their right, it is their duty, to throw off such government and to provide new guards for their future security. Such has been the patient sufferance of these colonies, and such is now the necessity which constrains them to alter their former systems of government. The history of the present King of Great Britain is a history of repeated injuries and usurpations, all having, in direct object, the establishment of an absolute tyranny over these States. To prove this, let facts be submitted to a candid world:

He has refused his assent to laws the most wholesome and necessary for the public good.

He has forbidden his governors to pass laws of immediate and pressing importance, unless suspended in their operation till his assent should be obtained; and, when so suspended, he has utterly neglected to attend to them.

He has refused to pass other laws for the accommodation of large districts of people, unless those people would relinquish the right of representation in the legislature; a right inestimable to them, and formidable to tyrants only.

He has called together legislative bodies at places unusual, uncomfortable, and distant from the depository of their public records, for the sole purpose of fatiguing them into compliance with his measures.

He has dissolved representative houses repeatedly for opposing, with manly firmness, his invasions on the rights of the people.

He has refused, for a long time after such dissolutions, to cause others to be elected; whereby the legislative powers, incapable of annihilation, have returned to the people at large for their exercise; the state remaining, in the meantime, exposed to all the danger of invasion from without, and convulsions within.

i

He has endeavored to prevent the population of these States; for that purpose, obstructing the laws for naturalization of foreigners, refusing to pass others to encourage their migration hither, and raising the conditions of new appropriations of lands.

He has obstructed the administration of justice, by refusing his assent to laws for establishing judiciary powers.

He has made judges dependent on his will alone, for the tenure of their offices, and the amount and payment of their salaries.

He has erected a multitude of new offices and sent hither swarms of officers to harass our people, and eat out their substance.

He has kept among us, in time of peace, standing armies, without the consent of our legislatures.

He has affected to render the military independent of, and superior to, the civil power.

He has combined, with others, to subject us to a jurisdiction foreign to our Constitution, and unacknowledged by our laws; giving his assent to their acts of pretended legislation:

For quartering large bodies of armed troops among us:

For protecting them by a mock trial, from punishment, for any murders which they should commit on the inhabitants of these States:

For cutting off our trade with all parts of the world:

For imposing taxes on us without our consent:

For depriving us, in many cases, of the benefit of trial by jury:

For transporting us beyond seas to be tried for pretended offences:

For abolishing the free system of English laws in a neighboring province, establishing therein an arbitrary government, and enlarging its boundaries, so as to render it at once an example and fit instrument for introducing the same absolute rule into these colonies:

For taking away our charters, abolishing our most valuable laws, and altering, fundamentally, the powers of our governments:

For suspending our own legislatures, and declaring themselves invested with power to legislate for us in all cases whatsoever.

He has abdicated government here, by declaring us out of his protection, and waging war against us.

He has plundered our seas, ravaged our coasts, burnt our towns, and destroyed the lives of our people.

He is, at this time, transporting large armies of foreign mercenaries to complete the works of death, desolation, and tyranny, already begun, with circumstances of cruelty and perfidy scarcely paralleled in the most barbarous ages, and totally unworthy the head of a civilized nation.

He has constrained our fellow citizens, taken captive on the high seas, to bear arms against their country, to become the executioners of their friends, and brethren, or to fall themselves by their hands.

He has excited domestic insurrections amongst us, and has endeavored to bring on the inhabitants of our frontiers, the merciless Indian savages, whose known rule of warfare is an undistinguished destruction of all ages, sexes, and conditions.

In every stage of these oppressions, we have petitioned for redress, in the most humble terms; our repeated petitions have been answered only by repeated injury. A prince, whose character is thus marked by every act which may define a tyrant, is unfit to be the ruler of a free people.

Nor have we been wanting in attention to our British brethren. We have warned them, from time to time, of attempts made by their legislature to extend an unwarrantable jurisdiction over us. We have reminded them of the circumstances of our emigration and settlement here. We have appealed to their native justice and magnanimity, and we have conjured them, by the ties of our common kindred, to disavow these usurpations, which would inevitably interrupt our connections and correspondence. They, too, have been deaf to the voice of justice and consanguinity. We must, therefore, acquiesce in the necessity which denounces our separation, and hold them as we hold the rest of mankind, enemies in war, in peace, friends.

We, therefore, the representatives of the United States of America, in general Congress assembled, appealing to the Supreme Judge of the world for the rectitude of our intentions, do, in the name, and by the authority of the good people of these colonies, solemnly publish and declare, that these united colonies are, and of right ought to be, free and independent states: that they are absolved from all allegiance to the British Crown, and that all political connection between them and the state of Great Britain is, and ought to be, totally dissolved; and that, as free and independent states, they have full power to levy war, conclude peace, contract alliances, establish commerce, and to do all other acts and things which independent states may of right do. And, for the support of this declaration, with a firm reliance on the protection of Divine Providence, we mutually pledge to each other our lives, our fortunes, and our sacred honor.

The foregoing Declaration was, by order of Congress, engrossed, and signed by the following members:

JOHN HANCOCK

New Hampshire
Josiah Bartlett
William Whipple
Matthew Thornton

Massachusetts Bay
Samuel Adams
John Adams
Robert Treat Paine
Elbridge Gerry

Rhode Island
Stephen Hopkins
William Ellery

Connecticut
Roger Sherman
Samuel Huntington
William Williams
Oliver Wolcott

New York
William Floyd
Philip Livingston
Francis Lewis
Lewis Morris

New Jersey
Richard Stockton
John Witherspoon
Francis Hopkinson
John Hart
Abraham Clark

Pennsylvania
Robert Morris
Benjamin Rush
Benjamin Franklin
John Morton
George Clymer
James Smith
George Taylor
James Wilson
George Ross

Delaware
Caesar Rodney
George Reed
Thomas M'Kean

Maryland
Samuel Chase
William Paca
Thomas Stone
Charles Carroll,
   of Carrollton

Virginia
George Wythe
Richard Henry Lee
Thomas Jefferson
Benjamin Harrison
Thomas Nelson, Jr.
Francis Lightfoot Lee
Carter Braxton

North Carolina
William Hooper
Joseph Hewes
John Penn

South Carolina
Edward Rutledge
Thomas Heyward, Jr.
Thomas Lynch, Jr.
Arthur Middleton

Georgia
Button Gwinnett
Lyman Hall
George Walton

Resolved, That copies of the Declaration be sent to the several assemblies, conventions, and committees, or councils of safety, and to the several commanding officers of the continental troops; that it be proclaimed in each of the United States, at the head of the army.

THE CONSTITUTION OF THE UNITED STATES OF AMERICA[1]

We the People of the United States, in Order to form a more perfect Union, establish Justice, insure domestic Tranquility, provide for the common defence, promote the general Welfare, and secure the Blessings of Liberty to ourselves and our Posterity, do ordain and establish this CONSTITUTION for the United States of America.

Article I

SECTION 1.

All legislative Powers herein granted shall be vested in a Congress of the United States, which shall consist of a Senate and House of Representatives.

SECTION 2.

The House of Representatives shall be composed of Members chosen every second Year by the People of the several States, and the Electors in each State shall have the Qualifications requisite for Electors of the most numerous Branch of the State Legislature.

No Person shall be a Representative who shall not have attained to the Age of twenty-five Years, and been seven Years a Citizen of the United States, and who shall not, when elected, be an Inhabitant of that State in which he shall be chosen.

[Representatives and direct Taxes[2] shall be apportioned among the several States which may be included within this Union, according to their respective Numbers, which shall be determined by adding to the whole Number of free Persons, including those bound to Service for a Term of Years, and excluding Indians not taxed, three fifths of all other Persons.][3] The actual Enumeration shall be made within three Years after the first Meeting of the Congress of the United States, and within every subsequent Term of ten Years, in such Manner as they shall by Law direct. The Number of Representatives shall not exceed one for every thirty Thousand, but each State shall have at Least one Representative; and until such enumeration shall be made, the State of New Hampshire shall be entitled to chuse three, Massachusetts eight, Rhode-Island and Providence Plantations one, Connecticut five, New York six, New Jersey four, Pennsylvania eight, Delaware one, Maryland six, Virginia ten, North Carolina five, South Carolina five, and Georgia three.

When vacancies happen in the Representation from any State, the Executive Authority thereof shall issue Writs of Election to fill such Vacancies.

The House of Representatives shall chuse their Speaker and other Officers; and shall have the sole Power of Impeachment.

SECTION 3.

The Senate of the United States shall be composed of two Senators from each State, chosen by the Legislature thereof, for six Years; and each Senator shall have one Vote.

Immediately after they shall be assembled in Consequence of the first Election, they shall be divided as equally as may be into three Classes. The Seats of the Senators of the first Class shall be vacated at the Expiration of the second Year, of the second Class at the Expiration of the fourth Year, and of the third Class at the Expiration of the sixth Year, so that one-third may be chosen every second Year; and if Vacancies happen by Resignation, or otherwise, during the Recess of the Legislature of any State, the Executive thereof may make temporary Appointments until the next Meeting of the Legislature, which shall then fill such Vacancies.

No Person shall be a Senator who shall not have attained to the Age of thirty Years, and been nine Years a Citizen of the United States, and who shall not, when elected, be an Inhabitant of that State for which he shall be chosen.

The Vice President of the United States shall be President of the Senate, but shall have no vote, unless they be equally divided.

---

[1] This version, which follows the original Constitution in capitalization and spelling, was published by the United States Department of the Interior, Office of Education, in 1935.

[2] Altered by the Sixteenth Amendment.

[3] Negated by the Fourteenth Amendment.

The Senate shall chuse their other Officers, and also a President pro tempore, in the absence of the Vice President, or when he shall exercise the Office of President of the United States.

The Senate shall have the sole Power to try all Impeachments. When sitting for that purpose they shall be on Oath or Affirmation. When the President of the United States is tried, the Chief Justice shall preside: And no person shall be convicted without the Concurrence of two thirds of the Members present.

Judgment in Cases of Impeachment shall not extend further than to removal from Office, and disqualification to hold and enjoy any Office of honor, Trust, or Profit under the United States: but the Party convicted shall nevertheless be liable and subject to Indictment, Trial, Judgment, and Punishment, according to Law.

SECTION 4.

The Times, Places and Manner of holding Elections for Senators and Representatives, shall be prescribed in each State by the Legislature thereof; but the Congress may at any time by Law make or alter such Regulations, except as to the Places of Chusing Senators.

The Congress shall assemble at least once in every Year, and such Meeting shall be on the first Monday in December, unless they shall by Law appoint a different Day.

SECTION 5.

Each House shall be the Judge of the Elections, Returns and Qualifications of its own Members, and a Majority of each shall constitute a Quorum to do Business; but a smaller number may adjourn from day to day, and may be authorized to compel the Attendance of absent Members, in such Manner, and under such Penalties, as each House may provide.

Each House may determine the Rules of its Proceedings, punish its Members for disorderly Behaviour, and, with the Concurrence of two thirds, expel a Member.

Each House shall keep a Journal of its Proceedings, and from time to time publish the same, excepting such Parts as may in their Judgment require Secrecy; and the Yeas and Nays of the Members of either House on any question shall, at the Desire of one fifth of those Present, be entered on the Journal.

Neither House, during the Session of Congress, shall, without the Consent of the other, adjourn for more than three days, nor to any other Place than that in which the two Houses shall be sitting.

SECTION 6.

The Senators and Representatives shall receive a Compensation for their Services, to be ascertained by Law, and paid out of the Treasury of the United States. They shall in all Cases, except Treason, Felony, and Breach of the Peace, be privileged from Arrest during their Attendance at the Session of their respective Houses, and in going to and returning from the same; and for any Speech or Debate in either House, they shall not be questioned in any other Place.

No Senator or Representative shall, during the Time for which he was elected, be appointed to any civil Office under the Authority of the United States, which shall have been created, or the Emoluments whereof shall have been increased, during such time; and no Person holding any Office under the United States shall be a Member of either House during his continuance in Office.

SECTION 7.

All Bills for raising Revenue shall originate in the House of Representatives; but the Senate may propose or concur with Amendments as on other bills.

Every Bill which shall have passed the House of Representatives and the Senate, shall, before it become a Law, be presented to the President of the United States; If he approve he shall sign it, but if not he shall return it, with his Objections, to that House in which it shall have originated, who shall enter the Objections at large on their Journal, and proceed to reconsider it. If after such Reconsideration two thirds of that House shall agree to pass the bill, it shall be sent, together with the objections, to the other House, by which it shall likewise be reconsidered, and if approved by two thirds of that House, it shall become a Law. But in all such Cases the Votes of both Houses shall be determined by Yeas and Nays, and the Names of the Persons voting for and against the Bill shall be entered on the Journal of each House respectively. If any Bill shall not be returned by the President within ten Days (Sundays excepted) after it shall have been presented to him, the Same shall be a Law, in like Manner as if he had signed it, unless the Congress by their Adjournment prevent its Return, in which Case it shall not be a Law.

Every Order, Resolution, or Vote to which the Concurrence of the Senate and House of Representatives may be necessary (except on a question of Adjournment) shall be presented to the President of the United States; and before the Same shall take Effect, shall be approved by him, or being disapproved by him, shall be repassed by two thirds of the Senate and House of Representatives, according to the Rules and Limitations prescribed in the Case of a Bill.

SECTION 8.

The Congress shall have Power To lay and collect Taxes, Duties, Imposts and Excises, to pay the Debts and provide for the common Defence and general Welfare of the United States; but all Duties, Imposts and Excises shall be uniform throughout the United States;

To borrow money on the credit of the United States;

To regulate Commerce with foreign Nations, and among the several States, and with the Indian Tribes;

To establish an uniform rule of Naturalization, and uniform Laws on the subject of Bankruptcies throughout the United States;

To coin Money, regulate the Value thereof, and of foreign Coin, and fix the Standard of Weights and Measures;

To provide for the Punishment of counterfeiting the Securities and current Coin of the United States;

To establish Post Offices and post Roads;

To promote the Progress of Science and useful Arts, by securing for limited Times to Authors and Inventors the exclusive Right to their respective Writings and Discoveries;

To constitute Tribunals inferior to the Supreme Court;

To define and punish Piracies and Felonies committed on the high Seas, and Offenses against the Law of Nations;

To declare War, grant Letters of Marque and Reprisal, and make Rules concerning Captures on Land and Water;

To raise and support Armies, but no Appropriation of Money to that Use shall be for a longer Term than two Years;

To provide and maintain a Navy;

To make Rules for the Government and Regulation of the land and naval forces;

To provide for calling forth the Militia to execute the Laws of the Union, suppress Insurrections and repel Invasions;

To provide for organizing, arming, and disciplining the Militia, and for governing such Part of them as may be employed in the Service of the United States, reserving to the States respectively, the Appointment of the Officers, and the Authority of training the Militia according to the discipline prescribed by Congress;

To exercise exclusive Legislation in all Cases whatsoever, over such District (not exceeding ten Miles square) as may, by Cession of particular States, and the acceptance of Congress, become the Seat of the Government of the United States, and to exercise like Authority over all Places purchased by the Consent of the Legislature of the State in which the Same shall be, for the Erection of Forts, Magazines, Arsenals, Dock-yards, and other needful Buildings;—And

To make all Laws which shall be necessary and proper for carrying into Execution the foregoing Powers, and all other Powers vested by this Constitution in the Government of the United States, or in any Department or Officer thereof.

SECTION 9.

The Migration or Importation of such Persons as any of the States now existing shall think proper to admit, shall not be prohibited by the Congress prior to the Year one thousand eight hundred and eight, but a tax or duty may be imposed on such Importation, not exceeding ten dollars for each Person.

The privilege of the Writ of Habeas Corpus shall not be suspended, unless when in Cases of Rebellion or Invasion the public Safety may require it.

No bill of Attainder or ex post facto Law shall be passed.

No capitation, or other direct, Tax shall be laid unless in Proportion to the Census or Enumeration herein before directed to be taken.

No Tax or Duty shall be laid on Articles exported from any State.

No Preference shall be given by any Regulation of Commerce or Revenue to the Ports of one State over those of another: nor shall Vessels bound to, or from, one State, be obliged to enter, clear, or pay Duties in another.

No Money shall be drawn from the Treasury, but in Consequence of Appropriations made by Law; and a regular Statement and Account of the Receipts and Expenditures of all public Money shall be published from time to time.

No Title of Nobility shall be granted by the United States: And no Person holding any Office of Profit or Trust under them, shall, without the Consent of the Congress, accept of any present, Emolument, Office, or Title, of any kind whatever, from any King, Prince, or foreign State.

SECTION 10.
No State shall enter into any Treaty, Alliance, or Confederation; grant Letters of Marque and Reprisal; coin Money; emit Bills of Credit; make any Thing but gold and silver Coin a Tender in Payment of Debts; pass any Bill of Attainder, ex post facto Law, or Law impairing the Obligation of Contracts, or grant any Title of Nobility.

No State shall, without the Consent of the Congress, lay any Imposts or Duties on Imports or Exports, except what may be absolutely necessary for executing its inspection Laws; and the net Produce of all Duties and Imposts, laid by any State on Imports or Exports, shall be for the Use of the Treasury of the United States; and all such Laws shall be subject to the Revision and Control of the Congress.

No state shall, without the Consent of Congress, lay any duty of Tonnage, keep Troops, or Ships of War in time of Peace, enter into any Agreement or Compact with another State, or with a foreign Power, or engage in War, unless actually invaded, or in such imminent Danger as will not admit of delay.

Article II

SECTION 1.
The executive Power shall be vested in a President of the United States of America. He shall hold his Office during the Term of four years, and, together with the Vice President, chosen for the same Term, be elected, as follows:

Each State shall appoint, in such Manner as the Legislature thereof may direct, a Number of Electors, equal to the whole Number of Senators and Representatives to which the State may be entitled in the Congress: but no Senator or Representative, or Person holding an Office of Trust or Profit under the United States, shall be appointed an Elector.

[The Electors shall meet in their respective States, and vote by Ballot for two persons, of whom one at least shall not be an Inhabitant of the same State with themselves. And they shall make a List of all the Persons voted for, and of the Number of Votes for each; which List they shall sign and certify, and transmit sealed to the Seat of the Government of the United States, directed to the President of the Senate. The President of the Senate shall, in the Presence of the Senate and House of Representatives, open all the Certificates, and the Votes shall then be counted. The Person having the greatest Number of Votes shall be the President, if such Number be a Majority of the whole Number of Electors appointed; and if there be more than one who have such Majority, and have an equal Number of Votes, then the House of Representatives shall immediately chuse by Ballot one of them for President; and if no Person have a Majority, then from the five highest on the List the said House shall in like Manner chuse the President. But in chusing the President, the Votes shall be taken by States, the Representation from each State having one Vote; a quorum for this Purpose shall consist of a Member or Members from two-thirds of the States, and a Majority of all the States shall be necessary to a Choice. In every Case, after the Choice of the President, the Person having the greatest Number of Votes of the Electors shall be the Vice President. But if there should remain two or more who have equal votes, the Senate shall chuse from them by Ballot the Vice President.][4]

The Congress may determine the Time of chusing the Electors, and the Day on which they shall give their Votes; which Day shall be the same throughout the United States.

No person except a natural-born Citizen, or a Citizen of the United States, at the time of the Adoption of this Constitution, shall be eligible to the Office of President; neither shall any Person be eligible to that Office who shall not have attained to the Age of thirty-five years, and been fourteen Years a Resident within the United States.

In Case of the Removal of the President from Office, or of his Death, Resignation, or Inability to discharge the Powers and Duties of the said Office, the same shall devolve on the Vice President, and the Congress may by Law provide for the Case of Removal, Death, Resignation, or Inability, both of the President and Vice President, declaring what Officer shall then act as President, and such Officer shall act accordingly, until the disability be removed, or a President shall be elected.

The President shall, at stated Times, receive for his Services a Compensation, which shall neither be increased nor diminished during the Period for which he shall have been elected, and he shall not receive within that Period any other Emolument from the United States, or any of them.

Before he enter on the execution of his Office, he shall take the following Oath or Affirmation:—"I do solemnly swear (or affirm) that I will faithfully execute the Office of President of the United States, and will, to the best of my Ability, preserve, protect, and defend the Constitution of the United States."

SECTION 2.

The President shall be Commander in Chief of the Army and Navy of the United States, and of the Militia of the several States, when called into the actual Service of the United States; he may require the Opinion, in writing, of the principal Officer in each of the executive Departments, upon any subject relating to the Duties of their respective Offices, and he shall have Power to Grant Reprieves

and Pardons for Offenses against the United States, except in Cases of Impeachment.

He shall have Power, by and with the Advice and Consent of the Senate, to make Treaties, provided two-thirds of the Senators present concur; and he shall nominate, and by and with the Advice and Consent of the Senate, shall appoint Ambassadors, other public Ministers and Consuls, Judges of the supreme Court, and all other Officers of the United States, whose Appointments are not herein otherwise provided for, and which shall be established by Law: but the Congress may by Law vest the Appointment of such inferior Officers, as they think proper, in the President alone, in the Courts of Law, or in the Heads of Departments.

The President shall have Power to fill up all Vacancies that may happen during the Recess of the Senate, by granting Commissions which shall expire at the End of their next Session.

SECTION 3.

He shall from time to time give to the Congress Information of the State of the Union, and recommend to their Consideration such Measures as he shall judge necessary and expedient; he may, on extraordinary occasions, convene both Houses, or either of them, and in Case of Disagreement between them, with respect to the Time of Adjournment, he may adjourn them to such Time as he shall think proper; he shall receive Ambassadors and other public Ministers; he shall take care that the Laws be faithfully executed, and shall Commission all the Officers of the United States.

SECTION 4.

The President, Vice President and all civil Officers of the United States, shall be removed from Office on Impeachment for, and Conviction of, Treason, Bribery, or other high Crimes and Misdemeanors.

Article III

SECTION 1.

The judicial Power of the United States, shall be vested in one supreme Court, and in such inferior Courts as the Congress may from time to time ordain and establish. The

---

[4] Revised by the Twelfth Amendment.

Judges, both of the supreme and inferior Courts, shall hold their Offices during good Behaviour, and shall, at stated Times, receive for their Services, a Compensation, which shall not be diminished during their Continuance in Office.

SECTION 2.

The judicial Power shall extend to all Cases, in Law and Equity, arising under this Constitution, the Laws of the United States, and Treaties made, or which shall be made, under their Authority;—to all Cases affecting ambassadors, other public ministers and consuls;—to all cases of admiralty and maritime Jurisdiction;—to Controversies to which the United States shall be a Party;—to Controversies between two or more States;—between a State and Citizens of another State;[5]—between Citizens of different States,—between Citizens of the same State claiming Lands under Grants of different States, and between a State, or the Citizens thereof, and foreign States, Citizens or Subjects.

In all Cases affecting Ambassadors, other public Ministers and Consuls, and those in which a State shall be Party, the supreme Court shall have original Jurisdiction. In all the other Cases before mentioned, the supreme Court shall have appellate Jurisdiction, both as to Law and Fact, with such Exceptions, and under such Regulations as the Congress shall make.

The trial of all Crimes, except in Cases of Impeachment, shall be by Jury; and such Trial shall be held in the State where the said Crimes shall have been committed; but when not committed within any State, the Trial shall be at such Place or Places as the Congress may by Law have directed.

SECTION 3.

Treason against the United States, shall consist only in levying War against them, or in adhering to their Enemies, giving them Aid and Comfort. No Person shall be convicted of Treason unless on the Testimony of two Witnesses to the same overt Act, or on Confession in open Court.

The Congress shall have power to declare

the Punishment of Treason, but no Attainder of Treason shall work Corruption of Blood, or Forfeiture except during the Life of the Person attainted.

Article IV

SECTION 1.

Full Faith and Credit shall be given in each State to the public Acts, Records, and judicial Proceedings of every other State. And the Congress may by general Laws prescribe the Manner in which such Acts, Records and Proceedings shall be proved, and the Effect thereof.

SECTION 2.

The Citizens of each State shall be entitled to all Privileges and Immunities of Citizens in the several States.

A Person charged in any State with Treason, Felony, or other Crime, who shall flee from Justice, and be found in another State, shall on demand of the executive Authority of the State from which he fled, be delivered up, to be removed to the State having Jurisdiction of the crime.

No Person held to Service or Labour in one State, under the Laws thereof, escaping into another, shall, in Consequence of any Law or Regulation therein, be discharged from such Service or Labour, but shall be delivered up on Claim of the Party to whom such Service or Labour may be due.

SECTION 3.

New States may be admitted by the Congress into this Union; but no new State shall be formed or erected within the Jurisdiction of any other State; nor any State be formed by the Junction of two or more States, or parts of States, without the Consent of the Legislatures of the States concerned as well as of the Congress.

The Congress shall have Power to dispose of and make all needful Rules and Regulations respecting the Territory or other Property belonging to the United States; and nothing in this Constitution shall be so construed as to Prejudice any Claims of the United States, or of any particular State.

---

[5] Qualified by the Eleventh Amendment.

SECTION 4.

The United States shall guarantee to every State in this Union a Republican Form of Government, and shall protect each of them against Invasion; and on Application of the Legislature, or of the Executive (when the Legislature cannot be convened) against domestic Violence.

Article V

The Congress, whenever two-thirds of both Houses shall deem it necessary, shall propose Amendments to this Constitution, or, on the Application of the Legislatures of two-thirds of the several States, shall call a Convention for proposing Amendments, which, in either Case, shall be valid to all Intents and Purposes, as part of this Constitution, when ratified by the Legislatures of three-fourths of the several States, or by Conventions in three-fourths thereof, as the one or the other Mode of Ratification may be proposed by the Congress; Provided that no Amendment which may be made prior to the Year One thousand eight hundred and eight shall in any Manner affect the first and fourth Clauses in the Ninth Section of the first Article; and that no State, without its Consent, shall be deprived of its equal Suffrage in the Senate.

Article VI

All Debts contracted and Engagements entered into, before the Adoption of this Constitution, shall be as valid against the United States under this Constitution, as under the Confederation.

This Constitution, and the Laws of the United States which shall be made in Pursuance thereof; and all Treaties made, or which shall be made, under the Authority of the United States, shall be the supreme Law of the Land; and the Judges in every State shall be bound thereby, and Thing in the Constitution or Laws of any State to the Contrary notwithstanding.

The Senators and Representatives before mentioned, and the Members of the several State Legislatures, and all executive and judicial Officers, both of the United States and of the several States, shall be bound by Oath or Affirmation to support this Constitution; but no religious Test shall ever be required as a qualification to any Office or public Trust under the United States.

Article VII

The Ratification of the Conventions of nine States shall be sufficient for the Establishment of this Constitution between the States so ratifying the same.

Done in Convention by the Unanimous Consent of the States present the Seventeenth Day of September in the Year of our Lord one thousand seven hundred and Eighty seven, and of the Independence of the United States of America the Twelfth. In Witness whereof We have hereunto subscribed our Names.[6]

George Washington
President and deputy from Virginia

New Hampshire	New Jersey	Delaware	North Carolina
John Langdon	William Livingston	George Read	William Blount
Nicholas Gilman	David Brearley	Gunning Bedford, Jr.	Richard Dobbs
	William Paterson	John Dickinson	Spaight
	Jonathan Dayton	Richard Bassett	Hugh Williamson
		Jacob Broom	

---

[6] These are the full names of the signers, which in some cases are not the signatures on the document.

Massachusetts

Nathaniel Gorham
Rufus King

Connecticut

William Samuel
   Johnson
Roger Sherman

New York

Alexander Hamilton

Pennsylvania

Benjamin Franklin
Thomas Mifflin
Robert Morris
George Clymer
Thomas FitzSimons
Jared Ingersoll
James Wilson
Gouverneur Morris

Maryland

James McHenry
Daniel of
   St. Thomas Jenifer
Daniel Carroll

Virginia

John Blair
James Madison, Jr.

South Carolina

John Rutledge
Charles Cotesworth
   Pinckney
Charles Pinckney
Pierce Butler

Georgia

William Few
Abraham Baldwin

Articles in Addition to, and Amendment of, the Constitution of the United States of America, Proposed by Congress, and Ratified by the Legislatures of the Several States, Pursuant to the Fifth Article of the Original Constitution[7]

[Article I]

Congress shall make no law respecting an establishment of religion, or prohibiting the free exercise thereof; or abridging the freedom of speech, or of the press; or the right of the people peaceably to assemble, and to petition the Government for a redress of grievances.

[Article II]

A well regulated Militia, being necessary to the security of a free State, the right of the people to keep and bear Arms shall not be infringed.

[Article III]

No Soldier shall, in time of peace, be quartered in any house, without the consent of the Owner, nor in time of war, but in a manner to be prescribed by law.

---

[7] This heading appears only in the joint resolution submitting the first ten amendments.

[Article IV]

The right of the people to be secure in their persons, houses, papers, and effects, against unreasonable searches and seizures, shall not be violated, and no Warrants shall issue, but upon probable cause, supported by Oath or affirmation, and particularly describing the place to be searched, and the persons or things to be seized.

[Article V]

No person shall be held to answer for a capital or otherwise infamous crime, unless on a presentment or indictment of a Grand Jury, except in cases arising in the land or naval forces, or in the Militia, when in actual service in time of War or public danger; nor shall any person be subject for the same offence to be twice put in jeopardy of life or limb; nor shall be compelled in any criminal case to be a witness against himself, nor be deprived of life, liberty, or property, without due process of law; nor shall private property be taken for public use, without just compensation.

[Article VI]

In all criminal prosecutions, the accused shall enjoy the right to a speedy and public trial, by an impartial jury of the State and district wherein the crime shall have been committed, which district shall have been previously ascertained by law, and to be informed of the nature and cause of the accusation; to be confronted with the witnesses against him; to have compulsory process for obtaining witnesses in his favour, and to have the Assistance of Counsel for his defence.

[Article VII]

In suits at common law, where the value in controversy shall exceed twenty dollars, the right of trial by jury shall be preserved, and no fact tried by a jury, shall be otherwise reexamined in any Court of the United States, than according to the rules of the common law.

[Article VIII]

Excessive bail shall not be required, nor excessive fines imposed, nor cruel and unusual punishments inflicted.

[Article IX]

The enumeration of the Constitution, of certain rights, shall not be construed to deny or disparage others retained by the people.

[Article X]

The powers not delegated to the United States by the Constitution, nor prohibited by it to the States, are reserved to the States respectively, or to the people.

[Amendments I-X, in force 1791.]

[Article XI][8]

The Judicial power of the United States shall not be construed to extend to any suit in law or equity, commenced or prosecuted against one of the United States by Citizens of another State, or by Citizens or Subjects of any Foreign State.

[Article XII][9]

The Electors shall meet in their respective States and vote by ballot for President and Vice-President, one of whom, at least, shall not be an inhabitant of the same State with themselves; they shall name in their ballots the person voted for as President, and in distinct ballots the person voted for as Vice-President, and they shall make distinct lists of all persons voted for as President, and of all persons voted for as Vice-President, and of the number of votes for each, which lists they shall sign and certify, and transmit sealed to the seat of the government of the United States, directed to the President of the Senate;—The President of the Senate shall, in the presence of the Senate and House of Representatives, open all the certificates and the votes shall then be counted;—The person having the greatest number of votes for President, shall be the President, if such number be a majority of the whole number of Electors appointed; and if no person have such majority, then from the persons having the highest numbers not exceeding three on the list of those voted for as President, the House of Representatives shall choose immediately, by ballot, the President. But in choosing the President, the votes shall be taken by states, the representation from each state having one vote; a quorum for this purpose shall consist of a member or members from two-thirds of the states, and a majority of all the states shall be necessary to a choice. And if the House of Representatives shall not choose a President whenever the right of choice shall devolve upon them, before the fourth day of March next following, then the Vice-President shall act as President, as in the case of the death or other constitutional disability of the President.—The person having the greatest number of votes as Vice-President, shall be the Vice-President, if such number be a majority of the whole number

---

[8] Adopted in 1798.

[9] Adopted in 1804.

of Electors appointed, and if no person have a majority, then from the two highest numbers on the list, the Senate shall choose the Vice-President; a quorum for the purpose shall consist of two-thirds of the whole number of Senators, and a majority of the whole number shall be necessary to a choice. But no person constitutionally ineligible to the office of President shall be eligible to that of Vice-President of the United States.

[Article XIII][10]

SECTION 1.
Neither slavery nor involuntary servitude, except as a punishment for crime whereof the party shall have been duly convicted, shall exist within the United States, or any place subject to their jurisdiction.

SECTION 2.
Congress shall have power to enforce this article by appropriate legislation.

[Article XIV][11]

SECTION 1.
All persons born or naturalized in the United States, and subject to the jurisdiction thereof, are citizens of the United States and of the State wherein they reside. No State shall abridge the privileges or immunities of citizens of the United States; nor shall any State deprive any person of life, liberty, or property, without due process of law; nor deny to any person within its jurisdiction the equal protection of the laws.

SECTION 2.
Representatives shall be apportioned among the several States according to their respective numbers, counting the whole number of persons in each State, excluding Indians not taxed. But when the right to vote at any election for the choice of electors for President and Vice-President of the United States, Representatives in Congress, the Executive and Judicial officers of a State, or the members of the Legislature thereof, is denied to any of the male inhabitants of such State, being twenty-one years of age, and citizens of the United States, or in any way abridged, except for participation in rebellion, or other crime, the basis of representation therein shall be reduced in the proportion which the number of such male citizens shall bear to the whole number of male citizens twenty-one years of age in such State.

SECTION 3.
No person shall be a Senator or Representative in Congress, or elector of President and Vice-President, or hold any office, civil or military, under the United States, or under any State, who, having previously taken an oath, as a member of Congress, or as an officer of the United States, or as a member of any State legislature, or as an executive or judicial officer of any State, to support the Constitution of the United States, shall have engaged in insurrection or rebellion against the same, or given aid or comfort to the enemies thereof. But Congress may by a vote of two-thirds of each House, remove such disability.

SECTION 4.
The validity of the public debt of the United States, authorized by law, including debts incurred for payment of pensions and bounties for services in suppressing insurrection or rebellion, shall not be questioned. But neither the United States nor any State shall assume or pay any debts or obligation incurred in aid of insurrection or rebellion against the United States, or any claim for the loss or emancipation of any slave; but all such debts, obligations, and claims shall be held illegal and void.

SECTION 5.
The Congress shall have the power to enforce, by appropriate legislation, the provisions of this article.

---

[10] Adopted in 1865.
[11] Adopted in 1868.

[Article XV][12]

SECTION 1.
The right of citizens of the United States to vote shall not be denied or abridged by the United States or by any State on account of race, color, or previous condition of servitude—

SECTION 2.
The Congress shall have power to enforce this article by appropriate legislation.

[Article XVI][13]

The Congress shall have power to lay and collect taxes on incomes, from whatever source derived, without apportionment among the several States, and without regard to any census or enumeration.

[Article XVII][14]

The Senate of the United States shall be composed of two Senators from each State, elected by the people thereof, for six years; and each Senator shall have one vote. The electors in each State shall have the qualifications requisite for electors of the most numerous branch of the State legislatures.

When vacancies happen in the representation of any State in the Senate, the executive authority of such State shall issue writs of election to fill such vacancies: *Provided,* That the legislature of any State may empower the executive thereof to make temporary appointments until the people fill the vacancies by election as the legislature may direct.

This amendment shall not be so construed as to affect the election or term of any Senator chosen before it becomes valid as part of the Constitution.

[Article XVIII][15]

SECTION 1.
After one year from the ratification of this article the manufacture, sale, or transportation of intoxicating liquors within, the importation thereof into, or the exportation thereof from the United States and all territory subject to the jurisdiction thereof for beverage purposes is hereby prohibited.

SECTION 2.
The Congress and the several States shall have concurrent power to enforce this article by appropriate legislation.

SECTION 3.
This article shall be inoperative unless it shall have been ratified as an amendment to the Constitution by the legislatures of the several States, as provided in the Constitution, within seven years from the date of the submission hereof to the States by the Congress.

[Article XIX][16]

The right of citizens of the United States to vote shall not be denied or abridged by the United States or by any State on account of sex.

Congress shall have power to enforce this article by appropriate legislation.

[Article XX][17]

SECTION 1.
The terms of the President and Vice-President shall end at noon on the 20th day of January, and the terms of Senators and Representatives at noon on the 3d day of January, of the years in which such terms would have ended if this article had not been

---

[12] Adopted in 1870.
[13] Adopted in 1913.
[14] Adopted in 1913.

[15] Adopted in 1918.
[16] Adopted in 1920.
[17] Adopted in 1933.

ratified; and the terms of their successors shall then begin.

SECTION 2.
The Congress shall assemble at least once in every year, and such meeting shall begin at noon on the 3d day of January, unless they shall by law appoint a different day.

SECTION 3.
If, at the time fixed for the beginning of the term of the President, the President elect shall have died, the Vice-President elect shall become President. If a President shall not have been chosen before the time fixed for the beginning of his term, or if the President elect shall have failed to qualify, then the Vice-President elect shall act as President until a President shall have qualified; and the Congress may by law provide for the case wherein neither a President elect nor a Vice-President elect shall have qualified, declaring who shall then act as President, or the manner in which one who is to act shall be selected, and such person shall act accordingly until a President or Vice-President shall have qualified.

SECTION 4.
The Congress may by law provide for the case of the death of any of the persons from whom the House of Representatives may choose a President whenever the right of choice shall have devolved upon them, and for the case of the death of any of the persons from whom the Senate may choose a Vice-President whenever the right of choice shall have devolved upon them.

SECTION 5.
Sections 1 and 2 shall take effect on the 15th day of October following the ratification of this article.

SECTION 6.
This article shall be inoperative unless it shall have been ratified as an amendment to the Constitution by the legislatures of three-fourths of the several States within seven years from the date of its submission.

[Article XXI][18]

SECTION 1.
The eighteenth article of amendment to the Constitution of the United States is hereby repealed.

SECTION 2.
The transportation or importation into any State, Territory, or possession of the United States for delivery or use therein of intoxicating liquors, in violation of the laws thereof, is hereby prohibited.

SECTION 3.
This article shall be inoperative unless it shall have been ratified as an amendment to the Constitution by conventions in the several States, as provided in the Constitution, within seven years from the date of the submission hereof to the States by the Congress.

[Article XXII][19]

No person shall be elected to the office of the President more than twice, and no person who has held the office of President, or acted as President, for more than two years of a term to which some other person was elected President shall be elected to the office of the President more than once.

But this Article shall not apply to any person holding the office of President when this Article was proposed by the Congress, and shall not prevent any person who may be holding the office of President, or acting as President, during the term within which this Article becomes operative from holding the office of President or acting as President during the remainder of such term.

This article shall be inoperative unless it shall have been ratified as an amendment to the Constitution by the legislatures of three-fourths of the several states within seven years from the date of its submission to the states by the Congress.

---

[18] Adopted in 1933.
[19] Adopted in 1951.

[Article XXIII][20]

SECTION 1.
The District constituting the seat of Government of the United States shall appoint in such manner as the Congress may direct:

A number of electors of President and Vice-President equal to the whole number of Senators and Representatives in Congress to which the District would be entitled if it were a State, but in no event more than the least populous State; they shall be in addition to those appointed by the States, but they shall be considered, for the purposes of the election of President and Vice-President, to be electors appointed by a State; and they shall meet in the District and perform such duties as provided by the twelfth article of amendment.

SECTION 2.
The Congress shall have power to enforce this article by appropriate legislation.

[Article XXIV][21]

SECTION 1.
The right of citizens of the United States to vote in any primary or other election for President or Vice President, for electors for President or Vice President, or for Senator or Representative in Congress, shall not be denied or abridged by the United States or any state by reason of failure to pay any poll tax or other tax.

SECTION 2.
The Congress shall have the power to enforce this article by appropriate legislation.

[Article XXV][22]

SECTION 1.
In case of the removal of the President from office or of his death or resignation, the Vice President shall become President.

SECTION 2.
Whenever there is a vacancy in the office of the Vice President, the President shall nominate a Vice President who shall take office upon confirmation by a majority vote of both Houses of Congress.

SECTION 3.
Whenever the President transmits to the President Pro Tempore of the Senate and the Speaker of the House of Representatives his written declaration that he is unable to discharge the powers and duties of his office, and until he transmits to them a written declaration to the contrary, such powers and duties shall be discharged by the Vice President as Acting President.

SECTION 4.
Whenever the Vice President and a majority of either the principal officers of the executive departments or of such other body as Congress may by law provide, transmit to the President Pro Tempore of the Senate and the Speaker of the House of Representatives their written declaration that the President is unable to discharge the powers and duties of his office, the Vice President shall immediately assume the powers and duties of the office as Acting President.

Thereafter, when the President transmits to the President Pro Tempore of the Senate and the Speaker of the House of Representatives his written declaration that no inability exists, he shall resume the powers and duties of his office unless the Vice President and a majority of either the principal officers of the executive departments or of such other body as Congress may by law provide, transmit within four days to the President Pro Tempore of the Senate and the Speaker of the House of Representatives their written declaration that the President is unable to discharge the powers and duties of his office. Thereupon Congress shall decide the issue, assembling within forty-eight hours for that purpose if not in session. If the Congress, within twenty-one days after receipt of the latter written declaration, or, if Congress is not in session, within twenty-one days after Congress is required to assemble, determines by two-thirds vote of both Houses that the

---

[20] Adopted in 1961.
[21] Adopted in 1964.
[22] Adopted in 1967.

President is unable to discharge the powers and duties of his office, the Vice President shall continue to discharge the same as Acting President; otherwise, the President shall resume the powers and duties of his office.

[Article XXVI][23]

SECTION 1.
The right of citizens of the United States,

[23] Adopted in 1971.

who are eighteen years of age or older, to vote shall not be denied or abridged by the United States or by any State on account of age.

SECTION 2.
The Congress shall have power to enforce this article by appropriate legislation.

ADMISSION OF STATES TO THE UNION*

1	Delaware	Dec. 7, 1787	26	Michigan	Jan. 26, 1837
2	Pennsylvania	Dec. 12, 1787	27	Florida	Mar. 3, 1845
3	New Jersey	Dec. 18, 1787	28	Texas	Dec. 29, 1845
4	Georgia	Jan. 2, 1788	29	Iowa	Dec. 28, 1846
5	Connecticut	Jan. 9, 1788	30	Wisconsin	May 29, 1848
6	Massachusetts	Feb. 6, 1788	31	California	Sept. 9, 1850
7	Maryland	Apr. 28, 1788	32	Minnesota	May 11, 1858
8	South Carolina	May 23, 1788	33	Oregon	Feb. 14, 1859
9	New Hampshire	June 21, 1788	34	Kansas	Jan. 29, 1861
10	Virginia	June 25, 1788	35	West Virginia	June 19, 1863
11	New York	July 26, 1788	36	Nevada	Oct. 31, 1864
12	North Carolina	Nov. 21, 1789	37	Nebraska	Mar. 1, 1867
13	Rhode Island	May 29, 1790	38	Colorado	Aug. 1, 1876
14	Vermont	Mar. 4, 1791	39	North Dakota	Nov. 2, 1889
15	Kentucky	June 1, 1792	40	South Dakota	Nov. 2, 1889
16	Tennessee	June 1, 1796	41	Montana	Nov. 8, 1889
17	Ohio	Mar. 1, 1803	42	Washington	Nov. 11, 1889
18	Louisiana	Apr. 30, 1812	43	Idaho	July 3, 1890
19	Indiana	Dec. 11, 1816	44	Wyoming	July 10, 1890
20	Mississippi	Dec. 10, 1817	45	Utah	Jan. 4, 1896
21	Illinois	Dec. 3, 1818	46	Oklahoma	Nov. 16, 1907
22	Alabama	Dec. 14, 1819	47	New Mexico	Jan. 6, 1912
23	Maine	Mar. 15, 1820	48	Arizona	Feb. 14, 1912
24	Missouri	Aug. 10, 1821	49	Alaska	Jan. 3, 1959
25	Arkansas	June 15, 1836	50	Hawaii	Aug. 21, 1959

* In the case of the first thirteen states, the date given is that of ratification of the Constitution.

PRESIDENTIAL ELECTIONS

Year	Candidates	Parties	Popular Vote	Percentage of Popular Vote	Electoral Vote
1789	GEORGE WASHINGTON (Va.)*				69
	John Adams				34
	Others				35
1792	GEORGE WASHINGTON (Va.)				132
	John Adams				77
	George Clinton				50
	Others				5
1796	JOHN ADAMS (Mass.)	Federalist			71
	Thomas Jefferson	Democratic-Republican			68
	Thomas Pinckney	Federalist			59
	Aaron Burr	Dem.-Rep.			30
	Others				48
1800	THOMAS JEFFERSON (Va.)	Dem.-Rep.			73
	Aaron Burr	Dem.-Rep.			73
	John Adams	Federalist			65
	C. C. Pinckney	Federalist			64
	John Jay	Federalist			1
1804	THOMAS JEFFERSON (Va.)	Dem.-Rep.			162
	C. C. Pinckney	Federalist			14
1808	JAMES MADISON (Va.)	Dem.-Rep.			122
	C. C. Pinckney	Federalist			47
	George Clinton	Dem.-Rep.			6
1812	JAMES MADISON (Va.)	Dem.-Rep.			128
	De Witt Clinton	Federalist			89
1816	JAMES MONROE (Va.)	Dem.-Rep.			183
	Rufus King	Federalist			34
1820	JAMES MONROE (Va.)	Dem.-Rep.			231
	John Quincy Adams	Dem.-Rep.			1
1824	JOHN Q. ADAMS (Mass.)	Dem.-Rep.	108,740	30.5	84
	Andrew Jackson	Dem.-Rep.	153,544	43.1	99
	William H. Crawford	Dem.-Rep.	46,618	13.1	41
	Henry Clay	Dem.-Rep.	47,136	13.2	37
1828	ANDREW JACKSON (Tenn.)	Democrat	647,286	56.0	178
	John Quincy Adams	National Republican	508,064	44.0	83
1832	ANDREW JACKSON (TENN.)	Democrat	687,502	55.0	219
	Henry Clay	National Republican ⎫	530,189	42.4	49
	John Floyd	Independent ⎬			11
	William Wirt	Anti-Mason	33,108	2.6	7
1836	MARTIN VAN BUREN (N.Y.)	Democrat	765,483	50.9	170
	W. H. Harrison	Whig ⎫			73
	Hugh L. White	Whig ⎬	739,795	49.1	26
	Daniel Webster	Whig ⎪			14
	W. P. Magnum	Independent ⎭			11

* State of residence at time of election.

Year	Candidates	Parties	Popular Vote	Percentage of Popular Vote	Electoral Vote
1840	**WILLIAM H. HARRISON (Ohio)**	Whig	1,274,624	53.1	234
	Martin Van Buren	Democrat	1,127,781	46.9	60
	J. G. Birney	Liberty	7,069		—
1844	**JAMES K. POLK (Tenn.)**	Democrat	1,338,464	49.6	170
	Henry Clay	Whig	1,300,097	48.1	105
	J. G. Birney	Liberty	62,300	2.3	—
1848	**ZACHARY TAYLOR (La.)**	Whig	1,360,967	47.4	163
	Lewis Cass	Democrat	1,222,342	42.5	127
	Martin Van Buren	Free-Soil	291,263	10.1	—
1852	**FRANKLIN PIERCE (N.H.)**	Democrat	1,601,117	50.9	254
	Winfield Scott	Whig	1,385,453	44.1	42
	John P. Hale	Free-Soil	155,825	5.0	—
1856	**JAMES BUCHANAN (Pa.)**	Democrat	1,832,955	45.3	174
	John C. Frémont	Republican	1,339,932	33.1	114
	Millard Fillmore	American	871,731	21.6	8
1860	**ABRAHAM LINCOLN (Ill.)**	Republican	1,865,593	39.8	180
	Stephen A. Douglas	Democrat	1,382,713	29.5	12
	John C. Breckinridge	Democrat	848,356	18.1	72
	John Bell	Union	592,906	12.6	39
1864	**ABRAHAM LINCOLN (Ill.)**	Republican	2,213,655	55.0	212
	George B. McClellan	Democrat	1,805,237	45.0	21
1868	**ULYSSES S. GRANT (Ill.)**	Republican	3,012,833	52.7	214
	Horatio Seymour	Democrat	2,703,249	47.3	80
1872	**ULYSSES S. GRANT (Ill.)**	Republican	3,597,132	55.6	286
	Horace Greeley	Democrat; Liberal Republican	2,834,125	43.9	66
1876	**RUTHERFORD B. HAYES (Ohio)**	Republican	4,036,298	48.0	185
	Samuel J. Tilden	Democrat	4,300,590	51.0	184
1880	**JAMES A. GARFIELD (Ohio)**	Republican	4,454,416	48.5	214
	Winfield S. Hancock	Democrat	4,444,952	48.1	155
1884	**GROVER CLEVELAND (N.Y.)**	Democrat	4,874,986	48.5	219
	James G. Blaine	Republican	4,851,981	48.2	182
1888	**BENJAMIN HARRISON (Ind.)**	Republican	5,439,853	47.9	233
	Grover Cleveland	Democrat	5,540,309	48.6	168
1892	**GROVER CLEVELAND (N.Y.)**	Democrat	5,556,918	46.1	277
	Benjamin Harrison	Republican	5,176,108	43.0	145
	James B. Weaver	People's	1,041,028	8.5	22
1896	**WILLIAM McKINLEY (Ohio)**	Republican	7,104,779	51.1	271
	William J. Bryan	Democrat-People's	6,502,925	47.7	176
1900	**WILLIAM McKINLEY (Ohio)**	Republican	7,207,923	51.7	292
	William J. Bryan	Dem.-Populist	6,358,133	45.5	155
1904	**THEODORE ROOSEVELT (N.Y.)**	Republican	7,623,486	57.9	336
	Alton B. Parker	Democrat	5,077,911	37.6	140
	Eugene V. Debs	Socialist	402,283	3.0	—
1908	**WILLIAM H. TAFT (Ohio)**	Republican	7,678,908	51.6	321
	William J. Bryan	Democrat	6,409,104	43.1	162
	Eugene V. Debs	Socialist	420,793	2.8	—

Year	Candidates	Parties	Popular Vote	Percentage of Popular Vote	Electoral Vote
1912	**WOODROW WILSON (N.J.)**	Democrat	6,293,454	41.9	435
	Theodore Roosevelt	Progressive	4,119,538	27.4	88
	William H. Taft	Republican	3,484,980	23.2	8
	Eugene V. Debs	Socialist	900,672	6.0	—
1916	**WOODROW WILSON (N.J.)**	Democrat	9,129,606	49.4	277
	Charles E. Hughes	Republican	8,538,221	46.2	254
	A. L. Benson	Socialist	585,113	3.2	—
1920	**WARREN G. HARDING (Ohio)**	Republican	16,152,200	60.4	404
	James M. Cox	Democrat	9,147,353	34.2	127
	Eugene V. Debs	Socialist	919,799	3.4	—
1924	**CALVIN COOLIDGE (Mass.)**	Republican	15,725,016	54.0	382
	John W. Davis	Democrat	8,386,503	28.8	136
	Robert M. LaFollette	Progressive	4,822,856	16.6	13
1928	**HERBERT HOOVER (Calif.)**	Republican	21,391,381	58.2	444
	Alfred E. Smith	Democrat	15,016,443	40.9	87
	Norman Thomas	Socialist	267,835	0.7	—
1932	**FRANKLIN D. ROOSEVELT (N.Y.)**	Democrat	22,821,857	57.4	472
	Herbert Hoover	Republican	15,761,841	39.7	59
	Norman Thomas	Socialist	881,951	2.2	—
1936	**FRANKLIN D. ROOSEVELT (N.Y.)**	Democrat	27,751,597	60.8	523
	Alfred M. Landon	Republican	16,679,583	36.5	8
	William Lemke	Union	882,479	1.9	—
1940	**FRANKLIN D. ROOSEVELT (N.Y.)**	Democrat	27,244,160	54.8	499
	Wendell L. Willkie	Republican	22,305,198	44.8	82
1944	**FRANKLIN D. ROOSEVELT (N.Y.)**	Democrat	25,602,504	53.5	432
	Thomas E. Dewey	Republican	22,006,285	46.0	99
1948	**HARRY S TRUMAN (Mo.)**	Democrat	24,105,695	49.5	304
	Thomas E. Dewey	Republican	21,969,170	45.1	189
	J. Strom Thurmond	State-Rights Democrat	1,169,021	2.4	38
	Henry A. Wallace	Progressive	1,156,103	2.4	—
1952	**DWIGHT D. EISENHOWER (N.Y.)**	Republican	33,936,252	55.1	442
	Adlai E. Stevenson	Democrat	27,314,992	44.4	89
1956	**DWIGHT D. EISENHOWER (N.Y.)**	Republican	35,575,420	57.6	457
	Adlai E. Stevenson	Democrat	26,033,066	42.1	73
	Other	—	—		1
1960	**JOHN F. KENNEDY (Mass.)**	Democrat	34,227,096	49.9	303
	Richard M. Nixon	Republican	34,108,546	49.6	219
	Other	—	—		15
1964	**LYNDON B. JOHNSON (Tex.)**	Democrat	43,126,506	61.1	486
	Barry M. Goldwater	Republican	27,176,799	38.5	52
1968	**RICHARD M. NIXON (N.Y.)**	Republican	31,770,237	43.4	301
	Hubert H. Humphrey	Democrat	31,270,533	42.7	191
	George Wallace	American Indep.	9,906,141	13.5	46

Year	Candidates	Parties	Popular Vote	Percentage of Popular Vote	Electoral Vote
1972	**RICHARD M. NIXON (N.Y.)**	Republican	47,169,911	60.7	520
	George S. McGovern	Democrat	29,170,383	37.5	17
	Other	—	—		1
1976	**JIMMY CARTER (Ga.)**	Democrat	40,828,587	50.0	297
	Gerald R. Ford	Republican	39,147,613	47.9	241
	Other	—	1,575,459	2.1	—
1980	**RONALD REAGAN (Calif.)**	Republican	43,901,812	50.7	489
	Jimmy Carter	Democrat	35,483,820	41.0	49
	John B. Anderson	Independent	5,719,722	6.6	—
	Ed Clark	Libertarian	921,188	1.1	—

PRESIDENTS, VICE PRESIDENTS, AND SECRETARIES OF STATE

President	Vice President	Secretary of State
1. George Washington, Federalist 1789	John Adams, Federalist 1789	T. Jefferson 1789 E. Randolph 1794 T. Pickering 1795
2. John Adams, Federalist 1797	Thomas Jefferson, Dem.-Rep. 1797	T. Pickering 1797 John Marshall 1800
3. Thomas Jefferson, Dem.-Rep. 1801	Aaron Burr, Dem.-Rep. 1801 George Clinton, Dem.-Rep. 1805	James Madison 1801
4. James Madison, Dem.-Rep. 1809	George Clinton, Dem.-Rep. 1809 Elbridge Gerry, Dem.-Rep. 1813	Robert Smith 1809 James Monroe 1811
5. James Monroe, Dem.-Rep. 1817	D. D. Tompkins, Dem.-Rep. 1817	J. Q. Adams 1817
6. John Quincy Adams, Dem.-Rep. 1825	John C. Calhoun, Dem.-Rep. 1825	Henry Clay 1825
7. Andrew Jackson, Democratic 1829	John C. Calhoun, Democratic 1829 Martin Van Buren, Democratic 1833	M. Van Buren 1829 E. Livingston 1831 Louis McLane 1833 John Forsyth 1834
8. Martin Van Buren, Democratic 1837	Richard M. Johnson, Democratic 1837	John Forsyth 1837
9. William H. Harrison, Whig 1841	John Tyler, Whig 1841	Daniel Webster 1841
10. John Tyler, Whig and Democratic 1841		Daniel Webster 1841 Hugh S. Legare 1843 Abel P. Upshur 1843 John C. Calhoun 1844
11. James K. Polk, Democratic 1845	George M. Dallas, Democratic 1845	James Buchanan 1845
12. Zachary Taylor, Whig 1849	Millard Fillmore, Whig 1848	John M. Clayton 1849
13. Millard Fillmore, Whig 1850		Daniel Webster 1850 Edward Everett 1852

President	Vice President	Secretary of State
14. Franklin Pierce, Democratic 1853	William R. D. King, Democratic 1853	W. L. Marcy 1853
15. James Buchanan, Democratic 1857	John C. Breckinridge, Democratic 1857	Lewis Cass 1857 J. S. Black 1860
16. Abraham Lincoln, Republican 1861	Hannibal Hamlin, Republican 1861 Andrew Johnson, Unionist 1865	W. H. Seward 1861
17. Andrew Johnson, Unionist 1865		W. H. Seward 1865
18. Ulysses S. Grant, Republican 1869	Schuyler Colfax, Republican 1869 Henry Wilson, Republican 1873	E. B. Washburne 1869 H. Fish 1869
19. Rutherford B. Hayes, Republican 1877	William A. Wheeler, Republican 1877	W. M. Evarts 1877
20. James A. Garfield, Republican 1881	Chester A. Arthur, Republican 1881	J. G. Blaine 1881
21. Chester A. Arthur, Republican 1881		F. T. Frelinghuysen 1881
22. Grover Cleveland, Democratic 1885	T. A. Hendricks, Democratic 1885	T. F. Bayard 1885
23. Benjamin Harrison, Republican 1889	Levi P. Morton, Republican 1889	J. G. Blaine 1889 J. W. Foster 1892
24. Grover Cleveland, Democratic 1893	Adlai E. Stevenson, Democratic 1893	W. Q. Gresham 1893 R. Olney 1895
25. William McKinley, Republican 1897	Garret A. Hobart, Republican 1897 Theodore Roosevelt, Republican 1901	J. Sherman 1897 W. R. Day 1897 J. Hay 1898
26. Theodore Roosevelt, Republican 1901	Chas. W. Fairbanks, Republican 1905	J. Hay 1901 E. Root 1905 R. Bacon 1909
27. William H. Taft, Republican 1909	James S. Sherman, Republican 1909	P. C. Knox 1909

POPULATION OF THE UNITED STATES

Division and State	1790	1800	1810	1820
UNITED STATES	3,929,214	5,308,483	7,239,881	9,638,453
GEOGRAPHIC DIVISIONS				
New England	1,009,408	1,233,011	1,471,973	1,660,071
Middle Atlantic	952,632	1,402,565	2,014,702	2,699,845
South Atlantic	1,851,806	2,286,494	2,674,891	3,061,063
East South Central	109,368	335,407	708,590	1,190,489
West South Central			77,618	167,680
East North Central		51,006	272,324	792,719
West North Central			19,783	66,586
Mountain				
Pacific				
NEW ENGLAND				
Maine	96,540	151,719	228,705	298,335
New Hampshire	141,885	183,858	214,460	244,161
Vermont	85,425	154,465	217,895	235,981
Massachusetts	378,787	422,845	472,040	523,287
Rhode Island	68,825	69,122	76,931	83,059
Connecticut	237,946	251,002	261,942	275,248

President	Vice President	Secretary of State
28. Woodrow Wilson, Democratic 1913	Thomas R. Marshall, Democratic 1913	W. J. Bryan 1913 R. Lansing 1915 B. Colby 1920
29. Warren G. Harding, Republican 1921	Calvin Coolidge, Republican 1921	C. E. Hughes 1921
30. Calvin Coolidge, Republican 1923	Charles G. Dawes, Republican 1925	C. E. Hughes 1923 F. B. Kellogg 1925
31. Herbert Hoover, Republican 1929	Charles Curtis, Republican 1929	H. L. Stimson 1929
32. Franklin D. Roosevelt, Democratic 1933	John Nance Garner, Democratic 1933 Henry A. Wallace, Democratic 1941 Harry S Truman, Democratic 1945	C. Hull 1933 E. R. Stettinius, Jr. 1944
33. Harry S Truman, Democratic 1945	Alben W. Barkley, Democratic 1949	J. F. Byrnes 1945 G. C. Marshall 1947 D. G. Acheson 1949
34. Dwight D. Eisenhower, Republican 1953	Richard M. Nixon, Republican 1953	J. F. Dulles 1953 C. A. Herter 1959
35. John F. Kennedy, Democratic 1961	Lyndon B. Johnson, Democratic 1961	D. Rusk 1961
36. Lyndon B. Johnson, Democratic 1963	Hubert H. Humphrey, Democratic 1965	D. Rusk 1963
37. Richard M. Nixon, Republican 1969	Spiro T. Agnew, Republican 1969 Gerald R. Ford, Republican 1973	W. P. Rogers 1969 H. A. Kissinger 1973
38. Gerald R. Ford, Republican 1974	Nelson Rockefeller, Republican 1974	H. A. Kissinger 1974
39. Jimmy Carter, Democratic 1977	Walter Mondale, Democratic 1977	C. Vance 1977 E. Muskie 1980
40. Ronald Reagan, Republican 1981	George Bush, Republican 1981	A. Haig 1981 G. Schultz 1982

1830	1840	1850	1860	1870	1880
12,866,020	17,069,453	23,191,876	31,443,321	39,818,449	50,155,783
1,954,717	2,234,822	2,728,116	3,135,283	3,487,924	4,010,529
3,587,664	4,526,260	5,898,735	7,458,985	8,810,806	10,496,878
3,645,752	3,925,299	4,679,090	5,364,703	5,853,610	7,597,197
1,815,969	2,575,445	3,363,271	4,020,991	4,404,445	5,585,151
246,127	449,985	940,251	1,747,667	2,029,965	3,334,220
1,470,018	2,924,728	4,523,260	6,926,884	9,124,517	11,206,668
140,455	426,814	880,335	2,169,832	3,856,594	6,157,443
		72,927	174,923	315,385	653,119
		105,871	444,053	675,125	1,114,578
399,455	501,793	583,169	628,279	626,915	648,936
269,328	284,574	317,976	326,073	318,300	346,530
280,652	291,948	314,120	315,098	330,551	332,286
610,408	737,699	994,514	1,231,066	1,457,351	1,783,085
97,199	108,830	147,545	174,620	217,353	276,531
297,675	309,978	370,792	460,147	537,454	622,700

Division and State	1790	1800	1810	1820
GEOGRAPHIC DIVISIONS				
MIDDLE ATLANTIC				
New York	340,120	589,051	959,049	1,372,812
New Jersey	184,139	211,149	245,562	277,575
Pennsylvania	434,373	602,365	810,091	1,049,458
SOUTH ATLANTIC				
Delaware	59,096	64,273	72,674	72,749
Maryland	319,728	341,548	380,546	407,350
Dist. of Columbia		14,093	24,023	33,039
Virginia	747,610	880,200	974,600	1,065,366
West Virginia				
North Carolina	393,751	478,103	555,500	638,829
South Carolina	249,073	345,591	415,115	502,741
Georgia	82,548	162,686	252,433	340,989
Florida				
EAST SOUTH CENTRAL				
Kentucky	73,677	220,955	406,511	564,317
Tennessee	35,691	105,602	261,727	422,823
Alabama				127,901
Mississippi		8,850	40,352	75,448
WEST SOUTH CENTRAL				
Arkansas			1,062	14,273
Louisiana			76,556	153,407
Texas				
EAST NORTH CENTRAL				
Ohio		45,365	230,760	581,434
Indiana		5,641	24,520	147,178
Illinois			12,282	55,211
Michigan			4,762	8,896
Wisconsin				
WEST NORTH CENTRAL				
Minnesota				
Iowa				
Missouri			19,783	66,586
North Dakota				
South Dakota				
Nebraska				
Kansas				
MOUNTAIN				
Montana				
Idaho				
Wyoming				
Colorado				
New Mexico				
Arizona				
Utah				
Nevada				
PACIFIC				
Washington				
Oregon				
California				

Division and State	1890	1900	1910	1920
UNITED STATES	62,947,714	75,994,575	91,972,266	105,710,620
GEOGRAPHIC DIVISIONS				
New England	4,700,749	5,592,017	6,552,681	7,400,909
Middle Atlantic	12,706,220	15,454,678	19,315,892	22,261,144
South Atlantic	8,857,922	10,443,480	12,194,895	13,990,272
East South Central	6,429,154	7,547,757	8,409,901	8,893,307
West South Central	4,740,983	6,532,290	8,784,534	10,242,224
East North Central	13,478,305	15,985,581	18,250,621	21,475,543
West North Central	8,932,112	10,347,423	11,637,921	12,544,249
Mountain	1,213,935	1,674,657	2,633,517	3,336,101
Pacific	1,888,334	2,416,692	4,192,304	5,566,871
Noncontiguous				

1830	1840	1850	1860	1870	1880
1,918,608	2,428,921	3,097,394	3,880,735	4,382,759	5,082,871
320,823	373,306	489,555	672,035	906,096	1,131,116
1,348,233	1,724,033	2,311,786	2,906,215	3,521,951	4,282,891
76,748	78,085	91,532	112,216	125,015	146,608
447,040	470,019	583,034	687,049	780,894	934,943
39,834	43,712	51,687	75,080	131,700	177,624
1,211,405	1,239,797	1,421,661	1,596,318	1,225,163	1,512,565
				442,014	618,457
737,987	753,419	869,039	992,622	1,071,361	1,399,750
581,185	594,398	668,507	703,708	705,606	995,577
516,823	691,392	906,185	1,057,286	1,184,109	1,542,180
34,730	54,477	87,445	140,424	187,748	269,493
687,917	779,828	982,405	1,155,684	1,321,011	1,648,690
681,904	829,210	1,002,717	1,109,801	1,258,520	1,542,359
309,527	590,756	771,623	964,201	996,992	1,262,505
136,621	375,651	606,526	791,305	827,922	1,131,597
30,388	97,574	209,897	435,450	484,471	802,525
215,739	352,411	517,762	708,002	726,915	939,946
		212,592	604,215	818,579	1,591,749
937,903	1,519,467	1,980,329	2,339,511	2,665,260	3,198,062
343,031	685,866	988,416	1,350,428	1,680,637	1,987,301
157,445	476,183	851,470	1,711,951	2,539,981	3,077,871
31,639	212,267	397,654	749,113	1,184,059	1,636,937
	30,945	305,391	775,881	1,054,670	1,315,497
		6,077	172,023	439,706	780,773
	43,112	192,214	674,913	1,194,020	1,624,615
140,455	383,702	682,044	1,182,012	1,721,295	2,168,380
				2,405	36,909
				11,776	98,268
			28,841	122,933	452,402
			107,206	364,399	996,096
				20,595	39,159
				14,999	32,610
				9,118	20,789
			34,277	39,864	194,327
		61,547	93,516	91,874	119,565
				9,658	40,440
		11,380	40,273	86,786	143,963
			6,857	42,491	62,266
			11,594	23,955	75,116
		13,294	52,465	90,923	174,768
		92,597	379,994	560,247	864,694

1930	1940	1950	1960	1970	1980
122,775,046	131,669,275	150,697,361	179,323,175	203,211,926	226,504,825
8,166,341	8,437,290	9,314,453	10,509,367	11,841,663	12,348,493
26,260,750	27,539,487	30,163,533	34,168,452	37,199,040	36,788,174
15,793,589	17,823,151	21,182,335	25,971,732	30,671,337	36,943,139
9,887,214	10,778,225	11,477,181	12,050,126	12,803,470	14,662,882
12,176,830	13,064,525	14,537,572	16,951,255	19,320,560	23,743,134
25,297,185	26,626,342	30,399,368	36,225,024	40,252,476	41,669,738
13,296,915	13,516,990	14,061,394	15,394,115	16,319,187	17,184,066
3,701,789	4,150,003	5,074,998	6,855,060	8,281,562	11,368,330
8,194,433	9,733,262	14,486,527	20,339,105	25,453,688	30,431,388
			858,939	1,068,943	1,365,481

Division and State	1890	1900	1910	1920
NEW ENGLAND				
Maine	661,086	694,466	742,371	768,014
New Hampshire	376,530	411,588	430,572	443,083
Vermont	332,422	343,641	355,956	352,428
Massachusetts	2,238,947	2,805,346	3,366,416	3,852,356
Rhode Island	345,506	428,556	542,610	604,397
Connecticut	746,258	908,420	1,114,756	1,380,631
MIDDLE ATLANTIC				
New York	6,003,174	7,268,894	9,113,614	10,385,227
New Jersey	1,444,933	1,883,669	2,537,167	3,155,900
Pennsylvania	5,258,113	6,302,115	7,665,111	8,720,017
SOUTH ATLANTIC				
Delaware	168,493	184,735	202,322	223,003
Maryland	1,042,390	1,188,044	1,295,346	1,449,661
Dist. of Columbia	230,392	278,718	331,069	437,571
Virginia	1,655,980	1,854,184	2,061,612	2,309,187
West Virginia	762,794	958,800	1,221,119	1,463,701
North Carolina	1,617,949	1,893,810	2,206,287	2,559,123
South Carolina	1,151,149	1,340,316	1,515,400	1,683,724
Georgia	1,837,353	2,216,331	2,609,121	2,895,832
Florida	391,422	528,542	752,619	968,470
EAST SOUTH CENTRAL				
Kentucky	1,858,635	2,147,174	2,289,905	2,416,630
Tennessee	1,767,518	2,020,616	2,184,789	2,337,885
Alabama	1,513,401	1,828,697	2,138,093	2,348,174
Mississippi	1,289,600	1,551,270	1,797,114	1,790,618
WEST SOUTH CENTRAL				
Arkansas	1,128,211	1,311,564	1,574,449	1,752,204
Louisiana	1,118,588	1,381,625	1,656,388	1,798,509
Oklahoma	258,657	790,391	1,657,155	2,028,283
Texas	2,235,527	3,048,710	3,896,542	4,663,228
EAST NORTH CENTRAL				
Ohio	3,672,329	4,157,545	4,767,121	5,759,394
Indiana	2,192,404	2,516,462	2,700,876	2,930,390
Illinois	3,826,352	4,821,550	5,638,591	6,485,280
Michigan	2,093,890	2,420,982	2,810,173	3,668,412
Wisconsin	1,693,330	2,069,042	2,333,860	2,632,067
WEST NORTH CENTRAL				
Minnesota	1,310,283	1,751,394	2,075,708	2,387,125
Iowa	1,912,297	2,231,853	2,224,771	2,404,021
Missouri	2,679,185	3,106,665	3,293,335	3,404,055
North Dakota	190,983	319,146	577,056	646,872
South Dakota	348,600	401,570	583,888	636,547
Nebraska	1,062,656	1,066,300	1,192,214	1,296,372
Kansas	1,428,108	1,470,495	1,690,949	1,769,257
MOUNTAIN				
Montana	142,924	243,329	376,053	548,889
Idaho	88,548	161,772	325,594	431,866
Wyoming	62,555	92,531	145,965	194,402
Colorado	413,249	539,700	799,024	939,629
New Mexico	160,282	195,310	327,301	360,350
Arizona	88,243	122,931	204,354	334,162
Utah	210,779	276,749	373,351	449,396
Nevada	47,355	42,335	81,875	77,407
PACIFIC				
Washington	357,232	518,103	1,141,990	1,356,621
Oregon	317,704	413,536	672,765	783,389
California	1,213,398	1,485,053	2,377,549	3,426,861
NONCONTIGUOUS				
Alaska				
Hawaii				

1930	1940	1950	1960	1970	1980
797,423	847,226	913,774	969,625	992,048	1,124,660
465,293	491,524	533,242	606,921	731,681	920,610
359,611	359,231	377,747	389,881	444,330	511,456
4,249,614	4,316,721	4,690,514	5,148,578	5,689,110	5,737,037
687,497	713,346	791,896	859,488	946,725	947,154
1,606,903	1,709,242	2,007,280	2,535,234	3,031,709	3,107,576
12,588,066	13,479,142	14,830,192	16,782,304	18,236,967	17,557,288
4,041,334	4,160,165	4,835,329	6,066,782	7,168,164	7,364,158
9,631,350	9,900,180	10,498,012	11,319,366	11,793,909	11,866,728
238,380	266,505	318,085	446,292	548,104	595,225
1,631,526	1,821,244	2,343,001	3,100,689	3,922,399	4,216,446
486,869	663,091	802,178	763,956	765,510	637,651
2,421,851	2,677,773	3,318,680	3,966,949	4,648,494	5,346,279
1,729,205	1,901,974	2,005,552	1,860,421	1,744,237	1,949,644
3,170,276	3,571,623	4,061,929	4,556,155	5,082,059	5,874,429
1,738,765	1,899,804	2,117,027	2,382,594	2,590,516	3,119,208
2,908,506	3,123,723	3,444,578	3,943,116	4,589,575	5,464,265
1,468,211	1,897,414	2,771,305	4,951,560	6,789,443	9,739,992
2,614,589	2,845,627	2,944,806	3,038,156	3,218,706	3,661,433
2,616,556	2,915,841	3,291,718	3,567,089	3,923,687	4,590,750
2,646,248	2,832,961	3,061,743	3,266,740	3,444,165	3,890,061
2,009,821	2,183,796	2,178,914	2,178,141	2,216,912	2,520,638
1,854,482	1,949,387	1,909,511	1,786,272	1,923,285	2,285,513
2,101,593	2,363,880	2,683,516	3,257,022	3,641,306	4,203,972
2,396,040	2,336,434	2,233,351	2,328,284	2,559,229	3,025,266
5,824,715	6,414,824	7,711,194	9,579,677	11,196,730	14,228,383
6,646,697	6,907,612	7,946,627	9,706,397	10,652,017	10,797,419
3,238,503	3,427,796	3,934,224	4,662,498	5,193,669	5,490,179
7,630,654	7,897,241	8,712,176	10,081,158	11,113,976	11,418,461
4,842,325	5,256,106	6,371,766	7,823,194	8,875,083	9,258,344
2,939,006	3,137,587	3,434,576	3,951,777	4,417,731	4,705,335
2,563,953	2,792,300	2,982,483	3,413,864	3,804,971	4,077,148
2,470,939	2,538,268	2,621,073	2,757,537	2,824,376	2,913,387
3,629,367	3,784,664	3,954,653	4,319,813	4,676,501	4,917,444
680,845	641,935	619,636	632,446	617,761	652,695
692,849	642,961	652,740	680,514	665,507	690,178
1,377,963	1,315,834	1,325,510	1,411,330	1,483,493	1,570,006
1,880,999	1,801,028	1,905,299	2,178,611	2,246,578	2,363,208
537,606	599,456	591,024	674,767	694,409	786,690
445,032	524,873	588,637	667,191	712,567	943,935
225,565	250,742	290,529	330,066	332,416	470,816
1,035,791	1,123,296	1,325,089	1,753,947	2,207,259	2,888,834
423,317	531,818	681,187	951,023	1,016,000	1,299,968
435,573	499,261	749,587	1,302,161	1,770,900	2,717,866
507,847	550,310	688,862	890,627	1,059,273	1,461,037
91,058	110,247	160,083	285,278	488,738	799,184
1,563,396	1,736,191	2,378,963	2,853,214	3,409,169	4,130,163
953,786	1,089,684	1,521,341	1,768,687	2,091,385	2,632,663
5,677,251	6,907,387	10,586,223	15,717,204	19,953,134	23,668,562
			226,167	300,382	400,481
			632,772	786,561	965,000

INDEX

Page references to illustrations, maps, and their captions appear in *italics*.

About the Authors

RICHARD N. CURRENT is University Distinguished Professor of History at the University of North Carolina at Greensboro. He is co-author of the Bancroft Prize–winning *Lincoln the President*. His books include: *Three Carpetbag Governors; The Lincoln Nobody Knows; Daniel Webster and the Rise of National Conservatism;* and *Secretary Stimson*. Professor Current has lectured on U.S. history in Europe, Asia, South America, Australia, and Antarctica. He has been a Fulbright Lecturer at the University of Munich and the University of Chile at Santiago and has served as Harmsworth Professor of American History at Oxford. He is past president of the Southern Historical Association.

T. HARRY WILLIAMS was Boyd Professor of History at Louisiana State University. He was awarded both the 1969 Pulitzer Prize and National Book Award for his biography of *Huey Long*. His books include: *Lincoln and His Generals; Lincoln and the Radicals; P. G. T. Beauregard; Americans at War; Romance and Realism in Southern Politics; Hayes of the Twenty-Third; McClellan, Sherman, and Grant; The Union Sundered;* and *The Union Restored*. Professor Williams was a Harmsworth Professor of American History at Oxford and President of both the Southern Historical Association and the Organization of American Historians.

FRANK FREIDEL is Bullitt Professor of American History at the University of Washington and Charles Warren Professor Emeritus of History at Harvard University. He is writing a six-volume biography of Franklin D. Roosevelt, four volumes of which have been published. Among his other books are: *Our Country's Presidents; F.D.R. and the South;* and *America in the Twentieth Century*. He is co-editor of the 1974 edition of the *Harvard Guide to American History* and past president of the Organization of American Historians. He is also a former president of the New England Historical Society.

ALAN BRINKLEY is Dunwalke Associate Professor of American History at Harvard University and has also taught at the Massachusetts Institute of Technology. He is a graduate of Princeton University, received his Ph.D. from Harvard, and has been awarded fellowships by the National Endowment for the Humanities and the American Council of Learned Societies. He is the author of *Voices of Protest: Huey Long, Father Coughlin, and the Great Depression*, co-author of *America in the Twentieth Century*, and the author of many articles and reviews.

A NOTE ON THE TYPE

The main text of this book was set via computer-driven cathode ray tube in Palatino, a type face designed by the noted German typographer Hermann Zapf. Named after Giovanbattista Palatino, a writing master of Renaissance Italy, Palatino was the first of Zapf's type faces to be introduced in America. The first designs for the face were made in 1948, and the fonts for the complete face were issued between 1950 and 1952. Like all Zapf-designed type faces, Palatino is beautifully balanced and exceedingly readable.

Other elements in this book were set via computer-driven cathode ray tube in Optima, a typeface designed by Hermann Zapf from 1952 to 1955 and issued in 1958. In designing Optima, Zapf created a truly new type form—a cross between the classic roman and a sans-serif face. So delicate are the stresses and balances in Optima that it rivals sans-serif faces in clarity and freshness and old-style faces in variety and interest.

Book design by Leon Bolognese

Cover design and construction by Jack Ribik

Cover photography by James McGuire

Composed by American–Stratford Graphic Services, Inc., Brattleboro, Vermont
Printed and bound by American Book–Stratford Press, Saddlebrook, N.J.